OFFICIAL OVERSTREET COMIC BOOK COMPANION

9th Edition

SELECTED COMICS FROM 1956–PRESENT INCLUDED
ILLUSTRATED CATALOGUE & EVALUATION GUIDE

by ROBERT M. OVERSTREET

GEMSTONE PUBLISHING

J.C. Vaughn, **Executive Editor**
Arnold T. Blumberg, **Editor** • Brenda Busick, **Creative Director**
Mark Huesman, **Production Coordinator** • Tom Gordon III, **Managing Editor**
Jamie David, **Director of Marketing** • Sara Ortt, **Marketing Assistant**
Stacia Brown, **Editorial Coordinator** • Heather Winter, **Office Manager**

SPECIAL CONTRIBUTORS TO THIS EDITION

J.C. Vaughn

SENIOR OVERSTREET ADVISORS FOR OVER 25 YEARS

Dave Alexander • Steve Geppi • Paul Levitz • Michelle Nolan • Ron Pussell
Rick Sloane • John K. Snyder Jr. • Doug Sulipa • Harry B. Thomas • Raymond S. True

SENIOR OVERSTREET ADVISORS FOR OVER 20 YEARS

Gary M. Carter • Bill Cole • Stan Gold • M. Thomas Inge
Phil Levine • Richard Olson • Gene Seger

SPECIAL ADVISORS

Tyler Alexander • Lon Allen • Dave Anderson • David J. Anderson, D.D.S. • Robert L. Beerbohm
Jon Berk • Brian Block • Steve Borock • Michael Browning • John Chruscinski • Gary Colabuono
Jack Copley • Carl De La Cruz • Peter Dixon • Gary Dolgoff • Bruce Ellsworth • Conrad Eschenberg
Michael Eury • Richard Evans • D'Arcy Farrell • Stephen Fishler • Dan Fogel • Chris Foss
Steve Gentner • Michael Goldman • Tom Gordon III • Jamie Graham • John Grasse • Daniel Greenhalgh
Eric Groves • Jim Halperin • Mark Haspel • John Hauser • Greg Holland • John Hone • George Huang
Bill Hughes • Rob Hughes • William Insignares • Ed Jaster • Paul Litch • Joe & Nadia Mannarino
Rick Manzella • Harry Matetsky • Jon McClure • Todd McDevitt • Mike McKenzie
Fred McSurley • Steve Mortensen • Michael Naiman • Josh Nathanson • Matt Nelson • Terry O'Neill
George Paniela • James Payette • John Petty • Jim Pitts • Yolanda Ramirez • Israel Rodriguez
Robert Rogovin • Chuck Rozanski • Matt Schiffman • Doug Schmell • Laura Sperber • Tony Starks
West Stephan • Al Stoltz • Ken Stribling • Joel Thingvall • Ted Van Liew • Joe Verenneault • Frank Verzyl • John Verzyl
Rose Verzyl • Bob Wayne • Jerry Weist • Mark Wilson • Anthony Yamada • Harley Yee • Vincent Zurzolo, Jr.

House of Collectibles
New York

Gemstone Publishing

THE OFFICIAL® OVERSTREET® COMIC BOOK COMPANION. Copyright ©2006 by Gemstone Publishing, Inc. All rights reserved. No part of this book may be used or reproduced in any manner whatsoever without written permission except in the case of brief quotations embodied in critical articles and reviews. For information, write to: Gemstone Publishing, 1966 Greenspring Drive, Timonium, Maryland 21093.

Front cover: Justice Society artwork by Mark Sparacio. Justice Society ©2006 DC Comics. All rights reserved.

THE OFFICIAL® OVERSTREET® COMIC BOOK COMPANION (9th Edition) is an original publication of Gemstone Publishing, Inc. and House of Collectibles. Distributed by Random House Information Group, a division of Random House, Inc., New York and simultaneously in Canada by Random House of Canada Limited, Toronto. This edition has never before appeared in book form.

House of Collectibles
Random House Information Group
1745 Broadway
New York, New York 10019

www.houseofcollectibles.com

Overstreet is a registered trademark of Gemstone Publishing, Inc.

House of Collectibles is a registered trademark and the colophon is a trademark of Random House, Inc.

Published by arrangement with Gemstone Publishing.

ISBN: 0-375-72110-X
ISBN: 978-0-375-72110-6
ISSN: 0891-8872

Printed in the United States of America

10 9 8 7 6 5 4 3 2 1

Ninth Edition: January 2006

Table of Contents

Acknowledgements

First of all, we thank Mark Sparacio for his inspiring Justice Society cover.

Comics Section: Thanks to those who supplied valuable comic data: Gary Carter (DC data); Gary Coddington (Superman data); Al Dellinges (Kubert data); David Gerstein (Walt Disney Comics data); Kevin Hancer (Tarzan data); Phil Levine (giveaway data); Paul Litch (Copper & Modern Age data); Jon McClure (Whitman data); Fred Nardelli (Frazetta data); Michelle Nolan (love comics); Chris Pedrin (DC War data); Matt Schiffman (Bronze Age data); Frank Scigliano (Little Lulu data); David R. Smith, Archivist, Walt Disney Productions (Disney data); Tony Starks (Silver and Bronze Age data); Al Stoltz (Promo data); Kim Weston (Disney and Barks data).

Credit is due my two grading advisors, Steve Borock and Mark Haspel of Comics Guaranty Corp., for their ongoing input on grading. A special "thanks" is also given to Chuck Rozanski for his many years of support.

Thanks again to Doug Sulipa, Jon McClure, Fred McSurley and Tony Starks for continuing to provide detailed Bronze Age data. To Dave Alexander, Tyler Alexander, Dave Anderson (Oklahoma), Dave Anderson (Virginia), Stephen Barrington, Lauren Becker, Michael Browning, John Chruscinski, Gary Dolgoff, Conrad Eschenberg, D'Arcy Farrell, Dan Fogel, Stephen Gentner, Jamie Graham, Dan Greenhalgh, Eric Groves, John Hauser, Jef Hinds, Greg Holland, Bill Hughes, William Insignares, Nadia Mannarino, Joe Mannarino, Todd McDevitt, Dale Moore, Steve Mortensen, Josh Nathanson, Terry O'Neill, Jim Payette, John Petty, Jim Pitts, Dave Robie, Ron Pussell, Israel Rodriguez, Rob Rogovin, Marnin Rosenberg, Matt Schiffman, West Stephan, Al Stoltz, Harry B. Thomas, Michael Tierney, John Verzyl, Frank Verzyl, Lon Webb and Vincent Zurzolo Jr., who supplied detailed pricing data or other material in this edition.

Toy Rings Section: The creation of this listing was made possible by the early inspiration of "Little" Jimmy Dempsey, who introduced me to the ring market years ago. But the inspiration to actually get the job done came from the constant encouragement and advice of John K. Snyder, Jr., Bruce Rosen, Steve Geppi, Ed Pragler, Don Maris, Harry Matetsky, R.C. Lettner, Mike Herz and Bob Hritz. These enthusiastic hobbyists gave freely of their time and knowledge in the early stages of compiling the needed information for this listing.

This edition includes most of the top collected rings of the 20th Century. Credit is given to Chris Smith for providing detailed descriptive information, prices and photos for the Phantom rings included in this and previous editions.

Evelyn Wilson, former archivist for General Mills, has supplied pages of detailed information used in this and previous editions, which includes dates, promoters for various giveaways as well as the quantities produced. We all owe her a debt of gratitude and thanks for keeping the record straight.

Special thanks is also due to Howard C. Weinberger for his help previously in compiling the flicker ring listings; to Howard's photographer, Jeff Kermath, for his excellent photographs of rings included in this and previous editions; to Bruce Rosen, who originally supplied hundreds of rings for photographing as well as the associated data; to Joe Statkus, who previously supplied photos of the header cards for Flicker rings in earlier listings; to Dave Eskenazi and Ed Pragler, who previously sent rings for photographing; to Ted Hake for his senior advice and continued support.

Finally, special credit is due our talented production staff for their assistance with this edition; to Mark Huesman (Production Coordinator), Arnold T. Blumberg (Editor), Brenda Busick (Creative Director), Tom Gordon III (Managing Editor), Jamie David (Director of Marketing), Sara Ortt (Marketing Assistant), Stacia Brown (Editorial Coordinator), and Heather Winter (Office Manager), as well as to our Executive Editor, J.C. Vaughn, for their valuable contributions to this edition. Thanks to my wife, Caroline, for her encouragement and support on such a tremendous project.

With this book you open the doorway to a whole universe of pop culture collecting! This handy volume contains detailed information on a selection of comics and toy rings that represent just a fraction of the myriad collectibles waiting out there for you to find. As you will see later, the comic book information is taken from our comprehensive annual publication, **The Official Overstreet Comic Book Price Guide**, now in its 36th consecutive year of publication. The toy ring information has been taken from another Gemstone book, **The Overstreet Toy Ring Price Guide**. Together these extensively researched guides cover over a hundred years of collectibles, with over 250,000 comics and thousands of toy rings. This book provides a glimpse into both collecting categories, but there's much more to be discovered.

Comics

In **The Official Overstreet Comic Book Price Guide**, the full story of the history of American comic books from 1842 to the present is reflected in hundreds of pages of listings for every comic from **Action Comics** to **Zot** and much, much more. In this book we've limited ourselves to just a small selection of titles from the Silver Age (beginning in 1956) to the present day, but you'll find the same attention to detail and dedication to accurate pricing here that also exists in our annual Guide.

Toy Rings

The Overstreet Toy Ring Price Guide traces the development of the toy ring hobby from just before the turn of the 20th century to the present, with thousands of metal and plastic rings drawn from decades of film, television, radio, comic book and advertising sources. In this book we've given you a small sampling of the plethora of rings you might find at conventions and through on-line venues.

Together, these two categories are just the tip of the iceberg, but every collector has to start somewhere, and we're glad you've chosen to start your pop culture journey with us. Turn the page and begin learning all about the amazing, exciting world of comic book and toy ring collecting, and at the end of the book we'll suggest a few other categories of collectibles that you might find interesting. Let the journey begin!

Collecting Comic Books

New comic books are available in many different venues, but principally in your local comic book shop and book store chains. However, comics can also be found in grocery stores; drug stores; newsstands; collectibles specialty shops; through mail order catalogs; and online from individual retailers and in some cases from the publishers themselves. Local flea markets and, of course, comic book conventions in your area, are also excellent sources for new and old comic books.

Many collectors begin by buying new issues in Near Mint condition directly from their local comic shop or off the newsstand, or perhaps they obtain comics via subscriptions with retailers and/or the publishers. Most collectors have to make use of several venues, from "brick and mortar" stores to online retailers, in order not to miss something they want.

Some collectors not only collect comics because they enjoy the stories or have fond memories of a particular title and/or character, but because they're interested in "playing the market" for investment purposes.

Today's comic books offer a wide variety of subjects, art styles and writers to satisfy even the most discriminating fan. Whether it's the latest new hot title or company, or one of many popular titles that have been around for a long time, the comic book fan has a broad range from which to pick. In terms of genre, "Bad Girl" and horror titles have often proven popular in addition to the ubiquitous superhero fare, but many series delving into less fanciful subjects, like crime comics and real-world relationship-based series, have also found some measure of success and a solid fan following. The collector should always stay informed about the new trends developing in this fast-moving market. Since the market fluctuates greatly, and there is a vast array of comics to choose from, it's recommended first and foremost that you collect what you enjoy reading; that way, despite any value changes, you will always maintain a sense of personal satisfaction with your collection.

Collecting on a Budget

Collectors usually check out their local comic shop or book store for the latest arrivals. Scores of brand new comic books are displayed each week for the collector. There are a few basic approaches to collecting comics on a budget, listed below, that may offer a solution.

Collecting Artists or Companies

Many collectors enjoy favorite artists and follow their work from issue to issue, title to title, or company to company. Over the years, some artists have achieved "star" status. Some collectors become loyal to a particular company and only collect its titles. Either approach is a convenient way to limit your spending and collect what you enjoy.

Collecting #1 Issues

For decades, comic enthusiasts have collected first (#1) issues. #1 issues have a lot going for them - some introduce new characters, while others are under-printed, creating a rarity factor. #1 issues cross many subjects as well as companies.

Back Issues

A back issue is any comic currently not available on the stands. Collectors of current titles often want to find the earlier issues in order to complete a run; thus a back issue collector is born. Today, there are hundreds of dealers that sell old comic books, and many of them advertise in **The Official Overstreet Comic Book Price Guide**. Call the Comic Shop Locator Service at 1-888-COMIC-BOOK, to see if you have a comic book store in your area. Of course, one of the best sources for information is the Internet. Search online for local comic shops, dealers with mailing lists and catalogs, or simply order from countless retailers who operate through the web. Auction sites like eBay also provide an enormous forum for finding desired comics, selling comics of your own, or just communicating with other collectors who share your interests.

Putting a quality collection of old comics together takes a lot of time, effort and money. Many old comics are not easy to find. Persistence and luck play a big part in acquiring needed issues. Most quality collections are put together over a long period of time by placing mail orders with dealers and other collectors, networking online and bidding in Internet auctions, and/or visiting conventions to find those elusive issues. Unless you have unlimited funds to invest in your hobby, you will find it necessary to restrict your collecting in certain ways. However you define your collection, you should be careful to set your goals well within affordable limits.

Comic book grading has evolved over the past several decades from a much looser interpretation of standards in the beginning to the very tight professional scrutiny in use by the market today. In recent years, grading criteria have become even tighter, especially in Silver and Bronze Age books, due to their higher survival rate.

For much more information on grading and restoration, as well as full-color photographs of many major defects and conditions, consult **The Official Overstreet Comic Book Grading Guide**. Copies are available through all normal distribution channels or can be ordered direct from Gemstone by sending $24 plus $4 postage and handling. You can also call Gemstone toll free at 1-888-375-9800.

How to Grade

Before a comic book's true value can be assessed, its condition or state of preservation must be determined. In all cases, the better the condition of the comic, the more desirable and valuable the book will be. Comic books in Mint condition will bring several times the price of the same book in Poor condition. Therefore, it is very important to be able to properly grade your books. Comics should be graded from the exterior (the covers) to the interior (the pages) and thoroughly examined before assigning a final grade.

Lay the comic down on a flat, clean surface. Under normal lighting, examine the exterior of the comic from front to back, identifying any defects or other significant attributes.

Check to make sure that the centerfold and all interior pages are still present. The whiteness level of the pages is of major importance in determining the final grade as well. Locate and identify interior defects such as chipping, flaking, possible brittleness, and other flaws.

After all the above steps have been taken, then the collector can begin to consider an overall grade for his or her book, which may range from absolutely perfect Gem Mint condition to Poor, where a comic is extremely worn, dirty and even falling apart.

NOTE: The + and - grades listed are similar to their primary grade except for an additional virtue or defect that raises or lowers them from the primary grade.

Grading Definitions

10.0 GEM MINT (GM): An exceptional example of a given book - the best ever seen. Cover is flat, corners square and sharp. Spine is tight and flat. Paper is white, supple and fresh. No interior autographs or owner signatures.

9.9 MINT (MT): Near perfect in every way. Cover is flat, corners square and sharp. Spine is tight and flat. Paper is white, supple and fresh.

9.8 NEAR MINT/MINT (NM/MT): Nearly perfect in every way with only minor imperfections that keep it from the next higher grade. Only the slightest interior tears are allowed.

9.6 NEAR MINT+ (NM+): Nearly perfect with a minor additional virtue or virtues that raise it from Near Mint. Cover is flat, corners almost sharp and square. Paper is off-white, supple and fresh.

9.4 NEAR MINT (NM): Nearly perfect with only minor imperfections that keep it from the next higher grade. Corners are square and sharp with ever-so-slight blunting. Paper is off-white to cream, supple and fresh.

9.2 NEAR MINT– (NM–): Nearly perfect with only a minor additional defect or defects that keep it from Near Mint. Ever-so-slight corner blunting.

9.0 VERY FINE/NEAR MINT (VF/NM): Nearly perfect with outstanding eye appeal. Cover is almost flat with almost imperceptible wear, corners blunted slightly. Paper is off-white to cream and supple. Very minor interior tears may be present.

8.5 VERY FINE+ (VF+)

8.0 VERY FINE (VF): An excellent copy with outstanding eye appeal. Cover is relatively flat with minimal surface wear. Spine is almost completely flat. Paper is cream to tan and supple.

7.5 VERY FINE– (VF–)

7.0 FINE/VERY FINE (FN/VF): An above-average copy that shows minor wear but is still relatively flat and clean with outstanding eye appeal. Paper is cream to tan.

6.5 FINE+ (FN+)

6.0 FINE (FN): An above-average copy that shows minor wear but is still relatively flat and clean with no significant creasing or other serious defects.

Blunted corners are more common, as is minor staining, soiling, discoloration, and/or foxing. A minor spine roll is allowed. Paper is tan to brown and fairly supple with no signs of brittleness. Centerfold may be loose.

5.5 FINE– (FN–)
5.0 VERY GOOD/FINE (VG/FN): An above-average but well-used comic book. Minor to moderate cover wear and spine roll apparent, staple tears, stress lines and a spine split possible. Paper is tan to brown with no signs of brittleness.

4.5 VERY GOOD+ (VG)
4.0 VERY GOOD (VG): The average used comic book. Cover shows moderate to significant wear, and may be loose but not completely detached. Some discoloration, fading, foxing, and even minor soiling is allowed. As much as a 1/4" triangle can be missing out of the corner or edge; a missing 1/8" square is also acceptable. Centerfold may be detached at one staple.

3.5 VERY GOOD– (VG–)
3.0 GOOD/VERY GOOD (GD/VG): A used comic book showing some substantial wear. Cover shows significant wear, and may be loose or even detached at one staple. Can have a book-length crease. Small chunks missing, tape and amateur repair possible. Paper is brown but not brittle.

2.5 GOOD+ (GD+)
2.0 GOOD (GD): Shows substantial wear; often considered a "reading copy." Cover shows significant wear and may even be detached. Cover reflectivity is low and in some cases absent. Book-length creases, rounded corners, soiling, staining, and discoloration may be present. Spine roll is likely. May have up to a 2" spine split. Paper is brown but not brittle.

1.8 GOOD– (GD–)
1.5 FAIR/GOOD (FR/GD): Shows substantial to heavy wear. Books in this grade are commonly creased, scuffed, abraded, soiled, and possibly unattractive, but still generally readable. Paper is brown and may show brittleness around the edges. Acidic odor may be present.
1.0 FAIR (FR): Shows heavy wear. Some collectors consider this the lowest

collectible grade because comic books in lesser condition are usually incomplete and/or brittle. Paper is brown and may show brittleness around the edges but not in the central portion of the pages. Acidic odor may be present. Accumulation of interior tears. Chunks may be missing. The centerfold may be missing if readability is generally preserved. Coupons may be cut.

0.5 POOR (PR): Sufficiently degraded to the point where there is little or no collector value; easily identified by a complete absence of eye appeal. Brittle almost to the point of turning to dust with a touch, and usually incomplete. Multiple pages, including the centerfold, may be missing that affect readability.

Scarcity of Comics

Silver Age and early Bronze Age comics (1956-1979): Early '60s comics are rare in Near Mint to Mint condition. Most copies of early '60s Marvels and DCs grade no higher than VF. Many early keys in NM or MT exist in numbers less than 10-20 of each. Mid-'60s to late '70s books in high grade are more common due to the hoarding of comics that began in the mid-'60s.

'80s and '90s comics (1980-1992): Collectors are only now beginning to discover that 10-15 years spent in quarter boxes have rendered many '80s comics scarce in NM condition, and as modern collecting shifts its focus ever closer to the present, these will become increasingly sought-after and harder to locate in high grade as a result, but not nearly as difficult as earlier era comics that are genuinely rare in high grade.

'90s and Modern Age comics (1992-Present): Comics of today are common in high grade. VF to NM is the standard rather than the exception.

Comic books were built to last but a short time. Some of the best advice for preserving a comic is simply to handle it carefully. When handling high grade comics, always wash your hands first, eliminating harmful oils from the skin. Lay the comic on a flat surface and slowly turn the pages. This will minimize the stress to the staples and spine.

Careful handling of an exceptional book can go a long way to preserving its condition, but careful storage is also key. Comics must be protected from the elements, as well as light, heat, and humidity.

Store comic books away from direct light sources, especially florescent light, which contains high levels of ultraviolet (UV) radiation. Tungsten filament lighting is safer than florescent lighting, but should still be used at brief intervals. Exposure to light accumulates damage, so store your collection in a cool, dark place away from windows.

Fungus and mold thrives in higher temperatures, so the lower the temperature, the longer the life of your collection. High relative humidity (rh) can also be damaging to paper. Maintaining a low and stable relative humidity, around 50%, is crucial. Varying humidity will damage your collection.

Atmospheric pollution is another problem associated with long term storage of paper. Sulfuric dioxide, which can occur from automobile exhaust, will cause paper to turn yellow over a period of time. For this reason, it is best not to store your valuable comics close to a garage.

Care must also be taken when choosing materials for storing your comics. Many common items such as plastic bags, boards, and boxes may not be as safe as they seem; some contain chemicals that actually help to destroy your collection. Always purchase materials designed for long-term storage, such as Mylar sleeves and acid-free backing boards and boxes. Polypropylene and polyethylene bags, while safe for temporary storage, should be changed every three to five years.

Comics are best stored vertically in boxes to preserve flatness. Never store comics on the floor; elevate them 6-10 inches to allow for flooding. Never store your collection directly against a wall, particularly an outside wall. Condensation and poor air circulation will encourage mold and fungus growth.

With some care in handling and attention to the materials used for comic book storage, your collection can enjoy a long life and maintain a reasonable condition for years to come.

Whether you're a new collector just starting to acquire comics or a long-time collector now interested in selling a collection, by purchasing this Guide you have begun the long process necessary to successfully buy and sell comics.

Selling Your Comics

You should never deal with a buyer without fully checking their references. For additional verification, consult The Better Business Bureau. **The Overstreet Comic Book Price Guide, Overstreet's Comic Price Review**, and **Comic Book Marketplace** are also recognized authorities. Advertised dealers will likely have a more established reputation.

Potential buyers will be most concerned with the retail value of your entire collection, which may be more or less than Guide depending on what you have and the current demand for many of the individual issues in your collection. Some rare early books in VF or NM may bring a price well over Guide while other titles in lower grades may sell for a price well under Guide. Most vintage books, though, will sell for around the Guide price.

However, since many '80s and '90s books that list at cover price may only be worth a percentage of that price, you must decide on what percentage you would be willing to accept for your collection, taking into account how the collection breaks down into fast, moderate and slow-moving books. To expect someone to pay full retail for books that usually sell at considerably lower prices is unrealistic. You will have to be flexible in order to close a deal.

Many buyers may want to purchase only certain key or high grade books from your collection, almost always favoring the buyer. While you may be paid a high percentage of retail for their selections, you will find that "cherry-picked" collections are much more difficult to sell, since all of the most desired books will be sold by the time the second or third potential buyer examines your collection. Furthermore, the percentage of retail that you will receive for a cherry-picked collection will be much lower than if the collection had been left intact. Remember, key issues and/or high grade issues make or break a collection and often set the value for the collection as a whole. Selling on consignment, another popular option, could become another breeding ground for cherry-pickers, so again, always check a dealer's references thoroughly.

Of course, while these rules apply to any transaction between collectors and potential buyers in most physical or "brick and mortar" retailer/dealer situations, there is a far more popular option available to collectors today who wish to sell part or all of their collection. With the advent of eBay and other online auction and store venues, collectors can now bypass the traditional routes and sell directly to other collectors rather than to retailers and/or dealers. As a result, realized prices for individual issues or entire collections can be much higher, since potential buyers are now often drawn from a pool of equally enthused collectors rather than dealers with a desire to resell their aquisitions for profit. On the other hand, even individual collectors seeking to buy comics on the web may be into the speculation game, so all the old rules about being a cautious buyer or seller still apply.

If you do choose to sell your comics on a piecemeal basis through eBay or other means, the process will require much greater care and detail in preparing an inventory list and grading comics for sale. As noted above, you will probably be able to realize a higher final price by selling your collection this way, but the key books will certainly sell first, leaving a significant portion of your collection unsold. You will need to keep repricing and discounting your books to encourage buyers on books that do not initially sell.

Entire books have been written about how best to achieve sales success through eBay and other Internet sites, so rather than dwell on all the possible strategies here, we will simply say that online auctions are the fastest-growing and most convenient venues for many private collectors to engage in the buying and selling of vintage comics of all Ages. It behooves anyone who chooses to use this method to educate themselves thoroughly about the intricacies of online auctions and transactions.

You can also advertise your collection in trade publications or through mass mailings, but whether selling books through the mail by traditional means or when shipping books at the close of an Internet auction, you should establish a reasonable return policy, as some books will unquestionably be returned. Close attention to detail when presenting accurate descriptions of the books in your sales information, and use of very clear pictures - particularly in Internet auction listings - will go a long way to preventing misunderstandings and arguments later on. Check the local post office and/or UPS regarding the various rates and services available for shipping your books.

Marketing your books at conventions is another option, but as a dealer, you will naturally also incur overhead expenses such as table rental if setting up at a show, postage, mailing and display supplies, advertising costs, etc.

In all cases, be willing to establish trust with a prospective buyer. By following the procedures outlined here, you will be able to sell your collection successfully, for a fair price, with both parties walking away satisfied. After all, collecting comic books is supposed to be fun; it only becomes a chore if you let it.

Comic Conventions

The first comic book conventions, or cons, were originally conceived as the comic book counterpart to science fiction fandom conventions. There were many attempts to form successful national cons, but they were all stillborn. It is interesting that after only three relatively organized years of existence, the first comic con was held. Of course, its magnitude was nowhere near as large as most established cons held today.

What is a comic con? Dealers, collectors, fans, publishers, distributors, manufacturers, and other enthusiasts can be found buying, selling and trading the adventures of their favorite characters for hours on end. Additionally, most cons have guests of honor, usually professionals in the field of comic art - writers, artists, editors, or other production personnel. The committees that run these conventions put together panels for the con attendees in which the assembled pros talk about certain aspects of comic book production and history, and often these guests field questions from the assembled audience as well.

At cons, one can usually find displays of various and sundry items for purchase, including toys, comic books of course, original art, and much more. Larger cons often serve as a launching platform for comic- or genre-related films and television shows, and there can be showings of movie trailers, video presentations, and special personal appearances by media stars. Of course, there is always the chance to get together with friends at cons and just talk about comics. One also has a good opportunity to make new friends who have similar interests and with whom one can correspond after the convention is over.

It is difficult to describe accurately what goes on at a con. The best way to find out is to go to one and see for yourself. The largest cons are WonderCon (April), Pittsburgh (April), Philadelphia (May), San Diego (July), Chicago (August), Baltimore (September), and Ohio (November). For accurate dates and addresses, visit the convention websites themselves for details.

The Justice Society of America, beginning with All Star Comics #3, has appeared at least semi-regularly since 1940, but between the end of their All Star run in 1951 and the launch of JSA in 1999, they were generally consigned to guest appearances and/or mini-series and one-shots. That's definitely not the case at present. JSA is a perennial best-seller in many comic shops, and the characters seem poised at the forefront of the DC Universe.

"I'm not sure what exactly it is that makes the JSA popular with readers," said Geoff Johns, the title's writer, who also scripts *JSA Classified*, *Infinite Crisis*, *Flash*, *Teen Titans* and other titles for DC Comics. "The characters have a very strong following, and always have, they just haven't had a very large opportunity to be seen on a monthly basis for awhile. I think part of what really works with the current team is the fact that many of the heroes are carrying on the legacies of previous members. They aren't all seasoned veterans, and I think the interaction between the characters is what readers respond to. It's also what makes the team members fun to write. Seeing Alan Scott talking to Stargirl, or Jakeem Thunder and Johnny Thunderbolt. This is what the JSA is to me today. The first super-hero team, carrying on with the help of the descendants of the originals."

Legacy is carrying on tradition, of learning what has come before and why, Johns said.

"It's about keeping an ideal alive. In this case, member by member. You can explore this in endless ways. The legacy may have not have been as perfect as one thought, one may not completely understand the weight of legacy, one may think they have learned all they need to have known," he said."It's really a terrific theme to explore, because we can all relate to it. We are all affected by our past peers and family, and we all have people we idolize."

GATHERED TOGETHER

When the superhero tide started in the late 1930s, it took no time at all for it to become a deluge of super-powered, mystically charged, and flat-out weirdly attired crime fighters to become the norm in comics publishing. From the first appearance of Superman in *Action Comics* #1 (June 1938) until the emergence of the Justice Society of America, the children of America found newsstands suddenly awash in superheroes.

It might not seem like the men behind the Junior Justice Society of America were taking a big risk. After all, they were following their highly successful formula of combining their top characters into the appropriately named *All Star Comics* and the equally profitable concept of their Supermen of America club. Between a world at war and corporate in-fighting, though, things weren't as easy as they looked.

Prior to the group's first appearance in *All Star Comics* #3 (November 1940) none of the publishers had cobbled their characters into a super team. In hindsight it's easy to wonder how it actually took someone so long to think of it. Numerous times during the preceding months publishers had put more than one feature character on the cover. By June 1940, Timely's Human Torch and Sub-Mariner, their two main mainstays, had done battle in a story, but it wasn't even close to the congregation of characters gathered together witnessed in *All Star*.

The Flash, Green Lantern, Sandman, Hourman, Spectre and Hawkman had already appeared in other comics and were off to a rousing start (Flash and Green Lantern even had their own titles). Dr. Fate and The Atom appeared for the first time in the same issue that featured the team's debut, but by then there was a solid formula in place.

Though replete with standard fantasy elements, superhero comics were among the vanguard in beginning to address the dark clouds then looming over America's future in 1940. Many yarns were filled with spies, saboteurs, action, adventure and patriotism. There were also numerous thinly disguised tales about the treatment of those trapped under the Nazi control. Though played delicately at the time, this would soon play an important role in the Junior Justice Society of America.

THE CLUB CONCEPT

By the time the Justice Society of America was born, comic character clubs for children were no longer a new idea. While the exploitation of the information they generated was limited by today's standards, they must be considered not only as pioneering efforts, but by and large as incredible successes.

The evolutionary course of the club concept became associated with comic characters as it developed through the newspaper comic strips, the pulps, comic books, and radio shows. A series of significant manifestations of the club concept corresponds directly with the marketing of aviation heroes (both real and fictitious) in the late '20s and through the '30s.

The Junior Birdmen of America, one of those aviation-themed clubs, was one of the most successful. Starting in 1934, Hearst Newspapers successfully invited the participation of the nation's youth through at least 22 of their papers. By the time DC's Supermen of America club rolled around there was already an art, if not a science, to getting kids involved.

On the trailing edge of the Great Depression, before America's involvement in the Second World War, the Supermen of America was simultaneously marketing at its most cynical and most inspired. The readers of the Superman comic books, unlike the readers of the newspaper strip or listeners to the radio show, were overwhelmingly children. This club recruited Superman fans and enlisted them to recruit others. In other words, it took the standard advertising tactic of going straight to the kids and getting them to pester the parents into buying a product one better: it got kids to not only work on their own beleaguered parents, it got them to get their friends to work on their own parents, too. For successfully recruiting others, members received the Supermen of America patch, today one of the most highly prized Superman collectibles. This successful club continued into the 1960s.

IDEALS IN A HOSTILE ENVIRONMENT

Text of the 1942 Junior Justice Society Certificate:

This Certifies that: [Name, Age, Address] has been duly elected a charter member of this organization upon his or her pledge to help keep our country united in the face of enemy attempts to make us think we

Americans are all different, because we are rich or poor; employer or worker; native or foreign-born; Gentile or Jew, Protestant or Catholic. And makes the further pledge to defeat this Axis propaganda, seeking to get us to fight among ourselves, so we cannot successfully fight our enemies - knowing that are all AMERICANS believing in DEMOCRACY and are resolved to do everything possible to help win the war!

It's next to impossible to understand the historic significance of the Junior Justice Society of America without placing it in its proper historic context. Rather than espousing a generic albeit genuine patriotism of many of their contemporaries, the JJSA certificate asked a few specifics of its members. Six months after the first class of Tuskegee Airmen graduated and six years before President Harry Truman ordered the integration of the U.S. military, the writers, editors, marketing men and their publisher all made a small but very significant stand. Half a year before race riots broke out in Detroit and more than two years before American troops came face-to-face with the realities of Hitler's "final solution" when they liberated the Buchenwald concentration camp, the folks behind the club not only wrapped themselves in the spirit of the flag, the Constitution and the Declaration of Independence, they asked America's kids to do the same.

What All-American Comics and DC did with the Junior Justice Society changed what could have been perceived as a cynical promotional ploy into something far more altruistic. And in doing so they took at least some risk, if not a great deal of it.

At that time and for decades to come it would not have been a prudent business decision in many parts of the country to suggest that "rich or poor; employer or worker; native or foreign-born; Gentile or Jew, Protestant or Catholic" would be on the same team. In an age when many of the men who created *All Star Comics* could not gain access to a country club on Long Island, New York, let alone one in Mobile, Alabama, they decided that in order to "provide for the common defense, promote the general Welfare, and secure the Blessings of Liberty to ourselves and our Posterity," we had to be better than what was being thrown at us from across the Atlantic and Pacific oceans. In the form of this simple certificate intended for children, they held that "with liberty and justice for all" meant something, even if we as a nation hadn't quite worked out exactly what it meant.

They had a roadmap, a great one, in the guise of Supermen of America. They went another direction. Thousands of kids joined. The Junior Justice Society of America was a smash hit.

THE CLUB KITS
Over the years the kits themselves have been documented and re-documented, researched, photocopied, theorized upon and written about. They've been the subjects of many "definitive" articles and much discussion amongst comic book fans and other collectors. Each of the kits had differences, some distinct, some subtle.

While it's been common to report otherwise, there were at least five distinct JJSA kits. *[Editors note: You can read more about this in The Official Hake's Price Guide to Character Toys, which features numerous JSA entries.]*

THE LONG, LEAN YEARS
With only Superman, Batman and handful of others surviving during the next very lean decade for superheroes, it would have been easy enough for the idea of a super-team to fade away as well. Superhero clubs and club kits quickly went the way of the superhero in post war years, which is to say they almost entirely disappeared. *All Star Comics* #57 was the last issue featuring the Justice Society. Following the then-current craze, the title became *All Star Western* with the next issue.

In 1960, DC debuted the Justice League of America in the pages of *Brave & The Bold* #28. After a three-issue smash hit run there, they got their own title. Clearly inspired by the Justice Society, it took less than three years for the Justice League to feature their elder counter-parts as guest-stars. This cross-time crossover was a big hit with the fans and became a regular event. Comics from the '60s and '70s featuring these crossovers are among the most fondly remembered of the period for many collectors, and the early Justice Society appearances in Justice League of America sparked not only

fan interest, but eventually a great deal of research into the history of the comics and the people behind them.

In 1976, DC took an odd step and revived *All Star Comics* featuring the Justice Society. The oddity was not in the revival of the characters, but the numbering of the series. They started with *All Star Comics* #58, as if the 61 subsequent issues of *All Star Western* never happened. This series lasted until 1978. The JSA appeared briefly in *Adventure Comics*, then was relegated to only the Justice League crossovers, one-shots, mini-series and other guest appearances until 1999.

AFTERMATH & REBIRTH

In the intervening years, those collectors with copies of the clubs kits should have started sending thank-you notes to all of the mothers and kids who discarded their kits. In many of the cases, particularly with the later kits, less than 10 copies are known to exist.

When the 1997 re-launch of the Justice League, entitled simply *JLA*, proved to be a major hit, it spawned the 1999 introduction of *JSA*, the first on-going title to feature the Justice Society in more than 20 years.

With the creation of their DC Direct label, DC Comics launched a line of toys based on their comic characters. They included many different Justice Society items featuring the team, its villains, and a number of the individual characters. It had been a half-century since the last JSA collectibles other than comics themselves had been produced.

Since the early DC Direct toys saw distribution limited to comic book specialty shops, many of these items will prove a worthy challenge to track down for JSA collectors who are only now becoming aware that their collection will no longer be complete if it ends with the club kits for Junior Justice Society of America.

This article appeared in different form in The Official Hake's Price Guide To Character Toys #5, also from Random House. J.C. Vaughn is the Executive Editor of Gemstone Publishing and the writer of numerous comic books, including Shi and 24.

Welcome to the hobby of comic book collecting! This section has an abbreviated version of the annual **The Official Overstreet Comic Book Price Guide**, now in its 36th consecutive year of publication. The **Guide** remains the most comprehensive reference work available on comic book pricing and history, and is respected and used by dealers and collectors everywhere. The Overstreet pricing and grading standards are the accepted foundations of the comic book marketplace around the world, and we have not earned this privilege easily. Through hard work, diligence and constant contact with the market for decades, Overstreet has become the most trusted name in comics.

How to Use This Book

This volume provides some selected listings for Silver Age through Modern Age comics from 1956 to the present. Comic books are listed by their title, regardless of company. Prices listed are shown in Good, Fine, and Near Mint- condition. Many of the comic books are listed in groups, i.e., 11-20, 21-30, 31-50, etc. The prices listed opposite these groupings represent the value of each issue in that group. More detailed information is given for individual comic books where warranted, such as publication dates, creators, and significant story and/or character notations.

Comic Book Values

Values listed in this book represent an average range of what one might expect to pay for the corresponding items. With input from a network of experienced advisors, we have undertaken significant effort to assemble this pricing information. We have earned our reputation for our cautious, conservative approach to pricing.

How Comics Are Listed

Comic books are listed alphabetically by title. The true title of a comic book can usually be found listed with the publisher's information, or indicia, often found at the bottom of the first page. Titles that appear on the front cover can vary from the official title listed inside.

Comic book titles, sequence of issues, dates of first and last issues, publishing companies, origin and special issues are listed when known. Prominent and collectible artists are also pointed out.

PRICING IN THIS GUIDE: Prices for **GD 2.0** (Good), **FN 6.0** (Fine) and **NM-9.2** (Near Mint-) are listed in whole U.S. dollars except for prices below $6 which show dollars and cents. **The minimum price listed is $2.25**, the cover price for current new comics. Many books listed at this price can be found in 25¢ boxes at conventions and dealers stores.

ABADAZAD
CrossGen (Code 6): Mar, 2004 - No. 3, May, 2004 ($2.95)

1-3-Ploog-a/c; DeMatteis-s			3.00
1-2nd printing with new cover			3.00

ABBOTT AND COSTELLO (TV)
Charlton Comics: Feb, 1968 - No. 22, Aug, 1971 (Hanna-Barbera)

1	9	27	120
2	5	15	60
3-10	4	12	45
11-22	3	10	35

ABC (See America's Best TV Comics)

ABSENT-MINDED PROFESSOR, THE
Dell Publishing Co.: Apr, 1961 (Disney)

Four Color #1199-Movie, photo-c	9	27	115

ABSOLUTE VERTIGO
DC Comics (Vertigo): Winter, 1995 (99¢, mature)

nn-1st app. Preacher. Previews upcoming titles including Jonah Hex: Riders of the Worm, The Invisibles & Preacher	1	3	9

ABYSS, THE (Movie)
Dark Horse Comics: June, 1989 - No. 2, July, 1989 ($2.25, limited series)

1,2-Adaptation of film; Kaluta & Moebius-a			3.00

ACME NOVELTY LIBRARY, THE
Fantagraphics Books: Winter 1993-94 - Present (quarterly, various sizes)

1-Introduces Jimmy Corrigan; Chris Ware-s/a in all	7.00
1-2nd and later printings	4.00
2,3: 2-Quimby	5.00
4-Sparky's Best Comics & Stories	6.00
5-12: Jimmy Corrigan in all	5.00
13,15-($10.95-c)	11.00
14-($12.95-c) Concludes Jimmy Corrigan saga	13.00
Jimmy Corrigan, The Smartest Kid on Earth (2000, Pantheon Books, Hardcover, $27.50, 380 pgs.) Collects Jimmy Corrigan stories; folded dust jacket	27.50
Jimmy Corrigan, The Smartest Kid on Earth (2003, Softcover, $17.95)	18.00

NOTE: *Multiple printings exist for most issues.*

ACTION COMICS (...Weekly #601-642) (Also see Promotional Comics)
DC Comics: No. 202, March, 1955 - Present

202-220,232: 212-(1/56)-Includes 1956 Superman calendar that is part of story. 232-1st Curt Swan-c in Action	42	126	525

	GD	FN	NM-

221-231,233-240: 221-1st S.A. issue. 224-1st Golden Gorilla story.
   228-(5/57)-Kongorilla in Congo Bill story (Congorilla try-out)

	39	117	425

241,243-251: 241-Batman x-over. 248-Origin/1st app. Congorilla; Congo Bill
   renamed Congorilla. 251-Last Tommy Tomorrow   33   99   360

242-Origin & 1st app. Brainiac (7/58); 1st mention of Shrunken City of Kandor

	139	417	2650

252-Origin & 1st app. Supergirl (5/59); intro new Metallo

	147	441	2800

253-2nd app. Supergirl	52	156	650
254-1st meeting of Bizarro & Superman-c/story	40	120	475

255-1st Bizarro Lois Lane-c/story & both Bizarros leave Earth to make
   Bizarro World; 3rd app. Supergirl   35   105   385

256-260: 259-Red Kryptonite used	22	66	240

261-1st X-Kryptonite which gave Streaky his powers; last Congorilla in Action;
   origin & 1st app. Streaky The Super Cat   24   72   260

262,264-266,268-270	20	60	210
263-Origin Bizarro World	25	75	270

267(8/60)-3rd Legion app; 1st app. Chameleon Boy, Colossal Boy, & Invisible
   Kid, 1st app. of Supergirl as Superwoman.   50   150   625

271-275,277-282: 274-Lois Lane as Superwoman; 282-Last 10¢ issue

	17	51	175

276(5/61)-6th Legion app; 1st app. Brainiac 5, Phantom Girl, Triplicate Girl,
   Bouncing Boy, Sun Boy, & Shrinking Violet; Supergirl joins Legion

	30	90	320

283(12/61)-Legion of Super-Villains app. 1st 12¢	12	36	180
284(1/62)-Mon-el app.	12	36	180

285(2/62)-12th Legion app; Brainiac 5 cameo; Supergirl's existence revealed
   to world; JFK & Jackie cameos   15   45   225

286-287,289-292,294-299: 286(3/62)-Legion of Super Villains app.
   287(4/62)-15th Legion app. (cameo). 289(6/62)-16th Legion app. (Adult);
   Lightning Man & Saturn Woman's marriage 1st revealed. 290(7/62)-Legion
   app. (cameo); Phantom Girl app. 1st Supergirl emergency squad.
   297-Mon-el app. 298-Legion cameo   10   30   140

288-Mon-el app.; r-origin Supergirl	11	33	150
293-Origin Comet (Superhorse)	13	39	185
300-(5/63)	12	36	170

301-303,305,307,308,310-312,315-320: 307-Saturn Girl app. 317-Death of
   Nor-Kan of Kandor. 319-Shrinking Violet app.   7   21   90

304,306,313: 304-Origin/1st app. Black Flame (9/63). 306-Brainiac 5, Mon-El
   app. 313-Batman app.   8   24   95

309-(2/64)-Legion app.;Batman & Robin-c & cameo; JFK app. (he died
   11/22/63; on stands last week of Dec, 1963)   8   24   100

314-Retells origin Supergirl; J.L.A. x-over	8	24	95
321-333,335-339: 336-Origin Akvar (Flamebird)	6	18	75

334-Giant G-20; origin Supergirl, Streaky, Superhorse & Legion (all-r)

	11	33	150

340-Origin, 1st app. of the Parasite	7	21	85

341,344,350,358: 341-Batman app. in Supergirl back-up story. 344-Batman

	GD	FN	NM-
x-over. 350-Batman, Green Arrow & Green Lantern app. in Supergirl back-up story. 358-Superboy meets Supergirl	5	15	60
342,343,345,346,348,349,351-357,359: 342-UFO story. 345-Allen Funt/ Candid Camera story	5	15	55
347,360-Giant Supergirl G-33,G-45; 347-Origin Comet-r plus Bizarro story. 360-Legion-r; r/origin Supergirl	8	24	95
361-364,367-372,374-378: 361-2nd app. Parasite. 363-366-Leper/Death story. 370-New facts about Superman's origin. 376-Last Supergirl in Action. 377-Legion begins (thru #392)	4	12	45
365,366: 365-JLA & Legion app. 366-JLA app.	4	12	50
373-Giant Supergirl G-57; Legion-r	7	21	85
379-399,401: 388-Sgt. Rock app. 392-Batman-c/app.; last Legion in Action; Saturn Girl gets new costume. 393-401-All Superman issues	3	9	30
400	4	12	42
402-Last 15¢ issue; Superman vs. Supergirl duel	3	10	35
403-413: All 52 pg. issues. 411-Origin Eclipso-(r). 413-Metamorpho begins, ends #418	4	12	38
414-424: 419-Intro. Human Target. 421-Intro Capt. Strong; Green Arrow begins. 422,423-Origin Human Target	2	6	16
425-Neal Adams-a(p); The Atom begins	3	9	24
426-431,433-436,438,439	2	6	12
432-1st S.A. Toyman app (2/74).	2	6	22
437,443-(100 pg. Giants)	4	12	50
440-1st Grell-a on Green Arrow	2	6	16
441,442,444-448: 441-Grell-a on Green Arrow continues	1	4	10
449-(68 pgs.)	2	6	16
450-465,467-483,486,489-499: 454-Last Atom. 456-Grell Jaws-c. 458-Last Green Arrow	1	3	7
466,485,487,488: 466-Batman, Flash app. 485-Adams-c. 487,488-(44 pgs.). 487-Origin Atom retold	1	3	9
481-483,485-492,495-498,501-508-Whitman variants (low print run; none show issue # on cover)	1	3	7
484-Earth II Superman & Lois Lane wed; 40th anniversary issue(6/78)	1	4	10
484-Variant includes 3-D Superman punchout doll in cello. pack; 4 different inserts; Canadian promo?)	2	6	15
500-($1.00, 68 pgs.)-Infinity-c; Superman life story; shows Legion statues in museum	1	4	10
501-543,545,547-551: 511-514-Airwave II solo stories. 513-The Atom begins. 517-Aquaman begins; ends #541. 521-1st app. The Vixen. 532,536-New Teen Titans cameo. 535,536-Omega Men app. 551-Starfire becomes Red-Star			3.00
504,505,507,508-Whitman variants (no cover price)			6.00
544-(6/83, Mando paper, 68 pgs.)-45th Anniversary issue; origins new Luthor & Brainiac; Omega Men cameo; Shuster-a (pin-up); article by Siegel	1	3	7
546-J.L.A., New Teen Titans app.	1	3	8

	GD	FN	NM-
552,553-Animal Man-c & app. (2/84 & 3/84)			5.00
554-582			3.00
583-Alan Moore scripts; last Earth 1 Superman story (cont'd from Superman #423)	1	4	10
584-Byrne-a begins; New Teen Titans app.			6.00
585-599: 586-Legends x-over. 596-Millennium x-over; Spectre app. 598-1st Checkmate			3.00
600-($2.50, 84 pgs., 5/88)			6.00
601-610,619-642: (#601-642 are weekly issues) ($1.50, 52 pgs.) 601-Re-intro The Secret Six; death of Katma Tui			3.00
611-618: 611-614-Catwoman stories (new costume in #611)			3.00
643-Superman & monthly issues begin again; Perez-c/a/scripts begin; swipes cover to Superman #1			4.00
644-649,651-661,663-673,675-683: 645-1st app. Maxima. 654-Part 3 of Batman storyline. 655-Free extra 8 pgs. 660-Death of Lex Luthor. 661-Begin $1.00-c. 667-($1.75, 52 pgs.). 675-Deathstroke cameo. 679-Last $1.00 issue. 683-Doomsday cameo			2.50
650-($1.50, 52 pgs.)-Lobo cameo (last panel)			3.00
662-Clark Kent reveals i.d. to Lois Lane; story cont'd in Superman #53			4.00
674-Supergirl logo & c/story (reintro)			5.00
683-685-2nd & 3rd printings			2.25
684-Doomsday battle issue			3.00
685,686-Funeral for a Friend issues; Supergirl app.			2.50
687-($1.95)-Collector's Ed.w/die-cut-c			2.50
687-($1.50)-Newsstand Edition with mini-poster			2.25
688-699,701-703-($1.50): 688-Guy Gardner-c/story. 697-Bizarro-c/story. 703-(9/94)-Zero Hour			2.25
695-($2.50)-Collector's Edition w/embossed foil-c			2.50
700-($2.95, 68 pgs.)-Fall of Metropolis Pt 1, Guice-a; Pete Ross marries Lana Lang and Smallville flashbacks with Curt Swan art & Murphy Anderson inks			3.00
700-Platinum			15.00
700-Gold			18.00
0(10/94), 704(11/94)-710-719,721-731: 710-Begin $1.95-c. 714-Joker app. 719-Batman-c/app. 721-Mr. Mxyzptlk app. 723-Dave Johnson-c. 727-Final Night x-over.			2.25
720-Lois breaks off engagement w/Clark			3.00
720-2nd print.			2.25
732-749,751-767: 732-New powers. 733-New costume, Ray app. 738-Immonen-s/a(p) begins. 741-Legion app. 745-747-70's-style Superman vs. Prankster. 753-JLA-c/app. 757-Hawkman-c. 760-1st Encantadora. 761-Wonder Woman app. 765-Joker & Harley-c/app. 766-Batman-c/app.			2.25
750-($2.95)			3.00
768,769,771-774: 768-Begin $2.25-c; Marvel Family-c/app. 771-Nightwing app. 772,773-Ra's al Ghul app. 774-Martian Manhunter-c/app.			2.25
770-($3.50) Conclusion of Emperor Joker x-over			3.50
775-($3.75) Bradstreet-c; intro. The Elite			3.75
776-799: 776-Farewell to Krypton; Rivoche-c. 780-782-Our Worlds at War			

	GD	FN	NM-

x-over. 781-Hippolyta and Major Lane killed. 782-War ends. 784-Joker:
Last Laugh; Batman & Green Lantern app. 793-Return to Krypton.
795-The Elite app. 798-Van Fleet-c 2.25
800-(4/03, $3.95) Struzan painted-c; guest artists include Ross, Jim Lee,
   Jurgens, Sale 4.00
801-811: 801-Raney-a. 809-The Creeper app. 811-Mr. Majestic app. 2.25
812-Godfall part 1; Turner-c; Caldwell-a(p) 4.00
812-2nd printing; B&W sketch-c by Turner 3.00
813-Godfall pt. 4; Turner-c; Caldwell-a(p) 3.00
814-822: 814-Reis-a/Art Adams-c; Darkseid app.; begin $2.50-c.
   815,816-Teen Titans-c/app. 820-Doomsday app. 2.50
#1,000,000 (11/98) Gene Ha-c; 853rd Century x-over 2.25
Annual 1-6('87-'94, $2.95)-1-Art Adams-c/a(p); Batman app. 2-Perez-c/a(i).
   3-Armageddon 2001. 4-Eclipso vs. Shazam. 5-Bloodlines; 1st app. Loose
   Cannon. 6-Elseworlds story 3.00
Annual 7,9 ('95, '97, $3.95)-7-Year One story. 9-Pulp Heroes sty 4.00
Annual 8 (1996, $2.95)-Legends of the Dead Earth story 3.00

ADAM-12 (TV)
Gold Key: Dec, 1973 - No. 10, Feb, 1976 (Photo-c)

1	8	24	95
2-10	4	12	42

ADDAMS FAMILY (TV cartoon)
Gold Key: Oct, 1974 - No. 3, Apr, 1975 (Hanna-Barbera)

1	10	30	140
2,3	7	21	85

ADVENTURE COMICS (...Presents Dial H For Hero #479-490)
National Periodical Publications/DC Comics: No. 200, May, 1954 - No. 503,
Sept, 1983

200 (5/54)	55	165	685
201-208: 207-Last Johnny Quick (not in 205)	40	120	440
209-Last pre-code issue; origin Speedy	40	120	460
210-1st app. Krypto (Superdog)-c/story (3/55)	294	882	5300
211-213,215-219	37	112	410
214-2nd app. Krypto	57	171	740
220-Krypto-c/sty	40	120	475

221-246: 229-1st S.A. issue. 237-1st Intergalactic Vigilante Squadron (6/57).
   239-Krypto-c   32   96   350
247(4/58)-1st Legion of Super Heroes app.; 1st app. Cosmic Boy, Saturn Girl
   & Lightning Boy (later Lightning Lad in #267) 364 1092 8000
248-252,254,255-Green Arrow in all: 255-Intro. Red Kryptonite in Superboy
   (used in #252 but with no effect)   27   81   290
253-1st meeting of Superboy & Robin; Green Arrow by Kirby in #250-255
   (also see World's Finest #96-99)   32   96   350
256-Origin Green Arrow by Kirby   65   195   850
257-259: 258-Green Arrow x-over in Superboy 22   66   240
260-1st Silver-Age origin Aquaman (5/59)   75   225   975
261-265,268,270: 262-Origin Speedy in Green Arrow. 270-Congorilla begins,

	GD	FN	NM-
ends #281,283	18	54	190
266-(11/59)-Origin & 1st app. Aquagirl (tryout, not same as later character)			
	19	57	200
267(12/59)-2nd Legion of Super Heroes; Lightning Boy now called Lightning Lad; new costumes for Legion	90	270	1175
269-Intro. Aqualad (2/60); last Green Arrow (not in #206)			
	31	93	340
271-Origin Luthor retold	35	105	375
272-274,277-280: 279-Intro White Kryptonite in Superboy. 280-1st meeting Superboy & Lori Lemaris	16	48	170
275-Origin Superman-Batman team retold (see World's Finest #94)			
	26	78	275
276-(9/60) Robinson Crusoe-like story	17	51	180
281,284,287-289: 281-Last Congorilla. 284-Last Aquaman in Adv.; Mooney-a. 287,288-Intro Dev-Em, the Knave from Krypton. 287-1st Bizarro Perry White & Jimmy Olsen. 288-Bizarro-c.	15	45	155
282(3/61)-5th Legion app; intro/origin Star Boy	28	84	300
283-Intro. The Phantom Zone	25	75	270
285-1st Tales of the Bizarro World-c/story (ends #299) in this title (see Action #255)	21	63	225
286-1st Bizarro Mxyzptlk; Bizarro-c	20	60	210
290(11/61)-9th Legion app; origin Sunboy in Legion (last 10¢ issue)			
	26	78	280
291,292,295-298: 291-1st 12¢ ish, (12/61). 292-1st Bizarro Lana Lang & Lucy Lane. 295-Bizarro-c; 1st Bizarro Titano	11	33	145
293(2/62)-13th Legion app; Mon-el & Legion of Super Pets (1st app./origin) (1st Superhorse). 1st Bizarro Luthor & Kandor.	16	48	240
294-1st Bizarro Marilyn Monroe, Pres. Kennedy.	12	36	180
299-1st Gold Kryptonite (8/62)	11	33	150
300-Tales of the Legion of Super-Heroes series begins (9/62); Mon-el leaves Phantom Zone (temporarily), joins Legion	38	114	600
301-Origin Bouncing Boy	15	45	220
302-305: 303-1st app. Matter-Eater Lad. 304-Death of Lightning Lad in Legion	11	33	160
306-310: 306-Intro. Legion of Substitute Heroes. 307-1st app. Element Lad in Legion. 308-1st app. Lightning Lass in Legion	11	33	145
311-320: 312-Lightning Lad back in Legion. 315-Last new Superboy story; Colossal Boy app. 316-Origins & powers of Legion given. 317-Intro. Dream Girl in Legion; Lightning Lass becomes Light Lass; Hall of Fame series begins. 320-Dev-Em 2nd app.	9	27	120
321-Intro. Time Trapper	8	24	105
322-330: 327-Intro/1st app. Lone Wolf in Legion. 329-Intro The Bizarro Legionnaires; intro. Legion flight rings	7	21	90
331-340: 337-Chlorophyll Kid & Night Girl app. 340-Intro Computo in Legion			
	7	21	80
341-Triplicate Girl becomes Duo Damsel	6	18	70
342-345,347-351: 345-Last Hall of Fame; returns in 356,371. 348-Origin Sunboy; intro Dr. Regulus in Legion. 349-Intro Universo & Rond Vidar. 351-1st app. White Witch	6	18	65

	GD	FN	NM-

346-1st app. Karate Kid, Princess Projectra, Ferro Lad, & Nemesis Kid.

	8	24	95

352,354-360: 354,355-Superman meets the Adult Legion. 355-Insect Queen
    joins Legion (4/67) | 5 | 15 | 60

353-Death of Ferro Lad in Legion | 7 | 21 | 80

361-364,366,368-370: 369-Intro Mordru in Legion | 4 | 12 | 50

365,367: 365-Intro Shadow Lass (memorial to Shadow Woman app. in #354's
    Adult Legion-s); lists origins & powers of L.S.H. 367-New Legion
    headquarters | 5 | 15 | 55

371,372: 371-Intro. Chemical King (mentioned in #354's Adult Legion-s).
    372-Timber Wolf & Chemical King join | 5 | 15 | 55

373,374,376-380: 373-Intro. Tornado Twins (Barry Allen Flash descendants).
    374-Article on comics fandom. 380-Last Legion in Adventure; last 12¢-c

	4	12	48

375-Intro Quantum Queen & The Wanderers | 5 | 15 | 55

381-Supergirl begins; 1st full length Supergirl story & her 1st solo book (6/69)

	10	30	135

382-389 | 4 | 12 | 45

390-Giant Supergirl G-69 | 6 | 18 | 75

391-396,398 | 3 | 10 | 35

397-1st app. new Supergirl | 4 | 12 | 50

399-Unpubbed G.A. Black Canary story | 4 | 12 | 40

400-New costume for Supergirl (12/70) | 4 | 12 | 50

401,402,404-408-(15¢-c) | 3 | 9 | 25

403-68 pg. Giant G-81; Legion-r/#304,305,308,312 | 6 | 18 | 75

409-411,413-415,417-420-(52 pgs.): 413-Hawkman by Kubert r/B&B #44;
    G.A. Robotman-r/Det. #178; Zatanna by Morrow. 414-r-2nd Animal
    Man/Str. Advs. #184. 415-Animal Man-r/Str. Adv.#190 (origin recap).
    417-Morrow Vigilante; Frazetta Shining Knight-r/Adv. #161; origin The
    Enchantress; no Zatanna. 418-Prev. unpub. Dr. Mid-Nite story from 1948;
    no Zatanna. 420-Animal Man-r/Str. Adv. #195 | 3 | 10 | 35

412-(52 pgs.) Reprints origin & 1st app. of Animal Man from Strange
    Adventures #180 | 3 | 10 | 35

416-Also listed as DC 100 Pg. Super Spectacular #10; Golden Age-r; r/1st
    app. Black Canary from Flash #86; no Zatanna | 11 | 33 | 145

421-424,427: 424-Last Supergirl in Adventure. 427-Last Vigilante

	2	6	15

425-New look, content change to adventure; Kaluta-c; Toth-a, origin
    Capt. Fear | 3 | 9 | 30

426-1st Adventurers Club | 2 | 6 | 15

428-Origin/1st app. Black Orchid (c/story, 6-7/73) | 6 | 18 | 70

429,430-Black Orchid-c/stories | 3 | 10 | 35

431-Spectre by Aparo begins, ends #440. | 6 | 18 | 75

432-439-Spectre app. 433-437-Cover title is Weird Adventure Comics.
    436-Last 20¢ issue | 4 | 12 | 38

440-New Spectre origin. | 4 | 12 | 50

441-458: 441-452-Aquaman app. 443-Fisherman app. 445-447-The Creeper
    app. 446-Flag-c. 449-451-Martian Manhunter app. 450-Weather Wizard
    app. in Aquaman story. 453-458-Superboy app. 453-Intro. Mighty Girl.

	GD	FN	NM-

457,458-Eclipso app.   1   3   9

459,460 (68 pgs.): 459-New Gods/Darkseid storyline concludes from New Gods #19 (#459 is dated 9-10/78) without missing a month. 459-Flash (ends #466), Deadman (ends #466), Wonder Woman (ends #464), Green Lantern (ends #460). 460-Aquaman (ends #478)   3   9   24

461,462 ($1.00, 68 pgs.): 461-Justice Society begins; ends 466. 461,462-Death Earth II Batman   3   10   35

463-466 ($1.00 size, 68 pgs.)   2   6   16

467-Starman by Ditko & Plastic Man begins; 1st app. Prince Gavyn (Starman)   2   6   12

468-490: 470-Origin Starman. 479-Dial 'H' For Hero begins, ends #490. 478-Last Starman & Plastic Man. 480-490: Dial 'H' For Hero   5.00

491-503: 491-100pg. Digest size begins; r/Legion of Super Heroes/Adv. #247, #267; Spectre, Aquaman, Superboy, S&K Sandman, Black Canary-r & new Shazam by Newton begin. 492,495,496,499-S&K Sandman-r/Adventure in all. 493-Challengers of the Unknown begins by Tuska w/brief origin. 493-495,497-499-G.A. Captain Marvel-r. 494-499-Spectre-r/Spectre 1-3, 5-7. 496-Capt. Marvel Jr. new-s, Cockrum-a. 498-Mary Marvel new-s; Plastic Man-r begin. 500-Legion-r (Digest size, 148 pgs.). 501-503: G.A.-r   2   6   16

... 80 Page Giant (10/98, $4.95) Wonder Woman, Shazam, Superboy, Supergirl, Green Arrow, Legion, Bizarro World stories   5.00

ADVENTURE COMICS (Also see All Star Comics 1999 crossover titles)
DC Comics: May, 1999 ($1.99, one-shot)

1-Golden Age Starman and the Atom; Snejbjerg-a   2.25

ADVENTURES IN THE DC UNIVERSE
DC Comics: Apr, 1997 - No. 19, Oct, 1998 ($1.75/$1.95/$1.99)

1-Animated style in all: JLA-c/app.   5.00

2-11,13-17,19: 2-Flash app. 3-Wonder Woman. 4-Green Lantern. 6-Aquaman. 7-Shazam Family. 8-Blue Beetle & Booster Gold. 9-Flash. 10-Legion. 11-Green Lantern & Wonder Woman. 13-Impulse & Martian Manhunter. 14-Superboy/Flash race   3.50

12,18-JLA-c/app   3.50

Annual 1(1997, $3.95)-Dr. Fate, Impulse, Rose & Thorn, Superboy, Mister Miracle app.   4.50

ADVENTURES INTO THE UNKNOWN
American Comics Group: No. 51, Jan, 1954 - No. 174, Aug, 1967 (1st continuous series Supernatural comic; see Eerie #1)

	GD	FN	NM-
51-(1/54)-(3-D effect-c/story)-Only white cover	38	114	420
52-58: (3-D effect-c/stories with black covers). 52-E.C. swipe of Haunt Of Fear #14	36	108	390
59-3-D effect story only; new logo	29	87	310
60-Woodesque-a by Landau	15	45	150
61-Last pre-code issue (1-2/55)	15	45	150
62-70	8	24	105
71-90	7	21	85
91,96(#95 on inside),107,116-All have Williamson-a	8	24	100

	GD	FN	NM-
92-95,97-99,101-106,108-115,117-128: 109-113,118-Whitney painted-c. 128-Williamson/Krenkel/Torres-a(r)/Forbidden Worlds #63; last 10¢ issue	6	18	65
100	6	18	70
129-153,157: 153,157-Magic Agent app.	4	12	50
154-Nemesis series begins (origin), ends #170	6	18	65
155,156,158-167,170-174	4	12	48
168-Ditko-a(p)	5	15	60
169-Nemesis battles Hitler	5	15	60

ADVENTURES OF BARRY WEEN, BOY GENIUS, THE (Also see Free Comic Book Day Edition in the Promotional Comics section)
Image Comics: Mar, 1999 - No. 3, May, 1999 ($2.95, B&W, limited series)

1-3-Judd Winick-s/a	3.00
TPB (Oni Press, 11/99, $8.95)	9.00

ADVENTURES OF BARRY WEEN, BOY GENIUS 2.0, THE
Oni Press: Feb, 2000 - No. 3, Apr, 2000 ($2.95, B&W, limited series)

1-3-Judd Winick-s/a	3.00
TPB (2000, $8.95)	9.00

ADVENTURES OF BARRY WEEN, BOY GENIUS 3, THE : MONKEY TALES
Oni Press: Feb, 2001 - No. 6, Feb, 2002 ($2.95, B&W, limited series)

1-6-Judd Winick-s/a	3.00
TPB (2001, $8.95) r/#1-3; intro. by Peter David	9.00
...4 TPB (5/02, $8.95) r/#4-6	9.00

ADVENTURES OF BOB HOPE, THE
National Per. Publ.: No. 32, April-May, 1952 - No. 109, Feb-Mar, 1968

32-40	11	33	150
41-50	9	27	120
51-70	7	21	90
71-93	5	15	60
94-Aquaman cameo	6	18	65
95-1st app. Super-Hip & 1st monster issue (11/65)	7	21	85
96-105: Super-Hip and monster stories in all. 103-Batman, Robin, Ringo Starr cameos	5	15	60
106-109-All monster-c/stories by N. Adams-c/a	7	21	90

ADVENTURES OF CAPTAIN AMERICA
Marvel Comics: Sept, 1991 - No. 4, Jan, 1992 ($4.95, 52 pgs., squarebound, limited series)

1-4: 1-Origin in WW2; embossed-c; Nicieza scripts; Maguire-c/a(p) begins, ends #3. 2-4-Austin-c/a(i). 3,4-Red Skull app.	5.00

ADVENTURES OF CYCLOPS AND PHOENIX
Marvel Comics: May, 1994 - No. 4, Aug, 1994 ($2.95, limited series)

1-4-Characters from X-Men; origin of Cable	4.00
Trade paperback ($14.95)-reprints #1-4	15.00

ADVENTURES OF JERRY LEWIS, THE (Adventures of Dean Martin & Jerry Lewis No. 1-40) (See Super DC Giant)

	GD	FN	NM-

National Periodical Publ.: No. 41, Nov, 1957 - No. 124, May-June, 1971

41	9	27	120
42-60	7	21	90
61-67,69-73,75-80	6	18	75
68,74-Photo-c (movie)	8	24	100
81,82,85-87,90,91,94,96,98,99	5	15	60

83,84,88: 83-1st Monsters-c/s. 84-Jerry as a Super-hero-c/s. 88-1st Witch,

Miss Kraft	6	18	70

89-Bob Hope app.; Wizard of Oz & Alfred E. Neuman in MAD parody

	7	21	80
92-Superman cameo	7	21	80
93-Beatles parody as babies	6	18	70
95-1st Uncle Hal Wack-A-Boy Camp-c/s	6	18	70

97-Batman/Robin/Joker-c/story; Riddler & Penguin app; Dick Sprang-c.

	10	30	130
100	6	18	75
101,103,104-Neal Adams-c/a	7	21	90
102-Beatles app.; Neal Adams c/a	9	27	120
105-Superman x-over	7	21	80
106-111,113-116	4	12	48
112,117: 112-Flash x-over. 117-W. Woman x-over	7	21	80
118-124	4	12	42

ADVENTURES OF MIGHTY MOUSE (2nd Series) (Becomes Mighty Mouse #161 on)(Two No. 144's; formerly Paul Terry's Comics; No. 129-137 have nn's)
St. John/Pines/Dell/Gold Key: No. 126, Aug, 1955 - No. 160, Oct, 1963

126(8/55), 127(10/55), 128(11/55)-St. John	9	27	80
nn(129, 4/56)-144(8/59)-Pines	5	15	60
144(10-12/59)-155(7-9/62) Dell	5	15	55
156(10/62)-160(10/63) Gold Key	5	15	55

ADVENTURES OF MIGHTY MOUSE (Formerly Mighty Mouse)
Gold Key: No. 166, Mar, 1979 - No. 172, Jan, 1980

166-172	1	3	8

ADVENTURES OF ROBIN HOOD, THE
Gold Key: Mar, 1974 - No. 7, Jan, 1975 (Disney cartoon) (36 pgs.)

1(90291-403)-Part-r of $1.50 editions	2	6	20
2-7: 1-7 are part-r	2	6	12

ADVENTURES OF SPIDER-MAN, THE (Based on animated TV series)
Marvel Comics: Apr, 1996 - No. 12, Mar, 1997 (99¢)

1-12: 1-Punisher app. 2-Venom cameo. 3-X-Men. 6-Fantastic Four			3.00

ADVENTURES OF SUPERBOY, THE (See Superboy, 2nd Series)

ADVENTURES OF SUPERMAN (Formerly Superman)
DC Comics: No. 424, Jan, 1987 - No. 499, Feb, 1993; No. 500, Early June, 1993 - Present

424-Ordway-c/a/Wolfman-s begin following Byrne's Superman revamp			3.00

425-435,437-462: 426-Legends x-over. 432-1st app. Jose Delgado who

	GD	FN	NM-

becomes Gangbuster in #434. 437-Millennium x-over. 438-New Brainiac
    app. 440-Batman app. 449-Invasion   3.00
436-Byrne scripts begin; Millennium x-over   3.50
463-Superman/Flash race; cover swipe/Superman #199   5.00
464-Lobo-c & app. (pre-dates Lobo #1)   4.00
465-495: 467-Part 2 of Batman story. 473-Hal Jordan, Guy Gardner x-over.
    477-Legion app. 491-Last $1.00-c. 480-($1.75, 52 pgs.). 495-Forever
    People-c/story; Darkseid app.   2.50
496,497: 496-Doomsday cameo. 497-Doomsday battle issue   3.00
496,497-2nd printings   2.25
498,499-Funeral for a Friend; Supergirl app.   2.50
498-2nd & 3rd printings   2.25
500-($2.95, 68 pgs.)-Collector's edition w/card   3.50
500-($2.50, 68 pgs.)-Regular edition w/different-c   2.50
500-Platinum edition   30.00
501-($1.95)-Collector's edition with die-cut-c   2.25
501-($1.50)-Regular edition w/mini-poster & diff.-c   2.25
502-516: 502-Supergirl-c/story. 508-Challengers of the Unknown app.
    510-Bizarro-c/story. 516-(9/94)-Zero Hour   2.25
505-($2.50)-Holo-grafx foil-c edition   2.50
0,517-523: 0-(10/94). 517-(11/94)   2.25
524-549,551-580: 524-Begin $1.95-c. 527-Return of Alpha Centurion (Zero
    Hour). 533-Impulse-c/app. 535-Luthor-c/app. 536-Brainiac app.
    537-Parasite app. 540-Final Night x-over. 541-Superboy-c/app.; Lois &
    Clark honeymoon. 545-New powers. 546-New costume. 555-Red & Blue
    Supermen battle. 557-Millennium Giants x-over. 558-560: Superman
    Silver Age-style story; Krypto app. 561-Begin $1.99-c. 565-JLA app. 2.25
550-($3.50)-Double sized   3.50
581-588: 581-Begin $2.25-c. 583-Emperor Joker. 588-Casey-s   2.25
589-595: 589-Return to Krypton; Rivoche-c. 591-Wolfman-s. 593-595-Our
    Worlds at War x-over. 594-Doomsday-c/app.   2.25
596-Aftermath of "War" x-over has panel showing damaged World Trade
    Center buildings; issue went on sale the day after the Sept. 11 attack 5.00
597-599,601-624: 597-Joker: Last Laugh. 604,605-Ultraman, Owlman,
    Superwoman app. 606-Return to Krypton. 612-616,619-623-Nowlan-c.
    624-Mr. Majestic app.   2.25
600-($3.95)-Wieringo-a; painted-c by Adel; pin-ups by various   4.00
625,626-Godfall parts 2,5; Turner-c; Caldwell-a(p)   3.00
627-634: 627-Begin $2.50-c, Rucka-s/Clark-a/Ha-c begin. 628-Wagner-c.
    631-Bagged with Sky Captain CD; Lois shot 634-Mxyzptlk visits DC offices
                                                    2.50
#1,000,000 (11/98) Gene Ha-c; 853rd Century x-over   3.00
Annual 1 (1987, $1.25, 52 pgs.)-Starlin-c & scripts   4.00
Annual 2,3 (1990, 1991, in $2.00, 68 pgs.): 2-Byrne-c/a(i); Legion '90 (Lobo)
    app. 3-Armageddon 2001 x-over   3.00
Annual 4-6 ('92-'94, $2.50, 68 pgs.): 4-Guy Gardner/Lobo-c/story; Eclipso
    storyline; Quesada-c(p). 5-Bloodlines storyline. 6-Elseworlds sty. 3.00
Annual 7,9('95, '97, $3.95)-7-Year One story. 9-Pulp Heroes sty 4.00
Annual 8 (1996, $2.95)-Legends of the Dead Earth story   3.00

	GD	FN	NM-

ADVENTURES OF THE FLY (The Fly #1-6; Fly Man No. 32-39)
Archie Publications/Radio Comics: Aug, 1959 - No. 30, Oct, 1964; No. 31, May, 1965

	GD	FN	NM-
1-Shield app.; origin The Fly; S&K-c/a	49	147	825
2-Williamson, S&K-a	29	87	425
3-Origin retold; Davis, Powell-a	24	72	350
4-Neal Adams-a(p)(1 panel); S&K-c; Powell-a; 2 pg. Shield story	14	42	210
5,6,9,10: 9-Shield app. 9-1st app. Cat Girl. 10-Black Hood app.	10	30	130
7,8: 7-1st S.A. app. Black Hood (7/60). 8-1st S.A. app. Shield (9/60)	11	33	160
11-13,15-20: 13-1st app. Fly Girl w/o costume. 16-Last 10¢ issue. 20-Origin Fly Girl retold	7	21	80
14-Origin & 1st app. Fly Girl in costume	8	24	100
21-30: 23-Jaguar cameo. 27-29-Black Hood 1 pg. strips. 30-Comet x-over (1st S.A. app.) in Fly Girl	5	15	55
31-Black Hood, Shield, Comet app.	5	15	60
Vol. 1 TPB ('04, $12.95) r/#1-4 & Double Life of Private Strong #1,2; foreward by Joe Simon			13.00

ADVENTURES OF THE OUTSIDERS, THE (Formerly Batman & The Outsiders; also see The Outsiders)
DC Comics: No. 33, May, 1986 - No. 46, June, 1987

33-46: 39-45-r/Outsiders #1-7 by Aparo			2.25

ADVENTURES OF THE X-MEN, THE (Based on animated TV series)
Marvel Comics: Apr, 1996 - No. 12, Mar, 1997 (99¢)

1-12: 1-Wolverine/Hulk battle. 3-Spider-Man-c. 5,6-Magneto-c/app.			3.00

ADVENTURES ON THE PLANET OF THE APES (See Planet of the Apes)
Marvel Comics Group: Oct, 1975 - No. 11, Dec, 1976

	GD	FN	NM-
1-Planet of the Apes magazine-r in color; Starlin-c; adapts movie thru #6	3	9	30
2-5: 5-(25¢-c edition)	2	6	16
5-7-(30¢-c variants, limited distribution)	3	9	30
6-10: 6,7-(25¢-c edition). 7-Adapts 2nd movie (thru #11)	2	6	18
11-Last issue; concludes 2nd movie adaptation	2	6	22

A.K.A. GOLDFISH
Caliber Comics: 1994 - 1995 (B&W, $3.50/$3.95)

...:Ace; ...:Jack; ...:Queen; ...:Joker; ...:King -Brian Michael Bendis-s/a			4.00
TPB (1996, $17.95)			20.00
Goldfish: The Definitive Collection (Image, 2001, $19.95) r/series plus promo art and new prose story; intro. by Matt Wagner			20.00
10th Anniversary HC (Image, 2002, $49.95)			50.00

AKIKO
Sirius: Mar, 1996 - Present ($2.50/$2.95, B&W)

1-Crilley-c/a/scripts in all			5.00

	GD	FN	NM-
2			4.00
3-39: 25-($2.95, 32 pgs.)-w/Asala back-up pages			3.00
40-49,51,52: 40-Begin $2.95-c			3.00
50-($3.50)			3.50
Flights of Fancy TPB (5/02, $12.95) r/various features, pin-ups and gags			13.00
TPB Volume 1,4 ('97, 2/00, $14.95) 1-r/#1-7. 4-r/#19-25			15.00
TPB Volume 2,3 ('98, '99, $11.95) 2-r/#8-13. 3- r/#14-18			12.00
TPB Volume 5 (12/01, $12.95) r/#26-31			13.00
TPB Volume 6,7 (6/03, 4/04, $14.95) 6-r/#32-38. 7-r/#40-47			15.00

AKIKO ON THE PLANET SMOO
Sirius: Dec, 1995 ($3.95, B&W)

V1#1-($3.95)-Crilley-c/a/scripts; gatefold-c			5.00
Ashcan ('95, mail offer)			3.00
Hardcover V1#1 (12/95, $19.95, B&W, 40 pgs.)			20.00
The Color Edition(2/00,$4.95)			5.00

AKIRA
Marvel Comics (Epic): Sept, 1988 - No. 38, Dec, 1995 ($3.50/$3.95/$6.95, deluxe, 68 pgs.)

	GD	FN	NM-
1-Manga by Katsuhiro Otomo	3	9	30
1,2-2nd printings (1989, $3.95)			5.00
2	2	6	15
3-5	2	6	12
6-16	1	3	9
17-33: 17-$3.95-c begins			6.00
34-37: 34-(1994)-$6.95-c begins. 35-37: 35-(1995). 37-Texeira back-up, Gibbons, Williams pin-ups	2	6	12
38-Moebius, Allred, Pratt, Toth, Romita, Van Fleet, O'Neill, Madureira pin-ups	2	6	14

ALF (TV) (See Star Comics Digest)
Marvel Comics: Mar, 1988 - No. 50, Feb, 1992 ($1.00)

	GD	FN	NM-
1-Photo-c			4.00
1-2nd printing			2.50
2-19: 6-Photo-c			2.50
20-22: 20-Conan parody. 21-Marx Brothers. 22-X-Men parody			3.00
23-30: 24-Rhonda-c/app. 29-3-D cover			2.50
31-43,46-49			3.00
44,45: 44-X-Men parody. 45-Wolverine, Punisher, Capt. America-c			4.00
50-($1.75, 52 pgs.)-Final issue; photo-c			4.00
Annual 1-3: 1-Rocky & Bullwinkle app. 2-Sienkiewicz-c. 3-TMNT parody			3.00
...Comics Digest 1,2: 1-(1988)-Reprints Alf #1,2	1	3	8
Holiday Special 1,2 ('88, Wint. '89, 68 pgs.): 2-X-Men parody-c			3.00
Spring Special 1 (Spr/89, $1.75, 68 pgs.) Invisible Man parody			3.00
TPB (68 pgs.) r/#1-3; photo-c			5.00

ALIAS (Also see The Pulse)
Marvel Comics (MAX Comics): Nov, 2001 - No. 28, Jan, 2004 ($2.99)

	GD	FN	NM-
1-Bendis-s/Gaydos-a/Mack-c; intro Jessica Jones; Luke Cage app.	1	3	8

	GD	FN	NM-

2-4 ..... 5.00
5-28: 7,8-Sienkiewicz-a (2 pgs.) 16-21-Spider-Woman app. 22,23-Jessica's origin. 24-28-Purple; Avengers app.; flashback-a by Bagley 3.00
HC (2002, $29.99) r/#1-9; intro. by Jeph Loeb 30.00
Vol. 1: TPB (2003, $19.99) r/#1-9 ..... 20.00
Vol. 2: Come Home TPB (2003, $13.99) r/#11-15 ..... 14.00
Vol. 3: The Underneath TPB (2003, $16.99) r/#10,16-21 ..... 17.00

ALIEN RESURRECTION (Movie)
Dark Horse Comics: Oct, 1997 - No. 2, Nov, 1997 ($2.50; limited series)

1,2-Adaptation of film; Dave McKean-c 3.00

ALIENS, THE (Captain Johner and...)(Also see Magnus Robot Fighter...)
Gold Key: Sept-Dec, 1967; No. 2, May, 1982

1-Reprints from Magnus #1,3,4,6-10; Russ Manning-a in all

	4	12	40
2-(Whitman) Same contents as #1	1	3	8

ALIENS (Movie) (See Alien: The Illustrated..., Dark Horse Comics & Dark Horse Presents #24)
Dark Horse Comics: May, 1988 - No. 6, July, 1989 ($1.95, B&W, lim. series)

1-Based on movie sequel;1st app. Aliens in comics	2	6	20
1-2nd - 6th printings; 4th w/new inside front-c			3.00
2	1	3	9
2-2nd & 3rd printing, 3-6-2nd printings			3.00
3	1	3	7
4-6			5.00

Mini Comic #1 (2/89, 4x6")-Was included with Aliens Portfolio 4.00
Collection 1 ($10.95,)-r/#1-6 plus Dark Horse Presents #24 plus new-a 12.00
Collection 1-2nd printing (1991, $11.95)-On higher quality paper than 1st print; Dorman painted-c 12.00
Hardcover ('90, $24.95, B&W)-r/1-6, DHP #24 ..... 30.00
Platinum Edition - (See Dark Horse Presents: Aliens Platinum Edition)

ALIENS
Dark Horse Comics: V2#1, Aug, 1989 - No. 4, 1990 ($2.25, limited series)

V2#1-Painted art by Denis Beauvais 5.00
1-2nd printing (1990), 2-4 ..... 3.00

ALIENS: (Series of titles, all Dark Horse)
--ALCHEMY, 10/97 - No. 3, 11/97 ($2.95),1-3-Corben-c/a, Arcudi-s 3.00
--APOCALYPSE - THE DESTROYING ANGELS, 1/99 - No. 4, 4/99 ($2.95)
1-4-Doug Wheatly-a/Schultz-s 3.00
--BERSERKERS, 1/95 - No. 4, 4/95 ($2.50) 1-4 ..... 3.00
--COLONIAL MARINES, 1/93 - No. 10, 7/94 ($2.50) 1-10 ..... 3.00
--EARTH ANGEL. 8/94 ($2.95) 1-Byrne-a/story; wraparound-c 3.00
--EARTH WAR, 6/90 - No. 4, 10/90 ($2.50) 1-All have Sam Kieth-a & Bolton painted-c 5.00
1-2nd printing, 3,4 ..... 3.00
2 ..... 4.00

	GD	FN	NM-

--GENOCIDE, 11/91 - No. 4, 2/92 ($2.50) 1-4-Suydam painted-c.

    4-Wraparound-c, poster   3.00

--GLASS CORRIDOR, 6/98 ($2.95) 1-David Lloyd-s/a   3.00

--HARVEST (See Aliens: Hive)

--HAVOC, 6/97 - No. 2, 7/97 ($2.95) 1,2: Schultz-s, Kent Williams-c, 40 artists

    including Art Adams, Kelley Jones, Duncan Fegredo, Kevin Nowlan   3.00

--HIVE, 2/92 - No. 4,5/92 ($2.50) 1-4: Kelley Jones-c/a in all   3.00

   ...Harvest TPB ('98, $16.95) r/series; Bolton-c   17.00

--KIDNAPPED, 12/97 - No. 3, 2/98 ($2.50) 1-3   3.00

--LABYRINTH, 9/93 - No. 4, 1/94 ($2.50)1-4: 1-Painted-c   3.00

--LOVESICK, 12/96 ($2.95) 1   3.00

--MONDO HEAT, 2/96 ($2.50) nn-Sequel to Mondo Pest   3.00

--MONDO PEST, 4/95 ($2.95, 44 pgs.)nn-r/Dark Horse Comics #22-24   3.00

--MUSIC OF THE SPEARS, 1/94 - No. 4, 4/94 ($2.50) 1-4   3.00

--NEWT'S TALE, 6/92 - No. 2, 7/92 ($4.95) 1,2-Bolton-c   5.00

--PIG, 3/97 ($2.95)1   3.00

--PREDATOR: THE DEADLIEST OF THE SPECIES, 7/93 - No. 12, 8/95 ($2.50)

   1-Bolton painted-c; Guice-a(p)   5.00

   1-Embossed foil platinum edition   10.00

   2-12: Bolton painted-c. 2,3-Guice-a(p)   3.00

--PURGE, 8/97 ($2.95) nn-Hester-a   3.00

--ROGUE, 4/993 - No. 4, 7/93 ($2.50)1-4: Painted-c   3.00

--SACRIFICE, 5/93 ($4.95, 52 pgs.) nn-P. Milligan scripts; painted-c/a   5.00

--SALVATION, 11/93 ($4.95, 52 pgs.) nn-Mignola-c/a(p); Gibbons script   5.00

--SPECIAL, 6/97 ($2.50) 1   3.00

--STALKER, 6/98 ($2.50)1-David Wenzel-s/a   3.00

--STRONGHOLD, 5/94 - No. 4, 9/94 ($2.50) 1-4   3.00

--SURVIVAL, 2/98 - No. 3, 4/98 ($2.95) 1-3-Tony Harris-c   3.00

--TRIBES, 1992 ($24.95, hardcover graphic novel) Bissette text-s with Dorman

    painted-a   25.00

   ...softcover ($9.95)   10.00

ALIENS VS. PREDATOR (See Dark Horse Presents #36)
Dark Horse Comics: June, 1990 - No. 4, Dec, 1990 ($2.50, limited series)

	GD	FN	NM-
1-Painted-c	1	3	8
1-2nd printing			3.00
0-(7/90, $1.95, B&W)-r/Dark Horse Pres. #34-36	1	3	9
2,3			5.00
4-Dave Dorman painted-c			4.00
Annual (7/99, $4.95) Jae Lee-c			5.00
... : Booty (1/96, $2.50) painted-c			3.00
... : Thrill of the Hunt (9/04, $6.95, digest-size TPB) Based on 2004 film			7.00

	GD	FN	NM-
... Wraith 1 (7/98, $2.95) Jay Stephens-s			3.00
--VS. PREDATOR: DUEL, 3/95 - No. 2, 4/95 ($2.50) 1,2			3.00
--VS. PREDATOR: ETERNAL, 6/98 - No. 4, 9/98 ($2.50)1-4: Edginton-s/ Maleev-a; Fabry-c			3.00
--VS. PREDATOR VS. THE TERMINATOR, 4/00 - No. 4, 7/00 ($2.95) 1-4: Ripley app.			3.00
--VS. PREDATOR: WAR, No. 0, 5/95 - No. 4, 8/95 ($2.50) 0-4: Corben painted-c			3.00
--VS. PREDATOR: XENOGENESIS, 12/99 - No. 4, 3/00 ($2.95) 1-4: Watson-s/Mel Rubi-a			3.00
--XENOGENESIS, 8/99 - No. 4, 11/99 ($2.95) 1-4: T&M Bierbaum-s			3.00

ALIEN: THE ILLUSTRATED STORY (Also see Aliens)
Heavy Metal Books: 1980 ($3.95, soft-c, 8x11")

nn-Movie adaptation; Simonson-a	3	9	24

ALIEN³ (Movie)
Dark Horse Comics: June, 1992 - No. 3, July, 1992 ($2.50, limited series)

1-3: Adapts 3rd movie; Suydam painted-c			3.00

ALL-AMERICAN COMICS (Also see All Star Comics 1999 crossover titles)
DC Comics: May, 1999 ($1.99, one-shot)

1-Golden Age Green Lantern and Johnny Thunder; Barreto-a			2.25

ALL-AMERICAN MEN OF WAR (Previously All-American Western)
National Periodical Publ.: No. 127, Aug-Sept, 1952 - No. 117, Sept-Oct, 1966

127 (#1, 1952)	84	252	1600
128 (1952)	51	153	900
2(12-1/'52-53)-5	44	132	750
6-Devil Dog story; Ghost Squadron story	35	105	560
7-10: 8-Sgt. Storm Cloud-s	35	105	560
11-16,18: 18-Last precode; 1st Kubert-c (2/55)	31	93	475
17-1st Frogman-s in this title	32	96	500
19,20,22-27	23	69	335
21-Easy Co. prototype	26	78	390
28 (12/55)-1st Sgt. Rock prototype; Kubert-a	33	99	525
29,30,32-Wood-a	24	72	350
31,33-38,40: 34-Gunner prototype-s. 35-Greytone-c. 36-Little Sure Shot prototype-s. 38-1st S.A. issue	19	57	275
39 (11/56)-2nd Sgt. Rock prototype; 1st Easy Co.?	29	87	425
41,43-47,49,50: 46-Tankbusters-c/s	15	45	225
42-Pre-Sgt. Rock Easy Co.-c/s	19	57	280
48-Easy Co.-c/s; Nick app.; Kubert-a	19	57	280
51-56,58-62,65,66: 61-Gunner-c/s	12	36	175
57(5/58),63,64 -Pre-Sgt. Rock Easy Co.-c/s	17	51	250
67-1st Gunner & Sarge by Andru & Esposito	33	99	535
68,69: 68-2nd app. Gunner & Sarge. 69-1st Tank Killer-c/s	15	45	225

	GD	FN	NM-
70	12	36	165
71-80: 71,72,76-Tank Killer-c/s. 74-Minute Commandos-c/s	10	30	130
81,84-88: 88-Last 10¢ issue	8	24	105
82-Johnny Cloud begins(1st app.), ends #117	14	42	200
83-2nd Johnny Cloud	10	30	130
89-100: 89-Battle Aces of 3 Wars begins, ends #98	6	18	75
101-111,113-116: 111,114,115-Johnny Cloud	5	15	55
112-Balloon Buster series begins, ends #114,116	5	15	60
117-Johnny Cloud-c & 3-part story	5	15	60

ALL-NEW COLLECTORS' EDITION (Formerly Limited Collectors' Edition: see for C-57, C-59)
DC Comics, Inc.: Jan, 1978 - Vol. 8, No. C-62, 1979 (No. 54-58: 76 pgs.)

C-53-Rudolph the Red-Nosed Reindeer	5	15	55
C-54-Superman Vs. Wonder Woman	4	12	45
C-55-Superboy & the Legion of Super-Heroes; Wedding of Lightning Lad & Saturn Girl; Grell-c/a	4	12	45
C-56-Superman Vs. Muhammad Ali: story & wraparound N. Adams-c/a	6	18	75
C-56-Superman Vs. Muhammad Ali (Whitman variant)-low print	7	21	90
C-57,C-59-(See Limited Collectors' Edition)			
C-58-Superman Vs. Shazam; Buckler-c/a	4	12	42
C-60-Rudolph's Summer Fun(8/78)	4	12	50
C-61-(See Famous First Edition-Superman #1)			
C-62-Superman the Movie (68 pgs.; 1979)-Photo-c from movie plus photos inside (also see DC Special Series #25)	3	9	25

ALL STAR COMICS
DC Comics: No. 58, Jan-Feb, '76 -No. 74, Sept-Oct, '78

V12 #58-(1976) JSA (Flash, Hawkman, Dr. Mid-Nite, Wildcat, Dr. Fate, Green Lantern, Robin & Star Spangled Kid) app.; intro. Power Girl	4	12	50
V12 #59,60: 59-Estrada & Wood-a	2	6	20
V12 #61-68: 62-65-Superman app. 64,65-Wood-c/a; Vandal Savage app. 66-Injustice Society app. 68-Psycho Pirate app.	2	6	20
V12 #69-1st Earth-2 Huntress (Helena Wayne)	3	10	35
V12 #70-73: 70-Full intro. of Huntress	2	6	20
V12 #74-(44 pgs.) Last issue, story continues in Adventure Comics #461 & 462 (death of Earth-2 Batman; Staton-c/a)	3	9	28

ALL STAR COMICS (Also see crossover 1999 editions of Adventure, All-American, National, Sensation, Smash, Star Spangled and Thrilling Comics)
DC Comics: May, 1999 - No. 2, May, 1999 ($2.95, bookends for JSA x-over)

1,2-Justice Society in World War 2; Robinson-s/Johnson-c		3.00
1-RRP Edition	(price will be based on future sales)	
...80-Page Giant (9/99, $4.95) Phantom Lady app.		5.00

ALL-STAR SQUADRON (See Justice League of America #193)
DC Comics: Sept, 1981 - No. 67, Mar, 1987

	GD	FN	NM-

1-Original Atom, Hawkman, Dr. Mid-Nite, Robotman (origin), Plastic Man, Johnny Quick, Liberty Belle, Shining Knight begin 1   3   7

2-10: 4,7-Spectre app. 8-Re-intro Steel, the Indestructable Man   5.00

11-46,48,49: 12-Origin G.A. Hawkman retold. 23-Origin/1st app. The Amazing Man. 24-Batman app. 25-1st app. Infinity, Inc. (9/83), 26-Origin Infinity, Inc. (2nd app.); Robin app. 27-Dr. Fate vs. The Spectre. 30-35-Spectre app. 33-Origin Freedom Fighters of Earth-X.

   36,37-Superman vs. Capt. Marvel; Ordway-c. 41-Origin Starman   4.00

47-Origin Dr. Fate; McFarlane-a (1st full story)/part-c (7/85)

                                               1   4   10

50-Double size; Crisis x-over   6.00

51-66: 51-56-Crisis x-over. 61-Origin Liberty Belle. 62-Origin The Shining Knight. 63-Origin Robotman. 65-Origin Johnny Quick. 66-Origin Tarantula   4.50

67-Last issue; retells first case of the Justice Society   6.00

Annual 1-3: 1(11/82)-Retells origin of G.A. Atom, Guardian & Wildcat; Jerry Ordway's 1st pencils for DC.(1st work was inking Carmine Infantino in Mystery in Space #94). 2(11/83)-Infinity, Inc. app. 3(9/84)   4.50

ALL-STAR WESTERN (Weird Western Tales No. 12 on)
National Periodical Publications: Aug-Sept, 1970 - No. 11, Apr-May, 1972

1-Pow-Wow Smith-r; Infantino-a   5   15   60

2-Outlaw begins; El Diablo by Morrow begins; has cameos by Williamson, Torres, Kane, Giordano & Phil Seuling   4   12   50

3-Origin El Diablo   4   12   50

4-6: 5-Last Outlaw issue. 6-Billy the Kid begins, ends #8

                                               3   10   35

7-9-(52 pgs.) 9-Frazetta-a, 3pgs.(r)   4   12   42

10-(52 pgs.) Jonah Hex begins (1st app., 2-3/72)   38   114   600

11-(52 pgs.) 2nd app. Jonah Hex; 1st cover   17   51   250

ALPHA FLIGHT (See X-Men #120,121 & X-Men/Alpha Flight)
Marvel Comics: Aug, 1983 - No. 130, Mar, 1994 (#52-on are direct sales only)

1-(52 pgs.) Byrne-a begins (thru #28) -Wolverine & Nightcrawler cameo   4.00

2-28: 2-Vindicator becomes Guardian; origin Marrina & Alpha Flight. 3-Concludes origin Alpha Flight. 6-Origin Shaman. 7-Origin Snowbird. 10,11-Origin Sasquatch. 12-(52 pgs.)-Death of Guardian. 13-Wolverine app. 16,17-Wolverine cameo. 17-X-Men x-over (mostly r-/X-Men #109); 20-New headquarters. 25-Return of Guardian. 28-Last Byrne issue   3.00

29-32,35-50: 39-47,49-Portacio-a(i). 50-Double size; Portacio-a(i)   2.50

33,34-1st & 2nd app. Lady Deathstrike; Wolverine app. 34-Origin Wolverine   3.00

51-Jim Lee's 1st work at Marvel (10/87); Wolverine cameo; 1st Lee Wolverine; Portacio-a(i)   5.00

52,53-Wolverine app.; Lee-a on Wolverine. 53-Lee/Portacio-a   3.00

54-73,76-86,91-99,101-105: 54,63,64-No Jim Lee-a. 54-Portacio-a(i). 55-62-Jim Lee-a(p). 71-Intro The Sorcerer (villain). 91-Dr. Doom app. 94-F.F. x-over. 99-Galactus, Avengers app. 102-Intro Weapon Omega   2.25

74,75,87-90,100: 74-Wolverine, Spider-Man & The Avengers app.

	GD	FN	NM-

75-($1.95, 52 pgs.). 87-90-Wolverine. 4 part story w/Lee-c. 89-Original
   Guardian returns. 100-($2.00, 52 pgs.)-Avengers & Galactus app.   3.00
106-Northstar revelation issue   2.50
106-2nd printing (direct sale only)   2.25
107-109,112-119,121-129: 107-X-Factor x-over. 112-Infinity War x-overs   2.25
110,111: Infinity War x-overs, Wolverine app. (brief). 111-Thanos cameo   3.00
120-($2.25)-Polybagged w/Paranormal Registration Act poster   2.50
130-($2.25, 52 pgs.)   3.00
Annual 1,2 (9/86, 12/87)   3.00
Special V2#1(6/92, $2.50, 52 pgs.)-Wolverine-c/story   2.50

AMAZING ADULT FANTASY (Formerly Amazing Adventures #1-6; becomes
Amazing Fantasy #15)
Marvel Comics Group (AMI): No. 7, Dec, 1961 - No. 14, July, 1962

7-Ditko-c/a begins, ends #14	50	150	850
8-Last 10¢ issue	41	123	660
9-13: 12-1st app. Mailbag. 13-Anti-communist sty	39	117	625
13-2nd printing (1994)	2	6	12
14-Prototype issue (Professor X)	41	123	675

AMAZING ADVENTURES (Becomes Amazing Adult Fantasy #7 on)
Atlas Comics (AMI)/Marvel Comics No. 3 on: June, 1961 - No. 6, Nov, 1961

1-Origin Dr. Droom (1st Marvel-Age Superhero) by Kirby; Kirby/Ditko-a			
(5 pgs.) Ditko & Kirby-a in all; Kirby-c on all	111	333	2100
2	48	144	825
3-6: 6-Last Dr. Droom	41	123	700

AMAZING ADVENTURES
Marvel Comics Group: Aug, 1970 - No. 39, Nov, 1976

1-Inhumans by Kirby(p) & Black Widow (1st app. in Tales of Suspense #52)			
double feature begins	6	18	70
2-4: 2-F.F. brief app. 4-Last Inhumans by Kirby	3	9	32
5-8: Adams-a(p); 8-Last Black Widow; last 15¢-c	4	12	50
9,10: Magneto app. 10-Last Inhumans (origin-r by Kirby)			
	3	9	30
11-New Beast begins(1st app. in mutated form; origin in flashback); X-Men			
cameo in flashback (#11-17 are X-Men tie-ins)	13	39	185
12-17: 12-Beast battles Iron Man. 13-Brotherhood of Evil Mutants x-over			
from X-Men. 15-X-Men app. 16-Rutland Vermont - Halloween x-over;			
Juggernaut app. 17-Last Beast (origin)	5	15	55
18-War of the Worlds begins (5/73); 1st app. Killraven; Neal Adams-a(p)			
	3	9	30
19-35,38,39: 19-Chaykin-a. 35-Giffen's first published story (art), along with			
Deadly Hands of Kung-Fu #22 (3/76)	1	4	10
36,37-(Regular 25¢ edition)(7-8/76)	1	4	10
36,37-(30¢-c variants, limited distribution)	3	9	25

AMAZING CHAN & THE CHAN CLAN, THE (TV)
Gold Key: May, 1973 - No. 4, Feb, 1974 (Hanna-Barbera)

1-Warren Tufts-a in all	4	12	38
2-4	3	9	26

	GD	FN	NM-

AMAZING FANTASY (Formerly Amazing Adult Fantasy #7-14)
Atlas Magazines/Marvel: #15, Aug, 1962 (Sept, 1962 shown in indicia); #16, Dec, 1995 - #18, Feb, 1996

	GD	FN	NM-
15-Origin/1st app. of Spider-Man by Steve Ditko (11 pgs.); 1st app. Aunt May & Uncle Ben; Kirby/Ditko-c	1400	4200	42,500
16-18 ('95-'96, $3.95): Kurt Busiek scripts; painted-c/a by Paul Lee			4.00

AMAZING FANTASY (Continues in Araña: The Heart of the Spider)
Marvel Comics: Aug, 2004 - No. 6, Jan, 2005 ($2.99)

1-Intro. Anya Corazon; Fiona Avery-s/Mark Brooks-c/a			4.00
2-6: 3,4-Roger Cruz-a			3.00

AMAZING SCARLET SPIDER
Marvel Comics: Nov, 1995 - No. 2, Dec, 1995 ($1.95, limited series)

1,2: Replaces "Amazing Spider-Man" for two issues. 1-Venom/Carnage cameos. 2-Green Goblin & Joystick-c/app.			2.25

AMAZING SPIDER-MAN, THE
Marvel Comics Group: March, 1963 - No. 441, Nov, 1998

	GD	FN	NM-
1-Spider-Man's 2nd app.; retells origin by Steve Ditko; 1st Fantastic Four x-over (ties with F.F. #12 as first Marvel x-over); intro. John Jameson & The Chameleon; Kirby/Ditko-c; Ditko-c/a #1-38	875	2625	32,500
1-Reprint from the Golden Record Comic set	14	42	200
With record (1966)	20	60	300
2-1st app. the Vulture & the Terrible Tinkerer	305	915	6700
3-1st app. Doc Octopus; 1st full-length story; Human Torch cameo; Spider-Man pin-up by Ditko	224	672	4700
4-Origin & 1st app. The Sandman (see Strange Tales #115 for 2nd app.); Intro. Betty Brant & Liz Allen	190	570	3800
5-Dr. Doom app.	160	480	3200
6-1st app. Lizard	153	459	3000
7,8,10: 7-Vs. The Vulture; 1st monthly issue. 8-Fantastic Four app. in back-up story by Kirby & Ditko	100	300	1900
9-Origin & 1st app. Electro (2/64)	106	318	2025
11,12: 11-1st app. Bennett Brant. 12-Doc Octopus unmasks Spider-Man-c	67	201	1275
13-1st app. Mysterio	92	276	1750
14-(7/64)-1st app. The Green Goblin (c/story)(Norman Osborn); Hulk x-over	175	525	3500
15-1st app. Kraven the Hunter; 1st mention of Mary Jane Watson (not shown)	76	228	1450
16-Spider-Man battles Daredevil (1st x-over 9/64); still in old yellow costume	58	174	1100
17-2nd app. Green Goblin (c/story); Human Torch x-over (also in #18 & #21)	72	216	1375
18-1st app. Ned Leeds who later becomes Hobgoblin; Fantastic Four cameo; 3rd app. Sandman	47	141	800
19-Sandman app.	41	123	650
20-Origin & 1st app. The Scorpion	54	162	1025
21-2nd app. The Beetle (see Strange Tales #123)	39	117	625

	GD	FN	NM-
22-1st app. Princess Python	33	99	525
23-3rd app. The Green Goblin-c/story; Norman Osborn app.			
	45	135	775
24	31	93	475
25-(6/65)-1st brief app. Mary Jane Watson (face not shown); 1st app. Spencer Smythe; Norman Osborn app.	36	108	575
26-4th app. The Green Goblin-c/story; 1st app. Crime Master; dies in #27			
	39	117	620
27-5th app. The Green Goblin-c/story; Norman Osborn app.			
	36	108	575
28-Origin & 1st app. Molten Man (9/65, scarcer in high grade)			
	63	189	1200
29,30	25	75	375
31-1st app. Harry Osborn who later becomes 2nd Green Goblin, Gwen Stacy & Prof. Warren.	30	90	450
32-38: 34-4th app. Kraven the Hunter. 36-1st app. Looter. 37-Intro. Norman Osborn. 38-(7/66)-2nd brief app. Mary Jane Watson (face not shown); last Ditko issue	23	69	340
39-The Green Goblin-c/story; Green Goblin's i.d. revealed as Norman Osborn; Romita-a begins (8/66; see Daredevil #16 for 1st Romita-a on Spider-Man)	32	96	500
40-1st told origin The Green Goblin-c/story	39	117	625
41-1st app. Rhino	31	93	480
42-(11/66)-3rd app. Mary Jane Watson (cameo in last 2 panels); 1st time face is shown	20	60	290
43-49: 44,45-2nd & 3rd app. The Lizard. 46-Intro. Shocker. 47-M. J. Watson & Peter Parker 1st date. 47-Green Goblin cameo; Harry & Norman Osborn app. 47,49-5th & 6th app. Kraven the Hunter	15	45	220
50-1st app. Kingpin (7/67)	50	150	950
51-2nd app. Kingpin; Joe Robertson 1-panel cameo	22	66	320
52-58,60: 52-1st app. Joe Robertson & 3rd app. Kingpin. 56-1st app. Capt. George Stacy. 57,58-Ka-Zar app.	11	33	160
59-1st app. Brainwasher (alias Kingpin); 1st-c app. M. J. Watson			
	11	33	160
61-74: 67-1st app. Randy Robertson. 69-Kingpin-c. 69,70-Kingpin app. 73-1st app. Silvermane. 74-Last 12¢ issue	9	27	120
75-83,87-89,91,92,95,99: 78,79-1st app. The Prowler. 83-1st app. Schemer & Vanessa (Kingpin's wife)	8	24	100
84-86,93: 84,85-Kingpin-c/story. 86-Re-intro & origin Black Widow in new costume. 93-1st app. Arthur Stacy	8	24	100
90-Death of Capt. Stacy	10	30	125
94-Origin retold	10	30	140
96-98-Green Goblin app. (97,98-Green Goblin-c); drug books not approved by CCA	11	33	145
100-Anniversary issue (9/71); Green Goblin cameo (2 pgs.)			
	17	51	250
101-1st app. Morbius the Living Vampire; Wizard cameo; last 15¢ issue (10/71)	17	51	250
101-Silver ink 2nd printing (9/92, $1.75)			2.25

	GD	FN	NM-
102-Origin & 2nd app. Morbius (25¢, 52 pgs.)	11	33	155
103-118: 104,111-Kraven the Hunter-c/stories. 108-1st app. Sha-Shan. 109-Dr. Strange-c/story (6/72). 110-1st app. Gibbon. 113-1st app. Hammerhead. 116-118-reprints story from Spectacular Spider-Man Mag. in color with some changes	5	15	60
119,120-Spider-Man vs. Hulk (4 & 5/73)	8	24	100
121-Death of Gwen Stacy (6/73) (killed by Green Goblin) (reprinted in Marvel Tales #98 & 192)	19	57	275
122-Death of The Green Goblin-c/story (7/73)	20	60	290
123,126-128: 123-Cage app. 126-1st mention of Harry Osborn becoming Green Goblin	5	15	60
124-1st app. Man-Wolf (9/73)	6	18	75
125-Man-Wolf origin	6	18	65
129-1st app. The Punisher (2/74); 1st app. Jackal	31	93	495
130-133: 131-Last 20¢ issue	4	12	45
134-(7/74); 1st app. Tarantula; Harry Osborn discovers Spider-Man's ID; Punisher cameo	5	15	55
135-2nd full Punisher app. (8/74)	7	21	90
136-1st app. Harry Osborn Green Goblin in costume	8	24	95
137-Green Goblin-c/story (2nd Harry Osborn Goblin)	5	15	60
138-141: 139-1st Grizzly. 140-1st app. Glory Grant	3	10	35
142,143-Gwen Stacy clone cameos: 143-1st app. Cyclone	4	12	38
144-147: 144-Full app. of Gwen Stacy clone. 145,146-Gwen Stacy clone storyline continues. 147-Spider-Man learns Gwen Stacy is clone	4	12	38
148-Jackal revealed	4	12	45
149-Spider-Man clone story begins, clone dies (?); origin of Jackal	6	18	70
150-Spider-Man decides he is not the clone	4	12	42
151-Spider-Man disposes of clone body	4	12	42
152-160-(Regular 25¢ editions). 159-Last 25¢ issue(8/76)	3	9	28
155-159-(30¢-c variants, limited distribution)	4	12	42
161-Nightcrawler app. from X-Men; Punisher cameo; Wolverine & Colossus app.	3	10	35
162-Punisher, Nightcrawler app.; 1st Jigsaw	3	10	35
163-168,181-188: 167-1st app. Will O' The Wisp. 181-Origin retold; gives life history of Spidey; Punisher cameo in flashback (1 panel). 182-(7/78)-Peter's first proposal to Mary Jane, but she declines	2	6	22
169-173-(Regular 30¢ edition). 169-Clone story recapped. 171-Nova app.	2	6	22
169-173-(35¢-c variants, limited dist.)(6-10/77)	3	9	35
174,175-Punisher app.	3	9	25
176-180-Green Goblin app.	3	9	28
189,190-Byrne-a	3	9	24
191-193,195-199: 193-Peter & Mary Jane break up. 196-Faked death of Aunt May	2	6	18

	GD	FN	NM-

NOTE: *Whitman 3-packs containing #192-194 exist.*

	GD	FN	NM-
194-1st app. Black Cat	4	12	40
200-Giant origin issue (1/80)	4	12	40
201,202-Punisher app.	2	6	18

203-205,207,208,210-219: 210-1st app. Madame Web. 212-1st app. Hydro
Man; origin Sandman

		2	6	12
206-Byrne-a		2	6	15
209-Origin & 1st app. Calypso (10/80)		2	6	20

220-237: 225-(2/82)-Foolkiller-c/story. 226,227-Black Cat returns.
236-Tarantula dies. 234-Free 16 pg. insert "Marvel Guide to Collecting
Comics". 235-Origin Will-'O-The-Wisp

			1	4	10

238-(3/83)-1st app. Hobgoblin (Ned Leeds); came with skin "Tattooz" decal.
NOTE: The same decal appears in the more common Fantastic Four #252 which is being
removed & placed in this issue as incentive to increase value
(Value listed is with or without tattooz)   8   24   95

239-2nd app. Hobgoblin & 1st battle w/Spidey	4	12	50

240-243,246-248: 241-Origin The Vulture. 242-Mary Jane Watson cameo
(last panel). 243-Reintro Mary Jane after 4 year absence

			1	3	9
244-3rd app. Hobgoblin (cameo)			2	6	15

245-(10/83)-4th app. Hobgoblin (cameo); Lefty Donovan gains powers of
Hobgoblin & battles Spider-Man   2   6   15

249-251: 3 part Hobgoblin/Spider-Man battle. 249-Retells origin & death of
1st Green Goblin. 251-Last old costume   2   6   16

252-Spider-Man dons new black costume (5/84); ties with Marvel Team-Up
#141 & Spectacular Spider-Man #90 for 1st new costume in regular title
(See Marvel Super-Heroes Secret Wars #8)   4   12   40

253-1st app. The Rose	2	6	12

254-258: 256-1st app. Puma. 257-Hobgoblin cameo; 2nd app. Puma; M.J.
Watson reveals she knows Spidey's i.d. 258-Hobgoblin app.

			1	3	9

259-Full Hobgoblin app.; Spidey back to old costume; origin Mary Jane
Watson   2   6   14

260-Hobgoblin app.	1	4	11
261-Hobgoblin-c/story; painted-c by Vess	2	6	12
262-Spider-Man unmasked; photo-c	1	3	9

263,264,266-274,277-280,282,283: 274-Zarathos (The Spirit of Vengeance)
app. 277-Vess back-up art. 279-Jack O'Lantern-c/story.
282-X-Factor x-over   1   3   7

265-1st app. Silver Sable (6/85)	2	6	16
265-Silver ink 2nd printing ($1.25)			2.25

275-($1.25, 52 pgs.)-Hobgoblin-c/story; origin-r by Ditko

			2	6	20
276-Hobgoblin app.			1	4	10
281-Hobgoblin battles Jack O'Lantern			1	4	10

284,285: 284-Punisher cameo; Gang War story begins; Hobgoblin-c/story.
285-Punisher app.; minor Hobgoblin app.   1   4   10

286-288: 286-Hobgoblin-c & app. (minor). 287-Hobgoblin app. (minor).
288-Full Hobgoblin app.; last Gang War   1   4   10

289-(6/87, $1.25, 52 pgs.)-Hobgoblin's i.d. revealed as Ned Leeds; death of

	GD	FN	NM-

Ned Leeds; Macendale (Jack O'Lantern) becomes new Hobgoblin
(1st app.)   3   9   24

290-292,295-297: 290-Peter proposes to Mary Jane. 292-She accepts; leads
   into wedding in Amazing Spider-Man Annual #21   1   3   7

293,294-Part 2 & 5 of Kraven story from Web of Spider-Man. 294-Death of
   Kraven   1   4   10

298-Todd McFarlane-c/a begins (3/88); 1st brief app. Eddie Brock who
   becomes Venom; (last pg.)   4   12   50

299-1st brief app. Venom with costume   3   9   30

300 ($1.50, 52 pgs.; 25th Anniversary)-1st full Venom app.; last black
   costume (5/88)   8   24   95

301-305: 301 ($1.00 issues begin). 304-1st bi-weekly issue
        2   6   16

306-311,313,314: 306-Swipes-c from Action #1   2   6   14

312-Hobgoblin battles Green Goblin   2   6   20

315-317-Venom app.   2   6   20

318-323,325: 319-Bi-weekly begins again   1   3   9

324-Sabretooth app.; McFarlane cover only   1   3   9

326,327,329: 327-Cosmic Spidey continues from Spectacular Spider-Man
   (no McFarlane-c/a)   5.00

328-Hulk x-over; last McFarlane issue   1   4   10

330,331-Punisher app. 331-Minor Venom app.   4.00

332,333-Venom-c/story   1   3   7

334-336,338-343: 341-Tarantula app.   4.00

337-Hobgoblin app.   4.00

344-1st app. Cletus Kasady (Carnage)   2   6   12

345-1st full app. Cletus Kasady; Venom cameo on last pg.
        2   6   12

346,347-Venom app.   1   3   7

348,349,351-359: 348-Avengers x-over. 351,352-Nova of New Warriors app.
   353-Darkhawk app.; brief Punisher app. 354-Punisher cameo & Nova,
   Night Thrasher (New Warriors), Darkhawk & Moon Knight app.
   357,358-Punisher, Darkhawk, Moon Knight, Night Thrasher, Nova x-over.
   358-3 part gatefold-c; last $1.00-c. 360-Carnage cameo   3.00

350-($1.50, 52pgs.)-Origin retold; Spidey vs. Dr. Doom; Uncle Ben app.   5.00

360-Carnage cameo   4.00

361-Intro Carnage (the Spawn of Venom); begin 3 part story; recap of how
   Spidey's alien costume became Venom   2   6   12

361-($1.25)-2nd printing; silver-c   2.50

362,363-Carnage & Venom-c/story   1   3   7

362-2nd printing   2.25

364,366-374,376-387: 364-The Shocker app. (old villain). 366-Peter's
   parents-c/story. 369-Harry Osborn back-up (Gr. Goblin II). 373-Venom
   back-up. 374-Venom-c/story. 376-Cardiac app. 378-Maximum Carnage
   part 3. 381,382-Hulk app. 383-The Jury app. 384-Venom/carnage app.
   387-New costume Vulture   2.50

365-($3.95, 84 pgs.)-30th anniversary issue w/silver hologram on-c;
   Spidey/Venom/Carnage pull-out poster; contains 5 pg. preview of
   Spider-Man 2099 (1st app.); Spidey's origin retold; Lizard app.; reintro

	GD	FN	NM-

Peter's parents in Stan Lee 3 pg. text w/illo (story cont. thru #370) — 5.00

375-($3.95, 68 pgs.)-Holo-grafx foil-c; vs. Venom story; ties into Venom: Lethal
  Protector #1; Pat Olliffe-a. — 5.00

388-($2.25, 68 pgs.)-Newsstand edition; Venom back-up & Cardiac & chance
  back-up — 2.25

388-($2.95, 68 pgs.)-Collector's edition w/foil-c — 3.00

389-396,398,399,401-420: 389-$1.50-c begins; bound-in trading card sheet;
  Green Goblin app. 394-Power & Responsibility Pt. 2. 396-Daredevil-c &
  app. 403-Carnage app. 406-1st New Doc Octopus. 407-Human Torch,
  Silver Sable, Sandman app. 409-Kaine, Rhino app. 410-Carnage app.
  414-The Rose app. 415-Onslaught story; Spidey vs. Sentinels.
  416-Epilogue to Onslaught; Garney-a(p); Williamson-a(i) — 2.25

390-($2.95)-Collector's edition polybagged w/16 pg. insert of new animated
  Spidey TV show plus animation cel — 3.00

394-($2.95, 48 pgs.)-Deluxe edition; flip book w/Birth of a Spider-Man Pt. 2;
  silver foil both-c; Power & Responsibility Pt. 2 — 3.00

397-($2.25)-Flip book w/Ultimate Spider-Man — 2.25

400-($2.95)-Death of Aunt May — 3.00

400-($3.95)-Death of Aunt May; embossed double-c — 5.00

400-Collector's Edition; white-c — 1 — 3 — 9

408-($2.95) Polybagged version with TV theme song cassette — 8.00

421-424,426,428-433: 426-Begin $1.99-c. 432-Spiderhunt pt. 2 — 2.25

425-($2.99)-48 pgs., wraparound-c — 3.00

427-($2.25) Return of Dr. Octopus; double gatefold-c — 2.50

434-440: 434-Double-c with "Amazing Ricochet #1". 438-Daredevil app.
  439-Avengers-c/app. 440-Byrne-s — 2.25

441-Final issue; Byrne-s — 4.00

**#500-up (See Amazing Spider-Man Vol. 2; series resumed original
numbering after Vol. 2 #58)**

#(-1) Flashback issue (7/97, $1.95-c) — 2.25

Annual 1 (1964, 72 pgs.)-Origin Spider-Man; 1st app. Sinister Six
  (Dr. Octopus, Electro, Kraven the Hunter, Mysterio, Sandman, Vulture)
  (new 41 pg. story); plus gallery of Spidey foes; early X-Men app.
  — 82 — 246 — 1550

Annual 2 (1965, 25¢, 72 pgs.)-Reprints from #1,2,5 plus new Doctor Strange
  story — 34 — 102 — 550

Special 3 (11/66, 25¢, 72 pgs.)-New Avengers story & Hulk x-over; Doctor
  Octopus-r from #11,12; Romita-a — 15 — 45 — 225

Special 4 (11/67, 25¢, 68 pgs.)-Spidey battles Human Torch (new 41 pg.
  story) — 13 — 39 — 185

Special 5 (11/68, 25¢, 68 pgs.)-New 40 pg. Red Skull story; 1st app. Peter
  Parker's parents; last annual with new-a — 12 — 36 — 175

Special 5-2nd printing (1994) — 2 — 6 — 12

Special 6 (11/69, 25¢, 68 pgs.)-Reprints 41 pg. Sinister Six story from
  annual #1 plus 2 Kirby/Ditko stories (r) — 6 — 18 — 65

Special 7 (12/70, 25¢, 68 pgs.)-All-r(#1,2) new Vulture-c
  — 6 — 18 — 65

Special 8 (12/71)-All-r — 6 — 18 — 65

King Size 9 ('73)-Reprints Spectacular Spider-Man (mag.) #2; 40 pg. Green

	GD	FN	NM-
Goblin-c/story (re-edited from 58 pgs.)	6	18	65
Annual 10 (1976)-Origin Human Fly (vs. Spidey); new-a begins			
		3	9	25
Annual 11-13 ('77-'79):12-Spidey vs. Hulk-r/#119,120. 13-New Byrne/Austin-a;			
Dr. Octopus x-over w/Spectacular S-M Ann. #1	2	6	15
Annual 14 (1980)-Miller-c/a(p); Dr. Strange app.	2	6	18
Annual 15 (1981)-Miller-c/a(p); Punisher app.	2	6	22
Annual 16-20:16 ('82)-Origin/1st app. new Capt. Marvel (female heroine).			
17 ('83)-Kingpin app. 18 ('84)-Scorpion app.; JJJ weds. 19 ('85).			
20 ('86)-Origin Iron Man of 2020	1	3	7
Annual 21 (1987)-Special wedding issue; newsstand & direct sale versions			
exist & are worth same	2	6	12
Annual 22 (1988, $1.75, 68 pgs.)-1st app. Speedball; Evolutionary War x-over;			
Daredevil app.			6.00
Annual 23 (1989, $2.00, 68 pgs.)-Atlantis Attacks; origin Spider-Man retold;			
She-Hulk app.; Byrne-c; Liefeld-a(p), 23 pgs.			4.00
Annual 24 (1990, $2.00, 68 pgs.)-Ant-Man app.			3.00
Annual 25 (1991, $2.00, 68 pgs.)-3 pg. origin recap; Iron Man app.; 1st Venom			
solo story; Ditko-a (6 pgs.)			5.00
Annual 26 (1992, $2.25, 68 pgs.)-New Warriors-c/story; Venom solo story			
cont'd in Spectacular Spider-Man Annual #12			4.00
Annual 27,28 ('93, '94, $2.95, 68 pgs.)-27-Bagged w/card; 1st app. Annex.			
28-Carnage-c/story; Rhino & Cloak and Dagger back-ups			3.00
'96 Special-($2.95, 64 pgs.)-"Blast From The Past"			3.00
'97 Special-($2.99)-Wraparound-c,Sundown app.			3.00
Marvel Graphic Novel - Parallel Lives (3/89, $8.95)	2	6	12
Marvel Graphic Novel - Spirits of the Earth (1990, $18.95, HC)			
	3	9	28
Super Special 1 (4/95, $3.95)-Flip Book			4.00
...: Skating on Thin Ice 1(1990, $1.25, Canadian)-McFarlane-c; anti-drug			
issue; Electro app.	1	3	9
...: Skating on Thin Ice 1 (2/93, $1.50, American)			4.00
...: Double Trouble 2 (1990, $1.25, Canadian)			6.00
...: Double Trouble 2 (2/93, $1.50, American)			3.00
...: Hit and Run 3 (1990, $1.25, Canadian)-Ghost Rider-c/story			
	1	3	9
...: Hit and Run 3 (2/93. $1.50, American)			3.00
... : Carnage (6/93, $6.95)-r/ASM #344,345,359-363	1	3	7
...: Chaos in Calgary 4 (Canadian; part of 5 part series)-Turbine,Night Rider,			
Frightful app.	2	6	14
...: Chaos in Calgary 4 (2/93, $1.50, American)			3.00
...: Deadball 5 (1993, $1.60, Canadian)-Green Goblin-c/story; features			
Montreal Expos	2	6	18
Note: Prices listed above are for English Canadian editions. French editions			
are worth double.			
...: Soul of the Hunter nn (8/92, $5.95, 52 pgs.)-Zeck-c/a(p)			6.00
Wizard #1 Ace Edition ($13.99) r/#1 w/ new Ramos acetate-c			14.00
Wizard #129 Ace Edition ($13.99) r/#129 w/ new Ramos acetate-c			14.00

AMAZING SPIDER-MAN (Volume 2) (Some issues reprinted in "Spider-Man,

	GD	FN	NM-

Best Of" hardcovers)
Marvel Comics: Jan, 1999 - Present ($2.99/$1.99/$2.25)

	GD	FN	NM-
1-($2.99)-Byrne-a			6.00
1-($6.95) Dynamic Forces variant-c by the Romitas	1	4	10
2-($1.99) Two covers -by John Byrne and Andy Kubert			4.00
3-11: 4-Fantastic Four app. 5-Spider-Woman-c			2.25
12-($2.99) Sinister Six return (cont. in Peter Parker #12)			3.00
13-17: 13-Mary Jane's plane explodes			2.25
18,19,21-24,26-28: 18-Begin $2.25-c. 19-Venom-c.			2.25
20-($2.99, 100 pgs.) Spider-Slayer issue; new story and reprints			3.00
25-($2.99) Regular cover; Peter Parker becomes the Green Goblin			3.00
25-($3.99) Holo-foil enhanced cover			4.00
29-Peter is reunited with Mary Jane			2.25
30-Straczynski-s/Campbell-c begin; intro. Ezekiel			6.00
31-35: Battles Morlun			4.00
36-Black cover; aftermath of the Sept. 11 tragedy in New York			6.00
37-49: 39-'Nuff Said issue 42-Dr. Strange app. 43-45-Doctor Octopus app.			
46-48-Cho-c			2.25
50-Peter and MJ reunite; Capt. America & Dr. Doom app.; Campbell-c			2.50
51-58: 51,52-Campbell-c. 55,56-Avery scripts. 57,58-Avengers, FF, Cyclops			
app.			2.25

(After #58 [Nov, 2003] numbering reverted back to original Vol. 1 with #500, Dec, 2003)

	GD	FN	NM-
500-($3.50) J. Scott Campbell-c; Romita Jr. & Sr.-a; Uncle Ben app.			3.50
501-514: 501-Harris-c. 503-504-Loki app. 506-508-Ezekiel app. 509-514-Sins			
Past; intro. Gabriel and Sarah Osborn; Deodato-a			2.25
1999, 2000 Annual (6/99, '00, $3.50) 1999-Buscema-a			3.50
2001 Annual ($2.99) Follows Peter Parker: S-M #29; last Mackie-s			3.00
Collected Edition #30-32 ($3.95) reprints #30-32 w/cover #30			4.00
... 500 Covers HC (2004, $49.99) reprints covers for #1-500 & Annuals;			
yearly re-caps			50.00
...Vol. 1: Coming Home (2001, $15.95) r/#30-35; J. Scott Campbell-c			16.00
...Vol. 2: Revelations (2002, $8.99) r/#36-39; Kaare Andrews-c			9.00
...Vol. 3: Until the Stars Turn Cold (2002, $12.99) r/#40-45; Romita Jr.-c			13.00
...Vol. 4: The Life and Death of Spiders (2003, $11.99) r/#46-50			12.00
...Vol. 5: Unintended Consequences (2003, $12.99) r/#51-56; Dodson-c			13.00
...Vol. 6: Happy Birthday (2003, $12.99) r/#57,58,500-502			13.00
...Vol. 7: The Book of Ezekiel (2004, $12.99) r/#503-508; Romita Jr.-c			13.00

AMAZING WORLD OF DC COMICS
DC Comics: Jul, 1974 - No. 17, 1978 ($1.50, B&W, mail-order DC Pro-zine)

	GD	FN	NM-
1-Kubert interview; unpublished Kirby-a; Infantino-c	7	21	85
2-4: 3-Julie Schwartz profile. 4-Batman; Robinson-c	5	15	55
5-Sheldon Mayer	4	12	45
6,8,13: 6-Joe Orlando; EC-r; Wrightson pin-up. 8-Infantino; Batman-r from			
Pop Tart giveaway. 13-Humor; Aragonés-c; Wood/Ditko-a; photos from			
serials of Superman, Batman, Captain Marvel	3	9	32
7,10-12: 7-Superman; r/1955 Pep comic giveaway. 10-Behind the scenes at			
DC; Showcase article. 11-Super-Villains; unpubl. Secret Society of S.V.			

	GD	FN	NM-
story. 12-Legion; Grell-c/interview;	3	10	35
9-Legion of Super-Heroes; lengthy bios and history; Cockrum-c			
	8	24	95
14-Justice League	4	12	38
15-Wonder Woman; Nasser-c	4	12	48
16-Golden Age heroes	4	12	45
17-Shazam; G.A., 70s, TV and Fawcett heroes	4	12	38
Special 1 (Digest size)	3	9	32

AMAZING WORLD OF SUPERMAN (See Superman)

AMAZING X-MEN
Marvel Comics: Mar, 1995 - No. 4, July, 1995 ($1.95, limited series)

1-Age of Apocalypse; Andy Kubert-c/a			3.50
2-4			2.50

AMAZON (Also see Marvel Versus DC #3 & DC Versus Marvel #4)
DC Comics (Amalgam): Apr, 1996 ($1.95, one-shot)

1-John Byrne-c/a/scripts			2.25

AMBUSH BUG (Also see Son of...)
DC Comics: June, 1985 - No. 4, Sept, 1985 (75¢, limited series)

1-4: Giffen-c/a in all			3.00
Nothing Special 1 (9/92, $2.50, 68pg.)-Giffen-c/a			3.00
Stocking Stuffer (2/86, $1.25)-Giffen-c/a			3.00

AMERICAN FLAGG! (See First Comics Graphic Novel 3,9,12,21 & Howard Chaykin's..)
First Comics: Oct, 1983 - No. 50, Mar, 1988

1,21-27: 1-Chaykin-c/a begins. 21-27-Alan Moore scripts			4.00
2-20,28-49: 31-Origin Bob Violence			3.00
50-Last issue			4.00
Special 1 (11/86)-Introduces Chaykin's Time[2]			4.00

AMERICAN TAIL: FIEVEL GOES WEST, AN
Marvel Comics: Early Jan, 1992 - No. 3, Early Feb, 1992 ($1.00, lim. series)

1-3-Adapts Universal animated movie; Wildman-a			3.00
1-($2.95-c, 69 pgs.) Deluxe squarebound edition			5.00

AMERICA'S BEST COMICS
America's Best Comics: 1999 - Present

Preview (1999, Wizard magazine supplement) - Previews Tom Strong, Top Ten, Promethea, Tomorrow Stories			2.25
Sketchbook (2002, $5.95, square-bound)-Design sketches by Sprouse, Ross, Adams, Nowlan, Ha and others			6.00
Special 1 (2/01, $6.95)-Short stories of Alan Moore's characters; art by various; Ross-c			7.00
TPB (2004, $17.95) Reprints short stories and sketch pages from ABC titles			18.00

AMERICA'S BEST TV COMICS (TV)
American Broadcasting Co. (Prod. by Marvel Comics): 1967 (25¢, 68 pgs.)

	GD	FN	NM-
1-Spider-Man, Fantastic Four (by Kirby/Ayers), Casper, King Kong, George of the Jungle, Journey to the Center of the Earth stories (promotes new TV cartoon show)	15	45	220

AMERICA VS. THE JUSTICE SOCIETY
DC Comics: Jan, 1985 - No. 4, Apr, 1985 ($1.00, limited series)

1-Double size; Alcala-a(i) in all	1	3	9
2-4: 3,4-Spectre cameo	1	3	7

ANDY GRIFFITH SHOW, THE (TV)(1st show aired 10/3/60)
Dell Publishing Co.: #1252, Jan-Mar, 1962; #1341, Apr-Jun, 1962

Four Color 1252(#1)	38	114	600
Four Color 1341-Photo-c	35	105	560

A-NEXT (See Avengers)
Marvel Comics: Oct, 1998 - No. 12, Sept, 1999 ($1.99)

1-Next generation of Avengers; Frenz-a	3.00
2-12: 2-Two covers. 3-Defenders app.	2.25

ANGEL (TV) (Also see Buffy the Vampire Slayer)
Dark Horse Comics: Nov, 1999 - No. 17, Apr, 2001 ($2.95/$2.99)

1-17: 1-3,5-7,10-14-Zanier-a. 16-Buffy-c/app.	3.00
...: Earthly Possessions TPB (4/01, $9.95) r/#5-7, photo-c	10.00
...: Surrogates TPB (12/00, $9.95) r/#1-3; photo-c	10.00

ANGEL (Buffy the Vampire Slayer)
Dark Horse Comics: Sept, 2001 - No. 4, May, 2002 ($2.99, limited series)

1-4-Joss Whedon & Matthews-s/Rubi-a; photo-c and Rubi-c on each	3.00

ANGEL AND THE APE (Meet Angel No. 7) (See Limited Collector's Edition C-34 & Showcase No. 77)
National Periodical Publications: Nov-Dec, 1968 - No. 6, Sept-Oct, 1969

1-(11-12/68)-Not Wood-a	5	15	60
2-5-Wood inks in all. 4-Last 12¢ issue	4	12	38
6-Wood inks	4	12	45

ANGEL AND THE APE (2nd Series)
DC Comics: Mar, 1991 - No. 4, June, 1991 ($1.00, limited series)

1-4	3.00

ANGEL AND THE APE (3rd Series)
DC Comics(Vertigo): Oct, 2001 - No. 4, Jan 2002 ($2.95, limited series)

1-4-Chaykin & Tischman-s/Bond-a/Art Adams-c	3.00

ANIMAL MAN (See Action Comics #552, 553, DC Comics Presents #77, 78, Secret Origins #39, Strange Adventures #180 & Wonder Woman #267, 268)
DC Comics (Vertigo imprint #57 on): Sept, 1988 - No. 89, Nov, 1995 ($1.25/$1.50/$1.75/$1.95/$2.25, mature)

1-Grant Morrison scripts begin, ends #26	1	4	10
2-10: 2-Superman cameo. 6-Invasion tie-in. 9-Manhunter-c/story			6.00
11-49,51-55,57-89: 24-Arkham Asylum story; Bizarro Superman app.			
25-Inferior Five app. 26-Morrison apps. in story; part photo-c			3.00

	GD	FN	NM-
50-($2.95, 52 pgs.)-Last issue w/Veitch scripts			5.00
56-($3.50, 68 pgs.)			5.00
Annual 1 (1993, $3.95, 68 pgs.)-Bolland-c; Children's Crusade Pt. 3			6.00
...: Deus Ex Machina TPB (2003, $19.95) r/#18-26; Morrison-a; new Bolland-c			20.00
...: Origin of the Species TPB (2002, $19.95) r/#10-17 & Secret Origins #39			20.00

ANIMANIACS (TV)
DC Comics: May, 1995 - No. 59, Apr, 2000 ($1.50/$1.75/$1.95/$1.99)

	GD	FN	NM-
1	1	3	7
2-20: 13-Manga issue. 19-X-Files parody; Kim-c; Adlard-a (4 pgs.)			4.00
21-59: 26-E.C. parody-c. 34-Xena parody. 43-Pinky & the Brain take over			3.00
A Christmas Special (12/94, $1.50, "1" on-c)			3.00

ANNETTE (Disney, TV)
Dell Publishing Co.: No. 905, May, 1958; No. 1100, May, 1960
(Mickey Mouse Club)

	GD	FN	NM-
Four Color 905-Annette Funicello photo-c	31	93	460
Four Color 1100-...'s Life Story (Movie); A. Funicello photo-c	25	75	375

ANNIE
Marvel Comics Group: Oct, 1982 - No. 2, Nov, 1982 (60¢)

	GD	FN	NM-
1,2-Movie adaptation			4.00
Treasury Edition ($2.00, tabloid size)	3	9	28

ANTHRO (See Showcase #74)
National Periodical Publications: July-Aug, 1968 - No. 6, July-Aug, 1969

	GD	FN	NM-
1-(7-8/68)-Howie Post-a in all	6	18	75
2-5: 5-Last 12¢ issue	4	12	42
6-Wood-c/a (inks)	4	12	48

APHRODITE IX
Image Comics (Top Cow): Sept, 2000 - No. 4, Mar, 2002 ($2.50)

	GD	FN	NM-
1-3: 1-Four covers by Finch, Turner, Silvestri, Benitez			4.00
1-Tower Record Ed.; Finch-c			3.00
1-DF Chrome ($14.99)			15.00
4-($4.95) Double-sized issue; Finch-c			5.00
Convention Preview			10.00
...: Time Out of Mind TPB (6/04, $14.99) r/#1-4, & #0; cover gallery			15.00
Wizard #0 (4/00, bagged w/Tomb Raider magazine) Preview & sketchbook			5.00
#0-(6/01, $2.95) r/Wizard #0 with cover gallery			3.00

AQUAMAN (1st Series)
National Periodical Publications/DC Comics: Jan-Feb, 1962 - #56, Mar-Apr, 1971; #57, Aug-Sept,1977 - #63, Aug-Sept, 1978

	GD	FN	NM-
1-(1-2/62)-Intro. Quisp	74	222	1400
2	32	96	500
3-5	19	57	275
6-10	13	39	185

	GD	FN	NM-

11,18: 11-1st app. Mera. 18-Aquaman weds Mera; JLA cameo

	10	30	140
12-17,19,20	10	30	130

21-32: 23-Birth of Aquababy. 26-Huntress app.(3-4/66). 29-1st app. Ocean
   Master, Aquaman's step-brother. 30-Batman & Superman-c & cameo

	7	21	80
33-1st app. Aqua-Girl (see Adventure #266)	7	21	90
34-40: 40-Jim Aparo's 1st DC work (8/68)	5	15	60
41-46,47,49: 45-Last 12¢-c	4	12	50
48-Origin reprinted	5	15	55
50-52-Deadman by Neal Adams	7	21	90
53-56('71): 56-1st app. Crusader; last 15¢-c	2	6	16
57('77)-63: 58-Origin retold	1	3	9

AQUAMAN (1st limited series)
DC Comics: Feb, 1986 - No. 4, May, 1986 (75¢, limited series)

1-New costume; 1st app. Nuada of Thierna Na Oge.	5.50
2-4: 3-Retelling of Aquaman & Ocean Master's origins.	4.00
Special 1 (1988, $1.50, 52 pgs.)	3.75

AQUAMAN (2nd limited series)
DC Comics: June, 1989 - No. 5, Oct, 1989 ($1.00, limited series)

1-5: Giffen plots/breakdowns; Swan-a(p).	3.00
Special 1 (Legend of..., $2.00, 1989, 52 pgs.)-Giffen plots/breakdowns; Swan-a(p)	3.00

AQUAMAN (2nd Series)
DC Comics: Dec, 1991 - No. 13, Dec, 1992 ($1.00/$1.25)

1-5	2.50
6-13: 6-Begin $1.25-c. 9-Sea Devils app.	2.50

AQUAMAN (3rd Series)(Also see Atlantis Chronicles)
DC Comics: Aug, 1994 - No. 75, Jan, 2001 ($1.50/$1.75/$1.95/$1.99/$2.50)

1-(8/94)-Peter David scripts begin; reintro Dolphin	6.00
2-(9/94)-Aquaman loses hand	6.50
0-(10/94)-Aquaman replaces lost hand with hook.	6.50
3-8: 3-(11/94)-Superboy-c/app. 4-Lobo app. 6-Deep Six app.	3.50
9-69: 9-Begin $1.75-c. 10-Green Lantern app. 11-Reintro Mera. 15-Re-intro	
Kordax. 16-vs. JLA. 18-Reintro Ocean Master & Atlan (Aquaman's father).	
19-Reintro Garth (Aqualad). 23-1st app. Deep Blue (Neptune Perkins &	
Tsunami's daughter). 23,24-Neptune Perkins, Nuada, Tsunami, Arion,	
Power Girl, & The Sea Devils app. 26-Final Night. 29-Black Manta-c/app.	
32-Swamp Thing-c/app. 37-Genesis x-over. 41-Maxima-c/app. 44-G.A.	
Flash & Sentinel app. 50-Larsen-s begins. 53-Superman app. 60-Tempest	
marries Dolphin; Teen Titans app. 63-Kaluta-c begin. 66-JLA app.	2.50
70-75: 70-Begin $2.50-c. 71-73-Warlord-c/app. 75-Final issue	2.50
#1,000,000 (11/98) 853rd Century x-over	3.00
Annual 1 (1995, $3.50)-Year One story	3.50
Annual 2 (1996, $2.95)-Legends of the Dead Earth story	3.00
Annual 3 (1997, $3.95)-Pulp Heroes story	4.00

	GD	FN	NM-
Annual 4,5 ('98, "99, $2.95)-4-Ghosts; Wrightson-c. 5-JLApe			3.00
...Secret Files 1 (12/98, $4.95) Origin-s and pin-ups			5.00

AQUAMAN (4th Series)(Also see JLA #69-75)
DC Comics: Feb, 2003 - Present ($2.50)

1-Veitch-s/Guichet-a/Maleev-c			3.00
2-14: 2-Martian Manhunter app. 8-11-Black Manta app.			2.50
15-25: 15-San Diego flooded; Pfeifer-s/Davis-c begin. 23,24-Sea Devils app.			2.50
...Secret Files 2003 (5/03, $4.95) background on Aquaman's new powers; pin-ups			5.00
...: The Waterbearer TPB (2003, $12.95) r/#1-4, stories from Aquaman Secret Files and JLA/JSA Secret Files #1; JG Jones-c			13.00

AQUAMAN: TIME & TIDE (3rd limited series) (Also see Atlantis Chronicles)
DC Comics: Dec, 1993 - No. 4, Mar, 1994 ($1.50, limited series)

1-4: Peter David scripts; origin retold.			3.00
Trade paperback ($9.95)			10.00

ARCHIE AS PUREHEART THE POWERFUL
Archie Publications (Radio Comics): Sept, 1966 - No. 6, Nov, 1967

1-Super hero parody	10	30	140
2	6	18	75
3-6	5	15	60

NOTE: *Evilheart cameos in all. Title: Archie As Pureheart the Powerful #1-3; ...As Capt. Pureheart-#4-6.*

ARCHIE MEETS THE PUNISHER (Same contents as The Punisher Meets Archie)
Marvel Comics & Archie Comics Publ.: Aug, 1994 ($2.95, 52 pgs., one-shot)

1-Batton Lash story, J. Buscema-a on Punisher, Goldberg-a on Archie			6.00

ARIA
Image Comics (Avalon Studios): Jan, 1999 - Present ($2.50)

Preview (11/98, $2.95)			5.00
1-Anacleto-c/a	1	3	8
1-Variant-c by Michael Turner	1	3	8
1-($10.00) Alternate-c by Turner	1	4	10
1,2-(Blanc & Noir) Black and white printing of pencil art			3.00
1-(Blanc & Noir) DF Edition			5.00
2-4: 2,4-Anacleto-c/a. 3-Martinez-a			3.00
4-($6.95) Glow in the Dark-c	1	4	10
Aria Angela 1 (2/00, $2.95) Anacleto-a; 4 covers by Anacleto, JG Jones, Portacio and Quesada			3.00
Aria Angela Blanc & Noir 1 (4/00, $2.95) Anacleto-c			3.00
Aria Angela European Ashcan			10.00
Aria Angela 2 (10/00, $2.95) Anacleto-a/c			3.00
...: A Midwinter's Dream 1 (1/02, $4.95, 7"x7") text-s w/Anacleto panels			5.00
...: The Enchanted Collection (5/04, $16.95) r/Summer's Spell & The Uses of Enchantment			17.00

ARISTOKITTENS, THE (...Meet Jiminy Cricket No. 1)(Disney)

	GD	FN	NM-

Gold Key: Oct, 1971 - No. 9, Oct, 1975

1	4	12	38
2-5,7-9	3	9	24
6-(52 pgs.)	3	9	28

ARMAGEDDON 2001
DC Comics: May, 1991 - No. 2, Oct, 1991 ($2.00, squarebound, 68 pgs.)

1-Features many DC heroes; intro Waverider		4.00
1-2nd & 3rd printings; 3rd has silver ink-c		2.25
2		3.00

ARMY ATTACK
Charlton Comics: July, 1964 - No. 4, Feb, 1965; V2#38, July, 1965 - No. 47, Feb, 1967

V1#1	5	15	55
2-4(2/65)	3	9	32
V2#38(7/65)-47 (formerly U.S. Air Force #1-37)	3	9	24

ARMY AT WAR (Also see Our Army at War & Cancelled Comic Cavalcade)
DC Comics: Oct-Nov, 1978

1-Kubert-c; all new story and art	2	6	14

ARMY OF DARKNESS (Movie)
Dark Horse Comics: Nov, 1992 - No. 2, Dec, 1992; No. 3, Oct, 1993 ($2.50, limited series)

1-3-Bolton painted-c/a	5.00

ARMY OF DARKNESS: ASHES 2 ASHES (Movie)
Devil's Due Publ.: July, 2004 - Present ($2.99, limited series)

1-3-Four covers for each; Bradshaw-a	3.00

ARMY WAR HEROES (Also see Iron Corporal)
Charlton Comics: Dec, 1963 - No. 38, June, 1970

1	5	15	60
2-10	3	9	35
11-21,23-30: 24-Intro. Archer & Corp. Jack series	3	9	25
22-Origin/1st app. Iron Corporal series by Glanzman	4	12	45
31-38	2	6	16
Modern Comics Reprint 36 ('78)			4.00

ARRGH! (Satire)
Marvel Comics Group: Dec, 1974 - No. 5, Sept, 1975 (25¢)

1-Dracula story; Sekowsky-a(p)	3	9	28
2-5: 2-Frankenstein. 3-Mummy. 4-Nightstalker(TV); Dracula-c/app., Hunchback. 5-Invisible Man, Dracula	2	6	18

ARSENAL (Teen Titans' Speedy)
DC Comics: Oct, 1998 - No. 4, Jan, 1999 ($2.50, limited series)

1-4: Grayson-s. 1-Black Canary app. 2-Green Arrow app.	2.50

ARSENAL SPECIAL (See New Titans, Showcase '94 #7 & Showcase '95 #8)
DC Comics: 1996 ($2.95, one-shot)

	GD	FN	NM-
1			3.00

ARTEMIS: REQUIEM (Also see Wonder Woman, 2nd Series #90)
DC Comics: June, 1996 - No. 6, Nov, 1996 ($1.75, limited series)

1-6: Messner-Loebs-s & Benes-c/a in all. 1,2-Wonder Woman app.			3.00

ASKANI'SON (See Adventures of Cyclops & Phoenix limited series)
Marvel Comics: Jan, 1996 - No. 4, May, 1996 ($2.95, limited series)

1-4: Story cont'd from Advs. of Cyclops & Phoenix; Lobdell/Loeb story; Gene Ha-c/a(p)			3.00
TPB (1997, $12.99) r/#1-4; Gene Ha painted-c			13.00

ASPEN (MICHAEL TURNER PRESENTS:...) (Also see Fathom)
Aspen MLT, Inc.: July, 2003 - Present ($2.99)

1-Fathom story; Turner-a/Johns-s; interviews w/Turner & Johns; two covers by Turner			3.00
2,3:2-Fathom story; Turner-a/Johns-s; two covers by Turner; pin-ups and interviews			3.00
Aspen Sketchbook 1 (2003, $2.99) sketch pages by Michael Turner and Talent Caldwell			3.00

ASTONISHING TALES (See Ka-Zar)
Marvel Comics Group: Aug, 1970 - No. 36, July, 1976 (#1-7: 15¢; #8: 25¢)

	GD	FN	NM-
1-Ka-Zar (by Kirby(p) #1,2; by B. Smith #3-6) & Dr. Doom (by Wood #1-4; by Tuska #5,6; by Colan #7,8; 1st Marvel villain solo series) double feature begins; Kraven the Hunter-c/story; Nixon cameo	6	18	70
2-Kraven the Hunter-c/story; Kirby, Wood-a	3	10	35
3-6: B. Smith-p; Wood-a-#3,4. 5,6-Red Skull 2-part story	4	12	42
7-Last 15¢ issue; Black Panther app.	3	9	24
8-(25¢, 52 pgs.)-Last Dr. Doom of series	4	12	38
9-All Ka-Zar issues begin; Lorna-r/Lorna #14	2	6	18
10-B. Smith/Sal Buscema-a.	3	9	24
11-Origin Ka-Zar & Zabu; death of Ka-Zar's father	2	6	20
12-2nd app.Man-Thing; by Neal Adams (see Savage Tales #1 for 1st app.)	4	12	40
13-3rd app.Man-Thing	3	9	30
14-20: 14-Jann of the Jungle-r (1950s); reprints censored Ka-Zar-s from Savage Tales #1. 17-S.H.I.E.L.D. begins. 19-Starlin-a(p). 20-Last Ka-Zar (continues into 1974 Ka-Zar series)	1	4	10
21-(12/73)-It! the Living Colossus begins, ends #24 (see Supernatural Thrillers #1)	3	9	32
22-24: 23,24-IT vs. Fin Fang Foom	2	6	22
25-1st app. Deathlok the Demolisher; full length stories begin, end #36; Perez's 1st work, 2 pgs. (8/74)	5	15	55
26-28,30	2	6	18
29-r/origin/1st app. Guardians of the Galaxy from Marvel Super-Heroes #18 plus-c w/4 pgs. omitted; no Deathlok story	1	4	10
31-34: 31-Watcher-r/Silver Surfer #3	2	6	14
35,36-(Regular 25¢ edition)(5,7/76)	2	6	14
35,36-(30¢-c, low distribution)	3	9	24

ASTONISHING X-MEN
Marvel Comics: Mar, 1995 - No. 4, July, 1995 ($1.95, limited series)

1-Age of Apocalypse; Magneto-c		4.00
2-4		3.00

ASTONISHING X-MEN
Marvel Comics: Sept, 1999 - No.3, Nov, 1999 ($2.50, limited series)

1-3-New team, Cable & X-Man app.; Peterson-a		2.50
TPB (11/00, $15.95) r/#1-3, X-Men #92 & #95, Uncanny X-Men #375		16.00

ASTONISHING X-MEN
Marvel Comics: July, 2004 - Present ($2.99)

1-Whedon-s/Cassaday-c/a; team of Cyclops, Beast, Wolverine, Emma Frost & Kitty Pryde		3.00
1-Director's Cut (2004, $3.99) different Cassaday partial sketch-c; cover gallery, sketch pages and script excerpt		4.00
1-Variant-c by Cassaday		5.00
1-Variant-c by Dell'Otto		5.00
2,3,5,6-X-Men battle Ord		3.00
4-Colossus returns		4.00
4-Variant Colossus cover by Cassaday		5.00

ASTRO BOY (TV) (See March of Comics #285 & The Original...)
Gold Key: August, 1965 (12¢)

	GD	FN	NM-
1(10151-508)-Scarce; 1st app. Astro Boy in comics	44	132	675

ASTRO CITY / ARROWSMITH (Flip book)
DC Comics (WildStorm Prods.): Jun, 2004 ($2.95, one-shot flip book)

1-Intro. Black Badge; Ross-c; Arrowsmith a/c by Pacheco		3.00

ASTRO CITY (Also see Kurt Busiek's Astro City)
DC Comics (WildStorm Productions): Dec, 2004 ($5.95, one-shot)

... A Visitor's Guide (12/04) short story, city guide and pin-ups; Ross-c		6.00

ASTRO CITY: LOCAL HEROES (Also see Kurt Busiek's Astro City)
DC Comics (WildStorm Productions): Apr, 2003 - No. 5, Feb, 2004 ($2.95, limited series)

1-5-Busiek-s/Anderson-a/Ross-c		3.00
HC (2005, $24.95) r/series; Kurt Busiek's Astro City V2 #21,22; stories from Astro City/Arrowsmith #1; and 9-11, The World's Finest... Vol. 2; Alex Ross sketch pages		25.00

ATARI FORCE (Also see Promotional comics section)
DC Comics: Jan, 1984 - No. 20, Aug, 1985 (Mando paper)

1-(1/84)-Intro Tempest, Packrat, Babe, Morphea, & Dart		4.00
2-20		3.00
Special 1 (4/86)		3.00

A-TEAM, THE (TV) (Also see Marvel Graphic Novel)
Marvel Comics Group: Mar, 1984 - No. 3, May, 1984 (limited series)

	GD	FN	NM-
1-3			5.00
1,2-(Whitman bagged set) w/75¢-c	1	4	10

	GD	FN	NM-
3-(Whitman, no bag) w/75¢-c	1	3	8

ATLANTIS CHRONICLES, THE (Also see Aquaman, 3rd Series & Aquaman: Time & Tide)
DC Comics: Mar, 1990 - No. 7, Sept, 1990 ($2.95, limited series, 52 pgs.)

1-7: 1-Peter David scripts. 7-True origin of Aquaman; nudity panels			3.25

ATOM, THE (...& the Hawkman No. 39 on)
National Periodical Publ.: June-July, 1962 - No. 38, Aug-Sept, 1968

	GD	FN	NM-
1-(6-7/62)-Intro Plant-Master; 1st app. Maya	74	222	1400
2	32	96	500
3-1st Time Pool story; 1st app. Chronos (origin)	22	66	330
4,5: 4-Snapper Carr x-over	17	51	250
6,9,10	12	36	180
7-Hawkman x-over (6-7/63; 1st Atom & Hawkman team-up); 1st app. Hawkman since Brave & the Bold tryouts	30	90	440
8-Justice League, Dr. Light app.	13	39	190
11-15: 13-Chronos-c/story	10	30	125
16-20: 19-Zatanna x-over	8	24	95
21-28,30: 28-Chronos-c/story	7	21	80
29-1st solo Golden Age Atom x-over in S.A.	15	45	220
31-35,37,38: 31-Hawkman x-over. 37-Intro. Major Mynah; Hawkman cameo	6	18	70
36-G.A. Atom x-over	7	21	90

ATOM & HAWKMAN, THE (Formerly The Atom)
National Periodical Publ: No. 39, Oct-Nov, 1968 - No. 45, Oct-Nov, 1969

	GD	FN	NM-
39-43: 40-41-Kubert/Anderson-a. 43-(7/69)-Last 12¢ issue; 1st app. Gentleman Ghost	6	18	65
44,45: 44-(9/69)-1st 15¢-c; origin Gentleman Ghost	6	18	65

ATOM ANT (TV) (See Golden Comics Digest #2) (Hanna-Barbera)
Gold Key: January, 1966 (12¢)

	GD	FN	NM-
1(10170-601)-1st app. Atom Ant, Precious Pup, and Hillbilly Bears	31	93	485

ATOMIC BUNNY (Formerly Atomic Rabbit)
Charlton Comics: No. 12, Aug, 1958 - No. 19, Dec, 1959

	GD	FN	NM-
12	12	36	125
13-19	8	24	65

ATOMICS, THE
AAA Pop Comics: Jan, 2000 - No. 15, Nov, 2001 ($2.95)

1-11-Mike Allred-s/a; 1-Madman-c/app.			3.00
12-15-($3.50): 13-15-Savage Dragon-c/app. 15-Afterword by Alex Ross; colored reprint of 1st Frank Einstein story			3.50
...King-Size Giant Spectacular: Jigsaw (2000, $10.00) r/#1-4			10.00
...King-Size Giant Spectacular: Lessons in Light, Lava, & Lasers (2000, $8.95) r/#5-8			9.00
...King-Size Giant Spectacular: Running With the Dragon ('02, $8.95) r/#13-15 and r/1st Frank Einstein app. in color			9.00
...King-Size Giant Spectacular: Worlds Within Worlds ('01, $8.95) r/#9-12			9.00

	GD	FN	NM-
...: Spaced Out & Grounded in Snap City TPB (10/03, $12.95) r/one-shots - It Girl, Mr. Gum, Spaceman and Crash Metro & the Star Squad			13.00

ATOM SPECIAL (See Atom & Justice League of America)
DC Comics: 1993/1995 ($2.50/$2.95)(68 pgs.)

	GD	FN	NM-
1,2: 1-Dillon-c/a. 2-McDonnell-a/Bolland-c/Peyer-s			3.00

ATOM THE CAT (Formerly Tom Cat; see Giant Comics #3)
Charlton Comics: No. 9, Oct, 1957 - No. 17, Aug, 1959

	GD	FN	NM-
9	9	27	85
10,13-17	6	18	48
11,12: 11(64 pgs)-Atomic Mouse app. 12(100 pgs.)	11	33	105

ATTACK
Charlton Comics: No. 54, 1958 - No. 60, Nov, 1959

	GD	FN	NM-
54 (25¢, 100 pgs.)	11	33	115
55-60	6	18	42

ATTACK!
Charlton Comics: 1962 - No. 15, 3/75; No. 16, 8/79 - No. 48, 10/84

	GD	FN	NM-
nn(#1)-('62) Special Edition	5	15	60
2('63), 3(Fall, '64)	3	10	35
V4#3(10/66), 4(10/67)-(Formerly Special War Series #2; becomes Attack At Sea V4#5)	3	9	25
1(9/71)	3	9	25
2-5: 4-American Eagle app.	2	6	15
6-15(3/75):	1	4	10
16(8/79) - 40			5.00
41-47 Low print run			7.00
48(10/84)-Wood-r; S&K-c (low print)	1	4	10
Modern Comics 13('78)-r			4.00

AUGIE DOGGIE (TV) (Also appears in Hanna-Barbera Band Wagon, Quick-Draw McGraw, Spotlight #2, Top Cat & Whitman Comic Books)
Gold Key: October, 1963 (12¢)

	GD	FN	NM-
1-Hanna-Barbera character	20	60	290

AUTHORITY, THE (See Stormwatch and Jenny Sparks: The Secret History...)
DC Comics (WildStorm): May, 1999 - No. 29, Jul, 2002 ($2.50)

	GD	FN	NM-
1-Wraparound-c; Warren Ellis-s/Bryan Hitch and Paul Neary-a	2	6	14
2-4	1	4	10
5-12: 12-Death of Jenny Sparks; last Ellis-s	1	3	8
13-Mark Millar-s/Frank Quitely-c/a begins	2	6	12
14-16-Authority vs. Marvel-esque villains	1	3	7
17-22: 17,18-Weston-a. 19,20,22-Quitely-a. 21-McCrea-a			5.00
23-29: 23-26-Peyer-s/Nguyen-a; new Authority. 24-Preview of "The Establishment." 25,26-Jenny Sparks app. 27,28-Millar-s/Adams-a/c			4.00
Annual 2000 ($3.50) Devil's Night x-over; Hamner-a/Bermejo-c	1	3	7
Absolute Authority Slipcased Hardcover (2002, $49.95) oversized r/#1-12			

	GD	FN	NM-
plus script pages by Ellis and sketch pages by Hitch			50.00
...: Earth Inferno and Other Stories TPB (2002, $14.95) r/#17-20, Annual 2000, and Wildstorm Summer Special; new Quitely-c			15.00
...: Human on the Inside HC (2004, $24.95, d.j.) Ridley-s/Oliver-a/c			25.00
...: Kev (10/02, $4.95) Ennis-s/Fabry-c/a			5.00
...: Relentless TPB (2000, $17.95) r/#1-8			18.00
...: Scorched Earth (2/03, $4.95) Robbie Morrison-s/Frazer Irving-a			5.00
...: Transfer of Power TPB (2002, $17.95) r/#22-29			18.00
...: Under New Management TPB (2000, $17.95) r/#9-16; new Quitely-c			18.00

AUTHORITY, THE (See previews in Sleeper, Stormwatch: Team Achilles and Wildcats Version 3.0)
DC Comics (WildStorm): Jul, 2003 - No. 14, Oct, 2004 ($2.95)

	GD	FN	NM-
1-14: 1-Robbie Morrison-s/Dwayne Turner-a. 5-Huat-a. 14-Portacio-a			3.00
#0 (10/03, $2.95) r/preview back-up-s listed above; Turner sketch pages			3.00
...: Harsh Realities TPB (2004, $14.95) r/#0-5; cover gallery			15.00
.../Lobo: Jingle Hell (2/04, $4.95) Bisley-c/a; Giffen & Grant-s			5.00

AUTHORITY, THE: MORE KEV
DC Comics (WildStorm): Jul, 2004 - No. 4, Dec, 2004 ($2.95, limited series)

	GD	FN	NM-
1-4-Garth Ennis-s/Glenn Fabry-c/a			3.00

AUTHORITY, THE: REVOLUTION
DC Comics (WildStorm): Dec, 2004 - Present ($2.95)

	GD	FN	NM-
1,2-3rubaker-s/Nguyen-a			3.00

AVENGERS, THE (TV)(Also see Steed and Mrs. Peel)
Gold Key: Nov, 1968 ("John Steed & Emma Peel" cover title) (15¢)

	GD	FN	NM-
1-Photo-c	25	75	375
1-(Variant with photo back-c)	31	93	460

AVENGERS, THE (The Mighty Avengers on cover only #63-69)
Marvel Comics Group: Sept, 1963 - No. 402, Sept, 1996

	GD	FN	NM-
1-Origin & 1st app. The Avengers (Thor, Iron Man, Hulk, Ant-Man, Wasp); Loki app.	257	771	5400
2-Hulk leaves Avengers	60	180	1150
3-2nd Sub-Mariner x-over outside the F.F. (see Strange Tales #107 for 1st); Sub-Mariner & Hulk team-up & battle Avengers; Spider-Man cameo (1/64)	41	123	700
4-Revival of Captain America who joins the Avengers; 1st Silver Age app. of Captain America & Bucky (3/64)	132	396	2500
4-Reprint from the Golden Record Comic set	11	33	150
With Record (1966)	16	48	230
5-Hulk app.	31	93	475
6,8: 6-Intro/1st app. original Zemo & his Masters of Evil. 8-Intro Kang	24	72	350
7-Rick Jones app. in Bucky costume	30	90	450
9-Intro Wonder Man who dies in same story	31	93	475
10-Intro/1st app. Immortus; early Hercules app. (11/64)	22	66	325
11-Spider-Man-c & x-over (12/64)	27	81	400

	GD	FN	NM-
12-15: 15-Death of original Zemo	15	45	225
16-New Avengers line-up (Hawkeye, Quicksilver, Scarlet Witch join; Thor, Iron Man, Giant-Man, Wasp leave)	20	60	290
17,18	12	36	170
19-1st app. Swordsman; origin Hawkeye (8/65)	13	39	185
20-22: Wood inks	9	27	110
23-30: 23-Romita Sr. inks (1st Silver Age Marvel work). 25-Dr. Doom-c/story. 28-Giant-Man becomes Goliath (5/66)	7	21	85
31-40	6	18	65
41-46,49-52,54-56: 43,44-1st app. Red Guardian. 46-Ant-Man returns (re-intro, 11/67). 52-Black Panther joins; 1st app. The Grim Reaper. 54-1st app. new Masters of Evil. 56-Zemo app; story explains how Capt. America became imprisoned in ice during WWII, only to be rescued in Avengers #4	5	15	55
47-Magneto-c/story	5	15	60
48-Origin/1st app. new Black Knight (1/68)	5	15	60
53-X-Men app.	7	21	85
57-1st app. S.A. Vision (10/68)	13	39	190
58-Origin The Vision	8	24	100
59-65: 59-Intro. Yellowjacket. 60-Wasp & Yellowjacket wed. 63-Goliath becomes Yellowjacket; Hawkeye becomes the new Goliath. 65-Last 12¢ issue	5	15	55
66,67-B. Smith-a	5	15	60
68-70: 70-Nighthawk on cover	4	12	45
71-1st app. The Invaders (12/69); 1st app. Nighthawk; Black Knight joins	7	21	80
72-79,81,82,84-86,89-91: 82-Daredevil app	4	12	42
80-Intro. Red Wolf (9/70)	4	12	45
83-Intro. The Liberators (Wasp, Valkyrie, Scarlet Witch, Medusa & the Black Widow)	4	12	50
87-Origin The Black Panther	4	12	50
88-Written by Harlan Ellison	4	12	40
88-2nd printing (1994)	2	6	12
92-Last 15¢ issue; Neal Adams-c	4	12	50
93-(52 pgs.)-Neal Adams-c/a	12	36	170
94-96-Neal Adams-c/a	6	18	75
97-G.A. Capt. America, Sub-Mariner, Human Torch, Patriot, Vision, Blazing Skull, Fin, Angel, & new Capt. Marvel x-over	4	12	50
98,99: 98-Goliath becomes Hawkeye; Smith c/a(i). 99-Smith-c, Smith/Sutton-a	4	12	42
100-(6/72)-Smith-c/a; featuring everyone who was an Avenger	9	27	110
101-Harlan Ellison scripts	3	9	32
102-106,108,109	3	9	28
107-Starlin-a(p)	3	9	32
110,111-X-Men app.	4	12	42
112-1st app. Mantis	4	12	38
113-115,119-124,126-130: 123-Origin Mantis	2	6	22
116-118-Defenders/Silver Surfer app.	4	12	38

	GD	FN	NM-
125-Thanos-c & brief app.	3	9	28
131-133,136-140: 136-Ploog-r/Amazing Advs. #12	2	6	15
134,135-Origin of the Vision revised (also see Avengers Forever mini-series)			
	2	6	22
141-143,145,152-163	1	4	11
144-Origin & 1st app. Hellcat	2	6	20
146-149-(Reg.25¢ editions)(4-7/76)	1	4	11
146-149-(30¢-c variants, limited distribution)	3	9	25
150-Kirby-a(r); new line-up: Capt. America, Scarlet Witch, Iron Man, Wasp, Yellowjacket, Vision & The Beast	2	6	14
150-(30¢-c variant, limited distribution)	3	9	28
151-Wonder Man returns w/new costume	2	6	12
160-164-(35¢-c variants, limited dist.)(6-10/77)	2	6	22
164-166: Byrne-a	2	6	12
167-180: 168-Guardians of the Galaxy app.	1	3	7
181-191-Byrne-a: 181-New line-up: Capt. America, Scarlet Witch, Iron Man, Wasp, Vision, Beast & The Falcon. 183-Ms. Marvel joins. 185-Origin Quicksilver & Scarlet Witch	1	3	9
192-199: 195-1st Taskmaster			6.00
200-(10/80, 52 pgs.)-Ms. Marvel leaves.	1	4	10
201-213,217-238: 211-New line-up: Capt. America, Iron Man, Tigra, Thor, Wasp & Yellowjacket. 213-Yellowjacket leaves. 217-Yellowjacket & Wasp return. 221-Hawkeye & She-Hulk join. 227-Capt. Marvel (female) joins; origins of Ant-Man, Wasp, Giant-Man, Goliath, Yellowjacket & Avengers. 230-Yellowjacket quits. 231-Iron Man leaves. 232-Starfox (Eros) joins. 234-Origin Quicksilver, Scarlet Witch. 238-Origin Blackout			4.50
214-Ghost Rider-c/story			6.00
215,216,239,240,250: 215,216-Silver Surfer app. 216-Tigra leaves. 239-(1/84) Avengers app. on David Letterman show. 240-Spider-Woman revived. 250-($1.00, 52 pgs.)			4.00
241-249, 251-262			3.50
263-1st app. X-Factor (1/86)(story continues in Fant. Four #286)			6.00
264-299: 272-Alpha Flight app. 291-$1.00 issues begin. 297-Black Knight, She-Hulk & Thor resign. 298-Inferno tie-in			3.00
300 (2/89, $1.75, 68 pgs.)-Thor joins; Simonson-a			4.00
301-304,306-313,319-325,327,329-343: 302-Re-intro Quasar. 320-324-Alpha Flight app. (320-cameo). 327-2nd app. Rage. 341,342-New Warriors app. 343-Last $1.00-c			3.00
305,314-318: 305-Byrne scripts begin. 314-318-Spider-Man x-over.			3.50
326-1st app. Rage (11/90)			4.00
328,344-349,351-359,361,362,364,365,367: 328-Origin Rage. 365-Contains coupon for Hunt for Magneto contest			3.00
350-($2.50, 68 pgs.)-Double gatefold-c showing-c to #1; r/#53 w/cover in flip book format; vs. The Starjammers			3.50
360-($2.95, 52 pgs.)-Embossed all-foil-c; 30th ann.			4.00
363-($2.95, 52 pgs.)-All silver foil-c			4.00
366-($3.95, 68 pgs.)-Embossed all gold foil-c			4.00
368,370-374,376-399: 368-Bloodties part 1; Avengers/X-Men x-over. 374-bound-in trading card sheet. 380-Deodato-a. 390,391-"The Crossing."			

	GD	FN	NM-

395-Death of "old" Tony Stark; wraparound-c. 3.00
369-($2.95)-Foil embossed-c; Bloodties part 5 4.00
375-($2.00, 52 pgs.)-Regular ed.; Thunderstrike returns; leads into Malibu
    Comics' Black September. 3.00
375-($2.50, 52 pgs.)-Collector's ed. w/bound-in poster; leads into Malibu
    Comics' Black September. 3.50
400-402: Waid-s; 402-Deodato breakdowns; cont'd in X-Men #56 &
    Onslaught: Marvel Universe. 4.00
**#500-503 (See Avengers Vol. 3; series resumed original numbering
after Vol. 3 #84)**
Special 1 (9/67, 25¢, 68 pgs.)-New-a; original & new Avengers team-up
                                     10   30   130
Special 2 (9/68, 25¢, 68 pgs.)-New-a; original vs. new Avengers
                                       6   18   70
Special 3 (9/69, 25¢, 68 pgs.)-r/Avengers #4 plus 3 Capt. America stories by
    Kirby (art); origin Red Skull   4   12   42
Special 4 (1/71, 25¢, 68 pgs.)-Kirby-r/Avengers #5,6 3   9   25
Special 5 (1/72, 52 pgs.)-Spider-Man x-over   3   9   25
Annual 6 (11/76) Peréz-a; Kirby-c   2   6   15
Annual 7 (11/77)-Starlin-c/a; Warlock dies; Thanos app.
                                       4   12   45
Annual 8 (1978)-Dr. Strange, Ms. Marvel app.   1   4   10
Annual 9 (1979)-Newton-a(p)   1   3   8
Annual 10 (1981)-Golden-p; X-Men cameo; 1st app. Rogue & Madelyne Pryor
                                       4   12   45
Annual 11-13: 11(1982)-Vs. The Defenders. 12('83), 13('84)   4.00
Annual 14-18: 14('85),15('86),16('87),17('88)-Evolutionary War x-over,
    18('89)-Atlantis Attacks   4.00
Annual 19-23 (90-'94, 68 pgs.). 22-Bagged/card   3.00
...Kree-Skrull War ('00, $24.95, TPB) new Neal Adams-c   25.00
...: Legends Vol. 3: George Perez ('03, $16.99)-r/#161,162,194-196,201,
    Ann. #6&8   17.00
Marvel Double Feature...Avengers/Giant-Man #379 ($2.50, 52 pgs.)-Same as
    Avengers #379 w/Giant-Man flip book   2.50
Marvel Graphic Novel - Deathtrap: The Vault (1991, $9.95) Venom-c/app.
                                       2   6   12
The Korvac Saga TPB (2003, $19.95)-r/#167,168,170-177; Perez-c   20.00
The Yesterday Quest ($6.95)-r/#181,182,185-187   1   3   7
Under Siege ('98, $16.95, TPB) r/#270,271,273-277   17.00
...: Visionaries ('99, $16.95)-r/early George Perez art   17.00

AVENGERS, THE (Volume Two)
Marvel Comics: V2#1, Nov. 1996 - No. 13, Nov, 1997 ($2.95/$1.95/$1.99)
(Produced by Extreme Studios)

    1-($2.95)-Heroes Reborn begins; intro new team (Captain America,
      Swordsman, Scarlet Witch, Vision, Thor, Hellcat & Hawkeye); 1st app.
      Avengers Island; Loki & Enchantress app.; Rob Liefeld-p & plot; Chap
      Yaep-p; Jim Valentino scripts; variant-c exists   5.00
    1-($1.95)-Variant-c   6.00
    2-13: 2,3-Jeph Loeb scripts begin, Kang app. 4-Hulk-c/app. 5-Thor/Hulk

	GD	FN	NM-

battle; 2 covers. 10,11,13-"World War 3"-pt. 2, x-over w/Image characters.
12-($2.99) "Heroes Reunited"-pt. 2   4.00

AVENGERS, THE (Volume Three)
Marvel Comics: Feb, 1998 - No. 84, Aug, 2004; No. 500, Sept, 2004 - No. 503, Dec, 2004 ($2.99/$1.99/$2.25)

1-($2.99, 48 pgs.) Busiek-s/Perez-a/wraparound-c; Avengers reassemble after Heroes Return			5.00
1-Variant Heroes Return cover	1	3	7
1-Rough Cut-Features original script and pencil pages			3.00
2-($1.99)Perez-c, 2-Lago painted-c			4.00
3,4: 3-Wonder Man-c/app. 4-Final roster chosen; Perez poster			3.00
5-11: 5,6-Squadron Supreme-c/app. 8-Triathlon-c/app.			2.50
12-($2.99) Thunderbolts app.			3.00
12-Alternate-c of Avengers w/white background; no logo			15.00
13-24,26,28: 13-New Warriors app. 16-18-Ordway-s/a. 19-Ultron returns. 26-Immonen-a			2.25
16-Variant-c with purple background			5.00
25,27-($2.99) 25-vs. the Exemplars; Spider-Man app. 27-100 pgs.			3.00
29-33,35-47: 29-Begin $2.25-c. 35-Maximum Security x-over; Romita Jr.-a. 36-Epting-a; poster by Alan Davis. 38-Davis-a begins ($1.99-c)			2.25
34-($2.99) Last Pérez-a; Thunderbirds app.			3.00
48-($3.50, 100 pgs.) new story w/Dwyer-a & r/#98-100			3.50
49,51-59: 49-'Nuff Said story. 51-Anderson-a. 57-Johns-s begin			2.25
50,60-($3.50): 50 Dwyer-a; Quasar app.			3.50
61-84: 61,62-Frank-a; new line-up. 63-Davis-a. 64-Reis-a. 65-70-Coipel-a. 75-Hulk-app. 76-Jack of Hearts dies; Jae Lee-c. 77-(50¢-c) Coipel-a/ Cassaday-c. 78,80,81Coipel-a. 83,84-New Invaders app.			2.25

(After #84 [Aug, 2004] numbering reverted back to original Vol. 1 with #500, Sept, 2004)

500-($3.50) "Avengers Disassembled" begins; Bendis-s/Finch-a; Ant-Man (Scott Lang) killed, Vision destroyed			3.50
500-Director's Cut ($4.99) Cassaday foil variant-c plus interviews and galleries			5.00
501, 502-($2.25): 502-Hawkeye killed			2.25
503-($3.50) "Avengers Disassembled" ends; reprint pages from Avengers V1#16			3.50
#11/2 (12/99, $2.50) Timm-c/a/Stern-s; 1963-style issue			2.50
.../ Squadron Supreme '98 Annual ($2.99)			3.00
1999, 2000 Annual (7/99, '00, $3.50) 1999-Manco-a. 2000-Breyfogle-a			3.50
2001 Annual ($2.99) Reis-a; back-up-s art by Churchill			3.00
... Assemble HC ('04, $29.95, oversized) r/#1-11 & '98 Annual; Busiek intro.; Pérez pencil art and Busiek script from Avengers #1			30.00
...: Clear and Present Dangers TPB ('01, $19.95) r/#8-15			20.00
...Finale 1 (1/05, $3.50) Epilogue to Avengers Disassembled; Neal Adams-c; art by various incl. Peréz, Maleev, Oeming, Powell, Mayhew, Mack, McNiven, Cheung, Frank			3.50
...: Living Legends TPB ('04, $19.99) r/#23-30; last Busiek/Pérez arc			20.00
...Supreme Justice TPB (4/01, $17.95) r/Squadron Supreme appearances in Avengers #5-7, '98 Annual, Iron Man #7, Capt. America #8,			

	GD	FN	NM-
Quicksilver #10; Pérez-c			18.00
The Kang Dynasty TPB ('02, $29.99) r/#41-55 & 2001 Annual			30.00
The Morgan Conquest TPB ('00, $14.95) r/#1-4			15.00
.../Thunderbolts Vol. 1: The Nefaria Protocols (2004, $19.99) r/#31-34, 42-44			20.00
Ultron Unleashed TPB (8/99, $3.50) reprints early app.			3.50
Ultron Unlimited TPB (4/01, $14.95) r/#19-22 & #0 prelude			15.00
Wizard #0-Ultron Unlimited prelude			2.50
Vol. 1: World Trust TPB ('03, $14.99) r/#57-62 & Marvel Double-Shot #2			15.00
Vol. 2: Red Zone TPB ('04, $14.99) r/#64-70			15.00
Vol. 3: The Search For She-Hulk TPB ('04, $12.99) r/#71-76			13.00
Vol. 4: The Lionheart of Avalon TPB ('04, $11.99) r/#77-81			12.00
Vol. 5: Once an Invader TPB ('04, $14.99) r/#82-84, V1 #71; Invaders #0 & Ann #1 ('77)			15.00

AVENGERS: CELESTIAL QUEST
Marvel Comics: Nov, 2001 - No. 8, June, 2002 ($2.50/$3.50, limited series)

1-7-Englehart-s/Santamaría-a; Thanos app.			2.50
8-($3.50)			3.50

AVENGERS COLLECTOR'S EDITION, THE
Marvel Comics: 1993 (Ordered through mail w/candy wrapper, 20 pgs.)

1-Contains 4 bound-in trading cards			5.00

AVENGERS: EARTH'S MIGHTIEST HEROES
Marvel Comics: Jan, 2005 - No. 8 ($3.50, limited series)

1,2-Retells origin; Casey-s/Kolins-a			3.50

AVENGERS FOREVER
Marvel Comics: Dec, 1998 - No. 12, Feb, 2000 ($2.99)

1-Busiek-s/Pacheco-a in all			4.00
2-12: 4-Four covers. 6-Two covers. 8-Vision origin revised. 12-Rick Jones becomes Capt. Marvel			3.00
TPB (1/01, $24.95) r/#1-12; Busiek intro.; new Pacheco-c			25.00

AVENGERS INFINITY
Marvel Comics: Sept, 2000 - No. 4, Dec, 2000 ($2.99, limited series)

1-4-Stern-s/Chen-a			3.00

AVENGERS/ JLA (See JLA/Avengers for #1 & #3)
DC Comics: No, 2, 2003; No. 4, 2003 ($5.95, limited series)

2-Busiek-s/Pérez-a; wraparound-c; Krona, Galactus app.			6.00
4-Busiek-s/Pérez-a; wraparound-c			6.00

AVENGERS LOG, THE
Marvel Comics: Feb, 1994 ($1.95)

1-Gives history of all members; Perez-c			2.25

AVENGERS SPOTLIGHT (Formerly Solo Avengers #1-20)
Marvel Comics: No. 21, Aug, 1989 - No. 40, Jan, 1991 (75¢/$1.00)

21-Byrne-c/a			3.00
22-40: 26-Acts of Vengeance story. 31-34-U.S. Agent series. 36-Heck-i.			

	GD	FN	NM-

37-Mortimer-i. 40-The Black Knight app. 2.25

AVENGERS STRIKEFILE
Marvel Comics: Jan, 1994 ($1.75, one-shot)

1 2.25

AVENGERS: THE CROSSING
Marvel Comics: July, 1995 ($4.95, one-shot)

1-Deodato-c/a; 1st app. Thor's new costume 5.00

AVENGERS: THE TERMINATRIX OBJECTIVE
Marvel Comics: Sept, 1993 - No. 4, Dec, 1993 ($1.25, limited series)

1 ($2.50)-Holo-grafx foil-c 3.00
2-4-Old vs. current Avengers 2.25

AVENGERS: THE ULTRON IMPERATIVE
Marvel Comics: Nov, 2001 ($5.99, one-shot)

1-Follow-up to the Ultron Unlimited ending in Avengers #42; BWS-c 6.00

AVENGERS/THUNDERBOLTS
Marvel Comics: May, 2004 - No. 6, Sept, 2004 ($2.99, limited series)

1-6: Busiek & Nicieza-s/Kitson-c. 1,2-Kitson-a. 3-6-Grummett-a 3.00
Vol. 2: Best Intentions (2004, $14.99) r/#1-6 15.00

AVENGERS: TIMESLIDE
Marvel Comics: Feb, 1996 ($4.95, one-shot)

1-Foil-c 5.00

AVENGERS TWO: WONDER MAN & BEAST
Marvel Comics: May, 2000 - No. 3, July, 2000 ($2.99, limited series)

1-3: Stern-s/Bagley-c/a 3.00

AVENGERS/ULTRAFORCE (See Ultraforce/Avengers)
Marvel Comics: Oct, 1995 ($3.95, one-shot)

1-Wraparound foil-c by Perez 4.00

AVENGERS UNITED THEY STAND
Marvel Comics: Nov, 1999 - No. 7, June, 2000 ($2.99/$1.99)

1-Based on the animated series 3.00
2-6-($1.99) 2-Avengers battle Hydra 2.25
7-($2.99) Devil Dinosaur-c/app.; reprints Avengers Action Figure Comic 3.00

AVENGERS UNIVERSE
Marvel Comics: Jun, 2000 - No. 3, Oct, 2000 ($3.99)

1-3-Reprints recent stories 4.00

AVENGERS UNPLUGGED
Marvel Comics: Oct, 1995 - No. 6, Aug, 1996 (99¢, bi-monthly)

1-6 2.25

AVENGERS WEST COAST (Formerly West Coast Avengers)
Marvel Comics: No. 48, Sept, 1989 - No. 102, Jan, 1994 ($1.00/$1.25)

48,49: 48-Byrne-c/a & scripts continue thru #57 3.00

	GD	FN	NM-

50-Re-intro original Human Torch 4.00
51-69,71-74,76-83,85,86,89-99: 54-Cover swipe/F.F. #1. 78-Last $1.00-c.
  79-Dr. Strange x-over. 93-95-Darkhawk app. 2.25
70,75,84,87,88: 70-Spider-Woman app. 75 (52 pgs.)-Fantastic Four x-over.
  84-Origin Spider-Woman retold; Spider-Man app. (also in #85,86).
  87,88-Wolverine-c/story 3.00
100-($3.95, 68 pgs.)-Embossed all red foil-c 4.00
101,102: 101-X-Men x-over 4.00
Annual 5-8 ('90- '93, 68 pgs.)-5,6-West Coast Avengers in indicia.
  7-Darkhawk app. 8-Polybagged w/card 3.00

AZRAEL (...Agent of the Bat #47 on)(Also see Batman: Sword of Azrael)
DC Comics: Feb, 1995 - No. 100, May, 2003 ($1.95/$2.25/$2.50/$2.95)

1-Dennis O'Neil scripts begin 5.00
2,3 3.00
4-46,48-62: 5,6-Ras Al Ghul app. 13-Nightwing-c/app. 15-Contagion Pt. 5
  (Pt. 4 on-c). 16-Contagion Pt. 10. 22-Batman-c/app. 23,27-Batman app.
  27,28-Joker app. 35-Hitman app. 36-39-Batman, Bane app. 50-New
  costume. 53-Joker-c/app. 56,57,60-New Batgirl app. 2.50
47-($3.95) Flip book with Batman: Shadow of the Bat #80 4.00
63-74,76-92: 63-Huntress-c/app.; Azrael returns to old costume. 67-Begin
  $2.50-c. 70-79-Harris-c. 83-Joker. 91-Bruce Wayne: Fugitive pt. 15 2.50
75-($3.95) New costume; Harris-c 4.00
93-100: 93-Begin $2.95-c. 95,96-Two-Face app. 100-Last issue; Zeck-c 3.00
#1,000,000 (11/98) Giarrano-a 2.50
Annual 1 (1995, $3.95)-Year One story 4.00
Annual 2 (1996, $2.95)-Legends of the Dead Earth story 3.00
Annual 3 (1997, $3.95)-Pulp Heroes story; Orbik-c 4.00
Plus (12/96, $2.95)-Question-c/app. 3.00

AZTEK: THE ULTIMATE MAN
DC Comics: Aug, 1996 - No. 10, May 1997 ($1.75)

1-1st app. Aztek & Synth; Grant Morrison & Mark Millar scripts in all 6.00
2-9: 2-Green Lantern app. 3-1st app. Death-Doll. 4-Intro The Lizard King.
  5-Origin. 6-Joker app.; Batman cameo. 7-Batman app. 8-Luthor app. 9-vs.
  Parasite-c/app. 4.00
10-JLA-c/app. 1 4 10

BABYLON 5 (TV)
DC Comics: Jan, 1995 - No. 11, Dec, 1995 ($1.95/$2.50)

1 2 6 14
2-5 1 3 9
6-11: 7-Begin $2.50-c 1 3 7
... The Price of Peace (1998, $9.95, TPB) r/#1-4,11 10.00

BABYLON 5: IN VALEN'S NAME
DC Comics: Mar, 1998 - No. 3, May, 1998 ($2.50, limited series)

1-3 4.00

BABY SNOOTS
Gold Key: Aug, 1970 - No. 22, Nov, 1975

	GD	FN	NM-
1	3	10	35
2-11	2	6	18
12-22: 22-Titled Snoots, the Forgetful Elefink	1	4	10

BACK TO THE FUTURE (Movie, TV cartoon)
Harvey Comics: Nov, 1991 - No. 4, June, 1992 ($1.25)

1-4: 1,2-Gil Kane-c; based on animated cartoon			3.00

BACK TO THE FUTURE: FORWARD TO THE FUTURE
Harvey Comics: Oct, 1992 - No. 3, Feb, 1993 ($1.50, limited series)

1-3			3.00

BALOO & LITTLE BRITCHES (Disney)
Gold Key: Apr, 1968

1-From the Jungle Book	4	12	45

BAMM BAMM & PEBBLES FLINTSTONE (TV)
Gold Key: Oct, 1964 (Hanna-Barbera)

1	10	30	135

BANANA SPLITS, THE (TV)
Gold Key: June, 1969 - No. 8, Oct, 1971 (Hanna-Barbera)

1-Photo-c on all	12	36	180
2-8	9	27	110

BARBIE
Marvel Comics: Jan, 1991 - No. 66, Apr, 1996 ($1.00/$1.25/$1.50)

1-Polybagged w/Barbie Pink Card; Romita-c	2	6	15
2-49,51-65	1	3	9
50,66: 50-(Giant). 66-Last issue (lower print)	2	6	12

BARBIE & KEN
Dell Publishing Co.: May-July, 1962 - No. 5, Nov-Jan, 1963-64

01-053-207(#1)-Based on Mattel toy dolls	39	117	625
2-4	31	93	485
5 (Rare)	33	99	525

BARBIE FASHION
Marvel Comics: Jan, 1991 - No. 63, Jan, 1996 ($1.00/$1.25/$1.50)

1-Polybagged w/doorknob hanger	2	6	15
2-49,51-62: 4-Contains preview to Sweet XVI. 14-Begin $1.25-c			
	1	3	9
50,63: 50-(Giant). 63-Last issue (lower print)	2	6	12

BARNEY AND BETTY RUBBLE (TV) (Flintstones' Neighbors)
Charlton Comics: Jan, 1973 - No. 23, Dec, 1976 (Hanna-Barbera)

1	4	12	50
2-11: 11(2/75)-1st Mike Zeck-a (illos)	3	9	25
12-23	2	6	18
Digest Annual (1972, B&W, 100 pgs.) (scarce)	3	10	35

BARTMAN (Also see Simpson's Comics & Radioactive Man)
Bongo Comics: 1993 - No. 6, 1994 ($1.95/$2.25)

	GD	FN	NM-
1-($2.95)-Foil-c; bound-in jumbo Bartman poster			6.00
2-6: 3-w/trading card			4.00

BART SIMPSON (See Simpsons Comics Presents Bart Simpson)

BATGIRL (See Batman: No Man's Land stories)
DC Comics: Apr, 2000 - Present ($2.50)

1-Scott & Campanella-a			6.00
1-(2nd printing)			2.50
2-10: 8-Lady Shiva app.			4.50
11-24: 15-Joker-c/app. 24-Bruce Wayne: Murderer pt. 2.			4.00
25-($3.25) Batgirl vs Lady Shiva			3.50
26-29: 27- Bruce Wayne: Fugitive pt. 5; Noto-a. 29-B.W.:F. pt. 13			3.50
30-49,51-58: 30-32-Connor Hawke app. 39-Intro. Black Wind. 41-Superboy-c/app. 53-Robin (Spoiler) app. 54-Bagged with Sky Captain CD. 55-57-War Games			2.50
50-($3.25) Batgirl vs Batman			3.25
Annual 1 ('00, $3.50) Planet DC; intro. Aruna			5.00
...: A Knight Alone (2001, $12.95, TPB) r/#7-11,13,14			13.00
...: Death Wish (2003, $14.95, TPB) r/#17-20,22,23,25 & Secret Files and Origins #1			15.00
...: Fists of Fury (2004, $14.95, TPB) r/#15,16,21,26-28			15.00
... Secret Files and Origins (8/02, $4.95) origin-s Noto-a; profile pages and pin-ups			5.00
...: Silent Running (2001, $12.95, TPB) r/#1-6			13.00

BATGIRL ADVENTURES (See Batman Adventures, The)
DC Comics: Feb, 1998 ($2.95, one-shot) (Based on animated series)

1-Harley Quinn and Poison Ivy app.; Timm-c			5.00

BATGIRL SPECIAL
DC Comics: 1988 ($1.50, one-shot, 52 pgs)

1-Kitson-a/Mignola-c	1	3	9

BATGIRL: YEAR ONE
DC Comics: Feb, 2003 - No. 9, Oct, 2003 ($2.95, limited series)

1-9-Barbara Gordon becomes Batgirl; Killer Moth app.; Beatty & Dixon-s			3.00
TPB (2003, $17.95) r/#1-9			18.00

BAT LASH (See DC Special Series #16, Showcase #76, Weird Western Tales)
National Periodical Publications: Oct-Nov, 1968 - No. 7, Oct-Nov, 1969
(All 12¢ issues)

1-(10-11/68)-2nd app. Bat Lash	5	15	60
2-7	3	10	35

BATMAN
National Per. Publ./Detective Comics/DC Comics: No. 90, March, 1955 - Present

90,91,93-99: 97-2nd app. Bat-Hound-c/story; Joker story. 99-(4/56)-Last G.A. Penguin app.	51	153	635
92-1st app. Bat-Hound-c/story	67	201	875
100-(6/56)	254	762	3300

	GD	FN	NM-
101-(8/56)-Clark Kent x-over who protects Batman's i.d. (3rd story)			
	52	156	650
102-104,106-109: 103-1st S.A. issue; 3rd Bat-Hound-c/story			
	45	135	560
105-1st Batwoman in Batman (2nd anywhere)	57	171	735
110-Joker story	46	138	570
111-120: 112-1st app. Signalman (super villain). 113-1st app. Fatman; Batman meets his counterpart on Planet X w/a chest plate similar to S.A. Batman's design (yellow oval w/black design inside)	40	120	450
121-Origin/1st app. of Mr. Zero (Mr. Freeze).	47	141	585
122,124-126,128,130: 122,126-Batwoman-c/story. 124-2nd app. Signal Man. 128-Batwoman cameo. 130-Lex Luthor app.	30	90	325
123,127: 123-Joker story; Bat-Hound app. 127-(10/59)-Batman vs. Thor the Thunder God c/story; Joker story; Superman cameo	32	96	350
129-Origin Robin retold; bondage-c; Batwoman-c/story (reprinted in Batman Family #8)	34	102	365
131-135,137-139,141-143: 131-Intro 2nd Batman & Robin series (see #66; also in #135,145,154,159,163). 133-1st Bat-Mite in Batman (3rd app. anywhere). 134-Origin The Dummy (not Vigilante's villain). 139-Intro 1st original Bat-Girl; only app. Signalman as the Blue Bowman. 141-2nd app. original Bat-Girl. 143-(10/61)-Last 10¢ issue	22	66	240
136-Joker-c/story	27	81	285
140-Joker story, Batwoman-c/s; Superman cameo	24	72	255
144-(12/61)-1st 12¢ issue; Joker story	17	51	250
145,148-Joker-c/stories	19	57	280
146,147,149,150	13	39	190
151-154,156-158,160-162,164-168,170: 152-Joker story. 156-Ant-Man/Robin team-up(6/63). 164-New Batmobile(6/64) new look & Mystery Analysts series begins	11	33	150
155-1st S.A. app. The Penguin (5/63)	31	93	485
159,163-Joker-c/stories. 159-Bat-Girl app.	13	39	190
169-2nd SA Penguin app.	14	42	200
171-1st Riddler app.(5/65) since Dec. 1948	38	114	610
172-175,177,178,180,184	9	27	115
176-(80-Pg. Giant G-17); Joker-c/story; Penguin app. in strip-r; Catwoman reprint	11	33	150
179-2nd app. Silver Age Riddler	15	45	220
181-Batman & Robin poster insert; intro. Poison Ivy	18	54	260
182,187-(80 Pg. Giants G-24, G-30); Joker-c/stories	10	30	125
183-2nd app. Poison Ivy	11	33	150
185-(80 Pg. Giant G-27)	9	27	120
186-Joker-c/story	9	27	120
188,191,192,194-196,199	6	18	75
189-1st S.A. app. Scarecrow; retells origin of G.A. Scarecrow from World's Finest #3(1st app.)	11	33	150
190-Penguin-c/app.	8	24	95
193-(80-Pg. Giant G-37)	8	24	105
197-4th S.A. Catwoman app. cont'd from Det. #369; 1st new Batgirl app. in			

	GD	FN	NM-
Batman (5th anywhere)	8	24	105
198-(80-Pg. Giant G-43); Joker-c/story-r/World's Finest #61; Catwoman-r/Det. #211; Penguin-r; origin-r/#47	9	27	115
200-(3/68)-Joker cameo; retells origin of Batman & Robin; 1st Neal Adams work this title (cover only)	12	36	170
201-Joker story	6	18	65
202,204-207,209-212: 210-Catwoman-c/app. 212-Last 12¢ issue	5	15	55
203-(80 Pg. Giant G-49); r/#48, 61, & Det. 185; Batcave Blueprints	7	21	80
208-(80 Pg. Giant G-55); New origin Batman by Gil Kane plus 3 G.A. Batman reprints w/Catwoman, Vicki Vale & Batwoman	7	21	80
213-(80-Pg. Giant G-61); 30th anniversary issue (7-8/69); origin Alfred (r/Batman #16), Joker(r/Det. #168), Clayface; new origin Robin with new facts	8	24	100
214-217: 214-Alfred given a new last name- "Pennyworth" (see Detective #96)	4	12	42
218-(80-Pg. Giant G-67)	6	18	70
219-Neal Adams-a	6	18	65
220,221,224-226,229-231	4	12	38
222-Beatles take-off; art lesson by Joe Kubert	5	15	58
223,228,233: 223,228-(80-Pg. Giants G-73,G-79). 233-G-85-(68 pgs., "64 pgs." on-c)	6	18	65
227-Neal Adams cover swipe of Detective #31	5	15	55
232-N. Adams-a. Intro/1st app. Ra's al Ghul; origin Batman & Robin retold; last 15¢ issue	13	39	185
234-(9/71)-1st modern app. of Harvey Dent/Two-Face; (see World's Finest #173 for Batman as Two-Face; only S.A. mention of character); Adams-a; 52 pg. issues begin, end #242	13	39	195
235,236,239-242: 239-XMas-c. 241-Reprint/#5	4	12	42
237-N. Adams-a. 1st Rutland Vermont - Bald Mountain Halloween x-over. G.A. Batman-r/Det. #37; 1st app. The Reaper; Wrightson/Ellison plots	8	24	100
238-Also listed as DC 100 Page Super Spectacular #8; Batman, Legion, Aquaman-r; G.A. Atom, Sargon (r/Sensation #57), Plastic Man stories; Doom Patrol origin-r; N. Adams wraparound-c	11	33	150
243-245-Neal Adams-a	6	18	65
246-250,252,253: 246-Scarecrow app. 253-Shadow-c & app.	3	10	35
251-(9/73)-N. Adams-c/a; Joker-c/story	8	24	95
254,256-259,261-All 100 pg. editions; part-r: 254-(2/74)-Man-Bat-c & app. 256-Catwoman app. 257-Joker & Penguin app. 258-The Cavalier-r. 259-Shadow-c/app.	5	15	60
255-(100 pgs.)-N. Adams-c/a; tells of Bruce Wayne's father who wore bat costume & fought crime (r/Det. #235); r/story Batman #22	6	18	75
260-Joker-c/story (100 pgs.)	6	18	75
262 (68pgs.)	4	12	38
263,264,266-285,287-290,292,293,295-299: 266-Catwoman back to old			

	GD	FN	NM-
costume	2	6	18
265-Wrightson-a(i)	2	6	20
286,291,294: 294-Joker-c/stories	3	9	25
300-Double-size	3	9	25
301-(7/78)-310,312-315,317-320,325-331,333-352: 304-(44 pgs.). 306-3rd app. Black Spider. 308-Mr. Freeze app. 310-1st modern app. The Gentleman Ghost in Batman; Kubert-c. 312,314,346-Two-Face-c/stories. 313-2nd app. Calendar Man. 318-Intro Firebug. 319-2nd modern age app. The Gentleman Ghost; Kubert-c. 344-Poison Ivy app. 345-1st app. new Dr. Death. 345,346,351-Catwoman back-ups	2	6	12
306-308,311-317,319,320,323,324,326-(Whitman variants; low print run; none show issue # on cover)	2	6	15
311,316,322-324: 311-Batgirl-c/story; Batgirl reteams w/Batman. 316-Robin returns. 322-324-Catwoman (Selina Kyle) app. 322,323-Cat-Man cameos (1st in Batman, 1 panel each). 323-1st meeting Catwoman & Cat-Man. 324-1st full app. Cat-Man this title	2	6	15
321,353,359-Joker-c/stories	2	6	18
332-Catwoman's 1st solo	2	6	18
354-356,358,360-365,369,370: 361-1st app Harvey Bullock	1	3	9
357-1st app. Jason Todd (3/83); see Det. #524; 1st brief app. Croc	2	6	15
366-Jason Todd 1st in Robin costume; Joker-c/story	2	6	18
367-Jason in red & green costume (not as Robin)	2	6	12
368-1st new Robin in costume (Jason Todd)	2	6	15
371-399,401-403: 371-Cat-Man-c/story; brief origin Cat-Man (cont'd in Det. #538). 386,387-Intro Black Mask (villain). 380-391-Catwoman app. 398-Catwoman & Two-Face app. 401-2nd app. Magpie (see Man of Steel #3 for 1st). 403-Joker cameo			6.00

NOTE: *Most issues between 397 & 432 were reprinted in 1989 and sold in multi-packs. Some are not identified as reprints but have newer ads copyrighted after cover dates. 2nd and 3rd printings exist.*

	GD	FN	NM-
400 ($1.50, 68pgs.)-Dark Knight special; intro by Stephen King; Art Adams/ Terry Austin-a	3	9	25
404-Miller scripts begin (end 407); Year 1; 1st modern app. Catwoman (2/87)	2	6	22
405-407: 407-Year 1 ends (See Detective Comics #575-578 for Year 2)	2	6	16
408-410: New Origin Jason Todd (Robin)	2	6	18
411-416,421-425: 411-Two-face app. 412-Origin/1st app. Mime. 414-Starlin scripts begin, end #429. 416-Nightwing-c/story. 423-McFarlane-c			5.00
417-420: "Ten Nights of the Beast" storyline	2	6	12
426-($1.50, 52 pgs.)- "A Death In The Family" storyline begins, ends #429	2	6	20
427- "A Death In The Family" part 2.	2	6	15
428-Death of Robin (Jason Todd)	2	6	20
429-Joker-c/story; Superman app.	2	6	12
430-432			3.00
433-435-Many Deaths of the Batman story by John Byrne-c/scripts			3.00
436-Year 3 begins (ends #439); origin original Robin retold by Nightwing			

	GD	FN	NM-

(Dick Grayson); 1st app. Timothy Drake (8/89) 4.00

436-441: 436-2nd printing. 437-Origin Robin cont. 440,441: "A Lonely Place of Dying" Parts 1 & 3 3.00

442-1st app. Timothy Drake in Robin costume 4.00

443-456,458,459,462-464: 445-447-Batman goes to Russia. 448,449-The Penguin Affair Pts 1 & 3. 450-Origin Joker. 450,451-Joker-c/stories. 452-454-Dark Knight Dark City storyline; Riddler app. 455-Alan Grant scripts begin, ends #466, 470. 464-Last solo Batman story; free 16 pg. preview of Impact Comics line 3.00

457-Timothy Drake officially becomes Robin & dons new costume 5.00

457-Direct sale edition (has #000 in indicia) 5.00

460,461,465-487: 460,461-Two part Catwoman story. 465-Robin returns to action with Batman. 470-War of the Gods x-over. 475,476-Return of Scarface-c/story. 476-Last $1.00-c. 477,478-Photo-c 3.00

488-Cont'd from Batman: Sword of Azrael #4; Azrael-c & app.
| | 1 | 3 | 8 |

489-Bane-c/story; 1st app. Azrael in Bat-costume 5.00

490-Riddler-c/story; Azrael & Bane app. 6.00

491,492: 491-Knightfall lead-in; Joker-c/story; Azrael & Bane app.; Kelley Jones-c begin. 492-Knightfall part 1; Bane app. 4.00

492-Platinum edition (promo copy) 10.00

493-496: 493-Knightfall Pt. 3. 494-Knightfall Pt. 5; Joker-c & app. 495-Knightfall Pt. 7; brief Bane & Joker apps. 496-Knightfall Pt. 9, Joker-c/story; Bane cameo 3.00

497-(Late 7/93)-Knightfall Pt. 11; Bane breaks Batman's back; B&W outer-c; Aparo-a(p); Giordano-a(i) 5.00

497-499: 497-2nd printing. 497-Newsstand edition w/o outer cover. 498-Knightfall part 15; Bane & Catwoman-c & app. (see Showcase 93 #7 & 8) 499-Knightfall Pt. 17; Bane app. 3.00

500-($2.50, 68 pgs.)-Knightfall Pt. 19; Azrael in new Bat-costume; Bane-c 3.00

500-($3.95, 68 pgs.)-Collector's Edition w/die-cut double-c w/foil by Joe Quesada & 2 bound-in post cards 5.00

501-508,510,511: 501-Begin $1.50-c. 501-508-Knightquest. 503,504-Catwoman app. 507-Ballistic app.; Jim Balent-a(p). 510-KnightsEnd Pt. 7. 511-(9/94)-Zero Hour; Batgirl-c/story 2.50

509-($2.50, 52 pgs.)-KnightsEnd Pt. 1 3.00

512-514,516-518: 512-(11/94)-Dick Grayson assumes Batman role 2.50

515-Special Ed.($2.50)-Kelley Jones-a begins; all black embossed-c 3.00

515-Regular Edition 2.50

519-534,536-549: 519-Begin $1.95-c. 521-Return of Alfred, 522-Swamp Thing app. 525-Mr. Freeze app. 527,528-Two Face app. 529-Contagion Pt. 6. 530-532-Deadman app. 533-Legacy prelude. 534-Legacy Pt. 5. 536-Final Night x-over; Man-Bat-c/app. 540,541-Spectre-c-app. 544-546-Joker & The Demon. 548,549-Penguin-c/app. 2.50

530-532 ($2.50)-Enhanced edition; glow-in-the-dark-c. 3.00

535-(10/96, $2.95)-1st app. The Ogre 3.00

535-(10/96, $3.95)-1st app. The Ogre; variant, cardboard, foldout-c 4.00

550-($3.50)-Collector's Ed., includes 4 collector cards; intro. Chase, return of Clayface; Kelley Jones-c 3.50

	GD	FN	NM-
550-($2.95)-Standard Ed.; Williams & Gray-c			3.00
551,552,554-562: 551,552-Ragman c/app. 554-Cataclysm pt. 12.			2.50
553-Cataclysm pt.3			4.00
563-No Man's Land; Joker-c by Campbell; Bob Gale-s			5.00
564-574: 569-New Batgirl-c/app. 572-Joker and Harley app.			2.50
575-579: 575-New look Batman begins; McDaniel-a			2.50
580-598: 580-Begin $2.25-c. 587-Gordon shot. 591,592-Deadshot-c/app.			2.50
599-Bruce Wayne: Murderer pt. 7			2.50
600-($3.95) Bruce Wayne: Fugitive pt. 1; back-up homage stories in '50s, 60's, & 70s styles; by Aragonés, Gaudiano, Shanower and others			5.00
600-(2nd printing)			4.00
601-604, 606,607: 601,603-Bruce Wayne: Fugitive pt.3,13. 606, 607-Deadshot-c/app.			2.50
605-($2.95) Conclusion to Bruce Wayne: Fugitive x-over; Noto-c			3.00
608-(12/02) Jim Lee-a/c & Jeph Loeb-s begin; Poison Ivy & Catwoman app.	1	3	8
608-2nd printing; has different cover with Batman standing on gargoyle			12.00
608-Special Edition; has different cover; 200 printed; used for promotional purposes (one ungraded copy sold for $930, and a CGC graded 9.8 copy sold for $2,751)			
609-Huntress app.			9.00
610,611: 610-Killer Croc-c/app.; Batman & Catwoman kiss			8.00
612-Batman vs. Superman; 1st printing with full color cover			9.00
612-2nd printing with B&W sketch cover			15.00
613,614: 614-Joker-c/app.			7.00
615-617: 615-Reveals ID to Catwoman. 616-Ra's al Ghul app.			5.00
618- Batman vs. "Jason Todd"			4.00
619-Newsstand cover; Hush story concludes; Riddler app.			5.00
619-Two variant tri-fold covers; one Heroes group, one Villains group			5.00
619-2nd printing with Riddler chess cover			5.00
620-Broken City pt. 1; Azzarello-s/Risso-a/c begin; Killer Croc app.			3.00
621-625-Azzarello-s/Risso-a/c			2.25
626-630,634-Winick-s/Nguyen-a/Wagner-c; Penguin & Scarecrow app.			2.25
631-633-War Games. 633-Conclusion to War Games x-over			3.00
#0 (10/94)-Zero Hour issue released between #511 & #512; Origin retold			2.50
#1,000,000 (11/98) 853rd Century x-over			2.50
Annual 1 (8-10/61)-Swan-c	57	171	1085
Annual 2	30	90	450
Annual 3 (Summer, '62)-Joker-c/story	31	93	460
Annual 4,5	14	42	210
Annual 6,7 (7/64, 25¢, 80 pgs.)	11	33	160
Annual V5#8 (1982)-Painted-c	1	3	8
Annual 9,10,12: 9(7/85). 10(1986). 12(1988, $1.50)			6.00
Annual 11 (1987, $1.25)-Penguin-c/story; Moore-s	1	3	8
Annual 13 (1989, $1.75, 68 pgs.)-Gives history of Bruce Wayne, Dick Grayson, Jason Todd, Alfred, Comm. Gordon, Barbara Gordon (Batgirl) & Vicki Vale; Morrow-i			5.00
Annual 14-17 ('90-'93, 68 pgs.)-14-Origin Two-Face. 15-Armageddon 2001 x-over; Joker app. 15 (2nd printing). 16-Joker-c/s; Kieth-c. 17 (1993, $2.50,			

	GD	FN	NM-

68 pgs.)-Azrael in Bat-costume; intro Ballistic	4.00
Annual 18 (1994, $2.95)	3.00
Annual 19 (1995, $3.95)-Year One story; retells Scarecrow's origin	4.00
Annual 20 (1996, $2.95)-Legends of the Dead Earth story; Giarrano-a	3.00
Annual 21 (1997, $3.95)-Pulp Heroes story	4.00
Annual 22,23 ('98, '99, $2.95)-22-Ghosts; Wrightson-c. 23-JLApe	3.00
Annual 24 ('00, $3.50) Planet DC; intro. The Boggart; Aparo-a	3.50

BATMAN (Hardcover books and trade paperbacks)

...: ABSOLUTION (2002, $24.95)-Hard-c.; DeMatteis-s/Ashmore painted-a	
	25.00
...: ABSOLUTION (2003, $17.95)-Soft-c.	18.00
...: A LONELY PLACE OF DYING (1990, $3.95, 132 pgs.)-r/Batman #440-442 & New Titans #60,61; Perez-a	4.00
...: ANARKY TPB (1999, $12.95) r/early appearances	13.00
...AND DRACULA: RED RAIN nn (1991, $24.95)-Hard-c.; Elseworlds	32.00
...AND DRACULA: Red Rain nn (1992, $9.95)-SC	12.00
ARKHAM ASYLUM Hard-c; Morrison-s/McKean-a (1989, $24.95)	30.00
ARKHAM ASYLUM Soft-c ($14.95)	15.00
ARKHAM ASYLUM 15TH ANNIVERSARY EDITION Hard-c (2004, $29.95) reprint with Morrison's script and annotations, original page layouts; Karen Berger afterword	30.00
...: AS THE CROW FLIES-(2004, $12.95) r/#626-630; Nguyen sketch pages	13.00
BIRTH OF THE DEMON Hard-c (1992, $24.95)-Origin of Ra's al Ghul	25.00
BIRTH OF THE DEMON Soft-c (1993, $12.95)	13.00
BLIND JUSTICE nn (1992, $7.50)-r/Det. #598-600	7.50
BLOODSTORM (1994, $24.95,HC) Kelley Jones-c/a	28.00
BRIDE OF THE DEMON Hard-c (1990, $19.95)	20.00
BRIDE OF THE DEMON Soft-c ($12.95)	13.00
...: BROKEN CITY HC-(2004, $24.95) r/#620-625; new Johnson-c; intro by Schreck	25.00
...: BRUCE WAYNE: FUGITIVE Vol. 1 ('02, $12.95)-r/ story arc	13.00
...: BRUCE WAYNE: FUGITIVE Vol. 2 ('03, $12.95)-r/ story arc	13.00
...: BRUCE WAYNE: FUGITIVE Vol. 3 ('03, $12.95)-r/ story arc	13.00
...: BRUCE WAYNE-MURDERER? ('02, $19.95)-r/ story arc	20.00
...: CASTLE OF THE BAT ($5.95)-Elseworlds story	6.00
...: CATACLYSM ('99, $17.95)-r/ story arc	18.00
...: CHILD OF DREAMS (2003, $24.95, B&W, HC) Reprint of Japanese manga with Kia Asamiya-s/a/c; English adaptation by Max Allan Collins; Asamiya interview	25.00
...: CHILD OF DREAMS (2003, $19.95, B&W, SC)	20.00
...: COLLECTED LEGENDS OF THE DARK KNIGHT nn (1994, $12.95)-r/Legends of the Dark Knight #32-34,38,42,43	13.00
...: CRIMSON MIST (1999, $24.95,HC)-Vampire Batman Elseworlds story Doug Moench-s/Kelley Jones-c/a	25.00
...: CRIMSON MIST (2001, $14.95,SC)	25.00
...: DARK JOKER-THE WILD (1993, $24.95,HC)-Elseworlds story; Moench-s/Jones-c/a	25.00
...: DARK JOKER-THE WILD (1993, $9.95,SC)	10.00

		GD	FN	NM-

...DARK KNIGHT DYNASTY nn (1997, $24.95)-Hard-c.; 3 Elseworlds stories;
    Barr-s/S. Hampton painted-a, Gary Frank, McDaniel-a(p)   25.00
...DARK KNIGHT DYNASTY Softcover (2000, $14.95) Hampton-c   15.00
...DEADMAN: DEATH AND GLORY nn (1996, $24.95)-Hard-c.; Robinson-s/
    Estes-c/a   25.00
...DEADMAN: DEATH AND GLORY ($12.95)-SC   13.00
DEATH IN THE FAMILY (1988, $3.95, trade paperback)-r/Batman #426-429
    by Aparo   5.00
DEATH IN THE FAMILY: (2nd - 5th printings)   4.00
...: DETECTIVE #27 HC (2003, $19.95)-Elseworlds; Uslan-s/Snejbjerg-a 20.00
...: DETECTIVE #27 SC (2004, $12.95)-Elseworlds   13.00
DIGITAL JUSTICE nn (1990, $24.95, Hard-c.)-Computer generated art 25.00
... :EVOLUTION (2001, $12.95, SC)-r/Detective Comics #743-750   13.00
... FACES (1995, $9.95, TPB)   10.00
...: FORTUNATE SON HC (1999, $24.95) Gene Ha-a   25.00
...: FORTUNATE SON SC (2000, $14.95) Gene Ha-a   15.00
FOUR OF A KIND TPB (1998, $14.95)-r/1995 Year One Annuals featuring
    Poison Ivy, Riddler, Scarecrow, & Man-Bat   15.00
...GOTHIC (1992, $12.95, TPB)-r/Legends of the Dark Knight #6-10   13.00
...: HARVEST BREED-(2000, $24.95) George Pratt-s/painted-a   25.00
...: HARVEST BREED-(2003, $17.95) George Pratt-s/painted-a   18.00
...: HAUNTED KNIGHT-(1997, $12.95) r/ Halloween specials   13.00
...: HONG KONG HC (2003, $24.95, with dustjacket) Doug Moench-s/Tony
    Wong-a   25.00
...: HONG KONG SC (2004, $17.95) Doug Moench-s/Tony Wong-a   18.00
...: HUSH DOUBLE FEATURE-(2003, $3.95) r/#608,609(1st 2 Jim Lee-a
    issues)   4.00
...: HUSH VOLUME 1 HC-(2003, $19.95) r/#608-612; & new 2 pg. origin
    w/Lee-a   20.00
...: HUSH VOLUME 1 SC-(2004, $12.95) r/#608-612; includes CD of DC GN
    art   13.00
...: HUSH VOLUME 2 HC-(2003, $19.95) r/#613-619; Lee intro & sketchpages
    20.00
...: HUSH VOLUME 2 SC-(2004, $12.95) r/#613-619; Lee intro & sketchpages
    13.00
...: ILLUSTRATED BY NEAL ADAMS VOL. 1 HC-(2003, $49.95) r/Batman,
    Brave and the Bold, and Detective Comics stories and cover   50.00
...: ILLUSTRATED BY NEAL ADAMS VOL. 2 HC-(2004, $49.95) r/Adams'
    Batman art from 1969-71; intro. by Dick Giordano   50.00
... IN THE FORTIES TPB ($19.95) Intro. by Bill Schelly   20.00
... IN THE FIFTIES TPB ($19.95) Intro. by Michael Uslan   20.00
... IN THE SIXTIES TPB ($19.95) Intro. by Adam West   20.00
... IN THE SEVENTIES TPB ($19.95) Intro. by Dennis O'Neil   20.00
... IN THE EIGHTIES TPB ($19.95) Intro. by John Wells   20.00
.../ JUDGE DREDD FILES (2004, $14.95) reprints cross-overs   15.00
... LEGACY-(1996,17.95) reprints Legacy   18.00
...: THE MANY DEATHS OF THE BATMAN (1992, $3.95, 84 pgs.)-r/Batman
    #433-435 w/new Byrne-c   4.00
...: THE MOVIES (1997, $19.95)-r/movie adaptations of Batman, Batman

	GD	FN	NM-

Returns, Batman Forever, Batman and Robin   20.00
...: NINE LIVES HC (2002, $24.95, sideways format) Motter-s/Lark-a   25.00
...: NINE LIVES SC (2003, $17.95, sideways format) Motter-s/Lark-a   18.00
...: OFFICER DOWN (2001, $12.95)-r/Commissioner shot x-over   13.00
...: PREY (1992, $12.95)-Gulacy/Austin-a   13.00
...: PRODIGAL (1997, $14.95)-Gulacy/Austin-a   15.00
SHAMAN (1993, $12.95)-r/Legends/D.K. #1-5   13.00
...: SON OF THE DEMON Hard-c (9/87, $14.95)   30.00
...: SON OF THE DEMON limited signed & numbered Hard-c (1,700)   45.00
...: SON OF THE DEMON Soft-c w/new-c ($8.95)   10.00
...: SON OF THE DEMON Soft-c (1989, $9.95, 2nd - 5th printings)   10.00
...: STRANGE APPARITIONS ($12.95) r/'77-'78 Englehart/Rogers stories
    from Detective #469-479; also Simonson-a   13.00
...: TALES OF THE DEMON (1991, $17.95, 212 pgs.)-Intro by Sam Hamm;
    reprints by Neal Adams(3) & Golden; contains Saga of Ra's al Ghul #1
    18.00
...: TEN NIGHTS OF THE BEAST (1994, $5.95)-r/Batman #417-420   6.00
...: TERROR (2003, $12.95, TPB)-r/Legends of the Dark Knight #137-141;
    Gulacy-c   13.00
...: THE CHALICE (HC, '99, $24.95) Van Fleet painted-a   25.00
...: THE CHALICE (SC, '00, $14.95) Van Fleet painted-a   15.00
...: THE LAST ANGEL (1994, $12.95, TPB) Lustbader-s   13.00
...: THE RING, THE ARROW AND THE BAT (2003, $19.95, TPB) r/Legends
    of the DCU #7-9 & Batman: Legends of the Dark Knight #127-131;
    Green Lantern & Green Arrow app.   20.00
...: THRILLKILLER (1998, $12.95, TPB)-r/series & Thrillkiller '62   13.00
...: VENOM (1993, $9.95, TPB)-r/Legends of the Dark Knight #16-20;
    embossed-c   10.00
... WAR DRUMS (2004, $17.95) r/Detective #790-796 & Robin #126-128
    18.00
YEAR ONE Hard-c (1988, $12.95)   18.00
YEAR ONE (1988, $9.95, TPB)-r/Batman #404-407 by Miller; intro by Miller
    10.00
YEAR ONE (TPB, 2nd & 3rd printings)   10.00
YEAR TWO (1990, $9.95, TPB)-r/Det. 575-578 by McFarlane; wraparound-c
    10.00

BATMAN (one-shots)
... ABDUCTION, THE (1998, $5.95)   6.00
... & ROBIN (1997, $5.95)-Movie adaptation   6.00
...: ARKHAM ASYLUM - TALES OF MADNESS (5/98, $2.95) Cataclysm
    x-over pt. 16   3.00
...: BANE (1997, $4.95)-Dixon-s/Burchett-a; Stelfreeze-c; cover art interlocks
    w/Batman:(Batgirl, Mr. Freeze, Poison Ivy)   5.00
...: BATGIRL (1997, $4.95)-Puckett-s/Haley,Kesel-a; Stelfreeze-c; cover art
    interlocks w/Batman:(Bane, Mr. Freeze, Poison Ivy)   5.00
...: BATGIRL (6/98, $1.95)-Girlfrenzy; Balent-a   2.50
...: BLACKGATE (1/97, $3.95) Dixon-s   4.00
...: BLACKGATE - ISLE OF MEN (4/98, $2.95) Cataclysm x-over pt. 8;
    Moench-s/Aparo-a   3.00

	GD	FN	NM-
... BOOK OF SHADOWS, THE (1999, $5.95)			6.00
BROTHERHOOD OF THE BAT (1995, $5.95)-Elseworlds-s			6.00
... BULLOCK'S LAW (8/99, $4.95) Dixon-s			5.00
.../CAPTAIN AMERICA (1996, $5.95, DC/Marvel) Elseworlds story; Byrne-c/s/a			6.00
... : CATWOMAN DEFIANT nn (1992, $4.95, prestige format)-Milligan scripts; cover art interlocks w/Batman: Penguin Triumphant; special foil logo			5.00
... /DAREDEVIL (2000, $5.95)-Barreto-a			6.00
...: DARK ALLEGIANCES (1996, $5.95)-Elseworlds story, Chaykin-c/a			6.00
...: DARK KNIGHT GALLERY (1/96, $3.50)-Pin-ups by Pratt, Balent, & others			3.50
...:DAY OF JUDGMENT (11/99, $3.95)			4.00
...:DEATH OF INNOCENTS (12/96, $3.95)-O'Neil-s/ Staton-a(p)			4.00
.../DEMON (1996, $4.95)-Alan Grant scripts			5.00
.../DEMON: A TRAGEDY (2000, $5.95)-Grant-s/Murray painted-a			6.00
...:D.O.A. (1999, $6.95)-Bob Hall-s/a			7.00
...:DREAMLAND (2000, $5.95)-Grant-s/Breyfogle-a			6.00
... : EGO (2000, $6.95)-Darwyn Cooke-s/a			7.00
... 80-PAGE GIANT (8/98, $4.95) Stelfreeze-c			6.00
... 80-PAGE GIANT 2 (10/99, $4.95) Luck of the Draw			6.00
... 80-PAGE GIANT 3 (7/00, $5.95) Calendar Man			6.00
... FOREVER (1995, $5.95, direct market)			6.00
... FOREVER (1995, $3.95, newsstand)			4.00
FULL CIRCLE nn (1991, $5.95, 68 pgs.)-Sequel to Batman: Year Two			6.00
...GALLERY, The 1 (1992, $2.95)-Pin-ups by Miller, N. Adams & others			3.00
...GOLDEN STREETS OF GOTHAM (2003, $6.95) Elseworlds Gotham City in early 1900s			7.00
...GOTHAM BY GASLIGHT (1989, $3.95)			4.00
...GOTHAM CITY SECRET FILES 1 (4/00, $4.95) Batgirl app.			5.00
...: GOTHAM NOIR (2001, $6.95)-Elseworlds; Brubaker-s/Phillips-c/a			7.00
.../GREEN ARROW: THE POISON TOMORROW nn (1992, $5.95, square-bound, 68 pgs.) Netzer-c/a			6.00
HOLY TERROR nn (1991, $4.95, 52 pgs.)-Elseworlds story			5.00
.../HOUDINI: THE DEVIL'S WORKSHOP (1993, $5.95)			6.00
... :HUNTRESS/SPOILER - BLUNT TRAUMA (5/98, $2.95) Cataclysm pt. 13; Dixon-s/Barreto & Sienkiewicz-a			3.00
...: I, JOKER nn (1998, $4.95)-Elseworlds story; Bob Hall-s/a			5.00
...: IN DARKEST KNIGHT nn (1994, $4.95, 52 pgs.)-Elseworlds story; Batman w/Green Lantern's ring.			5.00
...:JOKER'S APPRENTICE (5/99, $3.95) Von Eeden-a			4.00
.../ JOKER: SWITCH (2003, $6.95)-Bolton-a/Grayson-s			7.00
....:JUDGE DREDD: JUDGEMENT ON GOTHAM nn (1991, $5.95, 68 pgs.) Simon Bisley-c/a; Grant/Wagner scripts			6.00
...:JUDGE DREDD: JUDGEMENT ON GOTHAM nn (2nd printing)			6.00
...:JUDGE DREDD: THE ULTIMATE RIDDLE (1995, $4.95)			5.00
...:JUDGE DREDD: VENDETTA IN GOTHAM (1993, $5.95)			6.00
...: KNIGHTGALLERY (1995, $3.50)-Elseworlds sketchbook			3.50
.../ LOBO (2000, $5.95)-Elseworlds; Joker app.; Bisley-a			6.00
....: MASK OF THE PHANTASM (1994, $2.95)-Movie adapt.			3.00

	GD	FN	NM-
...: MASK OF THE PHANTASM (1994, $4.95)-Movie adapt.			5.00
...: MASQUE (1997, $6.95)-Elseworlds; Grell-c/s/a			7.00
...: MASTER OF THE FUTURE nn (1991, $5.95, 68 pgs.)-Elseworlds sequel to Gotham By Gaslight; embossed-c			6.00
...: MITEFALL (1995, $4.95)-Alan Grant script, Kevin O'Neill-a			5.00
... : MR. FREEZE (1997, $4.95)-Dini-s/Buckingham-a; Stelfreeze-c; cover art interlocks w/Batman:(Bane, Batgirl, Poison Ivy)			5.00
... /NIGHTWING: BLOODBORNE (2002, $5.95) Cypress-a; McKeever-c			6.00
...: NOSFERATU (1999, $5.95) McKeever-a			6.00
...: OF ARKHAM (2000, $5.95)-Elseworlds; Grant-s/Alcatena-a			6.00
...: OUR WORLDS AT WAR (8/01, $2.95)-Jae Lee-c			3.00
...: PENGUIN TRIUMPHANT nn (1992, $4.95)-Staton-a(p); foil logo			5.00
...•PHANTOM STRANGER nn (1997, $4.95) nn-Grant-s/Ransom-a			5.00
... : PLUS (2/97, $2.95) Arsenal-c/app.			3.00
... : POISON IVY (1997, $4.95)-J.F. Moore-s/Apthorp-a; Stelfreeze-c; cover art interlocks w/Batman:(Bane, Batgirl, Mr. Freeze)			5.00
.../POISON IVY: CAST SHADOWS (2004, $6.95) Van Fleet-c/a			7.00
.../PUNISHER: LAKE OF FIRE (1994, $4.95, DC/Marvel)			5.00
... :REIGN OF TERROR ('99, $4.95) Elseworlds			5.00
...-RETURNS MOVIE SPECIAL (1992, $3.95)			4.00
...RETURNS MOVIE PRESTIGE (1992, $5.95, squarebound)-Dorman painted-c			6.00
...:RIDDLER-THE RIDDLE FACTORY (1995, $4.95)-Wagner script			5.00
...: ROOM FULL OF STRANGERS (2004, $5.95) Scott Morse-s/c/a			6.00
...: SCARECROW 3-D (12/98, $3.95) w/glasses			4.00
.../ SCARFACE: A PSYCHODRAMA (2001, $5.95)-Adlard-a/Sienkiewicz-c			6.00
...: SCAR OF THE BAT nn (1996, $4.95)-Elseworlds; Max Allan Collins script; Barreto-a			5.00
... :SCOTTISH CONNECTION (1998, $5.95) Quitely-a			6.00
... :SEDUCTION OF THE GUN nn (1992, $2.50, 68 pgs.)			3.00
.../SPAWN: WAR DEVIL nn (1994, $4.95, 52 pgs.)			5.00
... SPECIAL 1 (4/84)-Mike W. Barr story; Golden-c/a	1	3	8
.../SPIDER-MAN (1997, $4.95) Dematteis-s/Nolan & Kesel-a			5.00
... : THE ABDUCTION ('98, $5.95)			6.00
...: THE BLUE, THE GREY, & THE BAT (1992, $5.95)-Weiss/Lopez-a			6.00
... :THE HILL (5/00, $2.95)-Priest-s/Martinbrough-a			3.00
... :THE KILLING JOKE (1988, deluxe 52 pgs., mature readers)-Bolland-c/a; Alan Moore scripts; Joker cripples Barbara Gordon	2	6	15
...: THE KILLING JOKE (2nd thru 10th printings)			4.00
...: THE OFFICIAL COMIC ADAPTATION OF THE WARNER BROS. MOTION PICTURE (1989, $2.50, regular format, 68 pgs.)-Ordway-c			3.00
...: THE OFFICIAL COMIC ADAPTATION OF THE WARNER BROS. MOTION PICTURE (1989, $4.95, prestige format, 68 pgs.)-same interiors but different-c			5.00
...: THE ORDER OF BEASTS (2004, $5.95)-Elseworlds; Eddie Campbell-a			6.00
...: THE 10-CENT ADVENTURE (3/02, 10¢) intro. to the "Bruce Wayne:			

	GD	FN	NM-

Murderer" x-over; Rucka-s/Burchett & Janson-a/Dave Johnson-c   2.25

NOTE: (Also see Promotional Comics section for alternate copies with special outer half-covers promoting local comic shops)

...: THE 12-CENT ADVENTURE (10/04, 12¢) intro. to the "War Games" x-over;
   Grayson-s/Bachs-a; Catwoman & Spoiler app.   2.25
...: TWO-FACE-CRIME AND PUNISHMENT-(1995, $4.95)-McDaniel-a   5.00
... : TWO FACES (11/98, $4.95) Elseworlds   5.00
...: VENGEANCE OF BANE SPECIAL 1 (1992, $2.50, 68 pgs.)-Origin & 1st
   app. Bane (see Batman #491)   2   6   12
...: VENGEANCE OF BANE SPECIAL 1 (2nd printing)   3.00
.....:VENGEANCE OF BANE II nn (1995, $3.95)-sequel   4.00
...Vs. THE INCREDIBLE HULK (1995, $3.95)-r/DC Special Series #27   4.00
...: VILLAINS SECRET FILES (10/98, $4.95) Origin-s   5.00

BATMAN ADVENTURES, THE (Based on animated series)
DC Comics: Oct, 1992 - No. 36, Oct, 1995 ($1.25/$1.50)

1-Penguin-c/story   4.00
1 ($1.95, Silver Edition)-2nd printing   2.25
2-6,8-19: 2,12-Catwoman-c/story. 3-Joker-c/story. 5-Scarecrow-c/story.
   10-Riddler-c/story. 11-Man-Bat/story. 12-Batgirl & Catwoman-c/story.
   16-Joker-c/story. 18-Batgirl-c/story. 19-Scarecrow-c/story   3.00
7-Special edition polybagged with Man-Bat trading card   5.00
20-24,26-32: 26-Batgirl app.   2.50
25-($2.50, 52 pgs.)-Superman app.   3.00
33-36: 33-Begin $1.75-c   2.25
Annual 1,2 ('94, '95): 2-Demon-c/story; Ra's al Ghul app.   3.50
...: Dangerous Dames & Demons (2003, $14.95, TPB) r/Annual 1,2, Mad
  Love & Adventures in the DC Universe #3; Bruce Timm painted-c   15.00
Holiday Special 1 (1995, $2.95)   4.00
The Collected Adventures Vol. 1,2 ('93, '95, $5.95)   6.00
TPB ('98, $7.95) r/#1-6; painted wraparound-c   8.00

BATMAN ADVENTURES (Based on animated series)
DC Comics: Jun, 2003 - No. 17, Oct, 2004 ($2.25)

1-Timm-c (2003 Free Comic Book Day edition is listed in Promotional
  Comics section)   2.25
2-17: 3,16-Joker-c/app. 4-Ra's al Ghul app. 6-8-Phantasm app. 14-Grey
  Ghost app.   2.25
Vol. 1: Rogues Gallery (2004, $6.95, digest size) r/#1-4 & Batman: Gotham
  Advs. #50   7.00
Vol. 2: Shadows & Masks (2004, $6.95, digest size) r/#5-9   7.00

BATMAN ADVENTURES, THE: MAD LOVE
DC Comics: Feb, 1994 ($3.95/$4.95)

1-Origin of Harley Quinn; Dini-s/Timm-c/a   2   6   12
1-($4.95, Prestige format) new Timm painted-c   1   3   8

BATMAN ADVENTURES, THE: THE LOST YEARS (TV)
DC Comics: Jan, 1998 - No. 5, May, 1998 ($1.95) (Based on animated
series)

1-5-Leads into Fall '97's new animated episodes. 4-Tim Drake becomes

	GD	FN	NM-

Robin. 5-Dick becomes Nightwing 2.25
TPB-(1999, $9.95) r/series 10.00

BATMAN/ALIENS
DC Comics/Dark Horse: Mar, 1997 - No. 2, Apr, 1997 ($4.95, limited series)

1,2: Wrightson-c/a. 5.00
TPB-(1997, $14.95) w/prequel from DHP #101,102 .... 15.00

BATMAN/ALIENS II
DC Comics/Dark Horse: 2003 - No. 3, 2003 ($5.95, limited series)

1-3-Edginton-s/Staz Johnson-a 6.00
TPB-(2003, $14.95) r/#1-3 .... 15.00

BATMAN AND ROBIN ADVENTURES (TV)
DC Comics: Nov, 1995 - No. 25, Dec, 1997 ($1.75) (Based on animated series)

1-Dini-s. 3.00
2-24: 2-4-Dini script. 4-Penguin-c/story. 5-Joker-c/story; Poison Ivy, Harley Quinn-c/app. 9-Batgirl & Talia-c/story. 10-Ra's al Ghul-c/story. 11-Man-Bat app. 12-Bane-c/app. 13-Scarecrow-c/app. 15 Deadman-c/app. 16-Catwoman-c/app. 18-Joker-c/app. 24-Poison Ivy app. 2.25
25-($2.95, 48 pgs.) 3.00
Annual 1,2 (11/96, 11/97): 1-Phantasm-c/app. 2-Zatara & Zatanna-c/app. 4.00
...: Sub-Zero(1998, $3.95) Adaptation of animated video 4.00

BATMAN AND SUPERMAN ADVENTURES: WORLD'S FINEST
DC Comics: 1997 ($6.95, square-bound, one-shot) (Based on animated series)

1-Adaptation of animated crossover episode; Dini-s/Timm-c 7.00

BATMAN AND SUPERMAN: WORLD'S FINEST
DC Comics: Apr, 1999 - No. 10, Jan, 2000 ($4.95/$1.99, limited series)

1,10-($4.95, squarebound) Taylor-a 5.00
2-9-($1.99) 5-Batgirl app. 8-Catwoman-c/app. 2.25
TPB (2003, $19.95) r/#1-10 .... 20.00

BATMAN AND THE OUTSIDERS (The Adventures of the Outsiders #33 on) (Also see Brave & The Bold #200 & The Outsiders) (Replaces The Brave and the Bold)
DC Comics: Aug, 1983 - No. 32, Apr, 1986 (Mando paper #5 on)

1-Batman, Halo, Geo-Force, Katana, Metamorpho & Black Lightning begin 4.00
2-32: 5-New Teen Titans x-over. 9-Halo begins. 11,12-Origin Katana. 18-More info on Metamorpho's origin. 28-31-Lookers origin. 32-Team disbands 2.50
Annual 1,2 (9/84, 9/85): 2-Metamorpho & Sapphire Stagg wed 3.00

BATMAN: BANE OF THE DEMON
DC Comics: Mar, 1998 - No. 4, June, 1998 ($1.95, limited series)

1-4-Dixon-s/Nolan-a; prelude to Legacy x-over 2.50

BATMAN BEYOND (Based on animated series)(Mini-series)
DC Comics: Mar, 1999 - No. 6, Aug, 1999 ($1.99)

	GD	FN	NM-

1-6: 1,2-Adaptation of pilot episode, Timm-c   2.25
TPB (1999, $9.95) r/#1-6   10.00

BATMAN BEYOND (Based on animated series)(Continuing series)
DC Comics: Nov, 1999 - No. 24, Oct, 2001 ($1.99)

1-24: 1-Rousseau-a; Batman vs. Batman. 14-Demon-c/app. 21,22-Justice
   League Unlimited-c/app.   2.25
...: Return of the Joker (2/01, $2.95) adaptation of video release   3.00

BATMAN: BLACK & WHITE
DC Comics: June, 1996 - No. 4, Sept, 1996 ($2.95, B&W, limited series)

1-Stories by McKeever, Timm, Kubert, Chaykin, Goodwin; Jim Lee-c;
   Allred inside front-c; Moebius inside back-c   4.00
2-4: 2-Stories by Simonson, Corben, Bisley & Gaiman; Miller-c. 3-Stories by
   M. Wagner, Janson, Sienkiewicz, O'Neil & Kristiansen; B. Smith-c; Russell
   inside front-c; Silvestri inside back-c. 4-Stories by Bolland, Goodwin &
   Gianni, Strnad & Nowlan, O'Neil & Stelfreeze; Toth-c; pin-ups by Neal
   Adams & Alex Ross   3.00
Hardcover ('97, $39.95) r/series w/new art & cover plate   40.00
Softcover ('00, $19.95) r/series   20.00
Volume 2 HC ('02, $39.95, 7 3/4"x12") r/B&W back-up-s from Batman:
   Gotham Knights #1-16; stories and art by various incl. Ross, Buscema,
   Byrne, Ellison, Sale; Mignola-c   40.00
Volume 2 SC ('03, $19.95, 7 3/4"x12") same contents as HC   20.00

BATMAN/ CATWOMAN: TRAIL OF THE GUN
DC Comics: 2004 - No. 2, 2004 ($5.95, limited series, prestige format)

1,2-Elseworlds; Van Sciver-a/Nocenti-s   6.00

BATMAN CHRONICLES, THE
DC Comics: Summer, 1995 - No. 23, Winter, 2001 ($2.95, quarterly)

1-3,5-19: 1-Dixon/Grant/Moench script. 3-Bolland-c. 5-Oracle Year One story,
   Richard Dragon app.,Chaykin-c. 6-Kaluta-c; Ra's al Ghul story.
   7-Superman-c/app.11-Paul Pope-s/a. 12-Cataclysm pt. 10   3.50
4-Hitman story by Ennis, Contagion tie-in; Balent-c   2   6   12
20-23: 20-Catwoman and Relative Heroes-c/app. 21-Pander Bros.-a   3.00
...Gallery (3/97, $3.50) Pin-ups   3.50
...Gauntlet, The (1997, $4.95, one-shot)   5.00

BATMAN: DARK VICTORY
DC Comics: 1999 - No. 13, 2000 ($4.95/$2.95, limited series)

Wizard #0 Preview   2.25
1-($4.95) Loeb-s/Sale-c/a   5.00
2-12-($2.95)   3.00
13-($4.95)   5.00
Hardcover (2001, $29.95) with dust jacket; r/#0,1-13   30.00
Softcover (2002, $19.95) r/#0,1-13   20.00

BATMAN: DEATH AND THE MAIDENS
DC Comics: Oct, 2003 - No. 9, Aug, 2004 ($2.95, limited series)

1-Ra's al Ghul app.; Rucka-s/Janson-a   4.00

	GD	FN	NM-

2-9: 9-Ra's al Ghul dies ... 3.00
TPB (2004, $19.95) r/#1-9 & Detective #783 ... 20.00

BATMAN/ DEATHBLOW: AFTER THE FIRE
DC Comics/WildStorm: 2002 - No. 3, 2002 ($5.95, limited series)

1-3-Azzarello-s/Bermejo & Bradstreet-a ... 6.00
TPB (2003, $12.95) r/#1-3; plus concept art ... 13.00

BATMAN FAMILY, THE
National Periodical Pub./DC Comics: Sept-Oct, 1975 - No. 20, Oct-Nov, 1978 (#1-4, 17-on: 68 pgs.) (Combined with Detective Comics with No. 481)

1-Origin/2nd app. Batgirl-Robin team-up (The Dynamite Duo); reprints plus one new story begins; N. Adams-a(r); r/1st app. Man-Bat from Det. #400 ... 3 ... 9 ... 32
2-5: 2-r/Det. #369. 3-Batgirl & Robin learn each's i.d.; r/Batwoman app. from Batman #105. 4-r/1st Fatman app. from Batman #113. 5-r/1st Bat-Hound app. from Batman #92 ... 2 ... 6 ... 18
6,9-Joker's daughter on cover (1st app?) ... 2 ... 6 ... 22
7,8,14-16: 8-r/Batwoman app.14-Batwoman app. 15-3rd app. Killer Moth. 16-Bat-Girl cameo (last app. in costume until New Teen Titans #47) ... 2 ... 6 ... 15
10-1st revival Batwoman; Cavalier app.; Killer Moth app. ... 3 ... 9 ... 24
11-13,17-20: 11-13-Rogers-a(p): 11-New stories begin; Man-Bat begins. 13-Batwoman cameo. 17-($1.00 size)-Batman, Huntress begin; Batwoman & Catwoman 1st meet. 18-20: Huntress by Staton in all. 20-Origin Ragman retold ... 2 ... 6 ... 22

BATMAN: FAMILY
DC Comics: Dec, 2002 - No. 8, Feb, 2003 ($2.95/$2.25, weekly lim. series)

1,8-($2.95). John Francis Moore-s/Hoberg & Gaudiano-a ... 3.00
2-7-($2.25). 3-Orpheus & Black Canary app. ... 2.25

BATMAN: GCPD
DC Comics: Aug, 1996 - No. 4, Nov, 1996 ($2.25, limited series)

1-4: Features Jim Gordon; Aparo/Sienkiewicz-a ... 2.50

BATMAN: GORDON OF GOTHAM
DC Comics: June, 1998 - No. 4, Sept, 1998 ($1.95, limited series)

1-4: Gordon's early days in Chicago ... 2.50

BATMAN: GOTHAM ADVENTURES (TV)
DC Comics: June, 1998 - No. 60, May, 2003 ($2.95/$1.95/$1.99/$2.25)

1-($2.95) Based on Kids WB Batman animated series ... 3.00
2-3-($1.95): 2-Two-Face-c/app. ... 2.50
4-22: 4-Begin $1.99-c. 5-Deadman-c. 13-MAD #1 cover swipe ... 2.50
23-60: 31,60-Joker-c/app. 50-Catwoman-c/app. 58-Creeper-c/app. ... 2.25
TPB (2000, $9.95) r/#1-6 ... 10.00

BATMAN: GOTHAM KNIGHTS
DC Comics: Mar, 2000 - Present ($2.50/$2.75)

1-Grayson-s; B&W back-up by Warren Eliis & Jim Lee ... 4.00

	GD	FN	NM-

2-10-Grayson-s; B&W back-ups by various — 2.75
11-($3.25) Bolland-c; Kyle Baker back-up story — 3.25
12-24: 13-Officer Down x-over; Ellison back-up-s. 15-Colan back-up.
 20-Superman-c/app. — 2.75
25,26-Bruce Wayne: Murderer pt. 4,10 — 3.00
27-31: 28,30,31-Bruce Wayne: Fugitive pt. 7,14,17 — 2.75
32-49: 32-Begin $2.75-c; Kaluta-a back-up. 33,34-Bane-c/app. 35-Mahfood-a
 back-up. 38-Bolton-a back-up. 43-Jason Todd & Batgirl app. 44-Jason
 Todd flashback — 2.75
50-54-Hush returns-Barrionuevo-a/Bermejo-c. 53,54-Green Arrow app. — 3.00
55-($3.75) Batman vs. Hush; Joker & Riddler app. — 4.00
56-60: 56-58-War Games; Jae Lee-c. 60-Hush app. — 2.50

BATMAN: GOTHAM NIGHTS II (First series listed under Gotham Nights)
DC Comics: Mar, 1995 - No. 4, June, 1995 ($1.95, limited series)

1-4 — 2.50

BATMAN/GRENDEL (1st limited series)
DC Comics: 1993 - No. 2, 1993 ($4.95, limited series, squarebound; 52 pgs.)

1,2: Batman vs. Hunter Rose. 1-Devil's Riddle; Matt Wagner-c/a/scripts.
 2-Devil's Masque; Matt Wagner-c/a/scripts — 6.00

BATMAN/GRENDEL (2nd limited series)
DC Comics: June, 1996 - No. 2, July, 1996 ($4.95, limited series, square-
bound)

1,2: Batman vs. Grendel Prime. 1-Devil's Bones. 2-Devil's Dance;
 Wagner-c/a/s — 5.00

BATMAN: HARLEY & IVY
DC Comics: Jun, 2004 - No. 3, Aug, 2004 ($2.50, limited series)

1-3-Paul Dini-s/Bruce Timm-c/a — 2.50

BATMAN: HARLEY QUINN
DC Comics: 1999 ($5.95, prestige format)

1-Intro. of Harley Quinn into regular DC continuity; Dini-s/Alex Ross-c — 9.00
1-(2nd printing) — 6.00

BATMAN: HAUNTED GOTHAM
DC Comics: 2000 - No. 4, 2000 ($4.95, limited series, squarebound)

1-4-Moench-s/Kelley Jones-c/a — 5.00

BATMAN/ HELLBOY/STARMAN
DC Comics/Dark Horse: Jan, 1999 - No. 2, Feb, 1999 ($2.50, limited series)

1,2: Robinson-s/Mignola-a. 2-Harris-c — 2.50

BATMAN: LEGENDS OF THE DARK KNIGHT (Legends of the Dark...#1-36)
DC Comics: Nov, 1989 - Present ($1.50/$1.75/$1.95/$1.99/$2.25/$2.50)

1- "Shaman" begins, ends #5; outer cover has four different color variations,
 all worth same — 4.00
2-10: 6-10- "Gothic" by Grant Morrison (scripts) — 3.00
11-15: 11-15-Gulacy/Austin-a. 13-Catwoman app. — 3.00
16-Intro drug Bane uses; begin Venom story — 5.00

	GD	FN	NM-
17-20			4.00
21-49,51-63: 38-Bat-Mite-c/story. 46-49-Catwoman app. w/Heath-c/a.			
51-Ragman app.; Joe Kubert-c. 59,60,61-Knightquest x-over.			
62,63-KnightsEnd Pt. 4 & 10			3.00
50-($3.95, 68 pgs.)-Bolland embossed gold foil-c; Joker-c/story; pin-ups by			
Chaykin, Simonson, Williamson, Kaluta, Russell, others			5.00
64-99: 64-(9/94)-Begin $1.95-c. 71-73-James Robinson-s,Watkiss-c/a.			
74,75-McKeever-c/a/s. 76-78-Scott Hampton-c/a/s. 81-Card insert.			
83,84-Ellis-s. 85-Robinson-s. 91-93-Ennis-s. 94-Michael T. Gilbert-s/a			3.00
100-($3.95) Alex Ross painted-c; gallery by various			5.00
101-115: 101-Ezquerra-a. 102-104-Robinson-s			2.50
116-No Man's Land stories begin; Huntress-c			4.00
117-119,121-126: 122-Harris-c			2.50
120-ID of new Batgirl revealed			4.00
127-131: Return to Legends stories; Green Arrow app.			2.50
132-186: 132-136 ($2.25-c) Archie Goodwin-s/Rogers-a. 137-141-Gulacy-a.			
142-145-Joker and Ra's al Ghul app. 146-148-Kitson-a. 158-Begin $2.50-c			
169-171-Tony Harris-c/a. 182-184-War Games. 182-Bagged with Sky			
Captain CD			2.50
#0-(10/94)-Zero Hour; Quesada/Palmiotti-c; released between #64&65			3.00
Annual 1-7 ('91-'97, $3.50-$3.95, 68 pgs.): 1-Joker app. 2-Netzer-c/a. 3-New			
Batman (Azrael) app. 4-Elseworlds story. 5-Year One; Man-Bat app.			
6-Legend of the Dead Earth story. 7-Pulp Heroes story			4.00
Halloween Special 1 (12/93, $6.95, 84 pgs.)-Embossed & foil stamped-c			

	1	3	7
Batman Madness-...Halloween Special (1994, $4.95)			5.00
Batman Ghosts-...Halloween Special (1995, $4.95)			5.00

BATMAN-LEGENDS OF THE DARK KNIGHT: JAZZ
DC Comics: Apr, 1995 - No. 3, June, 1995 ($2.50, limited series)

1-3			2.50

BATMAN: MANBAT
DC Comics: Oct, 1995 - No. 3, Dec, 1995 ($4.95, limited series)

1-3-Elseworlds-Delano-script; Bolton-a.			5.00
TPB-(1997, $14.95) r/#1-3			15.00

BATMAN: NEVERMORE
DC Comics: June, 2003 - No. 5, Oct, 2003 ($2.50, limited series)

1-5-Elseworlds Batman & Edgar Allan Poe; Wrightson-c/Guy Davis-a/			
Len Wein-s			2.50

BATMAN: NO MAN'S LAND (Also see 1999 Batman titles)
DC Comics: (one shots)

nn (3/99, $2.95) Alex Ross-c; Bob Gale-s; begins year-long story arc			3.00
Collector's Ed. (3/99, $3.95) Ross lenticular-c			5.00
#0 (: Ground Zero on cover) (12/99, $4.95) Orbik-c			5.00
...: Gallery (7/99, $3.95) Jim Lee-c			4.00
...: Secret Files (12/99, $4.95) Maleev-c			5.00
TPB ('99, $12.95) r/early No Man's Land stories; new Batgirl early app.			13.00
No Law and a New Order TPB(1999, $5.95) Ross-c			6.00

	GD	FN	NM-

Volume 2 ('00, $12.95) r/later No Man's Land stories; Batgirl(Huntress) app.;
  Deodato-c   13.00
Volume 3-5 ('00,'01 $12.95) 3-Intro. new Batgirl. 4-('00). 5-('01) Land-c   13.00

BATMAN/PREDATOR III: BLOOD TIES
DC Comics/Dark Horse Comics: Nov, 1997 - No. 4, Feb, 1998 ($1.95, lim. series)

1-4: Dixon-s/Damaggio-c/a   2.50
TPB-(1998, $7.95) r/#1-4   8.00

BATMAN RETURNS MOVIE SPECIAL (See Batman one-shots)

BATMAN: SECRET FILES
DC Comics: Oct, 1997 ($4.95)

1-New origin-s and profiles   5.00

BATMAN: SHADOW OF THE BAT
DC Comics: June, 1992 - No. 94, Feb, 2000 ($1.50/$1.75/$1.95/$1.99)

1-The Last Arkham-c/story begins; Alan Grant scripts in all   4.00
1-($2.50)-Deluxe edition polybagged w/poster, pop-up & book mark   5.00
2-7: 4-The Last Arkham ends. 7-Last $1.50-c   3.00
8-28: 14,15-Staton-a(p). 16-18-Knightfall tie-ins. 19-28-Knightquest tie-ins
  w/Azrael as Batman. 25-Silver ink-c; anniversary issue   2.50
29-($2.95, 52 pgs.)-KnightsEnd Pt. 2   3.00
30-72: 30-KnightsEnd Pt. 8. 31-(9.94)-Begin $1.95-c; Zero Hour. 32-(11/94).
  33-Robin-c. 35-Troika-Pt.2. 43,44-Cat-Man & Catwoman-c. 48-Contagion
  Pt. 1; card insert. 49-Contagion Pt.7. 56,57,58-Poison Ivy-c/app.
  62-Two-Face app. 69,70-Fate app.   2.50
35-($2.95)-Variant embossed-c   3.00
73,74,76-78: Cataclysm x-over pts. 1,9. 76-78-Orbik-c   2.50
75-($2.95) Mr. Freeze & Clayface app.; Orbik-c   3.00
79,81,82: 79-Begin $1.99-c; Orbik-c   2.50
80-($3.95) Flip book with Azrael #47   4.00
83-No Man's Land; intro. new Batgirl (Huntress)   12.00
84,85-No Man's Land   4.00
86-94: 87-Deodato-a. 90-Harris-c. 92-Superman app. 93-Joker and Harley
  app. 94-No Man's Land ends   3.00
#0 (10/94) Zero Hour; released between #31&32   3.00
#1,000,000 (11/98) 853rd Century x-over; Orbik-c   2.50
Annual 1-5 ('93-'97 $2.95-$3.95, 68 pgs.): 3-Year One story; Poison Ivy app.
  4-Legends of the Dead Earth story; Starman cameo. 5-Pulp Heroes story;
  Poison Ivy app.   4.00

BATMAN-SPAWN: WAR DEVIL (See Batman one-shots)

BATMAN SPECTACULAR (See DC Special Series No. 15)

BATMAN STRIKES!, THE (Based on the 2004 animated series)
DC Comics: Nov, 2004 - Present ($2.25)

1,2,4: 1-Penguin app. 2-Man-Bat app. 4-Bane app.   2.25
3-($2.95) Joker-c/app.; Catwoman & Wonder Woman-r from Advs. in the
  DCU   3.00

	GD	FN	NM-

BATMAN/ SUPERMAN/WONDER WOMAN: TRINITY
DC Comics: 2003 - No. 3, 2003 ($6.95, limited series, squarebound)

1-3-Matt Wagner-s/a/c. 1-Ra's al Ghul & Bizarro app.			7.00
HC (2004, $24.95, with dust-jacket) r/series; intro. by Brad Meltzer			30.00

BATMAN: SWORD OF AZRAEL (Also see Azrael & Batman #488,489)
DC Comics: Oct, 1992 - No. 4, Jan, 1993 ($1.75, limited series)

1-Wraparound gatefold-c; Quesada-c/a(p) in all; 1st app. Azrael	2	6	12
2-4: 4-Cont'd in Batman #488	1	3	8
Silver Edition 1-4 (1993, $1.95)-Reprints #1-4			2.25
Trade Paperback (1993, $9.95)-Reprints #1-4			10.00
Trade Paperback Gold Edition			15.00

BATMAN/ TARZAN: CLAWS OF THE CAT-WOMAN
Dark Horse Comics/DC Comics: Sept, 1999 - No. 4, Dec, 1999 ($2.95, limited series)

1-4: Marz-s/Kordey-a			3.00

BATMAN: THE CULT
DC Comics: 1988 - No. 4, Nov, 1988 ($3.50, deluxe limited series)

1-Wrightson-a/painted-c in all			6.00
2-4			5.00
Trade Paperback ('91, $14.95)-New Wrightson-c			15.00

BATMAN: THE DARK KNIGHT RETURNS (Also see Dark Knight Strikes Again)
DC Comics: Mar, 1986 - No. 4, 1986 ($2.95, squarebound, limited series)

1-Miller story & c/a(p); set in the future	5	15	55
1,2-2nd & 3rd printings, 3-2nd printing			6.00
2-Carrie Kelly becomes 1st female Robin	3	9	28
3-Death of Joker; Superman app.	2	6	22
4-Death of Alfred; Superman app.	2	6	18
Hardcover, signed & numbered edition ($40.00)(4000 copies)			250.00
Hardcover, trade edition			50.00
Softcover, trade edition (1st printing only)	2	6	18
Softcover, trade edition (2nd thru 8th printings)	1	3	9
10th Anniv. Slipcase set ('96, $100.00): Signed & numbered hard-c edition (10,000 copies), sketchbook, copy of script for #1, 2 color prints			100.00
10th Anniv. Hardcover ('96, $45.00)			45.00
10th Anniv. Softcover ('97, $14.95)			15.00
Hardcover 2nd printing ('02, $24.95) with 3 1/4" tall partial dustjacket			25.00

NOTE: *The #2 second printings can be identified by matching the grey background colors on the inside front cover and facing page. The inside front cover of the second printing has a dark grey background which does not match the lighter grey of the facing page. On the true 1st printings, the backgrounds are both light grey. All other issues are clearly marked.*

BATMAN: THE KILLING JOKE (See Batman one-shots)

BATMAN: THE LONG HALLOWEEN
DC Comics: Oct, 1996 - No. 13, Oct, 1997 ($2.95/$4.95, limited series)

1-($4.95)-Loeb-s/Sale-c/a in all	1	3	8

	GD	FN	NM-

2-5($2.95): 2-Solomon Grundy-c/app. 3-Joker-c/app., Catwoman,
Poison Ivy app. 6.00
6-10: 6-Poison Ivy-c. 7-Riddler-c/app. 5.00
11,12 .... 4.00
13-($4.95, 48 pgs.)-Killer revelations 5.00
HC-($29.95) r/series 30.00
SC-($19.95) 20.00

**BATMAN: THE OFFICIAL COMIC ADAPTATION OF THE WARNER BROS.
MOTION PICTURE** (See Batman one-shots)

BATMAN 3-D (Also see 3-D Batman)
DC Comics: 1990 ($9.95, w/glasses, 8-1/8x10-3/4")

nn-Byrne-a/scripts; Riddler, Joker, Penguin & Two-Face app. plus r/1953 3-D
Batman; pin-ups by many artists | 2 | 6 | 12 |

BATMAN: TWO-FACE STRIKES TWICE
DC Comics: 1993 - No. 2, 1993 ($4.95, 52 pgs.)

1,2-Flip book format w/Staton-a (G.A. side) 5.00

BATMAN VERSUS PREDATOR
DC Comics/Dark Horse Comics: 1991 - No. 3, 1992 ($4.95/$1.95, limited
series) (1st DC/Dark Horse x-over)

1 (Prestige format, $4.95)-1 & 3 contain 8 Batman/Predator trading cards;
Andy & Adam Kubert-a; Suydam painted-c 6.00
1-3 (Regular format, $1.95)-No trading cards 3.00
2,3-(Prestige)-2-Extra pin-ups inside; Suydam-c 5.00
TPB (1993, $5.95, 132 pgs.)-r/#1-3 w/new introductions & forward plus new
wraparound-c by Dave Gibbons 6.00

BATMAN VERSUS PREDATOR II: BLOODMATCH
DC Comics: Late 1994 - No. 4, 1995 ($2.50, limited series)

1-4-Huntress app.; Moench scripts; Gulacy-a 3.00
TPB (1995, $6.95)-r/#1-4 .... 7.00

BATMAN VS. THE INCREDIBLE HULK (See DC Special Series No. 27)

BATMAN: WAR ON CRIME
DC Comics: Nov, 1999 ($9.95, treasury size, one-shot)

nn-Painted art by Alex Ross; story by Alex Ross and Paul Dini 10.00

BATMAN/ WILDCAT
DC Comics: Apr, 1997 - No.3, June, 1997 ($2.25, mini-series)

1-3: Dixon/Smith-s: 1-Killer Croc app. 2.50

BATTLE CHASERS
Image Comics (Cliffhanger): Apr, 1998 - No. 4, Dec, 1998;
DC Comics (Cliffhanger): No. 5, May, 1999 - No. 8, May, 2001 ($2.50)
Image Comics: No. 9, Sept, 2001 ($3.50)

Prelude (2/98) | 1 | 4 | 10 |
Prelude Gold Ed. | 1 | 4 | 10 |
1-Madureira & Sharrieff-s/Madureira-a(p)/Charest-c | 1 | 3 | 9 |
1-American Ent. Ed. w/"racy" cover | 1 | 4 | 10 |

	GD	FN	NM-
1-Gold Edition			9.00
1-Chromium cover			40.00
1-2nd printing			3.00
2			5.00
2-Dynamic Forces BattleChrome cover	2	6	12
3-Red Monika cover by Madureira			4.00
4-8: 4-Four covers. 6-Back-up by Warren-s/a. 7-3 covers (Madureira, Ramos, Campbell)			3.00
9-($3.50, Image) Flip cover/story by Adam Warren			3.50
...: A Gathering of Heroes HC ('99, $24.95) r/#1-5, Prelude, Frank Frazetta Fantasy Ill.; cover gallery			25.00
...: A Gathering of Heroes SC ('99, $14.95)			15.00
...Collected Edition 1,2 (11/98, 5/99, $5.95) 1-r/#1,2. 2-r/#3,4			6.00

BATTLE OF THE PLANETS (Based on syndicated cartoon by Sandy Frank)
Gold Key/Whitman No. 6 on: 6/79 - No. 10, 12/80

	GD	FN	NM-
1: Mortimer a-1-4,7-10	3	9	32
2-6,10	2	6	22
7-Low print run	4	12	45
8,9-Low print run: 8(11/80). 9-(3-pack only?)	4	12	40

BATTLE OF THE PLANETS (Also see Thundercats/...)
Image Comics (Top Cow): Aug, 2002 - No. 12, Sept, 2003 ($2.95/$2.99)

	GD	FN	NM-
1-($2.95) Alex Ross-c & art director; Tortosa-a(p); re-intro. G-Force			3.00
1-($5.95) Holofoil-c by Ross			6.00
2-11-($2.99) Ross-c on all			3.00
12-($4.99)			5.00
#1/2 (7/03, $2.99) Benitez-c; Alex Ross sketch pages			3.00
... Battle Book 1 (5/03, $4.99) background info on characters, equipment, stories			5.00
... : Jason 1 (7/03, $4.99) Ross-c; Erwin David-a;			5.00
... : Mark 1 (5/03, $4.99) Ross-c; Erwin David-a; preview of BotP: Jason			5.00
.../Thundercats 1 (Image/WildStorm, 5/03, $4.99) 2 covers by Ross & Campbell			5.00
.../Witchblade 1 (2/03, $5.95) Ross-c; Christina and Jo Chen-a			6.00
Vol.1: Trial By Fire (2003, $7.99) r/#1-3			8.00
Vol.2: Blood Red Sky (9/03, $16.95) r/#4-9			17.00
Vol.3: Destroy All Monsters (11/03, $19.95) r/#10-12, ...: Jason, ...: Mark, .../Witchblade			20.00
Vol.1: Digest (1/04, $9.99, 7-3/8x5", B&W) r/#1-9 & ...: Mark			10.00
Vol.2: Digest (8/04, $9.99, B&W) r/#10-12, ...: Jason, ...: Manga #1-3, .../Witchblade			10.00

BATTLE OF THE PLANETS: MANGA
Image Comics (Top Cow): Nov, 2003 - No. 3, Jan, 2004 ($2.99, B&W)

	GD	FN	NM-
1-3-Edwin David-a/Wohl-s; previews for Wanted & Tomb Raider #35			3.00

BATTLE OF THE PLANETS: PRINCESS
Image Comics (Top Cow): Nov, 2004 - No. 6 ($2.99, B&W, limited series)

	GD	FN	NM-
1,2-Tortosa-a/Wohl-s. 1-Ross-c. 2-Tortosa-c			3.00

	GD	FN	NM-

BATTLESTAR GALACTICA (TV) (Also see Marvel Comics Super Special #8)
Marvel Comics Group: Mar, 1979 - No. 23, Jan, 1981

1: 1-5 adapt TV episodes	1	4	10
2-23: 1-3-Partial-r	1	3	7

BEAGLE BOYS, THE (Walt Disney)(See The Phantom Blot)
Gold Key: 11/64; No. 2, 11/65; No. 3, 8/66 - No. 47, 2/79 (See WDC&S #134)

1	6	18	65
2-5	3	9	32
6-10	3	9	26
11-20: 11,14,19-r	2	6	20
21-30: 27-r	2	6	14
31-47	1	4	10

BEAGLE BOYS VERSUS UNCLE SCROOGE
Gold Key: Mar, 1979 - No. 12, Feb, 1980

1	2	6	16
2-12: 9-r	1	3	8

BEAST BOY (See Titans)
DC Comics: Jan, 2000 - No. 4, Apr, 2000 ($2.95, mini-series)

1-4-Justiniano-c/a; Raab & Johns-s			3.00

BEATLES, THE (Life Story)
Dell Publishing Co.: Sept.-Nov, 1964 (35¢)

1-(Scarce)-Stories with color photo pin-ups; Paul S. Newman-s			
	42	126	715

BEAUTIFUL KILLER
Black Bull Comics: Sept., 2002 - No. 3, Jan, 2003 ($2.99, limited series)

...Limited Preview Edition (5/02, $5.00) preview pgs. & creator interviews	5.00
1-Noto-a/Palmiotti-s; Hughes-c; intro Brigit Cole	3.00
2,3: 2-Jusko-c. 3-Noto-c	3.00
TPB (5/03, $9.99) r/#1-3; cover gallery and Adam Hughes sketch pages	10.00

BEAUTY AND THE BEAST, THE
Marvel Comics Group: Jan, 1985 - No. 4, Apr, 1985 (limited series)

1-4: Dazzler & the Beast from X-Men; Sienkiewicz-c on all	3.00

BEAVIS AND BUTTHEAD (MTV's...)(TV cartoon)
Marvel Comics: Mar, 1994 - No. 28, June, 1996 ($1.95)

1-Silver ink-c. 1, 2-Punisher & Devil Dinosaur app.	4.00
1-2nd printing	2.25
2,3: 2-Wolverine app. 3-Man-Thing, Spider-Man, Venom, Carnage, Mary Jane & Stan Lee cameos; John Romita, Sr. art (2 pgs.)	2.50
4-28: 5-War Machine, Thor, Loki, Hulk, Captain America & Rhino cameos. 6-Psylocke, Daredevil & Bullseye app. 7-Ghost Rider & Sub-Mariner app. 8-Quasar & Eon app. 9-Prowler & Nightwatch app. 11-Black Widow app. 12-Thunderstrike & Bloodaxe app. 13-Night Thrasher app. 14-Spider-Man 2099 app. 15-Warlock app. 16-X-Factor app. 25-Juggernaut app.	2.50

BEEP BEEP, THE ROAD RUNNER (TV)(See Daffy & Kite Fun Book)

	GD	FN	NM-

Dell Publishing Co./Gold Key No. 1-88/Whitman No. 89 on: July, 1958 - No. 14, Aug-Oct, 1962; Oct, 1966 - No. 105, 1984

Four Color 918 (#1, 7/58)	11	33	160
Four Color 1008,1046 (11-1/59-60)	7	21	80
4(2-4/60)-14(Dell)	6	18	70
1(10/66, Gold Key)	6	18	75
2-5	4	12	45
6-14	3	9	32
15-18,20-40	3	9	24
19-With pull-out poster	4	12	42
41-50	2	6	18
51-70	2	6	12
71-88	1	3	8
89,90,94-101: 100(3/82), 101(4/82)	1	3	9
91(8/80), 92(9/80), 93 (3-pack) (low printing)	3	9	25
102-105 (All #90189 on-c; nd or date code; pre-pack) 102(6/83), 103(7/83), 104(5/84), 105(6/84)	2	6	18
#63-2970 (Now Age Books/Pendulum Pub. Comic Digest, 1971, 75¢, 100 pages, B&W) collection of one-page gags	3	9	36

BEFORE THE FANTASTIC FOUR: BEN GRIMM AND LOGAN
Marvel Comics: July, 2000 - No. 3, Sept, 2000 ($2.99, limited series)

1-3-The Thing and Wolverine app.; Hama-s			3.00

BEFORE THE FANTASTIC FOUR: REED RICHARDS
Marvel Comics: Sept, 2000 - No. 3, Dec, 2000 ($2.99, limited series)

1-3-Peter David-s/Duncan Fegredo-c/a			3.00

BEFORE THE FANTASTIC FOUR: THE STORMS
Marvel Comics: Dec, 2000 - No. 3, Feb, 2001 ($2.99, limited series)

1-3-Adlard-a			3.00

BEN CASEY (TV)
Dell Publishing Co.: June-July, 1962 - No. 10, June-Aug, 1965 (Photo-c)

12-063-207 (#1)	7	21	85
2(10/62),3,5-10	4	12	50
4-Marijuana & heroin use story	5	15	60

BEN CASEY FILM STORY (TV)
Gold Key: Nov, 1962 (25¢) (Photo-c)

30009-211-All photos	9	27	115

BEOWULF (Also see First Comics Graphic Novel #1)
National Periodical Publications: Apr-May, 1975 - No. 6, Feb-Mar, 1976

1	2	6	14
2,3,5,6: 5-Flying saucer-c/story	1	3	8
4-Dracula-c/s	1	3	9

BEST OF BUGS BUNNY, THE
Gold Key: Oct, 1966 - No. 2, Oct, 1968

1,2-Giants	6	18	70

	GD	FN	NM-

BEST OF DC, THE (Blue Ribbon Digest) (See Limited Coll. Ed. C-52)
DC Comics: Sept-Oct, 1979 - No. 71, Apr, 1986 (100-148 pgs; mostly reprints)

1-Superman, w/"Death of Superman"-r	2	6	20
2,5-9: 2-Batman 40th Ann. Special. 5-Best of 1979. 6,8-Superman.			
7-Superboy. 9-Batman, Creeper app.	2	6	12
3-Superfriends	2	6	15
4-Rudolph the Red Nosed Reindeer	2	6	16
10-Secret Origins of Super Villains; 1st ever Penguin origin-s			
	3	9	28
11-16,18-20: 11-The Year's Best Stories. 12-Superman Time and Space			
Stories.13-Best of DC Comics Presents. 14-New origin stories of Batman			
villains. 15-Superboy. 16-Superman Anniv. 18-Teen Titans new-s., Adams,			
Kane-a; Perez-c. 19-Superman. 20-World's Finest	1	3	9
17-Supergirl	2	6	12
21,22: 21-Justice Society. 22-Christmas; unpublished Sandman story			
w/Kirby-a	2	6	18
23-27: 23-(148 pgs.)-Best of 1981. 24 Legion, new story and 16 pgs. new			
costumes. 25-Superman. 26-Brave & Bold. 27-Superman vs. Luthor			
	2	6	15
28,29: 28-Binky, Sugar & Spike app. 29-Sugar & Spike, 3 new stories; new			
Stanley & his Monster story	2	6	16
30,32-36,38,40: 30-Detective Comics. 32-Superman. 33-Secret origins of			
Legion Heroes and Villains. 34-Metal Men; has #497 on-c from Adv.			
Comics. 35-The Year's Best Comics Stories (148 pgs.). 36-Superman vs.			
Kryptonite. 38-Superman. 40-World of Krypton	2	6	15
31-JLA	2	6	18
37,39: 37-"Funny Stuff", Mayer-a. 39-Binky	2	6	18
41,43,45,47,49,53,55,58,60,63,65,68,70: 41-Sugar & Spike new stories with			
Mayer-a. 43,49,55-Funny Stuff. 45,53,70-Binky. 47,58,65,68-Sugar & Spike.			
60-Plop!; Wood-c(r) & Aragonés-r (5/85). 63-Plop!; Wrightson-a(r)			
	3	9	24
42,44,46,48,50-52,54,56,57,59,61,62,64,66,67,69,71: 42,56-Superman vs.			
Aliens. 44,57,67-Superboy & LSH. 46-Jimmy Olsen. 48-Superman Team-			
ups. 50-Year's best Superman. 51-Batman Family. 52 Best of 1984.			
54,56,59-Superman. 61-(148 pgs.)Year's best. 62-Best of Batman 1985.			
69-Year's best Team stories. 71-Year's best	2	6	18

BEST OF DONALD DUCK, THE
Gold Key: Nov, 1965 (12¢, 36 pgs.)(Lists 2nd printing in indicia)

1-Reprints Four Color #223 by Barks	9	27	110

BEST OF DONALD DUCK & UNCLE SCROOGE, THE
Gold Key: Nov, 1964 - No. 2, Sept, 1967 (25¢ Giants)

1(30022-411)('64)-Reprints 4-Color #189 & 408 by Carl Barks; cover of F.C.			
#189 redrawn by Barks	10	30	125
2(30022-709)('67)-Reprints 4-Color #256 & "Seven Cities of Cibola" & U.S.			
#8 by Barks	9	27	110

BEST OF UNCLE SCROOGE & DONALD DUCK, THE

	GD	FN	NM-

Gold Key: Nov, 1966 (25¢)

1(30030-611)-Reprints part 4-Color #159 & 456 & Uncle Scrooge #6,7 by Carl Barks	9	27	110

BEVERLY HILLBILLIES (TV)
Dell Publishing Co.: 4-6/63 - No. 18, 8/67; No. 19, 10/69; No. 20, 10/70; No. 21, Oct, 1971

1-Photo-c	18	54	260
2-Photo-c	10	30	130
3-9: All have photo covers	8	24	100
10: No photo cover	6	18	65
11-21: All have photo covers. 18-Last 12¢ issue. 19-21-Reprint #1-3 (covers and insides)	6	18	75

BEWARE (Becomes Tomb of Darkness No. 9 on)
Marvel Comics Group: Mar, 1973 - No. 8, May, 1974 (All reprints)

1-Everett-c; Kirby & Sinnott-r ('54)	3	9	25
2-8: 2-Forte, Colan-r. 6-Tuska-a. 7-Torres-r/Mystical Tales #7	2	6	16

BEWARE THE CREEPER (See Adventure, Best of the Brave & the Bold, Brave & the Bold, 1st Issue Special, Flash #318-323, Showcase #73, World's Finest Comics #249)
National Periodical Publications: May-June, 1968 - No. 6, Mar-Apr, 1969 (All 12¢ issues)

1-(5-6/68)-Classic Ditko-c; Ditko-a in all	10	30	140
2-6: 2-5-Ditko-c. 2-Intro. Proteus. 6-Gil Kane-c	6	18	70

BEWITCHED (TV)
Dell Publishing Co.: 4-6/65 - No. 11, 10/67; No. 12, 10/68 - No. 13, 1/69; No. 14, 10/69

1-Photo-c	17	51	250
2-No photo-c	9	27	115
3-13-All have photo-c. 12-Rep. #1. 13-Last 12¢-c	8	24	95
14-No photo-c; reprints #2	6	18	65

BILLY THE KID (Formerly The Masked Raider; also see Doc Savage Comics & Return of the Outlaw)
Charlton Publ. Co.: No. 9, Nov, 1957 - No. 121, Dec, 1976; No. 122, Sept, 1977 - No. 123, Oct, 1977; No. 124, Feb, 1978 - No. 153, Mar, 1983

9	10	30	95
10,12,14,17-19: 12-2 pg Check-sty	7	21	55
11-(68 pgs.)-Origin & 1st app. The Ghost Train	9	27	75
13-Williamson/Torres-a	8	24	65
15-Origin; 2 pgs. Williamson-a	8	24	65
16-Williamson-a, 2 pgs.	8	24	60
20-26-Severin-a(3-4 each)	8	24	65
27-30: 30-Masked Rider app.	3	10	35
31-40	3	9	25
41-60	2	6	20
61-65	2	6	15

	GD	FN	NM-
66-Bounty Hunter series begins.	2	6	18
67-80: Bounty Hunter series; not in #79,82,84-86	2	6	14
81-90: 87-Last Bounty Hunter	1	3	9
91-123: 110-Dr. Young of Boothill app. 111-Origin The Ghost Train.			
117-Gunsmith & Co., The Cheyenne Kid app.			6.00
124(2/78)-153			4.00
Modern Comics 109 (1977 reprint)			4.00

BINKY (Formerly Leave It to…)
National Periodical Publ./DC Comics: No. 72, 4-5/70 - No. 81, 10-11/71; No. 82, Summer/77

72-76	3	9	30
77-79: (68pgs.). 77-Bobby Sherman 1pg. story w/photo. 78-1 pg. sty on			
Barry Williams of Brady Bunch. 79-Osmonds 1pg. story			
	5	15	55
80,81 (52pgs.)-Sweat Pain story	4	12	45
82 (1977, one-shot)	4	12	38

BINKY'S BUDDIES
National Periodical Publications: Jan-Feb, 1969 - No. 12, Nov-Dec, 1970

1	6	18	70
2-12: 3-Last 12¢ issue	3	10	35

BIONIC WOMAN, THE (TV)
Charlton Publications: Oct, 1977 - No. 5, June, 1978

1	3	9	25
2-5	2	6	15

BIRDS OF PREY (Also see Black Canary/Oracle: Birds of Prey)
DC Comics: Jan, 1999 - Present ($1.99/$2.50)

1-Dixon-s/Land-c/a	1	4	10
2-4			6.00
6,7,9-15: 15-Guice-a begins.			4.00
8-Nightwing-c/app.; Barbara & Dick's circus date	2	6	15
16-38: 23-Grodd-c/app. 26-Bane app. 32-Noto-c begin			2.50
39,40-Bruce Wayne: Murderer pt. 5,12			3.00
41-Bruce Wayne: Fugitive pt. 2			4.00
42-46: 42-Fabry-a. 45-Deathstroke-c/app.			2.50
47-74,76,77: 47-49-Terry Moore-s/Conner & Palmiotti-a; Noto-c. 50-Gilbert			
Hernandez-s begin. 52,54-Metamorpho app. 56-Simone-s/Benes-a begin.			
65,67,68,70-Land-c			2.50
75-($2.95) Pearson-c; back-up story of Lady Blackhawk			3.00
TPB (1999, $17.95) r/ previous series and one-shots			18.00
...: Batgirl 1 (2/98, $2.95) Dixon-s/Frank-c			5.00
...: Batgirl/Catwoman 1 ('03, $5.95) Robertson-a			6.00
...: Catwoman/Oracle 1 ('03, $5.95) Cont'd from BOP: Batgirl/Catwoman 1;			
David Ross-a			6.00
...: Of Like Minds TPB (2004, $14.95) r/#55-61			15.00
...: Old Friends, New Enemies TPB (2003, $17.95) r/#1-6, ...: Batgirl,			
...: Wolves			18.00
...: Revolution 1 (1997, $2.95) Frank-c/Dixon-s			5.00

	GD	FN	NM-
... Secret Files 2003 (8/03, $4.95) Short stories, pin-ups and profile pages; Noto-c			5.00
...: The Ravens 1 (6/98, $1.95)-Dixon-s; Girlfrenzy issue			4.00
...: Wolves 1 (10/97, $2.95) Dixon-s/Giordano & Faucher-a			5.00

BIRDS OF PREY: MANHUNT
DC Comics: Sept, 1996 - No. 4, Dec, 1996 ($1.95, limited series)

1-Features Black Canary, Oracle, Huntress, & Catwoman; Dixon scripts; Gary Frank-c on all. 1-Catwoman cameo only	1	3	8
2-4			6.00

BISHOP (See Uncanny X-Men & X-Men)
Marvel Comics: Dec, 1994 - No.4, Mar, 1995 ($2.95, limited series)

1-4: Foil-c; Shard & Mountjoy in all. 1-Storm app.			3.00

BISHOP THE LAST X-MAN
Marvel Comics: Oct, 1999 - No. 16, Jan, 2001 ($2.99/$1.99/$2.25)

1-($2.99)-Jeanty-a			3.50
2-8-($1.99): 2-Two covers			2.50
9-11,13-16: 9-Begin $2.25-c. 15-Maximum Security x-over; Xavier app.			2.50
12-($2.99)			3.00

BISHOP: XAVIER SECURITY ENFORCER
Marvel Comics: Jan, 1998 - No.3, Mar, 1998 ($2.50, limited series)

1-3: Ostrander-s			3.00

BIZARRE ADVENTURES (Formerly Marvel Preview)
Marvel Comics Group: No. 25, 3/81 - No. 34, 2/83 (#25-33: Magazine-$1.50)

25,26: 25-Lethal Ladies. 26-King Kull; Bolton-c/a	1	4	10
27,28: 27-Phoenix, Iceman & Nightcrawler app. 28-The Unlikely Heroes; Elektra by Miller; Neal Adams-a	2	6	16
29,30,32,33: 29-Stephen King's Lawnmower Man. 30-Tomorrow; 1st app. Silhouette. 32-Gods; Thor-c/s. 33-Horror; Dracula app.; photo-c	1	3	9
31-After The Violence Stops; new Hangman story; Miller-a	1	4	10
34 ($2.00, Baxter paper, comic size)-Son of Santa; Christmas special; Howard the Duck by Paul Smith	1	3	8

BLACK CANARY (See All Star Comics #38, Flash Comics #86, Justice League of America #75 & World's Finest #244)
DC Comics: Nov, 1991 - No. 4, Feb, 1992 ($1.75, limited series)

1-4			2.50

BLACK CANARY
DC Comics: Jan, 1993 - No. 12, Dec, 1993 ($1.75)

1-7			2.50
8-12: 8-The Ray-c/story. 9,10-Huntress-c/story			3.00

BLACK CANARY/ORACLE: BIRDS OF PREY (Also see Showcase '96 #3)
DC Comics: 1996 ($3.95, one-shot)

1-Chuck Dixon scripts & Gary Frank-c/a.	1	3	9

	GD	FN	NM-

BLACK GOLIATH (See Avengers #32-35,41,54)
Marvel Comics Group: Feb, 1976 - No. 5, Nov, 1976

1-Tuska-a(p) thru #3	2	6	14
2-5: 2-4-(Regular 25¢ editions). 4-Kirby-c/Buckler-a	1	3	9
2-4-(30¢-c variants, limited distribution)(4,6,8/76)	2	6	14

BLACKHAWK
National Periodical Pub./DC Comics: No. 108, Jan, 1957 - No. 243, Oct-Nov, 1968; No. 244, Jan-Feb, 1976 - No. 250, Jan-Feb, 1977; No. 251, Oct, 1982 - No. 273, Nov, 1984

	GD	FN	NM-
108-1st DC issue (1/57); re-intro. Blackie, the Hawk, their mascot; not in #115	41	123	675
109-117: 117-(10/57)-Mr. Freeze app.	16	48	235
118-(11/57)-Frazetta-r/Jimmy Wakely #4 (3 pgs.)	17	51	245
119-130 (11/58): 120-Robot-c	12	36	165
131-140 (9/59): 133-Intro. Lady Blackhawk	10	30	130
141-150,152-163,165,166: 141-Cat-Man returns-c/s. 143-Kurtzman-r/Jimmy Wakely #4. 150-(7/60)-King Condor returns. 166-Last 10¢ issue	8	24	95
151-Lady Blackhawk receives & loses super powers	8	24	100
164-Origin retold	8	24	105
167-180	5	15	60
181-190	4	12	45
191-196,199,201,202,204-210: 196-Combat Diary series begins.	3	10	35
197,198,200: 197-New look for Blackhawks. 198-Origin retold	4	12	40
203-Origin Chop Chop (12/64)	4	12	45
211-227,229-243(1968): 230-Blackhawks become superheroes; JLA cameo 242-Return to old costumes	3	9	30
228-Batman, Green Lantern, Superman, The Flash cameos.	3	10	35
244 ('76) -250: 250-Chuck dies	1	3	7
251-273: 251-Origin retold; Black Knights return. 252-Intro Domino. 253-Part origin Hendrickson. 258-Blackhawk's Island destroyed. 259-Part origin Chop-Chop. 265-273 (75¢ cover price)			3.00

BLACKHAWK
DC Comics: Mar, 1988 - No. 3, May, 1988 ($2.95, limited series, mature)

1-3: Chaykin painted-c/a/scripts			4.00

BLACKHAWK (Also see Action Comics #601)
DC Comics: Mar, 1989 - No. 16, Aug, 1990 ($1.50, mature)

1			3.50
2-6,8-16: 16-Crandall-c swipe			2.50
7-($2.50, 52 pgs.)-Story-r/Military #1			3.00
Annual 1 (1989, $2.95, 68 pgs.)-Recaps origin of Blackhawk, Lady Blackhawk, and others			3.50
Special 1 (1992, $3.50, 68 pgs.)-Mature readers			3.50

BLACK LIGHTNING (See The Brave & The Bold, Cancelled Comic

	GD	FN	NM-

Cavalcade, DC Comics Presents #16, Detective #490 and World's Finest #257)
National Periodical Publ./DC Comics: Apr, 1977 - No. 11, Sept-Oct, 1978

1-Origin Black Lightning	2	6	12
2,3,6-10			6.00
4,5-Superman-c/s. 4-Intro Cyclotronic Man	1	3	7
11-The Ray new solo story	1	3	9

BLACK LIGHTNING (2nd Series)
DC Comics: Feb, 1995 - No. 13, Feb, 1996 ($1.95/$2.25)

1-5-Tony Isabella scripts begin, ends #8			3.00
6-13: 6-Begin $2.25-c. 13-Batman-c/app.			3.00

BLACK ORCHID (See Adventure Comics #428 & Phantom Stranger)
DC Comics: Holiday, 1988-89 - No. 3, 1989 ($3.50, lim. series, prestige format)

Book 1,3: Gaiman scripts & McKean painted-a in all			6.00
Book 2-Arkham Asylum story; Batman app.	1	3	8
TPB (1991, $19.95) r/#1-3; new McKean-c			20.00

BLACK ORCHID
DC Comics: Sept, 1993 - No. 22, June, 1995 ($1.95/$2.25)

1-22: Dave McKean-c all issues			2.50
1-Platinum Edition			12.00
Annual 1 (1993, $3.95, 68 pgs.)-Children's Crusade			4.00

BLACK PANTHER, THE (Also see Avengers #52, Fantastic Four #52, Jungle
Action & Marvel Premiere #51-53)
Marvel Comics Group: Jan, 1977 - No. 15, May, 1979

1	3	9	30
2-13: 4,5-(Regular 30¢ editions). 8-Origin	2	6	12
4,5-(35¢-c variants, limited dist.)(7,9/77)	3	9	28
14,15-Avengers x-over. 14-Origin	2	6	18

BLACK PANTHER
Marvel Comics Group: July, 1988 - No. 4, Oct, 1988 ($1.25)

1-4-Gillis-s/Cowan & Delarosa-a			2.50

BLACK PANTHER (Marvel Knights)
Marvel Comics: Nov, 1998 - No. 62, Sept, 2003 ($2.50)

1-Texeira-a/c; Priest-s			6.00
1-($6.95) DF edition w/Quesada & Palmiotti-c	1	3	8
2-4: 2-Two covers by Texeira and Timm. 3-Fantastic Four app.			3.50
5-35,37-40: 5-Evans-a. 6-8-Jusko-a. 8-Avengers-c/app. 15-Hulk app. 22-Moon Knight app. 23-Avengers app. 25-Maximum Security x-over. 26-Storm-c/app. 28-Magneto & Sub-Mariner-c/app. 29-WWII flashback meeting w/Captain America. 35-Defenders-c/app. 37-Luke Cage and Falcon-c/app.			2.50
36-($3.50, 100 pgs.) 35th Anniversary issue incl. r/1st app. in FF #52			3.50
41-56: 41-44-Wolverine app. 47-Thor app. 48,49-Magneto app.			2.50
57-62: 57-Begin $2.99-c. 59-Falcon app.			3.00
...: The Client (6/01, $14.95, TPB) r/#1-5			15.00
... 2099 #1 (11/04, $2.99) Kirkman-s/Hotz-a/Pat Lee-c			3.00

	GD	FN	NM-

BLACK PANTHER: PANTHER'S PREY
Marvel Comics: May, 1991 - No. 4, Oct, 1991 ($4.95, squarebound, lim. series, 52 pgs.)

1-4: McGregor-s/Turner-a		5.00

BLACK WIDOW (Marvel Knights) (Also see Marvel Graphic Novel)
Marvel Comics: May, 1999 - No. 3, Aug, 1999 ($2.99, limited series)

1-(June on-c) Devin Grayson-s/J.G. Jones-c/a; Daredevil app.		5.00
1-Variant-c by J.G. Jones		6.00
2,3		4.00
...Web of Intrigue (6/99, $3.50) r/origin & early appearances		3.50
TPB (7/01, $15.95) r/Vol. 1 & 2; Jones-c		16.00

BLACK WIDOW (Marvel Knights) (Volume 2)
Marvel Comics: Jan, 2001 - No. 3, May, 2001 ($2.99, limited series)

1-3-Grayson & Rucka-s/Scott Hampton-c/a; Daredevil app.		3.00

BLACK WIDOW (Marvel Knights)
Marvel Comics: Nov, 2004 - No. 6 ($2.99, limited series)

1-3-Sienkiewicz-a/Land-c		3.00

BLACK WIDOW: PALE LITTLE SPIDER (Marvel Knights) (Volume 3)
Marvel Comics: Jun, 2002 - No. 3, Aug, 2002 ($2.99, limited series)

1-3-Rucka-s/Kordey-a/Horn-c		3.00

BLADE (The Vampire Hunter)
Marvel Comics

1-(3/98, $3.50) Colan-a(p)/Christopher Golden-s		3.50
... Black & White TPB (2004, $15.99, B&W) reprints from magazines Vampire Tales #8,9; Marvel Preview #3,6; Crescent City Blues #1 and Marvel Shadow and Light #1		16.00
San Diego Con Promo (6/97) Wesley Snipes photo-c		3.00
...Sins of the Father (10/98, $5.99) Sears-a; movie adaption		6.00
Blade 2: Movie Adaptation (5/02, $5.95) Ponticelli-a/Bradstreet-c		6.00

BLADE (The Vampire Hunter)
Marvel Comics: Nov, 1998 - No. 3, Jan, 1999 ($3.50/$2.99)

1-($3.50) Contains Movie insider pages; McKean-a		3.50
2,3-($2.99): 2-Two covers		3.00

BLADE (Volume 2)
Marvel Comics (MAX): May, 2002 -No. 6, Oct, 2002 ($2.99)

1-6-Bradstreet-c/Hinz-s. 1-5-Pugh-a. 6-Homs-a		3.00

BLADE RUNNER (Movie)
Marvel Comics Group: Oct, 1982 - No. 2, Nov, 1982

1,2-r/Marvel Super Special #22; 1-Williamson-c/a. 2-Williamson-a		3.50

BLADE: THE VAMPIRE-HUNTER
Marvel Comics: July, 1994 - No. 10, Apr, 1995 ($1.95)

1-($2.95)-Foil-c; Dracula returns; Wheatley-c/a		3.50
2-10: 2,3,10-Dracula-c/app. 8-Morbius app.		2.50

	GD	FN	NM-

BLADE: VAMPIRE-HUNTER
Marvel Comics: Dec, 1999 - No. 6, May, 2000 ($3.50/$2.50)

1-($3.50)-Bart Sears-s; Sears and Smith-a			3.50
2-6-($2.50): 2-Regular & Wesley Snipes photo-c			2.50

BLAZING COMBAT (Magazine)
Warren Publishing Co.: Oct, 1965 - No. 4, July, 1966 (35¢, B&W)

1-Frazetta painted-c on all	20	60	300
2	7	21	85
3,4: 4-Frazetta half pg. ad	6	18	75
nn-Anthology (reprints from No. 1-4) (low print)	7	21	85

BLIP
Marvel Comics Group: 2/1983 - 1983 (Video game mag. in comic format)

1-1st app. Donkey Kong & Mario Bros. in comics, 6pgs. comics; photo-c			
	1	3	8
2-Spider-Man photo-c; 6pgs. Spider-Man comics w/Green Goblin			
	1	4	10
3,4,6			5.00
5-E.T., Indiana Jones; Rocky-c			6.00
7-6pgs. Hulk comics; Pac-Man & Donkey Kong Jr. Hints	1	3	7

BLITZKRIEG
National Periodical Publications: Jan-Feb, 1976 - No. 5, Sept-Oct, 1976

1-Kubert-c on all	4	12	45
2-5	3	9	25

BLOODBATH
DC Comics: Early Dec, 1993 - No. 2, Late Dec, 1993 ($3.50, 68 pgs.)

1-Neon ink-c; Superman app.; new Batman-c /app.			3.50
2-Hitman 2nd app.	1	3	7

BLUE BEETLE (Unusual Tales #1-49; Ghostly Tales #55 on)
Charlton Comics: V2#1, June, 1964 - V2#5, Mar-Apr, 1965; V3#50, July, 1965 - V3#54, Feb-Mar, 1966; #1, June, 1967 - #5, Nov, 1968

V2#1-Origin/1st S.A. app. Dan Garrett-Blue Beetle	10	30	130
2-5: 5-Weiss illo; 1st published-a?	6	18	75
V3#50-54-Formerly Unusual Tales	6	18	70
1(1967)-Question series begins by Ditko	11	33	160
2-Origin Ted Kord-Blue Beetle (see Capt. Atom #83 for 1st Ted Kord Blue Beetle); Dan Garrett x-over	6	18	75
3-5 (All Ditko-c/a in #1-5)	6	18	65
1,3(Modern Comics-1977)-Reprints	1	3	7

NOTE: #6 only appeared in the fanzine 'The Charlton Portfolio.'

BLUE BEETLE (Also see Crisis On Infinite Earths, Justice League & Showcase '94 #2-4)
DC Comics: June, 1986 - No. 24, May, 1988

1-Origin retold; intro. Firefist			4.00
2-10,15-19,21-24: 2-Origin Firefist. 5-7-The Question app. 21-Millennium tie-in			2.25

	GD	FN	NM-
11-14-New Teen Titans x-over			3.00
20-Justice League app.; Millennium tie-in			3.00

BLUE MONDAY: ... (one-shots)
Oni Press: Feb, 2002 - Present (B&W, Chynna Clugston-Major-s/a/c in all)

	GD	FN	NM-
Dead Man's Party (10/02, $2.95) Dan Brereton painted back-c			3.00
Inbetween Days (9/03, $9.95, 8" x 5-1/2") r/Dead Man's Party, Lovecats, & Nobody's Fool			10.00
Lovecats (2/02, $2.95) Valentine's Day themed			3.00
Nobody's Fool (2/03, $2.95) April Fool's Day themed			3.00

BLUE MONDAY: ABSOLUTE BEGINNERS
Oni Press: Feb, 2001 - No. 4, Sept, 2001 ($2.95, B&W, limited series)

	GD	FN	NM-
1-4-Chynna Clugston-Major-s/a/c			3.00
TPB (12/01, $11.95, 8" x 6") r/series			12.00

BLUE MONDAY: PAINTED MOON
Oni Press: Feb, 2004 - No. 4 ($2.99, B&W, limited series)

	GD	FN	NM-
1-3-Chynna Clugston-Major-s/a/c			3.00

BLUE MONDAY: THE KIDS ARE ALRIGHT
Oni Press: Feb, 2000 - No. 3, May, 2000 ($2.95, B&W, limited series)

	GD	FN	NM-
1-3-Chynna Clugston-Major-s/a/c. 1-Variant-c by Warren. 2-Dorkin-c			3.00
3-Variant cover by J. Scott Campbell			4.00
TPB (12/00, $10.95, digest-sized) r/#1-3 & earlier short stories			11.00

BLUNTMAN AND CHRONIC TPB (Also see Jay and Silent Bob, Clerks, and Oni Double Feature)
Image Comics: Dec, 2001 ($14.95, TPB)

	GD	FN	NM-
nn-Tie-in for "Jay & Silent Bob Strike Back" movie; new Kevin Smith-s/Michael Oeming-a; r/app. from Oni Double Feature #12 in color; Ben Affleck & Jason Lee afterwords			15.00

BOBBY SHERMAN (TV)
Charlton Comics: Feb, 1972 - No. 7, Oct, 1972

	GD	FN	NM-
1-Based on TV show "Getting Together"	5	15	60
2-7: 2,4-Photo-c	4	12	38

BOMBA THE JUNGLE BOY (TV)
National Periodical Publ.: Sept-Oct, 1967 - No. 7, Sept-Oct, 1968 (12¢)

	GD	FN	NM-
1-Intro. Bomba; Infantino/Anderson-c	4	12	45
2-7	3	9	25

BONANZA (TV)
Dell/Gold Key: June-Aug, 1960 - No. 37, Aug, 1970 (All Photo-c)

	GD	FN	NM-
Four Color 1110 (6-8/60)	36	108	575
Four Color 1221,1283, & #01070-207, 01070-210	20	60	290
1(12/62-Gold Key)	21	63	305
2	11	33	160
3-10	10	30	125
11-20	8	24	95
21-37: 29-Reprints	7	21	80

	GD	FN	NM-

BONE
Cartoon Books #1-20, 28 on/Image Comics #21-27: Jul, 1991 - No. 55, Jun, 2004 ($2.95, B&W)

	GD	FN	NM-
1-Jeff Smith-c/a in all	7	21	90
1-2nd printing	2	6	12
1-3rd thru 5th printings			4.00
2-1st printing	4	12	45
2-2nd & 3rd printings			4.00
3-1st printing	3	10	35
3-2nd thru 4th printings			4.00
4,5	2	6	18
6-10	1	3	9
11-37: 21-1st Image issue			4.00
13 1/2 (1/95, Wizard)	1	4	10
13 1/2 (Gold)	2	6	12
38-($4.95) Three covers by Miller, Ross, Smith			5.00
39-55-($2.95)			3.00
1-27-($2.95): 1-Image reprints begin w/new-c. 2-Allred pin-up.			3.00
... Holiday Special (1993, giveaway)			3.00
... Reader -($9.95) Behind the scenes info			10.00
... Sourcebook-San Diego Edition			3.00
...10th Anniversary Edition (8/01, $5.95) r/#1 in color; came with figure			6.00
Complete Bone Adventures Vol 1,2 ('93, '94, $12.95, r/#1-6 & #7-12)			13.00
...: One Volume Ed. (2004, $39.95, 1300 pgs.) r/#1-54; extra material			40.00
Volume 1-($19.95, hard-c)-"Out From Boneville"			20.00
Volume 1-($12.95, soft-c)			13.00
Volume 2,5-($22.95, hard-c)-"The Great Cow Race" & "Rock Jaw"			23.00
Volume 2,5-($14.95, soft-c)			15.00
Volume 3,4-($24.95, hard-c)-"Eyes of the Storm" & "The Dragonslayer"			25.00
Volume 3,4,7-($16.95, soft-c)			17.00
Volume 6-($15.95, soft-c)-"Old Man's Cave"			16.00
Volume 7-($24.95, hard-c)-"Ghost Circles"			25.00
Volume 8-($23.95, hard-c)-"Treasure Hunters"			24.00

NOTE: *Printings not listed sell for cover price.*

BOOKS OF MAGIC
DC Comics: 1990 - No. 4, 1991 ($3.95, 52 pgs., limited series, mature)

	GD	FN	NM-
1-Bolton painted-c/a; Phantom Stranger app.; Gaiman scripts in all	1	4	10
2,3: 2-John Constantine, Dr. Fate, Spectre, Deadman app. 3-Dr. Occult app.; minor Sandman app.	1	3	7
4-Early Death-c/app. (early 1991)	1	3	8
Trade paperback-($19.95)-Reprints limited series			20.00

BOOKS OF MAGIC (Also see Hunter: The Age of Magic and Names of Magic)
DC Comics (Vertigo): May, 1994 - No. 75, Aug, 2000 ($1.95/$2.50, mature)

	GD	FN	NM-
1-Charles Vess-c	2	6	12
1-Platinum	2	6	22
2-4: 4-Death app.	1	3	7

	GD	FN	NM-
5-14; Charles Vess-c			4.00
15-50: 15-$2.50-c begins. 22-Kaluta-c. 25-Death-c/app; Bachalo-c			3.00
51-75: 51-Peter Gross-s/a begins. 55-Medley-a			2.50
Annual 1-3 (2/97, 2/98, '99, $3.95)			4.00
Bindings (1995, $12.95, TPB)-r/#1-4			13.00
Death After Death (2001, $19.95, TPB)-r/#42-50			20.00
Girl in the Box (1999, $14.95, TPB)-r/#26-32			15.00
Reckonings (1997, $12.95, TPB)-r/#14-20			13.00
Summonings (1996, $17.50, TPB)-r/#5-13, Vertigo Rave #1			17.50
The Burning Girl (2000, $17.95, TPB)-r/#33-41			18.00
Transformations (1998, $12.95, TPB)-r/#21-25			13.00

BOOKS OF MAGICK, THE : LIFE DURING WARTIME (See Books of Magic)
DC Comics (Vertigo): Sept, 2004 - Present ($2.50)

1-5-Spencer-s/Ormston-a/Quitely-c; Constantine app. 2-Bagged with Sky Captain CD			2.50

BOOSTER GOLD (See Justice League #4)
DC Comics: Feb, 1986 - No. 25, Feb, 1988 (75¢)

1-Dan Jurgens-s/a(p)			3.00
2-25: 4-Rose & Thorn app. 6-Origin. 6,7,23-Superman app. 8,9-LSH app. 22-JLI app. 24,25-Millennium tie-ins			2.50

BORN
Marvel Comics: 2003 - No. 4, 2003 ($3.50, limited series)

1-4-Frank Castle (the Punisher) in 1971 Vietnam; Ennis-s/Robertson-a			3.50
HC (2004, $17.99) oversized reprint of series; proposal, layout pages			18.00
Punisher: Born SC (2004, $13.99) r/series; proposal, layout pages			14.00

BRADY BUNCH, THE (TV)(See Kite Fun Book and Binky #78)
Dell Publishing Co.: Feb, 1970 - No. 2, May, 1970

1	12	36	175
2	9	27	115

BRAVE AND THE BOLD, THE (Replaced by Batman & The Outsiders)
National Periodical Publ./DC Comics: Aug-Sept, 1955 - No. 200, July, 1983

1-Viking Prince by Kubert, Silent Knight, Golden Gladiator begin; part Kubert-c	238	714	5000
2	105	315	2000
3,4	58	174	1100
5-Robin Hood begins (4-5/56, 1st DC app.), ends #15; see Robin Hood Tales #7	61	183	1150
6-10: 6-Robin Hood by Kubert; last Golden Gladiator app.; Silent Knight; no Viking Prince. 8-1st S.A. issue	46	138	775
11-22,24: 12,14-Robin Hood-c. 18,21-23-Grey tone-c. 22-Last Silent Knight. 24-Last Viking Prince (2nd solo book)	36	108	575
23-Viking Prince origin by Kubert; 1st B&B single theme issue & 1st Viking Prince solo book	46	138	775
25-1st app. Suicide Squad (8-9/59)	43	129	725
26,27-Suicide Squad	31	93	475
28-(2-3/60)-Justice League intro./1st app.; origin/1st app. Snapper Carr			

	GD	FN	NM-
	400	1200	8800

29-Justice League (4-5/60)-2nd app. battle the Weapons Master; robot-c

	175	525	3500

30-Justice League (6-7/60)-3rd app.; vs. Amazo | 142 | 426 | 2700

31-1st app. Cave Carson (8-9/60); scarce in high grade; 1st try-out series

	39	117	625

32,33-Cave Carson | 24 | 72 | 360

34-Origin/1st app. Silver-Age Hawkman, Hawkgirl & Byth (2-3/61); Gardner
Fox story, Kubert-c/a ; 1st S.A. Hawkman tryout series; 2nd in #42-44;
both series predate Hawkman #1 (4-5/64) | 185 | 555 | 3700

35-Hawkman by Kubert (4-5/61)-2nd app. | 47 | 141 | 800

36-Hawkman by Kubert; origin & 1st app. Shadow Thief (6-7/61)-3rd app.

	41	123	700

37-Suicide Squad (2nd tryout series) | 24 | 72 | 350

38,39-Suicide Squad. 38-Last 10¢ issue | 20 | 60 | 300

40,41-Cave Carson Inside Earth (2nd try-out series). 40-Kubert-a.
41-Meskin-a | 15 | 45 | 225

42-Hawkman by Kubert (2nd tryout series); Hawkman earns helmet wings;
Byth app. | 31 | 93 | 460

43-Hawkman by Kubert; more detailed origin | 35 | 105 | 560

44-Hawkman by Kubert; grey-tone-c | 29 | 87 | 425

45-49-Strange Sports Stories by Infantino | 10 | 30 | 125

50-The Green Arrow & Manhunter From Mars (10-11/63); 1st Manhunter
x-over outside of Detective Comics (pre-dates House of Mystery #143);
team-ups begin | 19 | 57 | 280

51-Aquaman & Hawkman (12-1/63-64); pre-dates Hawkman #1

	24	72	350

52-(2-3/64)-3 Battle Stars; Sgt. Rock, Haunted Tank, Johnny Cloud, & Mlle.
Marie team-up for 1st time by Kubert (c/a) | 20 | 60 | 300

53-Atom & The Flash by Toth | 10 | 30 | 125

54-Kid Flash, Robin & Aqualad; 1st app./origin Teen Titans (6-7/64)

	30	90	450

55-Metal Men & The Atom | 8 | 24 | 100

56-The Flash & Manhunter From Mars | 8 | 24 | 100

57-Origin & 1st app. Metamorpho (12-1/64-65) | 18 | 54 | 270

58-2nd app. Metamorpho by Fradon | 10 | 30 | 130

59-Batman & Green Lantern; 1st Batman team-up in Brave and the Bold
| 12 | 36 | 165

60-Teen Titans (2nd app.)-1st app. new Wonder Girl (Donna Troy), who joins
Titans (6-7/65) | 12 | 36 | 175

61-Origin Starman & Black Canary by Anderson | 13 | 39 | 190

62-Origin Starman & Black Canary cont'd. 62-1st S.A. app. Wildcat
(10-11/65); 1st S.A. app. of G.A. Huntress (W.W. villain)

	11	33	160

63-Supergirl & Wonder Woman | 8 | 24 | 100

64-Batman Versus Eclipso (see H.O.S. #61) | 8 | 24 | 105

65-Flash & Doom Patrol (4-5/66) | 6 | 18 | 65

66-Metamorpho & Metal Men (6-7/66) | 6 | 18 | 65

67-Batman & The Flash by Infantino; Batman team-ups begin, end #200

	GD	FN	NM-
(8-9/66)	7	21	85
68-Batman/Metamorpho/Joker/Riddler/Penguin-c/story; Batman as Bat-Hulk (Hulk parody)	9	27	120
69-Batman & Green Lantern	6	18	70
70-Batman & Hawkman; Craig-a(p)	6	18	70
71-Batman & Green Arrow	6	18	70
72-Spectre & Flash (6-7/67); 4th app. The Spectre; predates Spectre #1	6	18	75
73-Aquaman & The Atom	6	18	65
74-Batman & Metal Men	6	18	65
75-Batman & The Spectre (12-1/67-68); 6th app. Spectre; came out between Spectre #1 & #2	6	18	70
76-Batman & Plastic Man (2-3/68); came out between Plastic Man #8 & #9	6	18	65
77-Batman & The Atom	6	18	65
78-Batman, Wonder Woman & Batgirl	6	18	65
79-Batman & Deadman by Neal Adams (8-9/68); early Deadman app.	9	27	110
80-Batman & Creeper (10-11/68); N. Adams-a; early app. The Creeper; came out between Creeper #3 & #4	7	21	85
81-Batman & Flash; N. Adams-a	7	21	85
82-Batman & Aquaman; N. Adams-a; origin Ocean Master retold (2-3/69)	7	21	85
83-Batman & Teen Titans; N. Adams-a (4-5/69)	7	21	85
84-Batman (G.A., 1st S.A. app.) & Sgt. Rock; N. Adams-a; last 12¢ issue (6-7/69)	7	21	85
85-Batman & Green Arrow; 1st new costume for Green Arrow by Neal Adams (8-9/69)	7	21	90
86-Batman & Deadman (10-11/69); N. Adams-a; story concludes from Strange Adventures #216 (1-2/69)	7	21	85
87-Batman & Wonder Woman	4	12	48
88-Batman & Wildcat	4	12	48
89-Batman & Phantom Stranger (4-5/70); early Phantom Stranger app. (came out between Phantom Stranger #6 & 7	4	12	42
90-Batman & Adam Strange	4	12	42
91-Batman & Black Canary (8-9/70)	4	12	42
92-Batman; intro the Bat Squad	4	12	42
93-Batman-House of Mystery; N. Adams-a	6	18	75
94-Batman-Teen Titans	3	10	35
95-Batman & Plastic Man	3	10	35
96-Batman & Sgt. Rock; last 15¢ issue	4	12	38
97-Batman & Wildcat; 52 pg. issues begin, end #102; reprints origin & 1st app. Deadman from Strange Advs. #205	4	12	38
98-Batman & Phantom Stranger; 1st Jim Aparo Batman-a?	4	12	38
99-Batman & Flash	4	12	38
100-(2-3/72, 25¢, 52 pgs.)-Batman-Green Lantern-Green Arrow-Black Canary-Robin; Deadman-r by Adams/Str. Advs. #210	6	18	75

	GD	FN	NM-
101-Batman & Metamorpho; Kubert Viking Prince	3	10	35
102-Batman-Teen Titans; N. Adams-a(p)	4	12	50
103-107,109,110: Batman team-ups: 103-Metal Men. 104-Deadman. 105-Wonder Woman. 106-Green Arrow. 107-Black Canary. 109-Demon. 110-Wildcat	2	6	22
108-Sgt. Rock	3	9	24
111-Batman/Joker-c/story	3	9	28
112-117: All 100 pgs.; Batman team-ups: 112-Mr. Miracle. 113-Metal Men; reprints origin/1st Hawkman from Brave and the Bold #34; r/origin Multi-Man/Challengers #14. 114-Aquaman. 115-Atom; r/origin Viking Prince from #23; r/Dr. Fate/Hourman/Solomon Grundy/Green Lantern from Showcase #55. 116-Spectre. 117-Sgt. Rock; last 100 pg. issue	4	12	50
118-Batman/Wildcat/Joker-c/story	3	9	28
119,121-123,125-128,132-140: Batman team-ups: 119-Man-Bat. 121-Metal Men. 122-Swamp Thing. 123-Plastic Man/Metamorpho. 125-Flash. 126-Aquaman. 127-Wildcat. 128-Mr. Miracle. 132-Kung-Fu Fighter. 133-Deadman. 134-Green Lantern. 135-Metal Men. 136-Metal Men/Green Arrow. 137-Demon. 138-Mr. Miracle. 139-Hawkman. 140-Wonder Woman	2	6	12
120-Kamandi (68 pgs.)	3	9	24
124-Sgt. Rock	2	6	15
129,130-Batman/Green Arrow/Atom parts 1 & 2; Joker & Two Face-c/stories	2	6	22
131-Batman & Wonder Woman vs. Catwoman-c/sty	2	6	16
141-Batman/Black Canary vs. Joker-c/story	2	6	22
142-160: Batman team-ups: 142-Aquaman. 143-Creeper; origin Human Target (44 pgs.). 144-Green Arrow; origin Human Target part 2 (44 pgs.). 145-Phantom Stranger. 146-G.A. Batman/Unknown Soldier. 147-Supergirl. 148-Plastic Man; X-Mas-c. 149-Teen Titans. 150-Anniversary issue; Superman. 151-Flash. 152-Atom. 153-Red Tornado. 154-Metamorpho. 155-Green Lantern. 156-Dr. Fate. 157-Batman vs. Kamandi (ties into Kamandi #59). 158-Wonder Woman. 159-Ra's Al Ghul. 160-Supergirl.	1	3	9
145(11/79)-147,150-159,165(8/80)-(Whitman variants; low print run; none show issue # on cover)	2	6	12
161-181,183-190,192-195,198,199: Batman team-ups: 161-Adam Strange. 162-G.A. Batman/Sgt. Rock. 163-Black Lightning. 164-Hawkman. 165-Man-Bat. 166-Black Canary; Nemesis (intro) back-up story begins, ends #192; Penguin-c/story. 167-G.A. Batman/Blackhawk; origin Nemesis. 168-Green Arrow. 169-Zatanna. 170-Nemesis. 171-Scalphunter. 172-Firestorm. 173-Guardians of the Universe. 174-Green Lantern. 175-Lois Lane. 176-Swamp Thing. 177-Elongated Man. 178-Creeper. 179-Legion. 180-Spectre. 181-Hawk & Dove. 183-Riddler. 184-Huntress. 185-Green Arrow. 186-Hawkman. 187-Metal Men. 188,189-Rose & the Thorn. 190-Adam Strange. 192-Superboy vs. Mr. I.Q. 193-Nemesis. 194-Flash. 195-I...Vampire. 198-Karate Kid. 199-The Spectre			6.00
182-G.A. Robin; G.A. Starman app.; 1st modern app. G.A. Batwoman	1	3	7

	GD	FN	NM-
191-Batman/Joker-c/story; Nemesis app.	2	6	12
196-Ragman; origin Ragman retold.	1	3	8
197-Catwoman; Earth II Batman & Catwoman marry; 2nd modern app. of G.A. Batwoman	2	6	14
200-Double-sized (64 pgs.); printed on Mando paper; Earth One & Earth Two Batman app. in separate stories; intro/1st app. Batman & The Outsiders	1	4	10

BROTHER POWER, THE GEEK (See Saga of Swamp Thing Annual & Vertigo Visions)
National Periodical Publications: Sept-Oct, 1968 - No. 2, Nov-Dec, 1968

	GD	FN	NM-
1-Origin; Simon-c(i?)	6	18	75
2	4	12	38

BUCK ROGERS (...in the 25th Century No. 5 on) (TV)
Gold Key/Whitman No. 7 on: Oct, 1964; No. 2, July, 1979 - No. 16, May, 1982 (No #10; story was written but never released. #17 exists only as a press proof without covers and was never published)

	GD	FN	NM-
1(10128-410, 12¢)-1st S.A. app. Buck Rogers & 1st new B. R. in comics since 1933 giveaway; painted-c; back-c pin-up	10	30	130
2(7/79)-6: 3,4,6-Movie adaptation; painted-c	2	6	14
7,11 (Whitman)	2	6	18
8,9 (prepack)(scarce)	3	9	28
12-16: 14(2/82), 15(3/82), 16(5/82)	1	4	10
Giant Movie Edition 11296(64pp, Whitman, $1.50), reprints GK #2-4 minus cover; tabloid size; photo-c (See Marvel Treasury)	3	9	30
Giant Movie Edition 02489(Western/Marvel, $1.50), reprints GK #2-4 minus cover	3	9	28

BUFFY THE VAMPIRE SLAYER (Based on the TV series)(Also see Tales of the Vampires)
Dark Horse Comics: 1998 - No. 63, Nov, 2003 ($2.95/$2.99)

	GD	FN	NM-
1-Bennett-a/Watson-s; Art Adams-c	1	3	9
1-Variant photo-c	1	3	9
1-Gold foil logo Art Adams-c			15.00
1-Gold foil logo photo-c			20.00
2-15-Regular and photo-c. 4-7-Gomez-a. 5,8-Green-c			5.00
16-48: 29,30-Angel x-over. 43-45-Death of Buffy. 47-Lobdell-s begin. 48-Pike returns			3.00
50-($3.50) Scooby gang battles Adam; back-up story by Watson			3.50
51-63: 51-54-Viva Las Buffy; pre-Sunnydale Buffy & Pike in Vegas			3.00
Annual '99 ($4.95)-Two stories and pin-ups	1	3	7
...: A Stake to the Heart TPB (3/04, $12.95) r/#60-63			13.00
...: Chaos Bleeds (6/03, $2.99) Based on the video game; photo & Campbell-c			3.00
...: Creatures of Habit (3/02, $17.95) text with Horton & Paul Lee-a			18.00
...: Jonathan 1 (1/01, $2.99) two covers; Richards-a			3.00
...: Lost and Found 1 (3/02, $2.99) aftermath of Buffy's death; Richards-a			3.00
... Lovers Walk (2/01, $2.99) short stories by various; Richards & photo-c			3.00
...: Note From the Underground (3/03, $12.95) r/#47-50			13.00

	GD	FN	NM-

...: Reunion (6/02, $3.50) Buffy & Angel's; Espenson-s; art by various — 3.50
...: Slayer Interrupted TPB (2003, $14.95) r/#56-59 — 15.00
...: Tales of the Slayers (10/02, $3.50) art by Matsuda and Colan; art & photo-c — 3.50
...: The Death of Buffy TPB (8/02, $15.95) r/#43-46 — 16.00
...: Viva Las Buffy TPB (7/03, $12.95) r/#51-54 — 13.00
Wizard #1/2 — 1 — 3 — 9

BUFFY THE VAMPIRE SLAYER: ANGEL
Dark Horse Comics: May, 1999 - No. 3, July, 1999 ($2.95, limited series)

1-3-Gomez-a; Matsuda-c & photo-c for each — 3.00

BUFFY THE VAMPIRE SLAYER: GILES
Dark Horse Comics: Oct, 2000 ($2.95, one-shot)

1-Eric Powell-a; Powell & photo-c — 3.00

BUFFY THE VAMPIRE SLAYER: HAUNTED
Dark Horse Comics: Dec, 2001 - No. 4, Mar, 2002 ($2.99, limited series)

1-4-Faith and the Mayor app.; Espenson-s/Richards-a — 3.00
TPB (9/02, $12.95) r/series; photo-c — 13.00

BUFFY THE VAMPIRE SLAYER: OZ
Dark Horse Comics: July, 2001 - No. 3, Sept, 2001 ($2.99, limited series)

1-3-Totleben & photo-c; Golden-s — 3.00

BUFFY THE VAMPIRE SLAYER: SPIKE AND DRU
Dark Horse Comics: Apr, 1999; No. 2, Oct, 1999; No. 3, Dec, 2000 ($2.95)

1-3: 1,2-Photo-c. 3-Two covers (photo & Sook) — 3.00

BUFFY THE VAMPIRE SLAYER: THE ORIGIN (Adapts movie screenplay)
Dark Horse Comics: Jan, 1999 - No. 3, Mar, 1999 ($2.95, limited series)

1-3-Brereton-s/Bennett-a; reg & photo-c for each — 3.00

BUFFY THE VAMPIRE SLAYER: WILLOW & TARA
Dark Horse Comics: Apr, 2001 ($2.99, one-shot)

1-Terry Moore-a/Chris Golden & Amber Benson-s; Moore-c & photo-c — 3.00
TPB (4/03, $9.95) r/#1 & W&T - Wilderness; photo-c — 10.00

BUFFY THE VAMPIRE SLAYER: WILLOW & TARA - WILDERNESS
Dark Horse Comics: Jul, 2002 - No. 2, Sept, 2002 ($2.99, limited series)

1,2-Chris Golden & Amber Benson-s; Jothikaumar-c & photo-c — 3.00

BUGALOOS (TV)
Charlton Comics: Sept, 1971 - No. 4, Feb, 1972

1 — 5 — 15 — 55
2-4 — 3 — 9 — 32

BULLWINKLE (...and Rocky No. 22 on; See March of Comics #233 and Rocky & Bullwinkle) (TV) (Jay Ward)
Dell/Gold Key: 3-5/62 - #11, 4/74; #12, 6/76 - #19, 3/78; #20, 4/79 - #25, 2/80

Four Color 1270 (3-5/62) — 21 — 63 — 310
01-090-209 (Dell, 7-9/62) — 17 — 51 — 245
1(11/62, Gold Key) — 15 — 45 — 215

	GD	FN	NM-
2(2/63)	10	30	130
3(4/72)-11(4/74-Gold Key)	6	18	70
12-14: 12(6/76)-Reprints. 13(9/76), 14-New stories	3	9	30
15-25	2	6	18
Mother Moose Nursery Pomes 01-530-207 (5-7/62, Dell)			
	19	57	275

BULLWINKLE (…& Rocky No. 2 on)(TV)
Charlton Comics: July, 1970 - No. 7, July, 1971

1	7	21	90
2-7	5	15	60

BULLWINKLE AND ROCKY
Star Comics/Marvel Comics No. 3 on: Nov, 1987 - No. 9, Mar, 1989

1-9: Boris & Natasha in all. 3,5,8-Dudley Do-Right app. 4-Reagan-c			4.00
Marvel Moosterworks (1/92, $4.95)	1	4	10

CABLE (See Ghost Rider &…, & New Mutants #87) (Title becomes Soldier X)
Marvel Comics: May, 1993 - No. 107, Sept, 2002 ($3.50/$1.95/$1.50-$2.25)

1-($3.50, 52 pgs.)-Gold foil & embossed-c; Thibert a-1-4p; c-1-3			5.00
2-15: 3-Extra 16 pg. X-Men/Avengers ann. preview. 4-Liefeld-a assist; last Thibert-a(p). 6-8-Reveals that Baby Nathan is Cable; gives background on Stryfe. 9-Omega Red-c/story. 11-Bound-in trading card sheet			3.50
16-Newsstand edition			2.50
16-Enhanced edition			5.00
17-20-($1.95)-Deluxe edition, 20-w/bound in '95 Fleer Ultra cards			3.00
17-20-($1.50)-Standard edition			2.50
21-24, 26-44, -1(7/97): 21-Begin $1.95-c; return from Age of Apocalyse. 38-Weapon X-c/app; Psycho Man & Micronauts app.			3.00
25 ($3.95)-Foil gatefold-c			4.00
45-49,51-74: 45-Operation Zero Tolerance. 51-1st Casey-s. 54-Black Panther. 55-Domino-c/app. 62-Nick Fury-c/app.63-Stryfe-c/app. 67,68-Avengers-c/app. 71,73-Liefeld-a			2.50
50-($2.99) Double sized w/wraparound-c			3.00
75 -($2.99) Liefeld-c/a; Apocalypse: The Twelve x-over			3.00
76-79: 76-Apocalypse: The Twelve x-over			2.50
80-96: 80-Begin $2.25-c. 87-Mystique-c/app.			2.50
97-99,101-107: 97-Tischman-s/Kordey-a/c begin			2.25
100($3.99) Dialogue-free 'Nuff Said back-up story			4.00
…/Machine Man '98 Annual ($2.99) Wraparound-c			3.00
…/X-Force '96 Annual ($2.95) Wraparound-c			3.00
…'99 Annual ($3.50) vs. Sinister; computer photo-c			3.50

CAGE (Also see Hero for Hire, Power Man & Punisher)
Marvel Comics: Apr, 1992 - No. 20, Nov, 1993 ($1.25)

1,3,10,12: 3-Punisher-c & minor app. 10-Rhino & Hulk-c/app. 12-(52 pgs.)-Iron Fist app.			3.00
2,4-9,11,13-20: 9-Rhino-c/story; Hulk cameo			2.50

CAGE (Volume 3)
Marvel Comics (MAX): Mar, 2002 - No. 5, Sept, 2002 ($2.99, mature)

	GD	FN	NM-
1-5-Corben-c/a; Azzarello-s			3.00

HC (2002, $19.99, with dustjacket) r/#1-5; intro. by Darius James; sketch
  pages 20.00
SC (2003, $13.99) r/#1-5; intro. by Darius James 14.00

CAMP CANDY (TV)
Marvel Comics: May, 1990 - No. 6, Oct, 1990 ($1.00, limited series)

1-6: Post-c/a(p); featuring John Candy			4.00

CAPTAIN ACTION (Toy)
National Periodical Publications: Oct-Nov, 1968 - No. 5, June-July, 1969
(Based on Ideal toy)

	GD	FN	NM-
1-Origin; Wood-a; Superman-c app.	9	27	110
2,3,5-Kane/Wood-a	7	21	85
4	6	18	70

CAPTAIN AMERICA (Formerly Tales of Suspense #1-99) (Captain America
and the Falcon #134-223 & Steve Rogers: Captain America #444-454
appears on cover only)
Marvel Comics Group: No. 100, Apr, 1968 - No. 454, Aug, 1996

	GD	FN	NM-
100-Flashback on Cap's revival with Avengers & Sub-Mariner; story continued from Tales of Suspense #99; Kirby-c/a begins	28	84	420
101-The Sleeper-c/story; Red Skull app.	9	27	110
102-104: 102-Sleeper-c/s. 103,104-Red Skull-c/sty	7	21	80
105-108	6	18	65
109-Origin Capt. America retold	8	24	100
109-2nd printing (1994)	2	6	12
110-Rick becomes Cap's partner; Hulk x-over	10	30	130
111,113-Classic Steranko-c/a: 111-Death of Steve Rogers. 113-Cap's funeral	8	24	100
112-Origin retold; last Kirby-c/a	5	15	55
114-116,118-120: 115-Last 12¢ issue	4	12	38
117-1st app. The Falcon (9/69)	9	27	110
121-136,139,140: 121-Retells origin. 133-The Falcon becomes Cap's partner; origin Modok. 140-Origin Grey Gargoyle retold	3	9	25
137,138-Spider-Man x-over	3	9	32
141,142: 142-Last 15¢ issue	2	6	20
143-(52 pgs).	3	9	28
144-153: 144-New costume Falcon. 153-1st brief app. Jack Monroe	2	6	15
154-1st full app. Jack Monroe (Nomad)(10/72)	2	6	18
155-Origin; redrawn w/Falcon added; origin Jack Monroe	2	6	18
156-171,176-179: 155-158-Cap's strength increased. 160-1st app. Solarr. 164-1st app. Nightshade. 176-End of Capt. America	1	4	10
172-175: X-Men x-over	2	6	18
180-Intro/origin of Nomad (Steve Rogers)	2	6	20
181-Intro/origin new Cap.	2	6	16
182,184-192: 186-True origin The Falcon	1	3	8
183-Death of new Cap; Nomad becomes Cap	2	6	12

	GD	FN	NM-
193-Kirby-c/a begins	2	6	22
194-199-(Regular 25¢ edition)(4-7/76)	2	6	16
196-199-(30¢-c variants, limited distribution)	3	9	24
200-(Regular 25¢ edition)(8/76)	2	6	20
200-(30¢-c variant, limited distribution)	3	9	30
201-214-Kirby-c/a	2	6	14
210-214-(35¢-c variants, limited dist.)(6-10/77)	2	6	21

215,216,218-229,231-234,236-240,242-246: 215-Retells Cap's origin. 216-r/story from Strange Tales #114. 229-Marvel Man app. 233-Death of Sharon Carter. 234-Daredevil x-over. 244,245-Miller-c   5.00

217,230,235: 217-1st app. Marvel Man (later Quasar). 230-Battles Hulk-c/story cont'd in Hulk #232. 235-(7/79) Daredevil x-over; Miller-a(p)	1	3	7
241-Punisher app.; Miller-c.	3	9	30
241-2nd print			3.00
247-255-Byrne-a. 255-Origin; Miller-c.	1	3	9

256-281,284,285,289-322,324-326,328-331: 264-Old X-Men cameo in flashback. 265,266-Nick Fury & Spider-Man app. 267-1st app. Everyman. 269-1st Team America. 279-(3/83)-Contains Tattooz skin decals. 281-1950s Bucky returns. 284-Patriot (Jack Mace) app. 285-Death of Patriot. 298-Origin Red Skull. 328-Origin & 1st app. D-Man   3.00

282-Bucky becomes new Nomad (Jack Monroe)   5.00

282-Silver ink 2nd print ($1.75) w/original date (6/83)   2.25

283,327,333-340: 283-2nd app. Nomad. 327-Capt. Amer. battles Super Patriot. 333-Intro & origin new Captain (Super Patriot). 339-Fall of the Mutants tie-in   4.00

286-288-Deathlok app.   4.00

323-1st app. new Super Patriot (see Nick Fury)   4.00

332-Old Cap resigns   6.00

341-343,345-349   3.00

344-($1.50, 52 pgs.)-Ronald Reagan cameo   4.00

350-($1.75, 68 pgs.)-Return of Steve Rogers (original Cap) to original costume   4.00

351-382,384-396: 351-Nick Fury app. 354-1st app. U.S. Agent (6/89, see Avengers West Coast). 373-Bullseye app. 375-Daredevil app. 386-U.S. Agent app. 387-389-Red Skull back-up stories. 396-Last $1.00-c. 396,397-1st app. all new Jack O'Lantern   2.50

383-($2.00, 68 pgs.)-50th anniversary issue; Red Skull story; Lee-c(i)   4.00

397-399,401-424,425: 402-Begin 6 part Man-Wolf story w/Wolverine thru #407. 405-410-New Jack O'Lantern app. in back-up story. 406-Cable & Shatterstar cameo. 407-Capwolf vs. Cable-c/story. 408-Infinity War x-over; Falcon solo back-up. 423-Vs. Namor-c/story   2.25

400-($2.25, 84 pgs.)-Flip book format w/double gatefold-c; r/Avengers #4 plus-c; contains cover pin-ups.   3.00

425-($2.95, 52 pgs.)-Embossed Foil-c ed.n; Fighting Chance Pt. 1   3.00

426-443,446,447,449-453: 427-Begin $1.50-c; bound-in trading card sheet. 449-Thor app. 450-"Man Without A Country" storyline begins, ends #453; Bill Clinton app; variant-c exists. 451-1st app. Cap's new costume. 453-Cap gets old costume back; Bill Clinton app.   2.25

	GD	FN	NM-

444-Mark Waid scripts & Ron Garney-c/a(p) begins, ends #454; Avengers
  app.   5.00
445,454: 445-Sharon Carter & Red Skull return.   3.00
448-($2.95, double-sized issue)-Waid script & Garney-c/a; Red Skull "dies"
      4.00
Special 1(1/71)-Origin retold   5   15   55
Special 2(1/72, 52 pgs.)-Colan-r/Not Brand Echh; all-r 3   9   30
Annual 3('76, 52 pgs.)-Kirby-c/a(new)   2   6   22
Annual 4('77, 34 pgs.)-Magneto-c/story   2   6   22
Annual 5-7: (52 pgs.)('81-'83)   5.00
Annual 8(9/86)-Wolverine-c/story   3   10   35
Annual 9-13('90-'94, 68 pgs.)-9-Nomad back-up. 10-Origin retold (2 pgs.).
  11-Falcon solo story. 12-Bagged w/card. 13-Red Skull-c/story   3.00
...Ashcan Edition ('95, 75¢)   3.00
... and the Falcon: Madbomb TPB (2004, $16.99) r/#193-200; Kirby-s/a 17.00
...: Deathlok Lives! nn(10/93, $4.95)-r/#286-288   5.00
...Drug War 1-(1994, $2.00, 52 pgs.)-New Warriors app.   3.00
...Man Without a Country(1998, $12.99, TPB)-r/#450-453   13.00
...Medusa Effect 1 (1994, $2.95, 68 pgs.)-Origin Baron Zemo   3.00
...Operation Rebirth (1996, $9.95)-r/#445-448   10.00
...Streets of Poison ($15.95)-r/#372-378   16.00
...: The Movie Special nn (5/92, $3.50, 52 pgs.)-Adapts movie; printed on
  coated stock; The Red Skull app.   3.50

CAPTAIN AMERICA (Volume Two)
Marvel Comics: V2#1, Nov, 1996 - No. 13, Nov, 1997($2.95/$1.95/$1.99)
(Produced by Extreme Studios)

1-($2.95)-Heroes Reborn begins; Liefeld-c/a; reintro Nick Fury   6.00
1-($2.95)-(Variant-c)-Liefeld-c/a   6.00
1-(7/96, $2.95)-(Exclusive Comicon Ed.)-Liefeld-c/a. 1   3   8
2-11,13: 5-Two-c. 13-"World War 3"-pt. 4, x-over w/Image   3.00
12-($2.99) "Heroes Reunited"-pt. 4   4.00

CAPTAIN AMERICA (Vol. Three) (Also see Capt. America: Sentinel of
Liberty)
Marvel Comics: Jan, 1998 - No. 50, Feb, 2002 ($2.99/$1.99/$2.25)

1-($2.99) Mark Waid-s/Ron Garney-a   4.00
1-Variant cover   6.00
2-($1.99): 2-Two covers   3.00
3-11: 3-Returns to old shield. 4-Hawkeye app. 5-Thor-c/app. 7-Andy
  Kubert-c/a begin. 9-New shield   2.50
12-($2.99) Battles Nightmare; Red Skull back-up story   3.50
13-17,19-Red Skull returns   2.25
18-($2.99) Cap vs. Korvac in the Future   3.00
20-24,26-29: 20,21-Sgt. Fury back-up story painted by Evans   2.25
25-($2.99) Cap & Falcon vs. Hatemonger   3.00
30-49: 30-Begin $2.25-c. 32-Ordway-a. 33-Jurgens-s/a begins; U.S. Agent
  app. 36-Maximum Security x-over. 41,46-Red Skull app.   2.25
.../Citizen V '98 Annual ($3.50) Busiek & Kesel-s   3.50
50-($5.95) Stories by various incl. Jurgens, Quitely, Immonen; Ha-c   6.00

	GD	FN	NM-
1999 Annual ($3.50) Flag Smasher app.			3.50
2000 Annual ($3.50) Continued from #35 vs. Protocide; Jurgens-s			3.50
2001 Annual ($2.99) Golden Age flashback; Invaders app.			3.00
...: To Serve and Protect TPB (2/02, $17.95) r/Vol. 3 #1-7			18.00

CAPTAIN AMERICA (Volume 4)
Marvel Comics: Jun, 2002 - No. 32, Dec, 2004 ($3.99/$2.99)

1-Ney Rieber-s/Cassaday-c/a			4.00
2-9-($2.99) 3-Cap reveals Steve Rogers ID. 7-9-Hairsine-s			3.00
10-32: 10-16-Jae Lee-a. 17-20-Gibbons-s/Weeks-a. 21-26-Bachalo-a.			
26-Bucky flashback. 27,28-Eddie Campbell-a. 29-32-Red Skull app.			3.00
...Vol. 1: The New Deal HC (2003, $22.99) r/#1-6; foreward by Collins			23.00
...Vol. 2: The Extremists TPB (2003, $13.99) r/#7-11; Cassaday-c			14.00
...Vol. 3: Ice TPB (2003, $12.99) r/#12-16; Jae Lee-a; Cassaday-c			13.00
...Vol. 4: Cap Lives TPB (2004, $12.99) r/#17-22 & Tales of Suspense #66			
			13.00

CAPTAIN AMERICA
Marvel Comics: Jan, 2005 - Present ($2.99)

1-Brubaker-s/Epting-c/a; Red Skull app.			3.00

CAPTAIN AMERICA AND THE FALCON
Marvel Comics: May, 2004 - Present ($2.99, limited series)

1-4-Priest-s/Sears-a			3.00
5-7-Avengers Disassembled x-over. 6,7-Scarlet Witch app.			3.00
8-10-Modok app.			3.00

CAPTAIN AMERICA: DEAD MEN RUNNING
Marvel Comics: Mar, 2002 - No. 3, May, 2002 ($2.99, limited series)

1-3-Macan-s/Zezelj-a			3.00

CAPTAIN AMERICA: RED, WHITE & BLUE
Marvel Comics: Sept, 2002 ($29.99, one-shot, hardcover with dustjacket)

nn-Reprints from Lee & Kirby, Steranko, Miller and others; and new short stories and pin-ups by various incl. Ross, Dini, Timm, Waid, Dorkin, Sienkiewicz, Miller, Bruce Jones, Collins, Piers-Rayner, Pope, Deodato, Quitely, Nino; Stelfreeze-c			30.00

CAPTAIN AMERICA: SENTINEL OF LIBERTY
Marvel Comics: Sept, 1998 - No. 12, Aug, 1999 ($1.99)

1-Waid-s/Garney-a			3.00
1-Rough Cut ($2.99) Features original script and pencil pages			3.00
2-5: 2-Two-c; Invaders WW2 story			2.25
6-($2.99) Iron Man-c/app.			3.00
7-11: 8-Falcon-c/app. 9-Falcon poses as Cap			2.25
12-($2.99) Final issue; Bucky-c/app.			3.00

CAPTAIN AMERICA SPECIAL EDITION
Marvel Comics Group: Feb, 1984 - No. 2, Mar, 1984 ($2.00, Baxter paper)

1-Steranko-c/a(r) in both; r/ Captain America #110,111			6.00
2-Reprints the scarce Our Love Story #5, and C.A. #113			
	1	3	8

	GD	FN	NM-

CAPTAIN AMERICA: THE LEGEND
Marvel Comics: Sept, 1996 ($3.95, one-shot)

1-Tribute issue; wraparound-c   4.00

CAPTAIN AMERICA: WHAT PRICE GLORY
Marvel Comics: May, 2003 - No. 4, May, 2003 ($2.99, weekly limited series)

1-4-Bruce Jones-s/Steve Rude & Mike Royer-a   3.00

CAPTAIN ATOM (Formerly Strange Suspense Stories #77)
Charlton Comics: V2#78, Dec, 1965 - V2#89, Dec, 1967

V2#78-Origin retold; Bache-a (3 pgs.)	10	30	125
79-82: 79-1st app. Dr. Spectro; 3 pg. Ditko cut & paste /Space Adventures			
#24. 82-Intro. Nightshade (9/66)	6	18	75
83-86: Ted Kord Blue Beetle in all. 83-(11/66)-1st app. Ted Kord. 84-1st app.			
new Captain Atom	6	18	70
87-89: Nightshade by Aparo in all	6	18	70
83-85(Modern Comics-1977)-reprints	1	3	7

CAPTAIN ATOM (Also see Americomics & Crisis On Infinite Earths)
DC Comics: Mar, 1987 - No. 57, Sept, 1991 (Direct sales only #35 on)

1-(44 pgs.)-Origin/1st app. with new costume			4.00
2-49: 5-Firestorm x-over. 6-Intro. new Dr. Spectro. 11-Millennium tie-in.			
14-Nightshade app. 16-Justice League app. 17-$1.00-c begins; Swamp			
Thing app. 20-Blue Beetle x-over. 24,25-Invasion tie-in.			2.50
51-57: 50-($2.00, 52 pgs.). 57-War of the Gods x-over			2.50
Annual 1,2 ('88, '89)-1-Intro Major Force			3.00

CAPTAIN KANGAROO (TV)
Dell Publishing Co.: No. 721, Aug, 1956 - No. 872, Jan, 1958

Four Color 721 (#1)-Photo-c	18	54	270
Four Color 780, 872-Photo-c	15	45	215

CAPTAIN MARVEL (Becomes ...Presents the Terrible 5 No. 5)
M. F. Enterprises: April, 1966 - No. 4, Nov, 1966 (25¢ Giants)

nn-(#1 on pg. 5)-Origin; created by Carl Burgos	5	15	55
2-4: 3-(#3 on pg. 4)-Fights the Bat	3	9	32

CAPTAIN MARVEL (Marvel's Space-Born Super-Hero! Captain Marvel #1-6; see Giant-Size..., Life Of..., Marvel Graphic Novel #1, Marvel Spotlight V2#1 & Marvel Super-Heroes #12)
Marvel Comics Group: May, 1968 - No. 19, Dec, 1969; No. 20, June, 1970 - No. 21, Aug, 1970; No. 22, Sept, 1972 - No. 62, May, 1979

1	10	30	130
2-Super Skrull-c/story	4	12	50
3-5: 4-Captain Marvel battles Sub-Mariner	4	12	40
6-11: 11-Capt. Marvel given great power by Zo the Ruler; Smith/Trimpe-c;			
Death of Una	3	9	27
12,13,15-20: 16,17-New costume	2	6	18
14,21: 14-Capt. Marvel vs. Iron Man; last 12¢ issue. 21-Capt. Marvel battles			
Hulk; last 15¢ issue	3	9	30
22-24	2	6	16

	GD	FN	NM-

25,26: 25-Starlin-c/a begins; Starlin's 1st Thanos saga begins (3/73), ends #34; Thanos cameo (5 panels). 26-Minor Thanos app. (see Iron Man #55);

	GD	FN	NM-
1st Thanos-c	3	10	35
27,28-1st & 2nd full app. Thanos. 28-Thanos-c/s	3	9	30
29,30-Thanos cameos. 29-C.M. gains more powers	2	6	20
31,32: Thanos app. 31-Last 20¢ issue. 32-Thanos-c	2	6	22

33-Thanos-c & app.; Capt. Marvel battles Thanos; 1st origin Thanos

	GD	FN	NM-
	3	9	30

34-1st app. Nitro; C.M. contracts cancer which eventually kills him; last

	GD	FN	NM-
Starlin-c/a	2	6	20

35,37-40,42,46-48,50,53-56,58-62: 39-Origin Watcher. 58-Thanos cameo

	GD	FN	NM-
	1	3	8

36,41,43,49: 36-R-origin/1st app. Capt. Marvel from Marvel Super-Heroes #12. 41,43-Wrightson part inks; #43-c(i). 49-Starlin & Weiss-p assists

	GD	FN	NM-
	1	3	9
44,45-(Regular 25¢ editions)(5,7/76)	1	3	8
44,45-(30¢-c variants, limited distribution)	2	6	12
51,52-(Regular 30¢ editions)(7,9/77)	1	3	8
51,52-(35¢-c variants, limited distribution)	2	6	12
57-Thanos appears in flashback	1	4	10

CAPT. SAVAGE AND HIS LEATHERNECK RAIDERS (...And His Battlefield Raiders #9 on)
Marvel Comics Group (Animated Timely Features): Jan, 1968 - No. 19, Mar, 1970 (See Sgt. Fury No. 10)

	GD	FN	NM-
1-Sgt. Fury & Howlers cameo	5	15	55
2,7,11: 2-Origin Hydra. 1-5,7-Ayers/Shores-a. 7-Pre-"Thing" Ben Grimm			
story. 11-Sgt. Fury app.	3	9	28
3-6,8-10,12-14: 14-Last 12¢ issue	3	9	25
15-19	2	6	22

CAT, THE (Female hero)
Marvel Comics Group: Nov, 1972 - No. 4, June, 1973

	GD	FN	NM-
1-Origin & 1st app. The Cat (who later becomes Tigra); Mooney-a(i);			
Wood-c(i)/a(i)	4	12	45
2,3: 2-Marie Severin/Mooney-a. 3-Everett inks	2	6	22
4-Starlin/Weiss-a(p)	3	9	24

CATWOMAN (Also see Action Comics Weekly #611, Batman #404-407, Detective Comics, & Superman's Girlfriend Lois Lane #70, 71)
DC Comics: Feb, 1989 - No. 4, May, 1989 ($1.50, limited series, mature)

	GD	FN	NM-
1	1	4	10
2-4: 3-Batman cameo. 4-Batman app.	1	3	9
Her Sister's Keeper (1991, $9.95, trade paperback)-r/#1-4			10.00

CATWOMAN (Also see Batman #404-407)
DC Comics: Aug, 1993 - No. 94, Jul, 2001 ($1.50-$2.25)

0-(10/94)-Zero Hour; origin retold. Released between #14&15			3.00
1-($1.95)-Embossed-c; Bane app.; Balent c-1-10; a-1-10p			4.00
2-20: 3-Bane flashback cameo. 4-Brief Bane app. 6,7-Knightquest tie-ins;			
Batman (Azrael) app. 8-1st app. Zephyr. 12-KnightsEnd pt. 6. 13-new			

	GD	FN	NM-

Knights End Aftermath. 14-(9/94)-Zero Hour ... 3.00
21-24, 26-30, 33-49: 21-$1.95-c begins. 28,29-Penguin cameo app.
    36-Legacy pt. 2. 38-40-Year Two; Batman, Joker, Penguin & Two-Face app.
    46-Two-Face app. ... 2.50
25,31,32: 25-($2.95)-Robin app. 31,32-Contagion pt. 4 (Reads pt. 5 on-c)
    & pt. 9. ... 3.00
50-($2.95, 48 pgs.)-New armored costume ... 3.00
50-($2.95, 48 pgs.)-Collector's Ed.w/metallic ink-c ... 3.00
51-77: 51-Huntress-c/app. 54-Grayson-s begins. 56-Cataclysm pt.6.
    57-Poison Ivy-c/app. 63-65-Joker-c/app. 72-No Man's Land ... 2.50
78-82: 80-Catwoman goes to jail ... 2.25
83-94: 83-Begin $2.25-c. 83,84,89-Harley Quinn-c/app. ... 2.25
#1,000,000 (11/98) 853rd Century x-over ... 2.25
Annual 1 (1994, $2.95, 68 pgs.)-Elseworlds story; Batman app.; no Balent-a
     ... 3.00
Annual 2,4 ('95, '97, $3.95) 2-Year One story. 4-Pulp Heroes ... 4.00
Annual 3 (1996, $2.95)-Legends of the Dead Earth story ... 3.00
...Plus 1 (11/97, $2.95) Screamqueen (Scare Tactics) app. ... 3.00
TPB ($9.95) r/#15-19, Balent-c ... 10.00

CATWOMAN (Also see Detective Comics #759-762)
DC Comics: Jan, 2002 - Present ($2.50)

1-Darwyn Cooke & Mike Allred-a; Ed Brubaker-s ... 6.00
2-4 ... 3.00
5-37: 5-9-Rader-a/Paul Pope-c. 10-Morse-c. 16-JG Jones-c.
    22-Batman-c/app. 34-36-War Games ... 2.50
...: Crooked Little Town TPB (2003, $14.95) r/#5-10 & Secret Files; Oeming-c
     ... 15.00
... Secret Files and Origins (10/02, $4.95) origin-s Oeming-a; profiles and
    pin-ups ... 5.00
...Selina's Big Score HC (2002, $24.95) Cooke-s/a; pin-ups by various ... 25.00
...Selina's Big Score SC (2003, $17.95) Cooke-s/a; pin-ups by various ... 18.00
...: The Dark End of the Street TPB (2002, $12.95) r/#1-4 & Slam Bradley
    back-up stories from Detective Comics #759-762 ... 13.00

CATWOMAN/ GUARDIAN OF GOTHAM
DC Comics: 1999 - No. 2, 1999 ($5.95, limited series)

1,2-Elseworlds; Moench-s/Balent-a ... 6.00

CATWOMAN: THE MOVIE (2004 Halle Berry movie)
DC Comics: 2004 ($4.95/$9.95)

1-($4.95) Movie adaptation; Jim Lee-c and sketch pages; Derenick-a ... 5.00
... & Other Cat Tales TPB (2004, $9.95)-r/Movie adaptation; Jim Lee sketch
    pages, r/Catwoman #0, Catwoman (2nd series) #11 & 25; photo-c ... 10.00

CEREBUS THE AARDVARK (See A-V in 3-D, Nucleus, Power Comics)
Aardvark-Vanaheim: Dec, 1977 - No. 300, March, 2004 ($1.70/$2.00/$2.25,
B&W)

0 ... 3.00
0-Gold ... 20.00
1-1st app. Cerebus; 2000 print run; most copies poorly printed

	GD	FN	NM-
	41	123	650

Note: *There is a counterfeit version known to exist. It can be distinguished from the original in the following ways: inside cover is glossy instead of flat, black background on the front cover is blotted or spotty. Reports show that a counterfeit #2 also exists.*

	GD	FN	NM-
2-Dave Sim art in all	11	33	160
3-Origin Red Sophia	10	30	130
4-Origin Elrod the Albino	8	24	100
5,6	7	21	80
7-10	5	15	60
11,12: 11-Origin The Cockroach	4	12	40
13-15: 14-Origin Lord Julius	3	9	30
16-20	2	6	18
21-B. Smith letter in letter column	5	15	55
22-Low distribution; no cover price	3	9	28
23-30: 23-Preview of Wandering Star by Teri S. Wood. 26-High Society begins, ends #50	2	6	12
31-Origin Moonroach	2	6	15
32-40, 53-Intro. Wolveroach (brief app.)	1	3	9
41-50,52: 52-Church & State begins, ends #111; Cutey Bunny app.	1	3	8
51,54: 51-Cutey Bunny app. 54-1st full Wolveroach story	2	6	12
55,56-Wolveroach app.; Normalman back-ups by Valentino	1	3	9
57-100: 61,62: Flaming Carrot app. 65-Gerhard begins			4.00
101-160: 104-Flaming Carrot app. 112/113-Double issue. 114-Jaka's Story begins, ends #136. 139-Melmoth begins, ends #150. 151-Mothers & Daughters begins, ends #200			3.00
161-Bone app.	1	4	10
162-231: 175-($2.25, 44 pgs). 186-Strangers on Paradise cameo. 201-Guys storyline begins; Eddie Campbell's Bacchus app. 220-231-Rick's Story			2.50
232-265-Going Home			2.25
266-288,291-299-Latter Days: 267-Five-Bar Gate. 276-Spore (Spawn spoof)			2.25
289&290 ($4.50) Two issues combined			4.50
300-Final issue			2.25
Free Cerebus (Giveaway, 1991-92?, 36 pgs.)-All-r			4.00

CHALLENGERS OF THE UNKNOWN (See Showcase #6, 7, 11, 12, Super DC Giant, and Super Team Family)
National Per. Publ./DC Comics: 4-5/58 - No. 77, 12/1-70-71; No. 78, 2/73 - No. 80, 6-7/73; No. 81, 6-7/77 - No. 87, 6-7/78

	GD	FN	NM-
1-(4-5/58)-Kirby/Stein-a(2); Kirby-c	190	570	3800
2-Kirby/Stein-a(2)	67	201	1275
3-Kirby/Stein-a(2)	58	174	1100
4-8-Kirby/Wood-a plus cover to #8	46	138	775
9,10	29	87	425
11-Grey tone-c	20	60	300
12-15: 14-Origin/1st app. Multi-Man (villain)	19	57	285
16-22: 18-Intro. Cosmo, the Challengers Spacepet. 22-Last 10¢ issue			

	GD	FN	NM-
	13	39	190
23-30	8	24	100
31-Retells origin of the Challengers	8	24	105
32-40	5	15	60
41-47,49,50,52-60: 43-New look begins. 49-Intro. Challenger Corps.			
55-Death of Red Ryan. 60-Red Ryan returns	4	12	45
48,51: 48-Doom Patrol app. 51-Sea Devils app.	4	12	50
61-68: 64,65-Kirby origin-r, parts 1 & 2. 66-New logo. 68-Last 12¢ issue.			
	3	9	28
69-73,75-80: 69-1st app. Corinna. 77-Last 15¢ issue	2	6	16
74-Deadman by Tuska/Adams; 1 pg. Wrightson-a	4	12	50
81,83-87: 81-(6-7/77). 83-87-Swamp Thing app. 84-87-Deadman app.			
	1	4	10
82-Swamp Thing begins (thru #87, c/s	2	6	14

CHALLENGERS OF THE UNKNOWN
DC Comics: Mar, 1991 - No. 8, Oct, 1991 ($1.75, limited series)

1-Jeph Loeb scripts & Tim Sale-a in all (1st work together); Bolland-c			3.00
2-8: 2-Superman app. 3-Dr. Fate app. 6-G. Kane-c(p). 7-Steranko-c/swipe by			
Art Adams			2.50
... Must Die! (2004, $19.95, TPB) r/series; intro by Bendis; Sale sketch pages			
			20.00

NOTE: **Art Adams** c-7. **Hempel** c-5. **Gil Kane** c-6p. **Sale** a-1-8; c-3, 8. **Wagner** c-4.

CHAMBER OF CHILLS
Marvel Comics Group: Nov, 1972 - No. 25, Nov, 1976

1-Harlan Ellison adaptation	3	9	32
2-5: 2-1st app. John Jakes (Brak the Barbarian)	2	6	16
6-25: 22,23-(Regular 25¢ editions)	2	6	12
22,23-(30¢-c variants, limited distribution)(5,7/76)	2	6	18

CHAMBER OF DARKNESS (Monsters on the Prowl #9 on)
Marvel Comics Group: Oct, 1969 - No. 8, Dec, 1970

1-Buscema-a(p)	6	18	75
2,3: 2-Neal Adams scripts. 3-Smith, Buscema-a	4	12	38
4-A Conan-esque tryout by Smith (4/70); reprinted in Conan #16; Marie			
Severin/Everett-c	7	21	90
5,8: 5-H.P. Lovecraft adaptation. 8-Wrightson-c	3	9	30
6	3	9	25
7-Wrightson-c/a, 7pgs. (his 1st work at Marvel); Wrightson draws himself in			
1st & last panels; Kirby/Ditko-r; last 15¢-c	4	12	48
1-(1/72; 25¢ Special, 52 pgs.)	4	12	38

CHAMPIONS, THE
Marvel Comics Group: Oct, 1975 - No. 17, Jan, 1978

1-Origin & 1st app. The Champions (The Angel, Black Widow, Ghost Rider,			
Hercules, Iceman); Venus x-over	3	10	35
2-4,8-10,16: 2,3-Venus x-over	2	6	14
5-7-(Regular 25¢ edition)(4-8/76) 6-Kirby-c	2	6	14
5-7-(30¢-c variants, limited distribution)	2	6	20
11-14,17-Byrne-a. 14-(Regular 30¢ edition)	2	6	14

	GD	FN	NM-
14,15-(35¢-c variant, limited distribution)	2	6	20
15-(Regular 30¢ edition)(9/77)-Byrne-a	2	6	14

CHARLTON BULLSEYE
CPL/Gang Publications: 1975 - No. 5, 1976 ($1.50, B&W, bi-monthly, magazine format)

	GD	FN	NM-
1: 1 & 2 are last Capt. Atom by Ditko/Byrne intended for the never published Capt. Atom #90; Nightshade app.; Jeff Jones-a	5	15	65
2-Part 2 Capt. Atom story by Ditko/Byrne	4	12	42
3-Wrong Country by Sanho Kim	2	6	22
4-Doomsday + 1 by John Byrne	3	9	32
5-Doomsday + 1 by Byrne, The Question by Toth; Neal Adams back-c; Toth-c	4	12	48

CHARLTON BULLSEYE
Charlton Publications: June, 1981 - No. 10, Dec, 1982; Nov, 1986

	GD	FN	NM-
1-Blue Beetle, The Question app.; 1st app. Rocket Rabbit	1	3	9
2-5: 2-1st app. Neil The Horse; Rocket Rabbit app. 4-Vanguards			6.00
6-10: Low print run. 6-Origin & 1st app. Thunderbunny	1	3	9

NOTE: *Material intended for issue #11-up was published in Scary Tales #37-up.*

CHARLTON PREMIERE (Formerly Marine War Heroes)
Charlton Comics: V1#19, July, 1967; V2#1, Sept, 1967 - No. 4, May, 1968

	GD	FN	NM-
V1#19, V2#1,2,4: V1#19-Marine War Heroes. V2#1-Trio; intro. Shape, Tyro Team & Spookman. 2-Children of Doom; Boyette classic-a. 4-Unlikely Tales; Aparo, Ditko-a	3	9	28
V2#3-Sinistro Boy Fiend; Blue Beetle & Peacemaker x-over	3	10	35

CHASING DOGMA (See Jay and Silent Bob)

CHECKMATE (TV)
Gold Key: Oct, 1962 - No. 2, Dec, 1962

	GD	FN	NM-
1-Photo-c on both	7	21	80
2	6	18	70

CHECKMATE! (See Action Comics #598)
DC Comics: Apr, 1988 - No. 33, Jan, 1991 ($1.25)

	GD	FN	NM-
1-33: 13: New format begins			2.50

NOTE: *Gil Kane c-2, 4, 7, 8, 10, 11, 15-19.*

CHIP 'N' DALE (Walt Disney)(See Walt Disney's C&S #204)
Dell Publishing Co./Gold Key/Whitman No. 65 on: Nov, 1953 - No. 30, June-Aug, 1962; Sept, 1967 - No. 83, July, 1984

	GD	FN	NM-
Four Color 517(#1)	11	33	160
Four Color 581,636	7	21	80
4(12/55-2/56)-10	6	18	70
11-30	5	15	55
1(Gold Key, 1967)-Reprints	3	10	35
2-10	2	6	18

	GD	FN	NM-
11-20	2	6	12
21-40	1	3	9
41-64,70-77: 75(2/82), 76(2-3/82), 77(3/82)	1	3	7
65,66 (Whitman)	1	4	10
67-69 (3-pack? 1980): 67(8/80), 68(10/80) (scarce)	3	9	25
78-83 (All #90214; 3-pack, nd, nd code): 78(4/83), 79(5/83), 80(7/83), 81(8/83), 82(5/84), 83(7/84)	2	6	16

NOTE: All Gold Key/Whitman issues have reprints except No. 32-35, 38-41, 45-47. No. 23-28, 30-42, 45-47, 49 have new covers.

CHRISTMAS WITH THE SUPER-HEROES (See Limited Collectors' Edition)
DC Comics: 1988; No. 2, 1989 ($2.95)

1,2: 1-(100 pgs.)-All reprints; N. Adams-r, Byrne-c; Batman, Superman, JLA, LSH Christmas stories; r-Miller's 1st Batman/DC Special Series #21. 2-(68 pgs.)-Superman by Chadwick; Batman, Wonder Woman, Deadman, Green Lantern, Flash app.; Morrow-a; Enemy Ace by Byrne; all new-a   5.00

CLASSIC STAR WARS (Also see Star Wars)
Dark Horse Comics: Aug, 1992 - No. 20, June, 1994 ($2.50)

1-Begin Star Wars strip-r by Williamson; Williamson redrew portions of the panels to fit comic book format	6.00
2-10: 8-Polybagged w/Star Wars Galaxy trading card. 8-M. Schultz-c	4.00
11-19: 13-Yeates-c. 17-M. Schultz-c. 19-Evans-c	3.00
20-($3.50, 52 pgs.)-Polybagged w/trading card	3.50
Escape To Hoth TPB ($16.95) r/#15-20	17.00
The Rebel Storm TPB - r/#8-14	17.00
Trade paperback ($29.95, slip-cased)-Reprints all movie adaptations	30.00

NOTE: Williamson c-1-5,7,9,10,14,15,20.

CLASSIC STAR WARS: (Title series). **Dark Horse Comics**

--A NEW HOPE, 6/94 - No. 2, 7/94 ($3.95)
1,2: 1-r/Star Wars #1-3, 7-9 publ; 2-r/Star Wars #4-6, 10-12 publ. by Marvel Comics   4.00

--DEVILWORLDS, 8/96 - No.2, 9/96 ($2.50s)1,2: r/Alan Moore-s   2.50

--HAN SOLO AT STARS' END, 3/97 - No. 3, 5/97 ($2.95)
1-3: r/strips by Alfredo Alcala   3.00

--RETURN OF THE JEDI, 10/94 - No.2, 11/94 ($3.50)
1,2: 1-r/1983-84 Marvel series; polybagged with w/trading card   3.50

--THE EARLY ADVENTURES, 8/94 - No. 9, 4/95 ($2.50)1-9   2.50

--THE EMPIRE STRIKES BACK, 8/94 - No. 2, 9/94 ($3.95)
1-r/Star Wars #39-44 published by Marvel Comics   4.00

CLASSIC X-MEN (Becomes X-Men Classic #46 on)
Marvel Comics Group: Sept, 1986 - No. 45, Mar, 1990

1-Begins-r of New X-Men	5.00
2-10: 10-Sabretooth app.	4.00
11-45: 11-1st origin of Magneto in back-up story. 17-Wolverine-c. 27-r/X-Men #121. 26-r/X-Men #120; Wolverine-c/app. 35-r/X-Men #129. 39-New Jim Lee back-up story (2nd-a on X-Men). 43-$1.75-c, double-size	3.00

NOTE: Art Adams c(p)-1-10, 12-16, 18-23. Austin c-10,15-21,24-28i. Bolton back up stories

119

	GD	FN	NM-

in 1-28,30-35. **Williamson** *c-12-14i.*

CLAW THE UNCONQUERED (See Cancelled Comic Cavalcade)
National Periodical Publications/DC Comics: 5-6/75 - No. 9, 9-10/76; No. 10, 4-5/78 - No. 12, 8-9/78

	GD	FN	NM-
1-1st app. Claw	1	4	10
2-12: 3-Nudity panel. 9-Origin			6.00

CLERKS: THE COMIC BOOK (Also see Oni Double Feature #1)
Oni Press: Feb, 1998 ($2.95, B&W, one-shot)

	GD	FN	NM-
1-Kevin Smith-s	2	6	12
1-Second printing			4.00
...Holiday Special (12/98, $2.95) Smith-s			5.00
...The Lost Scene (12/99, $2.95) Smith-s/Hester-a			5.00

CLOSE SHAVES OF PAULINE PERIL, THE (TV cartoon)
Gold Key: June, 1970 - No. 4, March, 1971

	GD	FN	NM-
1	4	12	40
2-4	3	9	26

COLOSSUS (See X-Men)
Marvel Comics: Oct, 1997 ($2.99, 48 pgs., one-shot)

	GD	FN	NM-
1-Raab-s/Hitch & Neary-a, wraparound-c			3.00

COMBAT KELLY (...and the Deadly Dozen)
Marvel Comics Group: June, 1972 - No. 9, Oct, 1973

	GD	FN	NM-
1-Intro & origin new Combat Kelly; Ayers/Mooney-a; Severin-c (20¢)	3	9	28
2,5-8	2	6	15
3,4: 3-Origin. 4-Sgt. Fury-c/s	2	6	20
9-Death of the Deadly Dozen	2	6	22

COMIX INTERNATIONAL
Warren Magazines: Jul, 1974 - No. 5, Spring, 1977 (Full color, stiff-c, mail only)

	GD	FN	NM-
1-Low distribution; all Corben story remainders from Warren; Corben-c on all	9	27	110
2,4: 2-Two Dracula stories; Wood, Wrightson-r; Crandall-a; Maroto-a. 4-Printing w/ 3 Corben sty	4	12	50
3-5: 3-Dax story. 4-(printing without Corben story). 4-Crandall-a.			
4,5-Vampirella stories. 5-Spirit story; Eisner-a	4	12	40

NOTE: *No. 4 had two printings with extra* **Corben** *story in one. No. 3 may also have a variation. No. 3 has two Jeff Jones reprints from Vampirella.*

CONAN (The Legend)
Dark Horse Comics: Feb, 2004 - Present ($2.99)

	GD	FN	NM-
0-(11/03, 25¢-c) Busiek-s/Nord-a			2.25
1-Linsner-c/Busiek-s/Nord-a			5.00
1-(2nd printing) J. Scott Campell-c			3.00
1-(3rd printing) Nord-c			3.00
2-6			3.00

Vol. 1: The Frost Giant's Daughter and Other Stories (2005, $15.95) r/#1-6,

	GD	FN	NM-
partial #7			16.00

CONAN SAGA, THE
Marvel Comics: June, 1987 - No. 97, Apr, 1995 ($2.00/$2.25, B&W, magazine)

1-Barry Smith-r; new Smith-c	1	3	7
2-27: 2-9,11-new Barry Smith-c. 13,15-Boris-c. 17-Adams-r.18,25-Chaykin-r. 22-r/Giant-Size Conan 1,2			4.00
28-90: 28-Begin $2.25-c. 31-Red Sonja-r by N. Adams/SSOC #1; 1 pg. Jeff Jones-r. 32-Newspaper strip-r begin by Buscema. 33-Smith/Conrad-a. 39-r/Kull #1('71) by Andru & Wood. 44-Swipes-c/Savage Tales #1. 57-Brunner-r/SSOC #30. 66-r/Conan Annual #2 by Buscema. 79-r/Conan #43-45 w/Red Sonja. 85-Based on Conan #57-63			3.00
91-96			4.00
97-Last issue			5.00

CONAN THE BARBARIAN
Marvel Comics: Oct, 1970 - No. 275, Dec, 1993

1-Origin/1st app. Conan (in comics) by Barry Smith; 1st brief app. Kull; #1-9 are 15¢ issues	18	54	270
2	7	21	80
3-(Low distribution in some areas)	11	33	150
4,5	6	18	75
6-9: 8-Hidden panel message, pg. 14. 9-Last 15¢-c	4	12	50
10,11 (25¢ 52 pg. giants): 10-Black Knight-r; Kull story by Severin	6	18	70
12,13: 12-Wrightson-c(i)	4	12	40
14,15-Elric app.	5	15	55
16,19,20: 16-Conan-r/Savage Tales #1	4	12	40
17,18-No Barry Smith-a	3	9	25
21,22: 22-Has reprint from #1	3	9	30
23-1st app. Red Sonja (2/73)	4	12	40
24-1st full Red Sonja story; last Smith-a	4	12	38
25-John Buscema-c/a begins	2	6	22
26-30	2	6	16
31-36,38-40	1	4	10
37-Neal Adams-c/a; last 20¢ issue; contains pull-out subscription form	2	6	20
41-43,46-50: 48-Origin retold	1	3	8
44,45-N. Adams-i(Crusty Bunkers). 45-Adams-c	2	6	12
51-57,59,60: 59-Origin Belit			6.00
58-2nd Belit app. (see Giant-Size Conan #1)	1	3	8
61-65-(Regular 25¢ editions)(4-8/76)			5.00
61-65-(30¢-c variants, limited distribution)	1	3	7
66-99: 68-Red Sonja story cont'd from Marvel Feature #7. 75-79-(Reg. 30¢-c). 84-Intro. Zula. 85-Origin Zula. 87-r/Savage Sword of Conan #3 in color			4.00
75-79-(35¢-c variants, limited distribution)			6.00
100-(52 pg. Giant)-Death of Belit			6.00
101-114			2.25

	GD	FN	NM-
115-Double size			3.00
116-199,201-231,233-249: 116-r/Power Record Comic PR31. 244-Zula			
returns			2.25
200,232: 200-(52 pgs.). 232-Young Conan begins; Conan is born			4.00
250-(60 pgs.)			3.00
251-270: 262-Adapted from R.E. Howard story			3.00
271-274			5.00
275-($2.50, 68 pgs.)-Final issue; painted-c (low print)	1	3	8
King Size 1(1973, 35¢)-Smith-r/#2,4; Smith-c	3	9	25
Annual 2(1976, 50¢)-New full length story	2	6	12
Annual 3,4: 3('78)-Chaykin/N. Adams-r/SSOC #2. 4('78)-New full length story			
	1	3	8
Annual 5,6: 5(1979)-New full length Buscema story & part-c,			
6(1981)-Kane-c/a			5.00
Annual 7-12: 7('82)-Based on novel "Conan of the Isles" (new-a). 8(1984).			
9(1984). 10(1986). 11(1986). 12(1987)			4.00
Special Edition 1 (Red Nails)			4.00

CONAN THE BARBARIAN MOVIE SPECIAL (Movie)
Marvel Comics Group: Oct, 1982 - No. 2, Nov, 1982

1,2-Movie adaptation; Buscema-a			3.00

CONCRETE (Also see Dark Horse Presents & Within Our Reach)
Dark Horse Comics: March, 1987 - No. 10, Nov, 1988 ($1.50, B&W)

1-Paul Chadwick-c/a in all	1	4	10
1-2nd print			3.00
2			6.00
3-Origin			5.00
4-10			4.00
A New Life 1 (1989, $2.95, B&W)-r/#3,4 plus new-a (11 pgs.)			3.00
Celebrates Earth Day 1990 ($3.50, 52 pgs.)			6.00
Color Special 1 (2/89, $2.95, 44 pgs.)-r/1st two Concrete apps. from Dark			
Horse Presents #1,2 plus new-a			6.00
Land And Sea 1 (2/89, $2.95, B&W)-r/#1,2			6.00
Odd Jobs 1 (7/90, $3.50)-r/5,6 plus new-a			3.50

CONCRETE: (Title series), **Dark Horse Comics**

--ECLECTICA, 4/93 - No. 2, 5/93 ($2.95) 1,2			3.00
--FRAGILE CREATURE, 6/91 - No. 4, 2/92 ($2.50) 1-4			3.00
--KILLER SMILE, (Legend), 7/94 - No. 4, 10/94 ($2.9) 1-4			3.00
--STRANGE ARMOR, 12/97 - No. 5, 5/98 ($2.95, color) 1-5-Chadwick-s/c/a;			
retells origin			3.00
--THINK LIKE A MOUNTAIN, (Legend), 3/96 - No. 6, 8/96 ($2.95)			
1-6: Chadwick-a/scripts & Darrow-c in all			3.00

CONSTANTINE, JOHN (See Hellblazer)

CONTEST OF CHAMPIONS (See Marvel Super-Hero...)

CONTEST OF CHAMPIONS II
Marvel Comics: Sept, 1999 - No. 5 ($2.50, limited series)

	GD	FN	NM-
1-5-Claremont-s/Jimenez-a			2.50

COSMIC ODYSSEY
DC Comics: 1988 - No. 4, 1988 ($3.50, limited series, squarebound)

1-4: Reintro. New Gods into DC continuity; Superman, Batman, Green Lantern (John Stewart) app; Starlin scripts, Mignola-c/a in all. 2-Darkseid merges Demon & Jason Blood (separated in Demon limited series #4); John Stewart responsible for the death of a star system 5.00
Trade paperback-r/#1-4. 20.00

COSMIC POWERS
Marvel Comics: Mar, 1994 - No. 6, Aug, 1994 ($2.50, limited series)

1-6: 1-Ron Lim-c/a(p). 1,2-Thanos app. 2-Terrax. 3-Ganymede & Jack of Hearts app. 2.50

COSMIC POWERS UNLIMITED
Marvel Comics: May, 1995 - No. 5, May, 1996 ($3.95, quarterly)

1-5 4.00

COUNT DUCKULA (TV)
Marvel Comics: Nov, 1988 - No. 15, Jan, 1991 ($1.00)

1,8: 1-Dangermouse back-up. 8-Geraldo Rivera photo-c/& app.; Sienkiewicz-a(i) 5.00
2-7,9-15: Dangermouse back-ups in all 4.00

COURTNEY CRUMRIN & THE COVEN OF MYSTICS
Oni Press: Dec, 2002 - No. 4, March, 2003 ($2.95, B&W, limited series)

1-4-Ted Naifeh-s/a 3.00
TPB (9/03, $11.95, 8" x 5-1/2") r/#1-4 12.00

COURTNEY CRUMRIN & THE NIGHT THINGS (Also see Promotional Section for FCBD Ed.)
Oni Press: Mar, 2002 - No. 4, June, 2002 ($2.95, B&W, limited series)

1-4-Ted Naifeh-s/a 3.00
TPB (12/02, $11.95) r/#1-4 12.00

COURTNEY CRUMRIN IN THE TWILIGHT KINGDOM
Oni Press: Dec, 2003 - No. 4, May, 2004 ($2.99, B&W, limited series)

1-4-Ted Naifeh-s/a 3.00
TPB (9/04, $11.95, digest-size) r/#1-4 12.00

COURTSHIP OF EDDIE'S FATHER (TV)
Dell Publishing Co.: Jan, 1970 - No. 2, May, 1970

	GD	FN	NM-
1-Bill Bixby photo-c on both	6	18	70
2	4	12	50

CRAZY (Satire)
Marvel Comics Group: Feb, 1973 - No. 3, June, 1973

	GD	FN	NM-
1-Not Brand Echh-r; Beatles cameo (r)	3	9	25
2,3-Not Brand Echh-r; Kirby-a	2	6	16

CREATURES ON THE LOOSE (Formerly Tower of Shadows No. 1-9)
Marvel Comics: No. 10, March, 1971 - No. 37, Sept, 1975 (New-a & reprints)

	GD	FN	NM-
10-(15¢)-1st full app. King Kull; see Kull the Conqueror; Wrightson-a	6	18	75
11-15: 15-Last 15¢ issue	3	9	24
16-Origin Warrior of Mars (begins, ends #21)	2	6	18
17-20	2	6	12
21-Steranko-c	2	6	18
22-Steranko-c; Thongor stories begin	2	6	20
23-29-Thongor-c/stories	1	3	9
30-Manwolf begins	3	9	25
31-33	2	6	14
34-37	2	6	12

CREEPY (See Warren Presents)
Warren Publishing Co./Harris Publ. #146: 1964 - No. 145, Feb, 1983; No. 146, 1985 (B&W, magazine)

	GD	FN	NM-
1-Frazetta-a (his last story in comics?); Jack Davis-c; 1st Warren all comics magazine; 1st app. Uncle Creepy	11	33	160
2-Frazetta-c & 1 pg. strip	7	21	85
3-8,11-13,15-17: 3-7,9-11,15-17-Frazetta-c. 7-Frazetta 1 pg. strip. 15,16-Adams-a. 16-Jeff Jones-a	4	12	45
9-Creepy fan club sketch by Wrightson (1st published-a); has 1/2 pg. anti-smoking strip by Frazetta; Frazetta-c; 1st Wood and Ditko art on this tit'ɛ; Toth-a (low print)	7	21	80
10-E/unner fan club sketch (1st published work)	4	12	50
14-Neal Adams 1st Warren work	4	12	50
18-28,30,31: 27-Frazetta-c	3	10	35
29,34: 29-Jones-a	4	12	38
32-(scarce) Frazetta-c; Harlan Ellison sty	6	18	65
33,35,37,39,40,42-47,49: 35-Hitler/Nazi-s. 39-1st Uncle Creepy solo-s, Cousin Eerie app.; early Brunner-a. 42-1st San Julian-c. 44-1st Ploog-a. 46-Corben-a	3	9	30
36-(11/70)1st Corben art at Warren	4	12	40
38,41-(scarce): 38-1st Kelly-c. 41-Corben-a	4	12	45
48,55,65-(1972, 1973, 1974 Annuals) #55 & 65 contain an 8 pg. slick comic insert. 48-(84 pgs.). 55-Color poster bonus (1/2 price if missing). 65-(100 pgs.) Summer Giant	4	12	40
50-Vampirella/Eerie/Creepy-c	4	12	45
51,54,56-61,64: All contain an 8 pg. slick comic insert in middle. 59-Xmas horror. 54,64-Chaykin-a	3	10	35
52,53,66,71,72,75,76,78-80: 71-All Bermejo-a; Space & Time issue. 78-Fantasy issue. 79,80-Monsters issue	2	6	22
62,63-1st & 2nd full Wrightson story art; Corben-a; 8 pg. color comic insert	3	10	35
67,68,73	3	9	26
69,70-Edgar Allan Poe issues; Corben-a	3	9	24
74,77: 74-All Crandell-a. 77-Xmas Horror issue; Corben-a,Wrightson-a	3	9	30
81,84,85,88-90,92-94,96-99,102,104-112,114-118,120,122-130: 84,93-Sports issue. 85,97,102-Monster issue. 89-All war issue; Nino-a. 94-Weird Children issue. 96,109-Aliens issue. 99-Disasters. 103-Corben-a.			

	GD	FN	NM-
104-Robots issue. 106-Sword & Sorcery.107-Sci-fi. 116-End of Man.			
125-Xmas Horror	2	6	12
82,100,101: 82-All Maroto issue. 100-(8/78) Anniversary. 101-Corben-a			
	2	6	18
83,95-Wrightson-a. 83-Corben-a. 95-Gorilla/Apes.	2	6	14
86,87,91,103-Wrightson-a. 86-Xmas Horror	2	6	14
113-All Wrightson-r issue	3	9	24
119,121: 119-All Nino issue.121-All Severin-r issue	2	6	14
131,133-136,138,140: 135-Xmas issue	2	6	14
132,137,139: 132-Corben. 137-All Williamson-r issue. 139-All Toth-r issue			
	2	6	18
141,143,144 (low dist.): 144-Giant, $2.25; Frazetta-c	2	6	22
142,145 (low dist.): 142-(10/82, 100 pgs.) All Torres issue. 145-(2/83) last			
Warren issue	2	6	22
146 ($2.95)-1st from Harris; resurrection issue	7	21	85
Year Book '68-'70: '70-Neal Adams, Ditko-a(r)	4	12	50
Annual 1971,1972	4	12	45
1993 Fearbook ($3.95)-Harris Publ.; Brereton-c; Vampirella by Busiek-s/Art			
Adams-a; David-s; Paquette-a	4	12	40
....:The Classic Years TPB (Harris/Dark Horse,'91, $12.95) Kaluta-c; art by			
Frazetta,Torres, Crandall, Ditko, Morrow, Williamson, Wrightson		25.00	

CREEPY THINGS
Charlton Comics: July, 1975 - No. 6, June, 1976

1-Sutton-c/a	2	6	20
2-6: Ditko-a in 3,5. Sutton c-3,4. 6-Zeck-c	1	4	10
Modern Comics Reprint 2-6(1977)		4.00	

CRIMSON (Also see Cliffhanger #0)
Image Comics (Cliffhanger Productions): May, 1998 - No. 7, Dec, 1998;
DC Comics (Cliffhanger Prod.): No. 8, Mar, 1999 - No. 24, Apr, 2001 ($2.50)

1-Humberto Ramos-a/Augustyn-s	5.00
1-Variant-c by Warren	8.00
1-Chromium-c	20.00
2-Ramos-c with street crowd, 2-Variant-c by Art Adams	3.00
2-Dynamic Forces CrimsonChrome cover	15.00
3-7: 3-Ramos Moon background-c. 7-3 covers by Ramos, Madureira, &	
Campbell	3.50
8-23: 8-First DC issue	2.50
24-($3.50) Final issue; wraparound-c	3.50
DF Premiere Ed. 1998 ($6.95) covers by Ramos and Jae Lee	7.00
Crimson: Scarlet X Blood on the Moon (10/99, $3.95)	4.00
Crimson Sourcebook (11/99, $2.95) Pin-ups and info	3.00
Earth Angel TPB (2001, $14.95) r/#13-18	15.00
Heaven and Earth TPB (1/00, $14.95) r/#7-12	15.00
Loyalty and Loss TPB ('99, $12.95) r/#1-6	13.00
Redemption TPB ('01, $14.95) r/#19-24	15.00

CRISIS ON INFINITE EARTHS (Also see Official... Index and Legends of
the DC Universe)
DC Comics: Apr, 1985 - No. 12, Mar, 1986 (maxi-series)

	GD	FN	NM-

1-1st DC app. Blue Beetle & Detective Karp from Charlton; Pérez-c on all

	2	6	16

2-6: 6-Intro Charlton's Capt. Atom, Nightshade, Question, Judomaster, Peacemaker & Thunderbolt into DC Universe

	1	4	10

7-Double size; death of Supergirl

	2	6	22

8-Death of the Flash (Barry Allen)

	2	6	20

9-11: 9-Intro. Charlton's Ghost into DC Universe. 10-Intro. Charlton's Banshee, Dr. Spectro, Image, Punch & Jewellee into DC Universe; Starman (Prince Gavyn) dies

	1	4	10

12-(52 pgs.)-Deaths of Dove, Kole, Lori Lemaris, Sunburst, G.A. Robin & Huntress; Kid Flash becomes new Flash; 3rd & final DC app. of the 3 Lt. Marvels; Green Fury gets new look

	2	6	14

Slipcased Hardcover (1998, $99.95) Wraparound dust-jacket cover by Pérez and Alex Ross; sketch pages by Pérez; intro by Wolfman ... 125.00
TPB (2000, $29.95) Wraparound-c by Pérez and Ross ... 30.00

CRISIS ON MULTIPLE EARTHS
DC Comics: 2002, 2003, 2004 ($14.95, trade paperbacks)

TPB-(2003) Reprints 1st 4 Silver Age JLA/JSA crossovers from J.L.ofA. #21,22; 29,30; 37,38; 46,47; new painted-c by Alex Ross; intro. by Mark Waid ... 15.00
Volume 2 (2003, $14.95) r/J.L.ofA. #55,56; 64,65; 73,74; 82,83; new Ordway-c ... 15.00
Volume 3 (2004, $14.95) r/J.L.ofA. #91,92; 100-102; 107-108; 113; Wein intro., Ross-c ... 15.00

CROW, THE (Also see Caliber Presents)
Caliber Press: Feb, 1989 - No. 4, 1989 ($1.95, B&W, limited series)

	GD	FN	NM-
1-James O'Barr-c/a/scripts	5	15	60
1-3-2nd printing			6.00
2-4	3	9	32
2-3rd printing			4.00

CROW, THE
Tundra Publishing, Ltd.: Jan, 1992 - No. 3, 1992 ($4.95, B&W, 68 pgs.)

1-3: 1-r/#1,2 of Caliber series. 2-r/#3 of Caliber series w/new material. 3-All new material

	1	3	8

CROW, THE
Kitchen Sink Press: 1/96 - No. 3, 3/96 ($2.95, B&W)

1-3: James O'Barr-c/scripts ... 5.00
#0-A Cycle of Shattered Lives (12/98, $3.50) new story by O'Barr ... 4.00

CROW, THE
Image Comics (Todd McFarlane Prod.): Feb, 1999 - No. 10, Nov, 1999 ($2.50)

1-10: 1-Two covers by McFarlane and Kent Williams; Muth-s in all. 2-6, 10-Paul Lee-a ... 3.00
Book 1 - Vengeance (2000, $10.95, TPB) r/#1-3,5,6 ... 11.00
Book 2 - Evil Beyond Reach (2000, $10.95, TPB) r/#4,7-10 ... 11.00
Todd McFarlane Presents The Crow Magazine 1 (3/00, $4.95) ... 5.00

	GD	FN	NM-

CRUSADER RABBIT (TV)
Dell Publishing Co.: No. 735, Oct, 1956 - No. 805, May, 1957

	GD	FN	NM-
Four Color 735 (#1)	32	96	490
Four Color 805	26	78	380

CRY FOR DAWN
Cry For Dawn Pub.: 1989 - No. 9 ($2.25, B&W, mature)

	GD	FN	NM-
1	8	24	100
1-2nd printing	3	10	35
1-3rd printing	3	9	25
2	5	15	60
2-2nd printing	2	6	20
3	4	12	40
3a-HorrorCon Edition (1990, less than 400 printed, signed inside-c)			200.00
4-6	2	6	20
5-2nd printing	1	3	8
7-9	2	6	14
4-9-Signed & numbered editions	3	9	25
Angry Christ Comix HC (4/03, $29.99) reprints various stories; and 30pgs. new material			30.00
...Calendar (1993)			35.00

CRYPT OF SHADOWS
Marvel Comics Group: Jan, 1973 - No. 21, Nov, 1975 (#1-9 are 20¢)

	GD	FN	NM-
1-Wolverton-r/Advs. Into Terror #7	3	9	25
2-10: 2-Starlin/Everett-c	2	6	16
11-21: 18,20-Kirby-a	2	6	14

CSI: CRIME SCENE INVESTIGATION (Based on TV series)
IDW Publishing: Jan, 2003 - No. 5, May, 2003 ($3.99, limited series)

	GD	FN	NM-
1-Two covers (photo & Ashley Wood); Max Allan Collins-s			4.00
2-5			4.00
...: Serial TPB (2003, $19.99) r/#1-5; bonus short story by Collins/Wood			20.00
...: Thicker Than Blood (7/03, $6.99) Mariotte-s/Rodriguez-a			7.00

CSI: CRIME SCENE INVESTIGATION - BAD RAP
IDW Publishing: Aug, 2003 - No. 5, Dec, 2003 ($3.99, limited series)

	GD	FN	NM-
1-5-Two photo covers; Max Allan Collins-s/Rodriguez-a			4.00
TPB (3/04, $19.99) r/#1-5			20.00

CSI: CRIME SCENE INVESTIGATION - DEMON HOUSE
IDW Publishing: Feb, 2004 - No. 5, Jun, 2004 ($3.99, limited series)

	GD	FN	NM-
1-5-Photo covers on all; Max Allan Collins-s/Rodriguez-a			4.00
TPB (10/04, $19.99) r/#1-5			20.00

CSI: CRIME SCENE INVESTIGATION - DOMINOS
IDW Publishing: Aug, 2004 - No. 5 ($3.99, limited series)

	GD	FN	NM-
1-3-Photo covers on all; Oprisko-s/Rodriguez-a			4.00

CSI: MIAMI
IDW Publishing: Oct, 2003; Apr, 2004 ($6.99, one-shots)

	GD	FN	NM-
... - Blood Money (9/04)-Oprisko-s/Guedes & Perkins-a			7.00
... - Smoking Gun (10/03)-Mariotte-s/Avilés & Wood-a			7.00
... - Thou Shalt Not... (4/04)-Oprisko-s/Guedes & Wood-a			7.00

C•23 (Jim Lee's...) (Based on Wizards of the Coast card game)
Image Comics: Apr, 1998 - No. 8, Nov, 1998 ($2.50)

	GD	FN	NM-
1-8: 1,2-Choi & Mariotte-s/ Charest-c. 2-Variant-c by Jim Lee. 5,8-Corben var-c. 6-Flip book with Planetary preview; Corben-c			3.00

CURSE OF THE SPAWN
Image Comics (Todd McFarlane Prod.): Sept, 1996 - No. 29, Mar, 1999 ($1.95)

	GD	FN	NM-
1-Dwayne Turner-a(p)			6.00
1-B&W Edition	2	6	16
2-3			4.00
4-29: 12-Movie photo-c of Melinda Clarke (Priest)			2.50
Blood and Sutures ('99, $9.95, TPB) r/#5-8			10.00
Lost Values ('00, $10.95, TPB) r/#12-14,22; Ashley Wood-c			11.00
Sacrifice of the Soul ('99, $9.95, TPB) r/#1-4			10.00
Shades of Gray ('00, $9.95, TPB) r/#9-11,29			10.00

CYCLOPS (X-Men)
Marvel Comics: Oct, 2001 - No. 4, Jan, 2002 ($2.50, limited series)

	GD	FN	NM-
1-4-Texeira-c/a. 1,2-Black Tom and Juggernaut app.			2.50

DAISY AND DONALD (See Walt Disney Showcase No. 8)
Gold Key/Whitman No. 42 on: May, 1973 - No. 59, July, 1984 (no No. 48)

	GD	FN	NM-
1-Barks-r/WDC&S #280,308	4	12	40
2-5: 4-Barks-r/WDC&S #224	2	6	20
6-10	2	6	15
11-20	1	4	10
21-41: 32-r/WDC&S #308	1	3	8
42-44 (Whitman)	2	6	14
45 (8/80),46-(pre-pack?)(scarce)	4	12	40
47-(12/80)-Only distr. in Whitman 3-pack (scarce)	6	18	70
48(3/81)-50(8/81): 50-r/#3	2	6	18
51-54: 51-Barks-r/4-Color #1150. 52-r/#2. 53(2/82), 54(4/82)	2	6	16
55-59-(all #90284 on-c, nd, nd code, pre-pack): 55(5/83), 56(7/83), 57(8/83), 58(8/83), 59(7/84)	2	6	22

DANGER GIRL (Also see Cliffhanger #0)
Image Comics (Cliffhanger Productions): Mar, 1998 - No. 4, Dec, 1998;
DC Comics (Cliffhanger Prod.): No. 5, July, 1999 - No. 7, Feb, 2001

	GD	FN	NM-
Preview-Bagged in DV8 #14 Voyager Pack			4.00
Preview Gold Edition			8.00
1-($2.95) Hartnell & Campbell-s/Campbell/Garner-a	1	3	8
1-($4.95) Chromium cover			45.00
1-American Entertainment Ed.			8.00
1-American Entertainment Gold Ed., 1-Tourbook edition			10.00
1-"Danger-sized" ed.; over-sized format	3	9	30

	GD	FN	NM-

2-($2.50)   4.00

2-Smoking Gun variant cover, 2-Platinum Ed., 2-Dynamic Forces
  Omnichrome variant-c   2   6   16

2-Gold foil cover   9.00

2-Ruby red foil cover   90.00

3,4: 3-c by Campbell, Charest and Adam Hughes. 4-Big knife variant-c 3.00

3,5: 3-Gold foil cover. 5-DF Bikini variant-c   5.00

4-6   3.00

7-($5.95) Wraparound gatefold-c; Last issue   6.00

...: Hawaiian Punch (5/03, $4.95) Campbell-c; Phil Noto-a   5.00

San Diego Preview (8/98, B&W) flip book w/Wildcats preview   5.00

Sketchbook (2001, $6.95) Campbell-a; sketches for comics, toys, games 7.00

...Special (2/00, $3.50) art by Campbell, Chiodo, and Art Adams   3.50

... 3-D #1 (4/03, $4.95, bagged with 3-D glasses) r/ Preview & #1 in 3-D 5.00

...: Viva Las Danger (1/04, $4.95) Noto-a/Campbell-c   5.00

DANGER GIRL KAMIKAZE

DC Comics (Cliffhanger): Nov, 2001 - No. 2, Dec., 2001 ($2.95, lim. series)

1,2-Tommy Yune-s/a   3.00

DAREDEVIL (...& the Black Widow #92-107 on-c only; see Giant-Size...,
Marvel Advs., Marvel Graphic Novel #24 & Spider-Man &...)
Marvel Comics Group: Apr, 1964 - No. 380, Oct, 1998

	GD	FN	NM-
1-Origin/1st app. Daredevil; intro Foggy Nelson & Karen Page; death of Battling Murdock; Bill Everett-c/a	229	687	4800
2-Fantastic Four cameo; 2nd app. Electro (Spidey villain); Thing guest star	66	198	1250
3-Origin & 1st app. The Owl (villain)	43	129	725
4-Origin & 1st app. The Purple Man	36	108	575
5-Minor costume change; Wood-a begins	28	84	420
6-Mr. Fear app.	19	57	275
7-Daredevil battles Sub-Mariner & dons red costume for 1st time (4/65)	63	189	1200
8-10: 8-Origin/1st app. Stilt-Man	16	48	230
11-15: 12-1st app. Plunderer; Ka-Zar app. 13-Facts about Ka-Zar's origin; Kirby-a	10	30	140
16,17-Spider-Man x-over. 16-1st Romita-a on Spider-Man (5/66)	14	42	210
18-Origin & 1st app. Gladiator	10	30	125
19,20	8	24	95
21-26,28-30: 24-Ka-Zar app.	6	18	75
27-Spider-Man x-over	7	21	90
31-40: 38-Fantastic Four x-over; cont'd in F.F. #73. 39-1st Exterminator (later becomes Death-Stalker)	5	15	60
41,42,44-49: 41-Death Mike Murdock. 42-1st app. Jester. 45-Statue of Liberty photo-c	4	12	45
43-Daredevil battles Captain America; origin partially retold	6	18	70
50-53: 50-52-B. Smith-a. 53-Origin retold; last 12¢ issue	4	12	50

	GD	FN	NM-
54-56,58-60: 54-Spider-Man cameo. 56-1st app. Death's Head (9/69); story cont'd in #57 (not same as new Death's Head)	3	9	30
57-Reveals i.d. to Karen Page; Death's Head app.	4	12	38
61-76,78-80: 79-Stan Lee cameo. 80-Last 15¢ issue	3	9	28
77-Spider-Man x-over	4	12	40
81-(52 pgs.) Black Widow begins (11/71)	4	12	40
82,84-99: 87-Electro-c/story	2	6	22
83-B. Smith layouts/Weiss-p	3	9	25
100-Origin retold	3	9	32
101-104,106-120: 107-Starlin-c; Thanos cameo. 113-1st brief app. Deathstalker. 114-1st full app. Deathstalker	2	6	18
105-Origin Moondragon by Starlin (12/73); Thanos cameo in flashback (early app.)	2	6	22
121-130,137: 124-1st app. Copperhead; Black Widow leaves. 126-1st new Torpedo	2	6	14
131-Origin/1st app. new Bullseye (see Nick Fury #15)	6	18	65
132-2nd app. new Bullseye (Regular 25¢ edition)	4	12	40
132-(30¢-c variant, limited distribution)(4/76)	5	15	60
133-136-(Regular 25¢ editions)	2	6	12
133-136-(30¢-c variants, limited distribution)(5-8/76)	2	6	18
138-Ghost Rider-c/story; Death's Head is reincarnated; Byrne-a	2	6	18
139,140,142-145,147-157: 142-Nova cameo. 147,148-(Reg. 30¢-c). 150-1st app. Paladin. 151-Reveals i.d. to Heather Glenn. 155-Black Widow returns. 156-The '60s Daredevil app.	2	6	12
141,146-Bullseye app.	3	9	25
146-(35¢-c variant, limited distribution)	4	12	38
147,148-(35¢-c variants, limited distribution)	2	6	18
158-Frank Miller art begins (5/79); origin/death of Deathstalker (see Captain America #235 & Spectacular Spider-Man #27	7	21	90
159	4	12	42
160,161-Bullseye app.	3	10	35
162-Ditko-a; no Miller-a	1	4	10
163,164: 163-Hulk cameo. 164-Origin retold	3	9	24
165-167,170	2	6	20
168-Origin/1st app. Elektra; 1st Miller scripts	9	27	110
169-2nd Electra app.	4	12	40
171-173	2	6	18
174,175-Elektra app.	2	6	20
176-180-Elektra app. 178-Cage app. 179-Anti-smoking issue mentioned in the Congressional Record	2	6	18
181-(52 pgs.)-Death of Elektra; Punisher cameo out of costume	3	10	35
182-184-Punisher app. by Miller (drug issues)	2	6	15
185-191: 187-New Black Widow. 189-Death of Stick. 190-($1.00, 52 pgs.)-Elektra returns, part origin. 191-Last Miller Daredevil	1	4	10
192-195,198,199,201-207,209-218,220-226,234-237: 226-Frank Miller plots begin			3.50

	GD	FN	NM-

196-Wolverine-c/app.   2   6   14

197-Bullseye-c/app.; 1st app. Yuriko Oyama (who becomes Lady Deathstrike)
     5.00

200,238: 200-Bullseye app. 238-Mutant Massacre; Sabretooth app.   6.00

208,219,228-233: 208-Harlan Ellison scripts borrowed from Avengers TV
     episode "House that Jack Built". 219-Miller-c/script. 228-233-Last Miller
     scripts   4.00

227-Miller scripts begin   6.00

239,240,242-247   3.00

241-Todd McFarlane-a(p)   5.00

248,249-Wolverine app.   6.00

250,251,253,258: 250-1st app. Bullet. 258-Intro The Bengal (a villain)   3.00

252,260 (52 pgs.): 252-Fall of the Mutants. 260-Typhoid Mary app.   5.00

254-Origin & 1st app. Typhoid Mary (5/88)   1   3   8

255,256,258: 255,256-2nd/3rd app. Typhoid Mary. 259-Typhoid Mary app. 5.00

257-Punisher app. (x-over w/Punisher #10)   1   4   10

261-281,283-294,296-299,301-304,307-318: 270-1st app. Black Heart.
     272-Intro Shotgun (villain). 281-Silver Surfer cameo. 283-Capt. America
     app. 297-Typhoid Mary app.; Kingpin storyline begins. 292-D.G. Chichester
     scripts begin. 293-Punisher app. 303-Re-intro the Owl. 304-Garney-c/a.
     309-Punisher-c.; Terror app. 310-Calypso-c   2.50

282,295,300,305,306: 282-Silver Surfer app. 295-Ghost Rider app.
     300-($2.00, 52 pgs.) Kingpin story ends. 305,306-Spider-Man-c   3.00

319-Prologue to Fall From Grace; Elektra returns   6.00

319-2nd printing w/black-c   2.50

320-Fall From Grace Pt 1   5.00

321-Fall From Grace regular ed.; Pt 2; new costume; Venom app.   3.00

321-($2.00)-Wraparound Glow-in-the-dark-c ed.   5.00

322-Fall From Grace Pt 3; Eddie Brock app.   4.00

323,324-Fall From Grace Pt. 4 & 5: 323-Vs. Venom-c/story.   4.00

325-($2.50, 52 pgs.)-Fall From Grace ends; contains bound-in poster   4.00

326-349,351-353: 326-New logo. 328-Bound-in trading card sheet.
     330-Gambit app. 348-1st Cary Nord art in DD (1/96);"Dec" on-c. 353-Karl
     Kesel scripts; Nord-c/a begins; Mr. Hyde-c/app.   2.50

350-($2.95)-Double-sized   3.00

350-($3.50)-Double-sized; gold ink-c   3.50

354-374,376-379: Kesel scripts, Nord-c/a in all. 354-$1.50-c begins.
     355-Larry Hama layouts; Pyro app. 358-Mysterio-c/app. 359-Absorbing
     Man cameo. 360-Absorbing Man-c/app. 361-Black Widow-c/app.
     363,366-370-Gene Colan-a(p). 368-Omega Red-c/app. 372-Ghost Rider-
     c/app. 376-379-"Flying Blind", DD goes undercover for S.H.I.E.L.D.   2.50

375-($2.99) Wraparound-c; Mr. Fear-c/app.   3.00

380-($2.99) Final issue; flashback story   4.00

Special 1(9/67, 25¢, 68 pgs.)-New art/story   6   18   70

Special 2,3: 2(2/71, 25¢, 52 pgs.)-Entire book has Powell/Wood-r; Wood-c.
     3(1/72, 52 pgs.)-Reprints   3   9   25

Annual 4(10/76)   1   4   10

Annual 4(#5)-10: ('89-94 68 pgs.)-5-Atlantis Attacks. 6-Sutton-a. 7-Guice-a
     (7 pgs.). 8-Deathlok-c/story. 9-Polybagged w/card   3.00

	GD	FN	NM-

... :Born Again TPB ($17.95)-r/#227-233; Miller-s/Mazzucchelli-a & new-c 20.00

.../Deadpool- (Annual '97, $2.99)-Wraparound-c 3.00

....:Fall From Grace TPB ($19.95)-r/#319-325 20.00

... :Gang War TPB ($15.95)-r/#169-172,180; Miller-s/a(p) 16.00

...Legends: (Vol. 4) Typhoid Mary TPB (2003, $19.95) r/#254-257,259-263 20.00

... :Love's Labors Lost TPB ($19.99)-r/#215-217,219-222,225,226; Mazzucchelli-c 20.00

.../Punisher TPB (1988, $4.95)-r/D.D. #182-184 (all printings) 5.00

...Visionaries: Frank Miller Vol. 1 TPB ($17.95) r/#158-161,163-167 18.00

...Visionaries: Frank Miller Vol. 2 TPB ($24.95) r/#168-182; new Miller-c 25.00

...Visionaries: Frank Miller Vol. 3 TPB ($24.95) r/#183-191, What If? #28,35 & Bizarre Adventures #28; new Miller-c 25.00

... Vs. Bullseye Vol. 1 TPB (2004, $15.99) r/#131-132,146,169,181,191 16.00

Wizard Ace Edition: Daredevil (Vol. 1) #1 (4/03, $13.99) Acetate Campbell-c 14.00

DAREDEVIL (Volume 2) (Marvel Knights)
Marvel Comics: Nov, 1998 - Present ($2.50)

1-Kevin Smith-s/Quesada & Palmiotti-a 12.00

1-($6.95) DF Edition w/Quesada & Palmiotti var.-c 15.00

1-($6.00) DF Sketch Ed. w/B&W-c 10.00

2-Two covers by Campbell and Quesada/Palmiotti 9.00

3-8: 4,5-Bullseye app. 8-Spider-Man-c/app.; last Smith-s 6.00

9-15: 9-11-David Mack-s; intro Echo. 12-Haynes-a. 13,14-Quesada-a 3.00

16-19-Direct editions; Bendis-s/Mack-c/painted-a 3.00

18,19,21,22-Newsstand editions with variant cover logo "Marvel Unlimited Featuring..." 3.00

20-($3.50) Gale-s/Winslade-a; back-up by Stan Lee-s/Colan-a; Mack-c 3.50

21-40: 21-25-Gale-s. 26-38-Bendis-s/Maleev-a. 32-Daredevil's ID revealed. 35-Spider-Man-c/app. 38-Iron Fist & Luke Cage app. 40-Dodson-a 3.50

41-(25¢-c) Begins "Lowlife" arc; Maleev-a; intro Milla Donovan 2.25

41-(Newsstand edition with $2.99-c) 4.00

42-45-"Lowlife" arc; Maleev-a 2.25

46-50-($2.99). 46-Typhoid Mary returns. 49-Bullseye app. 50-Art panels by various incl.Romita, Colan, Mack, Janson, Oeming, Quesada 3.00

51-64,66,67: 51-55-Mack-s/a; Echo app. 54-Wolverine-c/app. 61-64-Black Widow app. 3.00

65-($3.99) 40th Anniversary issue; Land-c; art by Maleev, Horn, Bachalo and others 4.00

...2099 #1 (11/04, $2.99) Kirkman-s/Moline-a 3.00

TPB ($9.95) r/#1-3 10.00

...Vol. 1 HC (2001, $29.99, with dustjacket) r/#1-11,13-15 30.00

...Vol. 1 HC (2003, $29.99, with dustjacket) r/#1-11,13-15; larger page size 30.00

...Vol. 2 HC (2002, $29.99, with dustjacket) r/#26-37; Bendis afterword 30.00

...Vol. 3 HC (2004, $29.99, with dustjacket) r/#38-50; Maleev sketch pages 30.00

(Vol. 1) Visionaries TPB ($19.95) r/#1-8; Ben Affleck intro. 20.00

(Vol. 2) Parts of a Hole TPB (1/02, $17.95) r/#9-15; David Mack intro. 18.00

	GD	FN	NM-
(Vol. 3) Wake Up TPB (7/02, $9.99) r/#16-19			10.00
...Vol. 4: Underboss TPB (8/02, $14.99) r/#26-31			15.00
...Vol. 5: Out TPB (2003, $19.99) r/#32-40			20.00
...Vol. 6: Lowlife TPB (2003, $13.99) r/#41-45			14.00
...Vol. 7: Hardcore TPB (2003, $13.99) r/#46-50			14.00
...Vol. 8: Echo - Vision Quest TPB (2004, $13.99) r/#51-55; David Mack-s/a			
			14.00
...Vol. 9: King of Hell's Kitchen TPB (2004, $13.99) r/#56-60			14.00
...Vol. 10: The Widow TPB (2004, $16.99) r/#61-65 & Vol. 1 #81			17.00

DAREDEVIL/ BATMAN (Also see Batman/Daredevil)
Marvel Comics/ DC Comics: 1997 ($5.99, one-shot)

nn-McDaniel-c/a			6.00

DAREDEVIL/ ELEKTRA: LOVE AND WAR
Marvel Comics: 2003 ($29.99, hardcover with dust jacket)

HC-Larger-size reprints of Daredevil: Love and War (Marvel Graphic Novel #24) & Elektra: Assassin; Frank Miller-s; Bill Sienkiewicz-a			30.00

DAREDEVIL/ SPIDER-MAN
Marvel Comics: Jan, 2001 - No. 4, Apr, 2001 ($2.99, limited series)

1-4-Jenkins-s/Winslade-a/Alex Ross-c; Stilt Man app.			3.00
TPB (8/01, $12.95) r/#1-4; Ross-c			13.00

DAREDEVIL THE MAN WITHOUT FEAR
Marvel Comics: Oct, 1993 - No. 5, Feb, 1994 ($2.95, limited series) (foil embossed covers)

1-Miller scripts; Romita, Jr./Williamson-c/a			6.00
2-5			5.00
Hardcover			100.00
Trade paperback			20.00

DAREDEVIL: THE MOVIE (2003 movie adaptation)
Marvel Comics: March, 2003 ($3.50/$12.95, one-shot)

1-Photo-c of Ben Affleck; Bruce Jones-s/Manuel Garcia-a			3.50
TPB ($12.95) r/movie adaptation; Daredevil #32; Ultimate Daredevil & Elektra #1 and Spider-Man's Tangled Web #4; photo-c of Ben Affleck			13.00

DAREDEVIL: THE TARGET (Daredevil Bullseye on cover)
Marvel Comics: Jan, 2003 - No. 4, ($3.50, limited series)

1-Kevin Smith-s/Glenn Fabry-c/a			3.50

DAREDEVIL: YELLOW
Marvel Comics: Aug, 2001 - No. 6, Jan, 2002 ($3.50, limited series)

1-6-Jeph Loeb-s/Tim Sale-a/c; origin & yellow costume days retold			3.50
HC (5/02, $29.95) r/#1-6 with dustjacket; intro by Stan Lee; sketch pages			
			30.00
Daredevil Legends Vol. 1: Daredevil Yellow (2002, $14.99, TPB) r/#1-6			15.00

DARING NEW ADVENTURES OF SUPERGIRL, THE
DC Comics: Nov, 1982 - No. 13, Nov, 1983 (Supergirl No. 14 on)

1-Origin retold; Lois Lane back-ups in #2-12	1	3	8

	GD	FN	NM-
2-13: 8,9-Doom Patrol app. 13-New costume; flag-c			4.00

DARK CLAW ADVENTURES
DC Comics (Amalgam): June, 1997 ($1.95, one-shot)

1-Templeton-c/s/a & Burchett-a			2.50

DARK CRYSTAL, THE (Movie)
Marvel Comics Group: April, 1983 - No. 2, May, 1983

1,2-Adaptation of film			3.00

DARK DAYS (See 30 Days of Night)
IDW Publishing: June, 2003 - No. 6, Dec, 2003 ($3.99, limited series)

1-6-Sequel to 30 Days of Night; Niles-s/Templesmith-a			4.00
1-Retailer variant (Diamond/Alliance Fort Wayne 5/03 summit)			15.00
TPB (2004, $19.99) r/#1-6; cover gallery; intro. by Eric Red			20.00

DARKER IMAGE (Also see Deathblow, The Maxx, & Bloodwulf)
Image Comics: Mar, 1993 ($1.95, one-shot)

1-The Maxx by Sam Kieth begins; Bloodwulf by Rob Liefeld & Deathblow by Jim Lee begin (both 1st app.); polybagged w/1 of 3 cards by Kieth, Lee or Liefeld			2.50
1-B&W interior pgs. w/silver foil logo			6.00

DARK HORSE COMICS
Dark Horse Comics: Aug, 1992 - No. 25, Sept, 1994 ($2.50)

	GD	FN	NM-
1-Dorman double gategold painted-c; Predator, Robocop, Timecop (3-part) & Renegade stories begin			3.00
2-6,11-25: 2-Mignola-c. 3-Begin 3-part Aliens story; Aliens-c. 4-Predator-c. 6-Begin 4 part Robocop story. 12-Begin 2-part Aliens & 3-part Predator stories. 13-Thing From Another World begins w/Nino-a(i). 15-Begin 2-part Aliens: Cargo story. 16-Begin 3-part Predator story. 17-Begin 3-part Star Wars: Droids story & 3-part Aliens: Alien story; Droids-c. 19-Begin 2-part X story; X cover			2.50
7-Begin Star Wars: Tales of the Jedi 3-part story	1	3	7
8-1st app. X and begins; begin 4-part James Bond			6.00
9,10: 9-Star Wars ends. 10-X ends; Begin 3-part Predator & Godzilla stories			4.00

DARK HORSE MAVERICK
Dark Horse Comics: July, 2000; July, 2001; Sept, 2002 (B&W, annual)

2000-($3.95) Short stories by Miller, Chadwick, Sakai, Pearson			4.00
2001-($4.99) Short stories by Sakai, Wagner and others; Miller-c			5.00
...: Happy Endings (9/02, $9.95) Short stories by Bendis, Oeming, Mahfood, Mignola, Miller, Kieth and others; Miller-c			10.00

DARK HORSE PRESENTS
Dark Horse Comics: July, 1986 - No. 157, Sept, 2000 ($1.50-$2.95, B&W)

	GD	FN	NM-
1-1st app. Concrete by Paul Chadwick	2	6	14
1-2nd printing (1988, $1.50)			2.25
1-Silver ink 3rd printing (1992, $2.25)-Says 2nd printing inside			2.25
2-9: 2-6,9-Concrete app.			6.00
10-1st app. The Mask; Concrete app.	2	6	15

	GD	FN	NM-

11-19,21-23: 11-19,21-Mask stories. 12,14,16,18,22-Concrete app. 15(2/88).
  17-All Roachmill issue   6.00

20-(68 pgs.)-Concrete, Flaming Carrot, Mask   1   4   10

24-Origin Aliens-c/story (11/88); Mr. Monster app.   2   6   18

25-31,33,37-41,44,45,47-49: 28-(52 pgs.)-Concrete app.; Mr. Monster story
  (homage to Graham Ingels). 33-(44 pgs.). 38-Concrete. 40-(52 pgs.)-1st
  Argosy story. 44-Crash Ryan. 48,49-Contain 2 trading cards   3.00

32,34,35: 32-(68 pgs.)-Annual; Concrete, American. 34-Aliens-c/story.
  35-Predator-c/app.   4.00

36-1st Aliens Vs. Predator story; painted-c, 36-Variant line drawn-c   5.00

42,43,46: 42,43-Aliens-c/stories. 46-Prequel to new Predator II mini-series
    3.00

50-S/F story by Perez; contains 2 trading cards   4.00

51-53-Sin City by Frank Miller, parts 2-4; 51,53-Miller-c (see D.H.P. Fifth
  Anniversary Special for pt. 1)   4.00

54-62: 54-(9/91) The Next Men begins (1st app.) by Byrne; Miller-a/Morrow-c.
  Homocide by Morrow (also in #55). 55-2nd app. The Next Men; parts 5 & 6
  of Sin City by Miller; Miller-c. 56-(68 pg. annual)-part 7 of Sin City by Miller;
  part prologue to Aliens: Genocide; Next Men by Byrne. 57-(52 pgs.)-Part 8
  of Sin City by Miller; Next Men by Byrne; Byrne & Miller-c; Alien Fire story;
  swipes cover to Daredevil #1. 58,59-Alien Fire stories. 58-61- Part 9-12
  Sin City by Miller. 62-Last Sin City (entire book by Miller; 52 pgs.)   5.00

63-66,68-79,81-84-($2.25): 64-Dr. Giggles begins (1st app.), ends #66; Boris
  the Bear story. 66-New Concrete-c/story by Chadwick. 71-Begin 3 part
  Dominque story by Jim Balent; Balent-c. 72-(3/93)-Begin 3-part Eudaemon
  (1st app.) story by Nelson   3.00

67-($3.95, 68 pgs.)-Begin 3-part prelude to Predator: Race War mini-series;
  Oscar Wilde adapt. by Russell   4.00

80-Art Adams-c/a (Monkeyman & O'Brien)   4.00

85-87,92-99: 85-Begin $2.50-c. 92, 93, 95-Too Much Coffee Man   3.00

88-91-Hellboy by Mignola   4.00

NOTE: *There are 5 different Dark Horse Presents #100 issues*

100-1-Intro Lance Blastoff by Miller; Milk & Cheese by Evan Dorkin   4.00

100-2-100-5: 100-2-Hellboy-c by Wrightson; Hellboy story by Mignola;
  includes Roberta Gregory & Paul Pope stories. 100-3-Darrow-c, Concrete
  by Chadwick; Pekar story. 100-4-Gibbons-c; Miller story, Geary story/a.
  100-5-Allred-c, Adams, Dorkin, Pope   3.00

101-125: 101-Aliens c/a by Wrightson, story by Paul Pope. 103-Kirby
  gatefold-c. 106-Big Blown Baby by Bill Wray. 107-Mignola-c/a. 109-Begin
  $2.95-c; Paul Pope-c. 110-Ed Brubaker-a/s. 114-Flip books begin; Lance
  Blastoff by Miller; Star Slammers by Simonson. 115-Miller-c. 117-Aliens-
  c/app. 118-Evan Dorkin-c/a. 119-Monkeyman & O'Brien. 124-Predator.
  125-Nocturnals   3.00

126-($3.95, 48 pgs.)-Flip-book: Nocturnals, Starship Troopers   4.00

127-134,136-140: 127-Nocturnals. 129-The Hammer. 132-134-Warren-a   3.00

135-($3.50) The Mark   3.50

141-All Buffy the Vampire Slayer issue   4.00

142-149: 142-Mignola-c. 143-Tarzan. 146,147-Aliens vs. Predator. 148-Xena
    3.00

	GD	FN	NM-
150-($4.50) Buffy-c by Green; Buffy, Concrete, Fish Police app.			4.50
151-157: 151-Hellboy-c/app. 153-155-Angel flip-c. 156,157-Witch's Son			3.00
Annual 1997 ($4.95, 64 pgs.)-Flip book; Body Bags, Aliens. Pearson-c; stories by Allred & Stephens, Pope, Smith & Morrow	1	3	8
Annual 1998 ($4.95, 64 pgs.) 1st Buffy the Vampire Slayer comic app.; Hellboy story and cover by Mignola	1	3	7
Annual 1999 (7/99, $4.95) Stories of Xena, Hellboy, Ghost, Luke Skywalker, Groo, Concrete, the Mask and Usagi Yojimbo in their youth			5.00
Annual 2000 ($4.95) Girl sidekicks; Chiodo-c and flip photo Buffy-c			5.00
...Aliens Platinum Edition (1992)-r/DHP #24,43,46,56 & Special			11.00
...Fifth Anniversary Special nn (4/91, $9.95)-Part 1 of Sin City by Frank Miller (c/a); Aliens, Aliens vs. Predator, Concrete, Roachmill, Give Me Liberty & The American stories			10.00
The One Trick Rip-off (1997, $12.95, TPB)-r/stories from #101-112			13.00

NOTE: *Geary* a-59, 60. *Miller* a-Special, 51-53, 55-62; c-59-62, 100-1; c-51, 53, 55, 59-62, 100-1. *Moebius* a-63; c-63, 70. *Vess* a-78; c-75, 78.

DARK KNIGHT (See Batman: The Dark Knight Returns & Legends of the...)

DARK KNIGHT STRIKES AGAIN, THE (Also see Batman: The Dark Knight Returns)
DC Comics: 2001 - No. 3, 2002 ($7.95, prestige format, limited series)

1-Frank Miller-s/a/c; sequel 3 years after Dark Knight Returns; 2 covers	8.00
2,3	8.00
HC (2002, $29.95) intro. by Miller; sketch pages and exclusive artwork; cover has 3 1/4" tall partial dustjacket	30.00
SC (2002, $19.95) intro. by Miller; sketch pages	20.00

DARK MANSION OF FORBIDDEN LOVE, THE (Becomes Forbidden Tales of Dark Mansion No. 5 on)
National Periodical Publ.: Sept-Oct, 1971 - No. 4, Mar-Apr, 1972 (52 pgs.)

1	17	51	250
2-4: 2-Adams-c. 3-Jeff Jones-c	8	24	100

DARKMINDS
Image Comics (Dreamwave Prod.): July, 1998 - No. 8, Apr, 1999 ($2.50)

1-Manga; Pat Lee-s/a; 2 covers	1	4	10
1-2nd printing			2.50
2, 0-(1/99, $5.00) Story and sketch pages			5.00
3-8, 1/2-(5/99, $2.50) Story and sketch pages			2.50
... Collected 1,2 (1/99,3/99; $7.95) 1-r/#1-3. 2-r/#4-6			8.00
... Collected 3 (5/99; $5.95) r/#7,8			6.00

DARKMINDS (Volume 2)
Image Comics (Dreamwave Prod.): Feb, 2000 - No. 10, Apr, 2001 ($2.50)

1-10-Pat Lee-c	2.50
0-(7/00) Origin of Mai Murasaki; sketchbook	2.50

DARKNESS, THE (See Witchblade #10)
Image Comics (Top Cow Productions): Dec, 1996 - No. 40, Aug, 2001 ($2.50)

Special Preview Edition-(7/96, B&W)-Ennis script; Silvestri-a(p)

	GD	FN	NM-
	2	6	16
0	2	6	12
0-Gold Edition			16.00
1/2	1	4	10
1/2-Christmas-c	3	9	24
1/2-(3/01, $2.95) r/#1/2 w/new 6 pg. story & Silvestri-c			3.00
1-Ennis-s/Silvestri-a, 1-Black variant-c	2	6	15
1-Platinum variant-c			20.00
1-DF Green variant-c			12.00
1,2: 1-Fan Club Ed.	1	4	10
3-5			6.00
6-10: 9,10-Witchblade "Family Ties" x-over pt. 2,3			4.00
7-Variant-c w/concubine	1	3	9
8-American Entertainment			6.00
8-10-American Entertainment Gold Ed.			7.00
11-Regular Ed.; Ennis-s/Silverstri & D-Tron-c			3.00
11-Nine (non-chromium) variant-c (Benitez, Cabrera, the Hildebrandts, Finch, Keown, Peterson, Portacio, Tan, Turner			4.50
11-Chromium-c by Silvestri & Batt			20.00
12-19: 13-Begin Benitez-a(p)			3.00
20-24,26-40: 34-Ripclaw app.			2.50
25-($3.99) Two covers (Benitez, Silvestri)			4.00
25-Chromium-c variant by Silvestri			8.00
Holiday Pin-up-American Entertainment			5.00
Holiday Pin-up Gold Ed.-American Entertainment			7.00
Infinity #1 (8/99, $3.50) Lobdell-s			3.50
Prelude-American Entertainment			4.00
Prelude Gold Ed.-American Entertainment			9.00
Wizard ACE Ed.- Reprints #1	2	6	12
...Collected Editions #1-4 ($4.95,TPB) 1-r/#1,2. 2-r/#3,4. 3- r/#5,6. 4- r/#7,8			6.00
...Collected Editions #5,6 ($5.95, TPB)5- r/#11,12. 6-r/#13,14			6.00
Deluxe Collected Editions #1 (12/98, $14.95, TPB) r/#1-6 & Preview			15.00
...: Heart of Darkness (2001, $14.95, TPB) r/ #7,8, 11-14			15.00
...: Wanted Dead 1 (8/03, $2.99) Texiera-a/Tieri-s			3.00

DARKNESS (Volume 2)
Image Comics (Top Cow Productions): Dec, 2002 - Present ($2.99)

1-17: 1-6-Jenkins-s/Keown-a			3.00
...: Resurrection TPB (2/04, $16.99) r/#1-6 & Vol. 1 #40			17.00
.../ The Incredible Hulk (7/04, $2.99) Keown-a/Jenkins-s			3.00

DARKNESS/ BATMAN
Image Comics (Top Cow Productions): Aug, 1999 ($5.95, one-shot)

1-Silvestri, Finch, Lansing-a(p)			6.00

DARK SHADOWS (TV) (See Dan Curtis Giveaways)
Gold Key: Mar, 1969 - No. 35, Feb, 1976 (Photo-c: 1-7)

1(30039-903)-With pull-out poster (25¢)	28	84	410
1-With poster missing	11	33	145

	GD	FN	NM-
2	10	30	125
3-With pull-out poster	14	42	210
3-With poster missing	8	24	95
4-7: 7-Last photo-c	8	24	105
8-10	7	21	80
11-20	6	18	70
21-35: 30-Last painted-c	5	15	60
Story Digest 1 (6/70, 148pp.)-Photo-c (low print)	10	30	125

DAVID CASSIDY (TV)(See Partridge Family, Swing With Scooter #33 & Time For Love #30)
Charlton Comics: Feb, 1972 - No. 14, Sept, 1973

1-Most have photo covers	7	21	80
2-5	4	12	48
6-14	4	12	42

DAVY CROCKETT (...Frontier Fighter #1,2; Kid Montana #9 on)
Charlton Comics: Aug, 1955 - No. 8, Jan, 1957

1	10	30	95
2	7	21	50
3-8	5	15	35

DAY OF JUDGMENT
DC Comics: Nov, 1999 - No. 5, Nov, 1999 ($2.95/$2.50, limited series)

1-($2.95) Spectre possessed; Matt Smith-a			3.00
2-5: Parallax returns. 5-Hal Jordan becomes the Spectre			3.00
...Secret Files 1 (11/99, $4.95) Harris-c			5.00

DAZZLER, THE (Also see Marvel Graphic Novel & X-Men #130)
Marvel Comics Group: Mar, 1981 - No. 42, Mar, 1986

1,22,24,27,28,38,42: 1-X-Men app. 22 (12/82)-vs. Rogue Battle-c/sty. 24-Full app. Rogue w/Powerman (Iron Fist). 27-Rogue app. 28-Full app. Rogue; Mystique app. 38-Wolverine-c/app. 42-Beast-c/app			4.00
2-21,23,25,26,29-37,39-41: 2-X-Men app. 10,11-Galactus app. 21-Double size; photo-c. 23-Rogue/Mystique 1 pg. app. 26-Jusko-c. 33-Michael Jackson thriller swipe-c/sty. 40-Secret Wars II			3.00

DC COMICS PRESENTS
DC Comics: July-Aug, 1978 - No. 97, Sept, 1986 (Superman team-ups in all)

1-4th Superman/Flash race	2	6	22
1-(Whitman variant)	3	9	26
2-Part 2 of Superman/Flash race	2	6	15
2-4,10-12,14-16,19,21,22-(Whitman variants, low print run, none have issue # on cover)	2	6	15
3-10: 4-Metal Men. 6-Green Lantern. 8-Swamp Thing. 9-Wonder Woman	1	3	8
11-25,27-40: 13-Legion of Super-Heroes. 19-Batgirl. 35-Man-Bat			6.00
26-(10/80)-Green Lantern; intro Cyborg, Starfire, Raven (1st app. New Teen Titans in 16 pg. preview); Starlin-c/a; Sargon the Sorcerer back-up	3	9	30
41,72,77,78,97: 41-Superman/Joker-c/story. 72-Joker/Phantom Stranger-			

	GD	FN	NM-

c/story. 77,78-Animal Man app. (77-c also). 97-Phantom Zone   5.00
42-46,48-50,52-71,73-76,79-83: 42-Sandman. 43,80-Legion of Super-Heroes.
   52-Doom Patrol. 58-Robin. 82-Adam Strange. 83-Batman & Outsiders
                                                      4.00
  47-He-Man-c/s (1st app. in comics)   2   6   15
  51,84: 51-Preview insert (16 pgs.) of He-Man (2nd app.). 84-Challengers of
    the Unknown; Kirby-c/s.   6.00
  85-Swamp Thing; Alan Moore scripts   6.00
  86-96: 86-88-Crisis x-over. 88-Creeper   4.00
  Annual 1,4: 1(9/82)-G.A. Superman. 4(10/85)-Superwoman   4.00
  Annual 2,3: 2(7/83)-Intro/origin Superwoman. 3(9/84)-Shazam   4.00

DC COMICS PRESENTS: ...(Julie Schwartz tribute series of one-shots based
on classic covers)
DC Comics: Sept, 2004 - Oct, 2004 ($2.50)

The Atom -(Based on cover of Atom #10) Gibbons-s/Oliffe-a; Waid-s/Jurgens-a;
   Bolland-c   2.50
Batman -(Batman #183) Johns-s/Infantino-a; Wein-s/Kuhn-a; Hughes-c   2.50
The Flash -(Flash #163) Loeb-s/McGuinness-a; O'Neil-s/Mahnke-a; Ross-c
                                                    2.50
Green Lantern -(Green Lantern #31) Azzarello-s/Breyfogle-a; Pasko-s/McDaniel-a;
   Bolland-c   2.50
Hawkman -(Hawkman #6) Bates-s/Byrne-a; Busiek-s/Simonson-a;
   Garcia-Lopez-c   2.50
Justice League of America -(J.L. of A. #53) Ellison & David-s/Giella-a;
   Wolfman-s/Nguyen-a; Garcia-Lopez-c   2.50
Mystery in Space -(M.I.S. #82) Maggin-s/Williams-a; Morrison-s/Ordway-a;
   Ross-c   2.50
Superman -(Superman #264) Stan Lee-s/Cooke-a; Levitz-s/Giffen-a;
   Hughes-c   2.50

DC GRAPHIC NOVEL (Also see DC Science Fiction...)
DC Comics: Nov, 1983 - No. 7, 1986 ($5.95, 68 pgs.)

  1-3,5,7: 1-Star Raiders. 2-Warlords; not from regular Warlord series. 3-The
    Medusa Chain; Ernie Colon story/a. 5-Me and Joe Priest; Chaykin-c.
    7-Space Clusters; Nino-c/a   2   6   15
  4-The Hunger Dogs by Kirby; Darkseid kills Himon from Mister Miracle &
    destroys New Genesis   4   12   50
  6-Metalzoic; Sienkiewicz-c ($6.95)   2   6   15

DC/MARVEL: ALL ACCESS (Also see DC Versus Marvel & Marvel Versus DC)
DC Comics: 1996 - No. 4, 1997 ($2.95, limited series)

  1-4: 1-Superman & Spider-Man app. 2-Robin & Jubilee app. 3-Dr. Strange &
    Batman-c/app., X-Men, JLA app. 4-X-Men vs. JLA-c/app. rebirth of
    Amalgam   3.00

DC 100 PAGE SUPER SPECTACULAR
(Title is 100 Page... No. 14 on)(Square bound) (Reprints, 50¢)
National Periodical Publications: No. 4, Summer, 1971 - No. 13, 6/72; No.
14, 2/73 - No. 22, 11/73 (No #1-3)

  4-Weird Mystery Tales; Johnny Peril & Phantom Stranger; cover & splashes

	GD	FN	NM-
by Wrightson; origin Jungle Boy of Jupiter	18	54	260
5-Love Stories; Wood inks (7 pgs.)(scarcer)	44	132	750
6- "World's Greatest Super-Heroes"; JLA, JSA, Spectre, Johnny Quick, Vigilante & Hawkman; contains unpublished Wildcat story; N. Adams wrap-around-c; r/JLA #21,22	18	54	260
6-Replica Edition (2004, $6.95) complete reprint w/wraparound-c			7.00
7-(Also listed as Superman #245) Air Wave, Kid Eternity, Hawkman-r; Atom-r/Atom #3	9	27	115
8-(Also listed as Batman #238) Batman, Legion, Aquaman-r; G.A. Atom, Sargon (r/Sensation #57), Plastic Man (r/Police #14) stories; Doom Patrol origin-r; Neal Adams wraparound-c	11	33	150
9-(Also listed as Our Army at War #242) Kubert-c	9	27	120
10-(Also listed as Adventure Comics #416) Golden Age-reprints; r/1st app. Black Canary from Flash #86; no Zatanna	11	33	145
11-(Also listed as Flash #214) origin Metal Men-r/Showcase #37; never before published G.A. Flash story.	8	24	100
12,14: 12-(Also listed as Superboy #185) Legion-c/story; Teen Titans, Kid Eternity (r/Hit #46), Star Spangled Kid-r(S.S. #55). 14-Batman-r/Detective #31,32,156; Atom-r/Showcase #34	7	21	90
13-(Also listed as Superman #252) Ray(r/Smash #17), Black Condor, (r/Crack #18), Hawkman(r/Flash #24); Starman-r/Adv. #67; Dr. Fate & Spectre-r/More Fun #57; Neal Adams-c	9	27	120
15,16,18,19,21,22: 15-r/2nd Boy Commandos/Det. #64. 21-Superboy; r/Brave & the Bold #54. 22-r/All-Flash #13.	5	15	60
17,20: 17-JSA-r/All Star #37 (10-11/47, 38 pgs.), Sandman-r/Adv. #65 (8/41), JLA #23 (11/63) & JLA #43 (3/66). 20-Batman-r/Det. #66,68, Spectre; origin Two-Face	6	18	65
... : Love Stories Replica Edition (2000, $6.95) reprints #5			7.00

DC ONE MILLION (Also see crossover #1,000,000 issues and JLA One Million TPB)
DC Comics: Nov, 1998 - No. 4, Nov, 1998 ($2.95/$1.99, weekly lim. series)

1-($2.95) JLA travels to the 853rd century; Morrison-s			3.00
2-4-($1.99)			2.25
... Eighty-Page Giant (8/99, $4.95)			5.00
TPB ('99, $14.95) r/#1-4 and several x-over stories			15.00

DC SPECIAL (Also see Super DC Giant)
National Per. Publ.: 10-12/68 - No. 15, 11-12/71; No. 16, Spr/75 - No. 29, 8-9/77

1-All Infantino issue; Flash, Batman, Adam Strange-r; begin 68 pg. issues, end #21	8	24	100
2-Teen humor; Binky, Buzzy, Harvey app.	10	30	135
3-All-Girl issue; unpubl. GA Wonder Woman story	9	27	110
4,11: 4-Horror (1st Abel, brief). 11-Monsters	4	12	50
5-10,12-15: 5-All Kubert issue; Viking Prince, Sgt. Rock-r. 6-Western. 7,9,13-Strangest Sports. 12-Viking Prince; Kubert-c/a (r/B&B almost entirely). 15-G.A. Plastic Man origin-r/Police #1; origin Woozy by Cole; 14,15-(52 pgs.)	4	12	50
16-27: 16-Super Heroes Battle Super Gorillas; r/Capt. Storm #1, 1st Johnny			

	GD	FN	NM-

Cloud/All-Amer. Men of War #82. 17-Early S.A. Green Lantern-r. 22-Origin Robin Hood. 26-Enemy Ace. 27-Captain Comet story

	3	9	25

28,29: 28-Earth Shattering Disaster Stories; Legion of Super-Heroes story. 29-New "The Untold Origin of the Justice Society"; Staton-a

	3	9	28

DC SPECIAL BLUE RIBBON DIGEST
DC Comics: Mar-Apr, 1980 - No. 24, Aug, 1982

1,2,4,5: 1-Legion reprints. 2-Flash. 4-Green Lantern. 5-Secret Origins; new Zatara and Zatanna

	2	6	12

3-Justice Society

	2	6	16

6,8-10: 6-Ghosts. 8-Legion. 9-Secret Origins. 10-Warlord-"The Deimos Saga"-Grell-s/c/a

	2	6	12

7-Sgt. Rock's Prize Battle Tales

	2	6	20

11,16: 11-Justice League. 16-Green Lantern/Green Arrow-r; all Adams-a

	2	6	18

12-Haunted Tank; reprints 1st app.

	2	6	20

13-15,17-19: 13-Strange Sports Stories. 14-UFO Invaders; Adam Strange app. 15-Secret Origins of Super Villains; JLA app. 17-Ghosts. 18-Sgt. Rock; Kubert front & back-c. 19-Doom Patrol; new Perez-c

	2	6	15

20-Dark Mansion of Forbidden Love (scarce)

	5	15	55

21-Our Army at War

	3	9	25

22-24: 22-Secret Origins. 23-Green Arrow, w/new 7 pg. story. 24-House of Mystery; new Kubert wraparound-c

	2	6	20

DC SPECIAL SERIES
National Periodical Publications/DC Comics: 9/77 - No. 16, Fall, 1978; No. 17, 8/79 - No. 27, Fall, 1981 (No. 18, 19, 23, 24 - digest size, 100 pgs.; No. 25-27 - Treasury sized)

1-"5-Star Super-Hero Spectacular 1977"; Batman, Atom, Flash, Green Lantern, Aquaman, in solo stories, Kobra app.; N. Adams-c

	3	10	35

2(#1)-"The Original Swamp Thing Saga 1977"-r/Swamp Thing #1&2 by Wrightson; new Wrightson wraparound-c.

	2	6	14

3,4,6-8: 3-Sgt Rock. 4-Unexpected. 6-Secret Society of Super Villains, Jones-a. 7-Ghosts Special. 8-Brave and Bold w/ new Batman, Deadman & Sgt Rock team-up

	2	6	16

5-"Superman Spectacular 1977"-(84 pg, $1.00)-Superman vs. Brainiac & Lex Luthor, new 63 pg. story

	2	6	22

9-Wonder Woman; Ditko-a (11 pgs.)

	2	6	22

10-"Secret Origins of Superheroes Special 1978"-(52 pgs.)-Dr. Fate, Lightray & Black Canary on-c/new origin stories; Staton, Newton-a

	2	6	20

11-"Flash Spectacular 1978"-(84-pgs.) Flash, Kid Flash, GA Flash & Johnny Quick vs. Grodd; Wood-i on Kid Flash chapter

	2	6	16

12-"Secrets of Haunted House Special Spring 1978"

	2	6	16

13-"Sgt. Rock Special Spring 1978", 50 pg new story

	2	6	18

14,17,20-"Original Swamp Thing Saga", Wrightson-a: 14-Sum '78, r/#3,4.

	GD	FN	NM-

17-Sum '79 r/#5-7. 20-Jan/Feb '80, r/#8-10   1   4   10

15-"Batman Spectacular Summer 1978", Ra's Al Ghul-app.; Golden-a.
Rogers-a/front & back-c   3   9   25

16-"Jonah Hex Spectacular Fall 1978"; death of Jonah Hex, Heath-a; Bat
Lash and Scalphunter stories   6   18   70

18,19-Digest size: 18-"Sgt. Rock's Prize Battle Tales Fall 1979". 19-"Secret
Origins of Super-Heroes Fall 1979"; origins Wonder Woman (new-a),
r/Robin, Batman-Superman team,Aquaman, Hawkman and others
    2   6   16

21-"Super-Star Holiday Special Spring 1980", Frank Miller-a in "Batman--
Wanted Dead or Alive" (1st Batman story); Jonah Hex, Sgt. Rock,
Superboy & LSH and House of Mystery/Witching Hour-c/stories
    3   10   35

22-"G.I. Combat Sept. 1980", Kubert-c. Haunted Tank-s 2   6   18

23,24-Digest size: 23-World's Finest-r. 24-Flash   2   6   16

V5#25-($2.95)-"Superman II, the Adventure Continues Summer 1981";
photos from movie & photo-c (see All-New Coll. Ed. C-62)
    2   6   20

26-($2.50)-"Superman and His Incredible Fortress of Solitude Summer 1981"
    2   6   20

27-($2.50)-"Batman vs. The Incredible Hulk Fall 1981" 3   10   35

DC SUPER-STARS
National Periodical Publications/DC Comics: March, 1976 - No. 18, Winter, 1978 (No.3-18: 52 pgs.)

1-(68 pgs.)-Re-intro Teen Titans (predates T. T. #44 (11/76); tryout iss.) plus
r/Teen Titans   3   9   25

2-7,9,11,12,16: 2,4,6,8-Adam Strange; 2-(68 pgs.)-r/1st Adam Strange/
Hawkman team-up from Mystery in Space #90 plus Atomic Knights
origin-r. 3-Legion issue. 4-r/Tales/Unexpected #45 1   4   10

8-r/1st Space Ranger in Showcase #15, Adam Strange-r/Mystery in
Space #89 & Star Rovers-r/M.I.S. #80   2   6   12

10-Strange Sports Stories; Batman/Joker-c/story   2   6   14

13-Sergio Aragonés Special   2   6   22

14,15,18: 15-Sgt. Rock   2   6   12

17-Secret Origins of Super-Heroes (origin of The Huntress); origin Green
Arrow by Grell; Legion app.; Earth II Batman & Catwoman marry (1st
revealed; also see B&B #197 & Superman Family #211)
    4   12   50

DC: THE NEW FRONTIER
DC Comics: Mar, 2004 - No. 6, Nov, 2004 ($6.95, limited series)

1-6-DCU in the 1940s-60s; Darwyn Cooke-c/s/a in all. 1-Hal Jordan and
The Losers app. 2-Origin Martian Manhunter; Barry Allen app.
3-Challengers of the Unknown   7.00

DC VERSUS MARVEL (See Marvel Versus DC)
DC Comics: No. 1, 1996, No. 4, 1996 ($3.95, limited series)

1,4: 1-Marz script, Jurgens-a(p); 1st app. of Access.   4.00

.../Marvel Versus DC ($12.95, trade paperback) r/1-4   13.00

| | GD | FN | NM- |

DEADLIEST HEROES OF KUNG FU (Magazine)
Marvel Comics Group: Summer, 1975 (B&W)(76 pgs.)

1-Bruce Lee vs. Carradine painted-c; TV Kung Fu, 4pgs. photos/article;
   Enter the Dragon, 24 pgs. photos/article w/ Bruce Lee; Bruce Lee photo
   pinup   3   9   32

DEADLY HANDS OF KUNG FU, THE (See Master of Kung Fu)
Marvel Comics Group: April, 1974 - No. 33, Feb, 1977 (75¢) (B&W, magazine)

1(V1#4 listed in error)-Origin Sons of the Tiger; Shang-Chi, Master of Kung
   Fu begins (ties w/Master of Kung Fu #17 as 3rd app. Shang-Chi); Bruce
   Lee painted-c by Neal Adams; 2pg. memorial photo pinup w/8 pgs.
   photos/articles; TV Kung Fu, 9 pgs. photos/articles; 15 pgs. Starlin-a
       4   12   50

2-Adams painted-c; 1st time origin of Shang-Chi, 34 pgs. by Starlin. TV
   Kung Fu, 6 pgs. photos & article w/2 pg. pinup. Bruce Lee, 11 pgs. ph/a
       4   12   38

3,4,7,10: 3-Adams painted-c; Gulacy-a. Enter the Dragon, photos/articles,
   8 pgs. 4-TV Kung Fu painted-c by Neal Adams; TV Kung Fu 7 pg.
   article/art; Fu Manchu; Enter the Dragon, 10 pg. photos/article w/Bruce
   Lee. 7-Bruce Lee painted-c & 9 pgs. photos/articles-Return of Dragon
   plus 1 pg. photo pinup. 10-(3/75)-Iron Fist painted-c & 34 pg. sty-Early app.
       3   9   26

5,6: 5-1st app. Manchurian, 6 pgs. Gulacy-a. TV Kung Fu, 4 pg. article;
   reprints books w/Barry Smith-a. Capt. America-sty, 10 pgs. Kirby-a(r).
   6-Bruce Lee photos/article, 6 pgs.; 15 pgs. early Perez-a
       3   9   24

8,9,11: 9-Iron Fist, 2 pg. Preview pinup; Nebres-a. 11-Billy Jack painted-c
   by Adams; 17 pgs. photos/article   2   6   22

12,13: 12-James Bond painted-c by Adams; 14 pg. photos/article. 13-16 pgs.
   early Perez-a; Piers Anthony, 7 pgs. photos/article 2   6   20

14-Classic Bruce Lee painted-c by Adams. Lee pinup by Chaykin. Lee 16 pg.
   photos/article w/2 pgs. Green Hornet TV   5   15   60

15,19: 15-Sum, '75 Giant Annual #1. 20pgs. Starlin-a. Bruce Lee photo pinup
   & 3 pg. photos/article re book; Man-Thing app. Iron Fist-c/sty; Gulacy-a
   18 pgs. 19-Iron Fist painted-c & series begins; 1st White Tiger
       2   6   22

16,18,20: 16-1st app. Corpse Rider, a Samurai w/Sanho Kim-a. 20-Chuck
   Norris painted-c & 16 pgs. interview w/photos/article; Bruce Lee vs. C.
   Norris pinup by Ken Barr. Origin The White Tiger, Perez-a
       2   6   18

17-Bruce Lee painted-c by Adams; interview w/R. Clouse, director Enter the
   Dragon 7 pgs. w/B. Lee app. 1st Giffen-a (1pg. 11/75)
       3   10   35

21-Bruce Lee 1pg. photos/article   2   6   18

22,30-32: 22-1st brief app. Jack of Hearts. 1st Giffen sty-a (along w/Amazing
   Adv. #35, 3/76). 30-Swordquest-c/sty & conclusion; Jack of Hearts app.
   31-Jack of Hearts app; Staton-a. 32-1st Daughters of the Dragon-c/sty,
   21 pgs. Rogers-a/Claremont-sty;Iron Fist pinup 2   6   18

	GD	FN	NM-

23-26,29: 23-1st full app. Jack of Hearts. 24-Iron Fist-c & centerfold pinup;
early Zeck-a; Shang Chi pinup; 6 pgs. Piers Anthony text sty w/Perez &
Austin-a; Jack of Hearts app. early Giffen-a. 25-1st app. Shimuru,
"Samurai", 20 pgs. Mantlo-sty/Broderick-a; "Swordquest"-c & begins 17 pg.
sty by Sanho Kim; 11 pg. photos/article; partly Bruce Lee. 26-Bruce Lee
painted-c & pinup; 16 pgs. interviews w/Kwon & Clouse; talk about Bruce
Lee re-filming of Lee legend. 29-Ironfist vs. Shang Chi battle-c/sty; Jack of
Hearts app.   3   9   24

27   2   6   16

28-All Bruce Lee Special Issue; (1st time in comics). Bruce Lee painted-c by
Ken Barr & pinup. 36 pgs. comics chronicaling Bruce Lee's life; 15 pgs.
B. Lee photos/article (Rare in high grade)   7   21   80

33-Shang Chi-c/sty; Classic Daughters of the Dragon, 21 pgs. M. Rogers-a/
Claremont-story with nudity; Bob Wall interview, photos/article, 14 pgs.
    3   9   24

...Special Album Edition 1(Summer, '74)-Iron Fist-c/story (early app., 3rd?);
10 pgs. Adams-i; Shang Chi/Fu Manchu, 10 pgs.; Sons of Tiger, 11 pgs.;
TV Kung Fu, 6 pgs. photos/article   3   9   28

DEAD OF NIGHT
Marvel Comics Group: Dec, 1973 - No. 11, Aug, 1975

1-Horror reprints   3   9   28
2-10: 10-Kirby-a. 6-Jack the Ripper-c/s   2   6   16
11-Intro Scarecrow; Kane/Wrightson-c   3   10   35

DEADPOOL (See New Mutants #98)
Marvel Comics: Aug, 1994 - No. 4, Nov, 1994 ($2.50, limited series)

1-4: Mark Waid's 1st Marvel work; Ian Churchill-c/a   4.00

DEADPOOL (... : Agent of Weapon X on-c #57-60) (title becomes Agent X)
Marvel Comics: Jan, 1997 - No. 69, Sept, 2002 ($2.95/$1.95/$1.99)

1-($2.95)-Wraparound-c   1   3   7
2-Begin-$1.95-c.   5.00
3-10,12-22,24: 4-Hulk-c/app. 12-Variant-c. 14-Begin McDaniel-a   5.00
11-($3.99)-Deadpool replaces Spider-Man from Amazing Spider-Man #47;
Kraven, Gwen Stacy app.   6.00
23,25-($2.99); 23-Dead Reckoning pt. 1; wraparound-c   4.00
26-40: 27-Wolverine-c/app. 37-Thor app.   3.00
41-53,56-60: 41-Begin $2.25-c. 44-Black Panther-c/app. 46-49-Chadwick-a
51-Cover swipe of Detective #38. 57-60-BWS-c   3.00
54,55-Punisher-c/app. 54-Dillon-c. 55-Bradstreet-c   3.00
61-69: 61-64-Funeral For a Freak on cover. 65-69-Udon Studios-a.
67-Dazzler-c/app.   2.50
#(-1) Flashback (7/97) Lopresti-a; Wade Wilson's early days   3.00
.../Death '98 Annual ($2.99) Kelly-s, ... Team-Up (12/98, $2.99) Widdle
Wade-c/app., Baby's First Deadpool Book (12/98, $2.99), Encyclopædia
Deadpoolica (12/98, $2.99) Synopses   3.00
Mission Improbable TPB (9/98, $14.95) r/#1-5   15.00
Wizard #0 ('98, bagged with Wizard #87)   2.25

DEATH: AT DEATH'S DOOR (See Sandman: The Season of Mists)

	GD	FN	NM-

DC Comics: 2003 ($9.95, graphic novel one-shot, B&W, 7-1/2" x 5")

1-Jill Thompson-s/a/c; manga-style; Morpheus and the Endless app.   10.00

DEATHLOK (Also see Astonishing Tales #25)
Marvel Comics: July, 1990 - No. 4, Oct, 1990 ($3.95, limited series, 52 pgs.)

1-4: 1,2-Guice-a(p). 3,4-Denys Cowan-a, c-4   4.00

DEATHLOK
Marvel Comics: July, 1991 - No. 34, Apr, 1994 ($1.75)

1-Silver ink cover; Denys Cowan-c/a(p) begins   3.00
2-18,20-24,26-34: 2-Forge (X-Men) app. 3-Vs. Dr. Doom. 5-X-Men & F.F.
   x-over. 6,7-Punisher x-over. 9,10-Ghost Rider-c/story. 16-Infinity War
   x-over. 17-Jae Lee-c. 22-Black Panther app. 27-Siege app.   2.25
19-($2.25)-Foil-c   2.50
25-($2.95, 52 pgs.)-Holo-grafx foil-c   3.00
Annual 1 (1992, $2.25, 68 pgs.)-Guice-p; Quesada-c(p)   3.00
Annual 2 (1993, $2.95, 68 pgs.)-Bagged w/card; intro Tracer   3.00

DEATHLOK
Marvel Comics: Sept, 1999 - No. 11, June, 2000 ($1.99)

1-11: 1-Casey-s/Manco-a. 2-Two covers. 4-Canete-a   2.25

DEATHMATE
Valiant (Prologue/Yellow/Blue)/Image Comics (Black/Red/Epilogue):
Sept, 1993 - Epilogue (#6), Feb, 1994 ($2.95/$4.95, limited series)

Preview-(7/93, 8 pgs.)   2.25
Prologue (#1)–Silver foil; Jim Lee/Layton-c; B. Smith/Lee-a; Liefeld-a(p)   3.00
Prologue–Special gold foil ed. of silver ed.   4.00
Black (#2)-(9/93, $4.95, 52 pgs.)-Silvestri/Jim Lee-c; pencils by Peterson/
   Silvestri/Capullo/Jim Lee/Portacio; 1st story app. Gen 13 telling their
   rebellion against the Troika (see WildC.A.T.S. Trilogy)   6.00
Black-Special gold foil edition   7.00
Yellow (#3)-(10/93, $4.95, 52 pgs)-Yellow foil-c; Indicia says Prologue Sept
   1993 by mistake; 3rd app. Ninjak; Thibert-c(i)   5.00
Yellow-Special gold foil edition   6.00
Blue (#4)-(10/93, $4.95, 52 pgs.)-Thibert blue foil-c(i); Reese-a(i)   5.00
Blue-Special gold foil edition   6.00
Red (#5), Epilogue (#6)-(2/94, $2.95)-Silver foil Quesada/Silvestri-c;
   Silvestri-a(p)   3.00

DEATHSTROKE: THE TERMINATOR (Deathstroke: The Hunted #0-47;
Deathstroke #48-60) (Also see Marvel & DC Present, New Teen Titans #2,
New Titans, Showcase '93 #7,9 & Tales of the Teen Titans #42-44)
DC Comics: Aug, 1991 - No. 60, June, 1996 ($1.75-$2.25)

1-New Titans spin-off; Mike Zeck c-1-28   4.00
1-Gold ink 2nd printing ($1.75)   2.25
2   3.00
3-40,0(10/94),41(11/94)-49,51-60: 6,8-Batman cameo. 7,9-Batman-c/story.
   9-1st brief app. new Vigilante (female). 10-1st full app. new Vigilante;
   Perez-i. 13-Vs. Justice League; Team Titans cameo on last pg. 14-Total
   Chaos, part 1; TeamTitans-c/story cont'd in New Titans #90. 15-Total

	GD	FN	NM-

Chaos, part 4. 40-(9/94). 0-(10/94)-Begin Deathstroke, The Hunted, ends
#47.   2.50
50 ($3.50)   3.50
Annual 1-4 ('92-'95, 68 pgs.): 1-Nightwing & Vigilante app.; minor Eclipso app.
2-Bloodlines Deathstorm; 1st app. Gunfire. 3-Elseworlds story. 4-Year One
story   4.00

DEATH: THE HIGH COST OF LIVING (See Sandman #8) (Also see the
Books of Magic limited & ongoing series)
DC Comics (Vertigo): Mar, 1993 - No. 3, May, 1993 ($1.95, limited series)

1-Bachalo/Buckingham-a; Dave McKean-c; Neil Gaiman scripts in all   6.00
1-Platinum edition   40.00
2   3.50
3-Pgs. 19 & 20 had wrong placement   3.00
3-Corrected version w/pgs. 19 & 20 facing each other; has no-c & ads for
Sebastion O & The Geek added   4.00
Death Talks About Life-giveaway about AIDS prevention   5.00
Hardcover (1994, $19.95)-r/#1-3 & Death Talks About Life; intro. by Tori Amos
                                                                                      20.00
Trade paperback (6/94, $12.95, Titan Books)-r/#1-3 & Death Talks About Life;
prism-c   13.00

DEATH: THE TIME OF YOUR LIFE (See Sandman #8)
DC Comics (Vertigo): Apr, 1996 - No. 3, July, 1996 ($2.95, limited series)

1-3: Neil Gaiman story & Bachalo/Buckingham-a; Dave McKean-c. 2-(5/96)
                                                                                      3.00
Hardcover (1997, $19.95)-r/#1-3 w/3 new pages & gallery art by various   20.00
TPB (1997, $12.95)-r/#1-3 & Visions of Death gallery; Intro. by Claire Danes
                                                                                      13.00

DEFENDERS, THE (Also see Giant-Size..., Marvel Feature, Marvel Treasury
Edition, Secret Defenders & Sub-Mariner #34, 35; The New...#140-on)
Marvel Comics Group: Aug, 1972 - No. 152, Feb, 1986

	GD	FN	NM-
1-The Hulk, Doctor Strange, Sub-Mariner begin	11	33	150
2-Silver Surfer x-over	6	18	65
3-5: 3-Silver Surfer x-over. 4-Valkyrie joins	4	12	40
6,7: 6-Silver Surfer x-over	3	9	25
8,9,11: 8-11-Defenders vs. the Avengers (x-over with Avengers #115-118)			
8,11-Silver Surfer x-over	3	9	30
10-Hulk vs. Thor battle	7	21	80
12-14: 12-Last 20¢ issue	2	6	15
15,16-Magneto & Brotherhood of Evil Mutants app. from X-Men			
	2	6	16
17-20: 17-Power Man x-over (11/74)	1	4	10
21-25: 24,25-Son of Satan app.	1	3	7
26-29-Guardians of the Galaxy app. (#26 is 8/75; pre-dates Marvel Presents #3): 28-1st full app. Starhawk (1st brief app. #27). 29-Starhawk joins Guardians	1	3	9
30-33,39-50: 31,32-Origin Nighthawk. 44-Hellcat joins. 45-Dr. Strange leaves. 47-49-Early Moon Knight app. (5/77). 48-50-(Reg. 30¢-c)			5.00

	GD	FN	NM-

34-38-(Regular 25¢ editions): 35-Intro New Red Guardian   5.00
34-38-(30¢-c variants, limited distribution)(4-8/76)   1   3   7
48-52-(35¢-c variants, limited distribution)(6-10/77)   1   3   7
51-60: 51,52-(Reg. 30¢-c). 53-1st brief app. Lunatik (Lobo lookalike).
  55-Origin Red Guardian; Lunatik cameo. 56-1st full Lunatik story   4.00
61-75: 61-Lunatik & Spider-Man app. 70-73-Lunatik (origin #71).
  73-75-Foolkiller II app. (Greg Salinger). 74-Nighthawk resigns   3.00
76-93,95,97-99,102-119,123,124,126-149,151: 77-Origin Omega.
  78-Original Defenders return thru #101. 104-The Beast joins. 105-Son of
  Satan joins. 106-Death of Nighthawk. 129-New Mutants cameo (3/84,
  early x-over)   2.50
94,101,120-122: 94-1st Gargoyle. 101-Silver Surfer-c & app. 120,121-Son of
  Satan-c/stories. 122-Final app. Son of Satan (2 pgs.)   4.00
96-Ghost Rider app.   4.00
100-(52 pgs.)-Hellcat (Patsy Walker) revealed as Satan's daughter   5.00
125,150: 125-(52 pgs.)-Intro new Defenders. 150-(52 pgs.)-Origin Cloud   4.00
152-(52 pgs.)-Ties in with X-Factor & Secret Wars II   4.00
Annual 1 (1976, 52 pgs.)-New book-length story   3   9   25

DEFENDERS, THE (Volume 2) (Continues in The Order)
Marvel Comics: Mar, 2001 - No. 12, Feb, 2002 ($2.99/$2.25)

1-Busiek & Larsen-s/Larsen & Janson-a/c   3.00
2-11: 2-Two covers by Larsen & Art Adams; Valkyrie app. 4-Frenz-a   2.25
12-($3.50) 'Nuff Said issue; back-up-s Reis-a   3.50

DEMON, THE (See Detective Comics No. 482-485)
National Periodical Publications: Aug-Sept, 1972 - V3#16, Jan, 1974

1-Origin; Kirby-c/a in all   6   18   70
2-5   3   10   35
6-16   2   6   22

DEMON, THE (1st limited series)(Also see Cosmic Odyssey #2)
DC Comics: Nov, 1986 - No. 4, Feb, 1987 (75¢, limited series)(#2 has #4 of 4
on-c)

1-4: Matt Wagner-a(p) & scripts in all. 4-Demon & Jason Blood become
  separate entities.   3.00

DEMON, THE (2nd Series)
DC Comics: July, 1990 - No. 58, May, 1995 ($1.50/$1.75/$1.95)

1-Grant scripts begin, ends #39: 1-4-Painted-c   4.00
2-18,20-27,29-39,41,42: 3,8-Batman app. (cameo #4). 12-Bisley painted-c.
  12-15,21-Lobo app. (1 pg. cameo #11). 23-Robin app.
  29-Superman app. 31,33-39-Lobo app.   2.50
19,28,40: 19-($2.50, 44 pgs.)-Lobo poster stapled inside. 28-Superman-c/
  story; begin $1.75-c. 40-Garth Ennis scripts begin   4.00
43-45-Hitman app.   1   3   8
46-48 Return of The Haunted Tank-c/s. 48-Begin $1.95-c.   5.00
49,51,0-(10/94),55-58: 51-(9/94)   2.50
50 ($2.95, 52 pgs.)   3.00
52-54-Hitman-s   5.00
Annual 1 (1992, $3.00, 68 pgs.)-Eclipso-c/story   3.00

	GD	FN	NM-

Annual 2 (1993, $3.50, 68 pgs.)-1st app. of Hitman   2   6   16

DESTINY: A CHRONICLE OF DEATHS FORETOLD (See Sandman)
DC Comics (Vertigo): 1997 - No. 3, 1998 ($5.95, limited series)

1-3-Alisa Kwitney-s in all: 1-Kent Williams & Michael Zulli-a, Williams
painted-c. 2-Williams & Scott Hampton-painted-c/a. 3-Williams & Guay-a
    6.00
TPB (2000, $14.95) r/series   15.00

DETECTIVE COMICS (Also see other Batman titles)
National Periodical Publications/DC Comics: No. 225, Nov, 1955 - Present

225-(11/55)-1st app. Martian Manhunter, John Jones; later changed to J'onn
    J'onzz; origin begins; also see Batman #78   364   1092   8000
226-Origin Martian Manhunter cont'd (2nd app.)   138   414   1800
227-229: Martian Manhunter stories in all   55   165   700
230-1st app. Mad Hatter; brief recap origin of Martian Manhunter
    56   168   725
231-Brief origin recap Martian Manhunter   40   120   500
232,234,237-240: 239-Early DC grey tone-c   40   120   475
233-Origin & 1st app. Batwoman (7/56)   135   405   1750
235-Origin Batman & his costume; tells how Bruce Wayne's father (Thomas
    Wayne) wore Bat costume & fought crime (reprinted in Batman #255)
    65   195   840
236-1st S.A. issue; J'onn J'onzz talks to parents and Mars-1st since being
    stranded on Earth; 1st app. Bat-Tank?   43   129   535
241-260: 246-Intro. Diane Meade, John Jones' girl. 249-Batwoman-c/app.
    253-1st app. The Terrible Trio. 254-Bat-Hound-c/story. 257-Intro. & 1st app.
    Whirly Bats. 259-1st app. The Calendar Man   35   105   375
261-264,266,268-271: 261-J. Jones tie-in to sci/fi movie "Incredible Shrinking
    Man"; 1st app. Dr. Double X. 262-Origin Jackal. 268,271-Manhunter
    origin recap   27   81   290
265-Batman's origin retold with new facts   40   120   440
267-Origin & 1st app. Bat-Mite (5/59)   40   120   485
272,274,275,277-280   22   66   240
273-J'onn J'onzz i.d. revealed for 1st time   23   69   250
276-2nd app. Bat-Mite   25   75   270
281-292, 294-297: 285,286,292-Batwoman-c/app. 287-Origin J'onn J'onzz
    retold. 289-Bat-Mite-c/story. 292-Last Roy Raymond. 297-Last 10¢ issue
    (11/61)   18   54   190
293-(7/61)-Aquaman begins (pre #1); ends #300   19   57   200
298-(12/61)-1st modern Clayface (Matt Hagen)   25   75   375
299, 300-(2/62)-Aquaman ends   12   36   165
301-(3/62)-J'onn J'onzz returns to Mars (1st time since stranded on Earth
    six years before)   10   30   140
302-317,319-321,323,324,326,329,330: 302-315,311,321-Batwoman-c/app.
    311-Intro. Zook in John Jones; 1st app. Cat-Man. 321-2nd Terrible Trio.
    326-Last J'onn J'onzz, story cont'd in House of Mystery #143; intro.
    Idol-Head of Diabolu   9   27   115
318,322,325: 318,325-Cat-Man-c/story (2nd & 3rd app.); also 1st & 2nd app.
    Batwoman as the Cat-Woman. 322-Bat-Girl's 1st/only app. in Det. (6th in

	GD	FN	NM-

all); Batman cameo in J'onn J'onzz (only hero to app. in series)

	9	27	115

327-(5/64)-Elongated Man begins, ends #383; 1st new look Batman with new costume; Infantino/Giella new look-a begins; Batman with gun

	12	36	175
328-Death of Alfred; Bob Kane biog, 2 pgs.	11	33	160
331,333-340: 334-1st app. The Outsider	7	21	90

342-358,360,361,366-368: 345-Intro Block Buster. 347-"What If" theme story (1/66). 351-Elongated Man new costume. 355-Zatanna x-over in Elongated Man. 356-Alfred brought back in Batman, early SA app.

	6	18	75
332,341,365-Joker-c/stories	8	24	105

359-Intro/origin Batgirl (Barbara Gordon)-c/story (1/67); 1st Silver Age app. Killer Moth

	13	39	190

362-364: 362,364-S.A. Riddler app. (early). 363-2nd app. new Batgirl

	7	21	80

369(11/67)-N. Adams-a (Elongated Man); 3rd app. S.A. Catwoman (cameo; leads into Batman #197); 4th app. new Batgirl

	8	24	105
370-1st Neal Adams-a on Batman (cover only, 12/67)	7	21	80

371-(1/68) 1st new Batmobile from TV show; classic Batgirl-c

	8	24	95
372-376,378-386,389,390: 375-New Batmobile-c	6	18	65
377-S.A. Riddler-c/sty	6	18	70

387-r/1st Batman story from #27 (30th anniversary, 5/69); Joker-c;

	7	21	90
388-Joker-c/story; last 12¢ issue	7	21	80

391-394,396,398,399,401,403,405,406,409: 392-1st app. Jason Bard. 401-2nd Batgirl/Robin team-up

	4	12	50

395,397,402,404,407,408,410-Neal Adams-a. 404-Tribute to Enemy Ace

	6	18	70

400-(6/70)-Origin & 1st app. Man-Bat; 1st Batgirl/Robin team-up (cont'd in #401); Neal Adams-a

	13	39	190
411-413: 413-Last 15¢ issue	4	12	40

414-424: All-25¢, 52 pgs. 418-Creeper x-over. 424-Last Batgirl.

	4	12	45

425-436: 426,430,436-Elongated Man app. 428,434-Hawkman begins, ends #467

	3	9	28

437-New Manhunter begins (10-11/73, 1st app.) by Simonson, ends #443

	4	12	50

438-445 (All 100 Page Super Spectaculars): 438-Kubert Hawkman-r. 439-Origin Manhunter. 440-G.A. Manhunter(Adv. #79) by S&K, Hawkman, Dollman, Green Lantern; Toth-a. 441-G.A. Plastic Man, Batman, Ibis-r. 442-G.A. Newsboy Legion, Black Canary, Elongated Man, Dr. Fate-r. 443-Origin The Creeper-r; death of Manhunter; G.A. Green Lantern, Spectre-r; Batman-r/Batman #18. 444-G.A. Kid Eternity-r. 445-G.A. Dr. Midnite-r

	6	18	70
446-460: 457-Origin retold & updated	2	6	20

461-465,470,480: 480-(44 pgs.). 463-1st app. Black Spider. 464-2nd app. Black Spider

	2	6	16

	GD	FN	NM-

466-468,471-474,478,479-Rogers-a in all: 466-1st app. Signalman since
    Batman #139. 470,471-1st modern app. Hugo Strange. 474-1st app. new
    Deadshot. 478-1st app. 3rd Clayface (Preston Payne). 479-(44 pgs.)

	3	10	35

469-Intro/origin Dr. Phosphorous; Simonson-a   3   9   32

475,476-Joker-c/stories; Rogers-a   6   18   70

477-Neal Adams-a(r); Rogers-a (3 pgs.)   3   9   32

481-(Combined with Batman Family, 12-1/78-79, begin $1.00, 68 pg. issues,
    ends #495); 481-495-Batgirl, Robin solo stories   2   6   20

482-Starlin/Russell, Golden-a; The Demon begins (origin-r), ends #485 (by
    Ditko #483-485)   2   6   16

483-40th Anniversary issue; origin retold; Newton Batman begins

	2	6	20

484-495 (68 pgs): 484-Origin Robin. 485-Death of Batwoman. 487-The Odd
    Man by Ditko. 489-Robin/Batgirl team-up. 490-Black Lightning begins.
    491-(#492 on inside)   2   6   12

496-499   1   3   9

500-($1.50, 52 pgs.)-Batman/Deadman team-up; new Hawkman story by
    Joe Kubert; incorrectly says 500th anniv. of Det.   2   6   16

501-503,505-523: 512-2nd app. new Dr. Death. 519-Last Batgirl. 521-Green
    Arrow series begins. 523-Solomon Grundy app.   6.00

504-Joker-c/story   2   6   12

524-2nd app. Jason Todd (cameo)(3/83)   1   3   8

525-3rd app. Jason Todd (See Batman #357)   1   3   8

526-Batman's 500th app. in Detective Comics ($1.50, 68 pgs.); Death of
    Jason Todd's parents, Joker-c/story (55 pgs.); Bob Kane pin-up

	2	6	20

527-531,533,534,536-568,571,573: 538-Cat-Man-c/story cont'd from Batman
    #371. 542-Jason Todd quits as Robin (becomes Robin again #547).
    549, 550-Alan Moore scripts (Green Arrow). 554-1st new Black Canary
    (9/85). 566-Batman villains profiled. 567-Harlan Ellison scripts   5.00

532,569,570-Joker-c/stories   1   4   10

535-Intro new Robin (JasonTodd)-1st appeared in Batman.   6.00

572-(3/87, $1.25, 60 pgs.)-50th Anniv. of Det. Comics   6.00

574-Origin Batman & Jason Todd retold   6.00

575-Year 2 begins, ends #578   2   6   20

576-578: McFarlane-c/a. 578-Clay Face app.   2   6   20

579-597,599,601-610: 579-New bat wing logo. 583-1st app. villains Scarface
    & Ventriloquist. 589-595-(52 pgs.)-Each contain free 16 pg. Batman stories.
    604-607-Mudpack storyline; 604,607-Contain Batman mini-posters.
    610-Faked death of Penguin; artists names app. on tombstone on-c   3.00

598-($2.95, 84 pgs.)- "Blind Justice" storyline begins by Batman movie writer
    Sam Hamm, ends #600   4.00

600-(5/89, $2.95, 84 pgs.)-50th Anniv. of Batman in Det.; 1 pg. Neal Adams
    pin-up, among other artists   4.00

611-626,628-658: 612-1st new look Cat-Man; Catwoman app. 615- "The
    Penguin Affair" part 2 (See Batman #448,449). 617-Joker-c/story.
    624-1st new Catwoman (w/death) & 1st new Batwoman. 626-Batman's
    600th app. in Detective. 642-Return of Scarface, part 2. 644-Last $1.00-c.

	GD	FN	NM-

652,653-Huntress-c/story w/new costume plus Charest-c on both 3.00

627-($2.95, 84 pgs.)-Batman's 601st app. in Det.; reprints 1st story/#27 plus
3 versions (2 new) of same story 4.00

659-664: 659-Knightfall part 2; Kelley Jones-c. 660-Knightfall part 4; Bane-c
by Sam Kieth. 661-Knightfall part 6; brief Joker & Riddler app.
662-Knightfall part 8; Riddler app.; Sam Kieth-c. 663-Knightfall part 10;
Kelley Jones-c. 664-Knightfall part 12; Bane-c/story; Joker app.; continued
in Showcase 93 #7 & 8; Jones-c 3.00

665-675: 665,666-Knightfall parts 16 & 18; 666-Bane-c/story. 667-Knightquest:
The Crusade & new Batman begins (1st app. in Batman #500). 669-Begin
$1.50-c; Knightquest, cont'd in Robin #1. 671,673-Joker app. 2.75

675-($2.95)-Collectors edition w/foil-c 3.50

676-($2.50, 52 pgs.)-KnightsEnd pt. 3 3.00

677,678: 677-KnightsEnd pt. 9. 678-(9/94)-Zero Hour tie-in. 2.75

679-685: 679-(11/94). 682-Troika pt. 3 2.75

682-($2.50) Embossed-c Troika pt. 3 3.00

686-699,701-719: 686-Begin $1.95-c. 693,694-Poison Ivy-c/app.
695-Contagion pt. 2; Catwoman, Penguin app. 696-Contagion pt. 8.
698-Two-Face-c/app. 701-Legacy pt. 6; Batman vs. Bane-c/app.
702-Legacy Epilogue. 703-Final Night x-over. 705-707-Riddler-app.
714,715-Martian Manhunter-app. 2.75

700-($4.95, Collectors Edition)-Legacy pt. 1; Ra's Al Ghul-c/app; Talia & Bane
app; book displayed at shops in envelope 5.00

700-($2.95, Regular Edition)-Different-c 3.00

720-740: 720,721-Cataclysm pts. 5,14. 723-Green Arrow app. 730-740-No
Man's Land stories 2.75

741-($2.50) Endgame; Joker-c/app. 3.00

742-749,751-765: 742-New look Batman begins. 751,752-Poison Ivy app.
756-Superman-c/app. 759-762-Catwoman back-up; Cooke-a 2.75

750-($4.95, 64 pgs.) Ra's al Ghul-c 5.00

766-772: 766,767-Bruce Wayne: Murderer pt. 1,8. 769-772-Bruce Wayne:
Fugitive pts. 4,8,12,16 3.00

773,774,776-799,801: 773-Begin $2.75-c; Sienkiewicz-c. 777-784-Sale-c.
784-786-Alan Scott app. 787-Mad Hatter app. 793-Begin $2.95-c.
797-799-War Games. 801-Lapham-s 3.00

775-($3.50) Sienkiewicz-c 3.50

800-($3.50) Jock-c; aftermath of War Games; back-up by Lapham 3.50

#0-(10/94) Zero Hour tie-in 2.75

#1,000,000 (11/98) 853rd Century x-over 2.75

Annual 1 (1988, $1.50) 5.00

Annual 2-7,9 ('89-'94, '96, 68 pgs.)-4-Painted-c. 5-Joker-c/story (54 pgs.)
continued in Robin Annual #1; Sam Kieth-c; Eclipso app. 6-Azrael as
Batman in new costume; intro Geist the Twilight Man; Bloodlines storyline.
7-Elseworlds story. 9-Legends of the Dead Earth story 3.00

Annual 8 (1995, $3.95, 68 pgs.)-Year One story 4.00

Annual 10 (1997, $3.95)-Pulp Heroes story 4.00

DEVIL KIDS STARRING HOT STUFF
Harvey Publications (Illustrated Humor): July, 1962 - No. 107, Oct, 1981
(Giant-Size #41-55)

	GD	FN	NM-
1 (12¢ cover price #1-#41-9/69)	18	54	260
2	10	30	125
3-10 (1/64)	7	21	90
11-20	5	15	55
21-30	4	12	38
31-40: 40-(6/69)	3	9	28
41-50: All 68 pg. Giants	3	9	32
51-55: All 52 pg. Giants	3	9	28
56-70	2	6	15
71-90	1	3	9
91-107			6.00

DEXTER'S LABORATORY (Cartoon Network)
DC Comics: Sept, 1999 - No. 34, Apr, 2003 ($1.99/$2.25)

1			4.00
2-10: 2-McCracken-s			3.00
11-24			2.25
25-(50¢-c) Tartakovsky-s/a; Action Hank-c/app.			2.25
26-34: 31-Begin $2.25-c. 32-34-Wray-c			2.25

DISNEY COMIC ALBUM
Disney Comics: 1990(no month, year) - No. 8, 1991 ($6.95/$7.95)

1,2 ($6.95): 1-Donald Duck and Gyro Gearloose by Barks(r). 2-Uncle
Scrooge by Barks(r); Jr. Woodchucks app.   9.00
3-8: 3-Donald Duck-r/F.C. 308 by Barks; begin $7.95-c. 4-Mickey Mouse
Meets the Phantom Blot; r/M.M Club Parade (censored 1956 version of
story). 5-Chip `n' Dale Rescue Rangers; new-a. 6-Uncle Scrooge.
7-Donald Duck in Too Many Pets; Barks-r(4) including F.C. #29.
8-Super Goof; r/S.G. #1, D.D. #102   9.00

DISNEY COMIC HITS
Marvel Comics: Oct, 1995 - No. 16, Jan, 1997 ($1.50/$2.50)

1-16: 4-Toy Story. 6-Aladdin. 7-Pocahontas. 10-The Hunchback of Notre
Dame (Same story in Disney's The Hunchback of Notre Dame).
13-Aladdin and the Forty Thieves   4.00

DISNEY'S COLOSSAL COMICS COLLECTION
Disney Comics: 1991 - No. 10, 1993 ($1.95, digest-size, 96/132 pgs.)

1-10: Ducktales, Talespin, Chip 'n Dale's Rescue Rangers. 4-r/Darkwing
Duck #1-4. 6-Goofy begins. 8-Little Mermaid   5.00

DISNEY'S COMICS IN 3-D
Disney Comics: 1992 ($2.95, w/glasses, polybagged)

1-Infinity-c; Barks, Rosa, Gottfredson-r   5.00

DISNEY'S TALESPIN LIMITED SERIES: "TAKE OFF" (TV) (See Talespin)
W. D. Publications (Disney Comics): Jan, 1991 - No. 4, Apr, 1991 ($1.50,
lim. series, 52 pgs.)

1-4: Based on animated series; 4 part origin   2.50

DISNEY'S TARZAN (Movie)
Dark Horse Comics: June, 1999 - No. 2, July, 1999 ($2.95, limited series)

	GD	FN	NM-
1,2: Movie adaptation			3.00

DISNEY'S THE LION KING (Movie)
Marvel Comics: July, 1994 - No. 2, July, 1994 ($1.50, limited series)

1,2: 2-part movie adaptation			3.00
1-($2.50, 52 pgs.)-Complete story			5.00

DISNEY'S THE THREE MUSKETEERS (Movie)
Marvel Comics: Jan, 1994 - No. 2, Feb, 1994 ($1.50, limited series)

1,2-Morrow-c; Spiegle-a; Movie adaptation			2.25

DOCTOR MID-NITE (Also see All-American #25)
DC Comics: 1999 - No. 3, 1999 ($5.95, square-bound, limited series)

1-3-Matt Wagner-s/John K. Snyder III-painted art			6.00
TPB (2000, $19.95) r/series			20.00

DOCTOR OCTOPUS: NEGATIVE EXPOSURE
Marvel Comics: Dec, 2003 - No. 5, Apr, 2004 ($2.99, limited series)

1-5-Vaughan-s/Staz Johnson-a; Spider-Man app.			3.00
Spider-Man/Doctor Octopus: Negative Exposure TPB (2004, $13.99) r/series			14.00

DOCTOR SOLAR, MAN OF THE ATOM (See The Occult Files of Dr. Spektor #14 & Solar)
Gold Key/Whitman No. 28 on: 10/62 - No. 27, 4/69; No. 28, 4/81 - No. 31, 3/82 (1-27 have painted-c)

1-(#10000-210)-Origin/1st app. Dr. Solar (1st original Gold Key character)			
	21	63	305
2-Prof. Harbinger begins	10	30	125
3,4	7	21	80
5-Intro. Man of the Atom in costume	7	21	85
6-10	5	15	60
11-14,16-20	4	12	42
15-Origin retold	4	12	48
21-23: 23-Last 12¢ issue	3	10	35
24-27	3	9	32
28-31: 29-Magnus Robot Fighter begins. 31-(3/82)The Sentinel app.			
	2	6	20

DOCTOR STRANGE (Formerly Strange Tales #1-168) (Also see The Defenders, Giant-Size…, Marvel Fanfare, Marvel Graphic Novel, Marvel Premiere, Marvel Treasury Edition, Strange & Strange Tales, 2nd Series)
Marvel Comics Group: No. 169, 6/68 - No. 183, 11/69; 6/74 - No. 81, 2/87

169(#1)-Origin retold; panel swipe/M.D. #1-c	13	39	190
170-177: 177-New costume	4	12	45
178-183: 178-Black Knight app. 179-Spider-Man story-r. 180-Photo montage-c. 181-Brunner-c(part-i), last 12¢ issue	4	12	40
1(6/74, 2nd series)-Brunner-c/a	7	21	80
2	3	10	35
3-5	2	6	22
6-10	2	6	12

	GD	FN	NM-
11-13,15-20: 13,15-17-(Regular 25¢ editions)	1	3	7
13-17-(30¢-c variants, limited distribution)	1	4	10
14-(5/76) Dracula app.; (regular 25¢ edition)	1	4	10
21-40: 21-Origin-r/Doctor Strange #169. 23-25-(Regular 30¢ editions).			
31-Sub-Mariner-c/story			4.00
23-25-(35¢-c variants, limited distribution)(6,8,10/77)	1	3	8
41-57,63-77,79-81: 56-Origin retold			3.50
58-62: 58-Re-intro Hannibal King (cameo). 59-Hannibal King full app.			
59-62-Dracula app. (Darkhold storyline). 61,62-Doctor Strange, Blade,			
Hannibal King & Frank Drake team-up to battle. Dracula. 62-Death of			
Dracula & Lilith			5.00
78-New costume			3.00
Annual 1(1976, 52 pgs.)-New Russell-a (35 pgs.)	2	6	16
.../Silver Dagger Special Edition 1 (3/83, $2.50)-r/#1,2,4,5; Wrightson-c			3.00
...What Is It That Disturbs You, Stephen? #1 (10/97, $5.99, 48 pgs.)			
Russell-a/Andreyko & Russell-s, retelling of Annual #1 story			6.00

DOCTOR STRANGE (Volume 2)
Marvel Comics: Feb, 1999 - No. 4, May, 1999 ($2.99, limited series)

1-4: 1,2-Tony Harris-a/painted cover. 3,4-Chadwick-a			3.00

DOCTOR STRANGE, SORCERER SUPREME
Marvel Comics (Midnight Sons imprint #60 on): Nov, 1988 - No. 90, June, 1996 ($1.25/$1.50/$1.75/$1.95, direct sales only, Mando paper)

1 ($1.25)			4.00
2-9,12-14,16-25,27,29-40,42-49,51-64: 3-New Defenders app. 5-Guice-c/a			
begins. 14-18-Morbius story line. 31-36-Infinity Gauntlet x-overs. 31-Silver			
Surfer app. 33-Thanos-c & cameo. 36-Warlock app. 37-Silver Surfer app.			
40-Daredevil x-over. 41-Wolverine-c/story. 42-47-Infinity War x-overs.			
47-Gamora app. 52,53-Morbius-c/stories. 60,61-Siege of Darkness pt. 7			
& 15. 60-Spot varnish-c. 61-New Doctor Strange begins (cameo, 1st app).			
62-Dr. Doom & Morbius app.			2.50
10,11,26,28,41: 10-Re-intro Morbius w/new costume (11/89). 11-Hobgoblin			
app. 26-Werewolf by Night app. 28-Ghost Rider-s cont'd from G.R. #12;			
publ'd at same time as Doctor Strange/Ghost Rider Special #1(4/91)			3.00
15-Unauthorized Amy Grant photo-c			4.00
50-($2.95, 52 pgs.)-Holo-grafx foil-c; Hulk, Ghost Rider & Silver Surfer app.;			
leads into new Secret Defenders series			3.00
65-74, 76-90: 65-Begin $1.95-c; bound-in card sheet. 72-Silver ink-c.			
80-82- Ellis-s. 84-DeMatteis story begins. 87-Death of Baron Mordo			2.50
75 ($2.50)			3.00
75 ($3.50)-Foil-c			4.00
Annual 2-4 ('92-'94, 68 pgs.)-2-Defenders app. 3-Polybagged w/card			3.00
Ashcan (1995, 75¢)			2.25
.../Ghost Rider Special 1 (4/91, $1.50)-Same book as D.S.S.S. #28			2.50
...Vs. Dracula 1 (3/94, $1.75, 52 pgs.)-r/Tomb of Dracula #44 & Dr. Strange			
#14			2.50

NOTE: *See 1st series for Annual #1.*

DONALD DUCK (Walt Disney's...#262 on)
Gold Key #85-216/Whitman #217-245/Gladstone #246 on: No. 85, Dec,

	GD	FN	NM-

1962 - No. 245, July, 1984; No. 246, Oct, 1986 - No. 279, May, 1990; No. 280, Sept, 1993 - No. 307, Mar,1998

	GD	FN	NM-
85-97,99,100: 96-Donald Duck Album	5	15	60
98-Reprints #46 (Barks)	6	18	65
101,103-111,113-135: 120-Last 12¢ issue. 134-Barks-r/#52 & WDC&S 194.			
135-Barks-r/WDC&S 198, 19 pgs.	4	12	40
102-Super Goof. 112-1st Moby Duck	4	12	42
136-153,155,156,158: 149-20¢-c begin	3	9	24
154-Barks-r(#46)	3	9	30
157,159,160,164: 157-Barks-r(#45); 25¢-c begin. 159-Reprints/WDC&S #192			
(10 pgs.). 160-Barks-r(#26). 164-Barks-r/#79	3	9	24
161-163,165-173,175-187,189-191: 175-30¢-c begin. 187-Barks r/#68.			
	2	6	20
174,188: 174-r/4-Color #394.	2	6	22
192-Barks-r(40 pgs.) from Donald Duck #60 & WDC&S #226,234 (52 pgs.)			
	3	9	26
193-200,202-207,209-211,213-216	2	6	16
201,208,212: 201-Barks-r/Christmas Parade #26, 16pgs. 208-Barks-r/#60			
(6 pgs.). 212-Barks-r/WDC&S #130	2	6	16
217-219: 217 has 216 on-c. 219-Barks-r/WDC&S #106,107, 10 pgs. ea.			
	2	6	18
220,225-228: 228-Barks-r/F.C. #275	2	6	22
221,223,224: Scarce; only sold in pre-packs. 221(8/80), 223(11/80),			
224(12/80)	4	12	50
222-(9-10/80)-(Very low distribution)	17	51	250
229-240: 229-Barks-r/F.C. #282. 230-Barks-r/ #52 & WDC&S #194. 236(2/82),			
237(2-3/82), 238(3/82), 239(4/82), 240(5/82)	2	6	16
241-245: 241(4/83), 242(5/83), 243(3/84), 244(4/84), 245(7/84)(low print)			
	3	9	24
246-(1st Gladstone issue)-Barks-r/FC #422	3	9	25
247-249,251: 248,249-Barks-r/DD #54 & 26. 251-Barks-r/1945 Firestone			
	2	6	16
250-($1.50, 68 pgs.)-Barks-r/4-Color #9	2	6	18
252-277,280: 254-Barks-r/FC #328. 256-Barks-r/FC #147. 257-($1.50,			
52 pgs.)-Barks-r/Vacaction Parade #1. 261-Barks-r/FC #300.			
275-Kelly-r/FC #92. 280 (#1, 2nd Series)	1	3	8
278,279,286: 278,279 ($1.95, 68 pgs.): 278-Rosa-a; Barks-r/FC #263.			
279-Rosa-c; Barks-r/MOC #4. 286-Rosa-a	1	3	9
281,282,284	1	3	7
283-Don Rosa-a, part-c & scripts	1	3	8
285,287-307			5.00
286 ($2.95, 68 pgs.)-Happy Birthday, Donald			6.00
Mini-Comic #1(1976)-(3-1/4x6-1/2"); r/D.D. #150	2	6	14

DONALD DUCK ALBUM (See Comic Album No. 1,3 & Duck Album)
Dell Publishing Co./Gold Key: 5-7/59 - F.C. No. 1239, 10-12/61; 1962; 8/63 - No. 2, Oct, 1963

	GD	FN	NM-
Four Color 995 (#1)	7	21	85
Four Color 1182, 01204-207 (1962-Dell)	6	18	65

	GD	FN	NM-
Four Color 1099,1140,1239-Barks-c	8	24	95
1(8/63-Gold Key)-Barks-c	7	21	80
2(10/63)	6	18	65

DONALD DUCK AND THE CHRISTMAS CAROL
Whitman Publishing Co.: 1960 (A Little Golden Book, 6-3/8"x7-5/8", 28 pgs.)

nn-Story book pencilled by Carl Barks with the intended title "Uncle Scrooge's Christmas Carol." Finished art adapted by Norman McGary. (Rare)-Reprinted in Uncle Scrooge in Color.	30	90	270

DONALD DUCK BEACH PARTY (Also see Dell Giants)
Gold Key: Sept, 1965 (12¢)

1(#10158-509)-Barks-r/WDC&S #45; painted-c	8	24	95

DOOM PATROL, THE (Formerly My Greatest Adventure No. 1-85; see Brave and the Bold, DC Special Blue Ribbon Digest 19, Official... Index & Showcase No. 94-96)
National Periodical Publ.: No. 86, 3/64 - No. 121, 9-10/68; No. 122, 2/73 - No. 124, 6-7/73

	GD	FN	NM-
86-1 pg. origin (#86-121 are 12¢ issues)	11	33	150
87-98: 88-Origin The Chief. 91-Intro. Mento	8	24	105
99-Intro. Beast Boy (later becomes the Changeling in New Teen Titans	10	30	125
100-Origin Beast Boy; Robot-Maniac series begins (12/65)	10	30	125
101-110: 102-Challengers of the Unknown app. 105-Robot-Maniac series ends. 106-Negative Man begins (origin)	6	18	70
111-120	5	15	55
121-Death of Doom Patrol; Orlando-c.	10	30	140
122-124: All reprints	2	6	12

DOOM PATROL
DC Comics (Vertigo imprint #64 on): Oct, 1987 - No, 87, Feb, 1995 (75¢-$1.95, new format)

1-Wraparound-c; Lightle-a		5.00
2-18: 3-1st app. Lodestone. 4-1st app. Karma. 8,15,16-Art Adams-c(i). 18-Invasion tie-in		3.00
19-(2/89)-Grant Morrison scripts begin, ends #63; 1st app Crazy Jane; $1.50-c & new format begins. 1 3 8		
20-30: 29-Superman app. 30-Night Breed fold-out		5.00
31-49,51-56,58-60: 35-1st brief app. of Flex Mentallo. 36-1st full app. of Flex Mentallo. 39-World Without End preview.42-Origin of Flex Mentallo		2.50
50,57 ($2.50, 52 pgs.)		2.50
61-87: 61,70-Photo-c. 73-Death cameo (2 panels)		3.00
...And Suicide Squad 1 (3/88, $1.50, 52 pgs.)-Wraparound-c		2.50
Annual 1 (1988, $1.50, 52 pgs.)		2.50
Annual 2 (1994, $3.95, 68 pgs.)-Children's Crusade tie-in.		4.00
...: Crawling From the Wreckage TPB ('04, $19.95) r/#19-25; Morrison-s		20.00
...: The Painting That Ate Paris TPB ('04, $19.95) r/#26-34; Morrison-s		20.00

DRACULA (See Movie Classics for #1)(Also see Frankenstein & Werewolf)

	GD	FN	NM-

Dell Publ. Co.: No. 2, 11/66 - No. 4, 3/67; No. 6, 7/72 - No. 8, 7/73 (No #5)

2-Origin & 1st app. Dracula (11/66) (super hero)	4	12	50
3,4: 4-Intro. Fleeta ('67)	3	9	32
6-('72)-r/#2 w/origin	3	9	26
7,8-r/#3, #4	2	6	20

DROIDS (Based on Saturday morning cartoon) (Also see Dark Horse Comics)
Marvel Comics (Star Comics): April, 1986 - No. 8, June, 1987

1-R2D2 & C-3PO from Star Wars app. in all	2	6	20
2-8: 2,5,7,8-Williamson-a(i)	2	6	12

NOTE: *Romita* a-3p. *Sinnott* a-3i.

DUCKTALES
Gladstone Publ.: Oct, 1988 - No. 13, May, 1990 (1,2,9-11: $1.50; 3-8: 95¢)

1-Barks-r			6.00
2-11: 2-7,9-11-Barks-r			4.00
12,13 ($1.95, 68 pgs.)-Barks-r; 12-r/F.C. #495			5.00

DUCKTALES (TV)
Disney Comics: June, 1990 - No. 18, Nov, 1991 ($1.50)

1-All new stories			3.00
2-18			2.50
The Movie nn (1990, $7.95, 68 pgs.)-Graphic novel adapting animated movie			9.00

DUDLEY DO-RIGHT (TV)
Charlton Comics: Aug, 1970 - No. 7, Aug, 1971 (Jay Ward)

1	10	30	135
2-7	7	21	90

EARTH X
Marvel Comics: No. 0, Mar, 1999 - No. 12, Apr, 2000 ($3.99/$2.99, lim. series)

nn- (Wizard supplement) Alex Ross sketchbook; painted-c	1	4	10
Sketchbook (2/99) New sketches and previews			6.00
0-(3/99)-Prelude; Leon-a(p)/Ross-c	1	3	7
1-(4/99)-Leon-a(p)/Ross-c	1	3	7
1-2nd printing			3.00
2-12			3.50
#X (6/00, $3.99)			4.00
TPB (12/00, $24.95) r/#0,1-12, X; foreward by Joss Whedon			25.00

EERIE (Magazine)(See Warren Presents)
Warren Publ. Co.: No. 1, Sept, 1965; No. 2, Mar, 1966 - No. 139, Feb, 1983

1-24 pgs., black & white, small size (5-1/4x7-1/4"), low distribution; cover from inside back cover of Creepy No. 2; stories reprinted from Creepy No. 7, 8. At least three different versions exist.

First Printing - B&W, 5-1/4" wide x 7-1/4" high, evenly trimmed. On page 18, panel 5, in the upper left-hand corner, the large rear view of a bald headed man blends into solid black and is unrecognizable. Overall printing quality is poor.

	32	96	500

Second Printing - B&W, 5-1/4x7-1/4", with uneven, untrimmed edges (if one of these

	GD	FN	NM-

were trimmed evenly, the size would be less than as indicated). The figure of the bald headed man on page 18, panel 5 is clear and discernible. The staples have a 1/4" blue stripe.

	15	45	225

Other unauthorized reproductions for comparison's sake would be practically worthless. One known version was probably shot off a first printing copy with some loss of detail; the finer lines tend to disappear in this version which can be determined by looking at the lower right-hand corner of page one, first story. The roof of the house is shaded with straight lines. These lines are sharp and distinct on original, but broken on this version.

NOTE: *The Overstreet Comic Book Price Guide* recommends that, before buying a 1st issue, you consult an expert.

	GD	FN	NM-
2-Frazetta-c; Toth-a; 1st app. host Cousin Eerie	10	30	125
3-Frazetta-c & half pg. ad (rerun in #4); Toth, Williamson, Ditko-a	7	21	90
4-7: 4-Frazetta-a (1/2 pg. ad). 5,7-Frazetta-c. Ditko-a in all.	5	15	55
8-Frazetta-c; Ditko-a	6	18	65
9-11,25: 9,10-Neal Adams-a, Ditko-a. 11-Karloff Mummy adapt.-Wood-s/a. 25-Steranko-c	5	15	60
12-16,18-22,24,32-35,40,45: 12,13,20-Poe-s. 12-Bloch-s. 12,15-Jones-a. 13-Lovecraft-s. 14,16-Toth-a. 16,19,24-Stoker-s. 16,32,33,43-Corben-a. 34-Early Boris-c. 35-Early Brunner-a. 35,40-Early Ploog-a. 40-Frankestein; Ploog-a (6/72, 6 months before Marvel's series)	4	12	40
17-(low distribution)	10	30	140
23-Frazetta-c; Adams-a(reprint)	6	18	70
26-31,36-38,43,44	3	10	35
39,41: 39-1st Dax the Warrior; Maroto-a. 41-(low distribution)	4	12	48
42,51: 42-('73 Annual, 84 pgs.) Spooktacular; Williamson-a. 51-('74 Annual, 76 pgs.) Color poster insert; Toth-a	4	12	45
46,48: 46-Dracula series by Sutton begins; 2pgs. Vampirella. 48-Begin "Mummy Walks" and "Curse of the Werewolf" series (both continue in #49,50,52,53)	4	12	38
47,49,50,52,53: 47-Lilith. 49-Marvin the Dead Thing. 50-Satanna, Daughter of Satan. 52-Hunter by Neary begins. 53-Adams-a	3	10	35
54,55-Color insert Spirit story by Eisner, reprints sections 12/21/47 & 6/16/46 54-Dr. Archaeus series begins	3	9	30
56,57,59,63,69,77,78: All have 8 pg. slick color insert. 56,57,77-Corben-a. 59-(100 pgs.) Summer Special, all Dax issue. 69-Summer Special, all Hunter issue, Neary-a. 78-All Mummy issue	3	9	30
58,60,62,68,72,: 8 pg. slick color insert & Wrightson-a in all. 58,60,62-Corben-a. 60-Summer Giant (9/74, $1.25) 1st Exterminator One; Wood-a. 62-Mummies Walk. 68-Summer Special (84 pgs.)	3	10	35
61,64-67,71: 61-Mummies Walk-s, Wood-a. 64-Corben-a. 64,65,67-Toth-a. 65,66-El Cid. 67-Hunter II. 71-Goblin-c/1st app.	3	9	25
70,73-75	2	6	18
76-1st app. Darklon the Mystic by Starlin-s/a	3	9	32
79,80-Origin Darklon the Mystic by Starlin	3	9	26
81,86,97: 81-Frazetta-c, King Kong; Corben-a. 86-(92 pgs.) All Corben issue. 97-Time Travel/Dinosaur issue; Corben,Adams-a	3	9	24

	GD	FN	NM-
82-Origin/1st app. The Rook	3	9	30
83,85,88,89,91-93,98,99: 98-Rook (31 pgs.). 99-1st Horizon Seekers.			
	2	6	14
84,87,90,96,100: 84,100-Starlin-a. 87-Hunter 3; Nino-a. 87,90-Corben-a.			
96-Summer Special (92 pgs.). 100-(92 pgs.) Anniverary issue; Rook			
(30 pgs.)	2	6	18
94,95-The Rook & Vampirella team-up. 95-Vampirella-c; 1st MacTavish			
	3	9	28
101,106,112,115,118,120,121,128: 101-Return of Hunter II, Starlin-a.			
106-Hard John Nuclear Hit Parade Special, Corben-a. 112-All Maroto			
issue, Luana-s. 115-All José Ortiz issues. 118-1st Haggarth. 120-1st Zud			
Kamish. 121-Hunter/Darklon. 128-Starlin-a, Hsu-a			
	2	6	16
102-105,107-111,113,114,116,117,119,122-124,126,127,129: 104-Beast			
World. 103-105,109-111-Gulacy-a	2	6	14
125-(10/81, 84 pgs.) all Neal Adams issue	2	6	22
130-(76 pgs.) Vampirella-c/sty (54 pgs.); Pantha, Van Helsing, Huntress, Dax,			
Schreck, Hunter, Exterminator One, Rook app.	3	9	28
131-(Lower distr.); all Wood issue	3	9	24
132-134,136: 132-Rook returns. 133-All Ramon Torrents-a issue.			
134,136-Color comic insert	2	6	16
135-(Lower distr., 10/82, 100 pgs.) All Ditko issue	3	9	24
137-139 (lower distr.):137-All Super-Hero issue. 138-Sherlock Holmes.			
138,139-Color comic insert	2	6	20
Yearbook '70-Frazetta-c	5	15	60
Annual '71, '72-Reprints in both	4	12	45

80 PAGE GIANT (...Magazine No. 2-15)
National Periodical Publications: 8/64 - No. 15, 10/65; No. 16, 11/65 - No.
89, 7/71 (25¢)
(All reprints) (#1-56: 84 pgs.; #57-89: 68 pgs.)

	GD	FN	NM-
1-Superman Annual; originally planned as Superman Annual #9 (8/64)			
	41	123	700
2-Jimmy Olsen	25	75	370
3,4: 3-Lois Lane. 4-Flash-G.A.-r; Infantino-a	20	60	290
5-Batman; has Sunday newspaper strip; Catwoman-r; Batman's Life Story-r			
(25th anniversary special)	20	60	290
6-Superman	17	51	255
7-Sgt. Rock's Prize Battle Tales; Kubert-c/a	23	69	340
8-More Secret Origins-origins of JLA, Aquaman, Robin, Atom, & Superman;			
Infantino-a	35	105	560
9-15: 9-Flash (r/Flash #106,117,123 & Showcase #14); Infantino-a.			
10-Superboy. 11-Superman; all Luthor issue. 12-Batman; has Sunday			
newspaper strip. 13-Jimmy Olsen. 14-Lois Lane. 15-Superman and			
Batman; Joker-c/story	17	51	245

ELEKTRA (Also see Daredevil #319-325)
Marvel Comics: Mar, 1995 - No. 4, June, 1995 ($2.95, limited series)

1-4-Embossed-c; Scott McDaniel-a			3.00

ELEKTRA (Also see Daredevil)

	GD	FN	NM-

Marvel Comics: Nov, 1996 - No. 19, Jun, 1998 ($1.95)

1-Peter Milligan scripts; Deodato-c/a			3.00
1-Variant-c			5.00
2-19: 4-Dr. Strange-c/app. 10-Logan-c/app.			2.50
#(-1) Flashback (7/97) Matt Murdock-c/app.; Deodato-c/a			2.50
.../Cyblade (Image, 3/97,$2.95) Devil's Reign pt. 7			3.00

ELEKTRA (Vol. 2) (Marvel Knights)
Marvel Comics: Sept, 2001 - No. 35, Jun, 2004 ($3.50/$2.99)

1-Bendis-s/Austen-a/Horn-c			4.00
2-6: 2-Two covers (Sienkiewicz and Horn) 3,4-Silver Samurai app.			3.00
3-Initial printing with panel of nudity; most copies pulped			18.00
7-35: 7-Rucka-s begin. 9,10,17-Bennett-a. 19-Meglia-a. 23-25-Chen-a; Sienkiewicz-c			3.00
...Vol. 1: Introspect TPB (2002, $16.99) r/#10-15; Marvel Knights: Double Shot #3			17.00
...Vol. 2: Everything Old is New Again TPB (2003, $16.99) r/#16-22			17.00
...Vol. 3: Relentless TPB (2004, $14.99) r/#23-28			15.00
...Vol. 4: Frenzy TPB (2004, $17.99) r/#29-35			18.00

ELEKTRA: ASSASSIN (Also see Daredevil)
Marvel Comics (Epic Comics): Aug, 1986 - No. 8, June, 1987 (Limited series, mature)

1,8-Miller scripts in all; Sienkiewicz-c/a.			6.00
2-7			5.00
Signed & numbered hardcover (Graphitti Designs, $39.95, 2000 print run) reprints 1-8			50.00
TPB (2000, $24.95)			25.00

ELEKTRA LIVES AGAIN (Also see Daredevil)
Marvel Comics (Epic Comics): 1990 ($24.95, oversize, hardcover, 76 pgs.) (Produced by Graphitti Designs)

nn-Frank Miller-c/a/scripts; Lynn Varley painted-a; Matt Murdock & Bullseye app.			35.00
2nd printing (9/02, $24.99)			25.00

ELEKTRA MEGAZINE
Marvel Comics: Nov, 1996 - No. 2, Dec, 1996 ($3.95, 96 pgs., reprints, limited series)

1,2: Reprints Frank Miller's Elektra stories in Daredevil			4.00

EMERGENCY (Magazine)
Charlton Comics: June, 1976 - No. 4, Jan, 1977 (B&W)

1-Neal Adams-c/a; Heath, Austin-a	4	12	40
2,3: 2-N. Adams-c. 3-N. Adams-a.	3	10	35
4-Alcala-a	3	9	25

EMERGENCY (TV)
Charlton Comics: June, 1976 - No. 4, Dec, 1976

1-Staton-c; early Byrne-a (22 pages)	3	10	35
2-4: 2-Staton-c. 2,3-Byrne text illos.	3	9	24

	GD	FN	NM-

EMMA FROST
Marvel Comics: Aug, 2003 - Present ($2.50/$2.99)

1-7-Emma in high school; Bollers-s/Green-a/Horn-c			2.50
8-17-($2.99)			3.00
... Vol. 1: Higher Learning TPB (2004, $7.99, digest size) r/#1-6			8.00

ETERNALS, THE
Marvel Comics Group: July, 1976 - No. 19, Jan, 1978

1-(Regular 25¢ edition)-Origin & 1st app. Eternals	2	6	22
1-(30¢-c variant, limited distribution)	3	9	33
2-(Reg. 25¢ edition)-1st app. Ajak & The Celestials	1	4	10
2-(30¢-c variant, limited distribution)	2	6	15
3-19: 14,15-Cosmic powered Hulk-c/story	1	3	9
12-16-(35¢-c variants, limited distribution)	2	6	14
Annual 1(10/77)	1	3	9
NOTE: *Kirby c/a(p) in all.*

EWOKS (Star Wars) (TV) (See Star Comics Magazine)
Marvel Comics (Star Comics): June, 1985 - No. 14, Jul, 1987 (75¢/$1.00)

1,10: 10-Williamson-a (From Star Wars)	2	6	15
2-9	2	6	12
11-14: 14-($1.00-c)	2	6	14

EXCALIBUR (Also see Marvel Comics Presents #31)
Marvel Comics: Apr, 1988; Oct, 1988 - No. 125, Oct, 1998
($1.50/$1.75/$1.99)

Special Edition nn (The Sword is Drawn)(4/88, $3.25)-1st Excalibur comic			6.00
Special Edition nn (4/88)-no price on-c	1	4	10
Special Edition nn (2nd & print, 10/88, 12/89)			3.00
...The Sword is Drawn (Apr, 1992, $4.95)			5.00
1($1.50, 10/88)-X-Men spin-off; Nightcrawler, Shadowcat(Kitty Pryde), Capt. Britain, Phoenix & Meggan begin			5.00
2-4			4.00
5-10			3.00
11-49,51-70,72-74,76: 10,11-Rogers/Austin-a. 21-Intro Crusader X. 22-Iron Man x-over. 24-John Byrne app. in story. 26-Ron Lim-c/a. 27-B. Smith-a(p). 37-Dr. Doom & Iron Man app. 41-X-Men (Wolverine) app.; Cable cameo. 49-Neal Adams c-swipe. 52,57-X-Men (Cyclops, Wolverine) app. 53-Spider-Man-c/story. 58-X-Men (Wolverine, Gambit, Cyclops, etc.)-c/story. 61-Phoenix returns. 68-Starjammers-c/story			2.50
50-($2.75, 56 pgs.)-New logo			3.00
71-($3.95, 52 pgs.)-Hologram on-c; 30th anniversary			5.00
75-($3.50, 52 pgs.)-Holo-grafx foil-c			4.00
75-($2.25, 52 pgs.)-Regular edition			2.50
77-81,83-86: 77-Begin $1.95-c; bound-in trading card sheet. 83-86-Deluxe Editions and Standard Editions. 86-1st app. Pete Wisdom			2.50
82-($2.50)-Newsstand edition			3.00
82-($3.50)-Enhanced edition			4.00
87-89,91-99,101-110: 87-Return from Age of Apocalypse. 92-Colossus-c/app. 94-Days of Future Tense 95-X-Man-c/app. 96-Sebastian Shaw & the			

Hellfire Club app. 99-Onslaught app. 101-Onslaught tie-in. 102-w/card
insert. 103-Last Warren Ellis scripts; Belasco app. 104,105-Hitch &
Neary-c/a. 109-Spiral-c/app.   2.50
90,100-($2.95)-double-sized. 100-Onslaught tie-in; wraparound-c   4.00
111-124: 111-Begin $1.99-c, wraparound-c. 119-Calafiore-a   2.50
125-($2.99) Wedding of Capt. Britain and Meggan   4.00
Annual 1,2 ('93, '94, 68 pgs.)-1st app. Khaos. 2-X-Men & Psylocke app. 3.00
#(-1) Flashback (7/97)   2.50
...Air Apparent nn (12/91, $4.95)-Simonson-c   5.00
...Mojo Mayhem nn (12/89, $4.50)-Art Adams/Austin-c/a   5.00
...: The Possession nn (7/91, $2.95, 52 pgs.)   3.00
...: XX Crossing (7/92, 5/92-inside, $2.50)-vs. The X-Men   2.50

EXILES (Also see X-Men titles)
Marvel Comics: Aug, 2001 - Present ($2.99/$2.25)

	1	3	7
1-($2.99) Blink and parallel world X-Men; Winick-s/McKone & McKenna-a	1	3	7

2-10-($2.25) 2-Two covers (McKone & JH Williams III). 5-Alpha Flight app.
                                                                     3.00
11-24: 22-Blink leaves; Magik joins. 23,24-Alternate Weapon-X app. 2.25
25-55: 25-Begin $2.99-c; Inhumans app.; Walker-a. 26-30-Austen-s.
   33-Wolverine app. 35-37-Fantastic Four app. 37-Sunfire dies, Blink returns.
   38-40-Hyperion app.   3.00
TPB (3/02, $12.95) r/#1-4   13.00
...: A World Apart TPB (7/02, $14.99) r/#5-11   15.00
...: Vol. 3: Out of Time TPB (2003, $17.99) r/#12-19   18.00
...: Vol. 4: Legacy TPB (2003, $12.99) r/#20-25   13.00
...: Vol. 5: Unnatural Instinct TPB (2003, $14.99) r/#26-30   15.00
...: Vol. 6: Fantastic Voyage TPB (2004, $17.99) r/#31-37   18.00
...: Vol. 7: A Blink in Time TPB (2004, $19.99) r/#38-45   20.00
...: Vol. 8: Earn Your Wings TPB (2004, $14.99) r/#46-51   15.00

EX MACHINA
DC Comics: Aug, 2004 - Present ($2.95)

1-Intro. Mitchell Hundred; Vaughan-s/Harris-a/c   4.00
2-7   3.00

FABLES
DC Comics (Vertigo): July, 2002 - Present ($2.50)

1-Willingham-s/Medina-a; two covers by Maleev & Jean   8.00
2-Medina-a   5.00
3-5   4.00
6-32: 6-10-Buckingham-a. 11-Talbot-a. 18-Medley-a   2.50
6-RRP Edition wraparound variant-c; promotional giveaway for retailers
   (200 printed)   50.00
Animal Farm (2003, $12.95, TPB) r/#6-10; sketch pages by Buckingham &
   Jean   13.00
Legends in Exile (2002, $9.95, TPB) r/#1-5; new short story Willingham-s/a
                                                                     10.00
...: March of the Wooden Soldiers (2004, $17.95, TPB) r/#19-21 & ...: The

	GD	FN	NM-
Last Castle			18.00
...: Storybook Love (2004, $14.95, TPB) r/#11-18			15.00
...: The Last Castle (2003, $5.95) Hamilton-a/Willingham-s; prequel			6.00

FALCON (See Marvel Premiere #49, Avengers #181 & Captain America #117 & 133)
Marvel Comics Group: Nov, 1983 - No. 4, Feb, 1984 (Mini-series)

1-4: 1-Paul Smith-c/a(p). 2-Paul Smith-c/Mark Bright-a. 3-Kupperberg-c			3.00

FAMILY AFFAIR (TV)
Gold Key: Feb, 1970 - No. 4, Oct, 1970 (25¢)

1-With pull-out poster; photo-c	7	21	85
1-With poster missing	3	10	35
2-4: 3,4-Photo-c	4	12	42

FAMOUS FIRST EDITION (See Limited Collectors' Edition)
National Periodical Publications/DC Comics: ($1.00, 10x13-1/2", 72 pgs.)
(No.6-8, 68 pgs.) 1974 - No. 8, Aug-Sept, 1975; C-61, 1979
(Hardbound editions with dust jackets are from Lyle Stuart, Inc.)

C-26-Action Comics #1; gold ink outer-c	5	15	55
C-26-Hardbound edition w/dust jacket	17	51	250
C-28-Detective #27; silver ink outer-c	7	21	80
C-28-Hardbound edition w/dust jacket	22	66	320
C-30-Sensation #1(1974); bronze ink outer-c	5	15	55
C-30-Hardbound edition w/dust jacket	17	51	250
F-4-Whiz Comics #2(#1)(10-11/74)-Cover not identical to original (dropped "Gangway for Captain Marvel" from cover); gold ink on outer-c	5	15	55
F-4-Hardbound edition w/dust jacket	17	51	250
F-5-Batman #1(F-6 inside); silver ink on outer-c	6	18	65
F-5-Hardbound edition w/dust jacket	17	51	250
V2#F-6-Wonder Woman #1	5	15	55
F-6-Wonder Woman #1 Hardbound w/dust jacket	17	51	250
F-7-All-Star Comics #3	5	15	55
F-8-Flash Comics #1(8-9/75)	5	15	55
V8#C-61-Superman #1(1979, $2.00)	4	12	42
V8#C-61 (Whitman variant)	4	12	50

Warning: The above books are almost **exact** reprints of the originals that they represent except for the Giant-Size format. None of the originals are Giant-Size. The first five issues and C-61 were printed with two covers. Reprint information can be found on the outside cover, but not on the inside cover which was reprinted exactly like the original (inside and out).

FAN BOY
DC Comics: Mar, 1999 - No. 6, Aug, 1999 ($2.50, limited series)

1-6: 1-Art by Aragonés and various in all. 2-Green Lantern-c/a by Gil Kane. 3-JLA. 4-Sgt. Rock art by Heath, Marie Severin. 5-Batman art by Sprang, Adams, Miller, Timm. 6-Wonder Woman; art by Rude, Grell			2.50
TPB (2001, $12.95) r/#1-6			13.00

FANTASTIC FOUR
Marvel Comics Group: Nov, 1961 - No. 416, Sept, 1996 (Created by Stan Lee & Jack Kirby)

	GD	FN	NM-

1-Origin & 1st app. The Fantastic Four (Reed Richards: Mr. Fantastic, Johnny Storm: The Human Torch, Sue Storm: The Invisible Girl, & Ben Grimm: The Thing–Marvel's 1st super-hero group since the G.A.; 1st app. S.A. Human Torch); origin/1st app. The Mole Man.

	875	2625	35,000

1-Golden Record Comic Set Reprint (1966)-cover not identical to original

	16	48	240
with Golden Record	24	72	360
2-Vs. The Skrulls (last 10¢ issue)	318	954	7000

3-Fantastic Four don costumes & establish Headquarters; brief 1pg. origin; intro. The Fantasti-Car; Human Torch drawn w/two left hands on-c

	229	687	4800
4-1st S. A. Sub-Mariner app. (5/62)	252	756	5300
5-Origin & 1st app. Doctor Doom	327	981	7200

6-Sub-Mariner, Dr. Doom team up; 1st Marvel villain team-up (2nd S.A. Sub-Mariner app. | 147 | 441 | 2800

7-10: 7-1st app. Kurrgo. 8-1st app. Puppet-Master & Alicia Masters. 9-3rd Sub-Mariner app. 10-Stan Lee & Jack Kirby app. in story

	103	309	1950
11-Origin/1st app. The Impossible Man (2/63)	84	252	1600

12-Fantastic Four vs. The Hulk (1st meeting); 1st Hulk x-over & ties w/Amazing Spider-Man #1 as 1st Marvel x-over; (3/63)

	200	600	4000
13-Intro. The Watcher; 1st app. The Red Ghost	50	150	950

14-19: 14-Sub-Mariner x-over. 15-1st app. Mad Thinker. 16-1st Ant-Man x-over (7/63); Wasp cameo. 18-Origin/1st app. The Super Skrull. 19-Intro. Rama-Tut; Stan Lee & Jack Kirby cameo | 43 | 129 | 725

20-Origin/1st app. The Molecule Man | 44 | 132 | 750

21-Intro. The Hate Monger; 1st Sgt. Fury x-over (12/63)

	41	123	650
22-24: 22-Sue Storm gains more powers	26	78	390

25,26-The Hulk vs. The Thing (their 1st battle). 25-3rd Avengers x-over (1st time w/Captain America)(cameo, 4/64); 2nd S.A. app. Cap (takes place between Avengers #4 & 5. 26-4th Avengers x-over | 51 | 153 | 975

27-1st Doctor Strange x-over (6/64) | 32 | 96 | 500

28-Early X-Men x-over (7/64); same date as X-Men #6

	44	132	750
29,30: 30-Intro. Diablo	24	72	360

31-40: 31-Early Avengers x-over (10/64). 33-1st app. Attuma; part photo-c. 35-Intro/1st app. Dragon Man. 36-Intro/1st app. Madam Medusa & the Frightful Four (Sandman, Wizard, Paste Pot Pete). 39-Wood inks on Daredevil (early x-over) | 19 | 57 | 285

41-44,47: 41-43-Frightful Four app. 44-Intro. Gorgon 11 | 33 | 150

45-Intro/1st app. The Inhumans (c/story, 12/65); also see Incredible Hulk Special #1 & Thor #146, & 147 | 19 | 57 | 285

46-1st Black Bolt-c (Kirby) & 1st full app. | 12 | 36 | 180

48-Partial origin/1st app. The Silver Surfer & Galactus (3/66) by Lee & Kirby; Galactus brief app. in last panel; 1st of 3 part story 53 | 159 | 1000

	GD	FN	NM-
49-2nd app./1st cover Silver Surfer & Galactus	36	108	575
50-Silver Surfer battles Galactus; full S.S.-c	41	123	650
51-Classic "This Man...This Monster" story	16	48	240
52-1st app. The Black Panther (7/66)	29	87	425
53-Origin & 2nd app. The Black Panther	14	42	200
54-Inhumans cameo	10	30	130
55-Thing battles Silver Surfer; 4th app. Silver Surfer	16	48	240
56-Silver Surfer cameo	10	30	135
57-60: Dr. Doom steals Silver Surfer's powers (also see Silver Surfer: Loftier Than Mortals). 59,60-Inhumans cameo	9	27	110
61-65,68-71: 61-Silver Surfer cameo; Sandman-c/s	7	21	80
66-Begin 2 part origin of Him (Warlock); does not app. (9/67)	13	39	185
66,67-2nd printings (1994)	2	6	12
67-Origin/1st brief app. Him (Warlock); 1 page; see Thor #165,166 for 1st full app.	13	39	185
72-Silver Surfer-c/story (pre-dates Silver Surfer #1)	10	30	140
73-Spider-Man, D.D., Thor x-over; cont'd from Daredevil #38	10	30	125
74-77: Silver Surfer app.(#77 is same date/S.S. #1)	8	24	100
78-80	6	18	65
81-88: 81-Crystal joins & dons costume. 82,83-Inhumans app. 84-87-Dr. Doom app. 88-Last 12¢ issue	5	15	60
89-99,101: 94-Intro. Agatha Harkness.	4	12	45
100 (7/70) F.F. vs Thinker and Puppet-Master	10	30	130
102-104: F.F. vs. Sub-Mariner. 104-Magneto-c/story	4	12	45
105-109,111: 108-Last Kirby issue (not in #103-107)	4	12	48
110-Initial version w/green Thing and blue faces and pink uniforms on-c	5	15	55
110-Corrected-c w/accurately colored faces and uniforms and orange Thing	4	12	50
112-Hulk Vs. Thing (7/71)	11	33	160
113-115: 115-Last 15¢ issue	3	10	35
116 (52 pgs.)	5	15	55
117-120	3	9	32
121-123-Silver Surfer-c/stories. 122,123-Galactus	4	12	38
124,125,127,129-149: 129-Intro. Thundra. 130-Sue leaves F.F. 131-Quicksilver app. 132-Medusa joins. 133-Thundra Vs. Thing. 142-Kirbyish-a by Buckler begins. 143-Dr. Doom-c/story. 147-Sub-Mariner	3	9	24
126-Origin F.F. retold; cover swipe of F.F. #1	3	9	28
128-Four pg. insert of F.F. Friends & Foes	3	9	28
150-Crystal & Quicksilver's wedding	3	9	30
151-154,158-160: 151-Origin Thundra. 159-Medusa leaves; Sue rejoins	2	6	14
155-157: Silver Surfer in all	2	6	20
161-165,168,174-180: 164-The Crusader (old Marvel Boy) revived (origin #165); 1st app. Frankie Raye. 168-170-Cage app. 176-Re-intro Impossible Man; Marvel artists app. 180-r/#101 by Kirby	1	3	9
166,167-vs. Hulk	2	6	18

	GD	FN	NM-
169-173-(Regular 25¢ edition)(4-8/75)	1	3	9
169-173-(30¢-c, limited distribution)	2	6	14

181-199: 189-G.A. Human Torch app. & origin retold. 190,191-Fantastic Four
break up ... 1 ... 3 ... 8

| 183-187-(35¢-c variants, limited dist.)(6-10/77) | 2 | 6 | 12 |
| 200-(11/78, 52 pgs.)-F.F. re-united vs. Dr. Doom | 2 | 6 | 14 |

201-208,219,222-231: 207-Human Torch vs. Spider-Man-c/story. 211-1st app.
Terrax. 224-Contains unused alternate-c for FF #3 and pin-ups ... 5.00
209-216,218,220,221-Byrne-a. 209-1st Herbie the Robot. 220-Brief origin 6.00
217-Early app. Dazzler (4/80); by Byrne ... 6.00
232-Byrne-a begins ... 6.00
233-235,237-249,251-260: All Byrne-a. 238-Origin Frankie Raye. 244-Frankie
Raye becomes Nova, Herald of Galactus. 252-Reads sideways; Annihilus
app.; contains skin "Tattooz" decals ... 5.00
236-20th Anniversary issue(11/81, 68 pgs., $1.00)-Brief origin F.F.;
Byrne-c/a(p); new Kirby-a(p) ... 6.00
250-(52 pgs)-Spider-Man x-over; Byrne-a; Skrulls impersonate New X-Men
... 6.00
261-285: 261-Silver Surfer. 262-Origin Galactus; Byrne writes & draws himself
into story. 264-Swipes-c of F.F. #1. 274-Spider-Man's alien costume app.
(4th app., 1/85, 2 pgs.) ... 4.00
286-2nd app. X-Factor continued from Avengers #263; story continues in
X-Factor #1 ... 5.00
287-295: 291-Action Comcis #1 cover swipe. 292-Nick Fury app. 293-Last
Byrne-a ... 3.00
296-($1.50)-Barry Smith-c/a; Thing rejoins ... 4.00
297-318,321-330: 300-Johnny Storm & Alicia Masters wed. 306-New team
begins (9/87). 311-Re-intro The Black Panther. 327-Mr. Fantastic &
Invisible Girl return ... 3.00
319,320: 319-Double size. 320-Thing vs. Hulk ... 4.00
331-346,351-357,359,360: 334-Simonson-c/scripts begin. 337-Simonson-a
begins. 342-Spider-Man cameo. 356-F.F. vs. The New Warriors; Paul
Ryan-c/a begins. 360-Last $1.00-c ... 2.50
347-Ghost Rider, Wolverine, Spider-Man, Hulk-c/stories thru #349; Arthur
Adams-c/a(p) in each ... 4.00
347,348-Gold 2nd printing ... 2.50
348-350: 350-($1.50, 52 pgs.)-Dr. Doom app. ... 3.00
358-(11/91, $2.25, 88 pgs.)-30th anniversary issue; gives history of F.F.;
die cut-c; Art Adams back-up story-a ... 3.00
361-368,370,372-374,376-380,382-386: 362-Spider-Man app. 367-Wolverine
app. (brief). 370-Infinity War x-over; Thanos & Magus app. 374-Secret
Defenders (Ghost Rider, Hulk, Wolverine) x-over ... 2.25
369-Infinity War x-over; Thanos app. ... 2.50
371-All white embossed-c ($2.00) ... 4.00
371-All red 2nd printing ($2.00) ... 2.50
375-($2.95, 52 pgs.)-Holo-grafx foil-c; ann. issue ... 3.00
376-($2.95)-Variant polybagged w/Dirt Magazine #4 and music tape ... 5.00
381-Death of Reed Richards (Mister Fantastic) & Dr. Doom ... 4.00
387-Newsstand ed. ($1.25) ... 2.25

	GD	FN	NM-
387-($2.95)-Collector's Ed. w/Die-cut foil-c			3.00
388-393,395-397: 388-bound-in trading card sheet. 394-($1.50-c)			2.25
394,398,399: 394 ($2.95)-Collector's Edition-polybagged w/16 pg. Marvel Action Hour book and acetate print; pink logo. 398,399-Rainbow Foil-c			3.00
400-Rainbow-Foil-c			4.00
401-415: 401,402-Atlantis Rising. 407,408-Return of Reed Richards. 411-Inhumans app. 414-Galactus vs. Hyperstorm. 415-Onslaught tie-in; X-Men app.			2.25
416-($2.50)-Onslaught tie-in; Dr. Doom app.; wraparound-c			3.00

#500-up (See Fantastic Four Vol. 3; series resumed original numbering after Vol. 3 #70)

	GD	FN	NM-
Annual 1('63)-Origin F.F.; Ditko-i; early Spidey app.	68	204	1300
Annual 2('64)-Dr. Doom origin & c/story	38	114	600
Annual 3('65)-Reed & Sue wed; r/#6,11	17	51	250
Special 4(11/66)-G.A. Torch x-over (1st S.A. app.) & origin retold; r/#25,26 (Hulk vs. Thing). Torch vs. Torch battle	12	36	165
Special 5(11/67)-New art; Intro. Psycho-Man; early Black Panther, Inhumans & Silver Surfer (1st solo story) app.	12	36	170
Special 6(11/68)-Intro. Annihilus; birth of Franklin Richards; new 48 pg. movie length epic; last non-reprint annual	8	24	100
Special 7(11/69)-r/F.F. #1,2; Marvel staff photos	4	12	42
Special 8-10: All reprints. 8(12/70)-F.F. vs. Sub-Mariner plus gallery of F.F. foes. 9(12/71). 10('73)	3	9	28
Annual 11-14: 11(1976)-New art begins again. 12(1978). 13(1978). 14(1979)	1	3	9
Annual 15-17: 15('80-'94, 68 pgs.).17(1983)-Byrne-c/a			5.00
Annual 18-27: 21(1988)-Evolutionary War x-over. 22-Atlantis Attacks x-over; Sub-Mariner & The Avengers app.; Buckler-a. 23-Byrne-c; Guice-p. 24-2 pg. origin recap of Fantastic Four; Guardians of the Galaxy x-over. 25-Moondragon story. 26-Bagged w/card			3.00
Special Edition 1(5/84)-r/Annual #1; Byrne-c/a			3.00
...: Monsters Unleashed nn (1992, $5.95)-r/F.F. #347-349 w/new Arthur Adams-c			6.00
...: Nobody Gets Out Alive (1994, $15.95) TPB r/ #387-392			16.00
... Visionaries (11/01, $19.95) r/#232-240 by John Byrne			20.00
... Visionaries Vol. 2 (2004, $24.99) r/#241-250 by John Byrne			25.00

FANTASTIC FOUR (Volume Two)
Marvel Comics: V2#1, Nov, 1996 - No. 13, Nov, 1997 ($2.95/$1.95/$1.99)
(Produced by WildStorm Productions)

	GD	FN	NM-
1-($2.95)-Reintro Fantastic Four; Jim Lee-c/a; Brandon Choi scripts; Mole Man app.			5.00
1-($2.95)-Variant-c	1	3	7
2-9: 2-Namor-c/app. 3-Avengers-c/app. 4-Two covers; Dr. Doom cameo			3.00
10,11,13: All $1.99-c. 13-"World War 3"-pt. 1, x-over w/Image			3.00
12-($2.99) "Heroes Reunited"-pt. 1			4.00
...: Heroes Reborn (7/00, $17.95, TPB) r/#1-6			18.00

FANTASTIC FOUR (Volume Three)

	GD	FN	NM-

Marvel Comics: V3#1, Jan, 1998 - Present ($2.99/$1.99/$2.25)

1-($2.99)-Heroes Return; Lobdell-s/Davis & Farmer-a			5.00
1-Alternate Heroes Return-c	1	3	7
2-4,12: 2-Two covers. 4-Claremont-s/Larroca-a begin; Silver Surfer c/app.			
12-($2.99) Wraparound-c by Larroca			4.00
5-11: 6-Heroes For Hire app. 9-Spider-Man-c/app.			3.00
13-24: 13,14-Ronan-c/app.			2.50
25-($2.99) Dr. Doom returns			3.00
26-49: 27-Dr. Doom marries Sue. 30-Begin $2.25-c. 32,42-Namor-c/app.			
35-Regular cover; Pacheco-s/a begins. 37-Super-Skrull-c/app. 38-New			
Baxter Building			2.25
35-($3.25) Variant foil enhanced-c; Pacheco-s/a begins			3.25
50-($3.99, 64 pgs.) BWS-c; Grummett, Pacheco, Rude, Udon-a			4.00
51-53,55-59: 51-53-Bagley-a(p)/Wieringo-c; Inhumans app. 55,56-Immonen-a			
57-59-Warren-s/Grant-a			2.25
54-($3.50, 100 pgs.) Birth of Valeria; r/Annual #6 birth of Franklin			3.50
60-(9¢-c) Waid-s/Wieringo-a begin			2.25
60-($2.25 newsstand edition)(also see Promotional Comics section)			2.25
61-70: 62-64-FF vs. Modulus. 68-70-Dr. Doom app.			2.25

**(After #70 [Aug, 2003] numbering reverted back to original Vol. 1
with #500, Sept, 2003)**

500-($3.50) Regular edition; concludes Dr. Doom app.; Dr. Strange app.;			
Rivera painted-c			3.50
500-($4.99) Director's Cut Edition; chromium-c by Wieringo; sketch and			
script pages			8.00
501-516: 501,502-Casey Jones-a. 503-508-Porter-a. 509-Wieringo-c/a			
resumes. 512,513-Spider-Man app. 514-516-Ha-c/Medina-a			2.25
517-520: 517-Begin $2.99-c. 519,520-Galactus app.			3.00
...'98 Annual ($3.50) Immonen-a			3.50
...'99 Annual ($3.50) Ladronn-a			3.50
...'00 Annual ($3.50) Larocca-a; Marvel Girl back-up story			3.50
...'01 Annual ($2.99) Maguire-a; Thing back-up w/Yu-a			3.00
Fantastic 4th Voyage of Sinbad (9/01, $5.95) Claremont-s/Ferry-a			6.00
Flesh and Stone (8/01, $12.95, TPB) r/#35-39			13.00
... Vol. 1 HC (2004, $29.99, TPB) oversized reprint /#60-70, 500-502; Mark			
Waid intro and series proposal; cover gallery			30.00
... Vol. 1: Imaginauts (2003, $17.99, TPB) r/#56,60-66; Mark Waid's series			
proposal			18.00
... Vol. 2: Unthinkable (2003, $17.99, TPB) r/#67-70,500-502; #500 Director's			
Cut extras			18.00
... Vol. 3: Authoritative Action (2004, $12.99, TPB) r/#503-508			13.00
... Vol. 4: Hereafter (2004, $11.99, TPB) r/#509-513			12.00
Wizard #1/2 -Lim-a			10.00

FANTASTIC FOUR: 1 2 3 4
Marvel Comics: Oct, 2001 - No. 4, Jan, 2002 ($2.99, limited series)

1-4-Morrison-s/Jae Lee-a. 2-4-Namor-c/app.			3.00
TPB (2002, $9.99) r/#1-4			10.00

FANTASTIC FOUR ROAST

	GD	FN	NM-

Marvel Comics Group: May, 1982 (75¢, one-shot, direct sales)

1-Celebrates 20th anniversary of F.F.#1; X-Men, Ghost Rider & many others
   cameo; Golden, Miller, Buscema, Rogers, Byrne, Anderson art;
   Hembeck/Austin-c   4.00

FANTASTIC FOUR: WORLD'S GREATEST COMICS MAGAZINE
Marvel Comics: Feb, 2001 - No. 12 (Limited series)

1-12: Homage to Lee & Kirby era of F.F.; s/a by Larsen & various.
   5-Hulk-c/app. 10-Thor app.   3.00

FANTASTIC VOYAGES OF SINDBAD, THE
Gold Key: Oct, 1965 - No. 2, June, 1967

1-Painted-c on both	7	21	90
2	6	18	70

FAT ALBERT (...& the Cosby Kids) (TV)
Gold Key: Mar, 1974 - No. 29, Feb, 1979

1	4	12	42
2-10	2	6	22
11-29	2	6	16

FATHOM
Image Comics (Top Cow Prod.): Aug, 1998 - No. 14, May, 2002 ($2.50)

Preview	12.00
0-Wizard supplement	7.00
0-($6.95) DF Alternate	7.00
1/2 (Wizard) origin of Cannon; Turner-a	6.00
1/2 (3/03, $2.99) origin of Cannon	3.00
1-Turner-s/a; three covers; alternate story pages	6.00
1-Wizard World Ed.	9.00
2-14: 12-14-Witchblade app. 13,14-Tomb Raider app.	3.00
9-Green foil-c edition	15.00
9,12-Holofoil editions	18.00
12,13-DFE alternate-c	6.00
13,14-DFE Gold edition	8.00
14-DFE Blue	15.00
... Collected Edition 1 (3/99, $5.95) r/Preview & all three #1's	6.00
... Collected Edition 2-4 (3-12/99, $5.95) 2-r/#2,3. 3-r/#4,5. 4-r/#6,7	6.00
... Collected Edition 5 (4/00, $5.95) 5-r/#8,9	6.00
... Swimsuit Special (5/99, $2.95) Pin-ups by various	3.00
... Swimsuit Special 2000 (12/00, $2.95) Pin-ups by various; Turner-c	3.00
Michael Turner's Fathom HC ('01, $39.95) r/#1-9, black-c w/silver foil	40.00
Michael Turner's Fathom SC ('01, $24.95) r/#1-9, new Turner-c	25.00

FATMAN, THE HUMAN FLYING SAUCER
Lightning Comics(Milson Publ. Co.): April, 1967 - No. 3, Aug-Sept, 1967
(68 pgs.) (Written by Otto Binder)

1-Origin/1st app. Fatman & Tinman by Beck	7	21	80
2-C. C. Beck-a	4	12	50
3-(Scarce)-Beck-a	7	21	90

	GD	FN	NM-

FEAR (Adventure into…)
Marvel Comics Group: Nov, 1970 - No. 31, Dec, 1975

	GD	FN	NM-
1-Fantasy & Sci-Fi-r in early issues; 68 pg. Giant size; Kirby-a(r)	5	15	55
2-6: 2-4-(68 pgs.). 5,6-(52 pgs.) Kirby-a(r)	3	9	32
7-9-Kirby-a(r)	2	6	18
10-Man-Thing begins (10/72, 4th app.), ends #19; see Savage Tales #1 for 1st app.; 1st solo series; Chaykin/Morrow-c/a;	4	12	45
11,12: 11-N. Adams-c. 12-Starlin/Buckler-a	2	6	20
13,14,16-18: 17-Origin/1st app. Wundarr	2	6	16
15-1st full-length Man-Thing story (8/73)	2	6	20
19-Intro. Howard the Duck; Val Mayerik-a (12/73)	4	12	45
20-Morbius, the Living Vampire begins, ends #31; has history recap of Morbius with X-Men & Spider-Man	4	12	45
21-23,25	2	6	16
24-Blade-c/sty	3	9	30
26-31	2	6	12

FELICIA HARDY: THE BLACK CAT
Marvel Comics: July, 1994 - No. 4, Oct, 1994 ($1.50, limited series)

1-4: 1,4-Spider-Man app.			2.25

FINAL NIGHT, THE (See DC related titles and Parallax: Emerald Night)
DC Comics: Nov, 1996 - No. 4, Nov, 1996 ($1.95, weekly limited series)

1-4: Kesel-s/Immonen-a(p) in all. 4-Parallax's final acts			3.50
Preview			2.25
TPB-(1998, $12.95) r/#1-4, Parallax: Emerald Night #1, and preview			13.00

FIRESIDE BOOK SERIES (Hard and soft cover editions)
Simon and Schuster: 1974 - 1980 (130-260 pgs.), Square bound, color

		GD	FN	NM-
Amazing Spider-Man, The, 1979, 130 pgs., $3.95, Bob Larkin-c	HC	10	30	125
	SC	6	18	75
America At War–The Best of DC War Comics, 1979, $6.95, 260 pgs, Kubert-c	HC	13	39	185
	SC	9	27	110
Best of Spidey Super Stories (Electric Company) 1978, $3.95,	SC	7	21	90
Bring On The Bad Guys (Origins of the Marvel Comics Villains) 1976, $6.95, 260 pgs.; Romita-c	HC	9	27	120
	SC	6	18	70
Captain America, Sentinel of Liberty,1979, 130 pgs., $12.95, Cockrum-c	HC	10	30	125
	SC	6	18	75
Doctor Strange Master of the Mystic Arts, 1980, 130 pgs.	HC	10	30	125
	SC	6	18	75
Fantastic Four, The, 1979, 130 pgs.	HC	9	27	120
	SC	6		70
Heart Throbs–The Best of DC Romance Comics, 1979, 260 pgs., $6.,95	HC	18	54	260
	SC	11	33	150

		GD	FN	NM-
Incredible Hulk, The, 1978, 260 pgs. (8 1/4" x 11")	HC	9	27	120
	SC	6	18	70
Marvel's Greatest Superhero Battles, 1978, 260 pgs., $6.95, Romita-c	HC	11	33	155
	SC	7	21	90
Mysteries in Space, 1980, $7,95, Anderson-c. r-DC sci/fi stories	HC	10	30	140
	SC	7	21	80
Origins of Marvel Comics, 1974, 260 pgs., $5.95. r-covers & origins of Fantastic Four, Hulk, Spider-Man, Thor, & Doctor Strange	HC	9	27	120
	SC	6	18	70
Silver Surfer, The, 1978, 130 pgs., $4.95, Norem-c	HC	10	30	125
	SC	7	21	80
Son of Origins of Marvel Comics, 1975, 260 pgs., $6.95, Romita-c. Reprints covers & origins of X-Men, Iron Man, Avengers, Daredevil, Silver Surfer	HC	9	27	120
	SC	6	18	70
Superhero Women, The–Featuring the Fabulous Females of Marvel Comics, 1977, 260 pgs., $6.95, Romita-c	HC	11	33	155
	SC	7	21	90

Note: Prices listed are for 1st printings. Later printings have lesser value.

FIRESTORM (See Cancelled Comic Cavalcade, DC Comics Presents, Flash #289, The Fury of… & Justice League of America #179)
DC Comics: March, 1978 - No. 5, Oct-Nov, 1978

1,5: 1-Origin & 1st app.	1	4	10
2-4: 2-Origin Multiplex. 3-Origin & 1st app. Killer Frost. 4-1st app. Hyena			6.00

FIRESTORM
DC Comics: July, 2004 - Present ($2.50)

1-6: 1-Intro. Jason Rusch; Jolley-s/ChrisCross-a. 6-Identity Crisis tie-in. 7-Bloodhound x-over. 8-Killer Frost returns	2.50

FIRESTORM, THE NUCLEAR MAN (Formerly Fury of Firestorm)
DC Comics: No. 65, Nov, 1987 - No. 100, Aug, 1990

65-99: 66-1st app. Zuggernaut; Firestorm vs. Green Lantern. 71-Death of Capt. X. 67,68-Millennium tie-ins. 83-1st new look	2.50
100-($2.95, 68 pgs.)	4.00
Annual 5 (10/87)-1st app. new Firestorm	3.00

1ST ISSUE SPECIAL
National Periodical Publications: Apr, 1975 - No. 13, Apr, 1976 (Tryout series)

1,6: 1-Intro. Atlas; Kirby-c/a/script. 6-Dingbats	2	6	15
2,12: 2-Green Team (see Cancelled Comic Cavalcade). 12-Origin/1st app. "Blue" Starman (2nd app. in Starman, 2nd Series #3); Kubert-c	1	4	10
3-Metamorpho by Ramona Fradon	1	4	10
4,10,11: 4-Lady Cop. 10-The Outsiders. 11-Code Name: Assassin; Grell-c	1	3	9

	GD	FN	NM-
5-Manhunter; Kirby-c/a/script	2	6	18
7,9: 7-The Creeper by Ditko (c/a). 9-Dr. Fate; Kubert-c/Simonson-a.	2	6	15
8,13: 8-Origin/1st app. The Warlord; Grell-c/a (11/75). 13-Return of the New Gods; Darkseid app.; 1st new costume Orion; predates New Gods #12 by more than a year	3	9	26

FLASH, THE (1st Series)(Formerly Flash Comics)(See Showcase #4,8,13,14)
National Periodical Publ./DC: No. 105, Feb-Mar, 1959 - No. 350, Oct, 1985

	GD	FN	NM-
105-(2-3/59)-Origin Flash(retold), & Mirror Master (1st app.)	423	1269	9300
106-Origin Grodd & Pied Piper; Flash's 1st visit to Gorilla City; begin Grodd the Super Gorilla trilogy (Scarce)	145	435	2750
107-Grodd trilogy, part 2	75	225	1425
108-Grodd trilogy ends	63	189	1200
109-2nd app. Mirror Master	50	150	875
110-Intro/origin Kid Flash who later becomes Flash in Crisis On Infinite Earths #12; begin Kid Flash trilogy, ends #112 (also in #114,116,118); 1st app. & origin of The Weather Wizard	121	363	2300
111-2nd Kid Flash tryout; Cloud Creatures	41	123	650
112-Origin & 1st app. Elongated Man (4-5/60); also apps. in #115,119,130	46	138	775
113-Origin & 1st app. Trickster	41	123	650
114-Captain Cold app. (see Showcase #8)	32	96	500
115,116,118-120: 119-Elongated Man marries Sue Dearborn. 120-Flash & Kid Flash team-up for 1st time	25	75	375
117-Origin & 1st app. Capt. Boomerang; 1st & only S.A. app. Winky Blinky & Noddy	31	93	460
121,122: 122-Origin & 1st app. The Top	19	57	285
123-(9/61)-Re-intro. Golden Age Flash; origins of both Flashes; 1st mention of Earth II where DC Golden Age heroes live	116	348	2200
124-Last 10¢ issue	16	48	230
125-128,130: 127-Return of Grodd-c/story. 128-Origin & 1st app. Abra Kadabra. 130-(7/62)-1st Gauntlet of Super-Villains (Mirror Master, Capt. Cold, The Top, Capt. Boomerang & Trickster)	15	45	220
129-2nd G.A. Flash x-over; J.S.A. cameo in flashback (1st S.A. app. G.A. Green Lantern, Hawkman, Atom, Black Canary & Dr. Mid-Nite. Wonder Woman (1st S.A. app.?) appears)	29	87	435
131-136,138,140: 131-Early Green Lantern x-over (9/62). 135-1st app. of Kid Flash's yellow costume (3/63). 136-1st Dexter Miles. 140-Origin & 1st app. Heat Wave	13	39	190
137-G.A. Flash x-over; J.S.A. cameo (1st S.A. app.)(1st real app. since 2-3/51); 1st S.A. app. Vandal Savage & Johnny Thunder; JSA team decides to re-form	41	123	675
139-Origin & 1st app. Prof. Zoom	14	42	200
141-150: 142-Trickster app.	10	30	140
151-Engagement of Barry Allen & Iris West; G.A. Flash vs. The Shade.	13	39	185
152-159	9	27	120
160-(80-Pg. Giant G-21); G.A. Flash & Johnny Quick-r			

	GD	FN	NM-
	13	39	185
161-164,166,167: 167-New facts about Flash's origin	8	24	100
165-Barry Allen weds Iris West	9	27	110
168,170: 168-Green Lantern-c/app. 170-Dr. Mid-Nite, Dr. Fate, G.A. Flash			
x-over	8	24	100
169-(80-Pg. Giant G-34)-New facts about origin	10	30	130
171,172,174,176,177,179,180: 171-JLA, Green Lantern, Atom flashbacks.			
174-Barry Allen reveals I.D. to wife. 179-(5/68)-Flash travels to Earth-Prime			
and meets DC editor Julie Schwartz; 1st unnamed app. Earth-Prime (See			
Justice League of America #123 for 1st named app. & 3rd app. overall)			
	7	21	90
173-G.A. Flash x-over	8	24	100
175-2nd Superman/Flash race (12/67) (See Superman #199 & World's Finest			
#198,199); JLA cameo; gold kryptonite used (on J'onn J'onzz			
impersonating Superman)	16	48	240
178-(80-Pg. Giant G-46)	9	27	120
181-186,188,189: 186-Re-intro. Sargon. 189-Last 12¢-c			
	6	18	75
187,196: (68-Pg. Giants G-58, G-70)	7	21	90
190-195,197-199	5	15	55
200	6	18	65
201-204,206,207: 201-New G.A. Flash story. 206-Elongated Man begins			
207-Last 15¢ issue	4	12	40
205-(68-Pg. Giant G-82)	6	18	70
208-213-(52 pg.): 211-G.A. Flash origin-r/#104. 213-Reprints #137			
	4	12	45
214-DC 100 Page Super Spectacular DC-11; origin Metal Men-r/Showcase			
#37; never before published G.A. Flash story	8	24	100
215 (52 pgs.)-Flash-r/Showcase #4; G.A. Flash x-over, continued in #216			
	4	12	50
216,220: 220-1st app. Turtle since Showcase #4	3	9	30
217-219: Neal Adams-a in all. 217-Green Lantern/Green Arrow series begins			
(9/72); 2nd G.L. & G.A. team-up series (see Green Lantern #76).			
219-Last Green Arrow	4	12	50
221-225,227,228,230,231,233: 222-G. Lantern x-over. 228-(7-8/74)-Flash			
writer Cary Bates travels to Earth-One & meets Flash, Iris Allen &			
Trickster; 2nd unnamed app. Earth-Prime (See Justice League of America			
#123 for 1st named app. & 3rd app. overall)	2	6	20
226-Neal Adams-p	3	9	28
229,232-(100 pg. issues)-G.A. Flash-r & new-a	5	15	55
234-250: 235-Green Lantern x-over. 243-Death of The Top. 245-Origin The			
Floronic Man in Green Lantern back-up, ends #246. 246-Last Green			
Lantern. 247-Jay Garrick app. 250-Intro Golden Glider			
	2	6	15
251-274: 256-Death of The Top retold. 265-267-(44 pgs.). 267-Origin of			
Flash's uniform. 270-Intro The Clown	1	4	10
268,273-276,278,283,286-(Whitman variants; low print run; no issue #s			
shown on covers	2	6	12
275,276-Iris Allen dies	2	6	12

	GD	FN	NM-
277-288,290: 286-Intro/origin Rainbow Raider	1	3	7
289-1st Perez DC art (Firestorm); new Firestorm back-up series begins (9/80), ends #304	1	3	9
291-299,301-305: 291-1st app. Saber-Tooth (villain). 295-Gorilla Grodd-c/story. 298-Intro/origin new Shade. 301-Atomic bomb-c. 303-The Top returns. 304-Intro/origin Colonel Computron; 305-G.A. Flash x-over			5.00
300-(52 pgs.)-Origin Flash retold; 25th ann. issue	1	3	7
306-313-Dr. Fate by Giffen. 309-Origin Flash retold			5.00
314-340: 318-323-Creeper back-ups. 323,324-Two part Flash vs. Flash story. 324-Death of Reverse Flash (Professor Zoom). 328-Iris West Allen's death retold. 329-JLA app. 340-Trial of the Flash begins			4.00
341-349: 344-Origin Kid Flash			5.00
350-Double size ($1.25) Final issue			6.00
Annual 1 (10-12/63, 84 pgs.)-Origin Elongated Man & Kid Flash-r; origin Grodd; G.A. Flash-r	39	117	625
Annual 1 Replica Edition (2001, $6.95)-Reprints the entire 1963 Annual			7.00
The Flash Spectacular (See DC Special Series No. 11)			
The Life Story of the Flash (1997, $19.95, Hardcover) "Iris Allen's" chronicle of Barry Allen's life; comic panels w/additional text; Waid & Augustyn-s; Kane & Staton-a/Orbik painted-c			20.00
The Life Story of the Flash (1998, $12.95, Softcover) New Orbik-c			13.00

FLASH (2nd Series)(See Crisis on Infinite Earths #12 and Justice League Europe)

DC Comics: June, 1987 - Present (75¢-$2.25)

1-Guice-c/a begins; New Teen Titans app.	1	4	10
2-10: 3-Intro. Kilgore. 5-Intro. Speed McGee. 7-1st app. Blue Trinity. 8,9-Millennium tie-ins. 9-1st app. The Chunk			4.00
11-61: 12-Free extra 16 pg. Dr. Light story. 19-Free extra 16 pg. Flash story. 28-Capt. Cold app. 29-New Phantom Lady app. 40-Dr. Alchemy app. 50-($1.75, 52 pgs.)			3.00
62-78,80: 62-Flash: Year One begins, ends #65. 65-Last $1.00-c. 66-Aquaman app. 69,70-Green Lantern app. 70-Gorilla Grodd story ends. 73-Re-intro Barry Allen & begin saga ("Barry Allen's" true ID revealed in #78). 76-Re-intro of Max Mercury (Quality Comics' Quicksilver), not in uniform until #77. 80-($1.25-c) Regular Edition			4.00
79,80 ($2.50): 79-(68 pgs.) Barry Allen saga ends. 80-Foil-c			5.00
81-91,93,94,0,95-99,101: 81,82-Nightwing & Starfire app. 84-Razer app. 94-Zero Hour. 0-(10/94). 95-"Terminal Velocity" begins, ends #100. 96,98,99-Kobra app. 97-Origin Max Mercury; Chillblaine app.			4.00
92-1st Impulse	1	4	10
100 ($2.50)-Newstand edition; Kobra & JLA app.			4.00
100 ($3.50)-Foil-c edition; Kobra & JLA app.			5.00
102-131: 102-Mongul app.; begin-$1.75-c. 105-Mirror Master app. 107-Shazam app. 108-"Dead Heat" begins; 1st app. Savitar. 109-"Dead Heat" Pt. 2 (cont'd in Impulse #10). 110-"Dead Heat" Pt. 4 (cont'd in Impulse #11). 111-"Dead Heat" finale; Savitar disappears into the Speed Force; John Fox cameo (2nd app.). 112-"Race Against Time" begins, ends #118; re-intro John Fox. 113-Tornado Twins app. 119-Final Night x-over.			

                                                    GD   FN   NM-

127-129-Rogue's Gallery & Neron. 128,129-JLA-app.130-Morrison &
   Millar-s begin   3.00
132-150: 135-GL & GA app. 142-Wally almost marries Linda; Waid-s return.
   144-Cobalt Blue origin. 145-Chain Lightning begins.147-Professor Zoom
   app. 149-Barry Allen app. 150-($2.95) Final showdown with Cobalt Blue
                                                                          3.00
151-162: 151-Casey-s. 152-New Flash-c. 154-New Flash ID revealed.
   159-Wally marries Linda. 162-Last Waid-s.   2.50
163-187,189-196,198,199,201-206: 163-Begin $2.25-c. 164-186-Bolland-c.
   183-New Trickster. 196-Winslade-a. 205-Batman-c/app.   2.25
188-($2.95) Mirror Master, Weather Wizard, Trickster app.   3.00
197-Origin of Zoom (6/03)   6.00
200-($3.50) Flash vs. Zoom; Barry Allen & Hal Jordan app.; wraparound-c
                                                                          3.50

207-216: 207-211-Turner-c/Porter-a. 209-JLA app. 210-Nightwing app.
   212-Origin Mirror Master. 214-216-Identity Crisis x-over   2.25
#1,000,000 (11/98) 853rd Century x-over   2.50
Annual 1-7,9: 2-('87-'94,'96, 68 pgs), 3-Gives history of G.A.,S.A., & Modern
   Age Flash in text. 4-Armaggedon 2001. 5-Eclipso-c/story. 7-Elseworlds
   story. 9-Legends of the Dead Earth story; J.H. Williams-a(p)   3.00
Annual 8 (1995, $3.50)-Year One story   3.50
Annual 10 (1997, $3.95)-Pulp Heroes stories   4.00
Annual 11,12 ('98, '99)-11-Ghosts; Wrightson-c. 12-JLApe; Art Adams-c   3.00
Annual 13 ('00, $3.50) Planet DC; Alcatena-c/a   3.50
...: Blitz (2004, $19.95, TPB)-r/#192-200; Kolins-c   20.00
...: Blood Will Run (2002, $17.95, TPB)-r/#170-176, Secret Files #3   18.00
...: Crossfire (2004, $17.95, TPB)-r/#183-191 & parts of Flash Secret Files #3
                                                                         18.00
Dead Heat (2000, $14.95, TPB)-r/#108-111, Impulse #10,11   15.00
...80-Page Giant (8/98, $4.95) Flash family stories by Waid, Millar and others;
   Mhan-c   5.00
...80-Page Giant 2 (4/99, $4.95) Stories of Flash family, future Kid Flash,
   original Teen Titans and XS   5.00
...: Iron Heights (2001, $5.95)-Van Sciver-c/a; intro. Murmur   6.00
...: Our Worlds at War 1 (10/01, $2.95)-Jae Lee-c; Black Racer app.   3.00
...Plus 1 (1/1997, $2.95)-Nightwing-c/app.   3.00
Race Against Time (2001, $14.95, TPB)-r/#112-118   15.00
...: Rogues (2003, $14.95, TPB)-r/#177-182   15.00
...Secret Files 1 (11/97, $4.95) Origin-s & pin-ups   5.00
...Secret Files 2 (11/99, $4.95) Origin of Replicant   5.00
...Secret Files 3 (11/01; $4.95) Intro. Hunter Zolomon (who later becomes
   Zoom)   5.00
Special 1 (1990, $2.95, 84 pgs.)-50th anniversary issue; Kubert-c; 1st Flash
   story by Mark Waid; 1st app. John Fox (27th Century Flash)   3.00
Terminal Velocity (1996, $12.95, TPB)-r/#95-100.   13.00
The Return of Barry Allen (1996, $12.95, TPB)-r/#74-79.   13.00
...: Time Flies (2002, $5.95)-Seth Fisher-c/a; Rozum-s   6.00
TV Special 1 (1991, $3.95, 76 pgs.)-Photo-c plus behind the scenes photos
   of TV show; Saltares-a, Byrne scripts   4.00

	GD	FN	NM-

FLASH GORDON
Gold Key: June, 1965

1 (1947 reprint)-Painted-c	6	18	75

FLASH GORDON (Also see Comics Reading Libraries in the Promotional Comics section)
King #1-11/Charlton #12-18/Gold Key #19-23/Whitman #28 on:
9/66 - #11, 12/67; #12, 2/69 - #18, 1/70; #19, 9/78 - #37, 3/82 (Painted covers No. 19-30, 34)

1-1st S.A. app Flash Gordon; Williamson c/a(2); E.C. swipe/Incredible S.F. #32; Mandrake story	7	21	90
1-Army giveaway(1968)("Complimentary" on cover)(Same as regular #1 minus Mandrake story & back-c)	4	12	50
2-8: 2-Bolle, Gil Kane-c; Mandrake story. 3-Williamson-c. 4-Secret Agent X-9 begins, Williamson-c/a(3). 5-Williamson-c/a(2). 6,8-Crandall-a. 7-Raboy-a (last in comics?). 8-Secret Agent X-9-r	4	12	45
9-13: 9,10-Raymond-r. 10-Buckler's 1st pro work (11/67). 11-Crandall-a. 12-Crandall-c/a. 13-Jeff Jones-a (15 pgs.)	4	12	40
14,15: 15-Last 12¢ issue	3	9	30
16,17: 17-Brick Bradford story	3	9	24
18-Kaluta-a (3rd pro work?)(see Teen Confessions)	3	9	32
19(9/78, G.K.), 20-26	1	4	10
27-29,34-37: 34-37-Movie adaptation	2	6	12
30 (10/80) (scarce)	3	9	30
30 (7/81; re-issue), 31-33-single issues	2	6	12
31-33 (Bagged 3-pack): Movie adaptation; Williamson-a.			36.00

FLASH GORDON THE MOVIE
Western Publishing Co.: 1980 (8-1/4 x 11", $1.95, 68 pgs.)

11294-Williamson-c/a; adapts movie	2	6	16
13743-Hardback edition	3	9	24

FLINTSTONE KIDS, THE (TV) (See Star Comics Digest)
Star Comics/Marvel Comics #5 on: Aug, 1987 - No. 11, Apr, 1989

1-11			4.50

FLINTSTONES, THE (TV)(See Dell Giant #48 for No. 1)
Dell Publ. Co./Gold Key No. 7 (10/62) on: No. 2, Nov-Dec, 1961 - No. 60, Sept, 1970 (Hanna-Barbera)

2-2nd app. (TV debut was 9/30/60); 1st app. of Cave Kids; 15¢-c thru #5			
	12	36	170
3-6(7-8/62): 3-Perry Gunnite begins. 6-1st 12¢-c	8	24	100
7 (10/62; 1st GK)	8	24	100
8-10	7	21	80
11-1st app. Pebbles (6/63)	10	30	130
12-15,17-20	6	18	65
16-1st app. Bamm-Bamm (1/64)	9	27	120
21-23,25-30,33: 26,27-2nd & 3rd app. The Grusomes. 30-1st app. Martian Mopheads (10/65). 33-Meet Frankenstein & Dracula			
	5	15	60

	GD	FN	NM-
24-1st app. The Grusomes	7	21	85
31,32,35-40: 31-Xmas-c. 36-Adaptation of "the Man Called Flintstone" movie.			
39-Reprints	4	12	50
34-1st app. The Great Gazoo	7	21	85
41-60: 45-Last 12¢ issue	4	12	42
At N.Y. World's Fair ('64)-J.W. Books (25¢)-1st printing; no date on-c			
(29¢ version exists, 2nd print?) Most H-B characters app.; including Yogi			
Bear, Top Cat, Snagglepuss and the Jetsons	6	18	75
At N.Y. World's Fair (1965 on-c; re-issue; Warren Pub.)			
NOTE: Warehouse find in 1984	2	6	18
Bigger & Boulder 1(#30013-211) (Gold Key Giant, 11/62, 25¢, 84 pgs.)			
	10	30	125
Bigger & Boulder 2-(1966, 25¢)-Reprints B&B No. 1	6	18	70
...On the Rocks (9/61, $1.00, 6-1/4x9", cardboard-c, high quality paper,			
116 pgs.) B&W new material	10	30	140
...With Pebbles & Bamm Bamm (100 pgs.), G.K.)-30028-511 (paper-c, 25¢)			
(11/65)	10	30	125

FLINTSTONES, THE (TV)(...& Pebbles)
Charlton Comics: Nov, 1970 - No. 50, Feb, 1977 (Hanna-Barbera)

	GD	FN	NM-
1	9	27	120
2	5	15	60
3-7,9,10	4	12	40
8- "Flintstones Summer Vacation" (Summer, 1971, 52 pgs.)			
	6	18	75
11-20,36: 36-Mike Zeck illos (early work)	3	9	30
21-35,38-41,43-45	3	9	24
37-Byrne text illos (early work; see Nightmare #20)	3	9	30
42-Byrne-a (2 pgs.)	3	9	30
46-50	2	6	22
Digest nn (1972, B&W, 100 pgs.) (low print run)	4	12	40

FLINTSTONES, THE (TV)(See Yogi Bear, 3rd series) (Newsstand sales only)
Marvel Comics Group: October, 1977 - No. 9, Feb, 1979 (Hanna-Barbera)

	GD	FN	NM-
1,7-9: 1-(30¢-c). 7-9-Yogi Bear app.	4	12	40
1-(35¢-c variant, limited distribution)	4	12	50
2,3,5,6: Yogi Bear app.	3	9	28
4-The Jetsons app.	3	9	32

FOOM (Friends Of Ol' Marvel)
Marvel Comics: 1973 - No. 22, 1979 (Marvel fan magazine)

	GD	FN	NM-
1	6	18	65
2-Hulk-c by Steranko	4	12	42
3,4	4	12	38
5-11: 11-Kirby-a and interview	3	9	32
12-15: 12-Vision-c. 13-Daredevil-c. 14-Conan. 15-Howard the Duck			
	3	9	28
16-20: 16-Marvel bullpen. 17-Stan Lee issue. 19-Defenders			
	3	9	24
21-Star Wars	3	9	28

	GD	FN	NM-
22-Spider-Man-c; low print run final issue	5	15	55

FORBIDDEN TALES OF DARK MANSION (Formerly Dark Mansion of Forbidden Love #1-4)
National Periodical Publ.: No. 5, May-June, 1972 - No. 15, Feb-Mar, 1974

5-(52 pgs.)	5	15	60
6-15: 13-Kane/Howard-a	3	9	24

FOREVER PEOPLE, THE
National Periodical Publications: Feb-Mar, 1971 - No. 11, Oct-Nov, 1972 (Fourth World) (#1-3, 10-11 are 36 pgs; #4-9 are 52 pgs.)

1-1st app. Forever People; Superman x-over; Kirby-c/a begins; 1st full app. Darkseid (3rd anywhere, 3 weeks before New Gods #1); Darkseid storyline begins, ends #8 (app. in 1-4,6,8; cameos in 5,11)	8	24	100
2-9: 4-G.A. reprints thru #9. 9,10-Deadman app.	4	12	50
10,11	3	9	32
Jack Kirby's Forever People TPB ('99, $14.95, B&W&Grey) r/#1-11 plus cover gallery			15.00

FRACTURED FAIRY TALES (TV)
Gold Key: Oct, 1962 (Jay Ward)

1 (10022-210)-From Bullwinkle TV show	12	36	180

FRAGGLE ROCK (TV)
Marvel Comics (Star Comics)/Marvel V2#1 on: Apr, 1985 - No. 8, Sept, 1986; V2#1, Apr, 1988 - No. 6, Sept, 1988

1-6 (75¢-c)			5.00
7,8			6.00
V2#1-6-($1.00): Reprints 1st series			2.25

FRANKENSTEIN (The Monster of...; also see Monsters Unleashed #2, Power Record Comics, Psycho & Silver Surfer #7)
Marvel Comics Group: Jan, 1973 - No. 18, Sept, 1975

1-Ploog-c/a begins, ends #6	6	18	75
2	4	12	42
3-5	3	9	30
6,7,10: 7-Dracula cameo	3	9	24
8,9-Dracula c/sty. 9-Death of Dracula	4	12	48
11-17	2	6	18
18-Wrightson-c(i)	2	6	22

FRAY
Dark Horse Comics: June, 2001 - No. 8, July, 2003 ($2.99, limited series)

1-Joss Whedon-s/Moline & Owens-a	1	3	8
1-DF Gold edition	2	6	15
2-8: 6-(3/02). 7-(4/03)			4.00

FREEDOM FIGHTERS (See Justice League of America #107,108)
National Periodical Publ./DC Comics: Mar-Apr, 1976 - No. 15, July-Aug, 1978

1-Uncle Sam, The Ray, Black Condor, Doll Man, Human Bomb, & Phantom Lady begin (all former Quality characters)	2	6	20

	GD	FN	NM-

2-9: 4,5-Wonder Woman x-over. 7-1st app. Crusaders 2   6   12

10-15: 10-Origin Doll Man; Cat-Man-c/story (4th app; 1st revival since
Detective #325). 11-Origin The Ray. 12-Origin Firebrand. 13-Origin Black
Condor. 14-Batgirl & Batwoman app. 15-Batgirl & Batwoman app.; origin

Phantom Lady	2	6	14

FROM BEYOND THE UNKNOWN
National Periodical Publications: 10-11/69 - No. 25, 11-12/73

1	6	18	65
2-6	3	9	32
7-11: (64 pgs.) 7-Intro Col. Glenn Merrit	4	12	38
12-17: (52 pgs.) 13-Wood-a(i)(r). 17-Pres. Nixon-c	3	9	30
18-25: Star Rovers-r begin #18,19. Space Museum in #23-25			
	2	6	18

FUN-IN (TV)(Hanna-Barbera)
Gold Key: Feb, 1970 - No. 10, Jan, 1972; No. 11, 4/74 - No. 15, 12/74

1-Dastardly & Muttley in Their Flying Machines; Perils of Penelope Pitstop			
in #1-4; It's the Wolf in all	7	21	90
2-4,6-Cattanooga Cats in 2-4	4	12	42
5,7-Motormouse & Autocat, Dastardly & Muttley in both; It's the Wolf in #7			
	4	12	48
8,10-The Harlem Globetrotters, Dastardly & Muttley in #10			
	4	12	48
9-Where's Huddles?, Dastardly & Muttley, Motormouse & Autocat app.			
	4	12	48
11-Butch Cassidy	4	12	38
12-15: 12,15-Speed Buggy. 13-Hair Bear Bunch. 14-Inch High Private Eye			
	4	12	38

FUNKY PHANTOM, THE (TV)
Gold Key: Mar, 1972 - No. 13, Mar, 1975 (Hanna-Barbera)

1	6	18	70
2-5	3	10	35
6-13	3	9	26

FUNTASTIC WORLD OF HANNA-BARBERA, THE (TV)
Marvel Comics Group: Dec, 1977 - No. 3, June, 1978 ($1.25, oversized)

1-3: 1-The Flintstones Christmas Party(12/77). 2-Yogi Bear's Easter Parade			
(3/78). 3-Laff-a-lympics(6/78)	4	12	50

FURTHER ADVENTURES OF CYCLOPS AND PHOENIX (Also see
Adventures of Cyclops and Phoenix, Uncanny X-Men & X-Men)
Marvel Comics: June, 1996 - No. 4, Sept, 1996 ($1.95, limited series)

1-4: Origin of Mr. Sinister; Milligan scripts; John Paul Leon-c/a(p).			
2-4-Apocalypse app.			3.00
Trade Paperback (1997, $14.99) r/1-4			15.00

FURY OF FIRESTORM, THE (Becomes Firestorm The Nuclear Man on cover
with #50, in indicia with #65) (Also see Firestorm)
DC Comics: June, 1982 - No. 64, Oct, 1987 (75¢ on)

	GD	FN	NM-

1-Intro The Black Bison; brief origin 6.00
2-40,43-64: 4-JLA x-over. 17-1st app. Firehawk. 21-Death of Killer Frost.
   22-Origin. 23-Intro. Byte. 24-(6/84)-1st app. Blue Devil & Bug (origin);
   origin Byte. 34-1st app./origin Killer Frost II. 39-Weasel's ID revealed.
   48-Intro. Moonbow. 53-Origin/1st app. Silver Shade. 55,56-Legends x-over.
   58-1st app./origin new Parasite 2.50
41,42-Crisis x-over 3.00
61-Test cover variant; Superman logo   4   12   40
Annual 1-4: 1(1983), 2(1984), 3(1985), 4(1986) 3.00

FUTURAMA (TV)
Bongo Comics: 2000 - Present ($2.50, bi-monthly)

1-Based on the FOX-TV animated series; Groening/Morrison-c 3.50
1-San Diego Comic-Con Premiere Edition 5.00
2-19: 8-CGC cover spoof; X-Men parody 3.00
Futurama Adventures TPB (2004, $14.95) r/#5-9 15.00
Futurama-O-Rama TPB (2002, $12.95) r/#1-4; sketch pages of Fry's
   development 13.00

FUTURAMA/SIMPSONS INFINITELY SECRET CROSSOVER CRISIS (TV)
Bongo Comics: 2002 - No. 2, 2002 ($2.50, limited series)

1,2-Evil Brain Spawns put Futurama crew into the Simpsons' Springfield
    2.50

GAMBIT (See X-Men #266 & X-Men Annual #14)
Marvel Comics: Dec, 1993 - No. 4, Mar, 1994 ($2.00, limited series)

1-($2.50)-Lee Weeks-c/a in all; gold foil stamped-c. 5.00
1 (Gold)   2   6   15
2-4 3.00

GAMBIT
Marvel Comics: Sept, 1997 - No. 4, Dec, 1997 ($2.50, limited series)

1-4-Janson-a/ Mackie & Kavanagh-s 3.00

GAMBIT
Marvel Comics: Feb, 1999 - No. 25, Feb, 2001 ($2.99/$1.99)

1-($2.99) Five covers; Nicieza-a/Skroce-a 4.00
2-11,13-16-($1.99): 2-Two covers (Skroce & Adam Kubert) 2.50
12-($2.99) 3.50
17-24: 17-Begin $2.25-c. 21-Mystique-c/app. 2.25
25-($2.99) Leads into "Gambit & Bishop" 3.00
...1999 Annual ($3.50) Nicieza-s/McDaniel-a 3.50
...2000 Annual ($3.50) Nicieza-s/Derenick & Smith-a 3.50

GAMBIT
Marvel Comics: Nov, 2004 - Present ($2.99/)

1-4-Jeanty-a/Land-c/Layman-s 3.00

GARRISON'S GORILLAS (TV)
Dell Publishing Co.: Jan, 1968 - No. 4, Oct, 1968; No. 5, Oct, 1969 (Photo-c)

1   6   18   65
2-5: 5-Reprints #1   4   12   40

GEEKSVILLE (Also see 3 Geeks, The)
3 Finger Prints/ Image: Aug, 1999 - No. 6, Mar, 2001 ($2.75/$2.95, B&W)

1,2,4-6-The 3 Geeks by Koslowski; Innocent Bystander by Sassaman			3.00
3-Includes "Babes & Blades" mini-comic			5.00
0-(3/00) First Image issue			3.00
(Vol. 2) 1-4-($2.95) 3-Mini-comic insert by the Geeks. 4-Steve Borock app.			3.00

GEN ACTIVE
DC Comics (WildStorm): May, 2000 - No. 6, Aug, 2001 ($3.95)

1-6: 1-Covers by Campbell and Madureira; Gen 13 & DV8 app. 5-Mahfood-a; Quitely and Stelfreeze-c. 6-Portacio-a/c			4.00

GENERATION X (See Gen 13/ Generation X)
Marvel Comics: Oct, 1994 - No. 75, June, 2001 ($1.50/$1.95/$1.99/$2.25)

Collectors Preview ($1.75), "Ashcan" Edition			2.25
-1(7/97) Flashback story			3.00
1/2 (San Diego giveaway)	2	6	12
1-($3.95)-Wraparound chromium-c; Lobdell scripts & Bachalo-a begins			6.00
2-($1.95)-Deluxe edition, Bachalo-a			4.00
3,4-($1.95)-Deluxe Edition; Bachalo-a			3.00
2-10: 2-4-Standard Edition. 5-Returns from "Age of Apocalypse," begin $1.95-c. 6-Bachalo-a(p) ends, returns #17. 7-Roger Cruz-a(p). 10-Omega Red-c/app.			3.00
11-24, 26-28: 13,14-Bishop-app. 17-Stan Lee app. (Stan Lee scripts own dialogue); Bachalo/Buckingham-a; Onslaught update. 18-Toad cameo. 20-Franklin Richards app; Howard the Duck cameo. 21-Howard the Duck app. 22-Nightmare app.			2.50
25-($2.99)-Wraparound-c. Black Tom, Howard the Duck app.			3.50
29-37: 29-Begin $1.99-c, "Operation Zero Tolerance". 33-Hama-s			2.50
38-49: 38-Dodson-a begins. 40-Penance ID revealed. 49-Maggott app.			2.50
50,57-($2.99): 50-Crossover w/X-Man #50			3.50
51-56, 58-62: 59-Avengers & Spider-Man app.			2.25
63-74: 63-Ellis-s begin. 64-Begin $2.25-c. 69-71-Art Adams-c			2.25
75-($2.99) Final issue; Chamber joins the X-Men; Lim-a			3.00
'95 Special-($3.95)			4.00
'96 Special-($2.95)-Wraparound-c; Jeff Johnson-c/a			3.50
'97 Special-($2.99)-Wraparound-c;			3.50
'98 Annual-($3.50)-vs. Dracula			3.50
'99 Annual-($3.50)-Monet leaves			3.50
75¢ Ashcan Edition			3.00
...Holiday Special 1 (2/99, $3.50) Pollina-a			3.50
...Underground Special 1 (5/98, $2.50, B&W) Mahfood-a			2.50

GENERATION X/ GEN 13 (Also see Gen 13/ Generation X)
Marvel Comics: 1997 ($3.99, one-shot)

1-Robinson-s/Larroca-a(p)			4.00

GEN 13 (Also see Wild C.A.T.S. #1 & Deathmate Black #2)
Image Comics (WildStorm Productions): Feb, 1994 - No. 5, July 1994 ($1.95, limited series)

	GD	FN	NM-
0 (8/95, $2.50)-Ch. 1 w/Jim Lee-p; Ch.4 w/Charest-p			3.00
1/2	1	3	7
1-($2.50)-Created by Jim Lee	1	4	10
1-2nd printing			2.50
1-"3-D" Edition (9/97, $4.95)-w/glasses			5.00
2-($2.50)	1	3	7
3-Pitt-c & story			4.00
4-Pitt-c & story; wraparound-c			3.00
5			4.00
5-Alternate Portacio-c; see Deathblow #5			6.00
...Collected Edition ('94, $12.95)-r/#1-5			13.00
...Rave ($1.50, 3/95)-wraparound-c			3.00

NOTE: *Issues 1-4 contain coupons redeemable for the ashcan edition of Gen 13 #0. Price listed is for a complete book.*

GEN 13

Image Comics (WildStorm Productions): Mar, 1995 - No. 36, Dec, 1998;
DC Comics (WildStorm): No. 37, Mar, 1999 - No. 77, Jul, 2002 ($2.95/$2.50)

	GD	FN	NM-
1-A (Charge)-Campbell/Garner-c			4.50
1-B (Thumbs Up)-Campbell/Garner-c			4.50

1-C-1-F,1-I-1-M: 1-C (Lil' GEN 13)-Art Adams-c. 1-D (Barbari-GEN)-Simon Bisley-c. 1-E (Your Friendly Neighborhood Grunge)-Cleary-c. 1-F (GEN 13 Goes Madison Ave.)-Golden-c. 1-I (That's the way we became GEN 13)-Campbell/Gibson-c. 1-J (All Dolled Up)-Campbell/McWeeney-c. 1-K (Verti-GEN)-Dunn-c. 1-L (Picto-Fiction). 1-M (Do it Yourself Cover)

	GD	FN	NM-
	1	3	7
1-G (Lin-GEN-re)-Michael Lopez-c	2	6	12
1-H (GEN-et Jackson)-Jason Pearson-c	2	6	12
1-Chromium-c by Campbell			60.00
1-Chromium-c by Jim Lee			80.00
1-"3-D" Edition (2/98, $4.95)-w/glasses			5.00
2 ($1.95, Newsstand)-WildStorm Rising Pt. 4; bound-in card			2.50
2-12: 2-($2.50, Direct Market)-WildStorm Rising Pt. 4, bound-in card.			
6,7-Jim Lee-c/a(p). 9-Ramos-a. 10,11-Fire From Heaven Pt. 3. & Pt.9			3.00
11-($4.95)-Special European Tour Edition; chromium-c			
	2	6	18
13A,13B,13C-($1.30, 13 pgs.): 13A-Archie & Friends app. 13B-Bone-c/app.;			
Teenage Mutant Ninja Turtles, Madman, Spawn & Jim Lee app.			3.00
14-24: 20-Last Campbell-a			2.50
25-($3.50)-Two covers by Campbell and Charest			3.50
25-($3.50)-Voyager Pack w/Danger Girl preview			4.50
25-Foil-c			10.00
26-32,34: 26-Arcudi-s/Frank-a begins. 34-Back-up story by Art Adams			2.50
33-Flip book w/Planetary preview			4.00
35-49: 36,38,40-Two covers. 37-First DC issue. 41-Last Frank-a			2.50
50-($3.95) Two covers by Lee and Benes; art by various			4.00
51-76: 51-Moy-a; Fairchild loses her powers. 60-Warren-s/a. 66-Art by various			
incl. Campbell (3 pgs.). 70,75,76-Mays-a. 76-Original team dies			2.50
77-($3.50) Mays, Andrews, Warren-a			3.50
Annual 1 (1997, $2.95) Ellis-s/ Dillon-c/a.			3.50

	GD	FN	NM-
Annual 1999 ($3.50, DC) Slipstream x-over w/ DV8			3.50
Annual 2000 ($3.50) Devil's Night x-over w/WildStorm titles; Bermejo-c			3.50
...: A Christmas Caper (1/00, $5.95, one-shot) McWeeney-s/a			6.00
... Archives (4/98, $12.99) B&W reprints of mini-series, #0,1/2,1-13ABC; includes cover gallery and sourcebook			13.00
...: Carny Folk (2/00, $3.50) Collect back-up stories			3.50
... European Vacation TPB ($6.95) r/#6,7			7.00
.../ Fantastic Four (2001, $5.95) Maguire-s/c/a(p)			6.00
...: Going West (6/99, $2.50, one-shot) Pruett-s			2.50
...: Grunge Saves the World (5/99, $5.95, one-shot) Altieri-c/a			6.00
... I Love New York TPB ($9.95) r/part #25, 26-29; Frank-c			10.00
... London, New York, Hell TPB ($6.95) r/Annual #1 & Bootleg Ann. #1			7.00
... Lost in Paradise TPB ($6.95) r/#3-5			7.00
.../ Maxx (12/95, $3.50, one-shot) Messner-Loebs-s, 1st Coker-c/a.			3.50
...: Meanwhile (2003, $17.95) r/#43,44,66-70; all Warren-s; art by various			18.00
...: Medicine Song (2001, $5.95) Brent Anderson-c/a(p)/Raab-s			6.00
... Science Friction (2001, $5.95) Haley & Lopresti-a			6.00
... Starting Over TPB ($14.95) r/#1-7			15.00
... Superhuman Like You TPB ($12.95) r/#60-65; Warren-c			13.00
... #13 A,B&C Collected Edition ($6.95, TPB) r/#13A,B&C			7.00
... 3-D Special (1997, $4.95, one-shot) Art Adams-s/a(p)			5.00
...: The Unreal World (7/96, $2.95, one-shot) Humberto Ramos-c/a			3.00
... We'll Take Manhattan TPB ($14.95) r/#45-50; new Benes-c			15.00
...: Wired (4/99, $2.50, one-shot) Richard Bennett-c/a			2.50
... Yearbook 1997 (6/97, $2.50) College-themed stories and pin-ups			2.50
...: 'Zine (12/96, $1.95, B&W, digest size) Campbell/Garner-c			2.25
Variant Collection-Four editions (all 13 variants w/Chromium variant-limited, signed)			100.00

GEN 13
DC Comics (WildStorm): No. 0, Sept, 2002 - No. 16, Feb, 2004 ($2.95)

0-(13¢-c) Intro. new team; includes previews of 21 Down & The Resistance			2.50
1-Claremont-s/Garza-c/a; Fairchild app.			3.00
2-16: 8-13-Bachs-a. 16-Original team returns			3.00
...: September Song TPB (2003, $19.95) r/#0-6; Garza sketch pages			20.00

GEN 13 BOOTLEG
Image Comics (WildStorm): Nov, 1996 - No. 20, Jul, 1998 ($2.50)

1-Alan Davis-a; alternate costumes-c			2.50
1-Team falling variant-c			3.00
2-7: 2-Alan Davis-a. 5,6-Terry Moore-s. 7-Robinson-s/Scott Hampton-a			2.50
8-10-Adam Warren-s/a			4.00
11-20: 11,12-Lopresti-s/a & Simonson-s. 13-Wieringo-s/a. 14-Mariotte-s/ Phillips-a. 15,16-Strnad-s/Shaw-a. 18-Altieri-s/a(p)/c, 18-Variant-c by Bruce Timm			2.50
Annual 1 (2/98, $2.95) Ellis-s/Dillon-c/a			3.00
... Grunge: The Movie (12/97, $9.95) r/#8-10, Warren-c			10.00
...Vol. 1 TPB (10/98, $11.95) r/#1-4			12.00

GEN 13/ GENERATION X (Also see Generation X / Gen 13)

	GD	FN	NM-

Image Comics (WildStorm Publications): July, 1997 ($2.95, one-shot)

1-Choi-s/ Art Adams-p/Garner-i. Variant covers by Adams/Garner and Campbell/McWeeney			3.00
1-($4.95) 3-D Edition w/glasses; Campbell-c			5.00

GEN 13: ORDINARY HEROES
Image Comics (WildStorm Publications): Feb, 1996 - No. 2, July, 1996 ($2.50, limited series)

1,2-Adam Hughes-c/a/scripts			3.00
TPB (2004, $14.95) r/series, Gen13 Bootleg #1&2 and Wildstorm Thunderbook; new Hughes-c and art pages			15.00

GEORGE OF THE JUNGLE (TV)(See America's Best TV Comics)
Gold Key: Feb, 1969 - No. 2, Oct, 1969 (Jay Ward)

	GD	FN	NM-
1	14	42	200
2	10	30	125

GET SMART (TV)
Dell Publ. Co.: June, 1966 - No. 8, Sept, 1967 (All have Don Adams photo-c)

	GD	FN	NM-
1	11	33	160
2,3-Ditko-a	8	24	105
4-8: 8-Reprints #1 (cover and insides)	7	21	80

GHOST IN THE SHELL (Manga)
Dark Horse: Mar, 1995 - No. 8, Oct, 1995 ($3.95, B&W/color, lim. series)

	GD	FN	NM-
1,2	2	6	22
3	2	6	12
4-8	1	3	8

GHOST MANOR (Ghostly Haunts No. 20 on)
Charlton Comics: July, 1968 - No. 19, July, 1971

	GD	FN	NM-
1	6	18	65
2-6: 6-Last 12¢ issue	3	9	32
7-12,17: 17-Morisi-a	3	9	26
13,14,16-Ditko-a	3	9	32
15,18,19-Ditko-c/a	4	12	40

GHOST RIDER, THE (See Night Rider & Western Gunfighters)
Marvel Comics Group: Feb, 1967 - No. 7, Nov, 1967 (Western hero)(12¢)

	GD	FN	NM-
1-Origin & 1st app. Ghost Rider; Kid Colt-reprints begin	9	27	120
2	5	15	60
3-7: 6-Last Kid Colt-r; All Ayers-c/a(p)	4	12	50

GHOST RIDER (See The Champions, Marvel Spotlight #5, Marvel Team-Up #15, 58, Marvel Treasury Edition #18, Marvel Two-In-One #8, The Original Ghost Rider & The Original Ghost Rider Rides Again)
Marvel Comics Group: Sept, 1973 - No. 81, June, 1983 (Super-hero)

	GD	FN	NM-
1-Johnny Blaze, the Ghost Rider begins; 1st brief app. Daimon Hellstrom (Son of Satan)	9	27	110
2-1st full app. Daimon Hellstrom; gives glimpse of costume (1 panel); story			

	GD	FN	NM-
continues in Marvel Spotlight #12	4	12	45
3-5: 3-Ghost Rider gets new cycle; Son of Satan app.			
	3	10	35
6-10: 10-Reprints origin/1st app. from Marvel Spotlight #5; Ploog-a			
	2	6	22
11-16	2	6	14
17,19-(Reg. 25¢ editions)(4,8/76)	2	6	14
17,19-(30¢-c variants, limited distribution)	2	6	20
18-(Reg. 25¢ edition)(6/76). Spider-Man-c & app.	2	6	16
18-(30¢-c variant, limited distribution)	3	9	24
20-Daredevil x-over; ties into D.D. #138; Byrne-a	2	6	22
21-30: 22-1st app. Enforcer. 29,30-Vs. Dr. Strange	1	3	9
24-26-(35¢-c variants, limited distribution)	2	6	14
31-34,36-49	1	3	7
35-Death Race classic; Starlin-c/a/sty	2	6	12
50-Double size	1	3	9
51-76,78-80: 80-Brief origin recap. 68,77-Origin retold			5.00
81-Death of Ghost Rider (Demon leaves Blaze)	2	6	16

GHOST RIDER (Volume 2) (Also see Doctor Strange/Ghost Rider Special, Marvel Comics Presents & Midnight Sons Unlimited)
Marvel Comics (Midnight Sons imprint #44 on): V2#1, May, 1990 - No. 93, Feb, 1998 ($1.50/$1.75/$1.95)

1-($1.95, 52 pgs.)-Origin/1st app. new Ghost Rider; Kingpin app.	6.00
1-2nd printing (not gold)	2.50
2-5: 3-Kingpin app. 5-Punisher app.; Jim Lee-c	3.00
5-Gold background 2nd printing	2.50
6-14,16-24,29,30,32-39: 6-Punisher app. 6,17-Spider-Man/Hobgoblin-c/story. 9-X-Factor app. 10-Reintro Johnny Blaze on last pg. 11-Stroman-c/a(p). 12,13-Dr. Strange x-over cont'd in D.S. #28. 13-Painted-c. 14-Johnny Blaze vs. Ghost Rider; origin recap 1st Ghost Rider (Blaze). 18-Painted-c by Nelson. 29-Wolverine-c/story. 32-Dr. Strange x-over; Johnny Blaze app. 34-Williamson-a(i). 36-Daredevil app. 37-Archangel app.	2.50
15-Glow in the dark-c	3.00
25-27: 25-($2.75)-Contains pop-up scene insert. 26,27-X-Men x-over; Lee/Williams-c on both	3.00
28,31-($2.50, 52 pgs.)-Polybagged w/poster; part 1 & part 6 of Rise of the Midnight Sons storyline (see Ghost Rider/Blaze #1)	3.00
40-Outer-c is Darkhold envelope made of black parchment w/gold ink; Midnight Massacre; Demogoblin app.	3.00
41-48: 41-Lilith & Centurious app.; begin $1.75-c. 41-43-Neon ink-c. 43-Has free extra 16 pg. insert on Siege of Darkness. 44,45-Siege of Darkness parts 2 & 10. 44-Spot varnish-c. 46-Intro new Ghost Rider. 48-Spider-Man app.	2.25
49,51-60,62-74: 49-Begin $1.95-c; bound-in trading card sheet; Hulk app. 55-Werewolf by Night app. 65-Punisher app. 67,68-Gambit app. 68-Wolverine app. 73,74-Blaze, Vengeance app.	2.25
50,61: 50-($2.50, 52 pgs.)-Regular edition	2.50
50-($2.95, 52 pgs.)-Collectors Ed. die cut foil-c	3.00
75-92: 76-Vs. Vengeance. 77,78-Dr. Strange-app. 78-New costume	2.25

	GD	FN	NM-
93-($2.99)-Saltares & Texeira-a			3.00
#(-1) Flashback (7/97) Saltares-a			2.25
Annual 1,2 ('93, '94, $2.95, 68 pgs.) 1-Bagged w/card			3.00
...And Cable 1 (9/92, $3.95, stiff-c, 68 pgs.)-Reprints Marvel Comics			
Presents #90-98 w/new Kieth-c			4.00
...:Crossroads (11/95, $3.95) Die cut cover; Nord-a			5.00
Highway to Hell (2001, $3.50) Reprints origin from Marvel Spotlight #5			3.50
...: Resurrected TPB (2001, $12.95) r/#1-7			13.00

GHOST RIDER (Volume 3)
Marvel Comics: Aug, 2001 - No. 6, Jan, 2002 ($2.99, limited series)

	GD	FN	NM-
1-6-Grayson-s/Kaniuga-a/c			3.00
...: The Hammer Lane TPB (6/02, $15.95) r/#1-6			16.00

GHOSTS (Ghost No. 1)
National Periodical Publications/DC Comics: Sept-Oct, 1971 - No. 112, May, 1982 (No. 1-5: 52 pgs.)

	GD	FN	NM-
1-Aparo-a	13	39	190
2-Wood-a(i)	7	21	90
3-5-(52 pgs.)	6	18	70
6-10	3	9	32
11-20	2	6	22
21-39	2	6	14
40-(68 pgs.)	3	9	26
41-60	1	3	9
61-96	1	3	7
97-99-The Spectre vs. Dr. 13 by Aparo. 97,98-Spectre-c by Aparo.			
	2	6	14
100-Infinity-c	1	3	8
101-112			6.00

GIANT-SIZE...
Marvel Comics Group: May, 1974 - Dec, 1975 (35/50¢, 52/68 pgs.)
(Some titles quarterly) (Scarce in strict NM or better due to defective cutting, gluing and binding; warping, splitting and off-center pages are common)

	GD	FN	NM-
Avengers 1(8/74)-New-a plus G.A. H. Torch-r; 1st modern app. The Whizzer;			
1st & only modern app. Miss America; 2nd app. Invaders; Kang, Rama-Tut,			
Mantis app.	4	12	50
Avengers 2,3,5: 2(11/74)-Death of the Swordsman; origin of Rama-Tut.			
3(2/75). 5(12/75)-Reprints Avengers Special #1	3	9	30
Avengers 4 (6/75)-Vision marries Scarlet Witch.	4	12	40
Captain America 1(12/75)-r/stories T.O.S. 59-63 by Kirby (#63 reprints origin)			
	4	12	40
Captain Marvel 1(12/75)-r/Capt. Marvel #17, 20, 21 by Gil Kane (p)			
	3	9	28
Chillers 1(6/74, 52 pgs)-Curse of Dracula; origin/1st app. Lilith, Dracula's			
daughter; Heath-r; Colan-c/a(p); becomes Giant-Size Dracula #2 on			
	5	15	60
Chillers 1(2/75, 50¢, 68 pgs.)-Alcala-a	3	9	30
Chillers 2(5/75)-All-r; Everett-r from Advs. into Weird Worlds			

	GD	FN	NM-
	3	9	24

Chillers 3(8/75)-Wrightson-c(new)/a(r); Colan, Kirby, Smith-r

	3	9	30

Conan 1(9/74)-B. Smith-r/#3; start adaptation of Howard's "Hour of the Dragon" (ends #4); 1st app. Belit; new-a begins   3   9   32

Conan 2(12/74)-B. Smith-r/#5; Sutton-a(i)(#1 also); Buscema-c

	3	9	24

Conan 3-5: 3(4/75)-B. Smith-r/#6; Sutton-a(i). 4(6/75)-B. Smith-r/#7. 5(1975)-B. Smith-r/#14,15; Kirby-c   2   6   20

Creatures 1(5/74, 52 pgs.)-Werewolf app; 1st app. Tigra (formerly Cat); Crandall-r; becomes Giant-Size Werewolf w/#2   4   12   45

Daredevil 1(1975)-Reprints Daredevil Annual #1   3   9   26

Defenders 1(7/74)-Silver Surfer app.; Starlin-a; Ditko, Everett & Kirby reprints

	4	12	40

Defenders 2(10/74, 68 pgs.)-New G. Kane-c/a(p); Son of Satan app.; Sub-Mariner-r by Everett; Ditko-r/Strange Tales #119 (Dr. Strange); Maneely-r   3   9   28

Defenders 3-5: 3(1/75)-1st app. Korvac.; Newton, Starlin-a; Ditko, Everett-r. 4(4/75)-Ditko, Everett-r; G. Kane-c. 5-(7/75)-Guardians app.

	3	9	24

Doc Savage 1(1975, 68 pgs.)-r/#1,2; Mooney-r   2   6   20

Doctor Strange 1(11/75)-Reprints stories from Strange Tales #164-168; Lawrence, Tuska-r   3   9   24

Dracula 2(9/74, 50¢)-Formerly Giant-Size Chillers   3   9   28

Dracula 3(12/74)-Fox-r/Uncanny Tales #6   3   9   26

Dracula 4(3/75)-Ditko-r(2)   3   9   26

Dracula 5(6/75)-1st Byrne art at Marvel   4   12   50

Fantastic Four 2-4: 2(8/74)-Formerly Giant-Size Super-Stars; Ditko-r. 3(11/74). 4(2/75)-1st Madrox; 2-4-All have Buscema-a   3   9   30

Fantastic Four 5,6: 5(5/75)-All-r; Kirby, G. Kane-r. 6(10/75)-All-r; Kirby-r   2   6   22

Hulk 1(1975) r/Hulk Special #1   3   9   30

Invaders 1(6/75, 50¢, 68 pgs.)-Origin; G.A. Sub-Mariner-r/Sub-Mariner #1; intro Master Man   3   10   35

Iron Man 1(1975)-Ditko reprint   3   9   28

Kid Colt 1-3: 1(1/75). 2(4/75). 3(7/75)-new Ayers-a   6   18   70

Man-Thing 1(8/74)-New Ploog-c/a (25 pgs.); Ditko-r/Amazing Adv. #11; Kirby-r/Strange Tales Ann. #2 & T.O.S. #15; (#1-5 all have new Man-Thing stories, pre-hero-r & are 68 pgs.)   3   10   35

Man-Thing 2,3: 2(11/74)-Buscema-c/a(p); Kirby, Powell-r. 3(2/75)-Alcala-a; Ditko, Kirby, Sutton-r; Gil Kane-c   3   9   24

Man-Thing 4,5: 4(5/75)-Howard the Duck by Brunner-c/a; Ditko-r. 5(8/75)-Howard the Duck by Brunner (p); Dracula cameo in Howard the Duck; Buscema-a(p); Sutton-a(i); G. Kane-c   3   9   32

Marvel Triple Action 1,2: 1(5/75). 2(7/75)   2   6   22

Master of Kung Fu 1(9/74)-Russell-a; Yellow Claw-r in #1-4; Gulacy-a in #1,2   3   9   32

Master of Kung Fu 2-4: 2-(12/74)-r/Yellow Claw #1. 3(3/75)-Gulacy-a;

	GD	FN	NM-
Kirby-a. 4(6/75)-Kirby-a	3	9	24
Power Man 1(1975)	2	6	22
Spider-Man 1(7/74)-Spider-Man /Human Torch-r by Kirby/Ditko; Byrne-r plus new-a (Dracula-c/story)	6	18	75
Spider-Man 2,3: 2(10/74)-Shang-Chi-c/app. 3(1/75)-Doc Savage-c/app.; Daredevil/Spider-Man-r w/Ditko-a	4	12	42
Spider-Man 4(4/75)-3rd Punisher app.; Byrne, Ditko-r	10	30	140
Spider-Man 5,6: 5(7/75)-Man-Thing/Lizard-c. 6(9/75)	3	10	35
Super-Heroes Featuring Spider-Man 1(6/74, 35¢, 52 pgs.)-Spider-Man vs. Man-Wolf; Morbius, the Living Vampire app.; Ditko-r; G. Kane-a(p); Spidey villains app.	6	18	75
Super-Stars 1(5/74, 35¢, 52 pgs.)-Fantastic Four; Thing vs. Hulk; Kirbyish-c/a by Buckler/Sinnott; F.F. villains profiled; becomes Giant-Size Fantastic Four #2 on	5	15	55
Super-Villain Team-Up 1(3/75, 68 pgs.)-Craig-r(i) (Also see Fantastic Four #6 for 1st super-villain team-up)	3	9	28
Super-Villain Team-Up 2(6/75, 68 pgs.)-Dr. Doom, Sub-Mariner app.; Spider-Man-r from Amazing Spider-Man #8 by Ditko; Sekowsky-a(p)	2	6	22
Thor 1(7/75)	3	10	35
Werewolf 2(10/74, 68 pgs.)-Formerly Giant-Size Creatures; Ditko-r; Frankenstein app.	3	9	26
Werewolf 3,5: 3(1/75, 68 pgs.). 5(7/75, 68 pgs.)	3	9	26
Werewolf 4(4/75, 68 pgs.)-Morbius the Living Vampire app.	3	9	32
X-Men 1(Summer, 1975, 50¢, 68 pgs.)-1st app. new X-Men; intro. Nightcrawler, Storm, Colossus & Thunderbird; 2nd full app. Wolverine after Incredible Hulk #181	58	174	1100
X-Men 2 (11/75)-N. Adams-r (51 pgs)	8	24	105

G. I. COMBAT (See DC Special Series #22)
National Periodical Publ./DC Comics: No. 44, Jan, 1957 - No. 288, Mar, 1987

	GD	FN	NM-
44-Grey tone-c	50	150	875
45	27	81	400
46-50	22	66	320
51-Grey tone-c	23	69	335
52-54,59,60	18	54	268
55-Minor Sgt. Rock prototype by Finger	20	60	300
56-Sgt. Rock prototype by Kanigher/Kubert	24	72	360
57,58-Pre-Sgt. Rock Easy Co. stories	22	66	320
61-65,69-74: 74-American flag-c	14	42	200
66-Pre-Sgt. Rock Easy Co. story	20	60	290
67-1st Tank Killer	23	69	340
68-(1/59) Introduces "The Rock", Sgt. Rock prototype by Kanigher/Kubert; once considered his actual 1st app. (see Our Army at War #82,83)	55	165	1050
75-80: 75-Greytone-c begin, end #109	16	48	235
81,82,84-86	13	39	185

	GD	FN	NM-
83-1st Big Al, Little Al, & Charlie Cigar	15	45	225
87-1st Haunted Tank; series begins; classic-c	53	159	1000
88-2nd Haunted Tank	22	66	320
89,90: 90-Last 10¢ issue	13	39	185
91-1st Haunted Tank-c	17	51	250
92-99: 92-95,99-Grey tone-c	11	33	150
100,108: 108-1st Sgt. Rock x-over	12	36	165
101-107,109: 104,109-Grey tone-c	9	27	120
110-112,115-120: 119-Grey tone-c	7	21	90
113-Grey tone-c	9	27	110
114-Origin Haunted Tank	14	42	210
121-136: 121-1st app. Sgt. Rock's father. 125-Sgt. Rock app. 136-Last 12¢ issue	6	18	65
137,139,140	4	12	50
138-Intro. The Losers (Capt. Storm, Gunner/Sarge, Johnny Cloud) in Haunted Tank (10-11/69)	10	30	125
141-143	3	9	30
144-148 (68 pgs.)	4	12	40
149,151-154 (52 pgs.): 151-Capt. Storm story. 151,153-Medal of Honor series by Maurer	3	9	30
150- (52 pgs.) Ice Cream Soldier story (tells how he got his name); Death of Haunted Tank-c/s	4	12	40
155-167,169,170,200	2	6	15
168-Neal Adams-c	3	9	24
171-199	2	6	12
201,202 ($1.00 size) Neal Adams-c	2	6	20
203-210 ($1.00 size)	2	6	15
211-230 ($1.00 size)	2	6	12
231-259 ($1.00 size).232-Origin Kana the Ninja. 244-Death of Slim Stryker; 1st app. The Mercenaries. 246-(76 pgs., $1.50)-30th Anniversary issue. 257-Intro. Stuart's Raiders	1	3	9
260-281: 260-Begin $1.25, 52 pg. issues, end #281. 264-Intro Sgt. Bullet; origin Kana. 269-Intro. The Bravos of Vietnam. 274-Cameo of Monitor from Crisis on Infinite Earths			6.00
282-288 (75¢): 282-New advs. begin			6.00

G. I. JOE (America's Movable Fighting Man)
Custom Comics: 1967 (5-1/8x8-3/8", 36 pgs.)

	GD	FN	NM-
nn-Schaffenberger-a; based on Hasbro toy	4	12	40

G.I. JOE
Image Comics/Devil's Due Publishing: 2001 - Present ($2.95)

	GD	FN	NM-
1-Campbell-c; back-c painted by Beck; Blaylock-s	2	6	12
1-2nd printing with front & back covers switched			6.00
2,3			5.00
4-($3.50)			4.00
5-20,22-37: 6-SuperPatriot preview. 18-Brereton-c. 31-33-Wraith back-up; Caldwell-a			3.00
21-Silent issue; Zeck-a; two covers by Campbell and Zeck			3.00
...:Cobra Reborn (1/04, $4.95) Bradstreet-c/Jenkins-s			5.00

	GD	FN	NM-
...:G.I. Joe Reborn (2/04, $4.95) Bradstreet-c/Bennett & Saltares-a			5.00
...: Malfunction (2003, $15.95) r/#11-15			16.00
... M. I. A. (2002, $4.95) r/#1&2; Beck back-c from #1 on cover			5.00
...: Reborn (2004, $9.95) r/Cobra Reborn & G.I. Joe Reborn			10.00
...: Reckonings (2002, $12.95) r/#6-9; Zeck-c			13.00
...: Reinstated (2002, $14.95) r/#1-4			15.00

G. I. JOE AND THE TRANSFORMERS
Marvel Comics Group: Jan, 1987 - No. 4, Apr, 1987 (Limited series)

1-4			6.00

G. I. JOE, A REAL AMERICAN HERO (...Starring Snake-Eyes on-c #135 on)
Marvel Comics Group: June, 1982 - No. 155, Dec, 1994

	GD	FN	NM-
1-Printed on Baxter paper; based on Hasbro toy	3	9	28
2-Printed on reg. paper	3	9	25
3-10	2	6	18
11-20: 11-Intro Airborne	2	6	14
21-1st Storm Shadow; silent issue	3	9	28
22	2	6	12
23-25,28-30,60: 60-Todd McFarlane-a	1	3	8
26,27-Origin Snake-Eyes parts 1 & 2	2	6	16
31-50: 33-New headquarters			5.00
51-59,61-90			4.00
91,92,94-99			5.00
93-Snake-Eyes' face first revealed	2	6	16
100,135-138: 135-138-($1.75)-Bagged w/trading card	1	4	10
101-134: 110-1st Ron Garney-a	1	3	7
139-142-New Transformers app.	2	6	12
143,145-149	1	3	9
144-Origin Snake-Eyes	2	6	14
150-Low print thru #155	3	9	24
151-154	2	6	22
155-Last issue	4	12	38
All 2nd printings			2.25
Special #1 (2/95, $1.50) r/#60 w/McFarlane-a	4	12	40
Special Treasury Edition (1982)-r/#1	3	9	28
Volume 1 TPB (4/02, $24.95) r/#1-10; new cover by Michael Golden			25.00
Volume 2 TPB (6/02, $24.95) r/#11-20; new cover by J. Scott Campbell			25.00
Volume 3 TPB (2002, $24.99) r/#21-30; new cover by J. Scott Campbell			25.00
Volume 4 TPB (2002, $25.99) r/#31-40; new cover by J. Scott Campbell			26.00
Volume 5 TPB (2002, $24.99) r/#42-50; new cover by J. Scott Campbell			25.00
Yearbook 1-4: (3/85-3/88)-r/#1; Golden-c. 2-Golden-c/a			5.00

GOBBLEDYGOOK
Mirage Studios: 1984 - No. 2, 1984 (B&W)(1st Mirage comics, published at same time)

	GD	FN	NM-
1-(24 pgs.)-(distribution of approx. 50) Teenage Mutant Ninja Turtles app. on full page back-c ad; Teenage Mutant Ninja Turtles do not appear inside. 1st app of Fugitoid	47	141	800
2-(24 pgs.)-Teenage Mutant Ninja Turtles on full page back-c ad			

	GD	FN	NM-
	32	96	500

NOTE: Counterfeit copies exist. Originals feature both black & white covers and interiors. Signed and numbered copies do not exist.

GOBBLEDYGOOK
Mirage Studios: Dec, 1986 ($3.50, B&W, one-shot, 100 pgs.)

1-New 8 pg. TMNT story plus a Donatello/Michaelangelo 7 pg. story & a Gizmo story; Corben-i(r)/TMNT #7   6.00

GODZILLA (Movie)
Marvel Comics : August, 1977 - No. 24, July, 1979 (Based on movie series)

	GD	FN	NM-
1-(Regular 30¢ edition)-Mooney-i	3	9	25
1-(35¢-c variant, limited distribution)	4	12	38
2-(Regular 30¢ edition)-Tuska-i.	2	6	12
2,3-(35¢-c variant, limited distribution)	2	6	20
3-(30¢-c) Champions app.(w/o Ghost Rider)	2	6	14
4-10: 4,5-Sutton-a	1	4	10
11-23: 14-Shield app. 20-F.F. app. 21,22-Devil Dinosaur app.	1	3	9
24-Last issue	2	6	12

GO-GO
Charlton Comics: June, 1966 - No. 9, Oct, 1967

	GD	FN	NM-
1-Miss Bikini Luv begins w/Jim Aparo's 1st published work; Rolling Stones, Beatles, Elvis, Sonny & Cher, Bob Dylan, Sinatra, parody; Herman's Hermits pin-ups; D'Agostino-c/a in #1-8	9	27	110
2-Ringo Starr, David McCallum & Beatles photos on cover; Beatles story and photos	9	27	110
3,4: 3-Blooperman begins, ends #6; 1 pg. Batman & Robin satire; full pg. photo pin-ups Lovin' Spoonful & The Byrds	5	15	60
5,7,9: 5 (2/67)-Super Hero & TV satire by Jim Aparo & Grass Green begins. 6-8-Aparo-a. 7-Photo of Brian Wilson of Beach Boys on-c & Beach Boys photo inside f/b-c. 9-Aparo-c/a	5	15	60
6-Parody of JLA & DC heroes vs. Marvel heroes; Aparo-a; Elvis parody; Petula Clark photo-c	6	18	70
8-Monkees photo on-c & photo inside f/b-c	7	21	80

GOLDEN COMICS DIGEST
Gold Key: May, 1969 - No. 48, Jan, 1976

NOTE: *Whitman editions exist of many titles and are generally valued the same.*

	GD	FN	NM-
1-Tom & Jerry, Woody Woodpecker, Bugs Bunny	6	18	65
2-Hanna-Barbera TV Fun Favorites; Space Ghost, Flintstones, Atom Ant, Jetsons, Yogi Bear, Banana Splits, others app.	7	21	90
3-Tom & Jerry, Woody Woodpecker	3	9	26
4-Tarzan; Manning & Marsh-a	5	15	55
5,8-Tom & Jerry, W. Woodpecker, Bugs Bunny	3	9	24
6-Bugs Bunny	3	9	24
7-Hanna-Barbera TV Fun Favorites	6	18	65
9-Tarzan	5	15	55
10,12-17: 10-Bugs Bunny. 12-Tom & Jerry, Bugs Bunny, W. Woodpecker Journey to the Sun. 13-Tom & Jerry. 14-Bugs Bunny Fun Packed Funnies.			

	GD	FN	NM-
15-Tom & Jerry, Woody Woodpecker, Bugs Bunny. 16-Woody Woodpecker Cartoon Special. 17-Bugs Bunny	3	9	24
11-Hanna-Barbera TV Fun Favorites	6	18	70
18-Tom & Jerry; Barney Bear-r by Barks	3	9	26
19-Little Lulu	4	12	45
20-22: 20-Woody Woodpecker Falltime Funtime. 21-Bugs Bunny Showtime. 22-Tom & Jerry Winter Wingding	3	9	24
23-Little Lulu & Tubby Fun Fling	4	12	45
24-26,28: 24-Woody Woodpecker Fun Festival. 25-Tom & Jerry. 26-Bugs Bunny Halloween Hulla-Boo-Loo; Dr. Spektor article, also #25. 28-Tom & Jerry	2	6	22
27-Little Lulu & Tubby in Hawaii	4	12	42
29-Little Lulu & Tubby	4	12	42
30-Bugs Bunny Vacation Funnies	2	6	22
31-Turok, Son of Stone; r/4-Color #596,656; c-r/#9	4	12	48
32-Woody Woodpecker Summer Fun	2	6	22
33,36: 33-Little Lulu & Tubby Halloween Fun; Dr. Spektor app. 36-Little Lulu & Her Friends	4	12	42
34,35,37-39: 34-Bugs Bunny Winter Funnies. 35-Tom & Jerry Snowtime Funtime. 37-Woody Woodpecker County Fair. 39-Bugs Bunny Summer Fun	2	6	22
38-The Pink Panther	3	9	26
40,43: 40-Little Lulu & Tubby Trick or Treat; all by Stanley. 43-Little Lulu in Paris	4	12	42
41,42,44,47: 41-Tom & Jerry Winter Carnival. 42-Bugs Bunny. 44-Woody Woodpecker Family Fun Festival. 47-Bugs Bunny	2	6	20
45-The Pink Panther	3	9	26
46-Little Lulu & Tubby	4	12	38
48-The Lone Ranger	3	9	30

NOTE: #1-30, 164 pgs.; #31 on, 132 pgs..

GOMER PYLE (TV)
Gold Key: July, 1966 - No. 3, Jan, 1967

	GD	FN	NM-
1-Photo front/back-c	10	30	125
2,3	7	21	85

GOON, THE
Avatar Press: Mar, 1999 - No. 3, July, 1999 ($3.00, B&W)

1- Eric Powell-s/a		20.00
2		12.00
3		8.00
...: Rough Stuff (Albatross, 1/03, $15.95) r/Avatar Press series #1-3		16.00
...: Rough Stuff (Dark Horse, 2/04, $12.95) r/Avatar Press series #1-3 newly colored		13.00

GOON, THE
Albatross Exploding Funny Books: Oct, 2002 - No. 4, Feb, 2003 ($2.95)

1- Eric Powell-s/a	10.00
2-4	6.00
...Color Special 1 (8/02)	10.00
...: Nothin' But Misery Vol. 1 (Dark Horse, 7/03, $15.95, TPB) - Reprints The

	GD	FN	NM-

Goon #1-4 (Albatross series), Color Special, and story from DHP #157

16.00

GOON, THE
Dark Horse Comics: June, 2003 - Present ($2.99)

1-8-Eric Powell-s/a. 7-Hellboy-c/app; framing seq. by Mignola 3.00
...: My Murderous Childhood (And Other Grievous Yarns) (5/04, $13.95, TPB)
r/#1-4 and short story from Drawing on Your Nightmares one-shot; intro.
by Frank Cho 14.00

GORGO (Based on M.G.M. movie) (See Return of...)
Charlton Comics: May, 1961 - No. 23, Sept, 1965

1-Ditko-a, 22 pgs.	24	72	350
2,3-Ditko-c/a	12	36	175
4-Ditko-c	8	24	105
5-11,13-16: 11,13-16-Ditko-a	8	24	95
12,17-23: 12-Reptisaurus x-over; Montes/Bache-a-No. 17-23. 20-Giordano-c			
	5	15	55
Gorgo's Revenge('62)-Becomes Return of...	6	18	70

GOTHAM CENTRAL
DC Comics: Early Feb, 2003 - Present ($2.50)

1-26-Stories of Gotham City Police. 1-Brubaker & Rucka-s/Lark-c/a.
10-Two-Face app. 13,15-Joker-c. 18-Huntress app. 2.50
...: In The Line of Duty (2004, $9.95, TPB) r/#1-5, cover gallery & sketch
pages 10.00

GRAFIK MUSIK
Caliber Press: Nov, 1990 - No. 4, Aug, 1991 ($3.50/$2.50)

1-($3.50, 48 pgs., color) Mike Allred-c/a/scripts-1st app. in color of Frank			
Einstein (Madman)	3	9	25
2-($2.50, 24 pgs., color)	2	6	15
3,4-($2.50, 24 pgs., B&W)	2	6	12

GRAPHIQUE MUSIQUE
Slave Labor Graphics: Dec, 1989 - No. 3, May, 1990 ($2.95, 52 pgs.)

1-Mike Allred-c/a/scripts	4	12	40
2,3	3	9	30

GREAT GAZOO, THE (The Flintstones)(TV)
Charlton Comics: Aug, 1973 - No. 20, Jan, 1977 (Hanna-Barbera)

1	4	12	45
2-10	2	6	22
11-20	2	6	16

GREAT GRAPE APE, THE (TV)(See TV Stars #1)
Charlton Comics: Sept, 1976 - No. 2, Nov, 1976 (Hanna-Barbera)

1	3	9	32
2	2	6	18

GREEN ARROW
DC Comics: May, 1983 - No. 4, Aug, 1983 (limited series)

	GD	FN	NM-

1-Origin; Speedy cameo; Mike W. Barr scripts, Trevor Von Eeden-c/a 5.00
2-4 4.00

GREEN ARROW
DC Comics: Feb, 1988 - No. 137, Oct, 1998 ($1.00-$2.50) (Painted-c #1-3)

1-Mike Grell scripts begin, ends #80 5.00
2-49,51-74,76-86: 27,28-Warlord app. 35-38-Co-stars Black Canary; Bill
   Wray-i. 40-Grell-a. 47-Begin $1.50-c. 63-No longer has mature readers
   on-c. 63-66-Shado app. 81-Aparo-a begins, ends #100; Nuklon app.
   82-Intro & death of Rival. 83-Huntress-c/story. 84-Deathstroke cameo.
   85-Deathstroke-c/app. 86-Catwoman-c/story w/Jim Balent layouts 2.50
50,75-($2.50, 52 pgs.): Anniversary issues. 75-Arsenal (Roy Harper) &
   Shado app. 3.00
0,87-96: 87-$1.95-c begins. 88-Guy Gardner, Martian Manhunter, & Wonder
   Woman-c/app.; Flash-c. 89-Anarky app. 90-(9/94)-Zero Hour tie-in.
   0-(10/94)-1st app. Connor Hawke; Aparo-a(p). 91-(11/94). 93-1st app.
   Camorouge. 95-Hal Jordan cameo. 96-Intro new Force of July; Hal Jordan
   (Parallax) app; Oliver Queen learns that Connor Hawke is his son 2.50
97-99,102-109: 97-Begin $2.25-c; no Aparo-a. 97-99-Arsenal app.
   102,103-Underworld Unleashed x-over. 104-GL(Kyle Rayner)-c/app.
   105-Robin-c/app. 107-109-Thorn app. 109-Lois Lane cameo 2.50
100-($3.95)-Foil-c; Superman app. 1 4 10
101-Death of Oliver Queen; Superman app. 3 9 30
110,111-124: 110,111-GL x-over. 110-Intro Hatchet. 114-Final Night.
   115-117-Black Canary & Oracle app. 2.50
125-($3.50, 48 pgs)-GL x-over cont. in GL #92 3.50
126-136: 126-Begin $2.50-c. 130-GL & Flash x-over. 132,133-JLA app.
   134,135-Brotherhood of the Fist pts.1,5. 136-Hal Jordan-c/app. 2.50
137-Last issue; Superman app.; last panel cameo of Oliver Queen
                                                  2 6 15
#1,000,000 (11/98) 853rd Century x-over 2.50
Annual 1-6 ('88-'94, 68 pgs.)-1-No Grell scripts. 2-No Grell scripts; recaps
   origin Green Arrow, Speedy, Black Canary & others. 3-Bill Wray-a. 4-50th
   anniversary issue. 5-Batman, Eclipso app. 6-Bloodlines; Hook app. 3.50
Annual 7-('95, $3.95)-Year One story 4.00

GREEN ARROW
DC Comics: Apr, 2001 - Present ($2.50)

1-Oliver Queen returns; Kevin Smith-s/Hester-a/Wagner-painted-c
                                                  2 6 16
1-2nd-4th printings 3.00
2-Batman cameo 1 3 7
2-2nd printing 2.50
3-5: 4-JLA app. 5.00
6-15: 7-Barry Allen & Hal Jordan app. 9,10-Stanley & his Monster app.
   10-Oliver regains his soul. 12-Hawkman-c/app. 3.00
16-25: 16-Brad Meltzer-s begin; The Shade app. 18-Solomon Grundy-c/app.
   19-JLA app. 22-Beatty-s; Count Vertigo app. 23-25-Green Lantern app.;
   Raab-s/Adlard-a 2.50
26-44: 26-Winick-s begin. 35-37-Riddler app. 43-Mia learns she's HIV+ 2.50

	GD	FN	NM-

...: Quiver HC (2002, $24.95) r/#1-10; Smith intro.   25.00

...: Quiver SC (2003, $17.95) r/#1-10; Smith intro.   18.00

...Secret Files & Origins 1-(12/02, $4.95) Origin stories & profiles; Wagner-c
    5.00

...: Sounds of Violence HC (2003, $19.95) r/#11-15; Hester intro. & sketch
    pages   20.00

...: Sounds of Violence SC (2003, $12.95) r/#11-15; Hester intro. & sketch
    pages   13.00

...: Straight Shooter SC (2004, $12.95) r/#26-31   13.00

...: The Archer's Quest HC (2003, $19.95) r/#16-21; pitch, script and sketch
    pages   20.00

...: The Archer's Quest SC (2004, $14.95) r/#16-21; pitch, script and sketch
    pages   15.00

GREEN GOBLIN
Marvel Comics: Oct, 1995 - No. 13, Oct, 1996 ($2.95/$1.95)

1-($2.95)-Scott McDaniel-c/a begins, ends #7; foil-c   3.50
2-13: 2-Begin $1.95-c. 4-Hobgoblin-c/app. 6-Daredevil-c/app.
   8-Robertson-a; McDaniel-c. 12,13-Onslaught x-over. 13-Green Goblin
   quits; Spider-Man app.   2.25

GREEN LANTERN (2nd Series)(Green Lantern Corps #206 on)
National Periodical Publ./DC Comics: Jul/Aug. 1960 - No. 89, Apr/May
1972; No. 90, Aug/Sept. 1976 - No. 205, Oct, 1986

	GD	FN	NM-
1-(7-8/60)-Origin retold; Gil Kane-c/a continues; 1st app. Guardians of the Universe	327	981	7200
2-1st Pieface	74	222	1400
3-Contains readers poll	47	141	800
4,5: 5-Origin/1st app. Hector Hammond	38	114	600
6-Intro Tomar-Re the alien G.L.	33	99	520
7-Origin/1st app. Sinestro (7-8/61)	32	96	500
8-10: 8-1st 5700 A.D. story; grey tone-c. 9-1st Jordan Brothers; last 10¢ issue	27	81	400
11,12	19	57	275
13-Flash x-over	30	90	450
14-20: 14-Origin/1st app. Sonar. 16-Origin & 1st app. Star Sapphire. 20-Flash x-over	16	48	240
21-30: 21-Origin & 1st app. Dr. Polaris. 23-1st Tattooed Man. 24-Origin & 1st app. Shark. 29-JLA cameo; 1st Blackhand	13	39	190
31-39: 37-1st app. Evil Star (villain)	11	33	160
40-1st app. Crisis (10/65); 2nd solo G.A. Green Lantern in Silver Age (see Showcase #55); origin The Guardians; Doiby Dickles app.	46	138	775
41-44,46-50: 42-Zatanna x-over. 43-Flash x-over	10	30	130
45-2nd S.A. app. G.A. Green Lantern in title (6/66)	15	45	215
51,53-58	8	24	100
52-G.A. Green Lantern x-over	10	30	135
59-1st app. Guy Gardner (3/68)	17	51	255
60,62-69: 69-Wood inks; last 12¢ issue	6	18	75
61-G.A. Green Lantern x-over	8	24	95

	GD	FN	NM-
70-75	5	15	60
76-(4/70)-Begin Green Lantern/Green Arrow series (by Neal Adams #76-89) ends #122 (see Flash #217 for 2nd series)	32	96	500
77	9	27	110
78-80	7	21	90
81-84: 82-Wrightson-i(1 pg.). 83-G.L. reveals i.d. to Carol Ferris. 84-N. Adams/Wrightson-a (22 pgs.); last 15¢-c; partial photo-c	7	21	80
85,86-(52 pgs.)-Anti-drug issues. 86-G.A. Green Lantern-r; Toth-a	9	27	110
87-(12/71-1/72, 52 pgs.): 2nd app. Guy Gardner (cameo); 1st app. John Stewart (becomes 3rd Green Lantern in #182)	6	18	70
88-(2-3/72, 52 pgs.)-Unpubbed G.A. Green Lantern story; Green Lantern-r/Showcase #23. N. Adams-c/a (1 pg.)	4	12	45
89-(4-5/72, 52 pgs.)-G.A. Green Lantern-r; Green Lantern & Green Arrow move to Flash #217 (2nd team-up series)	6	18	70
90 (8-9/76)-Begin 3rd Green Lantern/Green Arrow team-up series; Mike Grell-c/a begins, ends #111	2	6	22
91-99	2	6	12
100-(1/78, Giant)-1st app. Air Wave II	2	6	20
101-107,111,113-115,117-119: 107-1st Tales of the G.L. Corps story	1	3	9
108-110-(44 pgs)-G.A. Green Lantern back-ups in each. 111-Origin retold; G.A. Green Lantern app.	1	4	10
112-G.A. Green Lantern origin retold	2	6	16
116-1st app. Guy Gardner as a G.L. (5/79)	4	12	45
117-119,121-(Whitman variants; low print run; none have issue # on cover)	2	6	12
120-122,124-150: 22-Last Green Lantern/Green Arrow team-up. 130-132-Tales of the G.L. Corps. 132-Adam Strange series begins, ends #147. 136,137-1st app. Citadel; Space Ranger app. 141-1st app. Omega Men (6/81). 142,143-Omega Men app.;Perez-c. 144-Omega Men cameo. 148-Tales of the G.L. Corps begins, ends #173. 150-Anniversary issue, 52 pgs.; no G.L. Corps			6.00
123-Green Lantern back to solo action; 2nd app. Guy Gardner as Green Lantern	1	4	10
151-180,183,184,186,187: 159-Origin Evil Star. 160,161-Omega Men			4.00
181,182,185,188: 181-Hal Jordan resigns as G.L. 182-John Stewart becomes new G.L.; origin recap of Hal Jordan as G.L. 185-Origin new G.L. (John Stewart).188-I.D. revealed; Alan Moore back-up scripts			5.00
189-193,196-199,201-205: 191-Re-intro Star Sapphire (cameo). 192-Re-intro & origin of Star Sapphire (1st full app.). 194,198-Crisis x-over. 199-Hal Jordan returns as a member of G.L. Corps (3 G.L.s now). 201-Green Lantern Corps begins (is cover title, says premiere issue); intro. Kilowog			3.50
194-Hal Jordan/Guy Gardner battle; Guardians choose Guy Gardner to become new Green Lantern			6.00
195-Guy Gardner becomes Green Lantern; Crisis on Infinite Earths x-over	2	6	12

	GD	FN	NM-
200-Double-size			4.00
Annual 1 (Listed as Tales Of The Green Lantern Corps Annual 1)			
Annual 2,3 (See Green Lantern Corps Annual #2,3)			3.50
Special 1 (1988), 2 (1989)-(Both $1.50, 52 pgs.)			3.50

GREEN LANTERN (3rd Series)
DC Comics: June, 1990 - No. 181, Nov, 2004
($1.00/$1.25/$1.50/$1.75/$1.95/$1.99/$2.25)

1-Hal Jordan, John Stewart & Guy Gardner return; Batman & JLA app. 5.00
2-26: 9-12-Guy Gardner solo story. 13-(52 pgs.). 18-Guy Gardner solo story.
   19-($1.75, 52 pgs.)-50th anniversary issue; Mart Nodell (original G.A.
   artist) part-p on G.A. Gr.Lantern; G. Kane-c. 25-($1.75, 52 pgs.)-Hal
   Jordan/Guy Gardner battle   4.00
27-45,47: 30,31-Gorilla Grodd-c/story(see Flash #69). 38,39-Adam Strange-
   c/story. 42-Deathstroke-c/s. 47-Green Arrow x-over   3.00
46,48,49,50: 46-Superman app. cont'd in Superman #82. 48-Emerald Twilight
   part 1. 50-($2.95, 52 pgs.)-Glow-in-the-dark-c   6.00
0, 51-62: 51-1st app. New Green Lantern (Kyle Rayner) with new costume.
   53-Superman-c/story. 55-(9/94)-Zero Hour. 0-(10/94). 56-(11/94)   4.00
63,64-Kyle Rayner vs. Hal Jordan.   4.00
65-80,82-92: 63-Begin $1.75-c. 65-New Titans app. 66,67-Flash app.
   71-Batman & Robin app. 72-Shazam!-c/app. 73-Wonder Woman-c/app.
   73-75-Adam Strange app. 76,77-Green Arrow x-over. 80-Final Night x-over.
   87-JLA app. 91-Genesis x-over. 92-Green Arrow x-over   3.00
81-(Regular Ed.)-Memorial for Hal Jordan (Parallax); most DC heroes app.
    5.00
81-($3.95, Deluxe Edition)-Embossed prism-c   6.00
93-99: 93-Begin $1.95-c; Deadman app. 94-Superboy app. 95-Starlin-a(p).
   98,99-Legion of Super-Heroes-c/app.   2.50
100-($2.95) Two covers (Jordan & Rayner); vs. Sinestro   5.00
101-106: 101-106-Hal Jordan-c/app. 103-JLA-c/app. 104-Green Arrow app.
   105,106-Parallax app.   3.00
107-126: 107-Jade becomes a Green Lantern. 119-Hal Jordan/Spectre app.
   125-JLA app.   2.25
127-149: 127-Begin $2.25-c. 129-Winick-s begin. 134-136-JLA-c/app.
   143-Joker: Last Laugh; Lee-c. 145-Kyle becomes The Ion   2.25
150-($3.50) Jim Lee-c; Kyle becomes Green Lantern again; new costume 3.50
151-181: 151-155-Jim Lee-c. 154-Terry attacked. 155-Spectre-c/app.
   162-164-Crossover with Green Arrow #23-25. 165-Raab-s begin.
   169-Kilowog returns   2.25
#1,000,000 (11/98) 853rd Century x-over; Hitch & Neary-a/c   3.00
Annual 1-3: ('92-'94, 68 pgs.)-1-Eclipso app. 2 -Intro Nightblade. 3-Elseworlds
   story   3.50
Annual 4 (1995, $3.50)-Year One story   4.00
Annual 5,7,8 ('96, '98, '99, $2.95): 5-Legends of the Dead Earth. 7-Ghosts;
   Wrightson-c. 8-JLApe; Art Adams-c   3.00
Annual 6 (1997, $3.95)-Pulp Heroes story   5.00
Annual 9 (2000, $3.50) Planet DC   3.50
...80 Page Giant (12/98, $4.95) Stories by various   5.00
...80 Page Giant 2 (6/99, $4.95) Team-ups   5.00

	GD	FN	NM-
...80 Page Giant 3 (8/00, \$5.95) Darkseid vs. the GL Corps			6.00
...: 1001 Emerald Nights (2001, \$6.95) Elseworlds; Guay-a/c; LaBan-s			7.00
...3-D #1 (12/98, \$3.95) Jeanty-a			4.00
...: A New Dawn TPB (1998, \$9.95)-r/#50-55			10.00
...: Baptism of Fire TPB (1999, \$12.95)-r/#59,66,67,70-75			13.00
...: Brother's Keeper (2003, \$12.95)-r/#151-155; Green Lantern Secret Files #3			13.00
...: Emerald Allies TPB (2000, \$14.95)-r/GL/GA team-ups			15.00
...: Emerald Knights TPB (1998, \$12.95)-r/Hal Jordan's return			13.00
...: Emerald Twilight nn (1994, \$5.95)-r/#48-50			6.00
...: Emerald Twilight/New Dawn TPB (2003, \$19.95)-r/#48-55			20.00
...: Ganthet's Tale nn (1992, \$5.95, 68 pgs.)-Silver foil logo; Niven scripts; Byrne-c/a			6.00
.../Green Arrow Vol. 1 (2004, \$12.95) -r/GL #76-82; intro. by O'Neil			13.00
.../Green Arrow Vol. 2 (2004, \$12.95) -r/GL #83-87,89 & Flash #217-219, 226; cover gallery with 1983-84 GL/GA covers #1-7; intro. by Giordano			13.00
.../Green Arrow Collection, Vol. 2-r/GL #84-87,89 & Flash #217-219 & GL/GA #5-7 by O'Neil/Adams/Wrightson			13.00
...: New Journey, Old Path TPB (2001, \$12.95)-r/#129-136			13.00
... : Our Worlds at War (8/01, \$2.95) Jae Lee-c; prelude to x-over			3.00
...: Passing The Torch (2004, \$12.95, TPB) r/#156,158-161 & GL Secret Files #2			13.00
...Plus 1 (12/1996, \$2.95)-The Ray & Polaris-c/app.			3.00
...Secret Files 1-3- (7/98-7/02, \$4.95)1- Origin stories/profiles. 2-Grell-c			5.00
.../Superman: Legend of the Green Flame (2000, \$5.95) 1988 unpub. Neil Gaiman story of Hal Jordan with new art by various; Frank Miller-c			6.00
...: The Power of Ion (2003, \$14.95, TPB) r/#142-150			15.00
...The Road Back nn (1992, \$8.95)-r/1-8 w/covers			9.00
...: Traitor TPB (2001, \$12.95) r/Legends of the DCU #20,21,28,29,37,38			13.00
...: Willworld (2001, \$24.95, HC) Seth Fisher-a/J.M. DeMatteis-s; Hal Jordan			25.00
...: Willworld (2003, \$17.95, SC)			18.00

GREEN LANTERN ANNUAL NO. 1, 1963
DC Comics: 1998 (\$4.95, one-shot)

1-Reprints Golden Age & Silver Age stories in 1963-style 80 pg. Giant format; new Gil Kane sketch art			5.00

GREEN LANTERN: BRIGHTEST DAY; BLACKEST NIGHT
DC Comics: 2002 (\$5.95, squarebound, one-shot)

nn-Alan Scott vs. Solomon Grundy in 1944; Snyder III-c/a; Seagle-s			6.00

GREEN LANTERN CORPS, THE (Formerly Green Lantern; see Tales of...)
DC Comics: No. 206, Nov. 1986 - No. 224, May, 1988

206-223: 212-John Stewart marries Katma Tui. 220,221-Millennium tie-ins			3.00
224-Double-size last issue			4.00
...Corps Annual 2,3- (12/86,8/87) 1-Formerly Tales of ...Annual #1; Alan Moore scripts. 3-Indicia says Green Lantern Annual #3; Moore scripts;			

	GD	FN	NM-
Byrne-a			3.00

GREEN LANTERN CORPS QUARTERLY
DC Comics: Summer, 1992 - No. 8, Spring, 1994 ($2.50/$2.95, 68 pgs.)

1,7,8: 1-G.A. Green Lantern story; Staton-a(p). 7-Painted-c; Tim Vigil-a. 8-Lobo-c/s			3.50
2-6: 2-G.A. G.L.-c/story; Austin-c(i); Gulacy-a(p). 3-G.A. G.L. story. 4-Austin-i			3.00

GREEN LANTERN: EMERALD DAWN (Also see Emerald Dawn)
DC Comics: Dec, 1989 - No. 6, May, 1990 ($1.00, limited series)

1-Origin retold; Giffen plots in all			5.00
2-6: 4-Re-intro. Tomar-Re			4.00

GREEN LANTERN: EMERALD DAWN II (Emerald Dawn II #1 & 2)
DC Comics: Apr, 1991 - No. 6, Sept, 1991 ($1.00, limited series)

1-6			2.50
TPB (2003, $12.95) r/#1-6; Alan Davis-c			13.00

GREEN LANTERN: MOSAIC (Also see Cosmic Odyssey #2)
DC Comics: June, 1992 - No. 18, Nov, 1993 ($1.25)

1-18: Featuring John Stewart. 1-Painted-c by Cully Hamner			2.25

GREEN LANTERN: REBIRTH
DC Comics: Dec, 2004 - No. 6, May, 2005 ($2.95, limited series)

1-Johns-s/Van Sciver-a; Hal Jordan as The Spectre on-c			5.00
1-2nd printing; Hal Jordan as Green Lantern on-c			3.00
1-3rd printing; B&W-c version of 1st printing			3.00
2-6: 2-Guy Gardner becomes a Green Lantern again; JLA app.			3.00

GREEN LANTERN VS. ALIENS
Dark Horse Comics: Sept, 2000 - No. 4, Dec, 2000 ($2.95, limited series)

1-4: 1-Hal Jordan and GL Corps vs. Aliens; Leonardi-p. 2-4-Kyle Rayner			3.00

GRENDEL (Also see Primer #2, Mage and Comico Collection)
Comico: Mar, 1983 - No. 3, Feb, 1984 ($1.50, B&W)(#1 has indicia to Skrog #1)

	GD	FN	NM-
1-Origin Hunter Rose	12	36	165
2,3: 2-Origin Argent	9	27	110

GRENDEL
Comico: Oct, 1986 - No. 40, Feb, 1990 ($1.50/$1.95/$2.50, mature)

	GD	FN	NM-
1	1	3	9
1,2: 2nd printings			3.00
2,3,5-15: 13-15-Ken Steacy-c.			4.00
4,16: 4-Dave Stevens-c(i). 16-Re-intro Mage (series begins, ends #19)			6.00
17-40: 24-25,27-28,30-31-Snyder-c/a			3.00
Devil by the Deed (Graphic Novel, 10/86, $5.95, 52 pgs.)-r/Grendel back-ups/ Mage 6-14; Alan Moore intro.	1	3	7
Devil's Legacy ($14.95, 1988, Graphic Novel)	2	6	15
Devil's Vagary (10/87, B&W & red)-No price; included in Comico Collection	2	6	12

GRENDEL (Title series): **Dark Horse Comics**

	GD	FN	NM-

--BLACK, WHITE, AND RED, 11/98 - No. 4, 2/99 ($3.95, anthology)
  1-Wagner-s in all. Art by Sale, Leon and others   5.00
  2-4: 2-Mack, Chadwick-a. 3-Allred, Kristensen-a. 4-Pearson, Sprouse-a   4.00

--CLASSICS, 7/95 - 8/95 ($3.95, mature) 1,2-reprints; new Wagner-c   4.00

--CYCLE, 10/95 ($5.95) 1-nn-history of Grendel by M. Wagner & others   6.00

--DEVIL BY THE DEED, 7/93 ($3.95, varnish-c) 1-nn-M. Wagner-c/a/scripts;
  r/Grendel back-ups from Mage #6-14   4.00
  Reprint (12/97, $3.95) w/pin-ups by various   4.00

--DEVIL CHILD, 6/99 - No. 2, 7/99 ($2.95, mature) 1,2-Sale & Kristiansen-a/
  Schutz-s   3.00

--DEVIL QUEST, 11/95 ($4.95) 1-nn-Prequel to Batman/Grendel II; M. Wagner
  story & art; r/back-up story from Grendel Tales series.   5.00

--DEVILS AND DEATHS, 10/94 - 11/94 ($2.95, mature) 1,2   3.00

: DEVIL'S LEGACY, 3/00 - No. 12, 2/01 ($2.95, reprints 1986 series,
  recolored) 1-12-Wagner-s/c; Pander Bros.-a   3.00

: DEVIL'S REIGN, 5/04 - No. 7 ($3.50, repr. 1989 series #34-40, recolored)
  1-4-Sale-c/a.   3.50

: GOD AND THE DEVIL, No. 0, 1/03 - No. 10, 12/03 ($3.50/$4.99, repr. 1986
  series, recolored) 0-9: 0-Sale-c/a; r/#23. 1-9-Snyder-c   3.50
  10-($4.99) Double-sized; Snyder-c   5.00

--RED, WHITE & BLACK, 9/02 - No. 4, 12/02 ($4.99, anthology)
  1-4-Wagner-s in all. 1-Art by Thompson, Sakai, Mahfood and others.
  2-Kelley Jones, Watson, Brereton, Hester & Parks-a. 3-Oeming, Noto,
  Cannon, Ashley Wood, Huddleston-a. 4-Chiang, Dalrymple, Robertson,
  Snyder III and Zulli-a   5.00

--TALES: DEVIL'S CHOICES, 3/95 - 6/95 ($2.95, mature) 1-4   3.00

--TALES: FOUR DEVILS, ONE HELL, 8/93 - 1/94 ($2.95, mature)
  1-6-Wagner painted-c   3.00
  TPB (12/94, $17.95) r/#1-6   18.00

--TALES: HOMECOMING, 12/94 - 2/95 ($2.95, mature) 1-3   3.00

--TALES: THE DEVIL IN OUR MIDST, 5/94 - 9/95 ($2.95, mature)
  1-5-Wagner painted-c   3.00

--TALES: THE DEVIL MAY CARE, 12/95 - No. 6, 5/96 ($2.95, mature)
  1-6-Terry LaBan scripts. 5-Batman/Grendel II preview   3.00

--TALES: THE DEVIL'S APPRENTICE, 9/97 - No. 3, 11/97 ($2.95, mature)
  1-3   3.00

: THE DEVIL INSIDE, 9/01 - No. 3, 11/01 ($2.99)
  1-3-r/#13-15 with new Wagner-c   3.00

GRENDEL: WAR CHILD
Dark Horse Comics: Aug, 1992 - No. 10, Jun, 1993 ($2.50, lim. series,
mature)
  1-9: 1-4-Bisley painted-c; Wagner-i & scripts in all   3.00
  10-($3.50, 52 pgs.) Wagner-c   4.00

	GD	FN	NM-
Limited Edition Hardcover ($99.95)			100.00

GRIMJACK (Also see Demon Knight & Starslayer)
First Comics: Aug, 1984 - No. 81, Apr, 1991 ($1.00/$1.95/$2.25)

	GD	FN	NM-
1-John Ostrander scripts & Tim Truman-c/a begins.			3.00
2-25: 20-Sutton-c/a begins. 22-Bolland-a.			2.25
26-2nd color Teenage Mutant Ninja Turtles			4.00
27-74,76-81 (Later issues $1.95, $2.25): 30-Dynamo Joe x-over; 31-Mandrake-c/a begins. 73,74-Kelley Jones-a			2.50
75-($5.95, 52 pgs.)-Fold-out map; coated stock			6.00

NOTE: *Truman c/a-1-17.*

GROOVY (Cartoon Comics - not CCA approved)
Marvel Comics Group: March, 1968 - No. 3, July, 1968

	GD	FN	NM-
1-Monkees, Ringo Starr, Sonny & Cher, Mamas & Papas photos	9	27	120
2,3	6	18	75

GUY GARDNER (Guy Gardner: Warrior #17 on)(Also see Green Lantern #59)
DC Comics: Oct, 1992 - No. 44, July, 1996 ($1.25/$1.50/$1.75)

	GD	FN	NM-
1-24,0,26-30: 1-Staton-c/a(p) begins. 6-Guy vs. Hal Jordan. 15-JLA x-over, begin $1.50-c. 18-Begin 4-part Emerald Fallout story; splash page x-over GL #50. 18-21-Vs. Hal Jordan. 24-(9/94)-Zero Hour. 0-(10/94)			2.50
25 (11/94, $2.50, 52 pgs.)			3.00
29 ($2.95)-Gatefold-c			3.50
29-Variant-c (Edward Hopper's Nighthawks)			2.50
31-44: 31-$1.75-c begins. 40-Grodd-c/app. 44-Parallax-app. (1 pg.)			2.50
Annual 1 (1995, $3.50)-Year One story			4.00
Annual 2 (1996, $2.95)-Legends of the Dead Earth story			3.00

HAIR BEAR BUNCH, THE (TV) (See Fun-In No. 13)
Gold Key: Feb, 1972 - No. 9, Feb, 1974 (Hanna-Barbera)

	GD	FN	NM-
1	4	12	48
2-9	3	9	30

HANNA-BARBERA BANDWAGON (TV)
Gold Key: Oct, 1962 - No. 3, Apr, 1963

	GD	FN	NM-
1-Giant, 84 pgs. 1-Augie Doggie app.; 1st app. Lippy the Lion, Touché Turtle & Dum Dum, Wally Gator, Loopy de Loop,	14	42	200
2-Giant, 84 pgs.; Mr. & Mrs. J. Evil Scientist (1st app.) in Snagglepuss story; Yakky Doodle, Ruff and Reddy and others app.	10	30	140
3-Regular size; Mr. & Mrs. J. Evil Scientist app. (pre-#1), Snagglepuss, Wally Gator and others app.	8	24	105

HANNA-BARBERA SUPER TV HEROES (TV)
Gold Key: Apr, 1968 - No. 7, Oct, 1969 (Hanna-Barbera)

	GD	FN	NM-
1-The Birdman, The Herculoids(ends #6; not in #3), Moby Dick, Young Samson & Goliath (ends #2,4), and The Mighty Mightor begin; Spiegle-a in all	19	57	275
2-The Galaxy Trio app.; Shazzan begins; 12¢ & 15¢ versions exist	13	39	185

	GD	FN	NM-
3,6,7-The Space Ghost app.	12	36	175
4,5	11	33	150

HARLEM GLOBETROTTERS (TV) (See Fun-In No. 8, 10)
Gold Key: Apr, 1972 - No. 12, Jan, 1975 (Hanna-Barbera)

	GD	FN	NM-
1	4	12	50
2-5	3	9	25
6-12	2	6	20

HAUNTED (Baron Weirwulf's Haunted Library on-c #21 on)
Charlton Comics: 9/71 - No. 30, 11/76; No. 31, 9/77 - No. 75, 9/84

	GD	FN	NM-
1-All Ditko issue	5	15	55
2-7-Ditko-c/a	3	9	28
8,12,28-Ditko-a	2	6	18
9,19	2	6	14
10,20,15,18: 10,20-Sutton-a. 15-Sutton-c	2	6	14
11,13,14,16-Ditko-c/a	2	6	20
17-Sutton-c/a; Newton-a	2	6	15
21-Newton-c/a; Sutton-a; 1st Baron Weirwulf	3	9	28
22-Newton-c/a; Sutton-a	2	6	16
23,24-Sutton-c; Ditko-a	2	6	16
25-27,29,32,33	1	4	10
30,41,47,49-52,74-Ditko-c/a: 51-Reprints #1	2	6	16
31,35,37,38-Sutton-a	1	4	10
34,36,39,40,42,57,60-Ditko-a	2	6	12
43-46,48,53-56,58,59,61-73: 59-Newton-a. 64-Sutton-c. 71-73-Low print	1	3	8
75-(9/84) Last issue; low print	2	6	16

HAUNT OF HORROR, THE (Digest)
Marvel Comics: Jun, 1973 - No. 2, Aug, 1973 (164 pgs.; text and art)

	GD	FN	NM-
1-Morrow painted skull-c; stories by Ellison, Howard, and Leiber; Brunner-a	4	12	40
2-Kelly Freas painted bondage-c; stories by McCaffrey, Goulart, Leiber, Ellison; art by Simonson, Brunner, and Buscema	3	9	28

HAWK AND THE DOVE, THE (See Showcase #75 & Teen Titans) (1st series)
National Periodical Publications: Aug-Sept, 1968 - No. 6, June-July, 1969

	GD	FN	NM-
1-Ditko-c/a	9	27	120
2-6: 5-Teen Titans cameo	6	18	70

HAWKMAN (1st Series) (Also see The Atom #7 & Brave & the Bold #34-36, 42-44, 51)
National Periodical Publications: Apr-May, 1964 - No. 27, Aug-Sept, 1968

	GD	FN	NM-
1-(4-5/64)-Anderson-c/a begins, ends #21	51	153	975
2	24	72	360
3,5: 5-2nd app. Shadow Thief	15	45	225
4-Origin & 1st app. Zatanna (10-11/64)	19	57	285
6	12	36	175
7	10	30	135
8-10: 9-Atom cameo; Hawkman & Atom learn each other's I.D.; 3rd app.			

	GD	FN	NM-

Shadow Thief 9 27 115
11-15 7 21 85
16,17-27: 18-Adam Strange x-over (cameo #19). 25-G.A. Hawkman-r by
    Moldoff. 26-Kirby-a(r). 27-Kubert-c 6 18 65

HAWKMAN (See JSA #23 for return)
DC Comics: May, 2002 - Present ($2.50)

1-Johns & Robinson-s/Morales-a 5.00
1-2nd printing 2.50
2-35: 2-4-Shadow Thief app. 5,6-Green Arrow-c/app. 8-Atom-c/app.
    13-Van Sciver-a. 14-Gentleman Ghost app. 15-Hawkwoman app. 16-Byth
    returns. 23-25-Black Reign x-over with JSA #56-58. 26-Byrne-c/a.
    27-Phillips-a. 28-Sook-a begins. 29,30-Land-c 2.50
...: Allies & Enemies TPB (2004, $14.95) r/#7-14 & pages fromSecret Files
    and Origins 15.00
...: Endless Flight TPB (2003, $12.95) r/#1-6 & Secret Files and Origins 13.00
... Secret Files and Origins (10/02, $4.95) profiles and pin-ups by various 5.00

HELLBLAZER (John Constantine) (See Saga of Swamp Thing #37)
(Also see Books of Magic limited series)
DC Comics (Vertigo #63 on): Jan, 1988 - Present
($1.25/$1.50/$1.95/$2.25/$2.50/$2.75)

1-(44 pgs.)-John Constantine; McKean-c thru #21 2 6 12
2-5 1 3 7
6-8,10: 10-Swamp Thing cameo 5.00
9,19: 9-X-over w/Swamp Thing #76. 19-Sandman app. 6.00
11-18,20 5.00
21-26,28-30: 22-Williams-c. 24-Contains bound-in Shocker movie poster.
    25,26-Grant Morrison scripts. 5.00
27-Gaiman scripts; Dave McKean-a; low print run 2 6 15
31-39: 36-Preview of World Without End. 4.00
40-($2.25, 52 pgs.)-Dave McKean-a & colors; preview of Kid Eternity 4.00
41-Ennis scripts begin; ends #83 5.00
42-120: 44,45-Sutton-a(i). 50-($3.00, 52 pgs.). 52-Glenn Fabry painted-c
    begin. 62-Special Death insert by McKean. 63-Silver metallic ink on-c.
    77-Totleben-c. 84-Sean Phillips-c/a begins; Delano story. 85-88-Eddie
    Campbell story. 75-($2.95, 52 pgs.). 89-Paul Jenkins scripts begin;
    108-Adlard-a. 100,120 ($3.50,48 pgs.) 3.50
121-199, 201,202: 129-Ennis-s. 141-Bradstreet-a. 146-150-Corben-a
    151-Azzarello-a begin. 175-Carey-s begin; Dillon-a. 176-Begin $2.75-c.
    182,183-Bermejo-a 2.75
200-($4.50) Carey-s/Dillon, Frusin, Manco-a 4.50
Annual 1 (1989, $2.95, 68 pgs.)-Bryan Talbot's 1st work in American comics
     5.00
Special 1 (1993, $3.95, 68 pgs.)-Ennis story; w/pin-ups. 4.00

HELLBLAZER/THE BOOKS OF MAGIC
DC Comics (Vertigo): Dec, 1997 - No. 2, Jan, 1998 ($2.50, mini-series)

1,2-John Constantine and Tim Hunter 2.50

HELLBOY (Also see Danger Unlimited #4, Dark Horse Presents, Gen[13] #13B,

	GD	FN	NM-

Ghost/Hellboy, John Byrne's Next Men, San Diego Comic Con #2, & Savage Dragon)

HELLBOY: ALMOST COLOSSUS
Dark Horse Comics (Legend): Jun, 1997 - No. 2, Jul, 1997 ($2.95, limited series)

1,2-Mignola-s/a	3.00

HELLBOY: BOX FULL OF EVIL
Dark Horse Comics: Aug, 1999 - No. 2, Sept, 1999 ($2.95, lim. series)

1,2-Mignola-s/a; back-up story w/ Matt Smith-a	3.00

HELLBOY CHRISTMAS SPECIAL
Dark Horse Comics: Dec, 1997 ($3.95, one-shot)

nn-Christmas stories by Mignola, Gianni, Darrow, Purcell	4.00

HELLBOY: CONQUEROR WORM
Dark Horse Comics: May, 2001 - No. 4, Aug, 2001 ($2.99, lim. series)

1-4-Mignola-s/a/c	3.00

HELLBOY, JR.
Dark Horse Comics: Oct, 1999 - No. 2, Nov, 1999 ($2.95, limited series)

1,2-Stories and art by various	3.00
TPB (1/04, $14.95) r/#1&2, Halloween; sketch pages; intro. by Steve Niles; Bill Wray-c	15.00

HELLBOY, JR., HALLOWEEN SPECIAL
Dark Horse Comics: Oct, 1997 ($3.95, one-shot)

nn-"Harvey" style renditions of Hellboy characters; Bill Wray, Mike Mignola & various-s/a; wraparound-c by Wray	4.00

HELLBOY PREMIERE EDITION
Dark Horse Comics (Wizard): 2004 (no price, one-shot)

nn-2 covers by Mignola & Davis; Mignola-s/a; BPRD story w/Arcudi-s/Davis-a	5.00
Wizard World Los Angeles-Movie photo-c; Mignola-s/a; BPRD story w/Arcudi-s/Davis-a	10.00

HELLBOY: SEED OF DESTRUCTION
Dark Horse Comics (Legend): Mar, 1994 - No. 4, Jun, 1994 ($2.50, lim. series)

1-4-Mignola-c/a w/Byrne scripts; Monkeyman & O'Brien back-up story (origin) by Art Adams.	4.00
Trade paperback (1994, $17.95)-collects all four issues plus r/Hellboy's 1st app. in San Diego Comic Con #2 & pin-ups	18.00
Limited edition hardcover (1995, $99.95)-includes everything in trade paperback plus additional material.	100.00

HELLBOY: THE CHAINED COFFIN AND OTHERS
Dark Horse Comics (Legend): Aug, 1998 ($17.95, TPB)

nn-Mignola-c/a/s; reprints out-of-print one shots; pin-up gallery	18.00

HELLBOY: THE CORPSE
Dark Horse Comics: Mar, 2004 (25¢, one-shot)

	GD	FN	NM-

nn-Mignola-c/a/scripts; reprints "The Corpse" serial from Capitol City's Advance Comics catalog; development sketches and photos of the Corpse from the Hellboy movie 2.25

HELLBOY: THE CORPSE AND THE IRON SHOES
Dark Horse Comics (Legend): Jan, 1996 ($2.95, one-shot)

nn-Mignola-c/a/scripts; reprints "The Corpse" serial w/new story 3.00

HELLBOY: THE RIGHT HAND OF DOOM
Dark Horse Comics (Legend): Apr, 2000 ($17.95, TPB)

nn-Mignola-c/a/s; reprints 18.00

HELLBOY: THE THIRD WISH
Dark Horse Comics (Maverick): July, 2002 - No. 2, Aug, 2002 ($2.99, limited series)

1,2-Mignola-c/a/s 3.00

HELLBOY: THE WOLVES OF ST. AUGUST
Dark Horse Comics (Legend): 1995 ($4.95, squarebound, one-shot)

nn-Mignola--c/a/scripts; r/Dark Horse Presents #88-91 with additional story 5.00

HELLBOY: WAKE THE DEVIL (Sequel to Seed of Destruction)
Dark Horse Comics (Legend): Jun, 1996 - No. 5, Oct, 1996 ($2.95, lim. series)

1-5: Mignola-c/a & scripts; The Monstermen back-up story by Gianni 3.00
TPB (1997, $17.95) r/#1-5 18.00

HELLBOY: WEIRD TALES
Dark Horse Comics: Feb, 2003 - No. 8, Apr, 2004 ($2.99, limited series, anthology)

1-8-Hellboy stories from other creators. 1-Cassaday-c/s/a; Watson-s/a.
6-Cho-c 3.00
... Vol. 1 (2004, 17.95) r/#1-4 18.00
... Vol. 2 (2004, 17.95) r/#5-8 and Lobster Johnson serial from #1-8 18.00

HERBIE (See Forbidden Worlds & Unknown Worlds)
American Comics Group: April-May, 1964 - No. 23, Feb, 1967 (All 12¢)

1-Whitney-c/a in most issues	17	51	250
2-4	10	30	125
5-Beatles parody (10 pgs.), Dean Martin, Frank Sinatra app.	11	33	150
6,7,9,10	8	24	100
8-Origin & 1st app. The Fat Fury	10	30	125
11-23: 14-Nemesis & Magicman app. 17-r/2nd Herbie from Forbidden Worlds #94. 23-r/1st Herbie from F.W. #73	6	18	75

HERCULES (See Charlton Classics)
Charlton Comics: Oct, 1967 - No. 13, Sept, 1969; Dec, 1968

1-Thane of Bagarth begins; Glanzman-a in all	4	12	45
2-13: 1-5,7-10-Aparo-a. 8-(12¢-c)	3	9	25
8-(Low distribution)(12/68, 35¢, B&W); magazine format; new Hercules story			

	GD	FN	NM-
plus-r story/#1; Thane-r/#1-3	6	18	70
Modern Comics reprint 10('77), 11('78)			6.00

HEROES
Marvel Comics: Dec, 2001 ($3.50, magazine-size, one-shot)

1-Pin-up tributes to the rescue workers of the Sept. 11 tragedy; art and text by various; cover by Alex Ross			3.50
1-2nd and 3rd printings			3.50

HEROES REBORN: THE RETURN
Marvel Comics: Dec, 1997 - No. 4 ($2.50, weekly mini-series)

	GD	FN	NM-
1-4-Avengers, Fantastic Four, Iron Man & Captain America rejoin regular Marvel Universe; Peter David-s/Larocca-c/a			4.00
1-4-Variant-c for each			6.00
Wizard 1/2	1	3	9
Return of the Heroes TPB ('98, $14.95) r/#1-4			15.00

HERO FOR HIRE (Power Man No. 17 on; also see Cage)
Marvel Comics Group: June, 1972 - No. 16, Dec, 1973

	GD	FN	NM-
1-Origin & 1st app. Luke Cage; Tuska-a(p)	8	24	95
2-Tuska-a(p)	4	12	40
3-5: 3-1st app. Mace. 4-1st app. Phil Fox of the Bugle	3	9	28
6-10: 8,9-Dr. Doom app. 9-F.F. app.	2	6	18
11-16: 14-Origin retold. 15-Everett Sub-Mariner-r('53). 16-Origin Stilletto; death of Rackham	2	6	12

HONG KONG PHOOEY (TV)
Charlton Comics: June, 1975 - No. 9, Nov, 1976 (Hanna-Barbera)

	GD	FN	NM-
1	6	18	70
2	3	10	35
3-9	3	9	26

HOT ROD RACERS (Grand Prix No. 16 on)
Charlton Comics: Dec, 1964 - No. 15, July, 1967

	GD	FN	NM-
1	9	27	115
2-5	6	18	65
6-15	4	12	48

HOT RODS AND RACING CARS
Charlton Comics (Motor Mag. No. 1): Nov, 1951 - No. 120, June, 1973

	GD	FN	NM-
1-Speed Davis begins; Indianapolis 500 story	30	90	320
2	15	45	160
3-10	11	33	110
11-20	10	30	90
21-33,36-40	8	24	70
34, 35 (? & 6/58, 68 pgs.)	11	33	105
41-60	7	21	55
61-80	4	12	38
81-100	3	9	28
101-120	2	6	22

	GD	FN	NM-

HOT STUFF, THE LITTLE DEVIL (Also see Devil Kids & Harvey Hits)
Harvey Publications (Illustrated Humor): 10/57 - No. 141, 7/77; No. 142, 2/78 - No. 164, 8/82; No. 165, 10/86 - 171, 11/87; No. 172, 11/88; No. 173, Sept, 1990 - No. 177, 1/91

	GD	FN	NM-
1	41	123	650
2-1st app. Stumbo the Giant (12/57)	21	63	310
3-5	15	45	220
6-10	10	30	130
11-20	7	21	90
21-40	5	15	60
41-60	4	12	38
61-80	3	9	30
81-105	2	6	22
106-112: All 52 pg. Giants	3	9	30
113-125	2	6	12
126-141	1	3	9
142-177: 172-177-($1.00)			6.00

HOT WHEELS (TV)
National Periodical Publications: Mar-Apr, 1970 - No. 6, Jan-Feb, 1971

	GD	FN	NM-
1	10	30	140
2,4,5	6	18	70
3-Neal Adams-c	7	21	80
6-Neal Adams-c/a	8	24	100

NOTE: *Toth a-1p, 2-5; c-1p, 5.*

HOUSE OF MYSTERY, THE
National Periodical Publications/DC Comics: Dec-Jan, 1951-52 - No. 321, Oct, 1983 (No. 194-203: 52 pgs.)

	GD	FN	NM-
1-DC's first horror comic	238	714	3100
2	92	276	1200
3	65	195	850
4,5	52	156	650
6-10	45	135	560
11-15	40	120	450
16(7/53)-25	31	93	335
26-35(2/55)-Last pre-code issue; 30-Woodish-a	24	72	260
36-50: 50-Text story of Orson Welles' War of the Worlds broadcast			
	14	42	200
51-60: 55-1st S.A. issue	11	33	160
61,63,65,66,69,70,72,76,85-Kirby-a	13	39	185
62,64,67,68,71,73-75,77-83,86-99	10	30	135
84-Prototype of Negative Man (Doom Patrol)	13	39	185
100 (7/60)	11	33	150
101-116: 109-Toth, Kubert-a. 116-Last 10¢ issue	10	30	125
117-130: 117-Swipes-c to HOS #20. 120-Toth-a	9	27	110
131-142	8	24	95
143-J'onn J'onzz, Manhunter begins (6/64), ends #173; story continues from			
Detective #326; intro. Idol-Head of Diabolu	22	66	320
144	10	30	130

	GD	FN	NM-
145-155,157-159: 149-Toth-a. 155-The Human Hurricane app. (12/65), Red Tornado prototype. 158-Origin Diabolu Idol-Head	7	21	85
156-Robby Reed begins (origin/1st app.), ends #173	9	27	115
160-(7/66)-Robby Reed becomes Plastic Man in this issue only; 1st S.A. app. Plastic Man; intro Marco Xavier (Martian Manhunter) & Vulture Crime Organization; ends #173	11	33	145
161-173: 169-Origin/1st app. Gem Girl	5	15	60
174-Mystery format begins.	9	27	115
175-1st app. Cain (House of Mystery host)	7	21	80
176,177	6	18	70
178-Neal Adams-a (2/69)	7	21	85
179-N. Adams/Orlando, Wrightson-a (1st pro work, 3 pgs.)	9	27	115
180,181,183: Wrightson-a (3,10, & 3 pgs.). 180-Last 12¢ issue; Kane/Wood-a(2). 183-Wood-a	6	18	70
182,184: 182-Toth-a. 184-Kane/Wood, Toth-a	4	12	45
185-Williamson/Kaluta-a; Howard-a (3 pgs.)	4	12	50
186-N. Adams-c/a; Wrightson-a (10 pgs.)	6	18	70
187,190: Adams-c. 187-Toth-a. 190-Toth-a(r)	4	12	40
188-Wrightson-a (8 & 3pgs.); Adams-c	5	15	55
189,192,197: Adams-c on all. 189-Wood-a(i). 192-Last 15¢-c	4	12	40
191-Wrightson-a (8 & 3pgs.); Adams-c	5	15	55
193-Wrightson-c	4	12	42
194-Wrightson-c; 52 pgs begin, end #203; Toth,Kirby-a	5	15	55
195: Wrightson-c. Swamp creature story by Wrightson similar to Swamp Thing (10 pgs.)(10/71)	7	21	80
196,198	4	12	42
199-Adams-c; Wood-a(8pgs.); Kirby-a	4	12	50
200-(25¢, 52 pgs.)-One third-r (3/72)	5	15	55
201-203-(25¢, 52 pgs.)-One third-r	4	12	42
204-Wrightson-c/a, 9 pgs.	4	12	38
205,206,208,210,212,215,216,218	3	9	24
207-Wrightson c/a; Starlin, Redondo-a	3	10	35
209,211,213,214,217,219-Wrightson-c	3	9	28
220,222,223	2	6	20
221-Wrightson/Kaluta-a(8 pgs.)	3	10	35
224-229: 224-Wrightson-r from Spectre #9; Dillin/Adams-r from House of Secrets #82; begin 100 pg. issues; Phantom Stranger-r. 225,227-(100 pgs.): 225-Spectre app. 226-Wrightson/Redondo-a Phantom Stranger-r. 228-N. Adams inks; Wrightson-r. 229-Wrightson-a(r); Toth-r; last 100 pg. issue	5	15	60
230,232-235,237-250	2	6	15
231-Classic Wrightson-c	3	9	30
236-Wrightson-c; Ditko-a(p); N. Adams-i	2	6	20
251-254-(84 pgs.)-Adams-c. 251-Wood-a	3	9	24
255,256-(84 pgs.)-Wrightson-c	3	9	24
257-259-(84 pgs.)	2	6	22

	GD	FN	NM-
260-289: 282-(68 pgs.)-Has extra story "The Computers That Saved Metropolis" Radio Shack giveaway by Jim Starlin	1	3	9
290-1st "I, Vampire"	3	9	24
291-299: 291,293,295-299- "I, Vampire"	2	6	14
300,319,321: Death of "I, Vampire"	2	6	16
301-318,320: 301-318-"I, Vampire"	2	6	14
Welcome to the House of Mystery (7/98, $5.95) reprints stories with new framing story by Gaiman and Aragonés			6.00

HOUSE OF SECRETS (Combined with The Unexpected after #154)
National Periodical Publications/DC Comics: 11-12/56 - No. 80, 9-10/66; No. 81, 8-9/69 - No. 140, 2-3/76; No. 141, 8-9/76 - No. 154, 10-11/78

	GD	FN	NM-
1-Drucker-a; Moreira-c	113	339	2150
2-Moreira-a	43	129	725
3-Kirby-c/a	38	114	600
4-Kirby-a	29	87	425
5-7	20	60	290
8-Kirby-a	23	69	340
9-11: 11-Lou Cameron-a (unsigned)	17	51	255
12-Kirby-c/a; Lou Cameron-a	19	57	280
13-15: 14-Flying saucer-c	13	39	190
16-20	12	36	170
21,22,24-30	11	33	145
23-1st app. Mark Merlin & begin series (8/59)	12	36	170
31-50: 48-Toth-a. 50-Last 10¢ issue	10	30	125
51-60: 58-Origin Mark Merlin	8	24	105
61-First Eclipso (7-8/63) and begin series	17	51	250
62	10	30	125
63-65-Toth-a on Eclipso (see Brave and the Bold #64)	8	24	95
66-1st Eclipso-c (also #67,70,78,79); Toth-a	10	30	125
67,73: 67-Toth-a on Eclipso. 73-Mark Merlin becomes Prince Ra-Man (1st app.)	8	24	95
68-72,74-80: 76-Prince Ra-Man vs. Eclipso. 80-Eclipso, Prince Ra-Man end	7	21	85
81-Mystery format begins; 1st app. Abel (House Of Secrets host); (cameo in DC Special #4)	9	27	115
82-84: 82-Neal Adams-c(i)	5	15	55
85,90: 85-N. Adams-a(i). 90-Buckler (early work)/N. Adams-a(i)	5	15	60
86,88,89,91	4	12	45
87-Wrightson & Kaluta-a	6	18	65
92-1st app. Swamp Thing-c/story (8 pgs.)(6-7/71) by Berni Wrightson(p) w/Jeff Jones/Kaluta/Weiss ink assists; classic-c.	50	150	850
93,94,96-(52 pgs.)-Wrightson-c. 94-Wrightson-a(i); 96-Wood-a	4	12	50
95,97,98-(52 pgs.)	4	12	50
99-Wrightson splash pg.	4	12	38
100-Classic Wrightson-c	5	15	55
101,102,104,105,108-120: 112-Grey tone-c	2	6	20

	GD	FN	NM-
103,106,107-Wrightson-c	3	9	28
121-133	2	6	14
134-136,139-Wrightson-a	2	6	18
137,138,141-154	1	4	10
140-1st solo origin of the Patchworkman (see Swamp Thing #3)			
	3	9	26

HOUSE OF SECRETS
DC Comics (Vertigo): Oct, 1996 - No. 25, Dec, 1998 ($2.50) (Creator-owned series)

1-Steven Seagle-s/Kristiansen-c/a.	3.50
2-25: 5,7-Kristiansen-c/a. 6-Fegrado-a	3.00
TPB-(1997, $14.95) r/1-5	15.00

HOWARD THE DUCK (See Bizarre Adventures #34, Crazy Magazine, Fear, Man-Thing, Marvel Treasury Edition & Sensational She-Hulk #14-17)
Marvel Comics Group: Jan, 1976 - No. 31, May, 1979; No. 32, Jan, 1986; No. 33, Sept, 1986

	GD	FN	NM-
1-Brunner-c/a; Spider-Man x-over (low distr.)	3	10	35
2-Brunner-c/a	2	6	15
3,4-(Regular 25¢ edition). 3-Buscema-a(p), (7/76)	1	4	10
3,4-(30¢-c, limited distribution)	2	6	15
5	1	4	10
6-11: 8-Howard The Duck for president. 9-1st Sgt. Preston Dudley of RCMP. 10-Spider-Man-c/sty	1	3	7
12-1st brief app. Kiss (3/77)	3	10	35
13-(30¢-c) 1st full app. Kiss (6/77); Daimon Hellstrom app. plus cameo of Howard as Son of Satan	4	12	40
13-(35¢-c, limited distribution)	5	15	60
14-32: 14-17-(Regular 30¢-c). 14-Howard as Son of Satan-c/story; Son of Satan app. 16-Album issue; 3 pgs. comics. 22,23-Man-Thing-c/stories; Star Wars parody. 30,32-P. Smith-a			4.00
14-17-(35¢-c, limited distribution)			6.00
33-Last issue; low print run	1	3	7
Annual 1(1977, 52 pgs.)-Mayerik-a	1	3	7

HOWARD THE DUCK (Magazine)
Marvel Comics Group: Oct, 1979 - No. 9, Mar, 1981 (B&W, 68 pgs.)

	GD	FN	NM-
1-Art by Colan, Janson, Golden. Kidney Lady app.	1	4	10
2,3,5-9 (nudity in most): 2-Mayerick-c. 3-Xmas issue; Jack Davis-c; Duck World flashback. 5-Dracula app. 6-1st Street People back-up story. 7-Has poster by Byrne; Man-Thing-c/s (46 pgs.). 8-Batman parody w/Marshall Rogers-a; Dave Sim-a (1 pg.). 9-Marie Severin-a; John Pound painted-c			5.00
4-Beatles, John Lennon, Elvis, Kiss & Devo cameos; Hitler app.	2	6	12

HOWARD THE DUCK: THE MOVIE
Marvel Comics Group: Dec, 1986 - No. 3, Feb, 1987 (Limited series)

1-3: Movie adaptation; r/Marvel Super Special	2.50

	GD	FN	NM-

H. R. PUFNSTUF (TV) (See March of Comics #360)
Gold Key: Oct, 1970 - No. 8, July, 1972

1-Photo-c	21	63	310
2-8-Photo-c on all. 6-8-Both Gold Key and Whitman editions exist			
	11	33	155

HUCKLEBERRY HOUND (TV)
Dell/Gold Key No. 18 (10/62) on: No. 990, 5-7/59 - No. 43, 10/70 (Hanna-Barbera)

Four Color 990(#1)-1st app. Huckleberry Hound, Yogi Bear, & Pixie & Dixie & Mr. Jinks	13	39	190
Four Color 1050,1054 (12/59)	9	27	120
3(1-2/60) - 7 (9-10/60), Four Color 1141 (10/60)	9	27	115
8-10	7	21	90
11,13-17 (6-8/62)	6	18	65
12-1st Hokey Wolf & Ding-a-Ling	6	18	75
18,19 (84pgs.; 18-20 titled ...Chuckleberry Tales)	9	27	115
20-Titled Chuckleberry Tales	5	15	60
21-30: 28-30-Reprints	4	12	48
31-43: 31,32,35,37-43-Reprints	4	12	38

HUCKLEBERRY HOUND (TV)
Charlton Comics: Nov, 1970 - No. 8, Jan, 1972 (Hanna-Barbera)

1	6	18	70
2-8	3	10	35

HUEY, DEWEY, AND LOUIE JUNIOR WOODCHUCKS (Disney)
Gold Key No. 1-61/Whitman No. 62 on: Aug, 1966 - No. 81, July, 1984
(See Walt Disney's Comics & Stories #125)

1	7	21	80
2,3(12/68)	4	12	45
4,5(4/70)-r/two WDC&S D.Duck stories by Barks	4	12	40
6-17	3	10	35
18,27-30	3	9	26
19-23,25-New storyboarded scripts by Barks, 13-25 pgs. per issue			
	4	12	38
24,26: 26-r/Barks Donald Duck WDC&S stories	3	9	30
31-57,60,61: 35,41-r/Barks J.W. scripts	2	6	14
58,59: 58-r/Barks Donald Duck WDC&S stories	2	6	16
62-64 (Whitman)	2	6	16
65-(9/80), 66 (Pre-pack? scarce)	3	9	32
67 (1/81),68	2	6	20
69-74: 72(2/82), 73(2-3/82), 74(3/82)	2	6	18
75-81 (all #90183; pre-pack; nd, nd code; scarce): 75(4/83), 76(5/83), 77(7/83), 78(8/83), 79(4/84), 80(5/84), 81(7/84)	2	6	22

HULK (Magazine)(Formerly The Rampaging Hulk)(Also see The Incredible Hulk)
Marvel Comics: No. 10, Aug., 1978 - No. 27, June, 1981 ($1.50)

10-18: 10-Bill Bixby interview. 11-Moon Knight begins. 12-15,17,18-Moon

	GD	FN	NM-

Knight stories. 12-Lou Ferrigno interview.   2   6   12
19-27: 20-Moon Knight story. 23-Last full color issue; Banner is attacked.
    24-Part color, Lou Ferrigno interview. 25-Part color. 26,27-are B&W
                                          1   3   8

HULK (Becomes Incredible Hulk Vol. 2 with issue #12)
Marvel Comics: Apr, 1999 - No. 11, Feb, 2000 ($2.99/$1.99)

1-($2.99) Byrne-s/Garney-a   5.00
1-Variant-c   9.00
1-DFE Remarked-c   50.00
1-Gold foil variant   10.00
2-7-($1.99): 2-Two covers. 5-Art by Jurgens, Buscema & Texeira.
    7-Avengers app.   4.00
8-Hulk battles Wolverine   7.00
9-11: 11-She-Hulk app.   3.00
1999 Annual ($3.50) Chapter One story; Byrne-s/Weeks-a   3.50
Hulk Vs. The Thing (12/99, $3.99, TPB) reprints their notable battles   4.00

HULK: THE MOVIE
Marvel Comics

...Adaptation (8/03, $3.50) Bruce Jones-s/Bagley-a/Keown-c   3.50
TPB (2003, $12.99) r/Adaptation, Ultimates #5, Inc. Hulk #34, Ult. Marvel
    Team-Up #2&3   13.00

HUMAN TORCH (From the Fantastic Four)
Marvel Comics: June, 2003 - No. 12, Jun, 2004 ($2.50/$2.99)

1-7-Skottie Young-c/a; Karl Kesel-s   2.50
8-12-($2.99) 8,10-Dodd-a. 9-Young-a. 11-Porter-a. 12-Medina-a   3.00

HUNTER: THE AGE OF MAGIC (See Books of Magic)
DC Comics (Vertigo): Sept, 2001 - No. 25, Sept, 2003 ($2.50/$2.75)

1-25: Horrocks-s/Case-a. 1-8-Bolton-c. 14-Begin $2.75-c. 19-Bachalo-c   2.75

IDENTITY CRISIS
DC Comics: Aug, 2004 - No. 7, Feb, 2005 ($3.95, limited series)

1-Meltzer-s/Morales-a/Turner-c in all; Sue Dibny murdered   6.00
1-(Second printing) black-c with white sketch lines   4.00
1-Diamond Retailer Summit Edition   100.00
2-7: 2-4-Deathstroke app. 5-Firestorm, Jack Drake, Capt. Boomerang killed
                                                 4.00

IDENTITY DISC
Marvel Comics: Aug, 2004 - No. 5, Dec, 2004 ($2.99, limited series)

1-5-Sabretooth, Bullseye, Sandman, Vulture, Deadpool, Juggernaut app.;
    Higgins-a   4.00

I DREAM OF JEANNIE (TV)
Dell Publishing Co.: Apr, 1965 - No. 2, Dec, 1966 (Photo-c)

1-Barbara Eden photo-c, each   17   51   250
2   13   39   185

IMPULSE (See Flash #92, 2nd Series for 1st app.) (Also see Young Justice)

	GD	FN	NM-

DC Comics: Apr, 1995 - No. 89, Oct, 2002 ($1.50/$1.75/$1.95/$2.25/$2.50)

1-Waid scripts & Ramos-c/a(p) begin; brief retelling of origin			6.00
2-12: 9-XS from Legion (Impulse's cousin) comes to the 20th Century, returns to the 30th Century in #12. 10-Dead Heat Pt. 3 (cont'd in Flash #110). 11-Dead Heat Pt. 4 (cont'd in Flash #111); Johnny Quick dies			3.00
13-25: 14-Trickster app. 17-Zatanna-c/app. 21-Legion-c/app. 22-Jesse Quick-c/app. 24-Origin; Flash app. 25-Last Ramos-a			2.50
26-55: 26-Rousseau-a begins. 28-1st new Arrowette (see World's Finest #113). 30-Genesis x-over. 47-Superman-c/app. 50-Batman & Joker-c/app. Van Sciver-a begins			2.50
56-62: 56-Young Justice app.			2.50
63-89: 63-Begin $2.50-c. 66-JLA,JSA-c/app. 68,69-Adam Strange, GL app. 77-Our Worlds at War x-over; Young Justice-c/app. 85-World Without Young Justice x-over pt. 2.			2.50
#1,000,000 (11/98) John Fox app.			2.50
Annual 1 (1996, $2.95)-Legends of the Dead Earth; Parobeck-a			4.00
Annual 2 (1997, $3.95)-Pulp Heroes stories; Orbik painted-c			4.00
.../Atom Double-Shot 1(2/98, $1.95) Jurgens-s/Mhan-a			3.00
...: Bart Saves the Universe (4/99, $5.95) JSA app.			6.00
...Plus (9/97, $2.95) w/Gross Out (Scare Tactics)-c/app.			3.00
...Reckless Youth (1997, $14.95, TPB) r/Flash #92-94, Impulse #1-6			15.00

INCREDIBLE HULK, THE
Marvel Comics: May, 1962 - No. 6, Mar, 1963; No. 102, Apr, 1968 - No. 474, Mar, 1999

	GD	FN	NM-
1-Origin & 1st app. (skin is grey colored); Kirby pencils begin, end #5	700	2100	25,000
2-1st green skinned Hulk; Kirby/Ditko-a	229	687	4800
3-Origin retold; 1st app. Ringmaster & Hercules (9/62)	147	441	2800
4,5: 4-Brief origin retold	137	411	2600
6-(3/63) Intro. Teen Brigade; all Ditko-a	170	510	3400
102-(4/68) (Formerly Tales to Astonish)-Origin retold; story continued from Tales to Astonish #101	24	72	350
103	10	30	140
104-Rhino app.	10	30	140
105-108: 105-1st Missing Link. 107-Mandarin app.(9/68). 108-Mandarin & Nick Fury app. (10/68)	8	24	95
109,110: 109-Ka-Zar app.	6	18	75
111-117: 117-Last 12¢ issue	5	15	60
118-Hulk vs. Sub-Mariner	6	18	75
119-121,123-125	4	12	45
122-Hulk battles Thing (12/69)	7	21	90
126-1st Barbara Norriss (Valkyrie)	4	12	45
127-139: 131-Hulk vs. Iron Man; 1st Jim Wilson, Hulk's new sidekick. 136-1st Xeron, The Star-Slayer	3	9	32
140-Written by Harlan Ellison; 1st Jarella, Hulk's love	3	10	35
140-2nd printing (1994)	2	6	12
141-1st app. Doc Samson (7/71)	10	30	125

	GD	FN	NM-
142-144: 144-Last 15¢ issue	3	9	30
145-(52 pgs.)-Origin retold	4	12	50
146-160: 149-1st app. The Inheritor. 155-1st app. Shaper. 158-Warlock cameo(12/72)	3	9	25
161-The Mimic dies; Beast app.	3	10	35
162-1st app. The Wendigo (4/73); Beast app.	7	21	80
163-171,173-176: 163-1st app. The Gremlin. 164-1st Capt. Omen & Colonel John D. Armbruster. 166-1st Zzzax. 168-1st The Harpy; nudity panels of Betty Brant. 169-1st app. Bi-Beast.176-Warlock cameo (2 panels only); same date as Strange Tales #178 (6/74)	2	6	20
172-X-Men cameo; origin Juggernaut retold	4	12	45
177-1st actual death of Warlock (last panel only)	2	6	20
178-Rebirth of Warlock	2	6	20
179	2	6	15
180-(10/74)-1st brief app. Wolverine (last pg.)	17	51	250
181-(11/74)-1st full Wolverine story; Trimpe-a	80	240	1300
182-Wolverine cameo; see Giant-Size X-Men #1 for next app.; 1st Crackajack Jackson	11	33	150
183-199: 185-Death of Col. Armbruster. 195,196-Abomination app. 197,198-Man-Thing-c/s	2	6	12
198,199, 201,202-(30¢-c variants, lim. distribution)	2	6	18
200-(25¢-c) Silver Surfer app.; anniversary issue	3	9	32
200-(30¢-c variant, limited distribution)(6/76)	4	12	48
201-220: 201-Conan swipe-c/sty. 212-1st app. The Constrictor			6.00
212-216-(35¢-c variant, limited distribution)	1	3	9
221-249: 227-Original Avengers app. 232-Capt. America x-over from C.A. #230. 233-Marvel Man app. 234-(4/79)-1st app. Quasar (formerly called Marvel Man. 243-Cage app.			5.00
250-Giant size; Silver Surfer app.	2	6	12
251-277,280-299: 271-Rocket Raccoon app. 272-Sasquatch & Wendigo app.; Wolverine & Alpha Flight cameo in flashback. 282-284-She-Hulk app. 293-F.F. app.			4.00
278,279-Most Marvel characters app. (Wolverine in both). 279-X-Men & Alpha Flight cameos			5.00
300-(11/84, 52 pgs.)-Spider-Man app in new black costume on-c & 2 pg. cameo			6.00
301-313: 312-Origin Hulk retold			3.00
314-Byrne-c/a begins, ends #319			5.00
315-319: 319-Bruce Banner & Betty Talbot wed			4.00
320-323,325,327-329			3.00
324-1st app. Grey Hulk since #1 (c-swipe of #1)	2	6	12
326-Grey vs. Green Hulk			5.00
330,331: 330-1st McFarlane ish (4/87); Thunderbolt Ross dies. 331-Grey Hulk series begins	3	9	25
332-334,336-339: 336,337-X-Factor app.	2	6	14
335-No McFarlane-a			5.00
340-Hulk battles Wolverine by McFarlane	4	12	45
341-346: 345-($1.50, 52 pgs.). 346-Last McFarlane issue	1	3	8

	GD	FN	NM-

347-349,351-358,360-366: 347-1st app. Marlo — 3.00

350-Hulk/Thing battle — 6.00

359-Wolverine app. (illusion only) — 3.00

367,372,377: 367-1st Dale Keown-a on Hulk (3/90). 372-Green Hulk app.; Keown-c/a. 377-1st all new Hulk; fluorescent-c; Keown-c/a

	1	3	8

368-371,373-376: 368-Sam Kieth-c/a, 1st app. Pantheon. 369,370-Dale Keown-c/a. 370,371-Original Defenders app. 371,373-376: Keown-c/a. 376-Green vs. Grey Hulk — 5.00

377-Fluorescent green logo 2nd printing — 3.00

378,380,389: No Keown-a. 380-Doc Samson app. — 3.00

379,381-388,390-392-Keown-a. 385-Infinity Gauntlet x-over. 389-Last $1.00-c. 392-X-Factor app. — 4.00

393-($2.50, 72 pgs.)-30th anniversary issue; green foil stamped-c; swipes-c to #1; has pin-ups of classic battles; Keown-c/a — 5.00

393-2nd printing — 2.50

394-399: 394-No Keown-c/a; intro Trauma. 395,396-Punisher-c/stories; Keown-c/a. 397-Begin "Ghost of the Past" 4-part sty; Keown c/a. 398-Last Keown-c/a — 2.50

400-($2.50, 68 pgs.)-Holo-grafx foil-c & r/TTA #63 — 3.00

400-416: 400-2nd print-Diff. color foil-c. 402-Return of Doc Samson — 2.50

417-424: 417-Begin $1.50-c; Rick Jones' bachelor party; Hulk returns from "Future Imperfect"; bound-in trading card sheet. 418-(Regular edition)-Rick Jones marries Marlo; includes cameo apps of various Marvel characters as well as DC's Death & Peter David. 420-Death of Jim Wilson — 2.50

418-($2.50)-Collector's Edition w/gatefold die-cut-c — 3.00

425 ($2.25, 52 pgs.) — 2.50

425 ($3.50, 52 pgs.)-Holographic-c — 4.00

426-434, 436-442: 426-Begin $1.95-c. 427, 428-Man-Thing app. 431, 432-Abomination app. 434-Funeral for Nick Fury. 436-Ghosts of the Future begins, ends #440. 439-Hulk becomes Maestro, Avengers app. 440-Thor-c/app. 441,442-She-Hulk-c/app. — 2.50

435 ($2.50)-Rhino-app; excerpt from "What Savage Beast" — 3.00

443,446-448: 443-Begin $1.50-c; re-app. of Hulk. 446-w/card insert. 447-Begin Deodato-c/a(p) — 2.50

444,445: 444-Cable-c/app.; "Onslaught". 445-"Onslaught" — 4.00

447-Variant cover — 4.00

449-1st app. Thunderbolts — 6.00

450-($2.95)-Thunderbolts app.; 2 stories; Heroes Reborn-c/app. — 5.00

451-470: 455-X-Men-c/app. 460-Bruce Banner returns. 464-Silver Surfer-c/app. 466,467: Betty dies. 467-Last Peter David-s/Kubert-a. 468-Casey-s/Pulido-a begin — 2.50

471-473 — 3.00

474-($2.99) Last issue; Abomination app. — 4.00

#(-1) Flashback (7/97) Kubert-a — 2.50

Special 1 (10/68, 25¢, 68 pg.)-New 51 pg. story, Hulk battles The Inhumans (early app.); Steranko-c — 10 — 30 — 140

Special 2 (10/69, 25¢, 68 pg.)-Origin retold — 6 — 18 — 70

Special 3,4: 3-(1/71, 25¢, 68 pg.). 4-(1/72, 52pgs.) — 3 — 9 — 30

	GD	FN	NM-
Annual 5 (1976)	2	6	16
Annual 6-8 ('77-79)-7-Byrne/Layton-c/a; Iceman & Angel app. in book-length			
story. 8-Book-length Sasquatch-c/sty	2	6	12
Annual 9,10: 9('80). 10 ('81)			6.00
Annual 11('82)-Doc Samson back-up by Miller(p)(5 pgs.); Spider-Man &			
Avengers app. Buckler-a(p)			6.00
Annual 12-17: 12 ('83). 13('84). 14('85). 15('86). 16('90, $2.00, 68 pgs.)-			
She-Hulk app. 17(1991, $2.00)-Origin retold			3.50
Annual 18-20 ('92-'94 68 pgs.)-18-Return of the Defenders, Pt. I;			
no Keown-c/a. 19-Bagged w/card			3.00
...'97 ($2.99) Pollina-c			3.00
...And Wolverine 1 (10/86, $2.50)-r/1st app. (#180-181)	1	4	10
...: Beauty and the Behemoth ('98, $19.95, TPB) r/Bruce & Betty stories			20.00
...Ground Zero ('95, $12.95) r/#340-346			13.00
...Hercules Unleashed (10/96, $2.50) David-s/Deodato-c/a			2.50
.../Sub-Mariner '98 Annual ($2.99)			3.00
...Versus Quasimodo 1 (3/83, one-shot)-Based on Saturday morning cartoon			
			4.00
...Vs. Superman 1 (7/99, $5.95, one-shot)-painted-c by Rude			6.00
...Versus Venom 1 (4/94, $2.50, one-shot)-Embossed-c; red foil logo			3.00
Wizard #1 Ace Edition - Reprints #1 with new Andy Kubert-c			14.00
Wizard #181 Ace Edition - Reprints #181 with new Chen-c			14.00
(Also see titles listed under **Hulk**)			

INCREDIBLE HULK (Vol. 2) (Formerly Hulk #1-11)
Marvel Comics: No. 12, Mar, 2000 - Present ($1.99-$3.50)

12-Jenkins-s/Garney & McKone-a		3.00
13,14-($1.99) Garney & Buscema-a		2.50
15-24,26-32: 15-Begin $2.25-c. 24-($1.99-c)		2.25
25-($2.99) Hulk vs. The Abomination; Romita Jr.-a		3.00
33-($3.50, 100 pgs.) new Bogdanove-a/Priest-s; reprints		3.50
34-Bruce Jones-s begin; Romita Jr.-a		5.00
35-49,51-54: 35-39-Jones-s/Romita Jr.-a. 40-43-Weeks-a. 44-49-Immonen-a		
		3.00
50-($3.50) Deodato-a begins; Abomination app. thru #54		3.50
55-74: 55(25¢-c) Absorbing Man returns; Fernandez-a. 60-65-Deodato-a.		
66-69-Braithwaite-a. 70-72-Deodato-a. 71-74-Iron Man app.		2.25
75,76-($3.50) The Leader app. 75-Robertson-a/Frank-c. 76-Braithwaite-a		
		3.50
Annual 2000 ($3.50) Texeira-a/Jenkins-s; Avengers app.		3.50
Annual 2001 ($2.99) Thor-c/app.; Larsen-s/Williams III-c		3.00
... : Boiling Point (Volume 2, 2002, $8.99, TPB) r/#40-43; Andrews-c		9.00
Dogs of War (6/01, $19.95, TPB) r/#12-20		20.00
... : Return of the Monster (7/02, $12.99, TPB) r/#34-39		13.00
...: The End (8/02, $5.95) David-s/Keown-a; Hulk in the far future		6.00
...Volume 1 HC (2002, $29.99, oversized) r/#34-43 & Startling Stories:		
Banner #1-4		30.00
...Volume 2 HC (2003, $29.99, oversized) r/#44-54; sketch pages and		
cover gallery		30.00
Volume 3: Transfer of Power (2003, $12.99, TPB) r/#44-49		13.00

	GD	FN	NM-

Volume 4: Abominable (2003, $11.99, TPB) r/#50-54; Abomination app.;
   Deodato-a   12.00
Volume 5: Hide in Plain Sight (2003, $11.99, TPB) r/#55-59; Fernandez-a
                                          12.00
Volume 6: Split Decisions (2004, $12.99, TPB) r/#60-65; Deodato-a   13.00
Volume 7: Dead Like Me (2004, $12.99, TPB) r/#66-69 & Hulk Smash #1&2
                                          13.00
Volume 8: Big Things (2004, $17.99, TPB) r/#70-76; Iron Man app.   18.00

INFERIOR FIVE, THE (Inferior 5 #11, 12) (See Showcase #62, 63, 65)
National Periodical Publications (#1-10: 12¢): 3-4/67 - No. 10, 9-10/68; No.
11, 8-9/72 - No. 12, 10-11/72

1-(3-4/67)-Sekowsky-a(p); 4th app.	6	18	70
2-5: 2-Plastic Man, F.F. app. 4-Thor app.	3	10	35
6-9: 6-Stars DC staff	3	9	26
10-Superman x-over; F.F., Spider-Man & Sub-Mariner app.			
	3	9	32
11,12: Orlando-c/a; both r/Showcase #62,63	2	6	20

INFINITY, INC. (See All-Star Squadron #25)
DC Comics: Mar, 1984 - No. 53, Aug, 1988 ($1.25, Baxter paper, 36 pgs.)

1-Brainwave, Jr., Fury, The Huntress, Jade, Northwind, Nuklon, Obsidian,
   Power Girl, Silver Scarab & Star Spangled Kid begin   4.00
2-13,38-49,51-53: 2-Dr. Midnite, G.A. Flash, W. Woman, Dr. Fate, Hourman,
   Green Lantern, Wildcat app. 5-Nudity panels. 46,47-Millennium tie-ins 3.00

14-Todd McFarlane-a (5/85, 2nd full story)	1	3	9

15-37-McFarlane-a (20,23,24: 5 pgs. only; 33: 2 pgs.); 18-24-Crisis x-over.
   21-Intro new Hourman & Dr. Midnight. 26-New Wildcat app. 31-Star
   Spangled Kid becomes Skyman. 32-Green Fury becomes Green Flame.
   33-Origin Obsidian. 35-1st modern app. G.A. Fury   4.00
50 ($2.50, 52 pgs.)   3.00
Annual 1,2: 1(12/85)-Crisis x-over. 2('88, $2.00), Special 1 ('87, $1.50) 3.00

INHUMANS, THE (See Amazing Adventures, Fantastic Four #54 & Special
#5, Incredible Hulk Special #1, Marvel Graphic Novel & Thor #146)
Marvel Comics Group: Oct, 1975 - No. 12, Aug, 1977

1: #1-4,6 are 25¢ issues	2	6	22
2-4-Peréz-a	1	4	10
5-12: 9-Reprints Amazing Adventures #1,2('70). 12-Hulk app.			
	1	3	9
4-(30¢-c variant, limited distribution)(4/76) Peréz-a	2	6	18
6-(30¢-c variant, limited distribution)(8/76)	2	6	18
11,12-(35¢-c variants, limited distribution)	2	6	18

Special 1(4/90, $1.50, 52 pgs.)-F.F. cameo   3.00
...: The Great Refuge (5/95, $2.95)   3.00

INHUMANS (Marvel Knights)
Marvel Comics: Nov, 1998 - No. 12, Oct, 1999 ($2.99, limited series)

1-Jae Lee-c/a; Paul Jenkins-s   10.00
1-($6.95) DF Edition; Jae Lee variant-c   7.00
2-Two covers by Lee and Darrow   4.00

	GD	FN	NM-
3-12			3.00
TPB (10/00, $24.95) r/#1-12			25.00

INHUMANS (Volume 3)
Marvel Comics: Jun, 2000 - No. 4, Oct, 2000 ($2.99, limited series)

	GD	FN	NM-
1-4-Ladronn-c/Pacheco & Marin-s. 1-3-Ladronn-a. 4-Lucas-a			3.00

INHUMANS (Volume 6)
Marvel Comics: Jun, 2003 - No. 12, Jun, 2004 ($2.50/$2.99)

	GD	FN	NM-
1-12: 1-6-McKeever-s/Clark-a/JH Williams III-c. 7-Begin $2.99-c			3.00

INVADERS, THE (TV)
Gold Key: Oct, 1967 - No. 4, Oct, 1968 (All have photo-c)

	GD	FN	NM-
1-Spiegle-a in all	11	33	160
2-4	8	24	105

INVADERS, THE (Also see The Avengers #71 & Giant-Size Invaders)
Marvel Comics Group: August, 1975 - No. 40, May, 1979; No. 41, Sept, 1979

	GD	FN	NM-
1-Captain America & Bucky, Human Torch & Toro, & Sub-Mariner begin; cont'd. from Giant Size Invaders #1; #1-7 are 25¢ issues	5	15	55
2-5: 2-1st app. Brain-Drain. 3-Battle issue; Cap vs. Namor vs. Torch; intro U-Man	2	6	22
6-10: 6,7-(Regular 25¢ edition). 6-(7/76) Liberty Legion app. 7-Intro Baron Blood & intro/1st app. Union Jack; Human Torch origin retold. 8-Union Jack-c/story. 9-Origin Baron Blood. 10-G.A. Capt. America-r/C.A #22	2	6	14
6,7-(30¢-c variants, limited distribution)	2	6	22
11-19: 11-Origin Spitfire; intro The Blue Bullet. 14-1st app. The Crusaders. 16-Re-intro The Destroyer. 17-Intro Warrior Woman. 18-Re-intro The Destroyer w/new origin. 19-Hitler-c/story	1	4	10
17-19,21-(35¢-c variants, limited distribution)	2	6	15
20-(Regular 30¢-c) Reprints origin/1st app. Sub-Mariner from Motion Picture Funnies Weekly with color added & brief write-up about MPFW; 1st app. new Union Jack II	2	6	14
20-(35¢-c variant, limited distribution)	2	6	22
21-(Regular 30¢ edition)-r/Marvel Mystery #10 (battle issue)	1	4	10
22-30,34-40: 22-New origin Toro. 24-r/Marvel Mystery #17 (team-up issue; all-r). 25-All new-a begins. 28-Intro new Human Top & Golden Girl. 29-Intro Teutonic Knight. 34-Mighty Destroyer joins. 35-The Whizzer app.	1	3	7
31-33: 31-Frankenstein-c/sty. 32,33-Thor app.	1	4	10
41-Double size last issue	2	6	16
Annual 1 (9/77)-Schomburg, Rico stories (new); Schomburg-c/a (1st for Marvel in 30 years); Avengers app.; re-intro The Shark & The Hyena	4	12	40

INVINCIBLE
Image Comics: Jan, 2003 - Present ($2.95)

	GD	FN	NM-
1-17: 1-7-Kirkman-s/Walker-a. 4-Preview of The Moth. 11-Origin of			

	GD	FN	NM-
Omni-Man. 14-Cho-c			3.00

Vol. 1: Family Matters TPB (8/03, $12.95) r/#1-4; intro. by Busiek; sketch
pages — 13.00
Vol. 2: Eight in Enough TPB (3/04, $12.95) r/#5-8; intro. by Larsen; sketch
pages — 13.00

INVISIBLES, THE (1st Series)
DC Comics (Vertigo): Sept, 1994 - No. 25, Oct, 1996 ($1.95/$2.50, mature)

1-($2.95, 52 pgs.)-Intro King Mob, Ragged Robin, Boy, Lord Fanny & Dane
(Jack Frost); Grant Morrison scripts in all — 6.00
2-8: 4-Includes bound-in trading cards. 5-1st app. Orlando; brown paper-c — 4.00
9-25: 10-Intro Jim Crow. 13-15-Origin Lord Fanny. 19-Origin King Mob;
polybagged. 20-Origin Boy. 21-Mister Six revealed. 25-Intro Division X — 2.50
Apocalipstick (2001, $19.95, TPB)-r/#9-16; Bolland-c — 20.00
Entropy in the U.K. (2001, $19.95, TPB)-r/#17-25; Bolland-c — 20.00
Say You Want A Revolution (1996, $17.50, TPB)-r/#1-8 — 18.00

INVISIBLES, THE (2nd Series)
DC Comics (Vertigo): V2#1, Feb, 1997 - No. 22, Feb, 1999 ($2.50, mature)

1-Intro Jolly Roger; Grant Morrison scripts, Phil Jimenez-a, & Brian
Bolland-c begins — 4.00
2-22: 9,14-Weston-a — 2.50
Bloody Hell in America TPB ('98, $12.95) r/#1-4 — 13.00
Counting to None TPB ('99, $19.95) r/#5-13 — 20.00
Kissing Mr. Quimper TPB ('00, $19.95) r/#14-22 — 20.00

INVISIBLES, THE (3rd Series) (Issue #'s go in reverse from #12 to #1)
DC Comics (Vertigo): V3#12, Apr, 1999 - No. 1, June, 2000 ($2.95, mature)

1-12-Bolland-c; Morrison-s on all. 1-Quitely-a. 2-4-Art by various.
5-8-Phillips-a. 9-12-Phillip Bond-a. — 3.00
The Invisible Kingdom TPB ('02, $19.95) r/#12-1; new Bolland-c — 20.00

IRON FIST (See Deadly Hands of Kung Fu, Marvel Premiere & Power Man)
Marvel Comics: Nov, 1975 - No. 15, Sept, 1977

		GD	FN	NM-
1-Iron Fist battles Iron Man (#1-6: 25¢)		6	18	65
2		3	9	32
3-10: 4-6-(Regular 25¢ edition)(4-6/76). 8-Origin retold		3	9	24
4-6-(30¢-c variant, limited distribution)		3	10	36
11,13: 13-(30¢-c)		2	6	18
12-Capt. America app.		2	6	22
13-(35¢-c variant, limited distribution)		3	9	28
14-1st app. Sabretooth (8/77)(see Power Man)		11	33	160
14-(35¢-c variant, limited distribution)		27	81	400
15-(Regular 30¢ ed.) X-Men app., Byrne-a		6	18	70
15-(35¢-c variant, limited distribution)		10	30	140

IRONJAW (Also see The Barbarians)
Atlas/Seaboard Publ.: Jan, 1975 - No. 4, July, 1975

	GD	FN	NM-
1,2-Neal Adams-c. 1-1st app. Iron Jaw; Sekowsky-a(p); Fleisher-s			
	2	6	12

	GD	FN	NM-
3,4-Marcos. 4-Origin	1	3	7

IRON MAN (Also see The Avengers #1, Giant-Size…, Marvel Collectors Item Classics, Marvel Double Feature, Marvel Fanfare & Tales of Suspense #39)
Marvel Comics: May, 1968 - No. 332, Sept, 1996

	GD	FN	NM-
1-Origin; Colan-c/a(p); story continued from Iron Man & Sub-Mariner #1	36	108	575
2	12	36	180
3	9	27	110
4,5	7	21	90
6-10: 9-Iron Man battles green Hulk-like android	6	18	70
11-15: 15-Last 12¢ issue	5	15	55
16-20	4	12	40
21-24,26-30: 22-Death of Janice Cord. 27-Intro Firebrand	3	9	30
25-Iron Man battles Sub-Mariner	3	10	35
31-42: 33-1st app. Spymaster. 35-Nick Fury & Daredevil x-over. 42-Last 15¢ issue	3	9	24
43-Intro The Guardsman; 25¢ giant (52 pgs.)	4	12	40
44-46,48-50: 43-Giant-Man back-up by Ayers. 44-Ant-Man by Tuska. 46-The Guardsman dies. 50-Princess Python app.	2	6	18
47-Origin retold; Barry Smith-a(p)	3	9	28
51-53: 53-Starlin part pencils	2	6	15
54-Iron Man battles Sub-Mariner; 1st app. Moondragon (1/73) as Madame MacEvil; Everett part-c	3	10	35
55-1st app. Thanos (brief), Drax the Destroyer, Mentor, Starfox & Kronos (2/73); Starlin-c/a	12	36	180
56-Starlin-a	3	9	32
57-65,67-70: 59-Firebrand returns. 65-Origin Dr. Spectrum. 67-Last 20¢ issue. 68-Sunfire & Unicorn app.; origin retold; Starlin-c	2	6	14
66-Iron Man vs. Thor.	3	9	26
71-84: 72-Cameo portraits of N. Adams. 73-Rename Stark Industries to Stark International; Brunner. 76-r/#9.	2	6	12
85-89-(Regular 25¢ editions): 86-1st app. Blizzard. 87-Origin Blizzard. 88-Thanos app. 89-Daredevil app.; last 25¢-c	2	6	12
85-89-(30¢-c variants, limited distribution)(4-8/76)	2	6	18
90-99: 96-1st app. new Guardsman	1	4	10
99,101-103-(35¢-c variants, limited dist.)	2	6	12
100-(7/77)-Starlin-c	3	9	28
100-(35¢-c variant, limited dist.)	4	12	42
101-117: 101-Intro DreadKnight. 109-1st app. new Crimson Dynamo; 1st app. Vanguard. 110-Origin Jack of Hearts retold; death of Count Nefaria. 114-Avengers app.	1	3	8
118-Byrne-a(p); 1st app. Jim Rhodes	1	4	10
119-127: 120,121-Sub-Mariner x-over. 122-Origin. 123-128-Tony Stark treated for alcohol problem. 125-Ant-Man app.	1	3	8
128-Classic Tony Stark alcoholism cover	2	6	15
129,130,133-149			6.00
131,132-Hulk x-over	1	3	8

	GD	FN	NM-

150-Double size   1   3   9

151-168: 152-New armor. 161-Moon Knight app. 167-Tony Stark alcohol problem resurfaces   4.00

169-New Iron Man (Jim Rhodes replaces Tony Stark)   6.00

170,171   4.00

172-199: 172-Captain America x-over. 186-Intro Vibro. 190-Scarlet Witch app. 191-198-Tony Stark returns as original Iron Man. 192-Both Iron Men battle   3.00

200-(11/85, $1.25, 52 pgs.)-Tony Stark returns as new Iron Man (red & white armor) thru #230   5.00

201-213,215-224: 213-Intro new Dominic Fortune   3.00

214,225,228,231,234,247: 214-Spider-Woman app. in new black costume (1/87). 225-Double size ($1.25). 228-vs. Capt. America. 231-Intro new Iron Man. 234-Spider-Man x-over. 247-Hulk x-over   4.00

226,227,229,230,232,233,235-243,245,246,248,249: 233-Ant-Man app. 243-Tony Stark loses use of legs   2.50

244-($1.50, 52 pgs.)-New Armor makes him walk   3.00

250-($1.50, 52 pgs.)-Dr. Doom-c/story   3.00

251-274,276-281,283,285-287,289,291-299: 258-277-Byrne scripts. 271-Fin Fang Foom app. 276-Black Widow-c/story; last $1.00-c. 281-1st brief app. War Machine. 283-2nd full app. War Machine   2.50

275-($1.50, 52 pgs.)   3.00

282-1st full app. War Machine (7/92)   4.00

284-Death of Iron Man (Tony Stark)   4.00

288-($2.50, 52pg.)-Silver foil stamped-c; Iron Man's 350th app. in comics 3.00

290-($2.95, 52pg.)-Gold foil stamped-c; 30th ann.   3.00

300-($3.95, 68 pgs.)-Collector's Edition w/embossed foil-c; anniversary issue; War Machine-c/story   4.00

300-($2.50, 68 pgs.)-Newsstand Edition   2.50

301-303: 302-Venom-c/story (cameo #301)   2.50

304-316,318-324,326-331: 304-Begin $1.50-c; bound-in trading card sheet; Thunderstrike-c/story. 310-Orange logo. 312-w/bound-in Power Ranger Card. 319-Prologue to "The Crossing." 326-New Tony Stark; Pratt-c. 330-War Machine & Stockpile app; return of Morgan Stark   2.50

310,325: 310 ($2.95)-Polybagged w/ 16 pg. Marvel Action Hour preview & acetate print; white logo. 325-($2.95)-Wraparound-c   3.00

317 ($2.50)-Flip book   2.50

332-Onslaught x-over   4.00

Special 1 (8/70)-Sub-Mariner x-over; Everett-c   4   12   42

Special 2 (11/71, 52 pgs.)-r/TOS #81,82,91 (all-r)   3   9   24

Annual 3 (1976)-Man-Thing app.   2   6   15

King Size 4 (8/77)-The Champions (w/Ghost Rider) app.; Newton-a(i)   1   4   10

Annual 5 ('82) New-a   6.00

Annual 6-8: ('83-"85) 6-New Iron Man (J. Rhodes) app. 8-X-Factor app. 5.00

Annual 9-15: ('86-'94) 10-Atlantis Attacks x-over; P. Smith-a; Layton/Guice-a; Sub-Mariner app. 11-(1990)-Origin of Mrs. Arbogast by Ditko (p&i). 12-1 pg. origin recap; Ant-Man back-up-s. 13-Darkhawk & Avengers West Coast app.; Colan/Williamson-a. 14-Bagged w/card   3.00

	GD	FN	NM-

Manual 1 (1993, $1.75)-Operations handbook   2.50
Graphic Novel: Crash (1988, $12.95, Adults, 72 pgs.)-Computer generated
    art & color; violence & nudity   13.00
...Collector's Preview 1(11/94, $1.95)-wraparound-c; text & illos-no comics
    2.50
...Vs. Dr. Doom (12/94, $12.95)-r/#149-150, 249,250. Julie Bell-c   13.00

IRON MAN (The Invincible...) (Volume Two)
Marvel Comics: Nov, 1996 - No. 13, Nov, 1997 ($2.95/$1.95/$1.99)
(Produced by WildStorm Productions)

V2#1-3-Heroes Reborn begins; Scott Lobdell scripts & Whilce Portacio-c/a
    begin; new origin Iron Man & Hulk. 2-Hulk app. 3-Fantastic Four app.   4.00
    1-Variant-c   5.00
    4-11: 4-Two covers. 6-Fantastic Four app.; Industrial Revolution; Hulk app.
       7-Return of Rebel. 11-($1.99) Dr. Doom-c/app.   3.00
    12-($2.99) "Heroes Reunited"-pt. 3; Hulk-c/app.   3.50
    13-($1.99) "World War 3"-pt. 3, x-over w/Image   3.00

IRON MAN (The Invincible...) (Volume Three)
Marvel Comics: Feb, 1998 - No. 89, Dec, 2004 ($2.99/$1.99/$2.25)

V3#1-($2.99)-Follows Heroes Return; Busiek scripts & Chen-c/a begin;
    Deathsquad app.   5.00
    1-Alternate Ed.   1   3   8
    2-12: 2-Two covers. 6-Black Widow-c/app. 7-Warbird-c/app. 8-Black Widow
       app. 9-Mandarin returns   3.00
    13-($2.99) battles the Controller   3.50
    14-24: 14-Fantastic Four-c/app.   3.00
    25-($2.99) Iron Man and Warbird battle Ultimo; Avengers app.   3.00
    26-30-Quesada-s. 28-Whiplash killed. 29-Begin $2.25-c.   2.50
    31-45,47-49,51-54: 35-Maximum Security x-over; FF-c/app. 41-Grant-a
       begins. 44-New armor debut. 48-Ultron-c/app.   2.25
    46-($3.50, 100 pgs.) Sentient armor returns; r/V1#78,140,141   3.50
    50-($3.50) Grell-s begin; Black Widow app.   3.50
    55-($3.50) 400th issue; Asamiya-c; back-up story Stark reveals ID; Grell-a
    3.50
    56-66: 56-Reis-a. 57,58-Ryan-a. 59-61-Grell-c/a. 62,63-Ryan-a. 64-Davis-a;
       Thor-c/app.   2.25
    67-89: 67-Begin $2.99-c; Gene Ha-c. 75-83-Granov-c. 84-Avengers
       Disassembled prologue. 85-89-Avengers Disassembled. 85-88-Harris-a.
       86-89-Pat Lee-c. 87-Rumiko killed   3.00
.../Captain America '98 Annual ($3.50) vs. Modok   3.50
1999, 2000 Annual ($3.50)   3.50
2001 Annual ($2.99) Claremont-s/Ryan-a   3.00
Mask in the Iron Man (5/01, $14.95, TPB) r/#26-30, #1/2   15.00

IRON MAN (The Invincible...)
Marvel Comics: Jan, 2005 - Present ($3.50)

    1-Warren Ellis-s/Adi Granov-c/a   3.50

IRON MAN & SUB-MARINER
Marvel Comics Group: Apr, 1968 (12¢, one-shot) (Pre-dates Iron Man #1 &

	GD	FN	NM-

Sub-Mariner #1)

1-Iron Man story by Colan/Craig continued from Tales of Suspense #99 &
continued in Iron Man #1; Sub-Mariner story by Colan continued from
Tales to Astonish #101 & continued in Sub-Mariner #1; Colan/Everett-c

	15	45	220

ISIS (TV) (Also see Shazam)
National Per.l Publ./DC Comics: Oct-Nov, 1976 - No. 8, Dec-Jan, 1977-78

1-Wood inks	2	6	16
2-8: 5-Isis new look. 7-Origin	1	3	9

JAY & SILENT BOB (See Clerks & Oni Double Feature)
Oni Press: July, 1998 - No. 4, Oct, 1999 ($2.95, B&W, limited series)

1-Kevin Smith-s/Fegredo-a; photo-c & Quesada/Palmiotti-c	8.00
1-San Diego Comic Con variant covers (2 different covers, came packaged with action figures)	10.00
1-2nd & 3rd printings, 2-4: 2-Allred-c. 3-Flip-c by Jaime Hernandez	3.00
Chasing Dogma TPB (1999, $11.95) r/#1-4; Alanis Morissette intro.	12.00
Chasing Dogma TPB (2001, $12.95) r/#1-4 in color; Morissette intro.	13.00
Chasing Dogma HC (1999, $69.95, S&N) r/#1-4 in color; Morissette intro.	70.00

JETSONS, THE (TV) (See March of Comics #276, 330, 348 & Spotlight #3)
Gold Key: Jan, 1963 - No. 36, Oct, 1970 (Hanna-Barbera)

1-1st comic book app.	27	81	395
2	13	39	185
3-10	10	30	140
11-22	8	24	105
23-36-Reprints	7	21	80

JETSONS, THE (TV) (Also see Golden Comics Digest)
Charlton Comics: Nov, 1970 - No. 20, Dec, 1973 (Hanna-Barbera)

1	10	30	130
2	6	18	65
3-10	4	12	42
11-20	3	9	32
nn (1973, 60¢, 100 pgs.) B&W one page gags	4	12	45

JINX
Caliber Press: 1996 - No. 7, 1996 ($2.95, B&W, 32 pgs.)

1-7: Brian Michael Bendis-c/a/scripts. 2-Photo-c	3.00

JINX (Volume 2)
Image Comics: 1997 - No. 5, 1998 ($2.95, B&W, bi-monthly)

1-4: Brian Michael Bendis-c/a/scripts.	3.00
5-($3.95) Brereton-c	4.00
...Buried Treasures ('98, $3.95) short stories, ...Confessions ('98, $3.95) short stories, ...Pop Culture Hoo-Hah ('98, $3.95) humor shorts	4.00
TPB (1997, $10.95) r/Vol 1,#1-4	11.00
...: The Definitive Collection ('01, $24.95) remastered #1-5, sketch pages, art gallery, script excerpts, Mack intro.	25.00

	GD	FN	NM-

JINX: TORSO
Image Comics: 1998 - No. 6, 1999 ($3.95/$4.95, B&W)

1-6-Based on Eliot Ness' pursuit of America's first serial killer; Brian Michael
   Bendis & Marc Andreyko-s/Bendis-a. 3-6-($4.95)   5.00
Softcover (2000, $24.95) r/#1-6; intro. by Greg Rucka; photo essay of the
   actual murders and police documents   25.00
Hardcover (2000, $49.95) signed & numbered   50.00

JLA (See Justice League of America and Justice Leagues)
DC Comics: Jan, 1997 - Present ($1.95/$1.99/$2.25)

1-Morrison-s/Porter & Dell-a. The Hyperclan app.	2	6	15
2	1	4	10
3,4	1	3	9

5-Membership drive; Tomorrow Woman app.   6.00
6-9: 8-Green Arrow joins.   6.00
10-21: 10-Rock of Ages begins. 11-Joker and Luthor-c/app. 15-($2.95) Rock
   of Ages concludes. 16-New members join; Prometheus app.
   17,20-Jorgensen-a. 18-21-Waid-s. 20,21-Adam Strange c/app.   5.00
22-40: 22-Begin $1.99-c; Sandman (Daniel) app. 27-Amazo app. 28-31-JSA
   app. 35-Hal Jordan/Spectre app. 36-40-World War 3   2.50
41-($2.99) Conclusion of World War 3; last Morrison-s   3.00
42-46: 43-Waid-s; Ra's al Ghul app. 44-Begin $2.25-c. 46-Batman leaves
        2.25
47-49: 47-Hitch & Neary-a begins; JLA battles Queen of Fables   2.25
50-($3.75) JLA vs. Dr. Destiny; art by Hitch & various   3.75
51-74: 52-55-Hitch-a. 59-Joker: Last Laugh. 61-68-Kelly-s/Mahnke-a.
   69-73-Hunt for Aquaman; bi-monthly with alternating art by Mahnke and
   Guichet   2.25
75-(1/03, $3.95) leads into Aquaman (4th series) #1   4.00
76-93: 76-Firestorm app. 77-Banks-a. 79-Kanjar Ro app. 91-93-O'Neil-s/
   Huat-a   2.25
94-99-Byrne & Ordway-a/Claremont-s; Doom Patrol app.   2.25
100-($3.50) Intro. Vera Black; leads into Justice League Elite #1   3.50
101-109: 101-106-Austen/Garney-a/c. 107-109-Crime Syndicate app.;
   Busiek-s   2.25
#1,000,000 (11/98) 853rd Century x-over   2.50
Annual 1 (1997, $3.95) Pulp Heroes; Augustyn-s/Olivetti & Ha-a   4.00
Annual 2 (1998, $2.95) Ghosts; Wrightson-c   4.00
Annual 3 (1999, $2.95) JLApe; Art Adams-c   3.00
Annual 4 (2000, $3.50) Planet DC x-over; Steve Scott-c/a   3.50
...80-Page Giant 1 (7/98, $4.95) stories & art by various   6.00
...80-Page Giant 2 (11/99, $4.95) Green Arrow & Hawkman app. Hitch-c 6.00
...80-Page Giant 3 (10/00, $5.95) Pariah & Harbinger; intro. Moon Maiden 6.00
...Foreign Bodies (1999, $5.95, one-shot) Kobra app.; Semeiks-a   6.00
...Gallery (1997, $2.95) pin-ups by various; Quitely-c   3.00
...God & Monsters (2001, $6.95, one-shot) Benefiel-a/c   7.00
.../ Haven: Anathema (2002, $6.95) Concludes the Haven: The Broken City
   series   7.00
.../ Haven: Arrival (2001, $6.95) Leads into the Haven: The Broken City series

	GD	FN	NM-

| | | | 7.00 |
...In Crisis Secret Files 1 (11/98, $4.95) recap of JLA in DC x-overs — 5.00

...: Island of Dr. Moreau, The (2002, $6.95, one-shot) Elseworlds; Pugh-c/a; Thomas-s — 7.00

.../ JSA Secret Files & Origins (1/03, $4.95) prelude to JLA/JSA: Virtue & Vice; short stories and pin-ups by various; Pacheco-c — 5.00

.../ JSA: Virtue and Vice HC (2002, $24.95) Teams battle Despero & Johnny Sorrow; Goyer & Johns-s/Pacheco-a/c — 25.00

.../ JSA: Virtue and Vice SC (2003, $17.95) — 18.00

...: Obsidian Age Book One, The (2003, $12.95) r/#66-71 — 13.00

...: Obsidian Age Book Two, The (2003, $12.95) r/#72-76 — 13.00

...: Our Worlds at War (9/01, $2.95) Jae Lee-c; Aquaman presumed dead — 3.00

...Primeval (1999, $5.95, one-shot) Abnett & Lanning-s/Olivetti-a — 6.00

...: Riddle of the Beast HC (2001, $24.95) Grant-s/painted-a by various; Sweet-c — 25.00

...: Riddle of the Beast SC (2003, $14.95) Grant-s/painted-a by various; Kaluta-c — 15.00

...: Seven Caskets (2000, $5.95, one-shot) Brereton-s/painted-c/a — 6.00

...Showcase 80-Page Giant (2/00, $4.95) Hitch-c — 5.00

...Superpower (1999, $5.95, one-shot) Arcudi-s/Eaton-a; Mark Antaeus joins — 6.00

...: Shogun of Steel (2002, $6.95, one-shot) Elseworlds; Justiniano-c/a — 7.00

...Vs. Predator (DC/Dark Horse, 2000, $5.95, one-shot) Nolan-c/a — 6.00

...: Welcome to the Working Week (2003, $6.95, one-shot) Patton Oswalt-s — 7.00

...: Zatanna's Search (2003, $12.95, TPB) rep. Zatanna's early app. & origin; Bolland-c — 13.00

American Dreams (1998, $7.95, TPB) r/#5-9 — 8.00

Divided We Fall (2001, $17.95, TPB) r/#47-54 — 18.00

Golden Perfect (2003, $12.95, TPB) r/#61-65 — 13.00

Justice For All (1999, $14.95, TPB) r/#24-33 — 15.00

New World Order (1997, $5.95, TPB) r/#1-4 — 6.00

One Million (2004, $19.95, TPB) r/#DC One Million #1-4 and other #1,000,000 issue x-overs — 20.00

Rock of Ages (1998, $9.95, TPB) r/#10-15 — 10.00

Rules of Engagement (2004, $12.95, TPB) r/#77-82 — 13.00

Strength in Numbers (1998, $12.95, TPB) r/#16-23, Secret Files #2 and Prometheus #1 — 13.00

Terror Incognita (2002, $12.95, TPB) r/#55-60 — 13.00

The Tenth Circle (2004, $12.95, TPB) r/#94-99 — 13.00

Tower of Babel (2001, $12.95, TPB) r/#42-46, Secret Files #3, 80-Page Giant #1 — 13.00

Trial By Fire (2004, $12.95, TPB) r/#84-89 — 13.00

World War III (2000, $12.95, TPB) r/#34-41 — 13.00

JLA/AVENGERS (See Avengers/JLA for #2 & #4)
Marvel Comics: Sept, 2003; No. 3, Dec, 2003 ($5.95, limited series)

1-Busiek-s/Pérez-a; wraparound-c; Krona, Starro, Grandmaster, Terminus app. — 6.00

3-Busiek-s/Pérez-a; wraparound-c; Phantom Stranger app. — 6.00

	GD	FN	NM-

JLA: CLASSIFIED
DC Comics: Jan, 2005 - Present ($2.95)

1-Morrison-s/McGuinness-a/c; Ultramarines app.			3.00

JLA: EARTH 2
DC Comics: 2000 (Graphic novel)

Hardcover ($24.95) Morrison-s/Quitely-a; Crime Syndicate app.			25.00
Softcover ($14.95)			15.00

JLA: HEAVEN'S LADDER
DC Comics: 2000 ($9.95, Treasury-size one-shot)

nn-Bryan Hitch & Paul Neary-c/a; Mark Waid-s			10.00

JLA: LIBERTY AND JUSTICE
DC Comics: Nov, 2003 ($9.95, Treasury-size one-shot)

nn-Alex Ross-c/a; Paul Dini-s; story of the classic Justice League			10.00

JLA SECRET FILES
DC Comics: Sept, 1997 - Present ($4.95)

1-Standard Ed. w/origin-s & pin-ups			5.00
1-Collector's Ed. w/origin-s & pin-ups; cardstock-c			6.00
2,3: 2-(8/98) origin-s of JLA #16's newer members. 3-(12/00)			5.00
... 2004 (11/04) Justice League Elite app.; Mahnke & Byrne-a; Crime Syndicate app.			5.00

JLA: SECRET ORIGINS
DC Comics: Nov, 2002 ($7.95, Treasury-size one-shot)

nn-Alex Ross 2-page origins of JLA members; text by Paul Dini			8.00

JLA: THE NAIL (Elseworlds) (Also see Justice League of America: Another Nail)
DC Comics: Aug, 1998 - No. 3, Oct, 1998 ($4.95, prestige format)

1-3-JLA in a world without Superman; Alan Davis-s/a(p)			5.00
TPB ('98, $12.95) r/series w/new Davis-c			13.00

JLA / TITANS
DC Comics: Dec, 1998 - No. 3, Feb, 1999 ($2.95, limited series)

1-3-Grayson-s; P. Jimenez-c/a			3.00
...:The Technis Imperative ('99, $12.95, TPB) r/#1-3; Titans Secret Files			13.00

JLA /WITCHBLADE
DC Comics/Top Cow: 2000 ($5.95, prestige format, one-shot)

1-Pararillo-c/a			6.00

JLA / WORLD WITHOUT GROWN-UPS (See Young Justice)
DC Comics: Aug, 1998 - No. 2, Sept, 1998 ($4.95, prestige format)

1,2-JLA, Robin, Impulse & Superboy app.; Ramos & McKone-a			6.00
TPB ('98, $9.95) r/series & Young Justice: The Secret #1			10.00

JLA: YEAR ONE
DC Comics: Jan, 1998 - No. 12, Dec, 1998 ($2.95/$1.95, limited series)

1-($2.95)-Waid & Augustyn-s/Kitson-a			5.00

	GD	FN	NM-
1-Platinum Edition			10.00
2-8-($1.95): 5-Doom Patrol-c/app. 7-Superman app.			4.00
9-12			3.00
TPB ('99, $19.95) r/#1-12; Busiek intro.			20.00

JOHN BYRNE'S NEXT MEN (See Dark Horse Presents #54)
Dark Horse Comics (Legend imprint #19 on): Jan, 1992 - No. 30, Dec, 1994 ($2.50, mature)

	GD	FN	NM-
1-Silver foil embossed-c; Byrne-c/a/scripts in all			4.00
1-4: 1-2nd printing with gold ink logo			2.50
0-(2/92)-r/chapters 1-4 from DHP w/new Byrne-c			2.50
5-20,22-30: 7-10-MA #1-4 mini-series on flip side. 16-Origin of Mark IV. 17-Miller-c. 19-22-Faith storyline. 23-26-Power storyline. 27-30-Lies storyline Pt. 1-4			2.50
21-(12/93) 1st Hellboy; cover and Hellboy pages by Mike Mignola; Byrne other pages	3	9	28
...Parallel, Book 2 ($16.95)-TPB; r/#7-12			17.00
...Fame, Book 3($16.95)-TPB r/#13-18			17.00
...Faith, Book 4($14.95)-TPB r/#19-22			15.00

NOTE: Issues 1 through 6 contain certificates redeemable for an exclusive Next Men trading card set by Byrne. Prices are for complete books. **Cody** painted c-23-26. **Mignola** a-21(part); c-21.

JOKER, THE (See Batman #1, Batman: The Killing Joke, Brave & the Bold, Detective, Greatest Joker Stories & Justice League Annual #2)
National Periodical Publications: May, 1975 - No. 9, Sept-Oct, 1976

	GD	FN	NM-
1-Two-Face app.	4	12	60
2,3: 3-The Creeper app.	3	9	30
4-9: 4-Green Arrow-c/sty. 6-Sherlock Holmes-c/sty. 7-Lex Luthor-c/story. 8-Scarecrow-c/story. 9-Catwoman-c/story	2	6	22

JONAH HEX (See All-Star Western, Hex and Weird Western Tales)
National Periodical Pub./DC Comics: Mar-Apr, 1977 - No. 92, Aug, 1985

	GD	FN	NM-
1	11	33	150
2	6	18	70
3,4,9: 9-Wrightson-c.	4	12	50
5,6,10: 5-Rep 1st app. from All-Star Western #10	4	12	40
7,8-Explains Hex's face disfigurement (origin)	5	15	55
11-20: 12-Starlin-c	3	9	25
21-32: 31,32-Origin retold	2	6	16
33-50	1	4	10
51-80			6.00
81-91: 89-Mark Texeira-a. 91-Cover swipe from Superman #243 (hugging a mystery woman)	1	3	7
92-Story cont'd in Hex #1	3	9	24

JONNY QUEST (TV)
Gold Key: Dec, 1964 (Hanna-Barbera)

	GD	FN	NM-
1 (10139-412)	35	105	560

JOURNEY INTO MYSTERY (1st Series) (Thor Nos. 126-502)
Atlas(CPS No. 1-48/AMI No. 49-68/Marvel No. 69 (6/61) on): 6/52 - No. 48,

	GD	FN	NM-

8/57; No. 49, 11/58 - No. 125, 2/66; 503, 11/96 - No. 521, June, 1998

	GD	FN	NM-
1-Weird/horror stories begin	300	900	4300
2	108	324	1400
3,4	81	243	1050
5-11	55	165	700
12-20,22: 15-Atomic explosion panel. 22-Davis*esque*-a; last pre-code issue			
(2/55)	43	129	540
21-Kubert-a; Tothish-a by Andru	44	132	550
23-32,35-38,40: 24-Torres?-a. 38-Ditko-a	32	96	350
33-Williamson-a; Ditko-a (his 1st for Atlas?)	35	105	385
34,39: 34-Krigstein-a. 39-1st S.A. issue; Wood-a	33	99	368
41-Crandall-a; Frazetta*esque*-a by Morrow	20	60	300
42,46,48: 42,48-Torres-a. 46-Torres & Krigstein-a	20	60	290
43,44-Williamson/Mayo-a in both	21	63	310
45,47,50,52-54: 50-Davis-a. 54-Williamson-a	19	57	280
49-Matt Fox, Check-a	20	60	290
51-Kirby/Wood-a	21	63	315
55-61,63-65,67-69,71,72,74,75: 74-Contents change to Fantasy.			
75-Last 10¢ issue	19	57	280
62-Prototype ish. (The Hulk); 1st app. Xemnu (Titan) called "The Hulk"			
	29	87	435
66-Prototype ish. (The Hulk)-Return of Xemnu "The Hulk"			
	26	78	380
70-Prototype ish. (The Sandman)(7/61); similar to Spidey villain			
	25	75	365
73-Story titled "The Spider" where a spider is exposed to radiation & gets			
powers of a human and shoots webbing; a reverse prototype of			
Spider-Man's origin	37	111	585
76,77,80-82: 80-Anti-communist propaganda story	15	45	225
76-(10¢ cover price blacked out, 12¢ printed on)	37	111	585
78-The Sorcerer (Dr. Strange prototype) app. (3/62)	25	75	365
79-Prototype issue. (Mr. Hyde)	21	63	310
83-Origin & 1st app. The Mighty Thor by Kirby (8/62) and begin series;			
Thor-c also begin	455	1365	10,000
83-Reprint from the Golden Record Comic Set	14	42	200
With the record (1966)	20	60	300
84-2nd app. Thor	142	426	2700
85-1st app. Loki & Heimdall; 1st brief app. Odin (1 panel)			
	89	267	1700
86-1st full app. Odin	55	165	1050
87-89: 89-Origin Thor retold	44	132	750
90-No Kirby-a	38	114	600
91,92,94,96-Sinnott-a	32	96	490
93,97-Kirby-a; Tales of Asgard series begins #97 (origin which concludes in			
#99); origin/1st app. Lava Man	38	114	600
95-Sinnott-a	32	96	490
98,99-Kirby/Heck-a. 98-Origin/1st app. The Human Cobra. 99-1st app.			
Surtur & Mr. Hyde	27	81	400
100-Kirby/Heck-a; Thor battles Mr. Hyde	27	81	400

	GD	FN	NM-

101,108: 101-(2/64)-2nd Avengers x-over (w/o Capt. America); see Tales Of Suspense #49 for 1st x-over. 108-(9/64)-Early Dr. Strange & Avengers x-over; ten extra pgs. Kirby-a   20   60   300

102,104-107,110: 102-Intro Sif. 105-109-Ten extra pgs. Kirby-a in each. 107-1st app. Grey Gargoyle   19   57   280

103-1st app. Enchantress   22   66   325

109-Magneto-c & app. (1st x-over, 10/64)   41   123   650

111,113: 113-Origin Loki   15   45   220

112-Thor Vs. Hulk (1/65); Origin Loki   41   123   700

114-Origin/1st app. Absorbing Man   22   66   325

115-Detailed origin of Loki   19   57   285

116-123,125: 118-1st app. Destroyer. 119-Intro Hogun, Fandral, Volstagg   13   39   190

124-Hercules-c/story   14   42   200

503-521: 503-(11/96, $1.50)-The Lost Gods begin; Tom DeFalco scripts & Deodato Studios-c/a. 505-Spider-Man-c/app. 509-Loki-c/app. 514-516-Shang-Chi   2.50

#(-1) Flashback (7/97) Tales of Asgard Donald Blake app.   2.50

Annual 1(1965, 25¢, 72 pgs.)-New Thor vs. Hercules(1st app.)-c/story (see Incredible Hulk #3); Kirby-c/a; r/#85,93,95,97   22   66   320

JOURNEY INTO MYSTERY (2nd Series)
Marvel Comics: Oct, 1972 - No. 19, Oct, 1975

1-Robert Howard adaptation; Starlin/Ploog-a   3   9   32

2-5: 2,3,5-Bloch adapt. 4-H. P. Lovecraft adapt.   2   6   22

6-19: Reprints   2   6   16

JSA (Justice Society of America) (Also see All Star Comics)
DC Comics: Aug, 1999 - Present ($2.50)

1-Robinson and Goyer-s; funeral of Wesley Dodds   2   6   12

2-5: 4-Return of Dr. Fate   6.00

6-24: 6-Black Adam-c/app. 11,12-Kobra. 16-20-JSA vs. Johnny Sorrow. 19,20-Spectre app. 22-Hawkgirl origin. 23-Hawkman returns   4.00

25-($3.75) Hawkman rejoins the JSA   1   3   9

26-36, 38-49: 27-Capt. Marvel app. 29-Joker: Last Laugh. 31,32-Snejbjerg-a. 33-Ultra-Humanite. 34-Intro. new Crimson Avenger and Hourman. 42-G.A. Mr. Terrific and the Freedom Fighters app. 46-Eclipso returns   3.00

37-($3.50) Johnny Thunder merges with the Thunderbolt; origin new Crimson Avenger   3.50

50-($3.95) Wraparound-c by Pacheco; Sentinel becomes Green Lantern again   4.00

51-68: 51-Kobra killed. 54-JLA app. 55-Ma Hunkle (Red Tornado) app. 56-58-Black Reign x-over with Hawkman #23-25. 64-Sand returns. 67-Identity Crisis tie-in; Gibbons-a. 68-Ross-c   2.50

Annual 1 (10/00, $3.50) Planet DC; intro. Nemesis   3.50

Darkness Falls TPB (2002, $19.95) r/#6-15   20.00

Fair Play TPB (2003, $14.95) r/#26-31 & Secret Files #2   15.00

Justice Be Done TPB (2000, $14.95) r/Secret Files & #1-5   15.00

...: Our Worlds at War 1 (9/01, $2.95) Jae Lee-c; Saltares-a   3.00

...: Savage Times TPB (2004, $14.95) r/#39-45   15.00

	GD	FN	NM-

... Secret Files 1 (8/99, $4.95) Origin stories and pin-ups; death of Wesley
   Dodds (G.A. Sandman); intro new Hawkgirl   5.00
... Secret Files 2 (9/01, $4.95) Short stories and profile pages   5.00
...: Stealing Thunder TPB (2003, $14.95) r/#32-38; JSA vs. The
   Ultra-Humanite   15.00
...: The Return of Hawkman TPB (2002, $19.95) r/#16-26 & Secret Files #1
                                                20.00

JSA: ALL STARS
DC Comics: July, 2003 - No. 8, Feb, 2004 ($2.50/$3.50, limited series, back-up stories in Golden Age style)

1-6,8-Goyer & Johns-s/Cassaday-c. 1-Velluto-a; intro. Legacy. 2-Hawkman
  by Loeb/Sale. 3-Dr. Fate by Cooke. 4-Starman by Robinson/Harris.
  5-Hourman by Chaykin. 6-Dr. Mid-nite by Azzarello/Risso   2.50
7-($3.50) Mr. Terrific back-up story by Chabon; Lark-a   3.50
TPB (2004, $14.95) r/#1-8   15.00

JUSTICE LEAGUE (...International #7-25; ...America #26 on)
DC Comics: May, 1987 - No. 113, Aug, 1996 (Also see Legends #6)

1-Batman, Green Lantern (Guy Gardner), Blue Beetle, Mr. Miracle, Capt.
  Marvel & Martian Manhunter begin   1   3   7
2,3: 3-Regular-c (white background)   5.00
3-Limited-c (yellow background, Superman logo)   4   12   50
4-10: 4-Booster Gold joins. 5-Origin Gray Man; Batman vs. Guy Gardner;
  Creeper app. 7-($1.25, 52 pgs.)-Capt. Marvel & Dr. Fate resign; Capt.
  Atom & Rocket Red join. 9,10-Millennium x-over.   3.00
11-17,22,23,25-49,51-68,71-82: 16-Bruce Wayne-c/story. 31,32-J. L. Europe
  x-over. 58-Lobo app. 61-New team begins; swipes-c to J.L. of A. #1('60).
  70-Newsstand version w/o outer-c. 71-Direct sales version w/black outer-c.
  71-Newsstand version w/o outer-c. 80-Intro new Booster Gold. 82,83-Guy
  Gardner-c/stories   2.50
18-21,24,50: 18-21-Lobo app. 24-($1.50)-1st app. Justice League Europe.
  50-($1.75, 52 pgs.)   3.00
69-Doomsday tie-in; takes place between Superman: The Man of Steel #18
  & Superman #74   5.00
69,70-2nd printings   2.25
70-Funeral for a Friend part 1; red 3/4 outer-c   4.00
83-99,101-113: 92-(9/94)-Zero Hour x-over; Triumph app. 113-Green Lantern,
  Flash & Hawkman app.   2.50
100 ($3.95)-Foil-c; 52 pgs.   4.00
100 ($2.95)-Newstand   3.00
#0-(10/94) Zero Hour (publ between #92 & #93); new team begins (Hawkman,
  Flash, Wonder Woman, Metamorpho, Nuklon, Crimson Fox, Obsidian &
  Fire)   2.50
Annual 1-8,10 ('87-'94, '96, 68 pgs.): 2-Joker-c/story; Batman cameo.
  5-Armageddon 2001 x-over; Silver ink 2nd print. 7-Bloodlines x-over.
  8-Elseworlds story. 10-Legends of the Dead Earth   3.00
Annual 9 (1995, $3.50)-Year One story   3.50
Special 1,2 ('90,'91, 52 pgs.): 1-Giffen plots. 2-Staton-a(p)   3.00
Spectacular 1 (1992, $1.50, 52 pgs.)-Intro new JLI & JLE teams; ties into JLI

	GD	FN	NM-

#61 & JLE #37; two interlocking covers by Jurgens   3.00
A New Beginning Trade Paperback (1989, $12.95)-r/#1-7   13.00

JUSTICE LEAGUE ADVENTURES (Based on Cartoon Network series)
DC Comics: Jan, 2002 - No. 34, Oct, 2004 ($1.99/$2.25)

1-Timm & Ross-c   3.00
2-32: 3-Nicieza-s. 5-Starro app. 10-Begin $2.25-c. 14-Includes 16 pg. insert
    for VERB with Haberlin CG-art. 15,29-Amancio-a. 16-McCloud-s.
    20-Psycho Pirate app. 25,26-Adam Strange-c/app. 28-Legion of Super-
    Heroes app. 30-Kamandi app.   2.25
Free Comic Book Day giveaway - (See Promotional Comics section)
TPB (2003, $9.95) r/#1,3,6,10-13; Timm/Ross-c from #1   10.00
...Vol. 1: The Magnificent Seven (2004, $6.95) digest-size reprints #3,6,10-12
    7.00
...Vol. 2: Friends and Foes (2004, $6.95) digest-size reprints #13,14,16,19,20
    7.00

JUSTICE LEAGUE: A MIDSUMMER'S NIGHTMARE
DC Comics: Sept, 1996 - No. 3, Nov, 1996 ($2.95, limited series, 38 pgs.)

1-3: Re-establishes Superman, Batman, Green Lantern, The Martian
    Manhunter, Flash, Aquaman & Wonder Woman as the Justice League;
    Mark Waid & Fabian Nicieza co-scripts; Jeff Johnson & Darick
    Robertson-a(p); Kevin Maguire-c   5.00
TPB-(1997, $8.95) r/1-3   9.00

JUSTICE LEAGUE ELITE (See JLA #100 and JLA Secret Files 2004)
DC Comics: Sept, 2004 - Present ($2.50)

1-6-Flash, Green Arrow, Vera Black and others; Kelly-s/Mahnke-a.
    5,6-JSA app.   2.50

JUSTICE LEAGUE EUROPE (Justice League International #51 on)
DC Comics: Apr, 1989 - No. 68, Sept., 1994 (75¢/ $1.00/$1.25/$1.50)

1-Giffen plots in all, breakdowns in #1-8,13-30; Justice League #1-c/swipe
    3.00
2-10: 7-9-Batman app. 7,8-JLA x-over. 8,9-Superman app.   2.50
11-49: 12-Metal Men app. 20-22-Rogers-c/a(p). 33,34-Lobo vs. Despero.
    37-New team begins; swipes-c to JLA #9; see JLA Spectacular   2.50
50-($2.50, 68 pgs.)-Battles Sonar   3.00
51-68: 68-Zero Hour x-over; Triumph joins Justice League Task Force (See
    JLTF #17)   2.25
Annual 1-5 ('90-'94, 68 pgs.)-1-Return of the Global Guardians; Giffen plots/
    breakdowns. 2-Armageddon 2001; Giffen-a(p); Rogers-a(p); Golden-a(i).
    3-Eclipso app. 4-Intro Lionheart. 5-Elseworlds story   3.00

JUSTICE LEAGUE INTERNATIONAL (See Justice League Europe)

JUSTICE LEAGUE OF AMERICA (See Brave & the Bold #28-30, Mystery In
Space #75 & Official... Index) (See Crisis on Multiple Earths TPBs for reprints
of JLA/JSA crossovers)
National Periodical Publ./DC Comics: Oct-Nov, 1960 - No. 261, Apr, 1987
(#91-99,139-157: 52 pgs.)

1-(10-11/60)-Origin & 1st app. Despero; Aquaman, Batman, Flash, Green

	GD	FN	NM-
Lantern, J'onn J'onzz, Superman & Wonder Woman continue from Brave and the Bold	364	1092	8000
2	92	276	1750
3-Origin/1st app. Kanjar Ro (see Mystery in Space #75)(scarce in high grade due to black-c)	74	222	1400
4-Green Arrow joins JLA	50	150	875
5-Origin & 1st app. Dr. Destiny	45	135	775
6-8,10: 6-Origin & 1st app. Prof. Amos Fortune. 7-(10-11/61)-Last 10¢ issue. 10-(3/62)-Origin & 1st app. Felix Faust; 1st app. Lord of Time	34	102	550
9-(2/62)-Origin JLA (1st origin)	42	126	725
11-15: 12-(6/62)-Origin & 1st app. Dr. Light. 13-(8/62)-Speedy app. 14-(9/62)-Atom joins JLA.	22	66	325
16-20: 17-Adam Strange flashback	19	57	280
21-(8/63)-"Crisis on Earth-One"; re-intro. of JSA in this title (see Flash #129) (1st S.A. app. Hourman & Dr. Fate)	34	102	540
22- "Crisis on Earth-Two"; JSA x-over (story continued from #21)	31	93	460
23-28: 24-Adam Strange app. 27-Robin app.	14	42	210
29-JSA x-over; 1st S.A. app. Starman; "Crisis on Earth-Three"	18	54	260
30-JSA x-over	16	48	235
31-Hawkman joins JLA, Hawkgirl cameo (11/64)	12	36	175
32,34: 32-Intro & Origin Brain Storm. 34-Joker-c/sty	10	30	140
33,35,36,40,41: 40-3rd S.A. Penguin app. 41-Intro & origin The Key	10	30	125
37-39: 37,38-JSA x-over. 37-1st S.A. app. Mr. Terrific; Batman cameo. 38-"Crisis on Earth-A". 39-Giant G-16; r/B&B #28,30 & JLA #5	12	36	175
42-45: 42-Metamorpho app. 43-Intro. Royal Flush Gang	8	24	100
46-JSA x-over; 1st S.A. app. Sandman; 3rd S.A. app. of G.A. Spectre (8/66)	13	39	185
47-JSA x-over; 4th S.A. app of G.A. Spectre.	10	30	125
48-Giant G-29; r/JLA #2,3 & B&B #29	9	27	120
49-54,57,59,60	7	21	90
55-Intro. Earth 2 Robin (1st G.A. Robin in S.A.)	10	30	125
56-JLA vs. JSA (1st G.A. Wonder Woman in S.A.)	8	24	105
58-Giant G-41; r/JLA #6,8,1	8	24	105
61-63,66,68-72: 69-Wonder Woman quits. 71-Manhunter leaves. 72-Last 12¢ issue	6	18	70
64,65-JSA story. 64-(8/68)-Origin/1st app. S.A. Red Tornado	7	21	80
67-Giant G-53; r/JLA #4,14,31	8	24	100
73-1st S.A. app. of G.A. Superman	7	21	80
74-Black Canary joins; 1st meeting of G.A. & S.A. Superman; Neal Adams-c	7	21	80
75-2nd app. Green Arrow in new costume (see Brave & the Bold #85)	6	18	75

	GD	FN	NM-
76-Giant G-65	7	21	80
77-80: 78-Re-intro Vigilante (1st S.A. app?)	4	12	45
81-84,86-90: 82-1st S.A. app. of G.A. Batman (cameo). 83-Apparent death of			
The Spectre. 90-Last 15¢ issue	4	12	40
85,93-(Giant G-77,G-89; 68 pgs.)	5	15	60
91,92: 91-1st meeting of the G.A. & S.A. Robin; begin 25¢, 52 pgs. issues,			
ends #99. 92-S.A. Robin tries on costume that is similar to that of G.A.			
Robin in All Star Comics #58	4	12	50
94-Reprints 1st Sandman story (Adv. #40) & origin/1st app. Starman			
(Adventure #61); Deadman x-over; N. Adams-a (4 pgs.)			
	9	27	120
95,96: 95-Origin Dr. Fate & Dr. Midnight -r/ More Fun #67, All-American #25).			
96-Origin Hourman (Adv. #48); Wildcat-r	5	15	55
97-99: 97-Origin JLA retold; Sargon, Starman-r. 98-G.A. Sargon, Starman-r.			
99-G.A. Sandman, Atom-r; last 52 pg. issue	4	12	45
100-(8/72)-1st meeting of G.A. & S.A.W. Woman	5	15	55
101,102: JSA x-overs. 102-Red Tornado dies	4	12	40
103-106,109: 103-Rutland Vermont Halloween x-over; Phantom Stranger			
joins. 105-Elongated Man joins. 106-New Red Tornado joins.			
109-Hawkman resigns	3	9	24
107,108-JSA x-over; 1st revival app. of G.A. Uncle Sam, Black Condor,			
The Ray, Dollman, Phantom Lady & The Human Bomb			
	3	9	26
110-116: All 100 pgs. 111-JLA vs. Injustice Gang; Shining Knight, Green			
Arrow-r. 112-Amazo app; Crimson Avenger, Vigilante-r; origin Starman-			
r/Adv. #81. 115-Martian Manhunter app.	4	12	50
117-122,125-134: 117-Hawkman rejoins. 120,121-Adam Strange app.			
125,126-Two-Face-app. 128-Wonder Woman rejoins. 129-Destruction of			
Red Tornado	2	6	18
123-(10/75),124: JLA/JSA x-over. DC editor Julie Schwartz & JLA writers			
Cary Bates & Elliot S! Maggin appear in story as themselves. 1st named			
app. Earth-Prime (3rd app. after Flash; 1st Series #179 & 228)			
	2	6	20
135-136: 135-137-G.A. Bulletman, Bulletgirl, Spy Smasher, Mr. Scarlet, Pinky			
& Ibis x-over, 1st appearances since G.A.	2	6	20
137-Superman battles G.A. Capt. Marvel	3	9	24
138,139-157: 138-Adam Strange app. w/c by Neal Adams; 1st app. Green			
Lantern of the 73rd Century. 139-157-(52 pgs.): 139-Adam Strange app.			
144-Origin retold; origin J'onn J'onzz. 145-Red Tornado resurrected.			
147,148-Legion of Super-Heroes x-over	2	6	15
158-160-(44 pgs.)	1	4	10
158,160-162,168,169,171,172,173,176-179,181-(Whitman variants; low print			
run, none show issue # on cover)	2	6	12
161-182: 161-Zatanna joins & new costume. 171-Mr. Terrific murdered.			
178-Cover similar to #1; J'onn J'onzz app. 179-Firestorm joins. 181-Green			
Arrow leaves JLA			6.00
183-185-JSA/New Gods/Darkseid/Mr.Miracle x-over	1	3	7
186-199: 192,193-Real origin Red Tornado. 193-1st app. All-Star Squadron			
as free 16 pg. insert			5.00

	GD	FN	NM-

200 ($1.50, Anniversary issue, 76pgs.)-JLA origin retold; Green Arrow rejoins;
    Bolland, Aparo, Giordano, Gil Kane, Infantino, Kubert-a; Perez-c/a   6.00
201-206,209-243,246-259: 203-Intro/origin new Royal Flush Gang. 219,220-
    True origin Black Canary. 228-Re-intro Martian Manhunter. 228-230-War
    of the Worlds storyline; JLA Satellite destroyed by Martians. 233-Story
    cont'd from Annual #2. 243-Aquaman leaves. 250-Batman rejoins.
    253-Origin Despero. 258-Death of Vibe. 258-261-Legends x-over   3.00
207,208-JSA, JLA, & All-Star Squadron team-up   4.00
244,245-Crisis x-over   4.00
260-Death of Steel   5.00
261-Last issue   1   3   7
Annual 1-3 ('83-'85), 2-Intro new J.L.A. (Aquaman, Martian Manhunter, Steel,
    Gypsy, Vixen, Vibe, Elongated Man, & Zatanna). 3-Crisis x-over   3.00

JUSTICE LEAGUE OF AMERICA : ANOTHER NAIL (Elseworlds) (Also see
JLA: The Nail)
DC Comics: 2004 - No. 3, 2004 ($5.95, prestige format)

1-3-Sequel to JLA: The Nail; Alan Davis-s/a(p)   6.00
TPB (2004, $12.95) r/series   13.00

JUSTICE LEAGUE QUARTERLY (...International Quarterly #6 on)
DC Comics: Winter, 1990-91 - No. 17, Winter, 1994 ($2.95/$3.50, 84 pgs.)

1-12,14-17: 1-Intro The Conglomerate (Booster Gold, Praxis, Gypsy, Vapor,
    Echo, Maxi-Man, & Reverb); Justice League #1-c/swipe. 1,2-Giffen
    plots/breakdowns. 3-Giffen plot; 72 pg. story. 4-Rogers/Russell-a in
    back-up. 5,6-Waid scripts. 8,17-Global Guardians app. 12-Waid script   3.50
13-Linsner-c   6.00
NOTE: *Phil Jimenez a-17p. Sprouse a-1p.*

JUSTICE LEAGUE TASK FORCE
DC Comics: June, 1993 - No. 37, Aug, 1996 ($1.25/$1.50/$1.75)

1-16,0,17-37: Aquaman, Nightwing, Flash, J'onn J'onzz, & Gypsy form team.
    5,6-Knight-quest tie-ins (new Batman cameo #5, 1 pg.). 15-Triumph
    cameo. 16-(9/94)-Zero Hour x-over; Triumph app. 0-(10/94).
    17-(11/94)-Triumph becomes part of Justice League TaskForce (See JLE
    #68). 26-Impulse app. 35-Warlord app. 37-Triumph quits team   2.25

JUSTICE LEAGUE UNLIMITED (Based on Cartoon Network animated series)
DC Comics: Nov, 2004 - Present ($2.25)

1-4: 1-Zatanna app. 2-Royal Flush Gang app. 4-Adam Strange app.   2.25

JUSTICE SOCIETY OF AMERICA (See Adventure #461 & All-Star #3)
DC Comics: April, 1991 - No. 8, Nov, 1991 ($1.00, limited series)

1-8: 1-Flash. 2-Black Canary. 3-Green Lantern. 4-Hawkman. 5-Flash/
    Hawkman. 6-Green Lantern/Black Canary. 7-JSA   2.50

JUSTICE SOCIETY OF AMERICA (Also see Last Days of the... Special)
DC Comics: Aug, 1992 - No. 10, May, 1993 ($1.25)

1-10   2.50

JUSTICE SOCIETY RETURNS, THE (See All Star Comics (1999) for related
titles)

	GD	FN	NM-

DC Comics: 2003 ($19.95, TPB)

TPB-Reprints 1999 JSA x-over from All-Star Comics #1,2 and related
   one-shots   20.00

JUST IMAGINE STAN LEE WITH... (Stan Lee re-invents DC icons)
DC Comics: 2001 - 2002 ($5.95, prestige format, one-shots)
(Adam Hughes back-c on all)(Michael Uslan back-up stories in all, diff. artists)

Scott McDaniel Creating **Aquaman**- Back-up w/Fradon-a			6.00
Joe Kubert Creating **Batman**- Back-up w/Kaluta-a			6.00
Chris Bachalo Creating **Catwoman**- Back-up w/Cooke & Allred-a			6.00
John Cassaday Creating **Crisis**- no back-up story			6.00
Kevin Maguire Creating **The Flash**- Back-up w/Aragonés-a			6.00
Dave Gibbons Creating **Green Lantern**- Back-up w/Giordano-a			6.00
Jerry Ordway Creating **JLA**			6.00
John Byrne Creating **Robin**- Back-up w/John Severin-a			6.00
Walter Simonson Creating **Sandman**- Back-up w/Corben-a			6.00
Gary Frank Creating **Shazam!**- Back-up w/Kano-a			6.00
John Buscema Creating **Superman**- Back-up w/Kyle Baker-a			6.00
Jim Lee Creating **Wonder Woman**- Back-up w/Gene Colan-a			6.00
Secret Files and Origins #1 (3/02, $4.95) Crisis prologue; Jurgens-a			5.00

TPB -Just Imagine Stan Lee Creating the DC Universe: Book One (2002,
   $19.95) r/Batman, Wonder Woman, Superman, Green Lantern   20.00
TPB -Just Imagine Stan Lee Creating the DC Universe: Book Two (2003,
   $19.95) r/Flash, JLA, Secret Files and Origins, Robin, Shazam; sketch
   pages   20.00
TPB -Just Imagine Stan Lee Creating the DC Universe: Book Three (2004,
   $19.95) r/Aquaman, Catwoman, Sandman, Crisis; profile pages   20.00

KABUKI
Caliber: Nov, 1994 ($3.50, B&W, one-shot)

nn-(Fear The Reaper) 1st app.; David Mack-c/a/s	1	3	8
Color Special (1/96, $2.95)-Mack-c/a/scripts; pin-ups by Tucci, Harris & Quesada			4.00
Gallery (8/95, $2.95)- pinups from Mack, Bradstreet, Paul Pope & others			3.00

KABUKI
Image Comics: Oct, 1997 - No. 9, Mar, 2000 ($2.95, color)

1-David Mack-c/s/a			5.00
1-($10.00)-Dynamic Forces Edition	1	4	10
2-5			4.00
6-9			3.00
#1/2 (9/01, $2.95) r/Wizard 1/2; Eklipse Mag. article; bio			3.00
...Classics (2/99, $3.95) Reprints Fear the Reaper			4.00
...Classics 2 (3/99, $3.95) Reprints Dance of Dance			4.00
...Classics 3-5 (3-6/99, $4.95) Reprints Circle of Blood-Acts 1-3			5.00
...Classics 6-12 (7/99-3/00, $3.25) Various reprints			3.25
...Images (6/98, $4.95) r/#1 with new pin-ups			5.00
...Images 2 (1/99, $4.95) r/#1 with new pin-ups			5.00
...Metamorphosis TPB (10/00, $24.95) r/#1-9; Sienkiewicz intro.			25.00
...Reflections 1-4 (7/98-5/02; $4.95) new story plus art techniques			5.00

	GD	FN	NM-
... The Ghost Play (11/02, $2.95) new story plus interview			3.00

KABUKI
Marvel Comics (Icon): July, 2004 - Present ($2.99, color)

1,2: 1-David Mack-c/s/a in all; variant-c by Alex Maleev			3.00

KABUKI: CIRCLE OF BLOOD
Caliber Press: Jan, 1995 - No. 6, Nov, 1995 ($2.95, B&W)

1-David Mack story/a in all			5.00
2-6: 3-#1 on inside indicia.			3.00
6-Variant-c			3.00
TPB ($16.95) r/#1-6, intro. by Steranko			17.00
TPB (1997, $17.95) Image Edition-r/#1-6, intro. by Steranko			18.00
TPB ($24.95) Deluxe Edition			25.00

KABUKI: DREAMS OF THE DEAD
Caliber: July, 1996 ($2.95, one-shot)

nn-David Mack-c/a/scripts			3.00

KABUKI FAN EDITION
Gemstone Publ./Caliber: Feb, 1997 (mail-in offer, one-shot)

nn-David Mack-c/a/scripts			4.00

KABUKI: MASKS OF THE NOH
Caliber: May, 1996 - No. 4, Feb, 1997 ($2.95, limited series)

1-4: 1-Three-c (1A-Quesada, 1B-Buzz, &1C-Mack). 3-Terry Moore pin-up			
			3.00
TPB-(4/98, $10.95) r/#1-4; intro by Terry Moore			11.00

KABUKI: SKIN DEEP
Caliber Comics: Oct, 1996 - No. 3, May, 1997 ($2.95)

1-3:David Mack-c/a/scripts. 2-Two-c (1-Mack, 1-Ross)			3.00
TPB-(5/98, $9.95) r/#1-3; intro by Alex Ross			10.00

KAMANDI: AT EARTH'S END
DC Comics: June, 1993 - No. 6, Nov, 1993 ($1.75, limited series)

1-6: Elseworlds storyline			2.50

KAMANDI, THE LAST BOY ON EARTH (Also see Alarming Tales #1, Brave
and the Bold #120 & 157 & Cancelled Comic Cavalcade)
National Periodical Publ./DC Comics: Oct-Nov, 1972 - No. 59, Sept-Oct,
1978

	GD	FN	NM-
1-Origin & 1st app. Kamandi	7	21	85
2,3	4	12	45
4,5: 4-Intro. Prince Tuftan of the Tigers	3	10	35
6-10	3	9	26
11-20	2	6	18
21-28,30,31,33-40: 24-Last 20¢ issue. 31-Intro Pyra.	2	6	16
29,32: 29-Superman x-over. 32-(68 pgs.)-r/origin from #1 plus one new			
story; 4 pg. biog. of Jack Kirby with B&W photos	2	6	20
41-57	2	6	12
58-(44 pgs.)-Karate Kid x-over from LSH	2	6	18

	GD	FN	NM-

59-(44 pgs.)-Cont'd in B&B #157; The Return of Omac back-up by
Starlin-c/a(p) — 2, 6, 18

KARATE KID (See Action, Adventure, Legion of Super-Heroes, & Superboy)
National Periodical Publications/DC Comics: Mar-Apr, 1976 - No. 15, July-Aug, 1978 (Legion of Super-Heroes spin-off)

1,15: 1-Meets Iris Jacobs; Estrada/Staton-a. 15-Continued into
Kamandi #58 — 2, 6, 14
2-14: 2-Major Disaster app. 14-Robin x-over — 1, 3, 8

KA-ZAR (Also see Marvel Comics #1, Savage Tales #6 & X-Men #10)
Marvel Comics Group: Aug, 1970 - No. 3, Mar, 1971 (Giant-Size, 68 pgs.)

1-Reprints earlier Ka-Zar stories; Avengers x-over in Hercules; Daredevil,
X-Men app.; hidden profanity-c — 4, 12, 38
2,3-Daredevil-r. 2-r/Daredevil #13 w/Kirby layouts; Ka-Zar origin, Angel-r
from X-Men by Tuska. 3-Romita & Heck-a (no Kirby) — 3, 9, 26

KA-ZAR
Marvel Comics Group: Jan, 1974 - No. 20, Feb, 1977 (Regular Size)

1 — 2, 6, 18
2-10 — 1, 3, 9
11-14,16,18-20 — 6.00
15,17-(Regular 25¢ edition)(8/76) — 6.00
15,17-(30¢-c variants, limited distribution) — 1, 3, 8

KA-ZAR (Volume 2)
Marvel Comics: May, 1997 - No. 20, Dec, 1998 ($1.95/$1.99)

1-Waid-s/Andy Kubert-c/a. thru #4 — 3.00
1-2nd printing; new cover — 2.25
2,4: 2-Two-c — 2.50
3-Alpha Flight #1 preview — 3.00
5-13,15-20: 8-Includes Spider-Man Cybercomic CD-ROM. 9-11-Thanos app.
15-Priest-s/Martinez & Rodriguez-a begin; Punisher app. — 2.25
14-($2.99) Last Waid/Kubert issue; flip book with 2nd story previewing new
creative team of Priest-s/Martinez & Rodriguez-a — 3.00
'97 Annual ($2.99)-Wraparound-c — 3.00

KA-ZAR THE SAVAGE (See Marvel Fanfare)
Marvel Comics Group: Apr, 1981 - No. 34, Oct, 1984 (Regular size)(Mando paper #10 on)

1 — 4.00
2-20,24,27,28,30-34: 11-Origin Zabu. 12-One of two versions with panel
missing on pg. 10. 20-Kraven the Hunter-c/story (also apps. in #21) — 2.50
12-Version with panel on pg. 10 (1600 printed) — 6.00
21-23, 25,26-Spider-Man app. 26-Photo-c. — 3.00
29-Double size; Ka-Zar & Shanna wed — 3.00

KILLING JOKE, THE (See Batman: The Killing Joke under Batman one-shots)

KING CONAN (Conan The King No. 20 on)
Marvel Comics Group: Mar, 1980 - No. 19, Nov, 1983 (52 pgs.)

	GD	FN	NM-
1			6.00
2-19: 4-Death of Thoth Amon. 7-1st Paul Smith-a, 1 pg. pin-up (9/81)			4.00

KINGDOM, THE
DC Comics: Feb, 1999 - No. 2, Feb, 1999 ($2.95/$1.99, limited series)

1,2-Waid-s; sequel to Kingdom Come; introduces Hypertime   4.00
...: Kid Flash 1 (2/99, $1.99) Waid-s/Pararillo-a, ...: Nightstar 1 (2/99, $1.99)
   Waid-s/Haley-a, ...: Offspring 1 (2/99, $1.99) Waid-s/Quitely-a, ...: Planet
   Krypton 1 (2/99, $1.99) Waid-s/Kitson-a, ...: Son of the Bat 1 (2/99, $1.99)
   Waid-s/Apthorp-a   2.25

KINGDOM COME
DC Comics: 1996 - No. 4, 1996 ($4.95, painted limited series)

1-Mark Waid scripts & Alex Ross-painted c/a in all; tells the last days of the			
DC Universe; 1st app. Magog	1	3	8
2-Superman forms new Justice League	1	3	7
3-Return of Captain Marvel			5.00
4-Final battle of Superman and Captain Marvel	1	3	7
Deluxe Slipcase Edition-($89.95) w/Revelations companion book, 12 new			
story pages, foil stamped covers, signed and numbered			120.00
Hardcover Edition-($29.95)-Includes 12 new story pages and artwork from			
Revelations, new cover artwork with gold foil inlay			35.00
Hardcover 2nd printing			30.00
Softcover Ed.-($14.95)-Includes 12 new story pgs. & artwork from			
Revelations, new c-artwork			15.00

KISS
Dark Horse Comics: June, 2002 - No. 13, Sept, 2003 ($2.99, limited series)

1-Photo-c and J. Scott Campbell-c; Casey-s   4.00
2-13: 2-Photo-c and J. Scott Campbell-c. 3-Photo-c and Leinil Yu-c   3.00
...: Men and Monsters TPB (9/03, $12.95) r/#7-10   13.00
...: Rediscovery TPB (2003, $9.95) r/#1-3   10.00
...: Return of the Phantom TPB (2003, $9.95) r/#4-6   10.00
...: Unholy War TPB (2004, $9.95) r/#11-13   10.00

KISS: THE PSYCHO CIRCUS
Image Comics: Aug, 1997 - No. 31, June, 2000 ($1.95/$2.25/$2.50)

1-Holguin-s/Medina-a(p)	1	3	8
1-2nd & 3rd printings			2.50
2			5.00
3,4: 4-Photo-c			4.00
5-8: 5-Begin $2.25-c			3.00
9-29			2.50
30,31: 30-Begin $2.50-c			2.50
Book 1 TPB ('98, $12.95) r/#1-6			13.00
Book 2 Destroyer TPB (8/99, $9.95) r/#10-13			10.00
Book 3 Whispered Scream TPB ('00, $9.95) r/#7-9,18			10.00
...Magazine 1 ($6.95) r/#1-3 plus interviews			7.00
...Magazine 2-5 ($4.95) 2-r/#4,5 plus interviews. 3-r/#6,7. 4-r/#8,9			5.00
Wizard Edition ('98, supplement) Bios, tour preview and interviews			2.25

	GD	FN	NM-

KOBRA (Unpublished #8 appears in DC Special Series No. 1)
National Periodical Publications: Feb-Mar, 1976 - No. 7, Mar-Apr, 1977

1-1st app.; Kirby-a redrawn by Marcos; only 25¢-c	1	4	10
2-7: (All 30¢ issues) 3-Giffen-a			6.00

KORAK, SON OF TARZAN (Edgar Rice Burroughs)(See Tarzan #139)
Gold Key: Jan, 1964 - No. 45, Jan, 1972 (Painted-c No. 1-?)

1-Russ Manning-a	9	27	110
2-5-Russ Manning-a	5	15	55
6-11-Russ Manning-a	4	12	50
12-23: 12,13-Warren Tufts-a. 14-Jon of the Kalahari ends. 15-Mabu, Jungle Boy begins. 21-Manning-a. 23-Last 12¢ issue	4	12	45
24-30	3	9	32
31-45	3	9	24

KORAK, SON OF TARZAN (Tarzan Family #60 on; see Tarzan #230)
National Periodical Publications: V9#46, May-June, 1972 - V12#56, Feb-Mar, 1974; No. 57, May-June, 1975 - No. 59, Sept-Oct, 1975 (Edgar Rice Burroughs)

46-(52 pgs.)-Carson of Venus begins (origin), ends #56; Pellucidar feature; Weiss-a	2	6	22
47-59: 49-Origin Korak retold	1	4	10

KROFFT SUPERSHOW (TV)
Gold Key: Apr, 1978 - No. 6, Jan, 1979

1-Photo-c	3	9	30
2-6: 6-Photo-c	2	6	20

KRUSTY COMICS (TV)(See Simpsons Comics)
Bongo Comics: 1995 - No. 3, 1995 ($2.25, limited series)

1-3			2.50

KRYPTON CHRONICLES
DC Comics: Sept, 1981 - No. 3, Nov, 1981

1-3: 1-Buckler-c(p)			4.00

KULL AND THE BARBARIANS
Marvel Comics: May, 1975 - No. 3, Sept, 1975 ($1.00, B&W, magazine)

1-(84 pgs.) Andru/Wood-r/Kull #1; 2 pgs. Neal Adams; Gil Kane(p), Marie & John Severin-a(r); Krenkel text illo.	2	6	20
2,3: 2-(84 pgs.) Red Sonja by Chaykin begins; Solomon Kane by Weiss/Adams; Gil Kane-a; Solomon Kane pin-up by Wrightson. 3-(76 pgs.) Origin Red Sonja by Chaykin; Adams-a; Solomon Kane app.	2	6	16

KULL THE CONQUEROR (...the Destroyer #11 on; see Conan #1, Creatures on the Loose #10, Marvel Preview, Monsters on the Prowl)
Marvel Comics Group: June, 1971 - No. 2, Sept, 1971; No. 3, July, 1972 - No. 15, Aug, 1974; No. 16, Aug, 1976 - No. 29, Oct, 1978

1-Andru/Wood-a; 2nd app. & origin Kull; 15¢ issue	4	12	50
2-5: 2-3rd Kull app. Last 15¢ iss. 3-13: 20¢ issues	2	6	20

	GD	FN	NM-
6-10	2	6	12
11-15: 11-15-Ploog-a. 14,15: 25¢ issues	1	3	9
16-(Regular 25¢ edition)(8/76)	1	3	7
16-(30¢-c variant, limited distribution)	1	4	10
17-29: 21-23-(Reg. 30¢ editions)	1	3	7
21-23-(35¢-c variants, limited distribution)	1	4	10

KUNG FU (See Deadly Hands of..., & Master of...)

KUNG FU FIGHTER (See Richard Dragon...)

KURT BUSIEK'S ASTRO CITY (Limited series) (Also see Astro City: Local Heroes)
Image Comics (Juke Box Productions): Aug, 1995 - No. 6, Jan, 1996 ($2.25)

1-Kurt Busiek scripts, Brent Anderson-a & Alex Ross front & back-c begins; 1st app. Samaritan & Honor Guard (Cleopatra, MHP, Beautie, The Black Rapier, Quarrel & N-Forcer)	2	6	12
2-6: 2-1st app. The Silver Agent, The Old Soldier, & the "original" Honor Guard (Max O'Millions, Starwoman, the "original" Cleopatra, the "original" N-Forcer, the Bouncing Beatnik, Leopardman & Kitkat). 3-1st app. Jack-in-the-Box & The Deacon. 4-1st app. Winged Victory (cameo), The Hanged Man & The First Family. 5-1st app. Crackerjack, The Astro City Irregulars, Nightingale & Sunbird. 6-Origin Samaritan; 1st full app. Winged Victory	1	4	10
Life In The Big City-(8/96, $19.95, trade paperback)-r/Image Comics limited series w/sketchbook & cover gallery; Ross-c			20.00
Life In The Big City-(8/96, $49.95, hardcover, 1000 print run)-r/Image Comics limited series w/sketchbook & cover gallery; Ross-c			50.00

KURT BUSIEK'S ASTRO CITY (1st Homage Comics series)
Image Comics (Homage Comics): V2#1, Sept, 1996 - No. 15, Dec, 1998;
DC Comics (Homage Comics): No. 16, Mar, 1999 - No. 22, Aug, 2000 ($2.50)

1/2-(10/96)-The Hanged Man story; 1st app. The All-American & Slugger, The Lamplighter, The Time-Keeper & Eterneon	1	4	10
1/2-(1/98) 2nd printing w/new cover			2.50
1- Kurt Busiek scripts, Alex Ross-c, Brent Anderson-p & Will Blyberg-i begin; intro The Gentleman, Thunderhead & Helia.	1	3	8
1-(12/97, $4.95) "3-D Edition" w/glasses			5.00
2-Origin The First Family; Astra story	1	3	7
3-5: 4-1st app. The Crossbreed, Ironhorse, Glue Gun & The Confessor (cameo)			6.00
6-10			5.00
11-22: 14-20-Steeljack story arc. 16-(3/99) First DC issue			2.50
TPB-($19.95) Ross-c, r/#4-9, #1/2 w/sketchbook			20.00
Family Album TPB ($19.95) r/#1-3,10-13			20.00
The Tarnished Angel HC ($29.95) r/#14-20; new Ross dust jacket; sketch pages by Anderson & Ross; cover gallery with reference photos			30.00
The Tarnished Angel SC ($19.95) r/#14-20; new Ross-c			20.00

LADY DEATH (See Evil Ernie)

	GD	FN	NM-

Chaos! Comics: Jan, 1994 - No. 3, Mar, 1994 ($2.75, limited series)

1/2-S. Hughes-c/a in all, 1/2 Velvet	1	3	7
1/2 Gold	1	4	10
1/2 Signed Limited Edition	2	6	12
1-($3.50)-Chromium-c	2	6	18
1-Commemorative	2	6	16
1-(9/96, $2.95) "Encore Presentation"; r/#1			3.00
2	1	3	8
3			5.00

LAFF-A-LYMPICS (TV)(See The Funtastic World of Hanna-Barbera)
Marvel Comics: Mar, 1978 - No. 13, Mar, 1979 (Newsstand sales only)

1-Yogi Bear, Scooby Doo, Pixie & Dixie, etc.	3	9	32
2-8	2	6	22
9-13: 11-Jetsons x-over; 1 pg. illustrated bio of Mighty Mightor, Herculoids, Shazzan, Galaxy Trio & Space Ghost	3	9	28

LANCELOT LINK, SECRET CHIMP (TV)
Gold Key: Apr, 1971 - No. 8, Feb, 1973

1-Photo-c	7	21	90
2-8: 2-Photo-c	4	12	48

LAND OF THE GIANTS (TV)
Gold Key: Nov, 1968 - No. 5, Sept, 1969 (All have photo-c)

1	7	21	90
2-5	4	12	50

LEAGUE OF EXTRAORDINARY GENTLEMEN, THE
America's Best Comics: Mar, 1999 - No. 6, Sept, 2000 ($2.95, lim. series)

1-Alan Moore-s/Kevin O'Neill-a	1	3	9
1-DF Edition ($10.00) O'Neill-c	2	6	12
2,3			5.00
4-6: 5-Revised printing with "Wonder Co. Syringe" parody ad			3.50
5-Initial printing recalled because of "Marvel Co. Syringe" parody ad			30.00
... Compendium 1,2: 1-r/#1,2. 2-r/#3,4			6.00
Hardcover (2000, $24.95) r/#1-6 plus cover gallery			25.00

LEAGUE OF EXTRAORDINARY GENTLEMEN, THE (Volume 2)
America's Best Comics: Sept, 2002 - No. 6, Nov, 2003 ($3.50, lim. series)

1-6-Alan Moore-s/Kevin O'Neill-a			3.50
... Bumper Compendium 1,2: 1-r/#1,2. 2-r/#3,4			6.00

LEGENDS
DC Comics: Nov, 1986 - No. 6, Apr, 1987 (75¢, limited series)

1-5: 1-Byrne-c/a(p) in all; 1st app. new Capt. Marvel. 3-1st app. new Suicide Squad; death of Blockbuster			4.00
6-1st app. new Justice League			6.00

LEGENDS OF THE DARK KNIGHT (See Batman: ...)

LEGENDS OF THE DC UNIVERSE
DC Comics: Feb, 1998 - No. 41, June, 2001 ($1.95/$1.99/$2.50)

	GD	FN	NM-

1-13,15-21: 1-3-Superman; Robinson-s/Semeiks-a/Orbik-painted-c.
   4,5-Wonder Woman; Deodato-a/Rude painted-c. 8-GL/GA, O'Neil-s.
   10,11-Batgirl; Dodson-a. 12,13-Justice League. 15-17-Flash. 18-Kid Flash;
   Guice-a. 19-Impulse; prelude to JLApe Annuals. 20,21-Abin Sur   3.00
14-($3.95) Jimmy Olsen; Kirby-esque-c by Rude   4.00
22-27,30: 22,23-Superman; Rude-c/Ladronn-a. 26,27-Aquaman/Joker   2.50
28,29: Green Lantern & the Atom; Gil Kane-a; covers by Kane and Ross   2.50
31,32: 32-Begin $2.50-c; Wonder Woman; Texeira-a   2.50
33-36-Hal Jordan as The Spectre; DeMatteis-s/Zulli-a; Hale painted-c   2.50
37-41: 37,38-Kyle Rayner. 39-Superman. 40,41-Atom; Harris-c   2.50
... Crisis on Infinite Earths 1 (2/99, $4.95) Untold story during and after Crisis
   on Infinite Earths #4; Wolfman-s/Ryan-a/Orbik-c   5.00
... 80 Page Giant 1 (9/98, $4.95) Stories and art by various incl. Ditko, Perez,
   Gibbons, Mumy; Joe Kubert-c   5.00
... 80 Page Giant 2 (1/00, $4.95) Stories and art by various incl. Challengers
   by Art Adams; Sean Phillips-c   5.00
... 3-D Gallery (12/98, $2.95) Pin-ups w/glasses   3.00

L.E.G.I.O.N. (The # to right of title represents year of print)(Also see Lobo &
R.E.B.E.L.S.)
DC Comics: Feb, 1989 - No. 70, Sept, 1994 ($1.50/$1.75)

1-Giffen plots/breakdowns in #1-12,28   5.00
2-22,24-47: 3-Lobo app. #3 on. 4-1st Lobo-c this title. 5-Lobo joins
   L.E.G.I.O.N. 13-Lar Gand app. 16-Lar Gand joins L.E.G.I.O.N., leaves #19.
   31-Capt. Marvel app. 35-L.E.G.I.O.N. '92 begins   3.00
23,70-($2.50, 52 pgs.)-L.E.G.I.O.N. '91 begins. 70-Zero Hour   4.00
48,49,51-69: 48-Begin $1.75-c. 63-L.E.G.I.O.N. '94 begins; Superman x-over
      3.00
50-($3.50, 68 pgs.)   4.00
Annual 1-5 ('90-94, 68 pgs.): 1-Lobo, Superman app. 2-Alan Grant scripts.
   5-Elseworlds story; Lobo app.   4.00

LEGION, THE (Continued from Legion Lost & Legion Worlds)
DC Comics: Dec, 2001 - No. 38, Oct, 2004 ($2.50)

1-Abnett & Lanning-s; Coipel & Lanning-c/a   4.00
2-24: 3-8-Ra's al Ghul app. 5-Snejbjerg-a. 9-DeStefano-a. 12-Legion vs. JLA.
   16-Fatal Five app.; Walker-a 17,18-Ra's al Ghul app. 20-23-Universo app.
      2.50
25-($3.95) Art by Harris, Cockrum, Rivoche; teenage Clark Kent app.;
   Harris-c   4.00
26-38-Superboy in classic costume. 26-30-Darkseid app. 31-Giffen-a.
   35-38-Jurgens-a   2.50
...Secret Files 3003 (1/04, $4.95) Kirk-a, Harris-c/a; Superboy app.   5.00
...Foundations TPB (2004, $19.95) r/#25-30 & Secret Files 3003; Harris-c
      20.00

LEGION LOST (Continued from Legion of Super-Heroes [4th series] #125)
DC Comics: May, 2000 - No. 12, Apr, 2001 ($2.50, limited series)

1-Abnett & Lanning-s. Coipel & Lanning-c/a	1	3	7
2-12-Abnett & Lanning-s. Coipel & Lanning-c/a in most. 4,9-Alixe-a			3.00

	GD	FN	NM-

LEGIONNAIRES (See Legion of Super-Heroes #40, 41 & Showcase 95 #6)
DC Comics: Apr, 1992 - No. 81, Mar, 2000 ($1.25/$1.50/$2.25)

0-(10/94)-Zero Hour restart of Legion; released between #18 & #19   2.50
1-49,51-77: 1-(4/92)-Chris Sprouse-c/a; polybagged w/SkyBox trading card.
    11-Kid Quantum joins. 18-(9/94)-Zero Hour. 19(11/94). 37-Valor (Lar Gand)
    becomes M'onel (5/96). 43-Legion tryouts; reintro Princess Projectra,
    Shadow Lass & others. 47-Forms one cover image with LSH #91.
    60-Karate Kid & Kid Quantum join. 61-Silver Age & 70's Legion app.
    76-Return of Wildfire. 79,80-Coipel-c/a; Legion vs. the Blight   2.50
50-($3.95) Pullout poster by Davis/Farmer   4.00
#1,000,000 (11/98) Sean Phillips-a   2.50
Annual 1,3 ('94,'96 $2.95)-1-Elseworlds-s. 3-Legends of the Dead Earth-s   3.00
Annual 2 (1995, $3.95)-Year One-s   4.50

LEGIONNAIRES THREE
DC Comics: Jan, 1986 - No. 4, May, 1986 (75¢, limited series)

1-4   3.00

LEGION OF MONSTERS (Also see Marvel Premiere #28 & Marvel Preview #8)
Marvel Comics Group: Sept, 1975 ($1.00, B&W, magazine, 76 pgs.)

1-Origin & 1st app. Legion of Monsters; Neal Adams-c; Morrow-a; origin &
    only app. The Manphibian; Frankenstein by Mayerik; Bram Stoker's Dracula
    adaptation; Reese-a; painted-c (#2 was advertised with Morbius & Satana,
    but was never published)   4   12   40

LEGION OF SUPER-HEROES (See Action Comics, Adventure, All New
Collectors Edition, Legionnaires, Superboy & Superman)
National Periodical Publications: Feb, 1973 - No. 4, July-Aug, 1973

1-Legion & Tommy Tomorrow reprints begin   3   9   32
2-4: 2-Forte-r. 3-r/Adv. #340. Action #240. 4-r/Adv. #341, Action #233;
    Mooney-r   2   6   16

LEGION OF SUPER-HEROES, THE (Formerly Superboy and...; Tales of The
Legion No. 314 on)
DC Comics: No. 259, Jan, 1980 - No. 313, July, 1984

259(#1)-Superboy leaves Legion   2   6   14
260-270,285-290,294: 265-Contains 28 pg. insert "Superman & the TRS-80
    computer"; origin Tyroc; Tyroc leaves Legion. 290-294-Great Darkness
    saga. 294-Double size (52 pgs.)   1   3   8
261,263,264,266-(Whitman variants; low print run; no cover #'s)
                                                                1   4   10
271-284,291-293: 272-Blok joins; origin; 20 pg. insert-Dial 'H' For Hero.
    277-Intro. Reflecto. 280-Superboy re-joins Legion. 282-Origin Reflecto.
    283-Origin Wildfire   5.00
295-299,301-313: 297-Origin retold. 298-Free 16pg. Amethyst preview.
    306-Brief origin Star Boy (Swan art). 311-Colan-a   3.00
300-(68 pgs., Mando paper)-Anniversary issue; has c/a by almost everyone
    at DC   5.00
Annual 1-3(82-84, 52 pgs.)-1-Giffen-c/a; 1st app./origin new Invisible Kid who

	GD	FN	NM-

joins Legion. 2-Karate Kid & Princess Projectra wed & resign   3.00
...The Great Darkness Saga (1989, $17.95, 196 pgs.)-r/LSH #287,290-294 &
   Annual #3; Giffen-c/a   2   6   18

LEGION OF SUPER-HEROES (3rd Series) (Reprinted in Tales of the Legion)
DC Comics: Aug, 1984 - No. 63, Aug, 1989 ($1.25/$1.75, deluxe format)

1-Silver ink logo   5.00
2-36,39-44,46-49,51-62: 4-Death of Karate Kid. 5-Death of Nemesis Kid.
   12-Cosmic Boy, Lightning Lad, & Saturn Girl resign. 14-Intro new
   members: Tellus, Sensor Girl, Quislet. 15-17-Crisis tie-ins. 18-Crisis x-over.
   25-Sensor Girl i.d. revealed as Princess Projectra. 35-Saturn Girl rejoins.
   42,43-Millennium tie-ins. 44-Origin Quislet   3.00
37,38-Death of Superboy   2   6   14
45,50: 45 ($2.95, 68 pgs.)-Anniversary ish. 50-Double size ($2.50-c)   4.00
63-Final issue   4.00
Annual 1-4 (10/85-'88, 52 pgs.)-1-Crisis tie-in   3.00

LEGION OF SUPER-HEROES (4th Series)
DC Comics: Nov, 1989 - No. 125, Mar, 2000 ($1.75/$1.95/$2.25)

0-(10/94)-Zero Hour restart of Legion; released between #61 & #62   2.50
1-Giffen-c/a(p)/scripts begin (4 pg.-a only #18)   4.00
2-20,26-49,51-53,55-58: 4-Mon-El (Lar Gand) destroys Time Trapper;
   changes reality. 5-Alt. reality story where Mordru rules all; Ferro Lad app.
   7-1st app. of Laurel Gand (Lar Gand's cousin). 8-Origin. 13-Free poster by
   Giffen showing new costumes. 15-(2/91)-1st reference of Lar Gand as
   Valor. 26-New map of headquarters. 34-Six pg. preview of TimberWolf
   mini-series. 40-Minor Legionnaires app. 41-(3/93)-SW6 Legion renamed
   Legionnaires w/new costumes and some new code-names   3.00
21-25: 21-24-Lobo & Darkseid storyline. 24-Cameo SW6 younger Legion
   duplicates. 25-SW6 Legion full intro.   3.50
50-($3.50, 68 pgs.)   4.00
54-($2.95)-Die-cut & foil stamped-c   4.00
59-99: 61-(9/94)-Zero Hour. 62-(11/94). 75-XS travels back to the 20th
   Century (cont'd in Impulse #9). 77-Origin of Brainiac 5. 81-Reintro Sun
   Boy. 85-Half of the Legion sent to the 20th century, Superman-c/app.
   86-Final Night. 87-Deadman-c/app. 88-Impulse-c/app. Adventure Comics
   #247 cover swipe. 91-Forms one cover image with Legionnaires #47.
   96-Wedding of Ultra Boy and Apparition. 99-Robin, Impulse, Superboy
   app.   2.50
100-($5.95, 96 pgs.)-Legionnaires return to the 30th Century; gatefold-c;
   5 stories-art by Simonson, Davis and others   1   3   7
101-121: 101-Armstrong-a(p) begins. 105-Legion past & present vs. Time
   Trapper. 109-Moder-a. 110-Thunder joins. 114,115-Bizarro Legion.
   120,121-Fatal Five.   2.50
122-124: 122,123-Coipel-c/a. 124-Coipel-c   3.00
125-Leads into "Legion Lost" maxi-series; Coipel-c   5.00
#1,000,000 (11/98) Giffen-a   2.50
Annual 1-5 (1990-1994, $3.50, 68 pgs.): 4-Bloodlines. 5-Elseworlds   3.50
Annual 6 (1995,$3.95)-Year One story   4.00
Annual 7 (1996, $3.50, 48 pgs.)-Legends of the Dead Earth story; intro 75th

	GD	FN	NM-
Century Legion of Super-Heroes; Wildfire app.			3.50
Legion: Secret Files 1 (1/98, $4.95) Retold origin & pin-ups			5.00
Legion: Secret Files 2 (6/99, $4.95) Story and profile pages			5.00
The Beginning of Tomorrow TPB ('99, $17.95) r/post-Zero Hour reboot			18.00

LEGION WORLDS (Follows Legion Lost series)
DC Comics: Jun, 2001 - No. 6, Nov, 2001 ($3.95, limited series)

1-6-Abnett & Lanning-s; art by various. 5-Dillon-a. 6-Timber Wolf app.			4.00

LIBERTY MEADOWS
Insight Studios Group/Image Comics #27 on: 1999 - Present ($2.95, B&W)

1-Frank Cho-s/a; reprints newspaper strips	3	9	25
2,3	2	6	14
4-10	1	3	7
11-25,27-36: 20-Adam Hughes-c. 22-Evil Brandy vs. Brandy. 27-1st Image issue, printed sideways			3.00
...: Eden Book 1 SC (Image, 2002, $14.95) r/#1-9; sketch gallery			15.00
...: Eden Book 1 SC 2nd printing (Image, 2004, $19.95) r/#1-9; sketch gallery			20.00
...: Eden Book 1 HC (Image, 2003, $24.95, with dustjacket) r/#1-9; sketch gallery			25.00
...: Creature Comforts Book 2 HC (Image, 2004, $24.95, with d.j.) r/#10-18; sketch gallery			25.00
... Sourcebook (5/04, $4.95) character info and unpublished strips			3.00
... Wedding Album (#26) (2002, $2.95)			3.00

LIDSVILLE (TV)
Gold Key: Oct, 1972 - No. 5, Oct, 1973

1-Photo-c	6	18	70
2-5	4	12	40

LIMITED COLLECTORS' EDITION (See Famous First Edition, Marvel Treasury #28, Rudolph The Red-Nosed Reindeer, & Superman Vs. The Amazing Spider-Man; becomes All-New Collectors' Edition for C-53 through C-56 & C-58 through C-60)
National Periodical Publications/DC Comics:
(#21-34,51-59: 84 pgs.; #35-41: 68 pgs.; #42-50: 60 pgs.)
C-21, Summer, 1973 - No. C-52, 1978; C-57, 1978; C-59, 1978 ($1.00) (10x13-1/2")

(Rudolph...C-20 (implied), 12/72)-See Rudolph The Red-Nosed Reindeer			
C-21: Shazam (TV); r/Captain Marvel Jr. #11 by Raboy; C.C. Beck-c, biog. & photo	4	12	38
C-22: Tarzan; complete origin reprinted from #207-210; all Kubert-c/a; Joe Kubert biography & photo inside	3	9	30
C-23: House of Mystery; Wrightson, N. Adams/Orlando, G. Kane/Wood, Toth, Aragones, Sparling reprints	4	12	45
C-24: Rudolph The Red-Nosed Reindeer	8	24	95
C-25: Batman; Neal Adams-c/a(r); G.A. Joker-r; Batman/Enemy Ace-r; Novick-a(r); has photos from TV show	4	12	50
C-26: See Famous First Edition C-26 (same contents)			
C-27,C-29,C-31: C-27: Shazam (TV); G.A. Capt. Marvel & Mary Marvel-r;			

	GD	FN	NM-

Beck-r. C-29: Tarzan; reprints "Return of Tarzan" from #219-223 by Kubert; Kubert-c. C-31: Superman; origin-r; Giordano-a; photos of George Reeves from 1950s TV show on inside b/c; Burnley, Boring-r

	3	9	28
C-32: Ghosts (new-a)	4	12	42
C-33: Rudolph The Red-Nosed Reindeer(new-a)	7	21	85

C-34: Christmas with the Super-Heroes; unpublished Angel & Ape story by Oksner & Wood; Batman & Teen Titans-r 3 9 28

C-35: Shazam (TV); photo cover features TV's Captain Marvel, Jackson Bostwick; Beck-r; TV photos inside b/c 3 9 25

C-36: The Bible; all new adaptation beginning with Genesis by Kubert, Redondo & Mayer; Kubert-c 3 9 25

C-37: Batman; r-1946 Sundays; inside b/c photos of Batman TV show villains (all villain issue; r/G.A. Joker, Catwoman, Penguin, Two-Face, & Scarecrow stories plus 1946 Sundays-r) 3 9 32

C-38: Superman; 1 pg. N. Adams; part photo-c; photos from TV show on inside back-c 3 9 25

C-39: Secret Origins of Super-Villains; N. Adams-i(r); collection reprints 1950's Joker origin, Luthor origin from Adv. Comics #271, Captain Cold origin from Showcase #8 among others; G.A. Batman-r; Beck-r 3 9 25

C-40: Dick Tracy by Gould featuring Flattop; newspaper-r from 12/21/43 - 5/17/44; biog. of Chester Gould 3 9 25

| C-41: Super Friends (TV); JLA-r(1965); Toth-c/a | 3 | 9 | 28 |
| C-42: Rudolph | 5 | 15 | 55 |

C-43-C-47: C-43: Christmas with the Super-Heroes; Wrightson, S&K, Neal Adams-a. C-44: Batman; N. Adams-p(r) & G.A.-r; painted-c. C-45: More Secret Origins of Super-Villains; Flash-r/#105; G.A. Wonder Woman & Batman/Catwoman-r. C-46: Justice League of America(1963-r); 3 pgs. Toth-a C-47: Superman Salutes the Bicentennial (Tomahawk interior); 2 pgs. new-a 3 9 24

C-48,C-49: C-48: Superman Vs. The Flash (Superman/Flash race); swipes-c to Superman #199; r/Superman #199 & Flash #175; 6 pgs. Neal Adams-a. C-49: Superboy & the Legion of Super-Heroes 3 9 28

C-50: Rudolph The Red-Nosed Reindeer; contains poster (1/2 price if poster is missing) 5 15 55

C-51: Batman; Neal Adams-c/a 3 9 30

C-52,C-57: C-52: The Best of DC; Neal Adams-c/a; Toth, Kubert-a. C-57: Welcome Back, Kotter-r(TV)(5/78) includes unpublished #11 3 9 25

C-59: Batman's Strangest Cases; N. Adams-r; Wrightson-r/Swamp Thing #7; N. Adams/Wrightson-c 3 9 25

NOTE: All-r with exception of some special features and covers. Aparo a-52r; c-37. Grell c-49. Infantino a-25, 39, 44, 45, 52. Bob Kane r-25. Robinson r-25, 44. Sprang r-44. Issues #21-31, 35-39, 45, 48 have back cover cut-outs.

LOGAN'S RUN
Marvel Comics Group: Jan, 1977 - No. 7, July, 1977

1: 1-5-Based on novel & movie	1	4	10
2-5,7: 6,7-New stories adapted from novel			6.00

	GD	FN	NM-
6-1st Thanos (also see Iron Man #55) solo story (back-up) by Zeck (6/77)			
	3	9	25
6-(35¢-c variant, limited distribution)	4	12	38
7-(35¢-c variant, limited distribution)	1	3	9

LOIS LANE (See Superman's Girlfriend...)

LONE WOLF AND CUB
First Comics: May, 1987 - No. 45, Apr, 1991 ($1.95-$3.25, B&W, deluxe size)

	GD	FN	NM-
1-Frank Miller-c & intro.; reprints manga series by Koike & Kojima			
	1	3	10
1-2nd print, 3rd print, 2-2nd print			3.25
2-12: 6-72 pgs. origin issue			5.50
13-38,40: 40-Ploog-c			4.00
39-($5.95, 120 pgs.)-Ploog-c			6.50
41-44: 41-($3.95, 84 pgs.)-Ploog-c. 42-Ploog-c			6.00
45-Last issue; low print	1	3	8
Deluxe Edition ($19.95, B&W)			20.00

LONE WOLF AND CUB (Trade paperbacks)
Dark Horse Comics: Aug, 2000 - No. 28 ($9.95, B&W, 4" x 6", approx. 300 pgs.)

1-Collects First Comics reprint series; Frank Miller-c	18.00
1-(2nd printing)	12.00
1-(3rd-5th printings)	10.00
2,3-(1st printings)	12.00
2,3-(2nd printings)	10.00
4-28	10.00

LOSERS
DC Comics (Vertigo): Aug, 2003 - Present ($2.95)

1-Andy Diggle-s/Jock-a	4.00
2-18: 15-Bagged with Sky Captain CD	3.00
...: Ante Up TPB (2004, $9.95) r/#1-6	10.00
...: Double Down TPB (2004, $12.95) r/#7-12	13.00

MADMAN (See Creatures of the Id #1)
Tundra Publishing: Mar, 1992 - No. 3, 1992 ($3.95, duotone, high quality, lim. series, 52 pgs.)

	GD	FN	NM-
1-Mike Allred-c/a in all	2	6	12
1-2nd printing			4.00
2,3			6.00

MADMAN ADVENTURES
Tundra Publishing: 1992 - No. 3, 1993 ($2.95, limited series)

	GD	FN	NM-
1-Mike Allred-c/a in all	1	3	9
2,3			5.00
TPB (Oni Press, 2002, $14.95) r/#1-3 & first app. of Frank Einstein from Creatures of the Id in color; gallery pages			15.00

MADMAN COMICS (Also see The Atomics)
Dark Horse Comics (Legend No. 2 on): Apr, 1994 - No. 20, Dec, 2000

	GD	FN	NM-

($2.95/$2.99)

1-Allred-c/a; F. Miller back-c.	1	3	8
2-3: 3-Alex Toth back-c.			5.00
4-11: 4-Dave Stevens back-c. 6,7-Miller/Darrow's Big Guy app. 6-Bruce Timm back-c. 7-Darrow back-c. 8-Origin?; Bagge back-c. 10-Allred/Ross-c; Ross back-c. 11-Frazetta back-c			4.00
12-16: 12-(4/99)			3.00
17-20: 17-The G-Men From Hell #1 on cover; Brereton back-c. 18-(#2). 19,20-($2.99-c). 20-Clowes back-c			3.00
... Boogaloo TPB (6/99, $8.95) r/Nexus Meets Madman & Madman/The Jam			9.00
Ltd. Ed. Slipcover (1997, $99.95, signed and numbered) w/Vol.1 & Vol. 2. Vol.1- reprints #1-5; Vol. 2- reprints #6-10			100.00
The Complete Madman Comics: Vol. 2 (11/96, $17.95, TPB) r/#6-10 plus new material			18.00
Madman King-Size Super Groovy Special (Oni Press, 7/03, $6.95) new short stories by Allred, Derington, Krall and Weissman			7.00
Madman Picture Exhibition No. 1-4 (4-7/02, $3.95) pin-ups by various			4.00
Madman Picture Exhibition Limited Edition (10/02, $29.95) Hardcover collects MPE #1-4			30.00
Yearbook '95 (1996, $17.95, TPB)-r/#1-5, intro by Teller			18.00

MAGILLA GORILLA (TV) (See Kite Fun Book)
Gold Key: May, 1964 - No. 10, Dec, 1968 (Hanna-Barbera)

1-1st comic app.	11	33	160
2-4: 3-Vs. Yogi Bear for President. 4-1st Punkin Puss & Mushmouse, Ricochet Rabbit & Droop-a-Long	8	24	95
5-10: 10-Reprints	7	21	80

MAGILLA GORILLA (TV)(See Spotlight #4)
Charlton Comics: Nov, 1970 - No. 5, July, 1971 (Hanna-Barbera)

1	6	18	70
2-5	4	12	40

MAGNUS, ROBOT FIGHTER (...4000 A.D.)(See Doctor Solar)
Gold Key: Feb, 1963 - No. 46, Jan, 1977 (All painted covers except #5,31)

1-Origin & 1st app. Magnus; Aliens (1st app.) series begins	25	75	365
2,3	11	33	160
4-10: 10-Simonson fan club illo (5/65, 1st-a?)	8	24	95
11-20	6	18	65
21,24-28: 28-Aliens ends	4	12	42
22,23: 22-Origin-r/#1; last 12¢ issue	4	12	45
29-46-Mostly reprints	2	6	20

MAN-BAT (See Batman Family, Brave & the Bold, & Detective #400)
National Periodical Publ./DC Comics: Dec-Jan, 1975-76 - No. 2, Feb-Mar, 1976; Dec, 1984

1-Ditko-a(p); Aparo-c; Batman app.; 1st app. She-Bat?	2	6	20

	GD	FN	NM-
2-Aparo-c	2	6	12
1 (12/84)-N. Adams-r(3)/Det.(Vs. Batman on-c)			4.00

MAN FROM U.N.C.L.E., THE (TV) (Also see The Girl From Uncle)
Gold Key: Feb, 1965 - No. 22, Apr, 1969 (All photo-c)

1	16	48	230
2-Photo back c-2-8	9	27	120
3-10: 7-Jet Dream begins (1st app., also see Jet Dream) (all new stories)			
	7	21	90
11-22: 19-Last 12¢ issue. 21,22-Reprint #10 & 7	7	21	80

MAN OF STEEL, THE (Also see Superman: The Man of Steel)
DC Comics: 1986 (June release) - No. 6, 1986 (75¢, limited series)

1-6: 1-Silver logo; Byrne-c/a/scripts in all; origin, 1-Alternate-c for newsstand sales,1-Distr. to toy stores by So Much Fun, 2-6: 2-Intro. Lois Lane, Jimmy Olsen. 3-Intro/origin Magpie; Batman-c/story. 4-Intro. new Lex Luthor			4.00
1-6-Silver Editions (1993, $1.95)-r/1-6			3.00
...The Complete Saga nn-Contains #1-6, given away in contest			26.00
Limited Edition, softcover	5	15	60

NOTE: *Issues 1-6 were released between Action #583 (9/86) & Action #584 (1/87) plus Superman #423 (9/86) & Advs. of Superman #424 (1/87).*

MAN-THING (See Fear, Giant-Size..., Marvel Comics Presents, Marvel Fanfare, Monsters Unleashed, Power Record Comics & Savage Tales)
Marvel Comics Group: Jan, 1974 - No. 22, Oct, 1975; V2#1, Nov, 1979 - V2#11, July, 1981

1-Howard the Duck(2nd app.) cont'd/Fear #19	5	15	60
2	3	9	25
3-1st app. original Foolkiller	2	6	20
4-Origin Foolkiller; last app. 1st Foolkiller	2	6	18
5-11-Ploog-a. 11-Foolkiller cameo (flashback)	2	6	18
12-22: 19-1st app. Scavenger. 20-Spidey cameo. 21-Origin Scavenger, Man-Thing. 22-Howard the Duck cameo	1	4	10
V2#1(1979)	1	3	8
V2#2-11: 4-Dr. Strange-c/app. 11-Mayerik-a			4.00

MANY LOVES OF DOBIE GILLIS (TV)
National Periodical Publications: May-June, 1960 - No. 26, Oct, 1964

1-Most covers by Bob Oskner	25	75	375
2-5	14	42	200
6-10: 10-Last 10¢-c	10	30	125
11-26: 20-Drucker-a. 24-(3-4/64). 25-(9/64)	9	27	110

M.A.R.S. PATROL TOTAL WAR (Formerly Total War #1,2)
Gold Key: No. 3, Sept, 1966 - No. 10, Aug, 1969 (All-Painted-c except #7)

3-Wood-a; aliens invade USA	7	21	85
4-10	4	12	48
Wally Wood's M.A.R.S. Patrol Total War TPB (Dark Horse, 9/04, $12.95) r/#3 & Total War #1&2; foreward by Batton Lash; afterword by Dan Adkins			13.00

MARTIAN MANHUNTER (See Detective Comics & Showcase '95 #9)
DC Comics: May, 1988 - No. 4, Aug,. 1988 ($1.25, limited series)

	GD	FN	NM-
1-4: 1,4-Batman app. 2-Batman cameo			2.50
Special 1-(1996, $3.50)			3.50

MARTIAN MANHUNTER (See JLA)
DC Comics: No. 0, Oct, 1998 - No. 36, Nov, 2001 ($1.99)

0-(10/98) Origin retold; Ostrander-s/Mandrake-c/a			3.00
1-36: 1-(12/98). 6-9-JLA app. 18,19-JSA app. 24-Mahnke-a			2.50
#1,000,000 (11/98) 853rd Century x-over			2.50
Annual 1,2 (1998,1999; $2.95) 1-Ghosts; Wrightson-c. 2-JLApe			3.00

MARVEL AND DC PRESENT FEATURING THE UNCANNY X-MEN AND THE NEW TEEN TITANS
Marvel Comics/DC Comics: 1982 ($2.00, 68 pgs., one-shot, Baxter paper)

	GD	FN	NM-
1-3rd app. Deathstroke the Terminator; Darkseid app.; Simonson/Austin-c/a	2	6	20

MARVEL CHILLERS (Also see Giant-Size Chillers)
Marvel Comics Group: Oct, 1975 - No. 7, Oct, 1976 (All 25¢ issues)

	GD	FN	NM-
1-Intro. Modred the Mystic, ends #2; Kane-c(p)	2	6	15
2,4,5,7: 4-Kraven app. 5,6-Red Wolf app. 7-Kirby-c; Tuska-p	1	3	9
3-Tigra, the Were-Woman begins (origin), ends #7 (see Giant-Size Creatures #1). Chaykin/Wrightson-c.	2	6	22
4-6-(30¢-c variants, limited distribution)(4-8/76)	2	6	18
6-Byrne-a(p); Buckler-c(p)	2	6	12

MARVEL COLLECTORS' ITEM CLASSICS (Marvel's Greatest #23 on)
Marvel Comics Group(ATF): Feb, 1965 - No. 22, Aug, 1969 (25¢, 68 pgs.)

	GD	FN	NM-
1-Fantastic Four, Spider-Man, Thor, Hulk, Iron Man-r begin	10	30	140
2 (4/66)	6	18	70
3,4	4	12	50
5-10	4	12	40
11-22: 22-r/The Man in the Ant Hill/TTA #27	3	9	30

NOTE: All reprints; **Ditko, Kirby** art in all.

MARVEL COMICS PRESENTS
Marvel Comics (Midnight Sons imprint #143 on): Early Sept, 1988 - No. 175, Feb, 1995 ($1.25/$1.50/$1.75, bi-weekly)

1-Wolverine by Buscema in #1-10			6.00
2-5			4.00
6-10: 6-Sub-Mariner app. 10-Colossus begins			3.00
11-47,51-71: 17-Cyclops begins. 19-1st app. Damage Control. 24-Havok begins. 25-Origin/1st app. Nth Man. 26-Hulk begins by Rogers. 29-Quasar app. 31-Excalibur begins by Austin (i). 32-McFarlane-a(p). 37-Devil-Slayer app. 33-Capt. America; Jim Lee-a. 38-Wolverine begins by Buscema; Hulk app. 39-Spider-Man app. 46-Liefeld Wolverine-c. 51-53-Wolverine by Rob Liefeld. 54-61-Wolverine/Hulk story: 54-Werewolf by Night begins; The Shroud by Ditko. 58-Iron Man by Ditko. 59-Punisher. 62-Deathlok & Wolverine stories. 63-Wolverine. 64-71-Wolverine/Ghost Rider 8-part story. 70-Liefeld Ghost Rider/Wolverine-c			2.50

	GD	FN	NM-

48-50-Wolverine & Spider-Man team-up by Erik Larsen-c/a. 48-Wasp app. 49,50-Savage Dragon prototype app. by Larsen. 50-Silver Surfer. 50-53-Comet Man; Mumy scripts   4.00

72-Begin 13-part Weapon-X story (Wolverine origin) by B. Windsor-Smith (prologue)   5.00

73-Weapon-X part 1; Black Knight, Sub-Mariner.   4.00

74-84: 74-Weapon-X part 2; Black Knight, Sub-Mariner. 76-Death's Head story. 77-Mr. Fantastic story. 78-Iron Man by Steacy. 80,81-Capt. America by Ditko/Austin. 81-Daredevil by Rogers/Williamson. 82-Power Man. 83-Human Torch by Ditko(a&scripts); $1.00-c direct, $1.25 newsstand. 84-Last Weapon-X (24 pg. conclusion)   3.00

85-Begin 8-part Wolverine story by Sam Kieth (c/a); 1st Kieth-a on Wolverine; begin 8-part Beast story by Jae Lee(p) with Liefeld part pencils #85,86; 1st Jae Lee-a (assisted w/Liefeld, 1991)   4.00

86-90: 86-89-Wolverine, Beast stories continue. 90-Begin 8-part Ghost Rider & Cable story, ends #97; begin flip book format with two-c   3.00

91-175: 93-Begin 6-part Wolverine story, ends #98. 98-Begin 2-part Ghost Rider story. 99-Spider-Man story. 101-Begin 6-part Ghost Rider/Dr. Strange story & begin 8-part Wolverine/Nightcrawler story by Colan/Williamson; Punisher story. 107-Begin 6-part Ghost Rider/Werewolf by Night story. 112-Demogoblin story by Colan/Williamson; Pip the Troll story w/Starlin scripts & Gamora cameo. 113-Begin 6-part Giant-Man & begin 6-part Ghost Rider/Iron Fist stories. 100-Full-length Ghost Rider/Wolverine story by Sam Kieth w/Tim Vigil assists; anniversary issue, non flip-book. 108-Begin 4 part Thanos story; Starlin scripts. 109-Begin 8 part Wolverine/Typhoid Mary story. 111-Iron Fist. 117-Preview of Ravage 2099 (1st app.); begin 6 part Wolverine/Venom story w/Kieth-a. 118-Preview of Doom 2099 (1st app.). 119-Begin Ghost Rider/Cloak & Dagger by Colan. 120,136,138-Spider-Man. 123-Begin 8-part Ghost Rider/Typhoid Mary story; begin 4-part She Hulk story; begin 8-part Wolverine/Lynx story. 125-Begin 6-part Iron Fist story. 129-Jae Lee back-c. 130-Begin 6-part Ghost Rider/ Cage story. 131-Begin 6-part Ghost Rider/Cage story. 132-Begin 5-part Wolverine story. 133-136-Iron Fist vs. Sabretooth. 136-Daredevil. 137-Begin 6-part Wolverine story & 6-part Ghost Rider story. 147-Begin 2-part Vengeance-c/story w/new Ghost Rider. 149-Vengeance-c/story w/new Ghost Rider. 150-Silver ink-c; begin 2-part Bloody Mary story w/Typhoid Mary,Wolverine, Daredevil, new Ghost Rider; intro Steel Raven. 152-Begin 4-part Wolverine, 4-part War Machine, 4-part Vengeance, 3-part Moon Knight stories; same date as War Machine #1. 143-146: Siege of Darkness parts 3,6,11,14; all have spot-varnished-c. 143-Ghost Rider/Scarlet Witch; intro new Werewolf. 144-Begin 2-part Morbius story. 145-Begin 2-part Nightstalkers story. 153-155-Bound-in Spider-Man trading card sheet   2.50

...Colossus: God's Country (1994, $6.95) r/#10-17   1   3   7

MARVEL COMICS SUPER SPECIAL, A (Marvel Super Special #5 on)
Marvel Comics: Sept, 1977 - No. 41(?), Nov, 1986 (nn 7) ($1.50, magazine)

1-Kiss, 40 pgs. comics plus photos & features; Simonson-a(p); also see Howard the Duck #12; ink contains real KISS blood; Dr. Doom, Spider-Man, Avengers, Fantastic Four, Mephisto app.   12   36   175

	GD	FN	NM-
2-Conan (1978)	2	6	20
3-Close Encounters of the Third Kind (1978); Simonson-a			
	2	6	14
4-The Beatles Story (1978)-Perez/Janson-a; has photos & articles			
	4	12	50
5-Kiss (1978)-Includes poster	12	36	175
6-Jaws II (1978)	2	6	14
7-Sgt. Pepper; Beatles movie adaptation; withdrawn from U.S. distribution (French ed. exists)			
8-Battlestar Galactica; tabloid size ($1.50, 1978); adapts TV show			
	2	6	18
8-Modern-r of tabloid size	2	6	18
8-Battlestar Galactica; publ. in regular magazine format; low distribution ($1.50, 8-1/2x11")			
	2	6	20
9-Conan	2	6	16
10-Star-Lord	2	6	12
11-13-Weirdworld begins #11; 25 copy special press run of each with gold seal and signed by artists (Proof quality), Spring-June, 1979			
	9	27	110
11-15: 11-13-Weirdworld (regular issues): 11-Fold-out centerfold. 14-Miller-c(p); adapts movie "Meteor." 15-Star Trek with photos & pin-ups ($1.50-c)			
	1	3	9
15-With $2.00 price; the price was changed at tail end of a 200,000 press run			
	2	6	12
16-Empire Strikes Back adaption; Williamson-a	2	6	12
17-20 (Movie adaptations):17-Xanadu. 18-Raiders of the Lost Ark. 19-For Your Eyes Only (James Bond). 20-Dragonslayer			6.00
21-26,28-30 (Movie adaptations): 21-Conan. 22-Blade Runner; Williamson-a; Steranko-c. 23-Annie. 24-The Dark Crystal. 25-Rock and Rule-w/photos; artwork is from movie. 26-Octopussy (James Bond). 28-Krull; photo-c. 29-Tarzan of the Apes (Greystoke movie). 30-Indiana Jones and the Temple of Doom	1	3	7
27,31-41: 27-Return of the Jedi. 31-The Last Star Fighter. 32-The Muppets Take Manhattan. 33-Buckaroo Banzai. 34-Sheena. 35-Conan The Destroyer. 36-Dune. 37-2010. 38-Red Sonja. 39-Santa Claus:The Movie. 40-Labyrinth. 41-Howard The Duck	1	3	9

MARVEL DOUBLE FEATURE
Marvel Comics Group: Dec, 1973 - No. 21, Mar, 1977

1-Capt. America, Iron Man-r/T.O.S. begin	2	6	16
2-10: 3-Last 20¢ issue	1	4	10
11-17,20,21:17-Story-r/Iron Man & Sub-Mariner #1; last 25¢ issue			6.00
15-17-(30¢-c variants, limited distribution)(4,6,8/76)	1	4	10
18,19-Colan/Craig-r from Iron Man #1 in both	1	3	8

MARVEL DOUBLE SHOT
Marvel Comics: Jan, 2003 - No. 4, April, 2003 ($2.99, limited series)

1-4: 1-Hulk by Haynes; Thor w/Asamiya-a; Jusko-c. 2-Dr. Doom by Rivera; Simpsons-style Avengers by Bill Morrison			3.00

MARVEL FANFARE (1st Series)

GD   FN   NM-

Marvel Comics Group: Mar, 1982 - No. 60, Jan, 1992 ($1.25/$2.25, slick paper, direct sales)

1-Spider-Man/Angel team-up; 1st Paul Smith-a (1st full story; see King Conan #7); Daredevil app. (many copies were printed missing the centerfold)   1   3   8

2-Spider-Man, Ka-Zar, The Angel. F.F. origin retold   6.00

3,4-X-Men & Ka-Zar. 4-Deathlok, Spidey app.   5.00

5-14: 5-Dr. Strange, Capt. America. 6-Spider-Man, Scarlet Witch. 7-Incredible Hulk; D.D. back-up(also 15). 8-Dr. Strange; Wolf Boy begins. 9-Man-Thing. 10-13-Black Widow. 14-The Vision   3.00

15,24,33: 15-The Thing by Barry Smith, c/a. 24-Weirdworld; Wolverine back-up. 33-X-Men, Wolverine app.; Punisher pin-up   4.00

16-23,25-32,34-44,46-50: 16,17-Skywolf. 16-Sub-Mariner back-up. 17-Hulk back-up. 18-Capt. America by Miller. 19-Cloak and Dagger. 20-Thing/Dr. Strange. 21-Thing/Dr. Strange /Hulk. 22,23-Iron Man vs. Dr. Octopus. 25,26-Weirdworld. 27-Daredevil/Spider-Man. 28-Alpha Flight. 29-Hulk. 30-Moon Knight. 31,32-Captain America. 34-37-Warriors Three. 38-Moon Knight/Dazzler. 39-Moon Knight/Hawkeye. 40-Angel/Rogue & Storm. 41-Dr. Strange. 42-Spider-Man. 43-Sub-Mariner/Human Torch. 44-Iron Man vs. Dr. Doom by Ken Steacy. 46-Fantastic Four. 47-Hulk. 48-She-Hulk/Vision. 49-Dr. Strange/Nick Fury. 50-X-Factor   2.50

45-All pin-up issue by Steacy, Art Adams & others   4.00

51-($2.95, 52 pgs.)-Silver Surfer; Fantastic Four & Capt. Marvel app.; 51,52-Colan/Williamson back-up (Dr. Strange)   3.00

52,53,56-60: 52,53-Black Knight; 53-Iron Man back up. 56-59-Shanna the She-Devil. 58-Vision & Scarlet Witch back-up. 60-Black Panther/Rogue/Daredevil stories   2.50

54,55-Wolverine back-ups. 54-Black Knight. 55-Power Pack   4.00

MARVEL FEATURE (See Marvel Two-In-One)

Marvel Comics Group: Dec, 1971 - No. 12, Nov, 1973 (1,2: 25¢, 52 pg. giants) (#1-3: quarterly)

1-Origin/1st app. The Defenders (Sub-Mariner, Hulk & Dr. Strange); see Sub-Mariner #34,35 for prequel; Dr. Strange solo story (predates Dr. Strange #1) plus 1950s Sub-Mariner-r; Neal Adams-c
                                                              15   45   225

2-2nd app. Defenders; 1950s Sub-Mariner-r. Rutland, Vermont Halloween x-over   8   24   100

3-Defenders ends   6   18   70

4-Re-intro Antman (1st app. since 1960s), begin series; brief origin; Spider-Man app.   3   9   30

5-7,9,10: 6-Wasp app. & begins team-ups. 9-Iron Man app. 10-Last Antman
                                                              2   6   14

8-Origin Antman & Wasp-r/TTA #44; Kirby-a   2   6   18

11-Thing vs. Hulk; 1st Thing solo book (9/73); origin Fantastic Four retold
                                                              6   18   65

12-Thing/Iron Man; early Thanos app.; occurs after Capt. Marvel #33; Starlin-a(p)   3   9   32

MARVEL FEATURE (Also see Red Sonja)

	GD	FN	NM-

Marvel Comics: Nov, 1975 - No. 7, Nov, 1976 (Story cont'd in Conan #68)

	GD	FN	NM-
1,7: 1-Red Sonja begins (pre-dates Red Sonja #1); adapts Howard short story; Adams-r/Savage Sword of Conan #1. 7-Battles Conan	1	4	10
2-6: Thorne-c/a in #2-7. 4,5-(Regular 25¢ edition)(5,7/76)			6.00
4,5-(30¢-c variants, limited distribution)	2	6	18

MARVEL GRAPHIC NOVEL
Marvel Comics Group (Epic Comics): 1982 - No. 38, 1990? ($5.95/$6.95)

	GD	FN	NM-
1-Death of Captain Marvel (2nd Marvel graphic novel); Capt. Marvel battles Thanos by Jim Starlin (c/a/scripts)	2	6	20
1 (2nd & 3rd printings)	1	3	8
2-Elric: The Dreaming City	2	6	12
3-Dreadstar; Starlin-c/a, 52 pgs.	2	6	14
4-Origin/1st app. The New Mutants (1982)	2	6	14
4,5-2nd printings	1	3	7
5-X-Men; book-length story (1982)	2	6	18
6-15,20,23,25,30,31: 6-The Star Slammers. 7-Killraven. 8-Super Boxers; Byrne scripts. 9-The Futurians. 10-Heartburst. 11-Void Indigo. 12-Dazzler. 13-Starstruck. 14-The Swords Of The Swashbucklers. 15-The Raven Banner (a Tale of Asgard). 20-Greenberg the Vampire. 23-Dr. Strange. 25-Alien Legion. 30-A Sailor's Story. 31-Wolfpack	1	3	9
16,17,21,29: 16-The Aladdin Effect (Storm, Tigra, Wasp, She-Hulk). 17-Revenge Of The Living Monolith (Spider-Man, Avengers, FF app.). 21-Marada the She-Wolf. 29-The Big Chance (Thing vs. Hulk)	1	3	9
18,19,26-28: 18-She Hulk. 19-Witch Queen of Acheron (Conan). 26-Dracula. 27-Avengers (Emperor Doom). 28-Conan the Reaver	2	6	13
22-Amaz. Spider-Man in Hooky by Wrightson	2	6	15
24-Love and War (Daredevil); Miller scripts	2	6	14
32-Death of Groo	2	6	15
32-2nd printing ($5.95)	1	3	8
33,34,36,37: 33-Thor. 34-Predator & Prey (Cloak & Dagger). 36-Willow (movie adapt.). 37-Hercules	1	4	10
35-Hitler's Astrologer (The Shadow, $12.95, HC)	2	6	16
35-Soft-c reprint (1990, $10.95)	2	6	12
38-Silver Surfer (Judgement Day)($14.95, HC)	2	6	18
38-Soft-c reprint (1990, $10.95)	2	6	14
nn-Abslom Daak: Dalak Killer (1990, $8.95) Dr. Who	1	4	10
nn-Arena by Bruce Jones (1989, $5.95) Dinosaurs	1	3	8
nn- A-Team Storybook Comics Illustrated (1983) r/ A-Team mini-series #1-3	1	4	10
nn-Ax (1988, $5.95) Ernie Colan-s/a	1	4	10
nn-Black Widow Coldest War (4/90, $9.95)	2	6	12
nn-Chronicles of Genghis Grimtoad (1990, $8.95)-Alan Grant-s	1	4	10
nn-Conan the Barbarian in the Horn of Azoth (1990, $8.95)	2	6	12

	GD	FN	NM-
nn-Conan of Isles ($8.95)	2	6	12
nn-Conan Ravagers of Time (1992, $9.95) Kull & Red Sonja app.			
	2	6	12
nn-Conan -The Skull of Set	2	6	12
nn-Doctor Strange and Doctor Doom Triumph and Torment (1989, $17.95, HC)			
	2	6	22
nn-Dreamwalker (1989, $6.95)-Morrow-a	1	3	9
nn-Excalibur Weird War III (1990, $9.95)	2	6	12
nn-G.I. Joe - The Trojan Gambit (1983, 68 pgs.)	2	6	12
nn-Harvey Kurtzman Strange Adventures (Epic, $19.95, HC) Aragonés, Crumb	3	9	25
nn-Hearts and Minds (1990, $8.95) Heath-a	1	4	10
nn-Inhumans (1988, $7.95)-Williamson-i	1	3	9
nn-Jhereg (Epic, 1990, $8.95)	1	4	10
nn-Kazar-Guns of the Savage Land (7/90, $8.95)	1	4	10
nn-Kull-The Vale of Shadow ('89, $6.95)	1	4	10
nn-Last of the Dragons (1988, $6.95) Austin-a(i)	1	3	7
nn-Nightraven: House of Cards (1991, $14.95)	2	6	15
nn-Nightraven: The Collected Stories (1990, $9.95) Bolton-r/British Hulk mag.; David Lloyd-c/a	2	6	12
nn-Original Adventures of Cholly and Flytrap (Epic, 1991, $9.95) Suydam-s/c/a	2	6	15
nn-Rick Mason Agent (1989, $9.95)	1	4	10
nn-Roger Rabbit In The Resurrection Of Doom (1989, $8.95)	1	4	10
nn-A Sailor's Story Book II: Winds, Dreams and Dragons ('86, $6.95, SC) Glansman-s/c/a	1	4	10
nn-Squadron Supreme: Death of a Universe (1989, $9.95) Gruenwald-s; Ryan & Williamson-a	1	4	10
nn-Who Framed Roger Rabbit (1989, $6.95)	1	4	10

MARVEL KNIGHTS (Volume 2)
Marvel Comics: May, 2002 - No. 6, Oct, 2002 ($2.99)

1-6-Daredevil, Punisher, Black Widow app.; Ponticelli-a			3.00

MARVEL KNIGHTS 4 (Fantastic Four) (Issues #1&2 are titled **Knights 4**)
Marvel Comics: Apr, 2004 - Present ($2.99)

1-12: 1-7-McNiven-c/a; Aguirre-Sacasa-a. 8,9-Namor app.			3.00

MARVEL KNIGHTS SPIDER-MAN
Marvel Comics: Jun, 2004 - Present ($2.99)

1-Wraparound-c by Dodson; Millar-s/Dodson-a; Green Goblin app.			3.00
2-7: 2-Avengers app. 2,3-Vulture & Electro app. 5,8-Cho-c/a. 6-8-Venom app.			3.00
...Vol. 1: Down Among the Dead Men (2004, $9.99, TPB) r/#1-4			10.00

MARVEL NO-PRIZE BOOK, THE (The Official... on-c)
Marvel Comics Group: Jan, 1983 (one-shot, direct sales only)

1-Golden-c; Kirby-a			4.00

MARVEL PREMIERE

	GD	FN	NM-

Marvel Comics Group: April, 1972 - No. 61, Aug, 1981 (A tryout book for new characters)

	GD	FN	NM-
1-Origin Warlock (pre-#1) by Gil Kane/Adkins; origin Counter-Earth; Hulk & Thor cameo (#1-14 are 20¢-c)	7	21	80
2-Warlock ends; Kirby Yellow Claw-r	3	10	35
3-Dr. Strange series begins (pre #1, 7/72), B. Smith-c/a(p)	6	18	70
4-Smith/Brunner-a	3	9	28
5-9: 8-Starlin-c/a(p)	2	6	18
10-Death of the Ancient One	3	9	24
11-14: 11-Dr. Strange origin-r by Ditko. 14-Last Dr. Strange (3/74), gets own title 3 months later	2	6	12
15-Origin/1st app. Iron Fist (5/74), ends #25	8	24	100
16,25: 16-2nd app. Iron Fist; origin cont'd from #15; Hama's 1st Marvel-a. 25-1st Byrne Iron Fist (moves to own title next)	3	10	35
17-24: Iron Fist in all	2	6	22
26-Hercules.	1	3	8
27-Satana	1	4	10
28-Legion of Monsters (Ghost Rider, Man-Thing, Morbius, Werewolf)	2	6	20
29-46,49: 29,30-The Liberty Legion. 29-1st modern app. Patriot. 31-1st app. Woodgod; last 25¢ issue. 32-1st app. Monark Starstalker. 33,34-1st color app. Solomon Kane (Robert E. Howard adaptation "Red Shadows".) 35-Origin/1st app. 3-D Man. 36,37-3-D Man. 38-1st Weirdworld. 39,40-Torpedo. 41-1st Seeker 3000! 42-Tigra. 43-Paladin. 44-Jack of Hearts (1st solo book, 10/78). 45,46-Man-Wolf. 49-The Falcon (1st solo book, 8/79)			4.00
29-31-(30¢-c variants, limited distribution)(4,6,8/76)	2	6	15
36-38-(35¢-c variants, limited distribution)(6,8,10/77)	2	6	15
47,48-Byrne-a: 47-Origin/1st app. new Ant-Man. 48-Ant-Man	1	3	9
50-1st app. Alice Cooper; co-plotted by Alice	2	6	15
51-56,58-61: 51-53-Black Panther. 54-1st Caleb Hammer. 55-Wonder Man. 56-1st color app. Dominic Fortune. 58-60-Dr. Who. 61-Star Lord			4.00
57-Dr. Who (2nd U.S. app.-see Movie Classics)			6.00

MARVEL PRESENTS

Marvel Comics: October, 1975 - No. 12, Aug, 1977 (#1-6 are 25¢ issues)

	GD	FN	NM-
1-Origin & 1st app. Bloodstone	2	6	12
2-Origin Bloodstone continued; Kirby-c	1	3	7
3-Guardians of the Galaxy (1st solo book, 2/76) begins, ends #12	2	6	16
4-7,9-12: 9,10-Origin Starhawk	1	3	8
4-6-(30¢-c variants, limited distribution)(4-8/76)	2	6	12
8-r/story from Silver Surfer #2 plus 4 pgs. new-a	1	3	8
11,12-(35¢-c variants, limited distribution)(6,8/77)	2	6	12

MARVEL PREVIEW (Magazine) (Bizarre Adventures #25 on)

Marvel Comics: Feb (no month), 1975 - No. 24, Winter, 1980 (B&W) ($1.00)

1-Man-Gods From Beyond the Stars; Crusty Bunkers (Neal Adams)-a(i) &

	GD	FN	NM-
cover; Nino-a	2	6	18
2-1st origin The Punisher (see Amaz. Spider-Man #129 & Classic Punisher); 1st app. Dominic Fortune; Morrow-c	9	27	120
3,8,10: 3-Blade the Vampire Slayer. 8-Legion of Monsters; Morbius app. 10-Thor the Mighty; Starlin frontispiece	2	6	22
4,5: 4-Star-Lord & Sword in the Star (origins & 1st app.). 5,6-Sherlock Holmes.	2	6	16
6,9: 6-Sherlock Holmes; N. Adams frontispiece. 9-Man-God; origin Star Hawk, ends #20	2	6	12
7-Satana, Sword in the Star app.	2	6	14
11,12,16,19: 11-Star-Lord; Byrne-a; Starlin frontispiece. 12-Haunt of Horror. 16-Masters of Terror. 19-Kull	1	3	8
13-15,17,18,20-24: 14,15-Star-Lord. 14-Starlin painted-c. 17-Blackmark by G. Kane (see SSOC #1-3). 18-Star-Lord. 20-Bizarre Advs. 21-Moon Knight (Spr/80)-Predates Moon Knight #1; The Shroud by Ditko. 22-King Arthur. 23-Bizarre Advs.; Miller-a. 24-Debut Paradox			5.00

MARVELS
Marvel Comics: Jan, 1994 - No. 4, Apr, 1994 ($5.95, painted lim. series) No. 1 (2nd Printing), Apr, 1996 - No. 4 (2nd Printing), July, 1996 ($2.95)

	GD	FN	NM-
1-4: Kurt Busiek scripts & Alex Ross painted-c/a in all; double-c w/acetate overlay	1	3	8
Marvel Classic Collectors Pack ($11.90)-Issues #1 & 2 boxed (1st printings).	2	6	16
0-(8/94, $2.95)-no acetate overlay.			4.00
1-4-(2nd printing): r/original limited series w/o acetate overlay			3.00
Hardcover (1994, $59.95)-r/#0-4; w/intros by Stan Lee, John Romita, Sr., Kurt Busiek & Scott McCloud.			60.00
...: 10th Anniversary Edition (2004, $49.99, hardcover w/dustjacket) r/#0-4; scripts and commentaries; Ross sketch pages, cover gallery, behind the scenes art			50.00
Trade paperback ($19.95)			20.00

MARVEL 1602
Marvel Comics: Nov, 2003 - No. 8, June, 2004 ($3.50, limited series)

1-8-Neil Gaiman-s; Andy Kubert & Richard Isanove-a			3.50
HC (2004, $24.99) r/series; script pages for #1, sketch pages and Gaiman afterword			25.00

MARVEL SPECIAL EDITION FEATURING... (Also see Special Collectors' Edition)
Marvel Comics Group: 1975 - 1978 (84 pgs.) (Oversized)

	GD	FN	NM-
1-The Spectacular Spider-Man ($1.50); r/Amazing Spider-Man #6,35, Annual 1; Ditko-a(r)	3	9	30
1,2-Star Wars ('77,'78; r/Star Wars #1-3 & #4-6; regular edition and Whitman variant exist	2	6	18
3-Star Wars ('78, $2.50, 116 pgs.); r/S. Wars #1-6; regular edition and Whitman variant exist	3	9	24
3-Close Encounters of the Third Kind (1978, $1.50, 56 pgs.)-Movie adaptation; Simonson-a(p)	2	6	16

	GD	FN	NM-

V2#2(Spring, 1980, $2.00, oversized)- "Star Wars: The Empire Strikes Back";
r/Marvel Comics Super Special #16   3   9   28

MARVEL SPOTLIGHT (...& Son of Satan #19, 20, 23, 24)
Marvel Comics Group: Nov, 1971 - No. 33, Apr, 1977; V2#1, July, 1979 -
V2#11, Mar, 1981 (A try-out book for new characters)

1-Origin Red Wolf (western hero)(1st solo book, pre-#1); Wood inks, Neal
Adams-c; only 15¢ issue   4   12   50
2-(25¢, 52 pgs.)-Venus-r by Everett; origin/1st app. Werewolf By Night
(begins) by Ploog; N. Adams-c   16   48   230
3,4: 4-Werewolf By Night ends (6/72); gets own title 9/72
    6   18   70
5-Origin/1st app. Ghost Rider (8/72) & begins   15   45   220
6-8: 6-Origin G.R. retold. 8-Last Ploog issue   5   15   55
9-11-Last Ghost Rider (gets own title next mo.)   4   12   42
12-Origin & 2nd full app. The Son of Satan (10/73); story cont'd from Ghost
Rider #2 & into #3; series begins, ends #24   4   12   40
13-24: 13-Partial origin Son of Satan. 14-Last 20¢ issue. 22-Ghost Rider-c
& cameo (5 panels). 24-Last Son of Satan (10/75); gets own title 12/75
    2   6   12
25,27,30,31: 27-(Regular 25¢-c), Sub-Mariner app. 30-The Warriors Three.
31-Nick Fury   6.00
26-Scarecrow   1   4   10
27-(30¢-c variant, limited distribution)   2   6   18
28-(Regular 25¢-c) 1st solo Moon Knight app.   3   10   35
28-(30¢-c variant, limited distribution)   6   18   70
29,32: 29-(Regular 25¢-c) (8/76) Moon Knight app.; last 25¢ issue. 32-1st
app./partial origin Spider-Woman (2/77); Nick Fury app.
    3   9   24
29-(30¢-c variant, limited distribution)   4   12   50
33-Deathlok; 1st app. Devil-Slayer   1   3   8
V2#1-7,9-11: 1-4-Capt. Marvel. 5-Dragon Lord. 6,7-StarLord; origin #6.
9-11-Capt. Universe (see Micronauts #8)   3.00
1-Variant copy missing issue #1 on cover   2   6   12
8-Capt. Marvel; Miller-c/a(p)   6.00

MARVEL SUPER ACTION (Magazine)
Marvel Comics Group: Jan, 1976 (B&W, 76 pgs.)

1-Origin/2nd app. Dominic Fortune(see Marvel Preview); early Punisher
app.; Weird World & The Huntress; Ploog-a   6   18   75

MARVEL SUPER ACTION
Marvel Comics Group: May, 1977 - No. 37, Nov, 1981

1-Reprints Capt. America #100 by Kirby   2   6   12
2-13: 2,3,5-13 reprint Capt. America #101,102,103-111. 4-Marvel Boy-r
(origin)/M. Boy #1. 11-Origin-r. 12,13-Classic Steranko-c/a(r).
    1   3   7
2,3-(35¢-c variants, limited distribution)(6,8/77)   1   3   10
14-20: r/Avengers #55,56, Annual 2, others   4.00
21-37: 30-r/Hulk #6 from U.K.   3.50

	GD	FN	NM-

MARVEL SUPER HERO CONTEST OF CHAMPIONS
Marvel Comics Group: June, 1982 - No. 3, Aug, 1982 (Limited series)

1-3: Features nearly all Marvel characters currently appearing in their comics; 1st Marvel limited series	1	3	8

MARVEL SUPER HEROES
Marvel Comics Group: October, 1966 (25¢, 68 pgs.) (1st Marvel one-shot)

1-r/origin Daredevil from D.D. #1; r/Avengers #2; G.A. Sub-Mariner-r/Marvel Mystery #8 (Human Torch app.). Kirby-a	11	33	160

MARVEL SUPER-HEROES (Formerly Fantasy Masterpieces #1-11)
(Also see Giant-Size Super Heroes) (#12-20: 25¢, 68 pgs.)
Marvel Comics: No. 12, 12/67 - No. 31, 11/71; No. 32, 9/72 - No. 105, 1/82

12-Origin & 1st app. Capt. Marvel of the Kree; G.A. Human Torch, Destroyer, Capt. America, Black Knight, Sub-Mariner-r (#12-20 all contain new stories and reprints)	13	39	190
13-2nd app. Capt. Marvel; G.A. Black Knight, Torch, Vision, Capt. America, Sub-Mariner-r	7	21	85
14-Amazing Spider-Man (5/68, new-a by Andru/Everett); G.A. Sub-Mariner, Torch, Mercury (1st Kirby-a at Marvel), Black Knight, Capt. America reprints	9	27	120
15-17: 15-Black Bolt cameo in Medusa (new-a); Black Knight, Sub-Mariner, Black Marvel, Capt. America-r. 16-Origin & 1st app. S. A. Phantom Eagle; G.A. Torch, Capt. America, Black Knight, Patriot, Sub-Mariner-r. 17-Origin Black Knight (new-a); G.A. Torch, Sub-Mariner-r; reprint from All-Winners Squad #21 (cover & story)	4	12	45
18-Origin/1st app. Guardians of the Galaxy (1/69); G.A. Sub-Mariner, All-Winners Squad-r	6	18	70
19-Ka-Zar (new-a); G.A. Torch, Marvel Boy, Black Knight, Sub-Mariner reprints; Smith-c(p); Tuska-a(r)	3	9	30
20-Doctor Doom (5/69); r/Young Men #24 w/-c	4	12	40
21-31: All-r issues. 21-X-Men, Daredevil, Iron Man-r begin, end #31. 31-Last Giant issue	2	6	16
32-50: 32-Hulk/Sub-Mariner-r begin from TTA.			6.00
51-70,100: 56-r/origin Hulk/Inc. Hulk #102; Hulk-r begin			4.00
57,58-(30¢-c variants, limited distribution)(5,7/76)			6.00
65,66-(35¢-c variants, limited distribution)(7,9/77)			6.00
71-99,101-105			3.00

MARVEL SUPER-HEROES SECRET WARS (See Secret Wars II)
Marvel Comics Group: May, 1984 - No. 12, Apr, 1985 (limited series)

1	1	3	8
1-3-(2nd printings, sold in multi-packs)			2.50
2-6,9-11: 6-The Wasp dies			6.00
7,12: 7-Intro. new Spider-Woman. 12-($1.00, 52 pgs.)	1	3	7
8-Spider-Man's new black costume explained as alien costume (1st app. Venom as alien costume)	3	9	28

NOTE: *Zeck* a-1-12; c-1,3,8-12. Additional artists (John Romita Sr., Art Adams and others) had uncredited art in #12.

MARVEL TALES (…Annual #1,2; …Starring Spider-Man #123 on)

	GD	FN	NM-

Marvel Comics Group (NPP earlier issues): 1964 - No. 291, Nov, 1994 (No. 1-32: 72 pgs.) (#1-3 have Canadian variants; back & inside-c are blank, same value)

	GD	FN	NM-
1-Reprints origins of Spider-Man/Amazing Fantasy #15, Hulk/Inc. Hulk#1, Ant-Man/T.T.A. #35, Giant Man/T.T.A. #49, Iron Man/T.O.S. #39,48, Thor/J.I.M. #83 & r/Sgt. Fury #1	30	90	450
2 ('65)-r/X-Men #1(origin), Avengers #1(origin), origin Dr. Strange-r/Strange Tales #115 & origin Hulk(Hulk #3)	11	33	160
3 (7/66)-Spider-Man, Strange Tales (H. Torch), Journey into Mystery (Thor), Tales to Astonish (Ant-Man)-r begin (r/Strange Tales #101)	6	18	75
4,5	4	12	50
6-8,10: 10-Reprints 1st Kraven/Amaz. S-M #15	3	9	30
9-r/Amazing Spider-Man #14 w/cover	3	10	35
11-33: 11-Spider-Man battles Daredevil-r/Amaz. Spider-Man #16. 13-Origin Marvel Boy-r from M. Boy #1. 22-Green Goblin-c/story/r/Amaz. Spider-Man #27. 30-New Angel story (x-over w/Ka-Zar #2,3). 32-Last 72 pg. iss. 33-(52 pgs.) Kraven-r	2	6	20
34-50: 34-Begin regular size issues	1	3	7
51-65			5.00
66-70-(Regular 25¢ editions)(4-8/76)			4.00
66-70-(30¢-c variants, limited distribution)			6.00
71-105: 75-Origin Spider-Man-r. 77-79-Drug issues-r/Amaz. Spider-Man #96-98. 98-Death of Gwen Stacy-r/Amaz. Spider-Man #121. 99-Death Green Goblin-r/Amaz. Spider-Man #122. 100-(52 pgs.)-New Hawkeye/Two Gun Kid story. 101-105-All Spider-Man-r			3.00
80-84-(35¢-c variants, limited distribution)(6-10/77)			5.00
106-r/1st Punisher-Amazing Spider-Man #129	1	3	8
107-136: 107-133-All Spider-Man-r. 111,112-r/Spider-Man #134,135 (Punisher). 113,114-r/Spider-Man #136,137(Green Goblin). 126-128-r/clone story from Amazing Spider-Man #149-151. 134-136-Dr. Strange-r begin; SpM stories continue.			3.00
137-Origin-r Dr. Strange; shows original unprinted-c & origin Spider-Man from Amazing Fantasy #15			6.00
137-Nabisco giveaway	1	3	7
138-Reprints all Amazing Spider-Man #1; begin reprints of Spider-Man with covers similar to originals			5.00
139-144: r/Amazing Spider-Man #2-7			3.00
145-149,151-190,193-199: Spider-Man-r continue w/#8 on. 149-Contains skin "Tattooz" decals. 153-r/1st Kraven/Spider-Man #15. 155-r/2nd Green Goblin/Spider-Man #17. 161,164,165-Gr. Goblin-c/stories-r/Spider-Man #23,26,27. 178,179-Green Goblin-c/story-r/Spider-Man #39,40. 187,189-Kraven-r. 193-Byrne-r/Marvel Team-Up begin w/scripts			2.50
150,191,192,200: 150-($1.00, 52pgs.)-r/Spider-Man Annual #1(Kraven app.). 191-($1.50, 68 pgs.)-r/Spider-Man #96-98. 192-($1.25, 52 pgs.)-r/Spider-Man #121,122. 200-Double size ($1.25)-Miller-c & r/Annual #14			4.00
201-257: 208-Last Byrne-r. 210,211-r/Spidey #134,135. 212,213-r/Giant-Size Spidey #4. 213-r/1st solo Silver Surfer story/F.F. Annual #5. 214,215-r/Spidey #161,162. 222-Reprints origin Punisher/Spectacular Spider-Man			

	GD	FN	NM-

#83; last Punisher reprint. 209-Reprints 1st app. The Punisher/Amazing Spider-Man #129; Punisher reprints begin, end #222. 223-McFarlane-c begins, end #239. 233-Spider-Man/X-Men team-ups begin; r/X-Men #35. 234-r/Marvel Team-Up #4. 235,236-r/M. Team-Up Annual #1. 237,238-r/M. Team-Up #150. 239,240-r/M. Team-Up #38,90(Beast). 242-r/M.Team-Up #89. 243-r/M. Team-Up #117 (Wolverine). 250-($1.50, 52pgs.)-r/1st Karma/M. Team-Up #100. 251-r/Spider-Man #100 (Green Goblin-c/story). 252-r/1st app. Morbius/Amaz. Spider-Man #101. 253-($1.50, 52 pgs.) - r/Amaz. S-M #102254-r/M. Team-Up #15(Ghost Rider); new painted-c. 255,256-Spider-Man & Ghost Rider-r/Marvel Team-Up #58,91.

257-Hobgoblin-r begin (r/Amazing Spider-Man #238) 2.25

258-291: 258-261-r/A. Spider-Man #239,249-251(Hobgoblin). 262,263-r/Marv. Team-Up #53,54. 262-New X-Men vs. Sunstroke story. 263-New Woodgod origin story. 264,265-r/Amazing Spider-Man Annual 5. 266-273-Reprints alien costume stories/A. S-M 252-259. 277-r/1st Silver Sable/A. S-M 265. 283-r/A. S-M 275 (Hobgoblin). 284-r/A. S-M 276 (Hobgoblin) 2.25

285-variant w/Wonder-Con logo on c-no price-giveaway 2.25
286-($2.95)-p/bagged w/16 page insert & animation print 3.00

MARVEL TEAM-UP (See Marvel Treasury Edition #18 & Official Marvel Index To...)(Replaced by Web of Spider-Man)
Marvel Comics Group: March, 1972 - No. 150, Feb, 1985
NOTE: *Spider-Man team-ups in all but Nos. 18, 23, 26, 29, 32, 35, 97, 104, 105, 137.*

	GD	FN	NM-
1-Human Torch	13	39	190
2-Human Torch	5	15	60

3-Spider-Man/Human Torch vs. Morbius (part 1); 3rd app. of Morbius (7/72)

	6	18	70

4-Spider-Man/X-Men vs. Morbius (part 2 of story); 4th app. of Morbius

	6	18	70

5-10: 5-Vision. 6-Thing. 7-Thor. 8-The Cat (4/73, came out between The Cat #3 & 4). 9-Iron Man. 10-H-T

	3	9	26

11,13,14,16-20: 11-Inhumans. 13-Capt. America. 14-Sub-Mariner. 16-Capt. Marvel. 17-Mr. Fantastic. 18-H-T/Hulk. 19-Ka-Zar. 20-Black Panther; last 20¢ issue

	2	6	16

12-Werewolf (8/73, 1 month before Werewolf #1).

	3	9	30

15-1st Spider-Man/Ghost Rider team-up (11/73)

	3	9	24

21-30: 21-Dr. Strange. 22-Hawkeye. 23-H-T/Iceman (X-Men cameo). 24-Brother Voodoo. 25-Daredevil. 26-H-T/Thor. 27-Hulk. 28-Hercules. 29-H-T/Iron Man. 30-Falcon

	1	4	10

31-45,47-50: 31-Iron Fist. 32-H-T/Son of Satan. 33-Nighthawk. 34-Valkyrie. 35-H-T/Dr. Strange. 36-Frankenstein. 37-Man-Wolf. 38-Beast. 39-H-T. 40-Sons of the Tiger/H-T. 41-Scarlet Witch. 42-The Vision. 43-Dr. Doom; retells origin. 44-Moondragon. 45-Killraven. 47-Thing. 48-Iron Man; last 25¢ issue. 49-Dr. Strange; Iron Man app. 50-Iron Man; Dr. Strange app.

	1	3	7
44-48-(30¢-c variants, limited distribution)(4-8/76)	2	6	18
46-Spider-Man/Deathlok team-up	1	3	8

51,52,56,57: 51-Iron Man; Dr. Strange app. 52-Capt. America. 56-Daredevil. 57-Black Widow 6.00

53-Hulk; Woodgod & X-Men app., 1st Byrne-a on X-Men (1/77)

	GD	FN	NM-
	3	9	32

54,55,58-60: 54,59,60: 54-Hulk; Woodgod app. 59-Yellowjacket/The Wasp.
60-The Wasp (Byrne-a in all). 55-Warlock-c/story; Byrne-a. 58-Ghost Rider

	1	3	8

58-62-(35¢-c variants, limited distribution)(6-10/77)   2   6   18

61-70: All Byrne-a; 61-H-T. 62-Ms. Marvel; last 30¢ issue. 63-Iron Fist.
64-Daughters of the Dragon. 65-Capt. Britain (1st U.S. app.). 66-Capt.
Britain; 1st app. Arcade. 67-Tigra; Kraven the Hunter app. 68-Man-Thing.
69-Havok (from X-Men). 70-Thor   1   3   7

71-74,76-78,80: 71-Falcon. 72-Iron Man. 73-Daredevil. 74-Not Ready for
Prime Time Players (Belushi). 76-Dr. Strange. 77-Ms. Marvel. 78-Wonder
Man. 80-Dr. Strange/Clea; last 35¢ issue   4.00

75,79,81: Byrne-a(p). 75-Power Man; Cage app. 79-Mary Jane Watson as
Red Sonja; Clark Kent cameo (1 panel, 3/79). 81-Death of Satana   6.00

82-99: 82-Black Widow. 83-Nick Fury. 84-Shang-Chi. 86-Guardians of the
Galaxy. 89-Nightcrawler (from X-Men). 91-Ghost Rider. 92-Hawkeye.
93-Werewolf by Night. 94-Spider-Man vs. The Shroud. 95-Mockingbird
(intro.); Nick Fury app. 96-Howard the Duck; last 40¢ issue. 97-Spider-
Woman/ Hulk. 98-Black Widow. 99-Machine Man. 85-Shang-Chi/Black
Widow/Nick Fury. 87-Black Panther. 88-Invisible Girl. 90-Beast   3.00

100-(Double-size)-Fantastic Four/Storm/Black Panther; origin/1st app. Karma,
one of the New Mutants; origin Storm; X-Men x-over; Miller-c/a(p); Byrne-a
(on X-Men app. only)   1   3   7

101-116: 101-Nighthawk(Ditko-a). 102-Doc Samson. 103-Ant-Man. 104-Hulk/
Ka-Zar. 105-Hulk/Powerman/Iron Fist. 106-Capt. America. 107-She-Hulk.
108-Paladin; Dazzler cameo. 109-Dazzler; Paladin app. 110-Iron Man.
111-Devil-Slayer. 112-King Kull; last 50¢ issue. 113-Quasar. 114-Falcon.
115-Thor. 116-Valkyrie   3.00

117-Wolverine-c/story   1   4   10

118-140,142-149: 118-Professor X; Wolverine app. (4 pgs.); X-Men cameo.
119-Gargoyle. 120-Dominic Fortune. 121-Human Torch. 122-Man-Thing.
123-Daredevil. 124-The Beast. 125-Tigra. 126-Hulk & Powerman/Son of
Satan. 127-The Watcher. 128-Capt. America; Spider-Man/Capt. America
photo-c. 129-The Vision. 130-Scarlet Witch. 131-Frogman. 132-Mr.
Fantastic. 133-Fantastic Four. 134-Jack of Hearts. 135-Kitty Pryde; X-Men
cameo. 136-Wonder Man. 137-Aunt May/Franklin Richards. 138-Sandman.
139-Nick Fury. 140-Black Widow. 142-Capt. Marvel. 143-Starfox. 144-Moon
Knight. 145-Iron Man. 146-Nomad. 147-Human Torch; Spider-Man back to
old costume. 148-Thor. 149-Cannonball   2.50

141-Daredevil; SpM/Black Widow app. (Spidey in new black costume; ties w/
Amazing Spider-Man #252 for 1st black costume)   1   4   10

150-X-Men ($1.00, double-size); B. Smith-c   5.00

Annual 1 (1976)-Spider-Man/X-Men (early app.)   3   9   30

Annual 2 (1979)-Spider-Man/Hulk   1   3   9

Annuals 3,4: 3 (1980)-Hulk/Power Man/Machine Man/Iron Fist; Miller-c(p).
4 (1981)-Spider-Man /Daredevil/Moon Knight/Power Man/Iron Fist; brief
origins of each; Miller-c; Miller scripts on Daredevil   6.00

Annuals 5-7: 5 (1982)-SpM/The Thing/Scarlet Witch/Dr. Strange/Quasar.
6 (1983)-Spider-Man/New Mutants (early app.), Cloak & Dagger.

	GD	FN	NM-

7(1984)-Alpha Flight; Byrne-c(i)   5.00

MARVEL TREASURY EDITION
Marvel Comics Group/Whitman #17,18: 1974; #2, Dec, 1974 - #28, 1981
($1.50/$2.50, 100 pgs., oversized, new-a &-r)(Also see Amazing Spider-Man,
The, Marvel Spec. Ed. Feat.--, Savage Fists of Kung Fu, Superman Vs. , &
2001, A Space Odyssey)

	GD	FN	NM-
1-Spectacular Spider-Man; story-r/Marvel Super-Heroes #14; Romita-c/a(r); G. Kane, Ditko-r; Green Goblin/Hulk-r	6	18	65
1-1,000 numbered copies signed by Stan Lee & John Romita on front-c & sold thru mail for $5.00; these were the1st 1,000 copies off the press	11	33	150
2-10: 2-Fantastic Four-r/F.F. 6,11,48-50(Silver Surfer). 3-The Mighty Thor-r/Thor #125-130. 4-Conan the Barbarian; Barry Smith-c/a(r)/Conan #11. 5-The Hulk (origin-r/Hulk #3). 6-Dr. Strange. 7-Mighty Avengers. 8-Giant Superhero Holiday Grab-Bag; Spider-Man, Hulk, Nick Fury. 9-Giant; Super-Hero Team-up. 10-Thor; r/Thor #154-157	3	9	25
11-20: 11-Fantastic Four. 12-Howard the Duck (r/#H. the Duck #1 & G.S. Man-Thing #4,5) plus new Defenders story. 13-Giant Super-Hero Holiday Grab-Bag. 14-The Sensational Spider-Man; r/1st Morbius from Amazing S-M #101,102 plus #100 & r/Not Brand Echh #6. 15-Conan; B. Smith, Neal Adams-i; r/Conan #24. 16-The Defenders (origin) & Valkyrie; r/Defenders #1,4,13,14. 17-The Hulk. 18-The Astonishing Spider-Man; r/Spider-Man's 1st team-ups with Iron Fist, The X-Men, Ghost Rider & Werewolf by Night; inside back-c has photos from 1978 Spider-Man TV show. 19-Conan the Barbarian. 20-Hulk	2	6	16
21-25,27: 21-Fantastic Four. 22-Spider-Man. 23-Conan. 24-Rampaging Hulk. 25-Spider-Man vs. The Hulk. 27-Spider-Man	2	6	16
26-The Hulk; 6 pg. new Wolverine/Hercules-s	2	6	20
28-Spider-Man/Superman; (origin of each)	4	12	50

MARVEL TREASURY OF OZ FEATURING THE MARVELOUS LAND OF OZ
Marvel Comics Group: 1975 ($1.50, oversized) (See MGM's Marvelous...)

	GD	FN	NM-
1-Buscema-a; Romita-c	3	9	24

MARVEL TREASURY SPECIAL (Also see 2001: A Space Odyssey)
Marvel Comics Group: 1974; 1976 ($1.50, oversized, 84 pgs.)

	GD	FN	NM-
Vol. 1-Spider-Man, Torch, Sub-Mariner, Avengers "Giant Superhero Holiday Grab-Bag"; Wood, Colan/Everett, plus 2 Kirby-r; reprints Hulk vs. Thing from Fantastic Four #25,26	3	9	24
Vol. 1-... Featuring Captain America's Bicentennial Battles (6/76)-Kirby-a; B. Smith inks, 11 pgs.	3	9	26

MARVEL TRIPLE ACTION (See Giant-Size...)
Marvel Comics Group: Feb, 1972 - No. 24, Mar, 1975; No. 25, Aug, 1975 -
No. 47, Apr, 1979

	GD	FN	NM-
1-(25¢ giant, 52 pgs.)-Dr. Doom, Silver Surfer, The Thing begin, end #4 ('66 reprints from Fantastic Four)	3	9	24
2-5	2	6	12
6-10	1	3	7
11-47: 45-r/X-Men #45. 46-r/Avengers #53(X-Men)			4.00

	GD	FN	NM-
29,30-(30¢-c variants, limited distribution)(5,7/76)			6.00
36,37-(35¢-c variants, limited distribution)(7,9/77)			6.00

MARVEL TWO-IN-ONE (...Featuring ... #82 on; also see The Thing)
Marvel Comics Group: January, 1974 - No. 100, June, 1983

	GD	FN	NM-
1-Thing team-ups begin; Man-Thing	6	18	75
2,3: 2-Sub-Mariner; last 20¢ issue. 3-Daredevil	3	9	25
4-6: 4-Capt. America. 5-Guardians of the Galaxy (9/74, 2nd app.?). 6-Dr. Strange (11/74)	2	6	18
7,9,10	2	6	12
8-Early Ghost Rider app. (3/75)	2	6	16
11-14,19,20: 13-Power Man. 14-Son of Satan (early app.)	1	3	8
15-18-(Regular 25¢ editions)(5-7/76) 17-Spider-Man.	1	3	8
15-18-(30¢-c variants, limited distribution)	2	6	18
21-29: 27-Deathlok. 29-Master of Kung Fu; Spider-Woman cameo			6.00
28,29,31-(35¢-c variants, limited distribution)	2	6	18
30-2nd full app. Spider-Woman (see Marvel Spotlight #32 for 1st app.)	1	4	10
30-(35¢-c variant, limited distribution)(8/77)	2	6	20
31-40: 31-33-Spider-Woman. 39-Vision			6.00
41,42,44,45,47-49: 42-Capt. America. 45-Capt. Marvel			4.00
43,50,53,55-Byrne-a(p). 53-Quasar(7/79, 2nd app.)			6.00
46-Thing battles Hulk-c/story	1	4	10
51-The Beast, Nick Fury, Ms. Marvel; Miller-p	1	3	7
52-Moon Knight app.			3.00
54-Death of Deathlok; Byrne-a	1	4	10
56-60,64-74,76-79,81,82: 60-Intro. Impossible Woman. 68-Angel. 69-Guardians of the Galaxy. 71-1st app. Maelstrom. 76-Iceman			3.00
61-63: 61-Starhawk (from Guardians); "The Coming of Her" storyline begins, ends #63; cover similar to F.F. #67 (Him-c). 62-Moondragon; Thanos & Warlock cameo in flashback; Starhawk app. 63-Warlock revived shortly; Starhawk & Moondragon app.			4.00
75-Avengers (52 pgs.)			4.00
80,90,100: 80-Ghost Rider. 90-Spider-Man. 100-Double size, Byrne-s			4.00
83-89,91-99: 83-Sasquatch. 84-Alpha Flight app. 93-Jocasta dies. 96-X-Men-c & cameo			3.00
Annual 1(1976, 52 pgs.)-Thing/Liberty Legion; Kirby-c	2	6	12
Annual 2(1977, 52 pgs.)-Thing/Spider-Man; 2nd death of Thanos; end of Thanos saga; Warlock app.; Starlin-c/a	4	12	40
Annual 3,4 (1978-79, 52 pgs.): 3-Nova. 4-Black Bolt			6.00
Annual 5-7 (1980-82, 52 pgs.): 5-Hulk. 6-1st app. American Eagle. 7-The Thing/Champion; Sasquatch, Colossus app.; X-Men cameo (1 pg.)			4.00

MARVEL VERSUS DC (See DC Versus Marvel)
Marvel Comics: No. 2, 1996 - No. 3, 1996 ($3.95, limited series)

2,3: 2-Peter David script. 3-Ron Marz script; Dan Jurgens-a(p). 1st app. of Super Soldier, Spider-Boy, Dr. Doomsday, Doctor Strangefate, The Dark Claw, Nightcreeper, Amazon, Wraith & others. Storyline continues in Amalgam books.   4.00

	GD	FN	NM-

MARY JANE (Spider-Man)
Marvel Comics: Aug, 2004 - No. 4, Nov, 2004 ($2.25)

	GD	FN	NM-
1-4-Marvel Age series with teen-age MJ Watson; Miyazawa-c/a; McKeever-s			2.25
... Vol. 1: Circle of Friends (2004, $5.99, digest-size) r/#1-4			6.00

MASTER OF KUNG FU (Formerly Special Marvel Edition; see Deadly Hands of Kung Fu & Giant-Size...)
Marvel Comics Group: No. 17, April, 1974 - No. 125, June, 1983

	GD	FN	NM-
17-Starlin-a; intro Black Jack Tarr; 3rd Shang-Chi (ties w/Deadly Hands #1)	3	9	30
18,20	2	6	15
19-Man-Thing-c/story	2	6	18
21-23,25-30	1	4	10
24-Starlin, Simonson-a	2	6	12
31-50: 33-1st Leiko Wu. 43-Last 25¢ issue			6.00
39-43-(30¢-c variants, limited distribution)(5-7/76)	2	6	15
51-99			4.00
53-57-(35¢-c variants, limited distribution)(6-10/77)	2	6	15
100,118,125-Double size			5.00
101-117,119-124			3.00
Annual 1(4/76)-Iron Fist app.	2	6	22

MASTERS OF THE UNIVERSE (See DC Comics Presents #47 for 1st app.)
DC Comics: Dec, 1982 - No. 3, Feb, 1983 (Mini-series)

	GD	FN	NM-
1			6.00
2,3: 2-Origin He-Man & Ceril			4.00

MASTERS OF THE UNIVERSE (Comic Album)
Western Publishing Co.: 1984 (8-1/2x11", $2.95, 64 pgs.)

	GD	FN	NM-
11362-Based on Mattel toy & cartoon	2	6	16

MASTERS OF THE UNIVERSE
Star Comics/Marvel #7 on: May 1986 - No. 13, May, 1988 (75¢/$1.00)

	GD	FN	NM-
1			6.00
2-11: 8-Begin $1.00-c			4.00
12-Death of He-Man (1st Marvel app.)	1	3	8
13-Return of He-Man & death of Skeletor	1	3	8
The Motion Picture (11/87, $2.00)-Tuska-p			5.00

MAUS: A SURVIVOR'S TALE (First graphic novel to win a Pulitzer Prize)
Pantheon Books: 1986, 1991 (B&W)

Vol. 1-(...: My Father Bleeds History)(1986) Art Spiegelman-s/a; recounts stories of Spiegelman's father in 1930s-40s Nazi-occupied Poland; collects first six stories serialized in Raw Magazine from 1980-1985	20.00
Vol. 2-(...: And Here My Troubles Began)(1991)	20.00
Complete Maus Survivor's Tale -HC Vols. 1& 2 w/slipcase	35.00
Hardcover Vol. 1 (1991)	24.00
Hardcover Vol. 2 (1991)	24.00
TPB (1992, $14.00) Vols. 1& 2	14.00

	GD	FN	NM-

MAXX (Also see Darker Image, Primer #5, & Friends of Maxx)
Image Comics (I Before E): Mar, 1993 - No. 35, Feb, 1998 ($1.95)

	GD	FN	NM-
1/2	1	4	10
1/2 (Gold)			20.00
1-Sam Kieth-c/a/scripts			4.00
1-Glow-in-the-dark variant	2	6	12
1-"3-D Edition" (1/98, $4.95) plus new back-up story			5.00
2-12: 6-Savage Dragon cameo(1 pg.). 7,8-Pitt-c & story			2.50
13-16			2.50
17-35: 21-Alan Moore-s			2.50

McHALE'S NAVY (TV) (See Movie Classics)
Dell Publ. Co.: May-July, 1963 - No. 3, Nov-Jan, 1963-64 (All have photo-c)

	GD	FN	NM-
1	8	24	100
2,3	6	18	70

MEN IN BLACK, THE (1st series)
Aircel Comics (Malibu): Jan, 1990 - No. 3 Mar, 1990 ($2.25, B&W, lim. series)

	GD	FN	NM-
1-Cunningham-s/a in all	4	12	50
2,3	3	9	28
Graphic Novel (Jan, 1991) r/#1-3	3	9	25

MEN IN BLACK (2nd series)
Aircel Comics (Malibu): May, 1991 - No. 3, Jul, 1991 ($2.50, B&W, lim. series)

	GD	FN	NM-
1-Cunningham-s/a in all	3	9	28
2,3	2	6	14

MEN OF WAR
DC Comics, Inc.: August, 1977 - No. 26, March, 1980 (#9,10: 44 pgs.)

	GD	FN	NM-
1-Enemy Ace, Gravedigger (origin #1,2) begin	2	6	20
2-4,8-10,12-14,19,20: All Enemy Ace stories. 4-1st Dateline Frontline.			
9-Unknown Soldier app.	1	4	10
5-7,11,15-18,21-25: 17-1st app. Rosa	1	3	8
26-Sgt. Rock & Easy Co.-c/s	2	6	15

METAL MEN (See Brave & the Bold, DC Comics Presents, and Showcase #37-40)
National Periodical Publications/DC Comics: 4-5/63 - No. 41, 12-1/69-70; No. 42, 2-3/73 - No. 44, 7-8/73; No. 45, 4-5/76 - No. 56, 2-3/78

	GD	FN	NM-
1-(4-5/63)-5th app. Metal Men	54	162	925
2	20	60	300
3-5	13	39	190
6-10	9	27	120
11-20: 12-Beatles cameo (2-3/65)	7	21	90
21-Batman, Robin & Flash x-over	6	18	70
22-26,28-30	5	15	60
27-Origin Metal Men retold	7	21	90
31-41(1968-70): 38-Last 12¢ issue. 41-Last 15¢	4	12	50
42-44(1973)-Reprints	2	6	15

	GD	FN	NM-
45('76)-49-Simonson-a in all: 48,49-Re-intro Eclipso	1	3	10
50-56: 50-Part-r. 54,55-Green Lantern x-over	1	3	10

METAMORPHO (See Brave & the Bold #57,58, 1st Issue Special, & World's Finest #217)
National Periodical Publications: July-Aug, 1965 - No. 17, Mar-Apr, 1968 (All 12¢ issues)

	GD	FN	NM-
1-(7-8/65)-3rd app. Metamorpho	12	36	180
2,3	7	21	85
4-6,10:10-Origin & 1st app. Element Girl (1-2/67)	6	18	65
7-9	5	15	55
11-17: 17-Sparling-c/a	4	12	45

MGM'S MARVELOUS WIZARD OF OZ (See Marvel Treasury of Oz)
Marvel Comics Group/National Periodical Publications: 1975 ($1.50, 84 pgs.; oversize)

	GD	FN	NM-
1-Adaptation of MGM's movie; J. Buscema-a	3	9	24

MICHAEL CHABON PRESENTS THE AMAZING ADVENTURES OF THE ESCAPIST
Dark Horse Comics: Feb, 2004 - Present ($8.95, squarebound)

1-4-Short stories by Chabon and various incl. Chaykin, Starlin, Brereton, Kyle Baker		9.00
... Vol. 1 (5/04, $17.95, digest-size) r/#1&2; wraparound-c by Chris Ware		18.00
... Vol. 2 (11/04, $17.95, digest-size) r/#3&4; wraparound-c by Matt Kindt		18.00

MICKEY MOUSE (...Secret Agent #107-109; Walt Disney's... #148-205?)
Gold Key #85-204/Whitman #204-218/Gladstone #219 on:
No. 85, Nov, 1962 - No. 256, Apr, 1990

	GD	FN	NM-
85-105: 93,95-titled "Mickey Mouse Club Album". 100-105: Reprint 4-Color #427,194,279, 170,343,214 in that order	4	12	38
106-120	3	9	28
121-130	2	6	22
131-146	2	6	20
147,148: 147-Reprints "The Phantom Fires" from WDC&S #200-202. 148-Reprints "The Mystery of Lonely Valley" from WDC&S #208-210	2	6	20
149-158	2	6	14
159-Reprints "The Sunken City" from WDC&S #205-207	2	6	14
160-178: 162-165,167-170-r	2	6	16
179-(52 pgs.)	1	4	10
180-203: 200-r/Four Color #371	1	3	9
204-(Whitman or G.K.), 205,206	2	6	14
207(8/80), 209(pre-pack?)	3	9	32
208-(8-12/80)-Only distr. in Whitman 3-pack	7	21	90
210(2/81),211-214	2	6	14
215-218: 215(2/82), 216(4/82), 217(3/84), 218(misdated 8/82; actual date 7/84)	2	6	16
219-1st Gladstone issue; The Seven Ghosts serial-r begins by Gottfredson	2	6	18

	GD	FN	NM-
220,221	1	3	9
222-225: 222-Editor-in Grief strip-r			4.00
226-230			4.00
231-243,246-254: 240-r/March of Comics #27. 245-r/F.C. #279. 250-r/F.C. #248			3.00
244 (1/89, $2.95, 100 pgs.)-Squarebound 60th anniversary issue; gives history of Mickey			4.00
245, 256: 245-r/F.C. #279. 256-$1.95, 68 pgs.			4.00
255 ($1.95, 68 pgs.)			3.00
Album 01-518-210(Dell), 1(10082-309)(9/63-Gold Key)	4	12	38
...Club 1(1/64-Gold Key)(TV)	4	12	42
Mini Comic 1(1976)(3-1/4x6-1/2")-Reprints 158	1	3	8
Surprise Party 1(30037-901, G.K.)(1/69)-40th Anniversary (see Walt Disney Showcase #47)	4	12	42
Surprise Party 1(1979)-r/1969 issue	1	3	8

MICKEY MOUSE ADVENTURES
Disney Comics: June, 1990 - No. 18, Nov, 1991 ($1.50)

1,8,9: 1-Bradbury, Murry-r/M.M. #45,73 plus new-a. 8-Byrne-c. 9-Fantasia 50th ann. issue w/new adapt. of movie			3.00
2-7,10-18: 2-Begin all new stories. 10-r/F.C. #214			2.50

MICKEY MOUSE COMICS DIGEST
Gladstone: 1986 - No. 5, 1987 (96 pgs.)

1 ($1.25-c)	1	3	8
2-5: 3-5 ($1.50-c)			5.00

MICKEY MOUSE MAGAZINE (Russian Version)
May 16, 1991 (1st Russian printing of a modern comic book)

1-Bagged w/gold label commemoration in English			10.00

MICKEY'S TWICE UPON A CHRISTMAS (Disney)
Gemstone Publishing: 2004 ($3.95, square-bound, one-shot)

nn-Christmas short stories with Mickey, Minnie, Donald, Uncle Scrooge, Goofy and others			4.00

MICRONAUTS (Toys)
Marvel Comics Group: Jan, 1979 - No. 59, Aug, 1984 (Mando paper #53 on)

1-Intro/1st app. Baron Karza			5.00
2-10,35,37,57: 7-Man-Thing app. 8-1st app. Capt. Universe (8/79). 9-1st app. Cilicia. 35-Double size; origin Microverse; intro Death Squad; Dr. Strange app. 37-Nightcrawler app.; X-Men cameo (2 pgs.). 57-(52 pgs.)			3.00
11-34,36,38-56,58,59: 13-1st app. Jasmine. 15-Death of Microtron. 15-17-Fantastic Four app. 17-Death of Jasmine. 20-Ant-Man app. 21-Microverse series begins. 25-Origin Baron Karza. 25-29-Nick Fury app. 27-Death of Biotron. 34-Dr. Strange app. 38-First direct sale. 40-Fantastic Four app. 48-Early Guice-a begins. 59-Golden painted-c			2.50
nn-Reprints #1-3; blank UPC; diamond on top			2.25
Annual 1,2 (12/79,10/80)-Ditko-c/a			3.00

MIGHTY CRUSADERS, THE (Also see Adventures of the Fly, The Crusaders

	GD	FN	NM-

& Fly Man)
Mighty Comics Group (Radio Comics): Nov, 1965 - No. 7, Oct, 1966 (All 12¢)

	GD	FN	NM-
1-Origin The Shield	7	21	80
2-Origin Comet	4	12	42
3,5-7: 3-Origin Fly-Man. 5-Intro. Ultra-Men (Fox, Web, Capt. Flag) & Terrific Three (Jaguar, Mr. Justice, Steel Sterling). 7-Steel Sterling feature; origin Fly-Girl	4	12	40
4-1st S.A. app. Fireball, Inferno & Fox; Firefly, Web, Bob Phantom, Blackjack, Hangman, Zambini, Kardak, Steel Sterling, Mr. Justice, Wizard, Capt. Flag, Jaguar x-over	4	12	45
Volume 1: Origin of a Super Team TPB (2003, $12.95) r/#1 & Fly Man #31-33			13.00

MIGHTY HEROES, THE (TV) (Funny)
Dell Publishing Co.: Mar, 1967 - No. 4, July, 1967

	GD	FN	NM-
1-Also has a 1957 Heckle & Jeckle-r	15	45	215
2-4: 4-Has two 1958 Mighty Mouse-r	10	30	140

MIGHTY MARVEL WESTERN, THE
Marvel Comics Group (LMC earlier issues): Oct, 1968 - No. 46, Sept, 1976 (#1-14: 68 pgs.; #15,16: 52 pgs.)

	GD	FN	NM-
1-Begin Kid Colt, Rawhide Kid, Two-Gun Kid-r	6	18	70
2-5: (2-14 are 68 pgs.)	4	12	45
6-16: (15,16 are 52 pgs.)	4	12	40
17-20	2	6	20
21-30,32,37: 24-Kid Colt-r end. 25-Matt Slade-r begin. 32-Origin-r/Rawhide Kid #23; Williamson-r/Kid Slade #7. 37-Williamson, Kirby-r/Two-Gun Kid #51	2	6	15
31,33-36,38-46: 31-Baker-r.	2	6	12
45-(30¢-c variant, limited distribution)(6/76)	2	6	18

MIGHTY MOUSE (TV)(3rd Series)(Formerly Adventures of Mighty Mouse)
Gold Key/Dell Publ. Co. No. 166-on: No. 161, Oct, 1964 - No. 172, Oct, 1968

	GD	FN	NM-
161(10/64)-165(9/65)-(Becomes Adventures of... No. 166 on)	6	18	65
166(3/66), 167(6/66)-172	4	12	42

MIGHTY SAMSON (Also see Gold Key Champion)
Gold Key/Whitman #32: July, 1964 - No. 20, Nov, 1969; No. 21, Aug, 1972; No. 22, Dec, 1973 - No. 31, Mar, 1976; No. 32, Aug, 1982 (Painted-c #1-31)

	GD	FN	NM-
1-Origin/1st app.; Thorne-a begins	10	30	130
2-5	6	18	65
6-10: 7-Tom Morrow begins, ends #20	4	12	42
11-20	3	9	32
21-31: 21,22-r	3	9	24
32(Whitman, 8/82)-r	2	6	14

MIGHTY THOR (See Thor)

MILK AND CHEESE (Also see Cerebus Bi-Weekly #20)

	GD	FN	NM-

Slave Labor: 1991 - Present ($2.50, B&W)

1-Evan Dorkin story & art in all	4	12	50
1-2nd-6th printings			4.00
2-"Other #1"	3	9	30
2-reprint			3.00
3-"Third #1"	2	6	20
4-"Fourth #1", 5-"First Second Issue"	1	4	10
6,7: 6-"#666"			5.00

NOTE: *Multiple printings of all issues exist and are worth cover price unless listed here.*

MIRACLEMAN

Eclipse Comics: Aug, 1985 - No. 15, Nov, 1988; No. 16, Dec, 1989 - No. 24, 1994

1-r/British Marvelman series; Alan Moore scripts in #1-16			
	1	3	9
1-Gold variant (edition of 400, signed by Alan Moore, came with signed & #'d certificate of authenticity)			1500.00
1-Blue variant (edition of 600, came with signed certificate of authenticity)			
			800.00
2-12: 8-Airboy preview. 9,10-Origin Miracleman. 9-Shows graphic scenes of childbirth. 10-Snyder-c	1	3	8
13,14	2	6	15
15-($1.75-c, scarce) end of Kid Miracleman	6	18	70
16-Last Alan Moore-s; 1st $1.95-c (low print)	2	6	22
17,18-($1.95): 17-"The Golden Age" begins, ends #22. Dave McKean-c begins, end #22; Neil Gaiman scripts in #17-24	2	6	14
19-23-($2.50); 23-"The Silver Age" begins; BWS-c	1	3	9
24-Last issue; B. Smith-c	2	6	15
3-D 1 (12/85)	1	3	8
Book One: A Dream of Flying (1988, $9.95, TPB) r/#1-5; Leach-c			22.00
Book One: A Dream of Flying-Hardcover (1988, $29.95) r/#1-5			70.00
Book Two: The Red King Syndrome (1990, $12.95, TPB) r/#6-10; Bolton-c			
			22.00
Book Two: The Red King Syndrome-Hardcover (1990, $30.95) r/#6-10			85.00
Book Three: Olympus (1990, $12.95, TPB) r/#11-16			100.00
Book Three: Olympus-Hardcover (1990, $30.95) r/#11-16			200.00
Book Four: The Golden Age (1992, $15.95, TPB) r/#17-22			30.00
Book Four: The Golden Age Hardcover (1992, $33.95) r/#17-22			50.00
Book Four: The Golden Age (1993, $12.99, TPB) new McKean-c			15.00

NOTE: **Chaykin** *c-3.* **Gulacy** *c-7.* **McKean** *c-17-22.* **B. Smith** *c-23, 24.* **Starlin** *c-4.* **Totleben** *a-11-13; c-9, 11-13.* **Truman** *c-6.*

MIRACLEMAN: APOCRYPHA

Eclipse Comics: Nov, 1991 - No. 3, Feb, 1992 ($2.50, limited series)

1-3: 1-Stories by Neil Gaiman, Mark Buckingham, Alex Ross & others. 3-Stories by James Robinson, Kelley Jones, Matt Wagner, Neil Gaiman, Mark Buckingham & others	1	3	7
TPB (12/92, $15.95) r/#1-3; Buckingham-c			20.00

MIRACLEMAN FAMILY

Eclipse Comics: May, 1988 - No. 2, Sept, 1988 ($1.95, lim. series, Baxter

	GD	FN	NM-

paper)

1,2: 2-Gulacy-c			5.00

MR. & MRS. J. EVIL SCIENTIST (TV)(See The Flintstones & Hanna-Barbera Band Wagon #3)
Gold Key: Nov, 1963 - No. 4, Sept, 1966 (Hanna-Barbera, all 12¢)

1	9	27	120
2-4	6	18	75

MISTER ED, THE TALKING HORSE (TV)
Dell Publishing Co./Gold Key: Mar-May, 1962 - No. 6, Feb, 1964 (All photo-c; photo back-c: 1-6)

Four Color 1295	14	42	210
1(11/62) (Gold Key)-Photo-c	10	30	140
2-6: Photo-c	7	21	80

MISTER MIRACLE (1st series) (See Cancelled Comic Cavalcade)
National Periodical Publications/DC Comics: 3-4/71 - V4#18, 2-3/74; V5#19, 9/77 - V6#25, 8-9/78; 1987 (Fourth World)

1-1st app. Mr. Miracle (#1-3 are 15¢)	8	24	95
2,3: 2-Intro. Granny Goodness. 3-Last 15¢ issue	4	12	50
4-8: 4-Intro. Barda; Boy Commandos-r begin; all 52 pgs.	4	12	50
9-18: 9-Origin Mr. Miracle; Darkseid cameo. 15-Intro/1st app. Shilo Norman. 18-Barda & Scott Free wed; New Gods app. & Darkseid cameo; Last Kirby issue.	3	9	24
19-25 (1977-78)	1	3	9
Special 1(1987, $1.25, 52 pgs.)			3.00
Jack Kirby's Fourth World TPB ('01, $12.95) B&W&Grey-toned reprint of #11-18; Mark Evanier intro.			13.00
Jack Kirby's Mister Miracle TPB ('98, $12.95) B&W&Grey-toned reprint of #1-10; David Copperfield intro.			13.00

MOD SQUAD (TV)
Dell Publishing Co.: Jan, 1969 - No. 3, Oct, 1969 - No. 8, April, 1971

1-Photo-c	8	24	95
2-4: 2-4-Photo-c	5	15	55
5-8: 8-Photo-c; Reprints #2	4	12	45

MOMENT OF SILENCE
Marvel Comics: Feb, 2002 ($3.50, one-shot)

1-Tributes to the heroes and victims of Sept. 11; s/a by various			3.50

MONKEES, THE (TV)(Also see Circus Boy, Groovy, Not Brand Echh #3, Teen-Age Talk, Teen Beam & Teen Beat)
Dell Publishing Co.: March, 1967 - No. 17, Oct, 1969

1-Photo-c	11	33	160
2-17: All photo-c. 17-Reprints #1	7	21	90

MONSTERS ON THE PROWL (Chamber of Darkness #1-8)
Marvel Comics Group (No. 13,14: 52 pgs.): No. 9, 2/71 - No. 27, 11/73; No. 28, 6/74 - No. 30, 10/74

	GD	FN	NM-
9-Barry Smith inks	4	12	38
10-12,15: 12-Last 15¢ issue	2	6	22
13,14-(52 pgs.)	3	9	28
16-(4/72)-King Kull 4th app.; Severin-c	3	9	25
17-30	2	6	18

MONSTERS UNLEASHED (Magazine)
Marvel Comics Group: July, 1973 - No. 11, Apr, 1975; Summer, 1975 (B&W)

1-Soloman Kane sty; Werewolf app.	4	12	42
2-4: 2-The Frankenstein Monster begins, ends #10. 3-Neal Adams-c/a; The Man-Thing begins (origin-r); Son of Satan preview. 4-Werewolf app.			
	3	10	35
5-7: Werewolf in all. 5-Man-Thing. 7-Williamson-a(r)	3	9	25
8-11: 8-Man-Thing; N. Adams-r. 9-Man-Thing; Wendigo app. 10-Origin Tigra			
	3	9	28
Annual 1 (Summer,1975, 92 pgs.)-Kane-a	3	9	25

MOONSHADOW (Also see Farewell, Moonshadow)
Marvel Comics (Epic Comics): 5/85 - #12, 2/87 ($1.50/$1.75, mature) (1st fully painted comic book)

1-Origin; J. M. DeMatteis scripts & Jon J. Muth painted-c/a.			6.00
2-12: 11-Origin			4.00
Trade paperback (1987?)-r/#1-12			14.00
Signed & numbered hard-c ($39.95, 1,200 copies)-r/#1-12			
	5	15	60

MS. MARVEL (Also see The Avengers #183)
Marvel Comics Group: Jan, 1977 - No. 23, Apr, 1979

1-1st app. Ms. Marvel; Scorpion app. in #1,2	2	6	12
2-10: 2-Origin. 5-Vision app. 6-10-(Reg. 30¢-c). 10-Last 30¢ issue			6.00
6-10-(35¢-c variants, limited dist.)(6/77)	1	3	9
11-15,19-23: 19-Capt. Marvel app. 20-New costume. 23-Vance Astro (leader of the Guardians) app.			5.00
16,17-1st brief app. Mystique	2	6	15
18-1st full app. Mystique; Avengers x-over	3	9	25

MUNSTERS, THE (TV)
Gold Key: Jan, 1965 - No. 16, Jan, 1968 (All photo-c)

1 (10134-501)	20	60	290
2	11	33	145
3-5	9	27	120
6-16	8	24	100

MY FAVORITE MARTIAN (TV)
Gold Key: 1/64; No.2, 7/64 - No. 9, 10/66 (No. 1,3-9 have photo-c)

1-Russ Manning-a	14	42	200
2	8	24	100
3-9	7	21	90

MY GREATEST ADVENTURE (Doom Patrol #86 on)
National Periodical Publications: Jan-Feb, 1955 - No. 85, Feb, 1964

	GD	FN	NM-
1-Before CCA	130	390	2200
2	50	150	850
3-5	36	108	575
6-10: 6-Science fiction format begins	31	93	475
11-14: 12-1st S.A. issue	23	69	340
15-17: Kirby in all	25	75	370
18-Kirby-c/a	29	87	425
19,22-25	19	57	280
20,21,28-Kirby-a	23	69	340
26,27,29,30	14	42	200
31-40	12	36	170
41,42,44-57,59	10	30	135
43-Kirby-a	11	33	150
58,60,61-Toth-a; Last 10¢ issue	10	30	140
62-76,78,79: 79-Promotes "Legion of the Strange" for next issue; renamed Doom Patrol for #80	8	24	95
77-Toth-a; Robotman prototype	8	24	100
80-(6/63)-Intro/origin Doom Patrol and begin series; origin & 1st app. Negative Man, Elasti-Girl & S.A. Robotman	45	135	775
81,85-Toth-a	18	54	265
82-84	16	48	240

MYSTERY IN SPACE (Also see Fireside Book Series and Pulp Fiction Library: ...)
National Periodical Pub.: 4-5/51 - No. 110, 9/66; No. 111, 9/80 - No. 117, 3/81 (#1-3: 52 pgs.)

	GD	FN	NM-
1-Frazetta-a, 8 pgs.; Knights of the Galaxy begins, ends #8	229	687	4800
2	89	267	1700
3	71	213	1350
4,5	59	177	1125
6-10: 7-Toth-a	48	144	825
11-15	38	114	600
16-18,20-25: Interplanetary Insurance feature by Infantino in all. 21-1st app. Space Cabbie. 24-Last pre-code issue	33	99	525
19-Virgil Finlay-a	36	108	585
26-40: 26-Space Cabbie feature begins. 34-1st S.A. issue	29	87	435
41-52: 47-Space Cabbie feature ends	22	66	325
53-Adam Strange begins (8/59, 10pg. sty); robot-c	153	459	2900
54	45	135	775
55-Grey tone-c	38	114	600
56-60: 59-Kane/Anderson-a	23	69	335
61-71: 61-1st app. Adam Strange foe Ulthoon. 62-1st app. A.S. foe Mortan. 63-Origin Vandor. 66-Star Rovers begin (1st app.). 68-1st app. Dust Devils (6/61). 69-1st Mailbag. 70-2nd app. Dust Devils. 71-Last 10¢ issue	18	54	260
72-74,76-80	12	36	180
75-JLA x-over in Adam Strange (5/62)(sequel to J.L.A. #3)	25	75	375

	GD	FN	NM-
81-86	11	33	145
87-(11/63)-Adam Strange/Hawkman double feat begins; 3rd Hawkman tryout series	19	57	280
88-Adam Strange & Hawkman stories	17	51	250
89-Adam Strange & Hawkman stories	16	48	240
90-Adam Strange & Hawkman team-up for 1st time (3/64); Hawkman moves to own title next month	19	57	275
91-102: 91-End Infantino art on Adam Strange; double-length Adam Strange story. 92-Space Ranger begins (6/64), ends #103. 92-94,96,98-Space Ranger-c. 94,98-Adam Strange/Space Ranger team-up. 102-Adam Strange ends (no Space Ranger)	7	21	80
103-Origin Ultra, the Multi-Alien; last Space Ranger	6	18	75
104-110: 110-(9/66)-Last 12¢ issue	5	15	55
V17#111(9/80)-117: 117-Newton-a(3 pgs.)	1	4	10

MYSTIQUE (See X-Men titles)
Marvel Comics: June, 2003 - Present ($2.99)

1-21: 1-6-Linsner-c/Vaughan-s/Lucas-a. 7-Ryan-a begins. 8-Horn-c. 9-21-Mayhew-c	3.00
... Vol. 1: Drop Dead Gorgeous TPB (2004, $14.99) r/#1-6	15.00
... Vol. 2: Tinker, Tailor, Mutant, Spy TPB (2004, $17.99) r/#7-13	18.00

'NAM, THE (See Savage Tales #1, 2nd series & Punisher Invades...)
Marvel Comics Group: Dec, 1986 - No. 84, Sept, 1993

1-Golden a(p)/c begins, ends #13	3.00
1 (2nd printing)	2.25
2-8,10-66,70-74: 7-Golden-a (2 pgs.). 32-Death R. Kennedy. 52,53-Frank Castle (The Punisher) app. 52,53-Gold 2nd printings. 58-Silver logo. 65-Heath-c/a. 70-Lomax scripts begin	2.25
9-1st app. Fudd Verzyl, Tunnel Rat	3.00
67-69,76-84: 67-69-Punisher 3 part story	3.00
75-($2.25, 52 pgs.)	2.50
Trade Paperback 1,2: 1-r/#1-4. 2-r/#5-8	5.00
TPB ('99, $14.95) r/#1-4; recolored	15.00

NAMOR, THE SUB-MARINER (See Prince Namor & Sub-Mariner)
Marvel Comics: Apr, 1990 - No. 62, May, 1995 ($1.00/$1.25/$1.50)

1-Byrne-c/a/scripts in 1-25 (scripts only #26-32)	4.00
2-5: 5-Iron Man app.	3.00
6-11,13-23,25,27-49,51-62: 16-Re-intro Iron Fist (8-cameo only). 18-Punisher cameo (1 panel); 21-23,25-Wolverine cameos. 22,23-Iron Fist app. 28-Iron Fist-c/story. 31-Dr. Doom-c/story. 33,34-Iron Fist cameo. 35-New Tiger Shark-c/story. 37-Aqua holografx foil-c. 48-The Thing app.	2.25
12,24: 12-(52pgs.)-Re-intro. The Invaders. 24-Namor vs. Wolverine	2.50
26-Namor w/new costume; 1st Jae Lee-c/a this title (5/92) & begins	3.00
50-($1.75, 52 pgs.)-Newsstand ed.; w/bound-in S-M trading card sheet (both versions)	2.25
50-($2.95, 52 pgs.)-Collector edition w/foil-c	3.00
Annual 1-4 ('91-'94, 68 pgs.): 1-3 pg. origin recap. 2-Return/Defenders.	

	GD	FN	NM-

3-Bagged w/card. 4-Painted-c   3.00

NEW ADVENTURES OF SUPERBOY, THE (Also see Superboy)
DC Comics: Jan, 1980 - No. 54, June, 1984

1			5.00
2-6,8-10			4.00

11-49,51-54: 11-Superboy gets new power. 14-Lex Luthor app. 15-Superboy
gets new parents. 28-Dial "H" For Hero begins, ends #49. 45-47-1st app.
Sunburst. 48-Begin 75¢-c   3.00

1,2,5,6,8 (Whitman variants; low print run; no issue # shown on cover)

		1	3	7

7,50: 7-Has extra story "The Computers That Saved Metropolis" by Starlin
(Radio Shack giveaway w/indicia). 50-Legion app.   5.00

NEW AVENGERS, THE
Marvel Comics: Jan, 2005 - Present ($2.25)

1-Bendis-s/Finch-a; Spider-Man app.; re-intro The Sentry; 4 covers by
McNiven, Quesada & Finch; variants from #1-6 combine for one team
image   3.00
1-Director's Cut ($3.99) includes alternate covers; script, villain gallery 4.00
2-6: Finch-a. 5-Wolverine app.   2.25

NEW GODS, THE (1st Series)(New Gods #12 on)(See Adventure #459, DC
Graphic Novel #4, 1st Issue Special #13 & Super-Team Family)
National Periodical Publications/DC Comics: 2-3/71 - V2#11, 10-11/72;
V3#12, 7/77 - V3#19, 7-8/78 (Fourth World)

	GD	FN	NM-
1-Intro/1st app. Orion; 4th app. Darkseid (cameo; 3 weeks after Forever People #1) (#1-3 are 15¢ issues)	10	30	130
2-Darkseid-c/story (2nd full app., 4-5/71)	6	18	65
3-1st app. Black Racer; last 15¢ issue	4	12	45
4-9: (25¢, 52 pg. giants): 4-Darkseid cameo; origin Manhunter-r. 5,7,8-Young Gods feature. 7-Darkseid app. (2-3/72); origin Orion; 1st origin of all New Gods as a group. 9-1st app. Forager	4	12	45
10,11: 11-Last Kirby issue.	3	9	30
12-19: Darkseid storyline w/minor apps. 12-New costume Orion (see 1st Issue Special #13 for 1st new costume). 19-Story continued in Adventure Comics #459,460	1	3	9

Jack Kirby's New Gods TPB ('98, $11.95, B&W&Grey) r/#1-11 plus cover
gallery of original series and "84 reprints   12.00

NEW GODS (Also see DC Graphic Novel #4)
DC Comics: June, 1984 - No. 6, Nov, 1984 ($2.00, Baxter paper)

1-5: New Kirby-c; r/New Gods #1-10.   4.00

6-Reprints New Gods #11 w/48 pgs of new Kirby story & art; leads into DC Graphic Novel #4	2	6	12

NEW MUTANTS, THE (See Marvel Graphic Novel #4 for 1st app.)(Also see
X-Force & Uncanny X-Men #167)
Marvel Comics Group: Mar, 1983 - No. 100, Apr, 1991

1			5.00
2-10: 3,4-Ties into X-Men #167. 10-1st app. Magma			3.00

	GD	FN	NM-

11-17,19,20: 13-Kitty Pryde app. 16-1st app. Warpath (w/out costume); see
   X-Men #193   2.50
18,21: 18-Intro. new Warlock. 21-Double size; origin new Warlock; newsstand
   version has cover price written in by Sienkiewicz   3.00
22-24,27-30: 23-25-Cloak & Dagger app.   2.50
25,26: 25-1st brief app. Legion. 26-1st full Legion app.   4.00
31-58: 35-Magneto intro'd as new headmaster. 43-Portacio-i. 50-Double size.
   58-Contains pull-out mutant registration form   2.50
59-61: Fall of The Mutants series. 60(52 pgs.)   3.00
62-85: 68-Intro Spyder. 63-X-Men & Wolverine clones app. 73-(52 pgs.).
   76-X-Factor & X-Terminator app. 85-Liefeld-c begin   2.50
86-Rob Liefeld-a begins; McFarlane-c(i) swiped from Ditko splash pg.; 1st
   brief app. Cable (last page teaser)   6.00
87-1st full app. Cable (3/90)   2   6   20
87-2nd printing; gold metallic ink-c ($1.00)   2.50
88-2nd app. Cable   1   3   7
92-No Liefeld-a; Liefeld-c   4.00
89,90,91,93-100: 89-3rd app. Cable. 90-New costumes. 90,91-Sabretooth
   app. 93,94-Cable vs. Wolverine. 95-97-X-Tinction Agenda x-over. 95-Death
   of new Warlock. 97-Wolverine & Cable-c, but no app. 98-1st app.
   Deadpool, Gideon & Domino (2/91); 2nd Shatterstar (cameo). 99-1st app.
   of Feral (of X-Force); Byrne-c/swipe (X-Men, 1st Series #138). 100-(52
   pgs.)-1st brief app. X-Force.   5.00
  95,100-Gold 2nd printing. 100-Silver ink 3rd printing   2.50
Annual 1 (1984)   4.00
Annual 2 (1986, $1.25)-1st Psylocke   1   3   8
Annual 3,4,6,7 ('87, '88,'90,'91, 68 pgs.): 4-Evolutionary War x-over.
   6-1st new costumes by Liefeld (3 pgs.); 1st brief app. Shatterstar (of
   X-Force). 7-Liefeld pin-up only; X-Terminators back-up story; 2nd app.
   X-Force (cont'd in New Warriors Annual #1)   3.00
Annual 5 (1989, $2.00, 68 pgs.)-Atlantis Attacks; 1st Liefeld-a on New
   Mutants   4.00
Special 1-Special Edition ('85, 68 pgs.)-Ties in w/X-Men Alpha Flight limited
   series; cont'd in X-Men Annual #9; Art Adams/Austin-a   5.00
Summer Special 1(Sum/90, $2.95, 84 pgs.)   3.00

NEW MUTANTS (Continues as New X-Men (Academy X))
Marvel Comics: July, 2003 - No. 13, June, 2004 ($2.50/$2.99)

1-7: 1-6-Josh Middleton-c. 7-Bachalo-c   2.50
8-13 ($2.99) 8-11-Bachalo-c   3.00

NEW TEEN TITANS, THE (See DC Comics Presents #26, Marvel and DC
Present & Teen Titans; Tales of the Teen Titans #41 on)
DC Comics: Nov, 1980 - No. 40, Mar, 1984

1-Robin, Kid Flash, Wonder Girl, The Changeling (1st app.), Starfire, The
   Raven, Cyborg begin; partial origin   1   4   10
2-1st app. Deathstroke the Terminator   6.00
3-10: 3-Origin Starfire; Intro The Fearsome Five. 4-Origin continues; J.L.A.
   app. 6-Origin Raven. 7-Cyborg origin. 8-Origin Kid Flash retold. 9-Minor
   app. Deathstroke on last pg. 10-2nd app. Deathstroke the Terminator (see

	GD	FN	NM-

Marvel & DC Present for 3rd app.); origin Changeling retold   5.00
11-40: 13-Return of Madame Rouge & Capt. Zahl; Robotman revived.
  14-Return of Mento; origin Doom Patrol. 15-Death of Madame Rouge &
  Capt. Zahl; intro. new Brotherhood of Evil. 16-1st app. Captain Carrot
  (free 16 pg. preview). 18-Return of Starfire. 19-Hawkman teams-up.
  21-Intro Night Force in free 16 pg. insert; intro Brother Blood. 23-1st app.
  Vigilante (not in costume), & Blackfire. 24-Omega Men app. 25-Omega
  Men cameo; free 16 pg. preview Masters of the Universe. 26-1st app.
  Terra. 27-Free 16 pg. preview Atari Force. 29-The New Brotherhood of Evil
  & Speedy app. 30-Terra joins the Titans. 34-4th app. Deathstroke the
  Terminator. 37-Batman & The Outsiders x-over. 38-Origin Wonder Girl.
  39-Last Dick Grayson as Robin; Kid Flash quits   3.00
Annual 1(11/82)-Omega Men app.   4.00
Annual V2#2(9/83)-1st app. Vigilante in costume   3.50
Annual 3 (See Tales of the Teen Titans Annual #3)
...: The Judas Contract TPB (2003, $19.95) r/#39,40 plus Tales of the Teen
  Titans #41-44 & Annual #3   20.00

NEW TEEN TITANS, THE (Becomes The New Titans #50 on)
DC Comics: Aug, 1984 - No. 49, Nov, 1988 ($1.25/$1.75; deluxe format)

1-New storyline; Perez-c/a begins   5.00
2,3: 2-Re-intro Lilith   4.00
4-10: 5-Death of Trigon. 7-9-Origin Lilith. 8-Intro Kole. 10-Kole joins   3.00
11-49: 13,14-Crisis x-over. 20-Robin (Jason Todd) joins; original Teen Titans
  return. 38-Infinity, Inc. x-over. 47-Origin of all Titans; Titans (East & West)
  pin-up by Perez   2.50
Annual 1-4 (9/85-'88): 1-Intro. Vanguard. 2-Byrne c/a(p); origin Brother Blood;
  intro new Dr. Light. 3-Intro. Danny Chase. 4-Perez-c   3.00
...: The Terror of Trigon TPB (2003, $17.95) r/#1-5; new cover by Phil Jimenez
     18.00

NEW TITANS, THE (Formerly The New Teen Titans)
DC Comics: No. 50, Dec, 1988 - No. 130, Feb, 1996 ($1.75/$2.25)

50-Perez-c/a begins; new origin Wonder Girl   6.00
51-59: 50-55-Painted-c. 55-Nightwing (Dick Grayson) forces Danny Chase to
  resign; Batman app. in flashback, Wonder Girl becomes Troia   3.00
60,61: 60-A Lonely Place of Dying Part 2 continues from Batman #440; new
  Robin tie-in; Timothy Drake app. 61-A Lonely Place of Dying Part 4   3.00
62-99,101-124,126-130: 62-65: 62-65: Deathstroke the Terminator app. 65-Tim
  Drake (Robin) app. 70-1st Deathstroke solo cover/sty. 71-(44 pgs.)-10th
  anniversary issue; Deathstroke cameo. 72-79-Deathstroke in all: 74-Intro.
  Pantha. 79-Terra brought back to life; 1 panel cameo Team Titans (1st
  app.). Deathstroke in #80-84,86. 80 'nd full app. Team Titans. 83,84-
  Deathstroke kills his son, Jericho. 85-Team Titans app. 86-Deathstroke vs.
  Nightwing-c/story; last Deathstroke app. 87-New costume Nightwing.
  90-92-Parts 2,5,8 Total Chaos (Team Titans). 115-(11/94)   2.50
100-($3.50, 52 pgs.)-Holo-grafx foil-c   3.50
125 (3.50)-wraparound-c   3.50
#0-(10/94) Zero Hour, released between #114 & 115   2.50
Annual 5-10 ('89-'94, 68 pgs.. 7-Armaggedon 2001 x-over; 1st full app. Teen

	GD	FN	NM-
(Team) Titans (new group). 8-Deathstroke app.; Eclipso app. (minor). 10-Elseworlds story			3.50
Annual 11 (1995, $3.95)-Year One story			4.00

NEW WARRIORS, THE (See Thor #411,412)
Marvel Comics: July, 1990 - No. 75, 1996 ($1.00/$1.25/$1.50)

1-Williamson-i; Bagley-c/a(p) in 1-13, Annual 1			5.00
1-Gold 2nd printing (7/91)			2.25
2-5: 1,3-Guice-c(i). 2-Williamson-c/a(i).			3.00
6-24,26-49,51-75: 7-Punisher cameo (last pg.). 8,9-Punisher app. 14-Darkhawk & Namor x-over. 17-Fantastic Four & Silver Surfer x-over. 19-Gideon (of X-Force) app. 28-Intro Turbo & Cardinal. 31-Cannonball & Warpath app. 42-Nova vs. Firelord. 46-Photo-c. 47-Bound-in S-M trading card sheet. 52-12 pg. ad insert. 62-Scarlet Spider-c/app. 70-Spider-Man-c/app. 72-Avengers-c/app.			2.25
25-($2.50, 52 pgs.)-Die-cut cover			2.50
40,60: 40-($2.25)-Gold foil collector's edition			2.50
50-($2.95, 52 pgs.)-Glow in the dark-c			3.00
Annual 1-4('91-'94,68 pgs.)-1-Origins all members; 3rd app. X-Force (cont'd from New Mutants Ann. #7 & cont'd in X-Men Ann. #15); x-over before X-Force #1. 3-Bagged w/card			3.00

NEW X-MEN (See X-Men 2nd series #114-156)

NICK FURY, AGENT OF SHIELD (See Fury, Marvel Spotlight #31 & Shield)
Marvel Comics Group: 6/68 - No. 15, 11/69; No. 16, 11/70 - No. 18, 3/71

1	10	30	140
2-4: 4-Origin retold	6	18	70
5-Classic-c	7	21	80
6,7: 7-Salvador Dali painting swipe	5	15	60
8-11,13: 9-Hate Monger begins, ends #11. 10-Smith layouts/pencil. 11-Smith-c. 13-1st app. Super-Patriot; last 12¢ issue	3	10	35
12-Smith-c/a	4	12	38
14-Begin 15¢ issues	3	9	30
15-1st app. & death of Bullseye-c/story(11/69); Nick Fury shot & killed; last 15¢ issue	7	21	85
16-18-(25¢, 52 pgs.)-r/Str. Tales #135-143	3	9	26
TPB (May 2000, $19.95) r/ Strange Tales #150-168			20.00
...: Who is Scorpio? TPB (11/00, $12.95) r/#1-3,5; Steranko-c			13.00

NIGHT NURSE
Marvel Comics Group: Nov, 1972 - No. 4, May, 1973

1	11	33	160
2-4	8	24	105

NIGHTWING (Also see New Teen Titans, New Titans, Showcase '93 #11,12, Tales of the New Teen Titans & Teen Titans Spotlight)
DC Comics: Sept, 1995 - No. 4, Dec, 1995 ($2.25, limited series)

1-Dennis O'Neil story/Greg Land-a in all			5.00
2-4			4.00

	GD	FN	NM-
...: Alfred's Return (7/95, $3.50) Giordano-a			4.00
...Ties That Bind (1997, $12.95, TPB) r/mini-series & Alfred's Return			13.00

NIGHTWING
DC Comics: Oct, 1996 - Present ($1.95/$1.99/$2.25)

	GD	FN	NM-
1-Chuck Dixon scripts & Scott McDaniel-c/a	2	6	12
2,3			6.00
4-10: 6-Robin-c/app.			4.00
11-20: 13-15-Batman app. 19,20-Cataclysm pts. 2,11			3.00
21-49,51-64: 23-Green Arrow app. 26-29-Huntress-c/app. 30-Superman-c/app. 35-39-No Man's Land. 41-Land/Geraci-a begins. 46-Begin $2.25-c. 47-Texiera-c. 52-Catwoman-c/app. 54-Shrike app.			2.50
50-($3.50) Nightwing battles Torque			3.50
65-74,76-99: 65,66-Bruce Wayne: Murderer x-over pt. 3,9. 68,69: B.W.: Fugitive pt. 6,9. 70-Last Dixon-s. 71-Devin Grayson-s begin. 81-Batgirl vs. Deathstroke. 93-Blockbuster killed. 94-Copperhead app. 96-Bagged w/CD. 96-98-War Games			2.50
75-(1/03, $2.95) Intro. Tarantula			3.00
100-(2/05, $2.95) Tarantula app.			3.00
#1,000,000 (11/98) teams with future Batman			2.25
Annual 1(1997, $3.95) Pulp Heroes			4.00
...Eighty Page Giant 1 (12/00, $5.95) Intro. of Hella; Dixon-s/Haley-c			6.00
...: Big Guns (2004, $14.95, TPB) r/#47-50; Secret Files 1, Eighty Page Giant 1			15.00
...: A Darker Shade of Justice (2001, $19.95, TPB) r/#30-39,Secret Files #1			20.00
...: A Knight in Blüdhaven (1998, $14.95, TPB) r/#1-8			15.00
...: Love and Bullets (2000, $17.95, TPB) r/#1/2, 19,21,22,24-29			18.00
...: Our Worlds at War (9/01, $2.95) Jae Lee-c			3.00
...: Rough Justice (1999, $17.95, TPB) r/#9-18			18.00
... Secret Files 1 (10/99, $4.95) Origin-s and pin-ups			5.00
...: The Hunt for Oracle (2003, $14.95, TPB) r/#41-46 & Birds of Prey #20,21			15.00
...: The Target (2001, $5.95) McDaniel-c/a			6.00
Wizard 1/2 (Mail offer)			5.00

9-11 - ARTISTS RESPOND
Dark Horse Comics: 2002 ($9.95, TPB, proceeds donated to charities)

	GD	FN	NM-
Volume 1-Short stories about the September 11 tragedies by various Dark Horse, Chaos! and Image writers and artists; Eric Drooker-c			10.00

9-11: EMERGENCY RELIEF
Alternative Comics: 2002 ($14.95, TPB, proceeds donated to the Red Cross)

	GD	FN	NM-
nn-Short stories by various inc. Pekar, Eisner, Oeming, Noto; Cho-c			15.00

9-11 - THE WORLD'S FINEST COMIC BOOK WRITERS AND ARTISTS TELL STORIES TO REMEMBER
DC Comics: 2002 ($9.95, TPB, proceeds donated to charities)

	GD	FN	NM-
Volume 2-Short stories about the September 11 tragedies by various DC, MAD, and WildStorm writers and artists ; Alex Ross-c			10.00

	GD	FN	NM-

NOT BRAND ECHH (Brand Echh #1-4; See Crazy, 1973)
Marvel Comics Group (LMC): Aug, 1967 - No. 13, May, 1969
(1st Marvel parody book)

1: 1-8 are 12¢ issues	7	21	80
2-8: 3-Origin Thor, Hulk & Capt. America; Monkees, Alfred E. Neuman			
cameo. 4-X-Men app. 5-Origin/intro. Forbush Man. 7-Origin Fantastical-4			
& Stuporman. Beatles cameo; X-Men satire; last 12¢-c	4	12	40
9-13 (25¢, 68 pgs., all Giants) 9-Beatles cameo. 10-All-r; The Old Witch,			
Crypt Keeper & Vault Keeper cameos. 12,13-Beatles cameo	5	15	55

NOVA (The Man Called... No. 22-25)(See New Warriors)
Marvel Comics Group: Sept, 1976 - No. 25, May, 1979

1-Origin/1st app. Nova	2	6	18
2-4,12: 4-Thor x-over. 12-Spider-Man x-over	1	3	9
5-11			6.00
10,11-(35¢-c variants, limited distribution)(6,7/77)	2	6	15
12-(35¢-c variant, limited distribution)(8/77)	2	6	20
13,14-(Regular 30¢ editions)(9/77) 13-Intro Crime-Buster.			5.00
13,14-(35¢-c variants, limited distribution)	2	6	15
15-24: 18-Yellow Claw app. 19-Wally West (Kid Flash) cameo			5.00
25-Last issue	1	3	8

NYX
Marvel Comics: Nov, 2003 - No. 5, Sept, 2004 ($2.99)

1,2: 1-Quesada-s/Middleton-a/c; intro. Kiden Nixon			3.00
3-1st app. X-23			4.00
4,5: 5-Teranishi-a			3.00

OCCULT FILES OF DR. SPEKTOR, THE
Gold Key/Whitman No. 25: Apr, 1973 - No. 24, Feb, 1977; No. 25, May, 1982
(Painted-c #1-24)

1-1st app. Lakota; Baron Tibor begins	4	12	48
2-5: 3-Mummy-c/s. 5-Jekyll & Hyde-c/s	2	6	22
6-10: 6,9-Frankenstein. 8,9-Dracula c/s. 9.-Jekyll & Hyde c/s.			
9,10-Mummy-c/s	2	6	16
11-13,15-17,19-22,24: 11-1st app. Spektor as Werewolf. 11-13-Werewolf-c/s.			
12,16-Frankenstein c/s. 17-Zombie/Voodoo-c. 19-Sea monster-c/s.			
20-Mummy-s. 21-Swamp monster-c/s. 24-Dragon-c/s	1	4	10
14-Dr. Solar app.	3	9	24
18,23-Dr. Solar cameo	2	6	15
22-Return of the Owl c/s	2	6	15
25(Whitman, 5/82)-r/#1 with line drawn-c	1	4	10

OMAC (One Man Army; ...Corps. #4 on; also see Kamandi #59 & Warlord)
(See Cancelled Comic Cavalcade)
National Periodical Publications: Sept-Oct, 1974 - No. 8, Nov-Dec, 1975

1-Origin	4	12	50

	GD	FN	NM-
2-8: 8-2 pg. Neal Adams ad	2	6	22

OMAC: ONE MAN ARMY CORPS
DC Comics: 1991 - No. 4, 1991 ($3.95, B&W, mini-series, mature, 52 pgs.)

Book One - Four: John Byrne-c/a & scripts			4.00

OMEGA MEN, THE (See Green Lantern #141)
DC Comics: Dec, 1982 - No. 38, May, 1986 ($1.00/$1.25/$1.50; Baxter paper)

1,20: 20-2nd full Lobo story			3.00
2,4-9,11-19,21-25,28-30,32,33,36,38: 2-Origin Broot. 5,9-2nd & 3rd app. Lobo (cameo, 2 pgs. each). 7-Origin The Citadel. 19-Lobo cameo. 30-Intro new Primus			2.50
3-1st app. Lobo (5 pgs.)(6/83); Lobo-c	1	3	7
10-1st full Lobo story			5.00
26,27,31,34,35: 26,27-Alan Moore scripts. 31-Crisis x-over. 34,35-Teen Titans x-over			3.00
37-1st solo Lobo story (8 pg. back-up by Giffen)			4.00
Annual 1(11/84, 52 pgs.), 2(11/85)			3.00

OMEGA THE UNKNOWN
Marvel Comics Group: March, 1976 - No. 10, Oct, 1977

1-1st app. Omega	2	6	12
2,3-(Regular 25¢ editions). 2-Hulk-c/story. 3-Electro-c/story.			6.00
2,3-(30¢-c variants, limited distribution)	2	6	15
4-10: 8-1st brief app. 2nd Foolkiller (Greg Salinger), 1 panel only.			
9,10-(Reg. 30¢ editions). 9-1st full app. 2nd Foolkiller			6.00
9,10-(35¢-c variants, limited distribution)	2	6	15

100 BULLETS
DC Comics (Vertigo): Aug, 1999 - Present ($2.50)

1-Azzarello-s/Risso-a/Dave Johnson-c	4.00
2-5	3.00
6-49,51-56: 26-Series summary; art by various. 45-Preview of Losers	2.50
50-($3.50) History of the Trust	3.50
...: A Foregone Tomorrow TPB (2002, $17.95) r/#20-30	18.00
...: First Shot, Last Call TPB (2000, $9.95) r/#1-5, Vertigo Winter's Edge #3	10.00
...: Hang Up on the Hang Low TPB (2001, $9.95) r/#15-19; Jim Lee intro.	10.00
...: Samurai TPB (2003, $12.95) r/#43-49	13.00
...: Six Feet Under the Gun TPB (2003, $12.95) r/#37-42	13.00
...: Split Second Chance TPB (2001, $14.95) r/#6-14	15.00
...: The Counterfifth Detective TPB (2003, $12.95) r/#31-36	13.00

100 PAGE SUPER SPECTACULAR (See DC 100 Page Super Spectacular)

ONI DOUBLE FEATURE (See Clerks: The Comic Book and Jay & Silent Bob)
Oni Press: Jan, 1998 - No. 13, Sept, 1999 ($2.95, B&W)

1-Jay & Silent Bob; Kevin Smith-s/Matt Wagner-a	1	4	10
1-2nd printing			3.00
2-11,13: 2,3-Paul Pope-s/a. 3,4-Nixey-s/a. 4,5-Sienkewicz-s/a. 6,7-Gaiman-s.			

	GD	FN	NM-
9-Bagge-c. 13-All Paul Dini-s; Jingle Belle			3.00
12-Jay & Silent Bob as Bluntman & Chronic; Smith-s/Allred-a			5.00

OUR ARMY AT WAR (Becomes Sgt. Rock #302 on; also see Army At War)
National Periodical Publications: Aug, 1952 - No. 301, Feb, 1977

	GD	FN	NM-
1	147	441	2800
2	63	189	1200
3,4: 4-Krigstein-a	50	150	900
5-7	41	123	700
8-11,14-Krigstein-a	41	123	650
12,15-20	33	99	525
13-Krigstein-c/a; flag-c	41	123	675
21-31: Last precode (2/55)	24	72	360
32-40	20	60	300
41-60: 51-1st S.A. issue	16	48	240
61-70: 67-Minor Sgt. Rock prototype	14	42	210
71-80	12	36	175
81- (4/59)-Sgt. <u>Rocky</u> of Easy Co. app. by Andru & Esposito-a/ Haney-s; (the last Sgt. Rock prototype)	200	600	4000
82-1st Sgt. Rock app., in name only, in Easy Co. story (6 panels) by Kanigher & Drucker	50	150	900
83-(6/59)-1st true Sgt. Rock app. in "The Rock and the Wall" by Kubert & Kanigher; (most similar to prototype in G.I. Combat #68)	160	480	3200
84-Kubert-c	30	90	440
85-Origin & 1st app. Ice Cream Soldier	38	114	600
86,87-Early Sgt. Rock; Kubert-a	28	84	420
88-1st Sgt. Rock-c; Kubert-c/a	31	93	475
89	25	75	375
90-Kubert-c/a; How Rock got his stripes	32	96	500
91-All-Sgt. Rock issue; Grandenetti-c/Kubert-a	58	174	1100
92,94,96-99: 97-Regular Kubert-c begin	18	54	260
93-1st Zack Nolan	18	54	270
95,100: 95-1st app. Bulldozer	19	57	285
101,105,108,113,115: 101-1st app. Buster. 105-1st app. Junior. 113-1st app. Wildman & Jackie Johnson. 115-Rock revealed as orphan; 1st x-over Mlle. Marie. 1st Sgt. Rock's battle family	14	42	200
102-104,106,107,109,110,114,116-120: 104-Nurse Jane-c/s. 109-Pre Easy Co. Sgt. Rock-s. 118-Sunny injured	12	36	175
111-1st app. Wee Willie & Sunny	15	45	225
112-Classic Easy Co. roster-c	16	48	240
121-125,130-133,135-139,141-150: 138-1st Sparrow. 141-1st Shaker. 147,148-Rock becomes a General	9	27	120
126,129,134: 126-1st app. Canary; grey tone-c	10	30	130
127-2nd all-Sgt. Rock issue; 1st app. Little Sure	11	33	150
128-Training & origin Sgt. Rock; 1st Sgt. Krupp	25	75	375
140-3rd all-Sgt. Rock issue	10	30	130
151-Intro. Enemy Ace by Kubert (2/65), black-c	38	114	600
152-4th all-Sgt. Rock issue	10	30	130
153-2nd app. Enemy Ace (4/65)	18	54	270

	GD	FN	NM-
154,156,157,159-161,165-167: 157-2 pg. pin-up: 159-1st Nurse Wendy			
Winston-c/s. 165-2nd Iron Major	8	24	100
155-3rd app. Enemy Ace (6/65)(see Showcase)	12	36	180
158-Origin & 1st app. Iron Major(9/65), formerly Iron Captain			
	9	27	120
162,163-Viking Prince x-over in Sgt. Rock	9	27	115
164-Giant G-19	14	42	200
168-1st Unknown Soldier app.; referenced in Star-Spangled War Stories			
#157; (Sgt. Rock x-over) (6/66)	12	36	180
169,170	7	21	90
171-176,178-181: 171-1st Mad Emperor	7	21	80
177-(80 pg. Giant G-32)	10	30	130
182,183,186-Neal Adams-a. 186-Origin retold	7	21	90
184-Wee Willie dies	8	24	100
185,187,188,193-195,197-199	6	18	65
189,191,192,196: 189-Intro. The Teen-age Underground Fighters of Unit 3.			
196-Hitler cameo	6	18	70
190-(80 pg. Giant G-44)	8	24	100
200-12 pg. Rock story told in verse; Evans-a	6	18	75
201,202,204-207: 201-Krigstein-r/#14. 204,205-All reprints; no Sgt. Rock.			
207-Last 12¢ cover	4	12	45
203-(80 pg. Giant G-56)-All-r, Sgt. Rock story	7	21	85
208-215	3	10	35
216,229-(80 pg. Giants G-68, G-80): 216-Has G-58 on-c by mistake			
	6	18	75
217-219: 218-1st U.S.S. Stevens	3	9	30
220-Classic dinosaur/Sgt. Rock-c/s	3	10	35
221-228,230-234: 231-Intro/death Rock's brother. 234-Last 15¢ issue			
	3	9	24
235-239,241: 52 pg. Giants	3	10	35
240-Neal Adams-a; 52 pg. Giant	4	12	45
242-DC 100 Page Super Spectacular #9	9	27	120
243-246: (All 52 pgs.) 244-No Adams-a	3	9	32
247-250,254-268,270: 247-Joan of Arc	2	6	18
251-253-Return of Iron Major	2	6	22
269,275-(100 pgs.)	4	12	50
271-274,276-279: 273-Crucifixion-c	2	6	16
280-(68 pgs.)-200th app. Sgt. Rock; reprints Our Army at War #81,83			
	3	9	32
281-299,301: 295-Bicentennial cover	2	6	15
300-Sgt. Rock-s by Kubert (2/77)	2	6	18

OUR FIGHTING FORCES
National Per. Publ./DC Comics: Oct-Nov, 1954 - No. 181, Sept-Oct, 1978

	GD	FN	NM-
1-Grandenetti-c/a	92	276	1750
2	41	123	700
3-Kubert-c; last precode issue (3/55)	36	108	575
4,5	30	90	450
6-9: 7-1st S.A. issue	25	75	375
10-Wood-a	26	78	385

	GD	FN	NM-
11-19	20	60	300
20-Grey tone-c (4/57)	23	69	340
21-30	14	42	210
31-40	13	39	185
41-Unknown Soldier tryout	16	48	240
42-44	12	36	165
45-Gunner & Sarge begins, end #94	38	114	600
46	16	48	240
47	12	36	170
48,50	11	33	150
49-1st Pooch	14	42	200
51-Grey tone-c	10	30	135
52-64: 64-Last 10¢ issue	9	27	115
65-70	7	21	85
71-Grey tone-c	7	21	80
72-80	6	18	65
81-90	5	15	60
91-98: 95-Devil-Dog begins, ends #98.	4	12	45
99-Capt. Hunter begins, ends #106	4	12	50
100	4	12	48
101-105,107-120: 116-Mlle. Marie app. 120-Last 12¢ issue			
	3	10	35
106-Hunters Hellcats begin	4	12	38
121,122: 121-Intro. Heller	3	9	30
123-The Losers (Capt. Storm, Gunner & Sarge, Johnny Cloud) begin			
	6	18	75
124-132: 132-Last 15¢ issue	3	9	24
133-137 (Giants). 134-Toth-a	3	9	32
138-145,147-150: 146-Toth-a	2	6	16
146-Classic Toth & Goodwin-a	2	6	20
151-162-Kirby a(p)	2	6	22
163-180	2	6	14
181-Last issue	2	6	16

OUTSIDERS, THE
DC Comics: Nov, 1985 - No. 28, Feb, 1988

1			3.00
2-17			2.25
18-28: 18-26-Batman returns. 21-Intro. Strike Force Kobra; 1st app. Clayface IV. 22-E.C. parody; Orlando-a. 21- 25-Atomic Knight app. 27,28-Millennium tie-ins			2.25
Annual 1 (12/86, $2.50), Special 1 (7/87, $1.50)			2.50

OUTSIDERS
DC Comics: Nov, 1993 - No. 24, Nov, 1995 ($1.75/$1.95/$2.25)

1-11,0,12-24: 1-Alpha; Travis Charest-c. 1-Omega; Travis Charest-c. 5-Atomic Knight app. 8-New Batman-c/story. 11-(9/94)-Zero Hour. 0-(10/94).12-(11/94). 21-Darkseid cameo. 22-New Gods app.			2.25

OUTSIDERS (See Titans/Young Justice: Graduation Day)
DC Comics: Aug, 2003 - Present ($2.50)

	GD	FN	NM-
1-Nightwing, Arsenal, Metamorpho app.; Winick-s/Raney-a			5.00
2-Joker and Grodd app.			3.00
3-18: 3-Joker-c. 5,6-ChrisCross-a. 8-Huntress app. 9,10-Capt. Marvel Jr. app.			
			2.50
... Double Feature (10/03, $4.95) r/#1,2			5.00
...: Looking For Trouble TPB (2004, $12.95) r/#1-7 & Teen Titans/Outsiders			
Secret Files & Origins 2003; intro. by Winick			13.00
...: Sum of All Evil TPB (2004, $14.95) r/#8-15			15.00

PARADISE X (Also see Earth X and Universe X)
Marvel Comics: Apr, 2002 - No. 11, July, 2003 ($4.50/$2.99)

0-Ross-c; Braithwaite-a			4.50
1-11-($2.99) Ross-c; Braithwaite-a. 7-Punisher on-c. 10-Kingpin on-c			3.00
...:A (10/03, $2.99) Braithwaite-a; Ross-c			3.00
...:Devils (11/02, $4.50) Sadowski-a; Ross-c			4.50
...:Ragnarok 1,2 (3/02, 4/03; $2.99) Yeates-a; Ross-c			3.00
...:X (11/03, $2.99) Braithwaite-a; Ross-c; conclusion of story			3.00
...:Xen (7/02, $4.50) Yeowell & Sienkiewicz-a; Ross-c			4.50
Earth X Vol. 4: Paradise X Book 1 (2003, $29.99, TPB) r/#0,1-5, ...: Xen;			
Heralds #1-3			30.00
Vol. 5: Paradise X Book 2 (2004, $29.99, TPB) r/#6-12, Ragnarok #1&2;			
Devils, A & X			30.00

PARADISE X: HERALDS (Also see Earth X and Universe X)
Marvel Comics: Dec, 2001 - No. 3, Feb, 2002 ($3.50)

1-3-Prelude to Paradise X series; Ross-c; Pugh-a			3.50
Special Edition (Wizard preview) Ross-c			2.25

PARALLAX: EMERALD NIGHT (See Final Night)
DC Comics: Nov, 1996 ($2.95, one-shot, 48 pgs.)

1-Final Night tie-in; Green Lantern (Kyle Rayner) app.			4.00

PARTRIDGE FAMILY, THE (TV)(Also see David Cassidy)
Charlton Comics: Mar, 1971 - No. 21, Dec, 1973

1	7	21	90
2-4,6-10	4	12	45
5-Partridge Family Summer Special (52 pgs.); The Shadow, Lone Ranger,			
Charlie McCarthy, Flash Gordon, Hopalong Cassidy, Gene Autry &			
others app.	8	24	105
11-21	4	12	38

PETER PARKER (See The Spectacular Spider-Man)

PETER PARKER: SPIDER-MAN
Marvel Comics: Jan, 1999 - No. 57, Aug, 2003 ($2.99/$1.99/$2.25)

1-Mackie-s/Romita Jr.-a; wraparound-c			3.00
1-($6.95) DF Edition w/variant cover by the Romitas			7.00
2-11,13-17-($1.99): 2-Two covers; Thor app. 3-Iceman-c/app.			
4-Marrow-c/app. 5-Spider-Woman app. 7,8-Blade app. 9,10-Venom app.			
11-Iron Man & Thor-c/app.			2.25
12-($2.99) Sinister Six and Venom app.			3.00
18-24,26-43: 18-Begin $2.25-c. 20-Jenkins-s/Buckingham-a start. 23-Intro			

	GD	FN	NM-
Typeface. 24-Maximum Security x-over. 29-Rescue of MJ. 30-Ramos-c.			
42,43-Mahfood-a			2.25
25-($2.99) Two covers; Spider-Man & Green Goblin			3.00
44-47-Humberto Ramos-c/a; Green Goblin-c/app.			3.00
48,49,51-57: 48,49-Buckingham-c/a. 51,52-Herrera-a. 56,57-Kieth-a;			
Sandman returns			2.25
50-($3.50) Buckingham-c/a			3.50
...'99 Annual (8/99, $3.50) Man-Thing app.			3.50
...'00 Annual ($3.50) Bounty app.; Joe Bennett-a; Black Cat back-up story			
			3.50
...'01 Annual ($2.99) Avery-s			3.00
...: A Day in the Life TPB (5/01, $14.95) r/#20-22,26; Webspinners #10-12			
			15.00
...: One Small Break TPB (2002, $16.95) r/#27,28,30-34; Andrews-c			17.00
Spider-Man: Return of the Goblin TPB (2002, $8.99) r/#44-47; Ramos-c			9.00
...Vol. 4: Trials & Tribulations TPB (2003, $11.99) r/#35,37,48-50; Cho-c			12.00

PHANTOM, THE (nn (#29)-Published overseas only)
Gold Key(#1-17)/King(#18-28)/Charlton(#30 on): Nov, 1962 - No. 17, Jul, 1966; No. 18, Sept, 1966 - No. 28, Dec, 1967; No. 30, Feb, 1969 - No. 74, Jan, 1977

	GD	FN	NM-
1-Origin revealed on inside-c & back-c	17	51	245
2-King, Queen & Jack begins, ends #11	9	27	120
3-5	8	24	105
6-10	8	24	100
11-17: 12-Track Hunter begins	7	21	80
18-Flash Gordon begins; Wood-a	6	18	65
19-24: 20-Flash Gordon ends (both by Gil Kane). 21-Mandrake begins.			
20,24-Girl Phantom app.	5	15	60
25-28: 25-Jeff Jones-a(4 pgs.); 1 pg. Williamson ad. 26-Brick Bradford app.			
28(nn)-Brick Bradford app.	4	12	50
30-33: 33-Last 12¢ issue	4	12	38
34-40: 36,39-Ditko-a	3	10	35
41-66: 46-Intro. The Piranha. 62-Bolle-c	3	9	24
67-Origin retold; Newton-c/a	3	9	32
68-73-Newton-c/a	2	6	22
74-Classic flag-c by Newton; Newton-a;	3	9	30

NOTE: *Aparo* a-31-34, 36-38; c-31-38, 60, 61. *Painted c-1-17.*

PHANTOM BLOT, THE (#1 titled New Adventures of...)
Gold Key: Oct, 1964 - No. 7, Nov, 1966 (Disney)

	GD	FN	NM-
1 (Meets The Mysterious Mr. X)	7	21	80
2-1st Super Goof	6	18	70
3-7	4	12	40

PHANTOM STRANGER, THE (1st Series)(See Saga of Swamp Thing)
National Periodical Publications: Aug-Sept, 1952 - No. 6, June-July, 1953

	GD	FN	NM-
1(Scarce)-1st app.	192	576	2500
2 (Scarce)	110	330	1425
3-6 (Scarce)	94	282	1225

	GD	FN	NM-

PHANTOM STRANGER, THE (2nd Series) (See Showcase #80)
National Periodical Publications: May-June, 1969 - No. 41, Feb-Mar, 1976

	GD	FN	NM-
1-2nd S.A. app. P. Stranger; only 12¢ issue	11	33	150
2,3	6	18	65
4-1st new look Phantom Stranger; N. Adams-a	6	18	70
5-7	4	12	50
8-14: 14-Last 15¢ issue	3	9	32
15-19: All 25¢ giants (52 pgs.)	4	12	38
20-Dark Circle begins, ends #24.	2	6	22
21,22	2	6	16
23-Spawn of Frankenstein begins by Kaluta	4	12	40
24,25,27-30-Last Spawn of Frankenstein	3	9	30
26- Book-length story featuring Phantom Stranger, Dr. 13 & Spawn of Frankenstein	3	9	32
31-The Black Orchid begins (6-7/74).	3	9	30
32,34-38: 34-Last 20¢ issue (#35 on are 25¢)	2	6	16
33,39-41: 33-Deadman-c/story. 39-41-Deadman app.	2	6	20

PINK PANTHER, THE (TV)(See The Inspector & Kite Fun Book)
Gold Key #1-70/Whitman #71-87: April, 1971 - No. 87, Mar, 1984

	GD	FN	NM-
1-The Inspector begins	6	18	70
2-5	3	9	30
6-10	2	6	22
11-30: Warren Tufts-a #16-on	2	6	15
31-60	2	6	12
61-70	1	3	8
71-74,81-83: 81(2/82), 82(3/82), 83(4/82)	1	4	10
75(8/80)-77 (Whitman pre-pack) (scarce)	3	9	24
78(1/81)-80 (Whitman pre-pack) (not as scarce)	2	6	16
84-87(All #90266 on-c, no date or date code): 84(6/83), 85(8/83), 87(3/84)			
	2	6	16
Mini-comic No. 1(1976)(3-1/4x6-1/2")	1	4	10

PIZZAZZ
Marvel Comics: Oct, 1977 - No. 16, Jan, 1979 (slick-color kids mag. w/puzzles, games, comics)

	GD	FN	NM-
1-Star Wars photo-c/article; origin Tarzan; KISS photos/article; Iron-On bonus; 2 pg. pin-up calendars thru #8	3	9	28
2-Spider-Man-c; Beatles pin-up calendar	2	6	16
3-8: 3-Close Encounters-s; Bradbury-s. 4-Alice Cooper, Travolta; Charlie's Angels/Fonz/Hulk/Spider-Man-c. 5-Star Trek quiz. 6-Asimov-s. 7-James Bond; Spock/Darth Vader-c. 8-TV Spider-Man photo-c/article			
	2	6	16
9-14: 9-Shaun Cassidy-c. 10-Sgt. Pepper-c/s. 12-Battlestar Galactica-s; Spider-Man app. 13-TV Hulk-c/s. 14-Meatloaf-c/s	2	6	14
15,16: 15-Battlestar Galactica-s. 16-Movie Superman photo-c/s, Hulk.			
	2	6	16

PLANETARY (See Preview in flip book Gen13 #33)
DC Comics (WildStorm Prod.): Apr, 1999 - Present ($2.50/$2.95)

	GD	FN	NM-
1-Ellis-s/Cassaday-a/c	1	4	10
2-5			6.00
6-10			5.00
11-15: 12-Fourth Man revealed			4.00
16-21-($2.95)			3.00
...: All Over the World and Other Stories (2000, $14.95) r/#1-6 & Preview			15.00
...: All Over the World and Other Stories-Hardcover (2000, $24.95) r/#1-6 & Preview; with dustjacket			25.00
.../Batman: Night on Earth 1 (8/03, $5.95) Ellis-s/Cassaday-a			6.00
...: Crossing Worlds (2004, $14.95) r/Batman, JLA, and The Authority x-overs			15.00
.../JLA: Terra Occulta (11/02, $5.95) Elseworlds; Ellis-s/Ordway-a			6.00
...: Leaving the 20th Century -HC (2004, $24.95) r/#13-18			25.00
.../The Authority: Ruling the World (8/00, $5.95) Ellis-s/Phil Jimenez-a			6.00
...: The Fourth Man -Hardcover (2001, $24.95) r/#7-12			25.00
...: The Planetary Reader (8/03, $5.95) r/#13-15			6.00

PLANET OF THE APES (Magazine) (Also see Adventures on the... & Power Record Comics)
Marvel Comics Group: Aug, 1974 - No. 29, Feb, 1977 (B&W) (Based on movies)

1-Ploog-a	4	12	40
2-Ploog-a	3	9	26
3-10	2	6	20
11-20	2	6	22
21-28 (low distribution)	3	9	26
29 (low distribution)	5	15	60

PLANET OF VAMPIRES
Seaboard Publications (Atlas): Feb, 1975 - No. 3, July, 1975

1-Neal Adams-c(i); 1st Broderick c/a(p); Hama-s	2	6	12
2,3: 2-Neal Adams-c. 3-Heath-c/a	1	3	9

PLASTIC MAN (See DC Special #15 & House of Mystery #160)
National Periodical Publications/DC Comics: 11-12/66 - No. 10, 5-6/68; V4#11, 2-3/76 - No. 20, 10-11/77

1-Real 1st app. Silver Age Plastic Man (House of Mystery #160 is actually tryout); Gil Kane-c/a; 12¢ issues begin	10	30	130
2-5: 4-Infantino-c; Mortimer-a	5	15	55
6-10('68): 7-G.A. Plastic Man & Woozy Winks (1st S.A. app.) app.; origin retold. 10-Sparling-a; last 12¢ issue	4	12	45
V4#11('76)-20: 11-20-Fradon-p. 17-Origin retold	1	3	9
...80-Page Giant (2003, $6.95) reprints origin and other stories in 80-Pg. Giant format			7.00
...Special 1 (8/99, $3.95)			4.00

PLOP! (Also see The Best of DC #60)
National Periodical Publications: Sept-Oct, 1973 - No. 24, Nov-Dec, 1976

1-Sergio Aragonés-a begins; Wrightson-a	4	12	38
2-4,6-20	2	6	20
5-Wrightson-a	2	6	22

	GD	FN	NM-
21-24 (52 pgs.). 23-No Aragonés-a	3	9	24

POWER MAN (Formerly Hero for Hire; ...& Iron Fist #50 on; see Cage & Giant-Size...)
Marvel Comics Group: No. 17, Feb, 1974 - No. 125, Sept, 1986

17-Luke Cage continues; Iron Man app.	2	6	18
18-20: 18-Last 20¢ issue	2	6	12
21-30	1	3	8
30-(30¢-c variant, limited distribution)(4/76)	2	6	12
31-46: 31-Part Neal Adams-i. 34-Last 25¢ issue. 36-r/Hero For Hire #12. 41-1st app. Thunderbolt. 45-Starlin-c.	1	3	7
31-34-(30¢-c variants, limited distribution)(5-8/76)	1	4	10
44-46-(35¢-c variants, limited distribution)(6-8/77)	1	4	10
47-Barry Smith-a	1	3	9
47-(35¢-c variant, limited distribution)(10/77)	2	6	14
48-50-Byrne-a(p); 48-Power Man/Iron Fist 1st meet. 50-Iron Fist joins Cage	2	6	12
51-56,58-65,67-77: 58-Intro El Aguila. 75-Double size. 77-Daredevil app.			4.00
57-New X-Men app. (6/79)	3	9	25
66-2nd app. Sabretooth (see Iron Fist #14)	4	12	40
78,84: 78-3rd app. Sabretooth (cameo under cloak). 84-4th app. Sabretooth	2	6	22
79-83,85-99,101-124: 87-Moon Knight app. 109-The Reaper app.			3.00
100,125-Double size: 100-Origin K'un L'un. 125-Death of Iron Fist			4.00
Annual 1(1976)-Punisher cameo in flashback	2	6	16

POWER OF SHAZAM!, THE (See SHAZAM!)
DC Comics: 1994 (Painted graphic novel) (Prequel to new series)

Hardcover-($19.95)-New origin of Shazam!; Ordway painted-c/a & script	3	9	25
Softcover-($7.50), Softcover-($9.95)-New-c.	2	6	12

POWER OF SHAZAM!, THE
DC Comics: Mar, 1995 - No. 47, Mar, 1999 ($1.50/$1.75/$1.95/$2.50)

1-Jerry Ordway scripts begin	4.00
2-20: 4-Begin $1.75-c. 6:Re-intro of Capt. Nazi. 8-Re-intro of Spy Smasher, Bulletman & Minuteman; Swan-a (7 pgs.). 11-Re-intro of Ibis, Swan-a (2 pgs.). 14-Gil Kane-a(p). 20-Superman-c/app.; "Final Night"	3.00
21-47: 21-Plastic Man-c/app. 22-Batman-c/app. 35,36-X-over w/Starman #39,40. 38-41-Mr. Mind. 43-Bulletman app. 45-JLA-c/app.	2.50
#1,000,000 (11/98) 853rd Century x-over; Ordway-c/s/a	3.00
Annual 1 (1996, $2.95)-Legends of the Dead Earth story; Jerry Ordway-c; Mike Manley-a	4.00

POWERPUFF GIRLS, THE (Also see Cartoon Network Starring... #1)
DC Comics: May, 2000 - Present ($1.99/$2.25)

1	4.00
2-55,57: 25-Pin-ups by Allred, Byrne, Baker, Mignola, Hernandez, Warren	2.25
56-($2.95) Bonus pages; Mojo Jojo-c	3.00
...Double Whammy (12/00, $3.95) r/#1,2 & a Dexter's Lab story	4.00

	GD	FN	NM-

...Movie: The Comic (9/02, $2.95) Adaptation; Phil Moy & Chris Cook-a   3.00

POWERS
Image Comics: 2000 - No. 37, Feb, 2004 ($2.95)

1-Bendis-s/Oeming-a; murder of Retro Girl	1	4	10
2-6: 6-End of Retro Girl arc.			5.00
7-14: 7-Warren Ellis app. 12-14-Death of Olympia			3.50
15-37: 31-36-Origin of the Powers			3.00
Annual 1 (2001, $3.95)			4.00

.....: Anarchy TPB (11/03, $14.95) r/#21-24; interviews, sketchbook, cover
    gallery   15.00
...Coloring/Activity Book (2001, $1.50, B&W, 8 x 10.5") Oeming-a   2.25
.....: Little Deaths TPB (2002, $19.95) r/#7,12-14, Ann. #1, Coloring/Activity
    Book; sketch pages, cover gallery   20.00
.....: Roleplay TPB (2001, $13.95) r/#8-11; sketchbook, cover gallery   14.00
... Scriptbook (2001, $19.95) scripts for #1-11; Oeming sketches   20.00
.....: Supergroup TPB (2003, $19.95) r/#15-20; sketchbook, cover gallery   20.00
..: Who Killed Retro Girl TPB (2000, $21.95) r/#1-6; sketchbook, cover gallery,
    and promotional strips from Comic Shop News   22.00

POWERS
Marvel Comics (Icon): Jul, 2004 - Present ($2.95)

1-6-Bendis-s/Oeming-a   3.00

PREACHER
DC Comics (Vertigo): Apr, 1995 - No. 66, Oct, 2000 ($2.50, mature)

	GD	FN	NM-
nn-Preview	2	6	20
1 ($2.95)-Ennis scripts, Dillon-a & Fabry-c in all; 1st app. Jesse, Tulip, &			
Cassidy	2	6	14
2,3: 2-1st app. Saint of Killers.	1	3	9
4,5	1	3	7
6-10			5.00

11-20: 12-Polybagged w/videogame w/Ennis text. 13-Hunters storyline
    begins; ends #17. 19-Saint of Killers app.; begin "Crusaders", ends #24
        4.00

21-25: 21-24-Saint of Killers app. 25-Origin of Cassidy.		3.00
26-49,52-64: 52-Tulip origin		2.50
50-($3.75) Pin-ups by Jim Lee, Bradstreet, Quesada and Palmiotti		3.75
51-Includes preview of 100 Bullets; Tulip origin		4.00
65,66-($3.75) 65-Almost everyone dies. 66-Final issue		5.00

Alamo (2001, $17.95, TPB) r/#59-66; Fabry-c   18.00
All Hell's a-Coming (2000, $17.95, TPB)-r/#51-58, ...:Tall in the Saddle   18.00
...: Dead or Alive HC (2000, $29.95) Gallery of Glenn Fabry's cover paintings
    for every Preacher issue; commentary by Fabry & Ennis   30.00
...: Dead or Alive SC (2003, $19.95)   20.00
Dixie Fried (1998, $14.95, TPB)-r/#27-33, Special: Cassidy   15.00
Gone To Texas (1996, $14.95, TPB)-r/#1-7; Fabry-c   15.00
Proud Americans (1997, $14.95, TPB)-r/#18-26; Fabry-c   15.00
Salvation (1999, $14.95, TPB)-r/#41-50; Fabry-c   15.00
Until the End of the World (1996, $14.95, TPB)-r/#8-17; Fabry-c   15.00

	GD	FN	NM-
War in the Sun (1999, $14.95, TPB)-r/#34-40			15.00

PREDATOR (Also see Aliens Vs. ..., Batman vs. ..., Dark Horse Comics, & Dark Horse Presents)
Dark Horse Comics: June, 1989 - No. 4, Mar, 1990 ($2.25, limited series)

	GD	FN	NM-
1-Based on movie; 1st app. Predator	1	3	7
1-2nd printing			3.00
2			5.00
3,4			4.00
Trade paperback (1990, $12.95)-r/#1-4			13.00

PREDATOR: (title series) **Dark Horse Comics**

	NM-
--**BAD BLOOD,** 12/93 - No. 4, 1994 ($2.50) 1-4	3.00
--**BIG GAME,** 3/91 - No. 4, 6/91 ($2.50) 1-4: 1-3-Contain 2 Dark Horse trading cards	3.00
--**BLOODY SANDS OF TIME,** 2/92 - No. 2, 2/92 ($2.50) 1,2-Dan Barry-c/a(p)/scripts	3.00
--**CAPTIVE,** 4/98 ($2.95, one-shot) 1	3.00
--**COLD WAR,** 9/91 - No. 4, 12/91 ($2.50) 1-4: All have painted-c	3.00
--**DARK RIVER,** 7/96 - No.4, 10/96 ($2.95)1-4: Miran Kim-c	3.00
--**HELL & HOT WATER,** 4/97 - No. 3, 6/97 ($2.95) 1-3	3.00
--**HELL COME A WALKIN',** 2/98 - No. 2, 3/98 ($2.95) 1,2-Civil War	3.00
--**HOMEWORLD,** 3/99 - No. 4, 6/99 ($2.95) 1-4	3.00
--**INVADERS FROM THE FOURTH DIMENSION,** 7/94 ($3.95, one-shot, 52 pgs.) 1	4.00
--**JUNGLE TALES.** 3/95 ($2.95t) 1-r/Dark Horse Comics	3.00
--**KINDRED,** 12/96 - No. 4, 3/97 ($2.50) 1-4	3.00
--**NEMESIS,** 12/97 - No. 2, 1/98 ($2.95) 1,2-Predator in Victorian England; Taggart-c	3.00
--**PRIMAL,** 7/97 - No. 2, 8/97 ($2.95) 1,2	3.00
--**RACE WAR** (See Dark Horse Presents #67), 2/93 - No. 4,10/93 ($2.50, color) 1-4,0: 1-4-Dorman painted-c #1-4, 0 (4/93)	3.00
--**STRANGE ROUX,** 11/96 ($2.95, one-shot) 1	3.00
--**XENOGENESIS** (Also see Aliens Xenogenesis), 8/99 - No. 4, 11/99 ($2.95) 1,2-Edginton-s	3.00

PREDATOR 2
Dark Horse Comics: Feb, 1991 - No. 2, June, 1991 ($2.50, limited series)

	NM-
1,2: 1-Adapts movie; both w/trading cards & photo-c	3.00

PREDATOR VS. JUDGE DREDD
Dark Horse Comics: Oct, 1997 - No. 3 ($2.50, limited series)

	NM-
1-3-Wagner-s/Alcatena-a/Bolland-c	3.00

PREDATOR VS. MAGNUS ROBOT FIGHTER
Dark Horse/Valiant: Oct, 1992 - No. 2, 1993 ($2.95, limited series)

	GD	FN	NM-

(1st Dark Horse/Valiant x-over)

	GD	FN	NM-
1,2: (Reg.)-Barry Smith-c; Lee Weeks-a. 2-w/trading cards			3.00
1 (Platinum edition, 11/92)-Barry Smith-c			10.00

PREZ (See Cancelled Comic Cavalcade, Sandman #54 & Supergirl #10)
National Periodical Publications: Aug-Sept, 1973 - No. 4, Feb-Mar, 1974

	GD	FN	NM-
1-Origin; Joe Simon scripts	3	9	30
2-4	2	6	18

PRIMER (Comico...)
Comico: Oct (no month), 1982 - No. 6, Feb, 1984 (B&W)

	GD	FN	NM-
1 (52 pgs.)	2	6	14
2-1st app. Grendel & Argent by Wagner	10	30	130
3,4	1	4	10
5-1st Sam Kieth art in comics ('83) & 1st The Maxx	4	12	38
6-Intro & 1st app. Evangeline	2	6	15

PROMETHEA
America's Best Comics: Aug, 1999 - No. 32, Apr, 2005 ($3.50/$2.95)

	GD	FN	NM-
1-Alan Moore-s/Williams III & Gray-a; Alex Ross painted-c			3.50
1-Variant-c by Williams III & Gray			3.50
2-31-($2.95): 7-Villarrubia photo-a. 10-"Sex, Stars & Serpents". 26-28-Tom Strong app. 27-Cover swipe of Superman vs. Spider-Man treasury ed.			3.00
32-($3.95) Final issue; pages can be assembled into 2-sided poster			4.00
Book 1 Hardcover ($24.95, dust jacket) r/#1-6			25.00
Book 1 TPB ($14.95) r/#1-6			15.00
Book 2 Hardcover ($24.95, dust jacket) r/#7-12			25.00
Book 2,3 TPB ($14.95) 2-r/#7-12. 3-r/#13-18			15.00
Book 3 Hardcover ($24.95, dust jacket) r/#13-18			25.00

PULSE, THE (Also see Alias and Deadline)
Marvel Comics: Apr, 2004 - Present ($2.99)

	GD	FN	NM-
1-6: 1-5-Bendis-s/Bagley-a; Jessica Jones, Ben Urich, Kat Farrell app. 3-5-Green Goblin app. 6-Brent Anderson-a			3.00
Vol. 1: Thin Air (2004, $13.99) r/#1-5, gallery of cover layouts and sketches			14.00

PUNISHER (The...)
Marvel Comics Group: Jan, 1986 - No. 5, May, 1986 (Limited series)

	GD	FN	NM-
1-Double size	2	6	18
2-5	1	4	10
Trade Paperback (1988)-r/#1-5			11.00
Circle of Blood TPB (8/01, $15.95) Zeck-c			16.00

PUNISHER (The...) (Volume 2)
Marvel Comics: July, 1987 - No. 104, July, 1995

	GD	FN	NM-
1	1	4	10
2-9: 8-Portacio/Williams-c/a begins, ends #18. 9-Scarcer, low dist.			6.00
10-Daredevil app; ties in w/Daredevil #257	1	4	10
11-74,76-85,87-89: 13-18-Kingpin app. 19-Stroman-c/a. 20-Portacio-c(p). 24-1st app. Shadowmasters. 25,50:($1.50,52 pgs.). 25-Shadowmasters			

	GD	FN	NM-

app. 57-Photo-c; came w/outer-c (newsstand ed. w/o outer-c). 59-Punisher
is severely cut & has skin grafts (has black skin). 60-62-Luke Cage app.
62-Punisher back to white skin. 68-Tarantula-c/story. 85-Prequel to Suicide
Run Pt. 0. 87,88-Suicide Run Pt. 6 & 9   2.50
75-($2.75, 52 pgs.)-Embossed silver foil-c   3.00
86-($2.95, 52 pgs.)-Embossed & foil stamped-c; Suicide Run part 3   3.00
90-99: 90-bound-in cards. 99-Cringe app.   2.50
100,104: 100-($2.95, 68 pgs.). 104-Last issue   4.00
100-($3.95, 68 pgs.)-Foil cover   5.00
101-103: 102-Bullseye   3.50
"Ashcan" edition (75¢)-Joe Kubert-c   3.00
Annual 1-7 ('88-'94, 68 pgs.) 1-Evolutionary War x-over. 2-Atlantis Attacks
   x-over; Jim Lee-a(p) (back-up story, 6 pgs.); Moon Knight app.
   4-Golden-c(p). 6-Bagged w/card.   3.00
...: A Man Named Frank (1994, $6.95, TPB)   7.00
...and Wolverine in African Saga nn (1989, $5.95, 52 pgs.)-Reprints Punisher
   War Journal #6 & 7; Jim Lee-c/a(r)   6.00
... Assassin Guild ('88, $6.95, graphic novel)   10.00
Back to School Special 1-3 (11/92-10/94, $2.95, 68 pgs.)   3.00
.../Batman: Deadly Knights (10/94, $4.95)   5.00
.../Black Widow: Spinning Doomsday's Web (1992, $9.95, GN)   12.00
...Bloodlines nn (1991, $5.95, 68 pgs.)   6.00
...: Die Hard in the Big Easy nn ('92, $4.95, 52 pgs.)   5.00
...: Empty Quarter nn ('94, $6.95)   7.00
...G-Force nn (1992, $4.95, 52 pgs.)-Painted-c   5.00
...Holiday Special 1-3 (1/93-1/95,, 52 pgs.,68pgs.)-1-Foil-c   3.00
...Intruder Graphic Novel (1989, $14.95, hardcover)   20.00
...Intruder Graphic Novel (1991, $9.95, softcover)   12.00
...Invades the 'Nam: Final Invasion nn (2/94, $6.95)-J. Kubert-c & chapter
   break art; reprints The 'Nam #84 & unpublished #85,86   7.00
...Kingdom Gone Graphic Novel (1990, $16.95, hardcover)   20.00
...Meets Archie (8/94, $3.95, 52 pgs.)-Die cut-c; no ads; same contents as
   Archie Meets The Punisher   5.00
...Movie Special 1 (6/90, $5.95, squarebound, 68 pgs.) painted-c; Brent
   Anderson-a; contents intended for a 3 issue series which was advertised
   but not published   6.00
...: No Escape nn (1990, $4.95, 52 pgs.)-New-a   5.00
...Return to Big Nothing Graphic Novel (Epic, 1989, $16.95, HC)   25.00
...Return to Big Nothing Graphic Novel (Marvel, 1989, $12.95, SC)   15.00
...The Prize nn (1990, $4.95, 68 pgs.)-New-a   5.00
Summer Special 1-4(8/91-7/94, 52 pgs.):1-No ads. 2-Bisley-c; Austin-a(i).
   3-No ads   3.00

PUNISHER (Also see Double Edge)
Marvel Comics: Nov, 1995 - No. 18, Apr, 1997 ($2.95/$1.95/$1.50)

1 ($2.95)-Ostrander scripts begin; foil-c.   3.00
2-18: 7-Vs. S.H.I.E.L.D. 11-"Onslaught." 12-17-X-Cutioner-c/app.
   17-Daredevil, Spider-Man-c/app.   2.50

PUNISHER (Marvel Knights)

	GD	FN	NM-

Marvel Comics: Nov, 1998 - No. 4, Feb, 1999 ($2.99, limited series)

1-4: 1-Wrightson-a; Wrightson & Jusko-c		3.00
1-($6.95) DF Edition; Jae Lee variant-c		7.00

PUNISHER (Marvel Knights) (Volume 3)
Marvel Comics: Apr, 2000 - No. 12, Mar, 2001 ($2.99, limited series)

1-Ennis-s/Dillon & Palmiotti-a/Bradstreet-c		5.00
1-Bradstreet white variant-c		10.00
1-($6.95) DF Edition; Jurgens & Ordway variant-c		7.00
2-Two covers by Bradstreet & Dillon		3.00
3-($3.99) Bagged with Marvel Knights Genesis Edition; Daredevil app.		4.00
4-12: 9-11-The Russian app.		3.00
HC (6/02, $34.95) r/#1-12, Punisher Kills the Marvel Universe, and Marvel Knights Double Shot #1		35.00
.../Painkiller Jane (1/01, $3.50) Jusko-c; Ennis-s/Jusko and Dave Ross-a(p)		3.50
...: Welcome Back Frank TPB (4/01, $19.95) r/#1-12		20.00

PUNISHER (Marvel Knights) (Volume 4)
Marvel Comics: Aug, 2001 - No. 37, Feb, 2004 ($2.99)

1-Ennis-s/Dillon & Palmiotti-a/Bradstreet-c; The Russian app.		4.00
2-Two covers (Dillon & Bradstreet) Spider-Man-c/app.		3.00
3-37: 3-7-Ennis-s/Dillon-a. 9-12-Peyer-s/Gutierrez-a. 13,14-Ennis-s/Dilllon-a. 16,17-Wolverine app.; Robertson-a. 18-23,32-Dillon-a. 24-27-Mandrake-a. 27-Elektra app. 33-37-Spider-Man, Daredevil, & Wolverine app. 36,37-Hulk app.		3.00
...Army of One TPB (2/02, $15.95) r/#1-7; Bradstreet-c		16.00
Vol. 2 HC (2003, $29.95) r/#1-7,13-18; intro. by Mike Millar		30.00
Vol. 3 HC (2004, $29.95) r/#19-27; script pages for #19		30.00
Vol. 3: Business as Usual TPB (2003, $14.99) r/#13-18; Bradstreet-c		15.00
Vol. 4: Full Auto TPB (2003, $17.99) r/#20-26; Bradstreet-c		18.00
Vol. 5: Streets of Laredo TPB (2003, $17.99) r/#19,27-32		18.00
Vol. 6: Confederacy of Dunces TPB (2004, $13.99) r/#33-37		14.00

PUNISHER (Marvel MAX)
Marvel Comics: Mar, 2004 - Present ($2.99)

1-13: 1-Ennis-s/Larosa-a/Bradstreet-c; flashback to his family's murder; Micro app. 6-Micro killed. 7-12-Fernandez-a. 13,14-Braithwaite-a		3.00
Vol. 1: In the Beginning TPB (2004, $14.99) r/#1-6		15.00
Vol. 2: Kitchen Irish TPB (2004, $14.99) r/#7-12		15.00

PUNISHER KILLS THE MARVEL UNIVERSE
Marvel Comics: Nov, 1995 ($5.95, one-shot)

1-Garth Ennis script/Doug Braithwaite-a		7.00
1-2nd printing (3/00) Steve Dillon-c		6.00

PUNISHER: OFFICIAL MOVIE ADAPTATION
Marvel Comics: May, 2004 - No. 3, May, 2004 ($2.99, limited series)

1-3-Photo-c of Thomas Jane; Milligan-s/Olliffe-a		3.00

PUNISHER: THE END

	GD	FN	NM-

Marvel Comics: June, 2004 ($4.50, one-shot)

1-Ennis-s/Corben-a/c   4.50

PUNISHER: THE MOVIE
Marvel Comics: 2004 ($12.99,TPB)

nn-Reprints Amazing Spider-Man #129; Official Movie Adaptation and
   Punisher V3 #1   13.00

PUNISHER WAR JOURNAL, THE
Marvel Comics: Nov, 1988 - No. 80, July, 1995 ($1.50/$1.75/$1.95)

1-Origin The Punisher; Matt Murdock cameo; Jim Lee inks begin   5.00
2-7: 2,3-Daredevil x-over; Jim Lee-c(i). 4-Jim Lee c/a begins. 6-Two part
   Wolverine story begins. 7-Wolverine-c, story ends   4.00
8-49,51-60,62,63,65: 13-16,20-22: No Jim Lee-a. 13-Lee-c only.
   13-15-Heath-i. 14,15-Spider-Man x-over. 19-Last Jim Lee-c/a.29,30-Ghost
   Rider app. 31-Andy & Joe Kubert art. 36-Photo-c. 47,48-Nomad/
   Daredevil-c/stories; see Nomad. 57,58-Daredevil & Ghost Rider-c/stories.
   62,63-Suicide Run Pt. 4 & 7.   3.00
50,61,64($2.95, 52 pgs.): 50-Preview of Punisher 2099 (1st app.);
   embossed-c. 61-Embossed foil cover; Suicide Run Pt. 1. 64-Die-cut-c;
   Suicide Run Pt. 10   3.00
64-($2.25, 52 pgs.)-Regular cover edition   2.25
66-74,76-80: 66-Bound-in card sheet   2.25
75 ($2.50, 52 pgs.)   2.50

PUNISHER: WAR ZONE, THE
Marvel Comics: Mar, 1992 - No. 41, July, 1995 ($1.75/$1.95)

1-($2.25, 40 pgs.)-Die cut-c; Romita, Jr.-c/a begins   3.00
2-22,24,26,27-41: 8-Last Romita, Jr.-c/a. 19-Wolverine app. 24-Suicide Run
   Pt. 5. 27-Bound-in card sheet   2.25
23-($2.95, 52 pgs.)-Embossed foil-c; Suicide Run part 2; Buscema-a(part)
                                           3.00
25-($2.25, 52 pgs.)-Suicide Run part 8; painted-c   2.50
Annual 1,2 ('93, '94, $2.95, 68 pgs.)-1-Bagged w/card; John Buscema-a 3.00

PUNISHER: YEAR ONE
Marvel Comics: Dec, 1994 - No. 4, Apr, 1995 ($2.50, limited series)

1-4   2.50

QUASAR (See Avengers #302, Captain America #217, Incredible Hulk #234,
Marvel Team-Up #113 & Marvel Two-in-One #53)
Marvel Comics: Oct, 1989 - No. 60, Jul, 1994 ($1.00/$1.25, Direct sales #17
on)

1-Origin; formerly Marvel Boy/Marvel Man   3.00
2-49,51-60: 3-Human Torch app. 6-Venom cameo (2 pgs.). 7-Cosmic Spidey.
   11-Excalibur x-over. 14-McFarlane-c. 16-($1.50, 52 pgs.). 17-Flash parody
   (Buried Alien). 20-Fantastic Four app. 23-Ghost Rider x-over. 25-($1.50,
   52 pgs.)-New costume Quasar. 26-Infinity Gauntlet x-over; Thanos-c/story.
   27-Infinity Gauntlet x-over. 30-Thanos cameo in flashback; last $1.00-c.
   31-Begin $1.25-c; D.P. 7 guest stars. 38-40-Infinity War x-overs. 38-Battles
   Warlock. 39-Thanos-c & cameo. 40-Thanos app. 42-Punisher-c/story.

	GD	FN	NM-

53-Warlock & Moondragon app. 58-w/bound-in card sheet 2.50
50-($2.95, 52 pgs.)-Holo-grafx foil-c; Silver Surfer, Man-Thing, Ren & Stimpy
   app. 3.00
Special #1-3 ($1.25, newsstand)-Same as #32-34 2.25

QUICK DRAW McGRAW (TV) (Hanna-Barbera)(See Whitman Comic Books)
Dell Publishing Co./Gold Key No. 12 on: No. 1040, 12-2/59-60 - No. 11, 7-
9/62; No. 12, 11/62; No. 13, 2/63; No. 14, 4/63; No. 15, 6/69 (1st show aired
9/29/59)

Four Color 1040(#1) 1st app. Quick Draw & Baba Looey, Augie Doggie &			
Doggie Daddy and Snooper & Blabber	15	45	215
2(4-6/60)-4,6: 2-Augie Doggie & Snooper & Blabber stories (8 pgs. each);			
pre-dates both of their #1 issues. 4-Augie Doggie & Snooper & Blabber			
stories	9	27	110
5-1st Snagglepuss app.; last 10¢ issue	9	27	120
7-11	7	21	80
12,13-Title change to ...Fun-Type Roundup (84pgs.)	9	27	120
14,15: 15-Reprints	6	18	70

QUICK DRAW McGRAW (TV)(See Spotlight #2)
Charlton Comics: Nov, 1970 - No. 8, Jan, 1972 (Hanna-Barbera)

1	6	18	70
2-8	4	12	38

RADIOACTIVE MAN (Simpsons TV show)
Bongo Comics: 1993 - No. 6, 1994 ($1.95/$2.25, limited series)

1-($2.95)-Glow-in-the-dark-c; bound-in jumbo poster; origin Radioactive Man;
   (cover dated Nov. 1952) 5.00
2-6: 2-Says #88 on-c & inside & dated May 1962; cover parody of Atlas
   Kirby monster-c; Superior Squad app.; origin Fallout Boy. 3-($1.95)-Cover
   "dated" Aug 1972 #216. 4-($2.25)-Cover "dated" Oct 1980 #412; w/trading
   card. 5-Cover "dated" Jan 1986 #679; w/trading card. 6-(Jan 1995 #1000)
    4.00
Colossal #1-($4.95) 7.00
#4 (2001, $2.50) Faux 1953 issue; Murphy Anderson-i (6 pgs.) 2.50
#100 (2000, $2.50) Comic Book Guy-c/app.; faux 1963 issue inside 2.50
#136 (2001, $2.50) Dan DeCarlo-c/a 2.50
#222 (2001, $2.50) Batton Lash-s; Radioactive Man in 1972-style 2.50
#575 (2002, $2.50) Chaykin-c; Radioactive Man in 1984-style 2.50
1963-106 (2002, $2.50) Radioactive Man in 1960s Gold Key-style; Groening-c
    2.50
#7 Bongo Super Heroes Starring... (2003, $2.50) Marvel Silver Age-style
   Superior Squad 2.50
#8 Official Movie Adaptation (2004, $2.99) starring Rainier Wolfcastle and
   Milhouse 3.00
#9 (#197 on-c) (2004, $2.50) Kirby-esque New Gods spoof; Golden Age
   Radio Man app. 2.50

RAGMAN (See Batman Family #20, The Brave & The Bold #196 & Cancelled
Comic Cavalcade)
National Per. Publ./DC Comics No. 5: Aug-Sept, 1976 - No. 5, Jun-Jul,

1977

		GD	FN	NM-
1-Origin & 1st app.		2	6	14
2-5: 2-Origin ends; Kubert-c. 4-Drug use story		1	3	8

RAMPAGING HULK (The Hulk #10 on; also see Marvel Treasury Edition)
Marvel Comics Group: Jan, 1977 - No. 9, June, 1978 ($1.00, B&W mag.)

	GD	FN	NM-
1-Bloodstone story w/Buscema & Nebres-a. Origin re-cap w/Simonson-a; Gargoyle, UFO story; Ken Barr-c	3	9	24
2-Old X-Men app; origin old w/Simonson-a & new X-Men in text w/Cockrum illos; Bloodstone story w/Brown & Nebres-a	2	6	18
3-9: 3-Iron Man app. 4-Gallery of villains w/Giffen-a. 5,6-Hulk vs. Sub-Mariner. 7-Man-Thing story. 8-Original Avengers app. 9-Thor vs. Hulk battle; Shanna the She-Devil story w/DeZuniga-a	2	6	14

RAMPAGING HULK
Marvel Comics: Aug, 1998 - No. 6, Jan, 1999 ($2.99/$1.99)

	NM-
1-($2.99) Flashback stories of Savage Hulk; Leonardi-a	3.00
2-6-($1.99): 2-Two covers	2.25

RAWHIDE KID
Atlas/Marvel Comics (CnPC No. 1-16/AMI No. 17-30): Mar, 1955 - No. 16, Sept, 1957; No. 17, Aug, 1960 - No. 151, May, 1979

	GD	FN	NM-
1-Rawhide Kid, his horse Apache & sidekick Randy begin; Wyatt Earp app.; #1 was not code approved; Maneely splash pg.	90	270	1175
2	40	120	475
3-5	31	93	340
6-10: 7-Williamson-a (4 pgs.)	24	72	260
11-16: 16-Torres-a	20	60	210
17-Origin by Jack Kirby; Kirby-a begins	33	99	525
18-21,24-30	13	39	185
22-Monster-c/story by Kirby/Ayers	16	48	230
23-Origin retold by Jack Kirby	20	60	290
31-35,40: 31,32-Kirby-a. 33-35-Davis-a. 34-Kirby-a. 35-Intro & death of The Raven. 40-Two-Gun Kid x-over.	11	33	145
36,37,39,41,42-No Kirby. 42-1st Larry Lieber issue	10	30	130
38-Red Raven-c/story; Kirby-c (2/64).	12	36	170
43-Kirby-a (beware: pin-up often missing)	12	36	170
44,46: 46-Toth-a. 46-Doc Holliday-c/s	9	27	120
45-Origin retold, 17 pgs.	11	33	150
47-49,51-60	6	18	75
50-Kid Colt x-over; vs. Rawhide Kid	7	21	80
61-70: 64-Kid Colt story. 66-Two-Gun Kid story. 67-Kid Colt story. 70-Last 12¢ issue	5	15	55
71-78,80-83,85	3	9	32
79,84,86,95: 79-Williamson-a(r). 84,86: Kirby-a. 86-Origin-r; Williamson-r/ Ringo Kid #13 (4 pgs.)	3	10	35
87-91: 90-Kid Colt app. 91-Last 15¢ issue	3	9	28
92,93 (52 pg.Giants). 92-Kirby-a	4	12	42
94,96-99	3	9	24
100 (6/72)-Origin retold & expanded	3	10	35

	GD	FN	NM-
101-120: 115-Last new story	2	6	18
121-151	2	6	12
133,134-(30¢-c variants, limited distribution)(5,7/76)	2	6	20
140,141-(35¢-c variants, limited distribution)(7,9/77)	2	6	20
Special 1(9/71, 25¢, 68 pgs.)-All Kirby/Ayers-r	4	12	50

RED SONJA (Also see Conan #23, Kull & The Barbarians, Marvel Feature & Savage Sword Of Conan #1)
Marvel Comics Group: 1/77 - No. 15, 5/79; V1#1, 2/83 - V2#2, 3/83; V3#1, 8/83 - V3#4, 2/84; V3#5, 1/85 - V3#13, 5/86

	GD	FN	NM-
1-Created by Robert E. Howard	2	6	15
2-10: 5-Last 30¢ issue	1	3	7
4,5-(35¢-c variants, limited distribution)(7,9/77)	1	3	10
11-15, V1#1,V2#2: 14-Last 35¢ issue			6.00
V3#1-13: #1-4 ($1.00, 52 pgs.)			3.50

RETURN OF GORGO, THE (Formerly Gorgo's Revenge)
Charlton Comics: No. 2, Aug, 1963; No. 3, Fall, 1964 (12¢)

	GD	FN	NM-
2,3-Ditko-c/a; based on M.G.M. movie	9	27	110

RETURN OF KONGA, THE (Konga's Revenge #2 on)
Charlton Comics: 1962

	GD	FN	NM-
nn	8	24	100

RICHARD DRAGON
DC Comics: July, 2004 - Present ($2.50)

	GD	FN	NM-
1-7: 1-Dixon-s/McDaniel-a/c; Ben Turner app. 2,3-Nightwing app. 4-6-Lady Shiva app.			2.50

RICHARD DRAGON, KUNG-FU FIGHTER (See The Batman Chronicles #5, Brave & the Bold, & The Question)
National Per. Publ./DC Comics: Apr-May, 1975 - No. 18, Nov-Dec, 1977

	GD	FN	NM-
1-Intro Richard Dragon, Ben Stanley & O-Sensei; 1st app. Barney Ling; adaptation of Jim Dennis novel "Dragon's Fists" begins, ends #4	2	6	18
2,3: 2-Intro Carolyn Woosan; Starlin/Weiss-c/a; bondage-c. 3-Kirby-a(p); Giordano bondage-c	1	4	10
4-8-Wood inks. 4-Carolyn Woosan dies. 5-1st app. Lady Shiva	1	3	7
9-13,15-18: 9-Ben Stanley becomes Ben Turner; intro Preying Mantis. 16-1st app. Prof Ojo. 18-1st app. Ben Turner as The Bronze Tiger	1	3	7
14-"Spirit of Bruce Lee"	2	6	18

RIMA, THE JUNGLE GIRL
National Periodical Publications: Apr-May, 1974 - No. 7, Apr-May, 1975

	GD	FN	NM-
1-Origin, part 1 (#1-5: 20¢; 6,7: 25¢)	2	6	16
2-7: 2-4-Origin, parts 2-4. 7-Origin & only app. Space Marshal	1	3	8

RIP HUNTER TIME MASTER (See Showcase #20, 21, 25, 26 & Time Masters)

	GD	FN	NM-
National Periodical Publications: Mar-Apr, 1961 - No. 29, Nov-Dec, 1965			
1-(3-4/61)	50	150	875
2	27	81	400
3-5: 5-Last 10¢ issue	16	48	240
6,7-Toth-a in each	11	33	160
8-15	9	27	120
16-20: 20-Hitler c/s	7	21	90
21-29: 29-Gil Kane-c	6	18	75

RISING STARS
Image Comics(Top Cow): Mar, 1999 - Present ($2.50/$2.99)

Preview-(3/99, $5.00) Straczynski-s			6.00
0-(6/00, $2.50) Gary Frank-a/c			2.50
1/2-(8/01, $2.95) Anderson-c; art & sketch pages by Zanier			3.00
1-Four covers; Keu Cha-c/a	1	3	9
1-($10.00) Gold Editions-four covers			10.00
1-($50.00) Holofoil-c			50.00
2-7: 5-7-Zanier & Lashley-a(p)	1	3	9
8-22: 8-13-Zanier & Lashley-a(p). 14-Immonen-a. 15-Flip book B&W preview of Universe. 15-22-Brent Anderson-a			3.00
Born In Fire TPB (11/00, $19.95) r/#1-8; foreword by Neil Gaiman			20.00
Power TPB (2002, $19.95) r/#9-16			20.00
Prelude-(10/00, $2.95) Cha-a/Lashley-c			3.00
...: Visitations (2002, $8.99) r/#0, 1/2, Preview; new Anderson-c; cover gallery			9.00
Wizard #0-(3/99) Wizard supplement; Straczynski-s			2.25
Wizard #1/2			10.00

ROBIN (See Batman #457)
DC Comics: Jan, 1991 - No. 5, May, 1991 ($1.00, limited series)

1-Free poster by N. Adams; Bolland-c on all			4.00
1-2nd & 3rd printings (without poster)			2.25
2-5			3.00
2-2nd printing			2.25
Annual 1,2 (1992-93, $2.50, 68 pgs.): 1-Grant/Wagner scripts; Sam Kieth-c. 2-Intro Razorsharp; Jim Balent-c(p)			3.00

ROBIN (See Detective #668)
DC Comics: Nov, 1993 - Present ($1.50/$1.95/$1.99/$2.25)

1-($2.95)-Collector's edition w/foil embossed-c; 1st app. Robin's car, The Redbird; Azrael as Batman app.			4.00
1-Newsstand ed.			2.25
0,2-49,51-66-Regular editions: 3-5-The Spoiler app. 6-The Huntress-c/story cont'd from Showcase '94 #5. 7-Knightquest: The Conclusion w/new Batman (Azrael) vs. Bruce Wayne. 8-KnightsEnd Pt. 5. 9-KnightsEnd Aftermath; Batman-c & app. 10-(9/94)-Zero Hour. 0-(10/94). 11-(11/94). 25-Green Arrow-c/app. 26-Batman app. 27-Contagion Pt. 3; Catwoman-c/app; Penguin & Azrael app. 28-Contagion Pt. 11. 29-Penguin app. 31-Wildcat-c/app. 32-Legacy Pt. 3. 33-Legacy Pt. 7. 35-Final Night. 46-Genesis. 52,53-Cataclysm pt. 7, conclusion. 55-Green Arrow app.			

	GD	FN	NM-
62-64-Flash-c/app.			2.50
14 ($2.50)-Embossed-c; Troika Pt. 4			3.00
50-($2.95)-Lady Shiva & King Snake app.			3.00
67-74,76-78: 67-72-No Man's Land			2.50
75-($2.95)			3.00
79-97: 79-Begin $2.25-c; Green Arrow app. 86-Pander Bros.-a			2.25
98,99-Bruce Wayne: Murderer x-over pt. 6, 11			2.50
100-($3.50) Last Dixon-s			3.50
101-125: 101-Young Justice x-over. 106-Kevin Lau-c. 121,122-Willingham-s/			
Mays-a. 125-Tim Drake quits			2.25
126-133: 126-Spoiler becomes the new Robin. 129-131-War Games.			
132-Robin moves to Bludhaven, Batgirl app.			2.25
#1,000,000 (11/98) 853rd Century x-over			2.50
Annual 3-5: 3-(1994, $2.95)-Elseworlds story. 4-(1995, $2.95)-Year One story.			
5-(1996, $2.95)-Legends of the Dead Earth story			3.00
Annual 6 (1997, $3.95)-Pulp Heroes story.			4.00
.../Argent 1 (2/98, $1.95) Argent (Teen Titans) app.			2.25
...Eighty-Page Giant 1 (9/00, $5.95) Chuck Dixon-s/Diego Barreto-a			6.00
...: Flying Solo (2000, $12.95, TPB) r/#1-6, Showcase '94 #5,6			13.00
...Plus 1 (12/96, $2.95) Impulse-c/app.; Waid-s			3.00
...Plus 2 (12/97, $2.95) Fang (Scare Tactics) app.			3.00
...: Unmasked (2004, $12.95, TPB) r/#121-125; Pearson-c			13.00

ROBIN II (The Joker's Wild)
DC Comics: Oct, 1991 - No. 4, Dec, 1991 ($1.50, mini-series)

1-(Direct sales, $1.50)-With 4 diff.-c; same hologram on each			3.00
1-(Newsstand, $1.00)-No hologram; 1 version			2.25
1-Collector's set ($10.00)-Contains all 5 versions bagged with hologram			
trading card inside			12.00
2-(Direct sales, $1.50)-With 3 different-c			2.50
2-4-(Newsstand, $1.00)-1 version of each			2.25
2-Collector's set ($8.00)-Contains all 4 versions bagged with hologram			
trading card inside			9.00
3-(Direct sale, $1.50)-With 2 different-c			2.50
3-Collector's set ($6.00)-Contains all 3 versions bagged with hologram			
trading card inside			7.00
4-(Direct sales, $1.50)-Only one version			2.50
4-Collector's set ($4.00)-Contains both versions bagged with Bat-Signal			
hologram trading card			5.00
Multi-pack (All four issues w/hologram sticker)			8.00
Deluxe Complete Set ($30.00)-Contains all 14 versions of #1-4 plus a new			
hologram trading card; numbered & limited to 25,000; comes with slipcase			
& 2 acid free backing boards			35.00

ROBIN: YEAR ONE
DC Comics: 2000 - No. 4, 2001 ($4.95, square-bound, limited series)

1-4: Earliest days of Robin's career; J. Pulido-c/a. 2,4-Two-Face app.			5.00
TPB (2002, $14.95) r/#1-4			15.00

ROCKY AND HIS FIENDISH FRIENDS (TV)(Bullwinkle)
Gold Key: Oct, 1962 - No. 5, Sept, 1963 (Jay Ward)

	GD	FN	NM-
1 (25¢, 80 pgs.)	22	66	325
2,3 (25¢, 80 pgs.)	15	45	215
4,5 (Regular size, 12¢)	10	30	140

ROCKY AND HIS FRIENDS (TV)
Dell Publishing Co.: No. 1128, 8-10/60 - No.1311,1962 (Jay Ward)

Four Color #1128 (#1) (8-10/60)	34	102	540
Four Color #1152 (12-2/61), 1166, 1208, 1275, 1311('62)	24	72	350

ROM (Based on the Parker Brothers toy)
Marvel Comics Group: Dec, 1979 - No. 75, Feb, 1986

1-Origin/1st app.	2	6	12
2-16,19-23,28-30: 5-Dr. Strange. 13-Saga of the Space Knights begins. 19-X-Men cameo. 23-Powerman & Iron Fist app.			4.00
17,18-X-Men app.	1	3	9
24-27: 24-F.F. cameo; Skrulls, Nova & The New Champions app. 25-Double size. 26,27-Galactus app.			5.00
31-49,51-60: 31,32-Brotherhood of Evil Mutants app. 32-X-Men cameo. 34,35-Sub-Mariner app. 41,42-Dr. Strange app. 56,57-Alpha Flight app. 58,59-Ant-Man app.			2.25
50-Skrulls app. (52 pgs.) Pin-ups by Konkle, Austin			3.00
61-74: 65-West Coast Avengers & Beta Ray Bill app. 65,66-X-Men app.			2.25
75-Last issue			6.00
Annual 1-4: (1982-85, 52 pgs.)			3.00

RUDOLPH, THE RED-NOSED REINDEER (Also see Limited Collectors' Edition C-20, C-24, C-33, C-42, C-50; and All-New Collectors' Edition C-53 & C-60)
National Per. Publ.: Christmas 1972 (Treasury-size)

nn-Precursor to Limited Collectors' Edition title (scarce) (implied to be Lim. Coll .Ed. C-20)	25	75	365

RUNAWAYS
Marvel Comics: July, 2003 - No. 18, Nov, 2004 ($2.95/$2.25/$2.99)

1-($2.95) Vaughan-s/Alphona-a/Jo Chen-c			3.00
2-9-($2.50)			2.50
10-18-($2.99) 11,12-Miyazawa-a; Cloak and Dagger app. 16-The mole revealed			3.00
Marvel Age Runaways Vol. 1: Pride and Joy (2004, $7.99, digest size) r/#1-6			8.00
...Vol. 2: Teenage Wasteland (2004, $7.99, digest size) r/#7-12			8.00
...Vol. 3: The Good Die Young (2004, $7.99, digest size) r/#13-18			8.00

SABRINA, THE TEEN-AGE WITCH (TV)(See Archie Giant Series, Archie's Madhouse 22, Archie's TV..., Chilling Advs. In Sorcery, Little Archie #59)
Archie Publications: April, 1971 - No. 77, Jan, 1983 (52 pg.Giants No. 1-17)

1-52 pgs. begin, end #17	15	45	220
2-Archie's group x-over	8	24	105
3-5: 3,4-Archie's Group x-over	6	18	70
6-10	5	15	60
11-17(2/74)	4	12	45

	GD	FN	NM-
18-30	3	9	30
31-40(8/77)	2	6	20
41-60(6/80)	2	6	14
61-70	1	4	10
71-76-low print run	2	6	14
77-Last issue; low print run	2	6	20

SAN DIEGO COMIC CON COMICS
Dark Horse Comics: 1992 - No.4, 1995 (B&W, promo comic for the San Diego Comic Con)

1-(1992)-Includes various characters published from Dark Horse including Concrete, The Mask, RoboCop and others; 1st app. of Sprint from John Byrne's Next Men; art by Quesada, Byrne, Rude, Burden, Moebius & others; pin-ups by Rude, Dorkin, Allred & others; Chadwick-c

	1	3	7

2-(1993)-Intro of Legend imprint; 1st app. of John Byrne's Danger Unlimited, Mike Mignola's Hellboy, Art Adams' Monkeyman & O'Brien; contains stories featuring Concrete, Sin City, Martha Washington & others; Grendel, Madman, & Big Guy pin-ups; Don Martin-c

	1	4	10

3-(1994)-Contains stories featuring Barb Wire, The Mask, The Dirty Pair, & Grendel by Matt Wagner; contains pin-ups of Ghost, Predator & Rascals In Paradise; The Mask-c   6.00

4-(1995)-Contains Sin City story by Miller (3 pg.), Star Wars, The Mask, Tarzan, Foot Soldiers; Sin City & Star Wars flip-c   6.00

SANDMAN, THE (1st Series) (Also see Adventure Comics #40, New York World's Fair & World's Finest #3)
National Periodical Publ.: Winter, 1974; No. 2, Apr-May, 1975 - No. 6, Dec-Jan, 1975-76

1-1st app. Bronze Age Sandman by Simon & Kirby (last S&K collaboration)	6	18	65
2-6: 6-Kirby/Wood-c/a	3	9	28

NOTE: *Kirby a-1p, 4-6p; c-1-5, 6p.*

SANDMAN (2nd Series) (See Books of Magic, Vertigo Jam & Vertigo Preview)
DC Comics (Vertigo imprint #47 on): Jan, 1989 - No. 75, Mar, 1996 ($1.50-$2.50, mature)

1 ($2.00, 52 pgs.)-1st app. Modern Age Sandman (Morpheus); Neil Gaiman scripts inc.; Sam Kieth-a(p) in #1-5; Wesley Dodds (G.A. Sandman) cameo	4	12	40
2-Cain & Abel app. (from HOM & HOS)	2	6	18
3-5: 3-John Constantine app.	2	6	15
6,7	1	4	10

8-Death-c/story (1st app.)-Regular ed. has Jeanette Kahn publishorial & American Cancer Society ad w/no indicia on inside front-c

	2	6	22

8-Limited ed. (600+ copies?); has Karen Berger editorial and next issue teaser on inside covers (has indicia)

	5	15	60

9-14: 10-Has explanation about #8 mixup; has bound-in Shocker movie poster. 14-(52 pgs.)-Bound-in Nightbreed fold-out

	1	3	9

15-20: 16-Photo-c. 17,18-Kelley Jones-a. 19-Vess-a.   6.00

	GD	FN	NM-
18-Error version w/1st 3 panels on pg. 1 in blue ink	3	9	25
19-Error version w/pages 18 & 20 facing each other	2	6	20

21,23-27: Seasons of Mist storyline. 22-World Without End preview. 24-Kelley
    Jones/Russell-a   6.00

| 22-1st Daniel (Later becomes new Sandman) | 2 | 6 | 12 |
| 28-30 | | | 5.00 |

31-49,51-74: 36-(52 pgs.). 41,44-48-Metallic ink on-c. 48-Cerebus appears
    as a doll. 54-Re-intro Prez; Death app.; Belushi, Nixon & Wildcat cameos.
    57-Metallic ink on c. 65-w/bound-in trading card. 69-Death of Sandman.
    70-73-Zulli-a. 74-Jon J. Muth-a.   4.00

50-($2.95, 52 pgs.)-Black-c w/metallic ink by McKean; Russell-a; McFarlane
    pin-up   5.00

50-($2.95)-Signed & limited (5,000) Treasury Edition with sketch of Neil			
Gaiman	1	3	8
50-Platinum			20.00
75-($3.95)-Vess-a.			5.00
Special 1 (1991, $3.50, 68 pgs.)-Glow-in-the-dark-c			5.00
...: A Gallery of Dreams ($2.95)-Intro by N. Gaiman			3.00
...: Preludes & Nocturnes ($29.95, HC)-r/#1-8.			30.00
...: The Doll's House (1990, $29.95, HC)-r/#8-16.			30.00
...: Dream Country ($29.95, HC)-r/#17-20.			30.00
...: Season of Mists ($29.95, Leatherbound HC)-r/#21-28.			50.00

...: A Game of You ($29.95, HC)-r/32-37, ...: Fables and Reflections ($29.95,
    HC)-r/Vertigo Preview #1, Sandman Special #1, #29-31, #38-40 & #50.
      ...: Brief Lives ($29.95, HC)-r/#41-49. ...: World's End ($29.95, HC)
    -r/#51-56   ...each   30.00

| ...: The Kindly Ones (1996, $34.95, HC)-r/#57-69 & Vertigo Jam #1 | | | 35.00 |
| ...: The Wake ($29.95, HC)-r/#70-75. | | | 30.00 |

NOTE: *A new set of hardcover printings with new covers was introduced in 1998-99. Multiple
printings exist of softcover collections. Bachalo a-12; Kelley Jones a-17, 18, 22, 23, 26, 27.
Vess a-19, 75.*

SANDMAN: ENDLESS NIGHTS
DC Comics (Vertigo): 2003 ($24.95, hardcover, with dust jacket)

HC-Neil Gaiman stories of Morpheus and the Endless illustrated by Fabry,			
Manara, Prado, Quitely, Russell, Sienkiewicz, and Storey; McKean-c			25.00
...Special (11/03, $2.95) Previews hardcover; Dream story w/Prado-a;			
McKean-c			3.00
SC (2004, $17.95)			18.00

SAVAGE DRAGON, THE (See Megaton #3 & 4)
Image Comics (Highbrow Entertainment): July, 1992 - No. 3, Dec, 1992
($1.95, lim. series)

1-Erik Larsen-c/a/scripts & bound-in poster in all; 4 cover color variations
    w/4 different posters; 1st Highbrow Entertainment title   4.00

2-Intro SuperPatriot-c/story (10/92)			3.00
3-Contains coupon for Image Comics #0			3.00
3-With coupon missing			2.25
...Vs. Savage Megaton Man 1 (3/93, $1.95)-Larsen & Simpson-c/a.			3.00
TPB-('93, $9.95) r/#1-3			10.00

GD   FN   NM-

SAVAGE DRAGON, THE
Image Comics (Highbrow Entertainment): June, 1993 - Present
($1.95/$2.50)

1-Erik Larsen-c/a/scripts   4.00
2-30: 2-(Wondercon Exclusive): 2-($2.95, 52 pgs.)-Teenage Mutant Ninja
    Turtles-c/story; flip book features Vanguard #0 (See Megaton for 1st app.).
    3-7: Erik Larsen-c/a/scripts. 3-Mighty Man back-up story w/Austin-a(i).
    4-Flip book w/Ricochet. 5-Mighty Man flip-c & back-up plus poster. 6-Jae
    Lee poster. 7-Vanguard poster. 8-Deadly Duo poster by Larsen.
    13A (10/94)-Jim Lee-c/a; 1st app. Max Cash (Condition Red).
    13B (6/95)-Larsen story. 15-Dragon poster by Larsen. 22-TMNT-c/a; Bisley
    pin-up. 27-"Wondercon Exclusive" new-c. 28-Maxx-c/app. 29-Wildstar-
    c/app. 30-Spawn app.   3.00
25 ($3.95)-variant-c exists.   4.00
31-49,51-71: 31-God vs. The Devil; alternate version exists w/o expletives
    (has "God Is Good" inside Image logo) 33-Birth of Dragon/Rapture's baby.
34,35-Hellboy-c/app. 51-Origin of She-Dragon. 70-Ann Stevens killed   2.50
50-($5.95, 100 pgs.) Kaboom and Mighty Man app.; Matsuda back-c; pin-ups
    by McFarlane, Simonson, Capullo and others   6.00
72-74: 72-Begin $2.95-c   3.00
75-($5.95)   6.00
76-99,101-106,108-114,116-118: 76-New direction starts. 83,84-Madman-
    c/app. 84-Atomics app. 97-Dragon returns home; Mighty Man app.   3.00
100-($8.95) Larsen-s/a; inked by various incl. Sienkiewicz, Timm, Austin,
    Simonson, Royer; plus pin-ups by Timm, Silvestri, Miller, Cho, Art Adams,
    Pacheco   9.00
107-($3.95) Firebreather, Invincible, Major Damage-c/app.; flip book w/Major
    Damage   4.00
115-($7.95, 100 pgs.) Wraparound-c; Freak Force app.; Larsen & Englert-a
                                    8.00
...Companion (7/02, $2.95) guide to issues #1-100, character backgrounds
                                    3.00
...Endgame (2/04, $15.95, TPB) r/#47-52   16.00
The Fallen (11/97, $12.95, TPB) r/#7-11, ...Possessed (9/98, $12.95, TPB)
    r/#12-16, ...Revenge (1998, $12.95, TPB) r/#17-21   ...each   13.00
...Gang War (4/00, $16.95, TPB) r/#22-26   17.00
.../Hellboy (10/02, $5.95) r/#34 & #35; Mignola-c   6.00
...Team-Ups (10/98, $19.95, TPB) r/team-ups   20.00
...: Terminated HC (2/03, $28.95) r/#34-40 & #1/2   29.00
...: This Savage World HC (2002, $24.95) r/#76-81; intro. by Larsen   25.00
...: This Savage World SC (2003, $15.95) r/#76-81; intro. by Larsen   16.00
...: Worlds at War SC (2004, $16.95) r/#41-46; intro. by Larsen; sketch pages
                                    17.00

SAVAGE SHE-HULK, THE (See The Avengers, Marvel Graphic Novel #18 &
The Sensational She-Hulk)
Marvel Comics Group: Feb, 1980 - No. 25, Feb, 1982

	GD	FN	NM-
1-Origin & 1st app. She-Hulk	2	6	12
2-5,25: 25-(52 pgs.)			6.00

	GD	FN	NM-

6-24: 6-She-Hulk vs. Iron Man. 8-Vs. Man-Thing   5.00

SAVAGE SWORD OF CONAN (The... #41 on; ...The Barbarian #175 on)
Marvel Comics Group: Aug, 1974 - No. 235, July, 1995 ($1.00/$1.25/$2.25, B&W magazine, mature)

	GD	FN	NM-
1-Smith-r; J. Buscema/N. Adams/Krenkel-a; origin Blackmark by Gil Kane (part 1, ends #3); Blackmark's 1st app. in magazine form-r/from paperback) & Red Sonja (3rd app.)	9	27	120
2-Neal Adams-c; Chaykin/N. Adams-a	4	12	50
3-Severin/B. Smith-a; N. Adams-a	3	10	35
4-Neal Adams/Kane-a(r)	3	9	25
5-10: 5-Jeff Jones frontispiece (r)	2	6	20
11-20	2	6	15
21-30	2	6	12
31-50: 34-3 pg. preview of Conan newspaper strip. 35-Cover similar to Savage Tales #1. 45-Red Sonja returns; begin $1.25-c	1	4	10
51-99: 63-Toth frontispiece. 65-Kane-a w/Chaykin/Miller/Simonson/Sherman finishes. 70-Article on movie. 83-Red Sonja-r by Neal Adams from #1	1	3	7
100	1	3	8
101-176: 163-Begin $2.25-c. 169-King Kull story. 171-Soloman Kane by Williamson (i). 172-Red Sonja story			6.00
177-199: 179,187,192-Red Sonja app. 190-193-4 part King Kull story. 196-King Kull story			5.00
200-220: 200-New Buscema-a; Robert E. Howard app. with Conan in story. 202-King Kull story. 204-60th anniversary (1932-92). 211-Rafael Kayanan's 1st Conan-a. 214-Sequel to Red Nails by Howard			6.00
221-230	1	3	8
231-234	1	4	10
235-Last issue	2	6	16
Special 1(1975, B&W)-B. Smith-r/Conan #10,13	3	9	25

SCARY TALES
Charlton Comics: 8/75 - #9, 1/77; #10, 9/77 - #20, 6/79; #21, 8/80 - #46, 10/84

	GD	FN	NM-
1-Origin/1st app. Countess Von Bludd, not in #2	3	9	30
2,4,6,9,10: 4-Sutton-c. 9-Sutton-c/a	2	6	12
3-Sutton painted-c; Ditko-a	2	6	16
5,11-Ditko-c/a.	2	6	18
7,8-Ditko-a	2	6	14
12,15,16,19,21,39-Ditko-a	2	6	12
13,17,20	1	3	9
14,18,30,32-Ditko-c/a	2	6	15
22-29,33-37,39,40: 37,38,40-New-a. 39-Reprints	1	3	8
31,38: 31-Newton-c/a. 38-Mr. Jigsaw app.	1	3	8
41-45-New-a. 41-Ditko-a(3). 42-45-(Low print)	1	3	9
46-Reprints (Low print)	2	6	14
1(Modern Comics reprint, 1977)			4.00

SCOOBY DOO (TV)(...Where are you? #1-16,26; ...Mystery Comics #17-25,

	GD	FN	NM-

27 on)

Gold Key: Mar, 1970 - No. 30, Feb, 1975 (Hanna-Barbera)

	GD	FN	NM-
1	14	42	200
2-5	8	24	105
6-10	7	21	85
11-20: 11-Tufts-a	6	18	65
21-30	4	12	48

SCOOBY DOO (TV)
Charlton Comics: Apr, 1975 - No. 11, Dec, 1976 (Hanna-Barbera)

	GD	FN	NM-
1	7	21	80
2-5	4	12	48
6-11	4	12	38
nn-(1976, digest, 68 pgs., B&W)	4	12	45

SECRET ORIGINS (1st Series) (See 80 Page Giant #8)
National Periodical Publications: Aug-Oct, 1961 (Annual) (Reprints)

1-Origin Adam Strange (Showcase #17), Green Lantern (Green Lantern
 #1), Challengers (partial-r/Showcase #6, 6 pgs. Kirby-a), J'onn J'onzz
 (Det. #225), The Flash (Showcase #4),Green Arrow (1 pg. text),
 Superman-Batman team (World's Finest #94), Wonder Woman
 (Wonder Woman #105)   49   147   825
Replica Edition (1998, $4.95) r/entire book and house ads   5.00
Even More Secret Origins (2003, $6.95) reprints origins of Hawkman, Eclipso,
 Kid Flash, Blackhawks, Green Lantern's oath, and Jimmy Olsen-Robin
 team in 80 pg. Giant style   7.00

SECRET ORIGINS (2nd Series)
National Periodical Publications: Feb-Mar, 1973 - No. 6, Jan-Feb, 1974; No.
7, Oct-Nov, 1974 (All 20¢ issues) (All origin reprints)

1-Superman (r/1 pg. origin/Action #1, 1st time since G.A.), Batman (Det. #33),
 Ghost (Flash #88), The Flash (Showcase #4)   5   15   55
2-7: 2-Green Lantern & The Atom (Showcase #22 & 34), Supergirl (Action
 #252). 3-Wonder Woman (W.W. #1), Wildcat (Sensation #1). 4-Vigilante
 (Action #42) by Meskin, Kid Eternity (Hit #25). 5-The Spectre by Baily
 (More Fun #52,53). 6-Blackhawk (Military #1) & Legion of Super-Heroes
 (Superboy #147). 7-Robin (Detective #38), Aquaman (More Fun #73)
                                                    3   9   30
NOTE: *Infantino* a-1. **Kane** a-2. *Kubert* a-1.

SECRET ORIGINS (3rd Series)
DC Comics: 4/86 - No. 50, 8/90 (All origins)(52 pgs. #6 on)(#27 on: $1.50)

1-Origin Superman   6.00
2-6: 2-Blue Beetle. 3-Shazam. 4-Firestorm. 5-Crimson Avenger. 6-Halo/G.A.
 Batman   3.00
7-9,11,12,14-20,22-26: 7-Green Lantern (Guy Gardner)/G.A. Sandman.
 8-Shadow Lass/Doll Man. 9-G.A. Flash/Skyman.11-G.A. Hawkman/Power
 Girl. 12-Challengers of Unknown/G.A. Fury (2nd modern app.). 14-Suicide
 Squad; Legends spin-off. 15-Spectre/Deadman. 16-G.A. Hourman/Warlord.
 17-Adam Strange story by Carmine infantino; Dr. Occult. 18-G.A. Green
 Lantern/The Creeper. 19-Uncle Sam/The Guardian. 20-Batgirl/G.A. Dr.

	GD	FN	NM-

Mid-Nite. 22-Manhunters. 23-Floronic Man/Guardians of the Universe.
    24-Blue Devil/Dr. Fate. 25-LSH/Atom. 26-Black Lightning/Miss America 2.50
10-Phantom Stranger w/Alan Moore scripts; Legends spin-off   2.50
13-Origin Nightwing; Johnny Thunder app.   2.50
21-Jonah Hex/Black Condor   2.50
27-30,36-38,40-49: 27-Zatara/Zatanna. 28-Midnight/Nightshade. 29-Power of
    the Atom/Mr. America; new 3 pg. Red Tornado story by Mayer (last app. of
    Scribbly, 8/88). 30-Plastic Man/Elongated Man. 36-Poison Ivy by Neil
    Gaiman & Mark Buckingham/Green Lantern. 37-Legion Of Substitute
    Heroes/Doctor Light. 38-Green Arrow/Speedy; Grell scripts. 40-All Ape
    issue. 41-Rogues Gallery of Flash. 42-Phantom Girl/GrimGhost.
    43-Original Hawk & Dove/Cave Carson/Chris KL-99. 44-Batman app.;
    story based on Det. #40. 45-Blackhawk/El Diablo. 46-JLA/LSH/New Titans.
    47-LSH. 48-Ambush Bug/Stanley & His Monster/Rex the Wonder Dog/
    Trigger Twins. 49-Newsboy Legion/Silent Knight/Bouncing Boy   2.50
31-35,39: 31-JSA. 32-JLA. 33-35-JLI. 39-Animal Man-c/story continued in
    Animal Man #10; Grant Morrison scripts; Batman app.   3.00
50-($3.95, 100 pgs.)-Batman & Robin in text, Flash of Two Worlds, Johnny
    Thunder, Dolphin, Black Canary & Space Museum   5.00
Annual 1 (8/87)-Capt. Comet/Doom Patrol   3.00
Annual 2 ('88, $2.00)-Origin Flash II & Flash III   3.00
Annual 3 ('89, $2.95, 84 pgs.)-Teen Titans; 1st app. new Flamebird who
    replaces original Bat-Girl   3.00
Special 1 (10/89, $2.00)-Batman villains: Penguin, Riddler, & Two-Face;
    Bolland-c; Sam Kieth-a; Neil Gaiman scripts(2)   3.00

SECRET SOCIETY OF SUPER-VILLAINS
National Per. Publ./DC Comics: May-June, 1976 - No. 15, June-July, 1978

	GD	FN	NM-
1-Origin; JLA cameo & Capt. Cold app.	2	6	18
2-5,15: 2-Re-intro/origin Capt. Comet; Green Lantern x-over. 5-Green Lantern, Hawkman x-over; Darkseid app. 15-G.A. Atom, Dr. Midnite, & JSA app.	1	4	10
6-14: 9,10-Creeper x-over. 11-Capt. Comet; Orlando-i	1	3	8

SECRETS OF HAUNTED HOUSE
National Periodical Publications/DC Comics: 4-5/75 - #5, 12-1/75-76; #6, 6-7/77 - #14, 10-11/78; #15, 8/79 - #46, 3/82

	GD	FN	NM-
1	5	15	55
2-4	3	9	24
5-Wrightson-c	3	9	30
6-14	2	6	16
15-30	1	4	10
31,44: 31-(12/80) Mr. E series begins (1st app.), ends #41. 44-Wrightson-c	2	6	12
32-(1/81) Origin of Mr. E	1	4	10
33-43,45,46: 34,35-Frankenstein Monster app.	1	3	7

SECRETS OF SINISTER HOUSE (Sinister House of Secret Love #1-4)
National Periodical Publ.: No. 5, June-July, 1972 - No. 18, June-July, 1974

	GD	FN	NM-
5-(52 pgs.).	5	15	55

	GD	FN	NM-
6-9: 7-Redondo-a	3	9	30
10-Neal Adams-a(i)	3	10	35
11-18: 15-Redondo-a. 17-Barry-a; early Chaykin 1 pg. strip	2	6	18

SECRET WARS II (Also see Marvel Super Heroes...)
Marvel Comics Group: July, 1985 - No. 9, Mar, 1986 (Maxi-series)

1,9: 9-(52 pgs.) X-Men app., Spider-Man app.			4.00
2-8: 2,8-X-Men app. 5-1st app. Boom Boom. 5,8-Spider-Man app.			3.00

SENSATIONAL SPIDER-MAN, THE
Marvel Comics: Jan, 1996 - No. 33, Nov, 1998 ($1.95/$1.99)

0 ($4.95)-Lenticular-c; Jurgens-a/scripts			5.00
1			5.00
1-($2.95) variant-c; polybagged w/cassette	1	3	8
2-5: 2-Kaine & Rhino app. 3-Giant-Man app.			4.00
6-18: 9-Onslaught tie-in; revealed that Peter & Mary Jane's unborn baby is a girl. 11-Revelations. 13-15-Ka-Zar app. 14,15-Hulk app.			3.00
19-24: Living Pharoah app. 22,23-Dr. Strange app.			2.50
25-($2.99) Spiderhunt pt. 1; Normie Osborne kidnapped			4.00
25-Variant-c	1	3	8
26-33: 26-Nauck-a. 27-Double-c with "The Sensational Hornet #1"; Vulture app. 28-Hornet vs. Vulture. 29,30-Black Cat-c/app. 33-Last issue; Gathering of Five concludes			2.50
#(-1) Flashback(7/97) Dezago-s/Wieringo-a			3.00
'96 Annual ($2.95)			3.00

SENTRY (Also see New Avengers)
Marvel Comics: Sept, 2000 - No. 5, Jan, 2001 ($2.99, limited series)

1-5-Paul Jenkins-s/Jae Lee-a. 3-Spider-Man-c/app. 4-X-Men, FF app.			3.00
.../Fantastic Four (2/01, $2.99) Continues story from #5; Winslade-a			3.00
.../Hulk (2/01, $2.99) Sienkiewicz-c/a			3.00
.../Spider-Man (2/01, $2.99) back story of the Sentry; Leonardi-a			3.00
.../The Void (2/01, $2.99) Conclusion of story; Jae Lee-a			3.00
.../X-Men (2/01, $2.99) Sentry and Archangel; Texeira-a			3.00
TPB (10/01, $24.95) r/#1-5 & all one-shots; Stan Lee interview			25.00

SGT. FURY (& His Howling Commandos)(See Fury & Special Marvel Edition)
Marvel Comics Group (BPC earlier issues): May, 1963 - No. 167, Dec, 1981

	GD	FN	NM-
1-1st app. Sgt. Nick Fury (becomes agent of Shield in Strange Tales #135); Kirby/Ayers-c/a; 1st Dum-Dum Dugan & the Howlers	132	396	2500
2-Kirby-a	38	114	600
3-5: 3-Reed Richards x-over. 4-Death of Junior Juniper. 5-1st Baron Strucker app.; Kirby-a	22	66	325
6-10: 8-Baron Zemo, 1st Percival Pinkerton app. 9-Hitler-c & app. 10-1st app. Capt. Savage (the Skipper)(9/64)	13	39	190
11,12,14-20: 14-1st Blitz Squad. 18-Death of Pamela Hawley	8	24	100
13-Captain America & Bucky app.(12/64); 2nd solo Capt. America x-over			

	GD	FN	NM-
outside The Avengers; Kirby-a	34	102	540
13-2nd printing (1994)	2	6	12
21-24,26,28-30	6	18	70
25,27: 25-Red Skull app. 27-1st app. Eric Koenig; origin Fury's eye patch			
	6	18	75
31-33,35-50: 35-Eric Koenig joins Howlers. 43-Bob Hope, Glen Miller app.			
44-Flashback on Howlers' 1st mission	4	12	40
34-Origin Howling Commandos	4	12	42
51-60	3	9	32
61-67: 64-Capt. Savage & Raiders x-over; peace symbol-c. 67-Last 12¢			
issue; flag-c	3	9	26
68-80: 76-Fury's Father app. in WWI story	3	9	24
81-91: 91-Last 15¢ issue	2	6	20
92-(52 pgs.)	3	9	26
93-99: 98-Deadly Dozen x-over	2	6	18
100-Capt. America, Fantastic 4 cameos; Stan Lee, Martin Goodman &			
others app.	3	9	26
101-120: 101-Origin retold	2	6	15
121-130: 121-123-r/#19-21	1	4	10
131-167: 167-Reprints (from 1963)	1	3	8
133,134-(30¢-c variants, limited dist.)(5,7/76)	2	6	12
141,142-(35¢-c variants, limited dist.)(7,9/77)	2	6	12
Annual 1(1965, 25¢, 72 pgs.)-r/#4,5 & new-a	15	45	220
Special 2(1966)	6	18	70
Special 3(1967) All new material	4	12	45
Special 4(1968)	3	9	32
Special 5-7(1969-11/71)	3	9	24

SGT. ROCK (Formerly Our Army at War; see Brave & the Bold #52 &
Showcase #45)
National Per. Publ./DC Comics: No. 302, Mar, 1977 - No. 422, July, 1988

302	3	10	35
303-310	2	6	18
311-320: 318-Reprints	2	6	12
321-350	1	3	9
329-Whitman variant (scarce)	1	4	10
351-399,401-421			6.00
400,422: 422-1st Joe, Adam, Andy Kubert-a team	1	3	9
Annual 2-4: 2(1982)-Formerly Sgt. Rock's Prize Battle Tales #1. 3(1983).			
4(1984)	1	3	9

SHADE, THE CHANGING MAN (See Cancelled Comic Cavalcade)
National Per. Publ./DC Comics: June July, 1977 - No. 8, Aug-Sept, 1978

1-1st app. Shade; Ditko-c/a in all	2	6	14
2-8	1	3	8

SHANNA, THE SHE-DEVIL (See Savage Tales #8)
Marvel Comics Group: Dec, 1972 - No. 5, Aug, 1973 (All are 20¢ issues)

1-1st app. Shanna; Steranko-c; Tuska-a(p)	3	9	32
2-Steranko-c; heroin drug story	3	9	24

	GD	FN	NM-
3-5	2	6	16

SHAZAM! (See Limited Collectors' Edition & The Power Of Shazam!)
National Periodical Publ./DC Comics: Feb, 1973 - No. 35, May-June, 1978

1-1st revival of original Captain Marvel since G.A. (origin retold), by C.C. Beck; Mary Marvel & Captain Marvel Jr. app.; Superman-c	4	12	50
2-5: 2-Infinity photo-c.; re-intro Mr. Mind & Tawny. 3-Capt. Marvel-r. (10/46). 4-Origin retold; Capt. Marvel-r. (1949). 5-Capt. Marvel Jr. origin retold; Capt. Marvel-r. (1948, 7 pgs.)	2	6	18
6,7,9-11: 6-photo-c; Capt. Marvel-r (1950, 6 pgs.). 9-Mr. Mind app. 10-Last C.C. Beck issue. 11-Schaffenberger-a begins.	2	6	15
8 (100 pgs.). 8-r/Capt. Marvel Jr. by Raboy; origin/C.M. #80; origin Mary Marvel/C.M.A. #18; origin Mr. Tawny/C.M.A. #79	6	18	65
12-17-(All 100 pgs.). 15-vs. Lex Luthor & Mr. Mind	5	15	55
18-24,26-30: 21-24-All reprints. 26-Sivana app. (10/76). 27-Kid Eternity teams up w/Capt. Marvel. 28-1st S.A. app. of Black Adam. 30-1st DC app. 3 Lt. Marvels	2	6	12
25-1st app. Isis	2	6	16
31-35: 31-1st DC app. Minuteman. 34-Origin Capt. Nazi & Capt. Marvel Jr. retold	2	6	16

SHAZAM!: POWER OF HOPE
DC Comics: Nov, 2000 ($9.95, treasury size, one-shot)

nn-Painted art by Alex Ross; story by Alex Ross and Paul Dini			10.00

SHOWCASE (See Cancelled Comic Cavalcade & New Talent...)
National Per. Publ./DC Comics: 3-4/56 - No. 93, 9/70; No. 94, 8-9/77 - No. 104, 9/78

	GD	FN	NM-
1-Fire Fighters; w/Fireman Farrell	262	786	5500
2-Kings of the Wild; Kubert-a (animal stories)	81	243	1550
3-The Frogmen by Heath; Heath greytone-c (early DC example, 7-8/56)	79	237	1500
4-Origin/1st app. The Flash (1st DC Silver Age hero, Sept-Oct, 1956); Kanigher-s; Infantino & Kubert-c/a; 1st app. Iris West and The Turtle; Flash shown reading G.A. Flash Comics #13; back-up story w/Broome-s/ Infantino & Kubert-a	1200	3600	42,000
5-Manhunters	80	240	1525
6-Origin/1st app. Challengers of the Unknown by Kirby, partly r/in Secret Origins #1 & Challengers #64,65 (1st S.A. hero team & 1st original concept S.A. series)(1-2/57)	286	858	6000
7-Challengers of the Unknown by Kirby (2nd app.) reprinted in Challengers of the Unknown #75	145	435	2750
8-The Flash (5-6/57, 2nd app.); origin & 1st app. Captain Cold	820	2460	17,000
9-Lois Lane (Pre-#1, 7-8/57) (1st Showcase character to win own series) Superman app. on-c	625	1875	11,000
10-Lois Lane; Jor-el cameo; Superman app. on-c	226	678	4750
11-Challengers of the Unknown by Kirby (3rd)	139	417	2650
12-Challengers of the Unknown by Kirby (4th)	139	417	2650

	GD	FN	NM-
13-The Flash (3rd app.); origin Mr. Element	314	942	6900
14-The Flash (4th app.); origin Dr. Alchemy, former Mr. Element (rare in NM)	329	987	7250
15-Space Ranger (7-8/58, 1st app.)	157	471	3150
16-Space Ranger (9-10/58, 2nd app.)	80	240	1525
17-(11-12/58)-Adventures on Other Worlds; origin/1st app. Adam Strange by Gardner Fox & Mike Sekowsky	190	570	3800
18-Adventures on Other Worlds (2nd A. Strange)	100	300	1900
19-Adam Strange; 1st Adam Strange logo	111	333	2100
20-Rip Hunter; origin & 1st app. (5-6/59); Moriera-a	84	252	1600
21-Rip Hunter (7-8/59, 2nd app.); Sekowsky-c/a	47	141	800
22-Origin & 1st app. Silver Age Green Lantern by Gil Kane and John Broome (9-10/59); reprinted in Secret Origins #2	341	1023	7500
23-Green Lantern (11-12/59, 2nd app.); nuclear explosion-c	129	387	2450
24-Green Lantern (1-2/60, 3rd app.)	129	387	2450
25,26-Rip Hunter by Kubert. 25-Grey tone-c	33	99	525
27-Sea Devils (7-8/60, 1st app.); Heath-c/a	71	213	1350
28-Sea Devils (9-10/60, 2nd app.); Heath-c/a	40	120	635
29-Sea Devils; Heath-c/a; grey tone c-27-29	40	120	635
30-Origin Silver Age Aquaman (1-2/61) (see Adventure #260 for 1st S.A. origin)	67	201	1275
31,32-Aquaman	40	120	635
33-Aquaman	41	123	655
34-Origin & 1st app. Silver Age Atom by Gil Kane & Murphy Anderson (9-10/61); reprinted in Secret Origins #2	116	348	2200
35-The Atom by Gil Kane (2nd); last 10¢ issue	63	189	1200
36-The Atom by Gil Kane (1-2/62, 3rd app.)	50	150	900
37-Metal Men (3-4/62, 1st app.)	56	168	1075
38-Metal Men (5-6/62, 2nd app.)	40	120	640
39-Metal Men (7-8/62, 3rd app.)	31	93	475
40-Metal Men (9-10/62, 4th app.)	29	87	425
41,42-Tommy Tomorrow (parts 1 & 2). 42-Origin	19	57	275
43-Dr. No (James Bond); Nodel-a; originally published as British Classics Illustrated #158A & as #6 in a European Detective series, all with diff. painted-c. This Showcase #43 version is actually censored, deleting all racial skin color and dialogue thought to be racially demeaning (1st DC S.A. movie adaptation)(based on Ian Fleming novel & movie)	41	123	675
44-Tommy Tomorrow	12	36	175
45-Sgt. Rock (7-8/63); pre-dates B&B #52; origin retold; Heath-c	30	90	450
46,47-Tommy Tomorrow	11	33	150
48,49-Cave Carson (3rd tryout series; see B&B)	9	27	120
50,51-I Spy (Danger Trail-r by Infantino), King Farady story (#50 has new 4 pg. story)	8	24	105
52-Cave Carson	8	24	105
53,54-G.I. Joe (11-12/64, 1-2/65); Heath-a	12	36	175
55-Dr. Fate & Hourman (3-4/65); origin of each in text; 1st solo app. G.A.			

	GD	FN	NM-
Green Lantern in Silver Age (pre-dates Gr. Lantern #40); 1st S.A. app. Solomon Grundy	26	78	380
56-Dr. Fate & Hourman	15	45	220
57-Enemy Ace by Kubert (7-8/65, 4th app. after Our Army at War #155)	22	66	325
58-Enemy Ace by Kubert (5th app.)	19	57	275
59-Teen Titans (11-12/65, 3rd app.)	12	36	180
60-1st S. A. app. The Spectre; Anderson-a (1-2/66); origin in text	30	90	440
61-The Spectre by Anderson (2nd app.)	15	45	225
62-Origin & 1st app. Inferior Five (5-6/66)	10	30	140
63,65-Inferior Five. 63-Hulk parody. 65-X-Men parody (11-12/66)	7	21	80
64-The Spectre by Anderson (5th app.)	15	45	215
66,67-B'wana Beast	5	15	55
68-Maniaks (1st app., spoof of The Monkees)	5	15	55
69,71-Maniaks. 71-Woody Allen-c/app.	5	15	55
70-Binky (9-10/67)-Tryout issue; 1950's Leave It To Binky reprints with art changes	6	18	70
72-Top Gun (Johnny Thunder-r)-Toth-a	5	15	55
73-Origin/1st app. Creeper; Ditko-c/a (3-4/68)	15	45	215
74-Intro/1st app. Anthro; Post-c/a (5/68)	10	30	130
75-Origin/1st app. Hawk & the Dove; Ditko-c/a	13	39	190
76-1st app. Bat Lash (8/68)	8	24	95
77-1st app. Angel & The Ape (9/68)	8	24	95
78-1st app. Jonny Double (11/68)	5	15	55
79-1st app. Dolphin (12/68); Aqualad origin-r	7	21	80
80-1st S.A. app. Phantom Stranger (1/69); Neal Adams-c	9	27	120
81-Windy & Willy; r/Many Loves of Dobie Gillis #26 with art changes	5	15	60
82-1st app. Nightmaster (5/69) by Grandenetti & Giordano; Kubert-c	8	24	95
83,84-Nightmaster by Wrightson w/Jones/Kaluta ink assist in each; Kubert-c. 83-Last 12¢ issue 84-Origin retold; begin 15¢	7	21	90
85-87-Firehair; Kubert-a	3	9	30
88-90-Jason's Quest: 90-Manhunter 2070 app.	3	9	25
91-93-Manhunter 2070: 92-Origin. 93-(9/70) Last 15¢ issue	3	9	25
94-Intro/origin new Doom Patrol & Robotman(8-9/77)	2	6	18
95,96-The Doom Patrol. 95-Origin Celsius	1	3	9
97-99-Power Girl; origin-97,98; JSA cameos	1	3	9
100-(52 pgs.)-Most Showcase characters featured	2	6	15
101-103-Hawkman; Adam Strange x-over	1	3	9
104-(52 pgs.)-O.S.S. Spies at War	1	3	9

SILVER SURFER, THE (Also see Essential Silver Surfer)
Marvel Comics Group: Aug, 1968 - No. 18, Sept, 1970; June, 1982

	GD	FN	NM-
1-More detailed origin by John Buscema (p); The Watcher back-up stories begin (origin), end #7; (No. 1-7: 25¢, 68 pgs.)	41	123	675

	GD	FN	NM-
2	19	57	275
3-1st app. Mephisto	16	48	235
4-Lower distribution; Thor & Loki app.	38	114	600
5-7-Last giant size. 5-The Stranger app.; Fantastic Four app. 6-Brunner inks.			
7-(8/69)-Early cameo Frankenstein's monster (see X-Men #40)			
	11	33	150
8-10: 8-18-(15¢ issues)	9	27	110
11-13,15-18: 15-Silver Surfer vs. Human Torch; Fantastic Four app. 17-Nick			
Fury app. 18-Vs. The Inhumans; Kirby-c/a.	8	24	100
14-Spider-Man x-over	12	36	165
V2#1 (6/82, 52 pgs.)-Byrne-c/a	1	4	10

SILVER SURFER (Volume 3) (See Marvel Graphic Novel #38)
Marvel Comics Group: V3#1, July, 1987 - No. 146, Nov, 1998

	GD	FN	NM-
1-Double size ($1.25)	1	3	9
2-17: 15-Ron Lim-c/a begins (9/88)			4.00
18-33,39-43: 25,31 ($1.50, 52 pgs.). 25-Skrulls app. 32,39-No Ron Lim-c/a.			
39-Alan Grant scripts			3.00
34-Thanos returns (cameo); Starlin scripts begin			5.00
35-38: 35-1st full Thanos app. in Silver Surfer (3/90); reintro Drax the			
Destroyer on last pg. (cameo). 36-Recaps history of Thanos; Capt. Marvel			
& Warlock app. in recap. 37-1st full app. Drax the Destroyer; Drax-c.			
38-Silver Surfer battles Thanos			6.00
44,45,49-Thanos stories (c-44,45)			4.00
46-48: 46-Return of Adam Warlock (2/91); re-intro Gamora & Pip the Troll.			
47-Warlock battles Drax. 48-Last Starlin scripts (also #50)			4.00
50-($1.50, 52 pgs.)-Embossed & silver foil-c; Silver Surfer has brief battle			
w/Thanos; story cont'd in Infinity Gauntlet #1	1	3	7
50-2nd & 3rd printings			2.50
51-59: 51-53: Infinity Gauntlet x-over . 54-57: Infinity Gauntlet x-overs.			
54-Rhino app. 55,56-Thanos-c & app. 57-Thanos-c & cameo. 58,59-Infinity			
Gauntlet x-overs; 58-Ron Lim-c only. 59-Thanos battles Silver			
Surfer-c/story; Thanos joins			3.00
60-74,76-99,101-124,126-139: 63-Capt. Marvel app. 67-69-Infinity War			
x-overs. 126-Dr. Strange-c/app. 128-Spider-Man & Daredevil-c/app.			
138-Thing-c			2.50
75-($2.50, 52 pgs.)-Embossed foil-c; Lim-c/a			3.00
100 ($2.25, 52 pgs.)-Wraparound-c			2.50
100 ($3.95, 52 pgs.)-Enhanced-c			4.00
125 ($2.95)-Wraparound-c; Vs. Hulk-c/app.			3.00
140-146: 140-142,144,145-Muth-c/a. 143,146-Cowan-a. 146-Last issue			2.50
#(-1) Flashback (7/97)			2.50
Annual 1 (1988, $1.75)-Evolutionary War app.; 1st Ron Lim-a on Silver Surfer			
(20 pg. back-up story & pin-ups)			5.00
Annual 2-7 ('89-'94, 68 pgs.): 2-Atlantis Attacks. 4-3 pg. origin story; Silver			
Surfer battles Guardians of the Galaxy. 5-Return of the Defenders, part 3;			
Lim-c/a (3 pgs. of pin-ups only). 6-Polybagged w/trading card; 1st app.			
Legacy; card is by Lim/Austin			3.00
Annual '97 ($2.99), .../Thor Annual '98 ($2.99)			3.00
Ashcan (1995, 75¢) reprints part of V1#3; Lim-c			2.25

	GD	FN	NM-
...Dangerous Artifacts-(1996, $3.95)-Ron Marz scripts; Galactus-c/app.			4.00
Graphic Novel (1988, HC, $14.95) Judgment Day; Lee-s/Buscema-a			15.00
The Enslavers Graphic Novel (1990, $16.95)			17.00
Homecoming Graphic Novel (1991, $12.95, softcover) Starlin-s			15.00
Inner Demons TPB (4/98, $3.50)r/#123,125,126			3.50
...: The First Coming of Galactus nn (11/92, $5.95, 68 pgs.)-Reprints			
Fantastic Four #48-50 with new Lim-c			6.00
Wizard 1/2	2	6	15

SIMPSONS COMICS (See Bartman, Futurama, Itchy & Scratchy & Radioactive Man)
Bongo Comics Group: 1993 - Present ($1.95/$2.50/$2.99)

1-($2.25)-FF#1-c swipe; pull-out poster; flip book	1	3	8
2-5: 2-Patty & Selma flip-c/sty. 3-Krusty, Agent of K.L.O.W.N. flip-c/story. 4-Infinity-c; flip-c of Busman #1; w/trading card. 5-Wraparound-c w/trading card			5.00
6-40: All Flip books. 6-w/Chief Wiggum's "Crime Comics". 7-w/"McBain Comics". 8-w/"Edna, Queen of the Congo". 9-w/"Barney Gumble". 10-w/"Apu". 11-w/"Homer". 12-w/"White Knuckled War Stories". 13-w/"Jimbo Jones' Wedgie Comics". 14-w/"Grampa". 15-w/"Itchy & Scratchy". 16-w/"Bongo Grab Bag". 17-w/"Headlight Comics". 18-w/"Milhouse". 19,20-w/"Roswell". 21,22-w/"Roswell". 23-w/"Hellfire Comics". 24-w/"Lil' Homey". 36-39-Flip book w/Radioactive Man			4.00
41-49,51-99: 43-Flip book w/Poochie. 52-Dini-s. 85-Begin $2.99-c.			3.00
50-($5.95) Wraparound-c; 80 pgs.; square-bound	1	3	7
100-($6.99) 100 pgs.; square-bound; clip issue of past highlights			7.00
... A Go-Go (1999, $11.95)-r/#32-35; ...Big Bonanza (1998, $11.95)-r/#28-31, ...Extravaganza (1994, $10.00)-r/#1-4; infinity-c, ...On Parade (1998, $11.95)-r/#24-27, ...Simpsorama (1996, $10.95)-r/#11-14			12.00
Simpsons Classics 1,2 (2004, $3.99, magazine-size) 1-r/#1&2; cover gallery			4.00
Simpsons Comics Belly Buster ('04, $14.95) r/#49,51,53-56			15.00
Simpsons Comics Madness ('03, $14.95) r/#43-48			15.00
Simpsons Comics Royale ('01, $14.95) r/various Bongo issues			15.00

SIMPSONS COMICS PRESENTS BART SIMPSON
Bongo Comics Group: 2000 - Present ($2.50/$2.99, quarterly)

1-20: 7-9-Dan DeCarlo-layouts. 13-Begin $2.99-c. 17-Bartman app.			3.00
The Big Book of Bart Simpson TPB (2002, $12.95) r/#1-4			13.00
The Big Bad Book of Bart Simpson TPB (2003, $12.95) r/#5-8			13.00
The Big Bratty Book of Bart Simpson TPB (2004, $12.95) r/#9-12			13.00

SIN CITY (See Dark Horse Presents, A Decade of Dark Horse, & San Diego Comic Con Comics #2,4)
Dark Horse Comics (Legend)

TPB ($15.00) Reprints early DHP stories			15.00
Booze, Broads & Bullets TPB ($15.00)			15.00

SIN CITY (FRANK MILLER'S...) (Reissued TPBs to coincide with the April 2005 movie)
Dark Horse Books: Feb, 2005 ($17.00/$19.00, 6" x 9" format with new Miller

GD   FN   NM-

covers)

Volume 1: The Hard Goodbye ($17.00) reprints stories from Dark Horse
    Presents #51-62 and DHP Fifth Anniv. Special; covers and publicity pieces
                                                                    17.00
Volume 2: A Dame to Kill For ($17.00) r/Sin City: A Dame to Kill For #1-6
                                                                    17.00
Volume 3: The Big Fat Kill ($17.00) r/Sin City: The Big Fat Kill #1-5; pin-up
    gallery   17.00
Volume 4: That Yellow Bastard ($19.00) r/Sin City: That Yellow Bastard #1-6;
    pin-up gallery by Mike Allred, Kyle Baker, Jeff Smith and Bruce Timm;
    cover gallery   19.00
Volume 5: Family Values ($12.00) r/Sin City: Family Values GN   12.00
Volume 6: Booze, Broads & Bullets ($15.00) r/Sin City: The Babe Wore Red
    and Other Stories; Silent Night; story from A Decade of Dark Horse; Lost
    Lonely & Lethal; Sex & Violence; and Just Another Saturday Night 15.00
Volume 7: Hell and Back ($28.00) r/Sin City: Hell and Back #1-9; pin-up
    gallery   28.00

SIN CITY: A DAME TO KILL FOR
Dark Horse Comics (Legend): Nov, 1993 - No. 6, May, 1994 ($2.95, B&W,
limited series)

1-6: Frank Miller-c/a & story in all. 1-1st app. Dwight.			5.00
Limited Edition Hardcover			85.00
Hardcover			25.00
TPB ($15.00)			15.00

SIN CITY: FAMILY VALUES
Dark Horse Comics (Legend): Oct, 1997 ($10.00, B&W, squarebound, one-
shot)

nn-Miller-c/a & story			10.00
Limited Edition Hardcover			75.00

SIN CITY: HELL AND BACK
Dark Horse (Maverick): Jul, 1999 - No. 9 ($2.95/$4.95, B&W, limited series)

1-8-Miller-c/a & story. 7-Color			3.00
9-($4.95)			5.00

SIN CITY: JUST ANOTHER SATURDAY NIGHT
Dark Horse Comics (Legend): Aug, 1997 (Wizard 1/2 offer, B&W, one-shot)

1/2-Miller-c/a & story	1	3	8
nn (10/98, $2.50) r/#1/2			2.50

SIN CITY: LOST, LONELY & LETHAL
Dark Horse Comics (Legend): Dec, 1996 ($2.95, B&W and blue, one-shot)

nn-Miller-c/s/a; w/pin-ups			4.00

SIN CITY: SEX AND VIOLENCE
Dark Horse Comics (Legend): Mar, 1997 ($2.95, B&W and blue, one-shot)

nn-Miller-c/a & story			4.00

SIN CITY: SILENT NIGHT
Dark Horse Comics (Legend): Dec, 1995 ($2.95, B&W, one-shot)

	GD	FN	NM-
1-Miller-c/a & story; Marv app.			4.00

SIN CITY: THAT YELLOW BASTARD (Second Ed. TPB listed under Sin City (Frank Miller's...)
Dark Horse Comics (Legend): Feb, 1996 - No. 6, July, 1996 ($2.95/$3.50, B&W and yellow, limited series)

1-5: Miller-c/a & story in all. 1-1st app. Hartigan.			5.00
6-($3.50) Error & corrected			5.00
Limited Edition Hardcover			25.00
TPB ($15.00)			15.00

SIN CITY: THE BABE WORE RED AND OTHER STORIES
Dark Horse Comics (Legend): Nov, 1994 ($2.95, B&W and red, one-shot)

1-r/serial run in Previews as well as other stories; Miller-c/a & scripts; Dwight app.			3.00

SIN CITY: THE BIG FAT KILL (Second Edition TPB listed under Sin City (Frank Miller's...)
Dark Horse Comics (Legend): Nov, 1994 - No. 5, Mar, 1995 ($2.95, B&W, limited series)

1-5-Miller story & art in all; Dwight app.			4.00
Hardcover			25.00
TPB ($15.00)			15.00

SINISTER HOUSE OF SECRET LOVE, THE (Becomes Secrets of Sinister House No. 5 on)
National Periodical Publ.: Oct-Nov, 1971 - No. 4, Apr-May, 1972

1 (all 52 pgs.)	16	48	240
2,4: 2-Jeff Jones-c	8	24	100
3-Toth-a	8	24	105

SIX MILLION DOLLAR MAN, THE (TV)
Charlton Comics: 6/76 - No. 4, 12/76; No. 5, 10/77; No. 6, 2/78 - No. 9, 6/78

1-Staton-c/a; Lee Majors photo on-c	2	6	22
2-9: 2-Neal Adams-c; Staton-a	2	6	16

SIX MILLION DOLLAR MAN, THE (TV)(Magazine)
Charlton Comics: July, 1976 - No. 7, Nov, 1977 (B&W)

1-Neal Adams-c/a	3	9	28
2-Neal Adams-c	2	6	22
3-N. Adams part inks; Chaykin-a	2	6	18
4-7	2	6	15

SPACE FAMILY ROBINSON (TV)(...Lost in Space #15-37, ...Lost in Space On Space Station One #38 on)(See Gold Key Champion)
Gold Key: Dec, 1962 - No. 36, Oct, 1969; No. 37, 10/73 - No. 54, 11/78; No. 55, 3/81 - No. 59, 5/82 (All painted covers)

1-(Low distribution); Spiegle-a in all	25	75	370
2(3/63)-Family becomes lost in space	13	39	185
3-5	9	27	110
6-10: 6-Captain Venture back-up stories begin	8	24	95
11-20: 14-(10/65). 15-Title change (1/66)	6	18	65

	GD	FN	NM-
21-36: 28-Last 12¢ issue. 36-Captain Venture ends	4	12	45
37-48: 37-Origin retold	2	6	18
49-59: Reprints #49,50,55-59	2	6	12

NOTE: *The TV show first aired on 9/15/65. Title changed after TV show debuted.*

SPACE GHOST (TV) (Also see Golden Comics Digest #2 & Hanna-Barbera Super TV Heroes #3-7)
Gold Key: March, 1967 (Hanna-Barbera) (TV debut was 9/10/66)

	GD	FN	NM-
1 (10199-703)-Spiegle-a	33	99	525

SPACE GHOST (TV cartoon)
Comico: Mar, 1987 ($3.50, deluxe format, one-shot) (Hanna-Barbera)

1-Steve Rude-c/a	1	3	8

SPACE GHOST (TV cartoon)
DC Comics: Jan, 2005 - No. 6, June, 2005 ($2.95, limited series)

1-6-Alex Ross-c/Ariel Olivetti-a/Joe Kelly-s; origin of Space Ghost		3.00

SPACE: 1999 (TV) (Also see Power Record Comics)
Charlton Comics: Nov, 1975 - No. 7, Nov, 1976

1-Origin Moonbase Alpha; Staton-c/a	2	6	20
2,7: 2-Staton-a	2	6	14
3-6: All Byrne-a; c-3,5,6	2	6	20

SPACE: 1999 (TV)(Magazine)
Charlton Comics: Nov, 1975 - No. 8, Nov, 1976 (B&W) (#7 shows #6 inside)

1-Origin Moonbase Alpha; Morrow-c/a	2	6	22
2-8: 2,3-Morrow-c/a. 4-6-Morrow-c. 5,8-Morrow-a	2	6	16

SPAWN (Also see Curse of the Spawn and Sam & Twitch)
Image Comics (Todd McFarlane Prods.): May, 1992 - Present ($1.95/$2.50)

1-1st app. Spawn; McFarlane-c/a begins; McFarlane/Steacy-c; 1st Todd McFarlane Productions title.	1	4	10
1-Black & white edition	2	6	20
2,3: 2-1st app. Violator; McFarlane/Steacy-c	1	3	9
4-Contains coupon for Image Comics #0	1	3	9
4-With coupon missing			3.00
4-Newsstand edition w/o poster or coupon			3.00
5-Cerebus cameo (1 pg.) as stuffed animal; Spawn mobile poster #1			6.00
6-8,10: 7-Spawn Mobile poster #2. 8-Alan Moore scripts; Miller poster. 10-Cerebus app.; Dave Sim scripts; 1 pg. cameo app. by Superman			4.00
9-Neil Gaiman scripts; Jim Lee poster; 1st Angela.			6.00
11-17,19,20,22-30: 11-Miller script; Darrow poster. 12-Bloodwulf poster by Liefeld. 14,15-Violator app. 16,17-Grant Morrison scripts; Capullo-c/a(p). 23,24-McFarlane-a/stories. 25-(10/94). 19-(10/94). 20-(11/94)			3.00
18-Grant Morrison script, Capullo-c/a(p); low distr.	1	3	9
21-low distribution	1	3	9
31-49: 31-1st app. The Redeemer; new costume (brief). 32-1st full app. new costume. 38-40,42,44,46,48-Tony Daniel-c/a(p). 38-1st app. Cy-Gor. 40,41-Cy-Gor & Curse app.			4.00
50-($3.95, 48 pgs.)			3.00
51-66: 52-Savage Dragon app. 56-w/ Darkchylde preview. 57-Cy-Gor-c/app.			

	GD	FN	NM-

64-Polybagged w/McFarlane Toys catalog. 65-Photo-c of movie Spawn
and McFarlane   3.00
67-97: 81-Billy Kincaid returns. 97-Angela-c/app.   2.50
98,99,101-140-($2.50): 98,99-Angela app.   2.50
100-($4.95) Angela dies; 6 covers by McFarlane, Ross, Miller, Capullo, Wood,
Mignola   5.00
Annual 1-Blood & Shadows ('99, $4.95) Ashley Wood-c/a; Jenkins-s   5.00
...Bible-(8/96, $1.95)-Character bios   4.00
...Simony (5/04, $7.95) English translation of French Spawn story; Briclot-a
    8.00

NOTE: *Posters come with issues 1, 4, 7-9, 11, 12. #25 was released before #19 & 20.*

SPAWN-BATMAN (See Batman/Spawn: War Devil under Batman: One-Shots)
Image Comics (Todd McFarlane Productions): 1994 ($3.95, one-shot)

1-Miller scripts; McFarlane-c/a   6.00

SPECIAL MARVEL EDITION (Master of Kung Fu #17 on)
Marvel Comics Group: Jan, 1971 - No. 16, Feb, 1974 (#1-3: 25¢, 68 pgs.;
#4: 52 pgs.; #5-16: 20¢, regular ed.)

1-Thor-r by Kirby; 68 pgs.	3	9	30
2-4: Thor-r by Kirby; 2,3-68 pg. Giant. 4-(52 pgs.)	2	6	18
5-14: Sgt. Fury-r; 11-r/Sgt. Fury #13 (Capt. America)	1	4	10
15-Master of Kung Fu (Shang-Chi) begins (1st app., 12/73); Starlin-a;			
origin/1st app. Nayland Smith & Dr. Petric	9	27	120
16-1st app. Midnight; Starlin-a (2nd Shang-Chi)	4	12	50

NOTE: *Kirby c-10-14.*

SPECTACULAR SPIDER-MAN, THE (Magazine)
Marvel Comics Group: July, 1968 - No. 2, Nov, 1968 (35¢)

1-(B&W)-Romita/Mooney 52 pg. story plus updated origin story with			
Everett-a(i)	11	33	160
1-Variation w/single c-price of 40¢	11	33	160
2-(Color)-Green Goblin-c & 58 pg. story; Romita painted-c (story reprinted in			
King Size Spider-Man #9); Romita/Mooney-a	12	36	180

SPECTACULAR SPIDER-MAN, THE (Peter Parker...#54-132, 134)
Marvel Comics Group: Dec, 1976 - No. 263, Nov, 1998

1-Origin recap in text; return of Tarantula	5	15	60
2-Kraven the Hunter app.	2	6	22
3-5: 3-Intro Lightmaster. 4-Vulture app.	2	6	16
6-8-Morbius app.; 6-r/Marvel Team-Up #3 w/Morbius			
	2	6	18
7,8-(35¢-c variants, limited distribution)(6,7/77)	3	9	27
9-20: 9,10-White Tiger app. 11-Last 30¢-c. 17,18-Angel & Iceman app. (from			
Champions); Ghost Rider cameo in flashback	2	6	12
9-11-(35¢-c variants, limited distribution)(8-10/77)	2	6	18
21,24-26: 21-Scorpion app. 26-Daredevil app.	1	3	9
22,23-Moon Knight app.	1	4	10
27-Miller's 1st art on Daredevil (2/79); also see Captain America #235			
	4	12	40
28-Miller Daredevil (p)	3	9	30

	GD	FN	NM-
29-55,57,59: 33-Origin Iguana. 38-Morbius app.			5.00
56-2nd app. Jack O'Lantern (Macendale) & 1st Spidey/Jack O'Lantern battle (7/81)			6.00
58-Byrne-a(p)			6.00
60-Double size; origin retold with new facts revealed			6.00
61-63,65-68,71-74: 65-Kraven the Hunter app.			4.00
64-1st app. Cloak & Dagger (3/82)	2	6	15
69,70-Cloak & Dagger app.	1	3	8
75-Double size			5.00
76-80: 78,79-Punisher cameo			4.00
81,82-Punisher, Cloak & Dagger app.			6.00
83-Origin Punisher retold (10/83)	1	4	10
84,86-89,91-99: 94-96-Cloak & Dagger app. 98-Intro The Spot			4.00
85-Hobgoblin (Ned Leeds) app. (12/83); gains powers of original Green Goblin (see Amazing Spider-Man #238)	1	4	10
90-Spider-Man's new black costume, last panel (ties w/Amazing Spider-Man #252 & Marvel Team-Up #141 for 1st app.)			4.00
100-(3/85)-Double size			5.00
101-115,117,118,120-129: 107-110-Death of Jean DeWolff. 111-Secret Wars II tie-in. 128-Black Cat new costume			3.00
116,119-Sabretooth-c/story	1	4	8
130-132: 30-Hobgoblin app. 131-Six part Kraven tie-in. 132-Kraven tie-in	1	3	7
133-140: 138-1st full app. Tombstone (origin #139). 140-Punisher cameo			3.00
141-143-Punisher app.			5.00
144-146,148-157: 151-Tombstone returns			3.00
147-1st brief app. new Hobgoblin (Macendale), 1 page; continued in Web of Spider-Man #48	2	6	12
158-Spider-Man gets new powers (1st Cosmic Spidey, cont'd in Web of Spider-Man #59)	1	3	7
159-Cosmic Spider-Man app.			6.00
160-170: 161-163-Hobgoblin app. 168-170-Avengers x-over. 169-1st app. The Outlaws			2.50
171-188,190-199: 180,181,183,184-Green Goblin app. 197-199-Original X-Men-c/story			2.50
189-($2.95, 52 pgs.)-Silver hologram on-c; battles Green Goblin; origin Spidey retold; Vess poster w/Spidey & Hobgoblin			4.00
189-(2nd printing)-Gold hologram on-c			3.00
195-(Deluxe ed.)-Polybagged w/"Dirt" magazine #2 & Beastie Boys/ Smithereens music cassette			4.00
200-($2.95)-Holo-grafx foil-c; Green Goblin-c/story			3.00
201-219,221,222,224,226-228,230-247: 233-Carnage-c/app. 240-Revelations storyline begins. 241-Flashback			2.50
213-Collectors ed. polybagged w/16 pg. preview & animation cel; foil-c; 1st meeting Spidey & Typhoid Mary			3.00
213-Version polybagged w/Gamepro #7; no-c date, price			2.50
217,219 ($2.95)-Deluxe edition foil-c; flip book			3.00
220 ($2.25, 52 pgs.)-Flip book, Mary Jane reveals pregnancy			3.00
223,229: ($2.50) 229-Spidey quits			3.00

	GD	FN	NM-
223,225: ($2.95)-223-Die Cut-c. 225-Newsstand ed.			3.00
225,229: ($3.95) 225-Direct Market Holodisk-c (Green Goblin). 229-Acetate-c, Spidey quits			4.00
240-Variant-c			3.00
248,249,251-254,256: 249-Return of Norman Osborn 256-1st app. Prodigy			2.50
250-($3.25) Double gatefold-c			3.25
255-($2.99) Spiderhunt pt. 4			3.00
257-262: 257-Double cover with "Spectacular Prodigy #1"; battles Jack O'Lantern. 258-Spidey is cleared. 259,260-Green Goblin & Hobgoblin app. 262-Byrne-s			2.50
263-Final issue; Byrne-c; Aunt May returns			4.00
#(-1) Flashback (7/97)			2.50
Annual 1 (1979)-Doc Octopus-c & 46 pg. story	2	6	12
Annual 2 (1980)-Origin/1st app. Rapier	1	3	7
Annual 3-5: ('81-'83) 3-Last Man-Wolf			4.00
Annual 6-14: 8 ('88,$ 1.75)-Evolutionary War x-over; Daydreamer returns Gwen Stacy "clone" back to real self (not Gwen Stacy). 9 ('89, $2.00, 68 pgs.)-Atlantis Attacks. 10 ('90, $2.00, 68 pgs.)-McFarlane-a 11 ('91, $2.00, 68 pgs.)-Iron Man app. 12 ('92, $2.25, 68 pgs.)-Venom solo story cont'd from Amazing Spider-Man Annual #26. 13 ('93, $2.95, 68 pgs.)-Polybagged w/trading card; John Romita, Sr. back-up-a			3.00
Special 1 (1995, $3.95)-Flip book			4.00

SPECTACULAR SPIDER-MAN
Marvel Comics: Sept, 2003 - Present ($2.25)

1-Jenkins-s/Ramos-a/c; Venom-c/app.			3.00
2-21: 2-5-Venom app. 6-9-Dr. Octopus app. 11-13-The Lizard app. 14-Rivera painted-a. 15,16-Capt. America app. 17,18-Ramos-a. 20-Spider-Man gets organic webshooters. 21-Caldwell-a; FF, Dr. Strange, Kingpin app.			2.25
Vol. 1: The Hunger TPB (2003, $11.99) r/#1-5			12.00
Vol. 2: Countdown TPB (2004, $11.99) r/#6-10			12.00
Vol. 3: Here There Be Monsters TPB (2004, $9.99) r/#11-14			10.00
Vol. 4: Disassembled TPB (2004, $14.99) r/#15-20			15.00

SPECTRE, THE (1st Series) (See Adventure Comics #431-440, More Fun & Showcase)
National Periodical Publ.: Nov-Dec, 1967 - No. 10, May-June, 1969 (All 12¢)

1-(11-12/67)-Anderson-c/a	13	39	195
2-5-Neal Adams-c/a; 3-Wildcat x-over	9	27	120
6-8,10: 6-8-Anderson inks. 7-Hourman app.	6	18	75
9-Wrightson-a	7	21	85

SPIDER-GIRL (See What If #105)
Marvel Comics: Oct, 1998 - Present ($1.99/$2.25)

0-($2.99)-r/1st app. Peter Parker's daughter from What If #105; previews regular series, Avengers-Next and J2	1	3	7
1-DeFalco-s/Olliffe & Williamson-s	1	3	7
2-Two covers			4.00
3-16,18-20: 3-Fantastic Five-c/app. 10,11-Spider-Girl time-travels to meet			

	GD	FN	NM-

teenaged Spider-Man 2.50
17-($2.99) Peter Parker suits up 3.00
21-24,26-49,51-59: 21-Begin $2.25-c. 31-Avengers app. 2.25
25-($2.99) Spider-Girl vs. the Savage Six 3.00
50-($3.50) 3.50
59-81-($2.99) 59-Avengers app.; Ben Parker born. 75-May in Black costume
3.00
1999 Annual ($3.99) 4.00
... A Fresh Start (1/99,$5.99, TPB) r/#1&2 6.00
TPB (10/01, $19.95) r/#0-8; new Olliffe-c 20.00
Marvel Age Spider-Girl Vol. 1: Legacy (2004, $7.99, digest size) r/#0-5 8.00
Marvel Age Spider-Girl Vol. 2: Like Father, Like Daughter (2004, $7.99, digest)
r/#6-11 8.00

SPIDER-MAN (See Amazing..., Giant-Size..., Marvel Age..., Marvel Knights..., Marvel Tales, Marvel Team-Up, Spectacular..., Spidey Super Stories, Ultimate Marvel Team-Up, Ultimate..., Venom, & Web Of...)

SPIDER-MAN
Marvel Comics: Aug, 1990 - No. 98, Nov, 1998 ($1.75/$1.95/ $1.99)

1-Silver edition, direct sale only (unbagged) 1 3 8
1-Silver bagged edition; direct sale, no price on comic, but $2.00 on plastic
bag (125,000 print run) 20.00
1-Regular edition w/Spidey face in UPC area (unbagged); green-c 6.00
1-Regular bagged edition w/Spidey face in UPC area; green cover (125,000)
12.00
1-Newsstand bagged w/UPC code 8.00
1-Gold edition, 2nd printing (unbagged) with Spider-Man in box
(400,000-450,000) 5.00
1-Gold 2nd printing w/UPC code; (less than 10,000 print run) intended for
Wal-Mart; much scarcer than originally believed 120.00
1-Platinum ed. mailed to retailers only (10,000 print run) stiff-c, has new
McFarlane-a & editorial material instead of ads; no cover price 120.00
2-26: 2-McFarlane-c/a/scripts continue. 6,7-Ghost Rider & Hobgoblin app.
8-Wolverine cameo; Wolverine storyline begins. 12-Wolverine storyline
ends. 13-Spidey's black costume returns; Morbius app. 14-Morbius app.
15-Erik Larsen-c/a; Beast c/s. 16-X-Force-c/story w/Liefeld assists;
continues in X-Force #4; reads sideways; last McFarlane issue.
17-Thanos-c/story; Leonardi/Williamson-c/a. 13,14-Spidey in black
costume. 18-Ghost Rider-c/story. 18-23-Sinister Six storyline w/Erik
Larsen-c/a/scripts. 19-Hulk & Hobgoblin-c & app. 20-22-Deathlok app.
22,23-Ghost Rider, Hulk, Hobgoblin app. 23-Wrap-around gatefold-c.
24-Infinity War x-over w/Demogoblin & Hobgoblin-c/story. 24-Demogoblin
dons new costume & battles Hobgoblin-c/story. 26-($3.50, 52 pgs.)-Silver
hologram on-c w/gatefold poster by Ron Lim; Spidey retells his origin 4.00
26-2nd printing; gold hologram on-c 3.50
27-45: 32-34-Punisher-c/story. 37-Maximum Carnage x-over.
39,40-Electro-c/s (cameo #38). 41-43-Iron Fist-c/stories w/Jae Lee-c/a.
42-Intro Platoon. 44-Hobgoblin app. 3.00
46-49,51-53, 55, 56,58-74,76-81: 46-Begin $1.95-c; bound-in card sheet.
51-Power & Responsibility Pt. 3. 52,53-Venom app. 60-Kaine revealed.

	GD	FN	NM-

61-Origin Kaine. 65-Mysterio app. 66-Kaine-c/app.; Peter Parker app.
67-Carnage-c/app. 68,69-Hobgoblin-c/app. 72-Onslaught x-over; Spidey
vs. Sentinels. 74-Daredevil-c/app. 77-80-Morbius-c/app.   2.50

46-($2.95)-Polybagged; silver ink-c w/16 pg. preview of cartoon series &
    animation style print; bound-in trading card sheet   3.00

50-($2.50)-Newsstand edition   2.50

50-($3.95)-Collectors edition w/holographic-c   4.00

51-($2.95)-Deluxe edition foil-c; flip book   3.00

54-($2.75, 52 pgs.)-Flip book   2.75

57-($2.50)   2.50

57-($2.95)-Die cut-c   3.00

65-($2.95)-Variant-c; polybagged w/cassette   3.00

75-($2.95)-Wraparound-c; return of the Green Goblin; death of Ben Reilly
    (who was the clone)   4.00

82-97: 84-Juggernaut app. 91-Double cover with "Dusk #1"; battles the
    Shocker. 93-Ghost Rider app.   2.50

98-Double cover; final issue   3.00

#(-1) Flashback (7/97)   2.50

Annual '97 ($2.99), '98 ($2.99)-Devil Dinosaur-c/app.   3.00

...and Batman ('95, $5.95) DeMatteis-s; Joker, Carnage app.   6.00

...and Daredevil ('84, $2.00) 1-r/Spect. Spider-Man #26-28 by Miller   3.00

...: Carnage nn (6/93, $6.95, TPB)-r/Amazing S-M #344,345,359-363;
    spot varnish-c   7.00

.../Daredevil (10/02, $2.99) Vatche Mavlian-c/a; Brett Matthews-s   3.00

.../Dr. Strange: "The Way to Dusty Death" nn (1992, $6.95, 68 pgs.)   7.00

.../Elektra '98-($2.99) vs. The Silencer   3.00

... Fear Itself Graphic Novel (2/92, $12.95)   18.00

Giant-Sized Spider-Man (12/98, $3.99) r/team-ups   4.00

Holiday Special 1995 ($2.95)   3.00

Identity Crisis (9/98, $19.95, TPB)   20.00

...Legends Vol. 1: Todd McFarlane ('03, $19.95, TPB)-r/Amaz. S-M #298-305
    20.00

...Legends Vol. 2: Todd McFarlane ('03, $19.99, TPB)-r/Amaz. S-M #306-314,
    & Spect. Spider-Man Annual #10   20.00

...Legends Vol. 3: Todd McFarlane ('04, $24.99, TPB)-r/Amaz. S-M #315-323,
    325,328   25.00

...Legends Vol. 4: Spider-Man & Wolverine ('03, $13.95, TPB) r/Spider-Man &
    Wolverine #1-4 and Spider-Man/Daredevil #1   14.00

.../Marrow (2/01, $2.99) Garza-a   3.00

..., Punisher, Sabretooth: Designer Genes (1993, $8.95)   9.00

...Return of the Goblin TPB (See Peter Parker: Spider-Man)

...Revelations ('97, $14.99, TPB) r/end of Clone Saga plus 14 new pages by
    Romita Jr.   15.00

...: Son of the Goblin (2004, $15.99, TPB) r/AS-M#136-137,312 & Spec. S-M
    #189,200   16.00

Special Edition 1 (12/92-c, 11/92 inside)-The Trial of Venom; ordered thru
    mail with $5.00 donation or more to UNICEF; embossed metallic ink;
    came bagged w/bound-in poster; Daredevil app.   1   4   10

Super Special (7/95, $3.95)-Planet of the Symbiotes   4.00

	GD	FN	NM-
The Complete Frank Miller Spider-Man (2002, $29.95, HC) r/Miller-s/a			30.00
The Death of Captain Stacy ($3.50) r/AS-M#88-90			3.50
The Death of Gwen Stacy ($14.95) r/AS-M#96-98,121,122			15.00
...: The Movie ($12.95) adaptation by Stan Lee-s/Alan Davis-a; plus r/Ultimate Spider-Man #8, Peter Parker #35, Tangled Web #10; photo-c			13.00
...: The Official Movie Adaptation ($5.95) Stan Lee-s/Alan Davis-a			6.00
Torment TPB (5/01$15.95) r/#1-5, Spec. S-M #10			16.00
... Vs. Doctor Octopus ($17.95) reprints early battles; Sean Chen-c			18.00
... Vs. Punisher (7/00, $2.99) Michael Lopez-c/a			3.00
...Vs. Venom (1990, $8.95, TPB)-r/Amaz. S-M #300,315-317 w/new McFarlane-c			9.00
...Visionaries (10/01, $19.95, TPB)-r/Amaz. S-M #298-305; McFarlane-a			20.00
...Visionaries: John Romita (8/01, $19.95, TPB)-r/Amaz. S-M #39-42,50,68, 69,108,109; new Romita-c			20.00
Wizard 1/2 ($10.00) Leonardi-a; Green Goblin app.			10.00

SPIDER-MAN: BLUE
Marvel Comics: July, 2002 - No. 6, Apr, 2003 ($3.50, limited series)

1-6: Jeph Loeb-s/Tim Sale-a/c; flashback to early MJ and Gwen Stacy			3.50
HC (2003, $21.99, with dust jacket) over-sized r/#1-6; intro. by John Romita			22.00
SC (2004, $14.99) r/#1-6; cover gallery			15.00

SPIDER-MAN: CHAPTER ONE
Marvel Comics: Dec, 1998 - No. 12, Oct, 1999 ($2.50, limited series)

1-Retelling/updating of origin; John Byrne-s/c/a			2.50
1-($6.95) DF Edition w/variant-c by Jae Lee			7.00
2-11: 2-Two covers (one is swipe of ASM #1); Fantastic Four app. 9-Daredevil. 11-Giant-Man-c/app.			2.50
12-($3.50) Battles the Sandman			3.50
0-(5/99) Origins of Vulture, Lizard and Sandman			2.50

SPIDER-MAN'S TANGLED WEB (Titled **"Tangled Web"** in indicia for #1-4)
Marvel Comics: Jun, 2001 - No. 22, Mar, 2003 ($2.99)

1-3: "The Thousand" on-c; Ennis-s/McCrea-a/Fabry-c			4.00
4-"Severance Package" on-c; Rucka-s/Risso-a; Kingpin-c/app.			5.00
5,6-Flowers for Rhino; Milligan-s/Fegredo-a			3.00
7-10,12,15-20,22: 7-9-Gentlemen's Agreement; Bruce Jones-s/Lee Weeks-a. 10-Andrews-s/a. 12-Fegredo-a. 15-Paul Pope-s/a. 18-Ted McKeever-s/a. 19-Mahfood-a. 20-Haspiel-a			3.00
11,13,21-($3.50) 11-Darwyn Cooke-s/a. 13-Phillips-a. 21-Christmas-s by Cooke & Bone			3.50
14-Azzarello & Scott Levy (WWE's Raven)-s about Crusher Hogan			4.00
TPB (10/01, $15.95) r/#1-6			16.00
Volume 2 TPB (4/02, $14.95) r/#7-11			15.00
Volume 3 TPB (2002, $15.99) r/#12-17; Jason Pearson-c			16.00
Volume 4 TPB (2003, $15.99) r/#18-22; Frank Cho-c			16.00

SPIDER-MAN 2: THE MOVIE
Marvel Comics: Aug, 2004 ($3.50/$12.99, one-shot)

1-($3.50) Movie adaptation; Johnson, Lim & Olliffe-a			3.50

	GD	FN	NM-

TPB-($12.99) Movie adaptation; r/Amazing Spider-Man #50, Ultimate
Spider-Man #14,15 ..... 13.00

SPIDER-WOMAN (Also see The Avengers #240, Marvel Spotlight #32,
Marvel Super Heroes Secret Wars #7 & Marvel Two-In-One #29)
Marvel Comics Group: April, 1978 - No. 50, June, 1983 (New logo #47 on)

1-New complete origin & mask added	2	6	18
2-5,7-18: 2-Excalibur app. 3,11,12-Brother Grimm app. 13,15-The Shroud.			
16-Sienkiewicz-c			5.00
6,19,20,28,29,32: 6-Morgan LeFay app. 6,19,32-Werewolf by Night-c/s.			
20,28,29-Spider-Man app. 32-Miller-c			6.00
21-27,30,31,33-36			5.00
37,38-X-Men x-over: 37-1st app. Siryn of X-Force; origin retold			
	1	4	10
39-49: 46-Kingpin app. 49-Tigra-c/story			4.00
50-(52 pgs.)-Death of Spider-Woman; photo-c	2	6	14

SPIDEY SUPER STORIES (Spider-Man) (Also see Fireside Books)
Marvel/Children's TV Workshop: Oct, 1974 - No. 57, Mar, 1982 (35¢, no ads)

1-Origin (stories simplified for younger readers)	4	12	50
2-Kraven	3	9	28
3-10,15: 6-Iceman. 15-Storm-c/sty	2	6	20
11-14,16-20: 19,20-Kirby-c	2	6	18
21-30: 24-Kirby-c	2	6	16
31-53: 31-Moondragon-c/app.; Dr. Doom app. 33-Hulk. 34-Sub-Mariner.			
38-F.F. 39-Thanos-c/story. 44-Vision. 45-Silver Surfer & Dr. Doom app.			
	2	6	14
54-57: 56-Battles Jack O'Lantern-c/sty (exactly one year after 1st app. in			
Machine Man #19)	2	6	20

SPIRIT, THE
Harvey Publications: Oct, 1966 - No. 2, Mar, 1967 (Giant Size, 25¢, 68 pgs.)

1-Eisner-r plus 9 new pgs.(origin Denny Colt, Take 3, plus 2 filler pgs.)			
(#3 was advertised, but never published)	9	27	110
2-Eisner-r plus 9 new pgs.(origin of the Octopus)	7	21	80

SQUADRON SUPREME (Also see Marvel Graphic Novel)
Marvel Comics Group: Aug, 1985 - No. 12, Aug, 1986 (Maxi-series)

1-Double size			3.00
2-12			2.50
TPB ($24.99) r/#1-12; Alex Ross painted-c; printing inks contain some of the			
cremated remains of late writer Mark Gruenwald			25.00
TPB-2nd printing ($24.99): Inks contain no ashes			25.00

STALKER (Also see All Star Comics 1999 and crossover issues)
National Periodical Publications: Jun-Jul, 1975 - No. 4, Dec-Jan, 1975-76

1-Origin & 1st app; Ditko/Wood-c/a	2	6	14
2-4-Ditko/Wood-c/a	1	3	8

STARMAN (1st Series) (Also see Justice League & War of the Gods)
DC Comics: Oct, 1988 - No. 45, Apr, 1992 ($1.00)

	GD	FN	NM-

1-25,29-45: 1-Origin. 4-Intro The Power Elite. 9,10,34-Batman app.
14-Superman app. 17-Power Girl app. 38-War of the Gods x-over.
42-45-Eclipso-c/stories   2.50
26-1st app. David Knight (G.A.Starman's son).   5.00
27,28: 27-Starman (David Knight) app. 28-Starman disguised as Superman;
leads into Superman #50   4.00

STARMAN (2nd Series) (Also see The Golden Age, Showcase 95 #12,
Showcase 96 #4,5)
DC Comics : No. 0, Oct, 1994 - No. 80, Aug, 2001 ($1.95/$2.25/$2.50)

0,1: 0-James Robinson scripts, Tony Harris-c/a(p) & Wade Von
Grawbadger-a(i) begins; Sins of the Father storyline begins, ends #3;
1st app. new Starman (Jack Knight); reintro of the G.A. Mist & G.A. Shade;
1st app. Nash; David Knight dies   1   3   7
2-7: 2-Reintro Charity from Forbidden Tales of Dark Mansion. 3-Reintro/2nd
app. "Blue" Starman (1st app. in 1st Issue Special #12); Will Payton app.
(both cameos). 5-David Knight app. 6-The Shade "Times Past" story; Teddy
Kristiansen-a. 7-The Black Pirate cameo   5.00
8-17: 8-Begin $2.25-c. 10-1st app. new Mist (Nash). 11-JSA "Times Past"
story; Matt Smith-a. 12-16-Sins of the Child. 17-The Black Pirate app. 4.00
18-37: 18-G.A. Starman "Times Past" story; Watkiss-a. 19-David Knight app.
20-23-G.A. Sandman app. 24-26-Demon Quest; all 3 covers make-up
triptych. 33-36-Batman-c/app. 37-David Knight and deceased JSA
members app.   3.00
38-49,51-56: 38-Nash vs. Justice League Europe. 39,40-Crossover w/Power
of Shazam! #35,36; Bulletman app. 42-Demon-c/app. 43-JLA-c/app.
44-Phantom Lady-c/app. 46-Gene Ha-a. 51-Jor-el app. 52,53-Adam
Strange-c/app.   2.50
50-($3.95) Gold foil logo on-c; Star Boy (LSH) app.   4.00
57-79: 57-62-Painted covers by Harris and Alex Ross. 72-Death of Ted Knight
2.50
80-($3.95) Final issue; cover by Harris & Robinson   4.00
#1,000,000 (11/98) 853rd Century x-over; Snejbjerg-a   2.50
Annual 1 (1996, $3.50)-Legends of the Dead Earth story; Prince Gavyn &
G.A. Starman stories; J.H. Williams III, Bret Blevins, Craig Hamilton-c/a(p)
4.00
Annual 2 (1997, $3.95)-Pulp Heroes story;   4.00
...80 Page Giant (1/99, $4.95) Harris-c   5.00
...Secret Files 1 (4/98, $4.95)-Origin stories and profile pages   5.00
...The Mist (6/98, $1.95) Girlfrenzy; Mary Marvel app.   2.50
A Starry Knight-($17.95, TPB) r/#47-53   18.00
Grand Guingnol-(2004, $19.95, TPB)-r/#61-73   20.00
Infernal Devices-($17.95, TPB) r/#29-35,37,38   18.00
Night and Day-($14.95, TPB)-r/#7-10,12-16   15.00
Sins of the Father-($12.95, TPB)-r/#0-5   13.00
Stars My Destination-(2003, $14.95, TPB)-r/#55-60   15.00
Times Past-($17.95, TPB)-r/stories of other Starmen   18.00

STARS AND S.T.R.I.P.E. (Also see JSA)
DC Comics: July, 1999 - No. 14, Sept, 2000 ($2.95/$2.50)

	GD	FN	NM-
0-($2.95) Moder and Weston-a; Starman app.			3.00
1-Johns and Robinson-s/Moder-a; origin new Star Spangled Kid			2.50
2-14: 4-Marvel Family app. 9-Seven Soldiers of Victory-c/app.			2.50

STAR SPANGLED WAR STORIES (Formerly Star Spangled Comics #1-130; Becomes The Unknown Soldier #205 on) (See Showcase)
National Periodical Publications: No. 131, 8/52 - No. 133, 10/52; No. 3, 11/52 - No. 204, 2-3/77

	GD	FN	NM-
131(#1)	100	300	1300
132	67	201	875
133-Used in **POP**, pg. 94	55	165	720
3-6: 4-Devil Dog Dugan app. 6-Evans-a	40	120	475
7-10	25	75	375
11-20	21	63	310
21-30: 30-Last precode (2/55)	18	54	265
31-33,35-40	12	36	180
34-Krigstein-a	13	39	185
41-44,46-50: 50-1st S.A. issue	12	36	170
45-1st DC grey tone war-c (5/56)	17	51	250
51,52,54-63,65,66, 68-83	10	30	125
53-"Rock Sergeant," 3rd Sgt. Rock prototype; inspired "P.I. & The Sand Fleas" in G.I. Combat #56 (1/57)	14	42	205
64-Pre-Sgt. Rock Easy Co. story (12/57)	12	36	170
67-2 Easy Co. stories without Sgt. Rock	12	36	180
84-Origin Mlle. Marie	18	54	260
85-89-Mlle. Marie in all	11	33	150
90-1st app. "War That Time Forgot" series; dinosaur issue-c/story (4-5/60) (also see Weird War Tales #94 & #99)	35	105	560
91,93-No dinosaur stories	10	30	130
92-2nd dinosaur-c/s	14	42	210
94 (12/60)- "Ghost Ace" story; Baron Von Richter as The Enemy Ace (predates Our Army at War #151)	18	54	270
95-99: Dinosaur-c/s	13	39	185
100-Dinosaur-c/story.	15	45	220
101-115: All dinosaur issues	11	33	150
116-125,127-133,135-137-Last dinosaur story; Heath Birdman-#129,131	10	30	130
126-No dinosaur story	8	24	105
134-Dinosaur story; Neal Adams-a	11	33	160
138-New Enemy Ace-c/stories begin by Joe Kubert (4-5/68), end #150 (also see Our Army at War #151 and Showcase #57)	12	36	175
139-Origin Enemy Ace (7/68)	10	30	125
140-143,145: 145-Last 12¢ issue (6-7/69)	7	21	85
144-Neal Adams/Kubert-a	8	24	100
146-Enemy Ace-c and cameo app.	5	15	55
147,148-New Enemy Ace stories	6	18	70
149,150-Last new Enemy Ace by Kubert. Viking Prince by Kubert	6	18	65
151-1st solo app. Unknown Soldier (6-7/70); Enemy Ace-r begin (from Our Army at War, Showcase & SSWS); end #161	15	45	220

	GD	FN	NM-
152-Reprints 2nd Enemy Ace app.	5	15	55
153,155-Enemy Ace reprints; early Unknown Soldier stories			
	4	12	42
154-Origin Unknown Soldier	11	33	160
156-1st Battle Album; Unknown Soldier story; Kubert-c/a			
	4	12	42
157-Sgt. Rock x-over in Unknown Soldier story.	4	12	38
158-163-(52 pgs.): New Unknown Soldier stories; Kubert-c/a. 161-Last Enemy Ace-r	3	9	28
164-183,200: 181-183-Enemy Ace vs. Balloon Buster serial app; Frank Thorne-a. 200-Enemy Ace back-up	2	6	16
184-199,201-204	2	6	12

STAR TREK (TV) (See Dan Curtis Giveaways, Dynabrite Comics & Power Record Comics)
Gold Key: 7/67; No. 2, 6/68; No. 3, 12/68; No. 4, 6/69 - No. 61, 3/79

	GD	FN	NM-
1-Photo-c begin, end #9	41	123	650
1 (rare variation w/photo back-c)	44	132	750
2	24	72	350
2 (rare variation w/photo back-c)	43	129	540
3-5	16	48	240
3 (rare variation w/photo back-c)	25	75	375
6-9	13	39	185
10-20	8	24	105
21-30	7	21	80
31-40	5	15	60
41-61: 52-Drug propaganda story	4	12	45
...the Enterprise Logs nn (8/76)-Golden Press, ($1.95, 224 pgs.)-r/#1-8 plus 7 pgs. by McWilliams (#11185)-Photo-c	5	15	60
...the Enterprise Logs Vol. 2 ('76)-r/#9-17 (#11187)-Photo-c	5	15	55
...the Enterprise Logs Vol. 3 ('77)-r/#18-26 (#11188); McWilliams-a (4 pgs.)-Photo-c	5	15	55
Star Trek Vol. 4 (Winter '77)-Reprints #27,28,30-34,36,38 (#11189) plus 3 pgs. new art	5	15	55
... : The Key Collection (Checker Book Publ. Group, 2004, $22.95) r/#1-8			23.00

STAR TREK
Marvel Comics Group: April, 1980 - No. 18, Feb, 1982

	GD	FN	NM-
1: 1-3-r/Marvel Super Special; movie adapt.	2	6	15
2-16: 5-Miller-c	1	3	8
17-Low print run	2	6	12
18-Last issue; low print run	2	6	18

STAR TREK (Also see Who's Who In Star Trek)
DC Comics: Feb, 1984 - No. 56, Nov, 1988 (75¢, Mando paper)

	GD	FN	NM-
1-Sutton-a(p) begins	1	4	10
2-5			6.00
6-10: 7-Origin Saavik			5.00
11-20: 19-Walter Koenig story			4.00

	GD	FN	NM-
21-32			3.50
33-($1.25, 52 pgs.)-20th anniversary issue			4.00
34-49: 37-Painted-c			3.00
50-($1.50, 52 pgs.)			4.00
51-56, Annual 1-3: 1(1985). 2(1986). 3(1988, $1.50)			3.00

STAR TREK
DC Comics: Oct, 1989 - No. 80, Jan, 1996 ($1.50/$1.75/$1.95/$2.50)

	GD	FN	NM-
1-Capt. Kirk and crew			6.00
2,3			4.00
4-23,25-30: 10-12-The Trial of James T. Kirk. 21-Begin $1.75-c			3.00
24-($2.95, 68 pgs.)-40 pg. epic w/pin-ups			3.50
31-49,51-60			2.50
50-($3.50, 68 pgs.)-Painted-c			3.50
61-74,76-80			2.50
75 ($3.95)			4.00
Annual 1-6('90-'95, 68 pgs.): 1-Morrow-a. 3-Painted-c			4.00
Special 1-3 ('9-'95, 68 pgs.)-1-Sutton-a.			4.00
...: The Ashes of Eden (1995, $14.95, 100 pgs.)-Shatner story			15.00
...Generations (1994, $3.95, 68 pgs.)-Movie adaptation			4.00
...Generations (1994, $5.95, 68 pgs.)-Squarebound			6.00

STAR TREK: DEEP SPACE NINE (TV)
Malibu Comics: Aug, 1993 - No. 32, Jan, 1996 ($2.50)

	GD	FN	NM-
1-Direct Sale Edition w/line drawn-c			4.00
1-Newsstand Edition with photo-c			3.00
0-(1/95, $2.95)-Terok Nor			3.00
2-30: 2-Polybagged w/trading card. 9-4 pg. prelude to Hearts & Minds			2.50
31-($3.95)			4.00
32-($3.50)			3.50
Annual 1 (1/95, $3.95, 68 pgs.)			4.00
Special 1 (1995, $3.50)			3.50
Ultimate Annual 1 (12/95, $5.95)			6.00
...:Lightstorm (12/94, $3.50)			3.50

STAR TREK: THE NEXT GENERATION (TV)
DC Comics: Feb, 1988 - No. 6, July, 1988 (limited series)

	GD	FN	NM-
1 ($1.50, 52 pgs.)-Sienkiewicz painted-c			6.00
2-6 ($1.00)			4.00

STAR TREK: THE NEXT GENERATION (TV)
DC Comics: Oct, 1989 -No. 80, 1995 ($1.50/$1.75/$1.95)

	GD	FN	NM-
1-Capt. Picard and crew from TV show	1	3	9
2,3			5.00
4-10			4.00
11-23,25-49,51-60			3.00
24,50: 24-($2.50, 52 pgs.). 50-($3.50, 68 pgs.)-Painted-c			5.00
61-74,76-80			2.50
75 ($3.95, 50 pgs.)			4.00
Annual 1-6 ('90-'95, 68 pgs.)			4.00
Special 1 -3('93-'95, 68 pgs.)-1-Contains 3 stories			4.00

	GD	FN	NM-

...-The Series Finale (1994, $3.95, 68 pgs.) 4.00

STAR TREK: VOYAGER
Marvel Comics (Paramount Comics): Nov, 1996 - No. 15, Mar, 1998 ($1.95/$1.99)

1-15: 13-"Telepathy War" pt. 5. 14-Seven of Nine joins crew 3.00

STAR TREK: VOYAGER
DC Comics/WildStorm: one-shots and trade paperbacks

- Elite Force (7/00, $5.95) The Borg app.; Abnett & Lanning-s 6.00
... Encounters With the Unknown TPB (2001, $19.95) reprints 20.00
- False Colors (1/00, $5.95) Photo-c and Jim Lee-c; Jeff Moy-a 6.00

STAR TREK/ X-MEN
Marvel Comics (Paramount Comics): Dec, 1996 ($4.99, one-shot)

1-Kirk's crew & X-Men; art by Silvestri, Tan, Winn & Finch; Lobdell-s 5.00

STAR TREK/ X-MEN: 2ND CONTACT
Marvel Comics (Paramount Comics): May, 1998 ($4.99, 64 pgs., one-shot)

1-Next Gen. crew & X-Men battle Kang, Sentinels & Borg following First Contact movie 5.00
1-Painted wraparound variant cover 5.00

STAR WARS (Movie) (See Classic…, Contemporary Motivators, Dark Horse Comics, The Droids, The Ewoks, Marvel Movie Showcase, Marvel Special Ed.)
Marvel Comics Group: July, 1977 - No. 107, Sept, 1986

	GD	FN	NM-
1-(Regular 30¢ edition)-Price in square w/UPC code; #1-6 adapt first movie; first issue on sale before movie debuted	6	18	70

1-(35¢-c; limited distribution - 1500 copies?)- Price in square w/UPC code (Prices vary widely on this book. In 2004, a CGC certified 9.2 sold for $4,050, a CGC 9.0 sold for $3,200 and a CGC 7.5 sold for $999.99)
NOTE: *The rare 35¢ edition has the cover price in a square box, and the UPC box in the lower left hand corner has the UPC code lines running through it.*

	GD	FN	NM-
2-4-(30¢ issues). 4-Battle with Darth Vader	3	10	35
2-4-(35¢ with UPC code; not reprints)	7	21	85
5,6- 5-Begin 35¢-c on all editions. 6-Stevens-a(i)	2	6	20
7-20	2	6	12
21-70: 39-44-The Empire Strikes Back-r by Al Williamson in all. 50-Giant. 68-Reintro Boba Fett.	1	3	9
71-80	1	4	10
81-90: 81-Boba Fett app.	2	6	12
91,93-99: 98-Williamson-a.	2	6	15
92,100-106: 92,100-($1.00, 52 pgs.).	2	6	20
107(low dist.); Portacio-a(i)	6	18	70
1-9: Reprints; has "reprint" in upper lefthand corner of cover or on inside or price and number inside a diamond with no date or UPC on cover; 30¢ and 35¢ issues published			4.00
Annual 1 (12/79, 52 pgs.)-Simonson-c	2	6	12
Annual 2 (11/82, 52 pgs.), 3(12/83, 52 pgs.)	1	4	10

STAR WARS (Monthly series)

	GD	FN	NM-

Dark Horse Comics: Dec, 1998 - Present ($2.50/$2.95/$2.99)

1-12: 1-6-Prelude To Rebellion; Strnad-s. 4-Brereton-c. 7-12-Outlander			3.00
5,6 (Holochrome-c variants)			6.00
13, 17-18-($2.95): 13-18-Emissaries to Malastare; Truman-s			3.00
14-16-($2.50) Schultz-c			3.00
19-67: 19-22-Twilight; Duursema-a. 23-26-Infinity's End. 51-65-Republic			3.00
#0 Another Universe.com Ed.($10.00) r/serialized pages from Pizzazz Magazine; new Dorman painted-c			10.00
... A Valentine Story (2/03, $3.50) Leia & Han Solo on Hoth; Winick-s/ Chadwick-a/c			3.50
...: Clone Wars Vol. 1 (2003, $14.95)			15.00
...: Clone Wars Vol. 2 (2003, $14.95) r/#51-53 & Star Wars: Jedi - Shaak Ti			15.00
...: Clone Wars Vol. 3 (2004, $14.95) r/#55-59			15.00
...: Clone Wars Vol. 4 (2004, $16.95) r/#54, 63 & Star Wars: Jedi - Aayla Secura & Dooku			17.00
...: Clone Wars Vol. 5 (2004, $17.95) r/#60-62, 64 & Star Wars: Jedi - Yoda			17.00
...: Rite of Passage (2004, $12.95) r/#42-45			13.00
...: The Stark Hyperspace War (903, $12.95) r/#36-39			13.00

STAR WARS: DARK EMPIRE
Dark Horse Comics: Dec, 1991 - No. 6, Oct, 1992 ($2.95, limited series)

	GD	FN	NM-
Preview-(99¢)			3.00
1-All have Dorman painted-c	1	3	9
1-3-2nd printing			4.00
2-Low print run	2	6	12
3			6.00
4-6			4.00
Gold Embossed Set (#1-6)-With gold embossed foil logo (price is for set)			90.00
Platinum Embossed Set (#1-6)			120.00
Trade paperback (4/93, 16.95)			17.00
Dark Empire 1 - TPB 3rd printing (2003, $16.95)			17.00
Ltd. Ed. Hardcover ($99.95) Signed & numbered			100.00

STAR WARS: DARK EMPIRE II
Dark Horse Comics: Dec, 1994 - No. 6, May, 1995 ($2.95, limited series)

1-Dave Dorman painted-c			5.00
2-6: Dorman-c in all.			4.00
Platinum Embossed Set (#1-6)			35.00
Trade paperback ($17.95)			18.00

STAR WARS: EMPIRE
Dark Horse Comics: Sept, 2002 - Present ($2.99)

1-24: 1-Benjamin-a; takes place weeks before SW: A New Hope. 7-Boba Fett-c. 14-Vader after the destruction of the Death Star. 15-Death of Biggs; Wheatley-a			3.00
... Volume 1 (2003, $12.95, TPB) r/#1-4			13.00
... Volume 2 (2004, $17.95, TPB) r/#8-12,15			18.00

	GD	FN	NM-

... Volume 3: The Imperial Perspective (2004, $17.95, TPB) r/#13,14,16-19
                                                            18.00

STAR WARS: EPISODE 1 THE PHANTOM MENACE
Dark Horse Comics: May, 1999 - No. 4 ($2.95, movie adaptation)

1-4-Regular and photo-c; Damaggio & Williamson-a   3.00
TPB ($12.95) r/#1-4   13.00
...Anakin Skywalker-Photo-c & Bradstreet-c, ...Obi-Wan Kenobi-Photo-c &
   Egeland-c, ...Queen Amidala-Photo-c & Bradstreet-c, ...Qui-Gon Jinn-
   Photo-c & Bradstreet-c   3.00
Gold foil covers; Wizard 1/2   10.00

STAR WARS: EPISODE II - ATTACK OF THE CLONES
Dark Horse Comics: Apr, 2002 - No. 4, May, 2002 ($3.99, movie adaptation)

1-4-Regular and photo-c; Duursema-a   4.00
TPB ($17.95) r/#1-4; Struzan-c   18.00

STAR WARS: RETURN OF THE JEDI (Movie)
Marvel Comics Group: Oct, 1983 - No. 4, Jan, 1984 (limited series)

1-4-Williamson-p in all; r/Marvel Super Special #27   1   4   10
Oversized issue (1983, $2.95, 10-3/4x8-1/4", 68 pgs., cardboard-c)-r/#1-4
                                                      2   6   16

STAR WARS TALES
Dark Horse Comics: Sept, 1999 - Present ($4.95/$5.95/$5.99, anthology)

1-4-Short stories by various   5.00
5-21 ($5.95/$5.99-c) Art and photo-c on each   6.00

STAR WARS: UNION
Dark Horse Comics: Nov, 1999 - No. 4, Feb, 2000 ($2.95, limited series)

1-4-Wedding of Luke and Mara Jade; Teranishi-a/Stackpole-s   3.00

STATIC (See Heroes)
DC Comics (Milestone): June, 1993 - No. 45, Mar, 1997 ($1.50/$1.75/$2.50)

1-($2.95)-Collector's Edition; polybagged w/poster & trading card & backing
   board (direct sales only)   4.00
1-24,26-45: 2-Origin. 8-Shadow War; Simonson silver ink-c. 14-($2.50,
   52 pgs.)-Worlds Collide Pt. 14. 27-Kent Williams-c   2.50
25 ($3.95)   4.00
...: Trial by Fire (2000, $9.95) r/#1-4; Leon-c   10.00

STATIC SHOCK!: REBIRTH OF THE COOL (TV)
DC Comics: Jan, 2001 - No. 4, Sept, 2001 ($2.50, limited series)

1-4: McDuffie-s/Leon-c/a   2.50

STEEL (Also see JLA)
DC Comics: Feb, 1994 - No. 52, July, 1998 ($1.50/$1.95/$2.50)

1-8,0,9-52: 1-From Reign of the Supermen storyline. 6,7-Worlds Collide
   Pt. 5 & 12. 8-(9/94). 0-(10/94). 9-(11/94). 46-Superboy-c/app. 50-Millennium
   Giants x-over   2.50
Annual 1 (1994, $2.95)-Elseworlds story   3.00
Annual 2 (1995, $3.95)-Year One story   4.00

	GD	FN	NM-
...Forging of a Hero TPB (1997, $19.95) r/ early app.			20.00

STRANGE ADVENTURES
National Per. Pubs: No. 54, 1955 - No. 244, Oct-Nov, 1973 (No. 1-12: 52 pgs.)

	GD	FN	NM-
54-70	18	54	260
71-99	14	42	200
100	16	48	230
101-110: 104-Space Museum begins by Sekowsky	11	33	150
111-116,118,119: 114-Star Hawkins begins, ends #185; Heath-a in Wood			
E.C. style	10	30	140
117-(6/60)-Origin/1st app. Atomic Knights.	50	150	850
120-2nd app. Atomic Knights	25	75	365
121,122,125,127,128,130,131,133,134: 134-Last 10¢ issue			
	9	27	120
123,126-3rd & 4th app. Atomic Knights	14	42	200
124-Intro/origin Faceless Creature	10	30	140
129,132,135,138,141,147-Atomic Knights app.	11	33	145
136,137,139,140,143,145,146,148,149,151,152,154,155,157-159:			
159-Star Rovers app.; Gil Kane/Anderson-a.	7	21	80
142-2nd app. Faceless Creature	8	24	100
144-Only Atomic Knights-c (by M. Anderson)	11	33	160
150,153,156,160: Atomic Knights in each. 153-(6/63)-3rd app. Faceless			
Creature; atomic explosion-c. 160-Last Atomic Knights			
	8	24	100
161-179: 161-Last Space Museum. 163-Star Rovers app. 170-Infinity-c.			
177-Intro/origin Immortal Man	5	15	60
180-Origin/1st app. Animal Man	19	57	275
181-183,185-189: 187-Intro/origin The Enchantress	4	12	50
184-2nd app. Animal Man by Gil Kane	12	36	170
190-1st app. Animal Man in costume	15	45	220
191-194,196-200,202-204	4	12	45
195-1st full app. Animal Man	8	24	105
201-Last Animal Man; 2nd full app.	6	18	70
205-(10/67)-Intro/origin Deadman by Infantino & begin series, ends #216			
	12	36	180
206-Neal Adams-a begins	9	27	120
207-210	9	27	110
211-216: 211-Space Museum-r. 216-(1-2/69)-Deadman story finally			
concludes in Brave & the Bold #86 (10-11/69); secret message panel by			
Neal Adams (pg. 13); tribute to Steranko	7	21	90
217-r/origin & 1st app. Adam Strange from Showcase #17, begin-r; Atomic			
Knights-r begin	3	9	24
218-221,223-225: 218-Last 12¢ issue. 225-Last 15¢ issue			
	2	6	22
222-New Adam Strange story; Kane/Anderson-a	3	10	36
226,227,230-236-(68-52 pgs.): 226, 227-New Adam Strange text story w/illos			
by Anderson (8,6 pgs.) 231-Last Atomic Knights-r. 235-JLA-c/s			
	2	6	22
228,229 (68 pgs.)	3	9	28
237-243	2	6	14

	GD	FN	NM-
244-Last issue	2	6	16

STRANGERS IN PARADISE
Antarctic Press: Nov, 1993 - No. 3, Feb, 1994 ($2.75, B&W, limited series)

1	6	18	65
1-2nd/3rd prints	1	3	8
2 (2300 printed)	4	12	45
3	3	9	30
Trade paperback (Antarctic Press, $6.95)-Red -c (5000 print run)			10.00
Trade paperback (Abstract Studios, $6.95)-Red-c (2000 print run)			15.00
Trade paperback (Abstract Studios, $6.95, 1st-4th printing)-Blue			7.00
Hardcover ('98, $29.95) includes first draft pages			30.00
Gold Reprint Series ($2.75) 1-3-r/#1-3			2.75

STRANGERS IN PARADISE
Abstract Studios: Sept, 1994 - No. 14, July, 1996 ($2.75, B&W)

1	2	6	16
1,3- 2nd printings			4.00
2,3: 2-Color dream sequence	1	3	8
4-10			4.00
4-6-2nd printings			2.75
11-14: 14-The Letters of Molly & Poo			3.00
Gold Reprint Series ($2.75) 1-13-r/#1-13			2.75
I Dream Of You ($16.95, TPB) r/#1-9			17.00
It's a Good Life ($8.95, TPB) r/#10-13			9.00

STRANGERS IN PARADISE (Volume Three)
Homage Comics #1-8/Abstract Studios #9-on: Oct, 1996 - Present ($2.75/$2.95, color #1-5, B&W #6-on):

1-Terry Moore-c/s/a in all; dream seq. by Jim Lee-a			4.00
1-Jim Lee variant-c	1	3	8
2-5			3.50
6-16: 6-Return to B&W. 13-15-High school flashback. 16-Xena Warrior Princess parody; two covers			3.00
17-66: 33-Color issue. 46-Molly Lane. 49-Molly & Poo			3.00
...Lyrics and Poems (2/99)			2.75
...Source Book (2003, $2.95) Background on characters & story arcs, checklists			3.00

STRANGE SPORTS STORIES (See Brave & the Bold #45-49, DC Special, and DC Super Stars #10)
National Periodical Publications: Sept-Oct, 1973 - No. 6, July-Aug, 1974

1	3	9	30
2-6: 2-Swan/Anderson-a	2	6	16

STRANGE TALES (...Featuring Warlock #178-181; Doctor Strange #169 on)
Atlas (CCPC #1-67/ZPC #68-79/VPI #80-85)/Marvel #86(7/61) on:
No. 51, Oct, 1956 - No. 168, May, 1968; No. 169, Sept, 1973 - No. 188, Nov, 1976

51-57,60: 51-1st S.A. issue. 53,56-Crandall-a. 60-(8/57)			
	18	54	265

	GD	FN	NM-
58,64-Williamson-a in each, with Mayo-#58	19	57	275
59,61-Krigstein-a; #61 (2/58)	21	63	310
62,63,65,66: 62-Torres-a. 66-Crandall-a	17	51	255
67-Prototype ish. (Quicksilver)	19	57	280
68,71,72,74,77,80: Ditko/Kirby-a in #67-80	18	54	265
69,70,73,75,76,78,79: 69-Prototype ish. (Prof. X). 70-Prototype ish. (Giant Man). 73-Prototype ish. (Ant-Man). 75-Prototype ish. (Iron Man). 76-Prototype ish. (Human Torch). 78-Prototype ish. (Ant-Man). 79-Prototype ish. (Dr. Strange) (12/60)	23	69	335
81-83,85-88,90,91-Ditko/Kirby-a in all: 86-Robot-c. 90-(11/61)-Atom bomb blast panel	17	51	245
84-Prototype ish. (Magneto)(5/61); has powers like Magneto of X-Men, but two years earlier; Ditko/Kirby-a	21	63	310
89-1st app. Fin Fang Foom (10/61) by Kirby	43	129	725
92-Prototype ish. (Ancient One); last 10¢ issue	18	54	265
93,95,96,98-100: Kirby-a	15	45	220
94-Prototype ish. (The Thing); Kirby-a	18	54	265
97-1st app. Aunt May & Uncle Ben by Ditko (6/62), before Amazing Fantasy #15; (see Tales Of Suspense #7); Kirby-a	38	114	600
101-Human Torch begins by Kirby (10/62); origin recap Fantastic Four & Human Torch; Human Torch-c begin	95	285	1800
102-1st app. Wizard; robot-c	36	108	575
103-105: 104-1st app. Trapster. 105-2nd Wizard	31	93	460
106,108,109: 106-Fantastic Four guests (3/63)	21	63	310
107-(4/63)-Human Torch/Sub-Mariner battle; 4th S.A. Sub-Mariner app. & 1st x-over outside of Fantastic Four	27	81	400
110-(7/63)-Intro Doctor Strange, Ancient One & Wong by Ditko	111	333	2100
111-2nd Dr. Strange	34	102	550
112,113	15	45	220
114-Acrobat disguised as Captain America, 1st app. since the G.A.; intro. & 1st app. Victoria Bentley; 3rd Dr. Strange app. & begin series (11/63)	39	117	625
115-Origin Dr. Strange; Human Torch vs. Sandman (Spidey villain; 2nd app. & brief origin); early Spider-Man x-over, 12/63	47	141	800
116-(1/64)-Human Torch battles The Thing; 1st Thing x-over	13	39	185
117,118,120: 120-1st Iceman x-over (from X-Men)	10	30	140
119-Spider-Man x-over (2 panel cameo)	12	36	165
121,122,124,126-134: Thing/Torch team-up in 121-134. 126-Intro Clea. 128-Quicksilver & Scarlet Witch app. (1/65). 130-The Beatles cameo. 134-Last Human Torch; The Watcher-c/story; Wood-a(i)	8	24	105
123-1st app. The Beetle (see Amazing Spider-Man #21 for next app.); 1st Thor app. (8/64); Loki app.	9	27	120
125-Torch & Thing battle Sub-Mariner (10/64)	9	27	120
135-Colonel (formerly Sgt.) Nick Fury becomes Nick Fury Agent of S.H.I.E.L.D (origin/1st app.) by Kirby (8/65); series begins	14	42	200

	GD	FN	NM-
136-140: 138-Intro Eternity	6	18	70

141-147,149: 145-Begins alternating-c features w/Nick Fury (odd #'s) & Dr. Strange (even #'s). 146-Last Ditko Dr. Strange who is in consecutive stories since #113; only full Ditko Dr. Strange-c this title. 147-Dr. Strange (by Everett #147-152) continues thru #168, then Dr. Strange #169

	5	15	55
148-Origin Ancient One	7	21	90
150(11/66)-John Buscema's 1st work at Marvel	6	18	65
151-Kirby/Steranko-c/a; 1st Marvel work by Steranko	8	24	95
152,153-Kirby/Steranko-a	6	18	65
154-158-Steranko-a/script	6	18	65

159-Origin Nick Fury retold; Intro Val; Captain America-c/story; Steranko-a

	7	21	80
160-162-Steranko-a/scripts; Capt. America app.	6	18	65

163-166,168-Steranko-a(p). 168-Last Nick Fury (gets own book next month) & last Dr. Strange who also gets own book

	5	15	60
167-Steranko pen/script; classic flag-c	7	21	80

169-1st app. Brother Voodoo (origin in #169,170) & begin series, ends #173

	2	6	20
170-174: 174-Origin Golem	2	6	14
175-177: 177-Brunner-c	1	4	10

178-(2/75)-Warlock by Starlin begins; origin Warlock & Him retold; 1st app. Magus; Starlin-c/a/scripts in #178-181 (all before Warlock #9)

	3	9	25

179-181-All Warlock. 179-Intro/1st app. Pip the Troll. 180-Intro Gamora. 181-(8/75)-Warlock story continued in Warlock #9

	2	6	16
182-188: 185,186-(Regular 25¢ editions)			6.00
185,186-(30¢-c variants, limited distribution)(5,7/76)	2	6	18

Annual 1(1962)-Reprints from Strange Tales #73,76,78, Tales of Suspense #7,9, Tales to Astonish #1,6,7, & Journey Into Mystery #53,55,59; (1st Marvel annual?)

	48	144	825

Annual 2(7/63)-Reprints from Strange Tales #67, Strange Worlds (Atlas) #1-3, World of Fantasy #16; new Human Torch vs. Spider-Man story by Kirby/Ditko (1st Spidey x-over; 4th app.); Kirby-c

	66	198	1250

SUB-MARINER, THE (2nd Series)(Sub-Mariner #31 on)
Marvel Comics Group: May, 1968 - No. 72, Sept, 1974 (No. 43: 52 pgs.)

	17	51	250
1-Origin Sub-Mariner; story continued from Iron Man & Sub-Mariner #1			
2-Triton app.	8	24	100
3-5: 5-1st Tiger Shark (9/68)	6	18	75

6,7,9,10: 6-Tiger Shark-c & 2nd app., cont'd from #5. 7-Photo-c. (1968). 9-1st app. Serpent Crown (origin in #10 & 12)

	5	15	55
8-Sub-Mariner vs. Thing	9	27	115
8-2nd printing (1994)	2	6	12
11-13,15: 15-Last 12¢ issue	4	12	42

14-Sub-Mariner vs. G.A. Human Torch; death of Toro (1st modern app. & only app. Toro, 6/69)

	5	15	60

16-20: 19-1st Sting Ray (11/69); Stan Lee, Romita, Heck, Thomas, Everett & Kirby cameos. 20-Dr. Doom app.

	3	9	28

	GD	FN	NM-
21,23-33,37-39,41,42: 25-Origin Atlantis. 30-Capt. Marvel x-over. 37-Death of Lady Dorma. 38-Origin retold. 42-Last 15¢ issue	2	6	22
22,40: 22-Dr. Strange x-over. 40-Spider-Man x-over	3	9	24
34-Prelude (w/#35) to 1st Defenders story; Hulk & Silver Surfer x-over	7	21	85
35-Namor/Hulk/Silver Surfer team-up to battle The Avengers-c/story (3/71); hints at teaming up again	6	18	65
36-Wrightson-a(i)	3	9	28
43-King Size Special (52 pgs.)	3	9	28
44,45-Sub-Mariner vs. Human Torch	3	9	25
46-49,56,62,64-72: 47,48-Dr. Doom app. 49-Cosmic Cube story. 62-1st Tales of Atlantis, ends #66. 64-Hitler cameo. 67-New costume; F.F. x-over. 69-Spider-Man x-over (6 panels)	1	4	10
50-1st app. Nita, Namor's niece (later Namorita in New Warriors)	2	6	15
51-55,57,58,60,61,63-Everett issues: 61-Last artwork by Everett; 1st 4 pgs. completed by Mortimer; pgs. 5-20 by Mooney	2	6	14
59-1st battle with Thor; Everett-a	3	9	25
Special 1 (1/71)-r/Tales to Astonish #70-73	3	9	30
Special 2 (1/72)-(52 pgs.)-r/T.T.A. #74-76; Everett-a	2	6	22

SUGAR & SPIKE (Also see The Best of DC & DC Silver Age Classics)
National Periodical Publications: Apr-May, 1956 - No. 98, Oct-Nov, 1971

1 (Scarce)	277	831	3600
2	96	288	1250
3-5: 3-Letter column begins	67	201	875
6-10	42	126	525
11-20	38	114	420
21-29: 26-Christmas-c	26	78	275
30-Scribbly & Scribbly, Jr. x-over	27	81	285
31-40	15	45	215
41-60	10	30	125
61-80: 69-1st app. Tornado-Tot-c/story. 72-Origin & 1st app. Bernie the Brain	8	24	95
81-84,86-95: 84-Bernie the Brain apps. as Superman in 1 panel (9/69)	6	18	75
85 (68 pgs.)-r/#72	7	21	85
96 (68 pgs.)	8	24	95
97,98 (52 pgs.)	7	21	85
No. 1 Replica Edition (2002, $2.95) reprint of #1			3.00

SUPERBOY (1st Series)(...& the Legion of Super-Heroes with #231)
(Becomes The Legion of Super-Heroes No. 259 on)
National Periodical Publications/DC Comics: Mar-Apr, 1949 - No. 258, Dec, 1979 (#1-16: 52 pgs.)

1-Superman cover; intro in More Fun #101 (1-2/45)	774	2322	12,000
2-Used in **SOTI**, pg. 35-36,226	212	636	2750
3	162	486	2100

	GD	FN	NM-
4,5: 5-1st pre-Supergirl tryout (c/story, 11-12/49)	108	324	1400
6-10: 8-1st Superbaby. 10-1st app. Lana Lang	94	282	1225
11-15	73	219	950
16-20: 20-2nd Jor-El cover	50	150	625
21-26,28-30: 21-Lana Lang app.	40	120	475
27-Low distribution	40	120	500
31-38: 38-Last pre-code issue (1/55)	35	105	385
39-48,50 (7/56)	31	93	335
49 (6/56)-1st app. Metallo (Jor-El's robot)	33	99	360
51-60: 52-1st S.A. issue. 56-Krypto-c	22	66	230
61-67	18	54	185
68-Origin/1st app. original Bizarro (10-11/58)	56	168	725
69-77,79: 76-1st Supermonkey	14	42	145
78-Origin Mr. Mxyzptlk & Superboy's costume	22	66	240
80-1st meeting Superboy/Supergirl (4/60)	20	60	210
81,83-85,87,88: 83-Origin/1st app. Kryptonite Kid	10	30	135
82-1st Bizarro Krypto	11	33	145
86-(1/61)-4th Legion app; Intro Pete Ross	18	54	270
89-(6/61)-1st app. Mon-el; 2nd Phantom Zone	28	84	410
90-92: 90-Pete Ross learns Superboy's I.D. 92-Last 10¢ issue			
	10	30	135
93-10th Legion app.(12/61); Chameleon Boy app.	11	33	145
94-97,99	8	24	105
98-(7/62)-18th Legion app; origin & 1st app. Ultra Boy; Pete Ross joins Legion	11	33	160
100-(10/62)-Ultra Boy app; 1st app. Phantom Zone villains, Dr. Xadu & Erndine. 2 pg. map of Krypton; origin Superboy retold; r-cover of Superman #1	19	57	275
101-120: 104-Origin Phantom Zone. 115-Atomic bomb-c. 117-Legion app.	7	21	90
121-128: 124-(10/65)-1st app. Insect Queen (Lana Lang). 125-Legion cameo. 126-Origin Krypto the Super Dog retold with new facts	7	21	80
129-(80-pg. Giant G-22)-Reprints origin Mon-el	9	27	110
130-137,139,140: 131-Legion statues cameo in Dog Legionnaires story. 133-Superboy meets Robin	6	18	65
138 (80-pg. Giant G-35)	7	21	85
141-146,148-155,157: 145-Superboy's parents regain their youth. 148-Legion app. 157-Last 12¢ issue	4	12	45
147(6/68)-Giant G-47; 1st origin of L.S.H. (Saturn Girl, Lightning Lad, Cosmic Boy); origin Legion of Super-Pets-r/Adv. #293	6	18	70
147 Replica Edition (2003, $6.95) reprints entire issue; cover recreation by Ordway			7.00
156,165,174 (Giants G-59,71,83): 165-r/1st app. Krypto the Superdog from Adventure Comics #210	4	12	50
158-164,166-171,175: 171-1st app. Aquaboy	3	9	28
172,173,176-Legion app.: 172-Origin Yango (Super Ape). 176-Partial photo-c; last 15¢ issue	3	9	30
177-184,186,187 (All 52 pgs.): 182-All new origin of the classic World's Finest			

	GD	FN	NM-

team (Superman & Batman) as teenagers (2/72, 22pgs).

184-Origin Dial H for Hero-r 3 9 32

185-Also listed as DC 100 Pg. Super Spectacular #12; Legion-c/story;
Teen Titans, Kid Eternity(r/Hit #46), Star Spangled Kid-r(S.S. #55)

7 21 90

188-190,192,194,196: 188-Origin Karkan. 196-Last Superboy solo story

2 6 16

191,193,195: 191-Origin Sunboy retold; Legion app. 193-Chameleon Boy &
Shrinking Violet get new costumes. 195-1st app. Erg-1/Wildfire; Phantom
Girl gets new costume 2 6 18

197-Legion series begins; Lightning Lad's new costume

3 10 35

198,199: 198-Element Lad & Princess Projectra get new costumes

2 6 22

200-Bouncing Boy & Duo Damsel marry; J'onn J'onzz cameo

3 9 26

201,204,206,207,209: 201-Re-intro Erg-1 as Wildfire. 204-Supergirl resigns
from Legion. 206-Ferro Lad & Invisible Kid app. 209-Karate Kid gets new
costume 2 6 18

202,205-(100 pgs.): 202-Light Lass gets new costume; Mike Grell's 1st comic
work-i (5-6/74) 5 15 60

203-Invisible Kid killed by Validus 3 9 26

208,210: 208-(68 pgs.). 208-Legion of Super-Villains app. 210-Origin Karate
Kid 3 9 24

211-220: 212-Matter-Eater Lad resigns. 216-1st app. Tyroc, who joins the
Legion in #218 2 6 14

221-230,246-249: 226-Intro. Dawnstar. 228-Death of Chemical King

1 4 10

231-245: (Giants). 240-Origin Dawnstar. 242-(52 pgs.). 243-Legion of
Substitute Heroes app. 243-245-(44 pgs.). 2 6 16

244,245-(Whitman variants; low print run, no issue# shown on cover)

2 6 20

246-248-(Whitman variants; low ...) 2 6 15

250-258: 253-Intro Blok. 257-Return of Bouncing Boy & Duo Damsel by Ditko

1 3 8

251-258-(Whitman variants; low print run) 2 6 12

Annual 1 (Sum/64, 84 pgs.)-Origin Krypto-r 19 57 275

Spectacular 1 (1980, Giant)-1st comic distributed only through comic stores;
mostly-r 1 3 9

SUPERBOY (TV)(2nd Series)(The Adventures of...#19 on)
DC Comics: Feb, 1990 - No. 22, Dec, 1991 ($1.00/$1.25)

1-22: Mooney-a(p) in 1-8,18-20; 1-Photo-c from TV show. 8-Bizarro-c/story;
Arthur Adams-a(i). 9-12,14-17-Swan-p 3.00

...Special 1 (1992, $1.75) Swan-a 3.00

SUPERBOY (3rd Series)
DC Comics: Feb, 1994 - No. 100, Jul, 2002 ($1.50/$1.95/$1.99/$2.25)

1-Metropolis Kid from Reign of the Supermen 4.00

2-8,0,9-24,26-76: 6,7-Worlds Collide Pts. 3 & 8. 8-(9/94)-Zero Hour x-over.

	GD	FN	NM-

0-(10/94). 9-(11/94)-King Shark app. 21-Legion app. 28-Supergirl-c/app.
33-Final Night. 38-41-"Meltdown". 45-Legion-c/app. 47-Green Lantern app.
50-Last Boy on Earth begins. 60-Crosses Hypertime. 68-Demon-c/app.
$\qquad$ 2.50

25-($2.95)-New Gods & Female Furies app.; w/pin-ups $\qquad$ 3.50
77-99: 77-Begin $2.25-c. 79-Superboy's powers return. 80,81-Titans app.
83-New costume. 85-Batgirl app. 90,91-Our Worlds at War x-over $\qquad$ 2.25
100-($3.50) Sienkiewicz-c; Grummett & McCrea-a; Superman cameo $\qquad$ 3.50
#1,000,000 (11/98) 853rd Century x-over $\qquad$ 2.50
Annual 1 (1994, $2.95, 68 pgs.)-Elseworlds story, Pt. 2 of The Super Seven
$\quad$ (see Adventures Of Superman Annual #6) $\qquad$ 3.00
Annual 2 (1995, $3.95)-Year One story $\qquad$ 4.00
Annual 3 (1996, $2.95)-Legends of the Dead Earth $\qquad$ 3.00
Annual 4 (1997, $3.95)-Pulp Heroes story $\qquad$ 4.00
...Plus 1 (Jan, 1997, $2.95) w/Capt. Marvel Jr. $\qquad$ 3.00
...Plus 2 (Fall, 1997, $2.95) w/Slither (Scare Tactics) $\qquad$ 3.00
.../Risk Double-Shot 1 (Feb, 1998, $1.95) w/Risk (Teen Titans) $\qquad$ 2.50

SUPER DC GIANT (25-50¢, all 68-52 pg. Giants)
National Per. Publ.: No. 13, 9-10/70 - No. 26, 7-8/71; V3#27, Summer, 1976
(No #1-12)

	GD	FN	NM-
S-13-Binky	11	33	160
S-14-Top Guns of the West; Kubert-c; Trigger Twins, Johnny Thunder, Wyoming Kid-r; Moreira-r (9-10/70)	5	15	60
S-15-Western Comics; Kubert-c; Pow Wow Smith, Vigilante, Buffalo Bill-r; new Gil Kane-a (9-10/70)	5	15	60
S-16-Best of the Brave & the Bold; Batman-r & Metamorpho origin-r from Brave & the Bold; Spectre pin-up.	4	12	45
S-17-Love 1970 (scarce)	25	75	375
S-18-Three Mouseketeers; Dizzy Dog, Doodles Duck, Bo Bunny-r; Sheldon Mayer-a	10	30	135
S-19-Jerry Lewis; Neal Adams pin-up	10	30	145
S-20-House of Mystery; N. Adams-c; Kirby-r(3)	7	21	85
S-21-Love 1971 (scarce)	29	87	450
S-22-Top Guns of the West; Kubert-c	4	12	40
S-23-The Unexpected	4	12	50
S-24-Supergirl	4	12	40
S-25-Challengers of the Unknown; all Kirby/Wood-r	3	10	38
S-26-Aquaman (1971)-r/S.A. Aquaman origin story from Showcase #30	3	10	38
27-Strange Flying Saucers Adventures (Sum, 1976)	3	9	35

SUPER FRIENDS (TV) (Also see Best of DC & Limited Collectors' Edition)
National Periodical Publications/DC Comics: Nov, 1976 - No. 47, Aug, 1981
(#14 is 44 pgs.)

	GD	FN	NM-
1-Superman, Batman, Robin, Wonder Woman, Aquaman, Atom, Wendy, Marvin & Wonder Dog begin (1st Super Friends)	4	12	40
2-Penquin-c/sty	2	6	20
3-5	2	6	18

6-10,14: 7-1st app. Wonder Twins & The Seraph. 8-1st app. Jack O'Lantern.

	GD	FN	NM-

9-1st app. Icemaiden. 14-Origin Wonder Twins   2   6   14

11-13,15-30: 13-1st app. Dr. Mist. 25-1st app. Fire as Green Fury. 28-Bizarro
   app.   1   4   10

13-16,20-23,25,32-(Whitman variants; low print run, no issue# on cover)
                                          2   6   12

31,47: 31-Black Orchid app. 47-Origin Fire & Green Fury
                                          2   6   12

32-46: 36,43-Plastic Man app.   1   3   9

TBP (2001, $14.95) r/#1,6-9,14,21,27 & L.C.E. C-41; Alex Ross-c   15.00

...: Truth, Justice and Peace TPB (2003, $14.95) r/#10,12,13,25,28,29,31,36,37
                                               15.00

SUPERGIRL
National Periodical Publ.: Nov, 1972 - No. 9, Dec-Jan, 1973-74; No. 10,
Sept-Oct, 1974 (1st solo title)(20¢)

1-Zatanna back-up stories begin, end #5   6   18   70

2-4,6,7,9   3   9   30

5,8,10: 5-Zatanna origin-r. 8-JLA x-over; Batman cameo. 10-Prez
                                        3   9   32

SUPERGIRL (See Showcase '96 #8)
DC Comics: Sept, 1996 - No. 80, May, 2003 ($1.95/$1.99/$2.25/$2.50)

1-Peter David scripts & Gary Frank-c/a; DC cover logo in upper left is blue
                                          1   3   8

1-2nd printing-DC cover logo in upper left is red   3.00

2,4-9: 4-Gorilla Grodd-c/app. 6-Superman-c/app. 9-Last Frank-a   4.00

3-Final Night, Gorilla Grodd app.   5.00

10-19: 14-Genesis x-over. 16-Power Girl app.   3.50

20-35: 20-Millennium Giants x-over; Superman app. 23-Steel-c/app.
   24-Resurrection Man x-over. 25-Comet ID revealed; begin $1.99-c   3.00

36-46: 36,37-Young Justice x-over   2.50

47-49,51-74: 47-Begin $2.25-c. 51-Adopts costume from animated series.
   54-Green Lantern app. 59-61-Our Worlds at War x-over.
   68-74-Mary Marvel app. 70-Nauck-a. 73-Begin $2.50-c   2.50

50-($3.95) Supergirl's final battle with the Carnivore   4.00

75-80: 75-Re-intro. Kara Zor-El; cover swipe of Action #252 by Haynes;
   Benes-a. 78-Spectre app. 80-Last issue; Romita-c   2.50

#1,000,000 (11/98) 853rd Century x-over   3.00

Annual 1 (1996, $2.95)-Legends of the Dead Earth   3.00

Annual 2 (1997, $3.95)-Pulp Heroes; LSH app.; Chiodo-c   4.00

...: Many Happy Returns TPB (2003, $14.95) r/#75-80; intro. by Peter David
                                           15.00

...Plus (2/97, $2.95) Capt.(Mary) Marvel-c/app.; David-s/Frank-a   3.00

.../Prysm Double-Shot 1 (Feb, 1998, $1.95) w/Prysm (Teen Titans)   2.50

...: Wings (2001, $5.95) Elseworlds; DeMatteis-s/Tolagson-a   6.00

TPB-('98, $14.95) r/Showcase '96 #8 & Supergirl #1-9   15.00

SUPERMAN (Becomes Adventures of...#424 on)
National Periodical Publ./DC Comics: No. 100, Sept-Oct, 1955 - No. 423,
Sept, 1986

	GD	FN	NM-
100 (9-10/55)-Shows cover to #1 on-c	208	624	2700
101-105,107-110: 109-1st S.A. issue	40	120	475
106 (7/56)-Retells origin	40	120	500
111-120	37	111	400
121,122,124-127,129: 127-Origin/1st app. Titano. 129-Intro/origin Lori Lemaris, The Mermaid	31	93	340
123-Pre-Supergirl tryout-c/story (8/58)	39	117	425
128-(4/59)-Red Kryptonite used. Bruce Wayne x-over who protects Superman's i.d. (3rd story)	33	99	360
130-(7/59)-2nd app, Krypto, the Superdog with Superman (see Sup.'s Pal Jimmy Olsen #29)(all other previous app. w/Superboy)	33	99	360
131-139: 135-2nd Lori Lemaris app. 139-Lori Lemaris app.;	25	75	265
140-1st Blue Kryptonite & Bizarro Supergirl; origin Bizarro Jr. #1	26	78	275
141-145,148: 142-2nd Batman x-over	20	60	215
146-(7/61)-Superman's life story; back-up hints at Earth II. Classic-c	26	78	280
147(8/61)-7th Legion app; 1st app. Legion of Super-Villains; 1st app. Adult Legion; swipes-c to Adv. #247	25	75	265
149(11/61)-8th Legion app. (cameo); "The Death of Superman" imaginary story; last 10¢ issue	22	66	240
150,151,153,154,157,159,160: 157-Gold Kryptonite used (see Adv. #299); Mon-el app.; Lightning Lad cameo (11/62)	10	30	140
152,155,156,158,162: 152(4/62)-15th Legion app. 155-(8/62)-Legion app; Lightning Man & Cosmic Man, & Adult Legion app. 156,162-Legion app.			
158-1st app. Flamebird & Nightwing & Nor-Kan of Kandor(12/62)	11	33	145
161-1st told death of Ma and Pa Kent	11	33	145
161-2nd printing (1987, $1.25)-New DC logo; sold thru So Much Fun Toy Stores (cover title: Superman Classic)			3.00
163-166,168-180: 166-XMas-c. 168-All Luthor issue; JFK tribute/memorial. 169-Bizarro Invasion of Earth-c/story; last Sally Selwyn. 170-Pres. Kennedy story is finally published after delay from #168 due to assassination. 172,173-Legion cameos. 174-Super-Mxyzptlk; Bizarro app.	9	27	110
167-New origin Brainiac & Brainiac 5; intro Tharla (later Luthor's wife)	11	33	145
181,182,184-186,188-192,194-196,198,200: 181-1st 2965 story/series. 182-1st S.A. app. of The Toyman (1/66). 189-Origin/destruction of Krypton II	7	21	90
183 (Giant G-18)	10	30	130
187,193,197 (Giants G-23,G-31,G-36)	8	24	105
199-1st Superman/Flash race (8/67): also see Flash #175 & World's Finest #198,199 (r-in Limited Coll. Ed. C-48)	26	78	385
201,203-206,208-211,213-216: 213-Brainiac-5 app. 216-Last 12¢ issue	5	15	60
202 (80-pg. Giant G-42)-All Bizarro issue	7	21	80

	GD	FN	NM-

207,212,217 (Giants G-48,G-54,G-60): 207-30th anniversary Superman (6/68)

	7	21	80
218-221,223-226,228-231	4	12	50
222,239(Giants, G-66,G-84)	6	18	75
227,232(Giants, G-72,G-78)-All Krypton issues	6	18	70

233-2nd app. Morgan Edge; Clark Kent switches from newspaper reporter to
   TV newscaster; all Kryptonite on earth destroyed; classic Neal Adams-c

	7	21	90
234-238	4	12	45
240-Kaluta-a; last 15¢ issue	3	10	35

241-244 (All 52 pgs.): 241-New Wonder Woman app. 243-G.A.-r/#38

	4	12	38

245-Also listed as DC 100 Pg. Super Spectacular #7; Air Wave, Kid Eternity,
   Hawkman-r; Atom-r/Atom #3

	9	27	115

246-248,250,251,253 (All 52 pgs.): 246-G.A.-r/#40. 248-World of Krypton
   story. 251-G.A.-r/#45. 253-Finlay-a, 2 pgs., G.A.-r/#1

	4	12	38

249,254-Neal Adams-a. 249-(52 pgs.); origin & 1st app. Terra-Man by Neal
   Adams (inks)

	5	15	55

252-Also listed as DC 100 Pg. Super Spectacular #13; Ray(r/Smash #17),
   Black Condor, (r/Crack #18), Hawkman(r/Flash #24); Starman-r/Adv. #67;
   Dr. Fate & Spectre-r/More Fun #57; N. Adams-c

	9	27	120

255-271,273-277,279-283: 263-Photo-c. 264-1st app. Steve Lombard.
   276-Intro Capt. Thunder. 279-Batman, Batgirl app.

	2	6	15
272,278,284-All 100 pgs. G.A.-r in all	5	15	55

285-299: 289-Partial photo-c. 292-Origin Lex Luthor retold

	1	3	10
300-(6/76) Superman in the year 2001	3	9	32

301-350: 301,320-Solomon Grundy app. 323-Intro. Atomic Skull.
   327-329-(44 pgs.). 327-Kobra app. 330-More facts revealed about I.D.
   338-The bottled city of Kandor enlarged. 344-Frankenstein & Dracula app.

			6.00

321-323,325-327,329-332,335-345,348,350 (Whitman variants;
   low print run; no issue # on cover)

	1	3	9

351-399: 353-Brief origin. 354,355,357-Superman 2020 stories (354-Debut of
   Superman III). 356-World of Krypton story (also #360,367,375). 366-Fan
   letter by Todd McFarlane. 372-Superman 2021 story. 376-Free 16 pg.
   preview Daring New Advs. of Supergirl. 377-Free 16 pg. preview Masters
   of the Universe

			5.00

400 (10/84, $1.50, 68 pgs.)-Many top artists featured; Chaykin painted cover,
   Miller back-c; Steranko-s/a (10 pages)

			6.00

401-422: 405-Super-Batman story. 408-Nuclear Holocaust-c/story.
   411-Special Julius Schwartz tribute issue. 414,415-Crisis x-over.
   422-Horror-c

			4.00

423-Alan Moore scripts; Perez-a(i); last Earth I Superman story, cont'd in
   Action #583

	1	4	10

Annual 1(10/60, 84 pgs.)-Reprints 1st Supergirl story/Action #252; r/Lois
   Lane #1; Krypto-r (1st Silver Age DC annual)

	86	258	1650

Annual 2(Win, 1960-61)-Super-villain issue; Brainiac, Titano, Metallo, Bizarro

	GD	FN	NM-
origin-r	41	123	675
Annual 3(Sum, 1961)-Strange Lives of Superman	29	87	435
Annual 4(Win, 1961-62)-11th Legion app; 1st Legion origins (text & pictures); advs. in time, space & on alien worlds	24	72	350
Annual 5(Sum, 1962)-All Krypton issue	19	57	275
Annual 6(Win, 1962-63)-Legion-r/Adv. #247	17	51	250
Annual 7(Sum, 1963)-Origin-r/Superman-Batman team/Adv. 275; r/1955 Superman dailies	13	39	190
Annual 8(Win, 1963-64)-All origins issue	12	36	165
Annual 9(8/64)-Was advertised but came out as 80 Page Giant #1 instead			
Annual 9(1983)-Toth/Austin-a			6.00
Annuals 10-12: 10(1984, $1.25)-M. Anderson inks. 11(1985)-Moore scripts. 12(1986)-Bolland-c			4.00
Special 1-3('83-'85): 1-G. Kane-c/a; contains German-r			4.00
The Amazing World of Superman "Official Metropolis Edition" (1973, $2.00, treasury-size)-Origin retold; Wood-r(i) from Superboy #153,161; poster incl. (half price if poster missing)	4	12	50
11195 (2/79, $1.95, 224 pgs.)-Golden Press	4	12	40

SUPERMAN (2nd Series)
DC Comics: Jan, 1987 - Present (75¢/$1.00/$1.25/$1.50/$1.95/$1.99)

	GD	FN	NM-
0-(10/94) Zero Hour; released between #93 & #94			2.50
1-Byrne-c/a begins; intro new Metallo			5.00
2-8,10: 3-Legends x-over; Darkseid-c & app. 7-Origin/1st app. Rampage. 8-Legion app.			3.00
9-Joker-c			4.50
11-15,17-20,22-49,51,52,54-56,58-67: 11-1st new Mr. Mxyzptlk. 12-Lori Lemaris revived. 13-1st app. new Toyman. 13,14-Millennium x-over. 20-Doom Patrol app.; Supergirl cameo. 31-Mr. Mxyzptlk app. 37-Newsboy Legion app. 41-Lobo app. 44-Batman storyline, part 1. 45-Free extra 8 pgs. 54-Newsboy Legion story. 63-Aquaman x-over. 67-Last $1.00-c			2.50
16,21: 16-1st app. new Supergirl (4/88). 21-Supergirl-c/story; 1st app. Matrix who becomes new Supergirl			4.00
50-($1.50, 52 pgs.)-Clark Kent proposes to Lois			5.00
50-2nd printing			2.25
53-Clark reveals i.d. to Lois (Cont'd from Action #662)			3.00
53-2nd printing			2.25
57-($1.75, 52 pgs.)			3.00
68-72: 65,66,68-Deathstroke-c/stories. 70-Superman & Robin team-up			2.50
73-Doomsday cameo			5.00
74-Doomsday Pt. 2 (Cont'd from Justice League #69); Superman battles Doomsday			6.00
73,74-2nd printings			2.25
75-($2.50)-Collector's Ed.; Doomsday Pt. 6; Superman dies; polybagged w/poster of funeral, obituary from Daily Planet, postage stamp & armband premiums (direct sales only)	2	6	18
75-Direct sales copy (no upc code, 1st print)	1	3	8
75-Direct sales copy (no upc code, 2nd-4th prints)			2.25
75-Newsstand copy w/upc code	1	3	8
75-Platinum Edition; given away to retailers			55.00

	GD	FN	NM-
76,77-Funeral For a Friend parts 4 & 8			3.00
78-($1.95)-Collector's Edition with die-cut outer-c & mini poster; Doomsday cameo			3.00
78-($1.50)-Newsstand Edition w/poster and different-c; Doomsday-c & cameo			2.25
79-81,83-89: 83-Funeral for a Friend epilogue; new Batman (Azrael) cameo. 87,88-Bizarro-c/story			2.50
82-($3.50)-Collector's Edition w/all chromium-c; real Superman revealed; Green Lantern x-over from G.L. #46; no ads			6.00
82-($2.00, 44 pgs.)-Regular Edition w/different-c			2.50
90-99: 93-(9/94)-Zero Hour. 94-(11/94). 95-Atom app. 96-Brainiac app.			2.50
100-Death of Clark Kent foil-c			4.00
100-Newsstand			3.00
101-122: 101-Begin $1.95-c; Black Adam app. 105-Green Lantern app. 110-Plastic Man-c/app. 114-Brainiac app; Dwyer-c. 115-Lois leaves Metropolis. 116-(10/96)-1st app. Teen Titans by Jurgens & Perez in 8 pg. preview. 117-Final Night. 118-Wonder Woman app.119-Legion app. 122-New powers			2.50
123-Collector's Edition w/glow in the dark-c, new costume			6.00
123-Standard ed., new costume			4.00
124-149: 128-Cyborg-c/app. 131-Birth of Lena Luthor. 132-Superman Red/ Superman Blue. 134-Millennium Giants. 136,137-Superman 2999. 139-Starlin-a. 140-Grindberg-a			2.50
150-($2.95) Standard Ed.; Brainiac 2.0 app.; Jurgens-s			3.00
150-($3.95) Collector's Ed. w/holo-foil enhanced variant-c			4.00
151-158: 151-Loeb-s begins; Daily Planet reopens			2.25
159-174: 159-$2.25-c begin. 161-Joker-c/app. 162-Aquaman-c/app. 163-Young Justice app. 165-JLA app.; Ramos; Madureira, Liefeld, A. Adams, Wieringo, Churchill-a. 166-Collector's and reg. editions. 167-Return to Krypton. 168-Batman-c/app.(cont'd in Detective #756). 171-173-Our Worlds at War. 173-Sienkiewicz-a (2 pgs.). 174-Adopts black & red "S" logo			2.25
175-($3.50) Joker: Last Laugh x-over; Doomsday-c/app.			3.50
176-189,191-199: 176,180-Churchill-a. 180-Dracula app. 181-Bizarro-c/app. 184-Return to Krypton II. 189-Van Fleet-c. 192,193,195,197-199-New Supergirl app.			2.25
190-($2.25) Regular edition			2.25
190-($3.95) Double-Feature Issue; included reprint of Superman: The 10¢ Adventure			4.00
200-($3.50) Gene Ha-c/art by various; preview art by Yu & Bermejo			3.50
201-Mr Majestic-c/app.; cover swipe of Action #1			2.25
202,203-Godfall parts 3,6; Turner-c; Caldwell-a(p). 203-Jim Lee sketch pages			2.25
204-Jim Lee-c/a begins; Azzarello-s			3.00
204-Diamond Retailer Summit edition with sketch cover			100.00
205-211: 205-Two covers by Jim Lee and Michael Turner. 208-JLA app. 211-Battles Wonder Woman			2.50
#1,000,000 (11/98) 853rd Century x-over; Gene Ha-c			2.25
Annual 1,2: 1 (1987)-No Byrne-a. 2 (1988)-Byrne-a; Newsboy Legion;			

	GD	FN	NM-
Guardian returns			4.00

Annual 3-6 ('91-'94 68 pgs.): 1-Armageddon 2001 x-over; Batman app.;
   Austin-c(i) & part inks. 4-Eclipso app. 6-Elseworlds sty   3.00
Annual 3-2nd & 3rd printings; 3rd has silver ink   2.25
Annual 7 (1995, $3.95, 69 pgs.)-Year One story   4.00
Annual 8 (1996, $2.95)-Legends of the Dead Earth story   3.00
Annual 9 (1997, $3.95)-Pulp Heroes story   4.00
Annual 10 (1998, $2.95)-Ghosts; Wrightson-c   3.00
Annual 11 (1999, $2.95)-JLApe; Art Adams-c   3.00
Annual 12 (2000, $3.50)-Planet DC   3.50
...: Critical Condition ('03, $14.95, TPB) r/2000 Kryptonite poisoning storyline   15.00
...: 80 Page Giant (2/99, $4.95) Jurgens-c   5.00
...: 80 Page Giant 2 (6/99, $4.95) Harris-c   5.00
...: 80 Page Giant 3 (11/00, $5.95) Nowlan-c; art by various   6.00
...: Endgame (2000, $14.95, TPB)-Reprints Y2K and Brainiac story line 15.00
...: Eradication! The Origin of the Eradicator (1996, $12.95, TPB)   13.00
...: Exile (1998, $14.95, TPB)-Reprints space exile following execution of
   Kryptonian criminals; 1st Eradicator   15.00
...: Godfall HC (2004, $19.95, dustjacket) r/Action #812-813, Advs. of
   Superman #625-626, Superman #202-203; Caldwell sketch pages;
   Turner cover gallery; new Turner-c   20.00
... In the Fifties ('02, $19.95, TPB) Intro. by Mark Waid   20.00
... In the Seventies ('00, $19.95, TPB) Intro. by Christopher Reeve   20.00
... No Limits ('00, $14.95, TPB) Reprints early 2000 stories   15.00
...: Our Worlds at War Book 1 ('02, $19.95, TPB) r/1st half of x-over   20.00
...: Our Worlds at War Book 2 ('02, $19.95, TPB) r/2nd half of x-over   20.00
...Plus 1(2/97, $2.95)-Legion of Super-Heroes-c/app.   3.00
...: President Lex TPB (2003, $17.95) r/Luthor's run for the White House;
   Harris-c   18.00
...: Return to Krypton (2004, $17.95, TPB) r/2001-2002 x-over   18.00
Special 1 (1992, $3.50, 68 pgs.)-Simonson-c/a   5.00
The Death of Clark Kent (1997, $19.95, TPB)-Reprints Man of Steel #43
   (1 page), Superman #99 (1 page),#100-102, Action #709 (1 page), #710,
   #711, Advs. of Superman #523-525, Superman:The Man of Tomorrow #1   20.00

The Death of Superman (1993, $4.95, TPB)-Reprints Man of Steel #17-19,
   Superman #73-75, Advs. of Superman #496,497, Action #683,684, &
   Justice League #69   1   3   8
The Death of Superman, 2nd & 3rd printings   5.00
The Death of Superman Platinum Edition   15.00
...: The Greatest Stories Ever Told ('04, $19.95, TPB) Ross-c, Uslan intro.   20.00
...: The Man of Steel Vol. 2 ('03, $19.95, TPB) r/Superman #1-3,
   Action #584-586, Advs. of Superman #424-426 & Who's Who Update '87   20.00
...: The Man of Steel Vol. 3 ('04, $19.95, TPB) r/Superman #4-6, Action #587-
   #589, Advs. of Superman #427-429; intro. by Ordway; new Ordway-c   20.00

	GD	FN	NM-

The Trial of Superman ('97, $14.95, TPB) reprints story arc   15.00
...: They Saved Luthor's Brain ('00, $14.95) r/ "death" and return of Luthor
      15.00
...: 'Til Death Do Us Part ('01, $17.95) reprints; Mahnke-c   18.00
...: Time and Time Again (1994, $7.50, TPB)-Reprints   8.00
....: Transformed ('98, $12.95, TPB) r/post Final Night powerless Superman to
    Electric Superman   13.00
... Vs. The Revenge Squad (1999, $12.95, TPB)   13.00

SUPERMAN (one-shots)
Daily News Magazine Presents DC Comics' Superman nn-(1987, 8 pgs.)-
    Supplement to New York Daily News; Perez-c/a   5.00
...: A Nation Divided (1999, $4.95)-Elseworlds Civil War story   5.00
... & Savage Dragon: Chicago (2002, $5.95) Larsen-a; Ross-c   6.00
... & Savage Dragon: Metropolis (11/99, $4.95) Bogdanove-a   5.00
...: At Earth's End (1995, $4.95)-Elseworlds story   5.00
...: Blood of My Ancestors (2003, $6.95)-Gil Kane & John Buscema-a   7.00
...: Distant Fires (1998, $5.95)-Elseworlds; Chaykin-s   6.00
...: Emperor Joker (10/00, $3.50)-Follows Action #769   3.50
...: End of the Century (2/00, $24.95, HC)-Immonen-s/a   25.00
...: End of the Century (2003, $17.95, SC)-Immonen-s/a   18.00
... For Earth (1991, $4.95, 52 pgs, printed on recycled paper)-Ordway
    wraparound-c   5.00
...IV Movie Special (1987, $2.00)-Movie adaptation; Heck-a   3.00
...Gallery, The 1 (1993, $2.95)-Poster-a   3.00
..., Inc. (1999, $6.95)-Elseworlds Clark as a sports hero; Garcia-Lopez-a   7.00
...: Kal (1995, $5.95)-Elseworlds story   6.00
...: Lex 2000 (1/01, $3.50)-Election night for the Luthor Presidency   3.50
...: Monster (1999, $5.95)-Elseworlds story; Anthony Williams-a   6.00
... Movie Special-(9/83)-Adaptation of Superman III; other versions exist with
    store logos on bottom 1/3 of-c   4.00
...: Our Worlds at War Secret Files 1-(8/01, $5.95)-Stories & profile pages   6.00
...'s Metropolis-(1996, $5.95, prestige format)-Elseworlds; McKeever-c/a   6.00
...: Speeding Bullets-(1993, $4.95, 52 pgs.)-Elseworlds   5.00
.../Spider-Man-(1995, $3.95)-r/DC and Marvel Presents...   4.00
... 10-Cent Adventure 1 (3/02, 10¢) McDaniel-a; intro. Cir-El Supergirl   2.25
...: The Earth Stealers 1-(1988, $2.95, 52 pgs, prestige format) Byrne script;
    painted-c   4.00
...: The Earth Stealers 1-2nd printing   3.00
...: The Legacy of Superman #1 (3/93, $2.50, 68 pgs.)-Art Adams-c;
    Simonson-a   4.00
...: The Last God of Krypton ('99,$4.95) Hildebrandt Bros.-a/Simonson-s   5.00
...: The Odyssey ('99, $4.95) Clark Kent's post-Smallville journey   5.00
...: 3-D (12/98, $3.95)-with glasses   4.00
.../Thundercats (1/04, $5.95) Winick-s/Garza-a; two covers by Garza &
    McGuinness   6.00
.../Toyman-(1996, $1.95)   2.50
...: True Brit (2004, $24.95, HC w/dust jacket) Elseworlds; Kal-El's rocket
    lands in England; co-written by John Cleese and Kim Howard Johnson;
    John Byrne-a   25.00

| | GD | FN | NM- |

...: Under A Yellow Sun (1994, $5.95, 68 pgs.)-A Novel by Clark Kent;
   embossed-c   6.00
... Vs. Darkseid: Apokolips Now! 1 (3/03, $2.95) McKone-a; Kara (Supergirl
   #75) app.   3.00
...: War of the Worlds (1999, $5.95)-Battles Martians   6.00
...: Where is thy Sting? (2001, $6.95)-McCormack-Sharp-c/a   7.00
...: Y2K (2/00, $4.95)-1st Brainiac 13 app.; Guice-c/a   5.00

SUPERMAN ADVENTURES, THE (Based on animated series)
DC Comics: Oct, 1996 - No. 66, Apr, 2002 ($1.75/$1.95/$1.99)

1-Rick Burchett-c/a begins; Paul Dini script; Lex Luthor app.; silver ink,
   wraparound-c   3.00
2-20,22: 2-McCloud scripts begin; Metallo-c/app. 3-Brainiac-c/app.
   6-Mxyzptlk-c/app.   2.50
21-($3.95) 1st animated Supergirl   5.00
23-66: 23-Begin $1.99-c; Livewire app. 25-Batgirl-c/app. 28-Manley-a.
   54-Retells Superman #233 "Kryptonite Nevermore" 58-Ross-c   2.25
Annual 1 (1997, $3.95)-Zatanna and Bruce Wayne app.   4.00
Special 1 (2/98, $2.95) Superman vs. Lobo   3.00
TPB (1998, $7.95) r/#1-6   8.00
... Vol 1: Up, Up and Away (2004, $6.95, digest-size) r/#16,19,22-24;
   Amancio-a   7.00
... Vol 2: The Never-Ending Battle (2004, $6.95, digest-size) r/#25-29   7.00

SUPERMAN & BATMAN: WORLD'S FUNNEST (Elseworlds)
DC Comics: 2000 ($6.95, square-bound, one-shot)

nn-Mr. Mxyzptlk and Bat-Mite destroy each DC Universe; Dorkin-s/ art by
   various incl. Ross, Timm, Miller, Allred, Moldoff, Cho, Jimenez   7.00

SUPERMAN/BATMAN
DC Comics: Oct, 2003 - Present ($2.95)

1-Two covers (Superman or Batman in foreground) Loeb-s/McGuinness-a;
   Metallo app.   5.00
1-2nd printing (Batman cover)   3.00
1-3rd printing; new McGuinness cover   3.00
1-Diamond/Alliance Retailer Summit Edition-variant cover   100.00
2-6: 2,5-Future Superman app. 6-Luthor in battlesuit   3.00
7-Pat Lee-c/a; Superboy & Robin app.   3.00
8-Michael Turner-c/a; intro. new Kara Zor-El   5.00
8-Second printing with sketch cover   3.00
8-Third printing with new Turner cover   3.00
9-13-Turner-c/a; Wonder Woman app. 10,13-Variant-c by Jim Lee   3.00
14,15-Pacheco-a; Lightning Lord, Saturn Queen & Cosmic King app.   3.00
...Public Enemies HC (2004, $19.95) r/#1-6 & Secret Files 2003   20.00
...Secret Files 2003 (11/03, $4.95) Reis-a; pin-ups by various; Loeb/Sale
   short-s   5.00

SUPERMAN: BIRTHRIGHT
DC Comics: Sept, 2003 - No. 12, Sept, 2004 ($2.95, limited series)

1-12-Waid-s/Leinil Yu-a; retelling of origin and early Superman years   3.00
HC (2004, $29.95, dustjacket) r/series; cover gallery; Waid proposal with Yu

	GD	FN	NM-
concept art			30.00

SUPERMAN FAMILY, THE (Formerly Superman's Pal Jimmy Olsen)
National Per. Publ./DC Comics: No. 164, Apr-May, 1974 - No. 222, Sept, 1982

	GD	FN	NM-
164-(100 pgs.) Jimmy Olsen, Supergirl, Lois Lane begin	5	15	55
165-169 (100 pgs.)	3	10	35
170-176 (68 pgs.)	2	6	22
177-190 (52 pgs.): 177-181-52 pgs. 182-Marshall Rogers-a; $1.00 issues begin; Krypto begins, ends #192. 183-Nightwing-Flamebird begins, ends #194. 189-Brainiac 5, Mon-el app.	2	6	15
191-193,195-199: 191-Superboy begins, ends #198	1	3	9
194,200: 194-Rogers-a. 200-Book length sty	1	4	10
201-222: 211-Earth II Batman & Catwoman marry	1	3	7

SUPERMAN FOR ALL SEASONS
DC Comics: 1998 - No, 4, 1998 ($4.95, limited series, prestige format)

1-Loeb-s/Sale-a/c; Superman's first year in Metropolis			6.00
2-4			5.00
Hardcover (1999, $24.95) r/#1-4			25.00

SUPERMAN: PEACE ON EARTH
DC Comics: Jan, 1999 ($9.95, Treasury-sized, one-shot)

1-Alex Ross painted-c/a; Paul Dini-s			12.00

SUPERMAN: RED SON
DC Comics: 2003 - No. 3, 2003 ($5.95, limited series, prestige format)

1-Elseworlds; Superman's rocket lands in Russia; Mark Millar-s/Dave Johnson-c/a			10.00
2,3			6.00
TPB (2004, $17.95) r/#1-3; intro. by Tom DeSanto; sketch pages			18.00

SUPERMAN'S GIRLFRIEND LOIS LANE (See Showcase #9,10)
National Periodical Publ.: Mar-Apr, 1958 - No. 136, Jan-Feb, 1974; No. 137, Sept-Oct, 1974

	GD	FN	NM-
1-(3-4/58)	300	900	6300
2	78	234	1475
3	51	153	975
4,5	44	132	750
6,7	35	105	560
8-10: 9-Pat Boone-c/story	30	90	450
11-13,15-19: 12-(10/59)-Aquaman app.	19	57	275
14-Supergirl x-over; Batman app. on-c only	19	57	285
20-Supergirl-c/sty	18	57	285
21-28: 23-1st app. Lena Thorul, Lex Luthor's sister; 1st Lois as Elastic Lass. 27-Bizarro-c/story	14	42	210
29-Aquaman, Batman, Green Arrow cover app. and cameo; last 10¢ issue	15	45	220
30-32,34-46,48,49	9	27	120
33(5/62)-Mon-el app.	10	30	130
47-Legion app.	10	30	130

	GD	FN	NM-
50(7/64)-Triplicate Girl, Phantom Girl & Shrinking Violet app.			
	10	30	125
51-55,57-67,69: 59-Jor-el app.; Batman back-up sty	7	21	90
56-Saturn Girl app.	8	24	95
68-(Giant G-26)	9	27	115
70-Penguin & Catwoman app. (1st S.A. Catwoman, 11/66; also see Detective			
#369 for 3rd app.); Batman & Robin cameo	25	75	375
71-Batman & Robin cameo (3 panels); Catwoman story cont'd from #70			
(2nd app.); see Detective #369 for 3rd app	14	42	210
72,73,75,76,78	6	18	70
74-1st Bizarro Flash (5/67); JLA cameo	6	18	75
77-(Giant G-39)	8	24	95
79-Neal Adams-c or c(i) begin, end #95,108	6	18	75
80-85,87,88,90-92: 92-Last 12¢ issue	4	12	48
86,95 (Giants G-51,G-63)-Both have Neal Adams-c	7	21	80
89,93: 89-Batman x-over; all N. Adams-c. 93-Wonder Woman-c/story			
	4	12	50
94,96-99,101-103,107-110	4	12	38
100	4	12	42
104-(Giant G-75)	6	18	70
105-Origin/1st app. The Rose & the Thorn.	6	18	70
106-"Black Like Me" sty; Lois changes her skin color to black			
	6	18	65
111-Justice League-c/s; Morrow-a; last 15¢ issue	4	12	42
112,114-123 (52 pgs.): 122-G.A. Lois Lane-r/Superman #30. 123-G.A.			
Batman-r/Batman #35 (w/Catwoman)	4	12	40
113-(Giant G-87) Kubert-a (previously unpublished G.A. story)(scarce in NM)			
	7	21	80
124-135: 130-Last Rose & the Thorn. 132-New Zatanna story			
	3	9	24
136,137: 136-Wonder Woman x-over	3	9	28
Annual 1(Sum, 1962)-r/L. Lane #12; Aquaman app.	22	66	330
Annual 2(Sum, 1963)	15	45	215

SUPERMAN'S PAL JIMMY OLSEN (Superman Family #164 on)
(See Action Comics #6 for 1st app. & 80 Page Giant)
National Periodical Publ.: Sept-Oct, 1954 - No. 163, Feb-Mar, 1974 (Fourth
World #133-148)

	GD	FN	NM-
1	409	1227	9000
2	129	387	2450
3-Last pre-code issue	70	210	1325
4,5	50	150	900
6-10	38	114	600
11-20: 15-1st S.A. issue	26	78	390
21-30: 29-(6/58) 1st app. Krypto with Superman	17	51	250
31-Origin & 1st app. Elastic Lad (Jimmy Olsen)	15	45	225
32-40: 33-One pg. biography of Jack Larson (TV Jimmy Olsen). 36-Intro Lucy			
Lane. 37-2nd app. Elastic Lad & 1st cover app.	12	36	180
41-50: 41-1st J.O. Robot. 48-Intro/origin Superman Emergency Squad			
	10	30	140

	GD	FN	NM-
51-56: 56-Last 10¢ issue	9	27	110
57-62,64-70: 57-Olsen marries Supergirl. 62-Mon-el & Elastic Lad app. but not as Legionnaires. 70-Element Boy (Lad) app.	7	21	80
63(9/62)-Legion of Super-Villains app.	7	21	85
71,74,75,78,80-84,86,89,90: 86-Jimmy Olsen Robot becomes Congorilla	6	18	65
72,73,76,77,79,85,87,88: 72(10/63)-Legion app; Elastic Lad (Olsen) joins. 73-Ultra Boy app. 76,85-Legion app. 76-Legion app. 77-Olsen with Colossal Boy's powers & costume; origin Titano retold. 79-(9/64)-Titled The Red-headed Beatle of 1000 B.C. 85-Legion app. 87-Legion of Super-Villains app. 88-Star Boy app.	6	18	70
91-94,96-98	5	15	55
95 (Giant G-25)	8	24	95
99-Olsen w/powers & costumes of Lightning Lad, Sun Boy & Element Lad	5	15	60
100-Legion cameo	6	18	65
101-103,105-112,114-120: 106-Legion app. 110-Infinity-c. 117-Batman & Legion cameo. 120-Last 12¢ issue	4	12	40
104 (Giant G-38)	6	18	75
113,122,131,140 (Giants G-50,G-62,G-74,G-86)	6	18	65
121,123-130,132	3	10	35
133-(10/70)-Jack Kirby story & art begins; re-intro Newsboy Legion; 1st app. Morgan Edge	7	21	85
134-1st app. Darkseid (1 panel, 12/70)	8	24	100
135-2nd app. Darkseid (1 pg. cameo; see New Gods & Forever People); G.A. Guardian app.	5	15	60
136-139: 136-Origin new Guardian. 138-Partial photo-c. 139-Last 15¢ issue	4	12	45
141-150: (25¢,52 pgs.). 141-Photo-c; Newsboy Legion-r by S&K begin; full pg. self-portrait of Jack Kirby; Don Rickles cameo. 149,150-G.A. Plastic Man-r in both; 150-Newsboy Legion app.	4	12	40
151-163	3	9	24

SUPERMAN: THE MAN OF STEEL (Also see Man of Steel, The)
DC Comics: July, 1991 - No. 134, Mar, 2003
($1.00/$1.25/$1.50/$1.95/$2.25)

	GD	FN	NM-
0-(10/94) Zero Hour; released between #37 & #38			2.50
1-($1.75, 52 pgs.)-Painted-c			5.00
2-16: 3-War of the Gods x-over. 5-Reads sideways. 10-Last $1.00-c. 14-Superman & Robin team-up			3.00
17-1st brief app. Doomsday	1	3	7
17,18: 17-2nd printing. 18-2nd & 3rd printings			2.25
18-1st full app. Doomsday	1	3	9
19-Doomsday battle issue (c/story)			6.00
20-22: 20,21-Funeral for a Friend. 22-($1.95)-Collector's Edition w/die-cut outer-c & bound-in poster; Steel-c/story			2.50
22-($1.50)-Newsstand Ed. w/poster & different-c			2.25
23-49,51-99: 30-Regular edition. 32-Bizarro-c/story. 35,36-Worlds Collide Pt. 1 & 10. 37-(9/94)-Zero Hour x-over. 38-(11/94). 48-Aquaman app. 54-Spectre-c/app; Lex Luthor app. 56-Mxyzptlk-c/app. 57-G.A. Flash app.			

	GD	FN	NM-

58-Supergirl app. 59-Parasite-c/app.; Steel app. 60-Reintro Bottled City of
    Kandor. 62-Final Night. 64-New Gods app. 67-New powers. 75-"Death" of
    Mxyzptlk. 78,79-Millennium Giants. 80-Golden Age style. 92-JLA app.
    98-Metal Men app. 2.50
30-($2.50)-Collector's Edition; polybagged with Superman & Lobo vinyl clings
    that stick to wraparound-c; Lobo-c/story 3.00
50 ($2.95)-The Trial of Superman 4.00
100-($2.99) New Fortress of Solitude revealed 3.00
100-($3.99) Special edition with fold out cardboard-c 4.00
101,102-101-Batman app. 2.25
103-133: 103-Begin $2.25. 105-Batman-c/app. 111-Return to Krypton.
    115-117-Our Worlds at War. 117-Maxima killed. 121-Royal Flush Gang
    app. 128-Return to Krypton II 2.25
134-($2.75) Last issue; Steel app.; Bogdanove-c 2.75
#1,000,000 (11/98) 853rd Century x-over; Gene Ha-c 2.50
Annual 1-5 ('92-'96,68 pgs.): 1-Eclipso app.; Joe Quesada-c(p). 2-Intro Edge.
    3 -Elseworlds; Mignola-c; Batman app. 4-Year One story. 5-Legends of
    the Dead Earth story 3.00
Annual 6 (1997, $3.95)-Pulp Heroes story 4.00
...Gallery (1995, $3.50) Pin-ups by various 3.50

SUPERMAN: THE MAN OF TOMORROW
DC Comics: 1995 - No. 15, Fall, 1999 ($1.95, quarterly)

1-15: 1-Lex Luthor app. 3-Lex Luthor-c/app; Joker app. 4-Shazam! app.
    5-Wedding of Lex Luthor. 10-Maxima-c/app. 13-JLA-c/app. 2.50
#1,000,000 (11/98) 853rd Century x-over; Gene Ha-c 2.50

SUPERMAN: THE WEDDING ALBUM
DC Comics: Dec, 1996 ($4.95, 96 pgs, one-shot)

1-Standard Edition-Story & art by past and present Superman creators;
    gatefold back-c. Byrne-a 5.00
1-Collector's Edition-Embossed cardstock variant-c w/ metallic silver ink
    and matte and gloss varnishes 5.00
TPB ('97, $14.95) r/Wedding and honeymoon stories 15.00

SUPERMAN VS. MUHAMMAD ALI (See All-New Collectors' Edition C-56)

SUPERMAN VS. THE AMAZING SPIDER-MAN (Also see Marvel Treasury Edition No. 28)
National Periodical Publications/Marvel Comics Group: 1976
($2.00, Treasury sized, 100 pgs.)

1-Superman and Spider-Man battle Lex Luthor and Dr. Octopus; Andru/
    Giordano-a; 1st Marvel/DC x-over.   7   21   90
1-2nd printing; 5000 numbered copies signed by Stan Lee & Carmine
    Infantino on front cover & sold through mail   13   39   185
nn-(1995, $5.95)-r/#1 6.00

SUPER-TEAM FAMILY
National Per. Publ./DC Comics: Oct-Nov, 1975 - No. 15, Mar-Apr, 1978

1-Reprints by Neal Adams & Kane/Wood; 68 pgs. begin, ends #4.
    New Gods app.   2   6   22

	GD	FN	NM-
2,3: New stories	2	6	16
4-7: Reprints. 4-G.A. JSA-r & Superman/Batman/Robin-r from World's Finest. 5-52 pgs. begin	2	6	12
8-14: 8-10-New Challengers of the Unknown stories. 9-Kirby-a. 11-14: New stories	2	6	16
15-New Gods app. New stories	2	6	18

SUPER-VILLAIN TEAM-UP (See Fantastic Four #6 & Giant-Size...)
Marvel Comics Group: 8/75 - No. 14, 10/77; No. 15, 11/78; No. 16, 5/79; No. 17, 6/80

	GD	FN	NM-
1-Giant-Size Super-Villain Team-Up #2; Sub-Mariner & Dr. Doom begin, end #10	4	12	40
2-5: 5-1st app. The Shroud	2	6	15
5-(30¢-c variant, limited distribution)(4/76)	2	6	22
6,7-(25¢ editions) 6-(6/76)-F.F., Shroud app. 7-Origin Shroud	1	3	9
6,7-(30¢-c, limited distribution)(6,8/76)	2	6	14
8-17: 9-Avengers app. 11-15-Dr. Doom & Red Skull app.	1	3	9
12-14-(35¢-c variants, limited distribution)(6,8,10/77)	2	6	14

SWAMP THING (See Brave & the Bold, Challengers of the Unknown #82, DC Comics Presents #8 & 85, DC Special Series #2, 14, 17, 20, House of Secrets #92, Limited Collectors' Edition C-59, & Roots of the...)

SWAMP THING
National Per. Publ./DC Comics: Oct-Nov, 1972 - No. 24, Aug-Sept, 1976

	GD	FN	NM-
1-Wrightson-c/a begins; origin	12	36	180
2-1st brief app. Patchwork Man (1 panel)	6	18	75
3-1st full app. Patchwork Man (see House of Secrets #140)	4	12	50
4-6,	4	12	45
7-Batman-c/story	4	12	50
8-10: 10-Last Wrightson issue	3	10	35
11-20: 11-19-Redondo-a. 13-Origin retold (1 pg.)	2	6	18
21-24: 23,24-Swamp Thing reverts back to Dr. Holland. 23-New logo	2	6	18

SWAMP THING (Saga Of The... #1-38,42-45) (See Essential Vertigo:...)
DC Comics (Vertigo imprint #129 on): May, 1982 - No. 171, Oct, 1996
(Direct sales #65 on)

	GD	FN	NM-
1-Origin retold; Phantom Stranger series begins; ends #13; Yeates-c/a begins			6.00
2-15: 2-Photo-c from movie. 13-Last Yeates-a			4.00
16-19: Bissette-a.			5.00
20-1st Alan Moore issue	2	6	22
21-New origin	2	6	18
22,23,25: 25-John Constantine 1-panel cameo	2	6	12
24-JLA x-over; Last Yeates-c.	2	6	14
26-30	1	3	7
31-33,35,36: 33-r/1st app. from House of Secrets #92			5.00

	GD	FN	NM-
34	1	3	8
37-1st app. John Constantine (Hellblazer) (6/85)	2	6	15
38-40: John Constantine app.	1	3	8

41-52,54-64: 44-Batman cameo. 44-51-John Constantine app. 46-Crisis x-over; Batman cameo. 49-Spectre app. 50-($1.25, 52 pgs.)-Deadman, Dr. Fate, Demon. 52-Arkham Asylum-c/story; Joker-c/cameo. 58-Spectre preview. 64-Last Moore issue   3.50

53-($1.25, 52 pgs.)-Arkham Asylum; Batman-c/story   4.50

65-83,85-99,101-124,126-149,151-153: 65-Direct sales only begins. 66-Batman & Arkham Asylum story. 70,76-John Constantine x-over; 76-X-over w/Hellblazer #9. 79-Superman-c/story. 85-Jonah Hex app. 102-Preview of World Without End. 116-Photo-c. 129-Metallic ink on-c. 140-Millar scripts begin, end #171   3.00

84-Sandman (Morpheus) cameo.   4.00

100,125,150: 100 ($2.50, 52 pgs.). 125-($2.95, 52 pgs.)-20th anniversary issue. 150 (52 pgs.)-Anniversary issue   3.00

154-171: 154-$2.25-c begins. 165-Curt Swan-a(p). 166,169,171-John Constantine & Phantom Stranger app. 168-Arcane returns   2.50

Annual 1,3-6('82-91): 1-Movie Adaptation; painted-c. 3-New format; Bolland-c. 4-Batman-c/story. 5-Batman cameo; re-intro Brother Power (Geek),1st app. since 1968   4.00

Annual 2 (1985)-Moore scripts; Bissette-a(p); Deadman, Spectre app.   7.00

Annual 7(1993, $3.95)-Children's Crusade   4.00

...A Murder of Crows (2001, $19.95)-r/#43-50; Moore-s   20.00

...: Earth To Earth (2002, $17.95)-r/#51-56; Batman app.   18.00

...Love and Death (1990, $17.95)-r/#28-34 & Annual #2; Totleben painted-c   18.00

...: Regenesis (2004, $17.95, TPB) r/#65-70; Veitch-s   18.00

...: Reunion (2003, $19.95, TPB) r/#57-64; Moore-s   20.00

...: Roots (1998, $7.95) Jon J Muth-s/painted-a/c   8.00

Saga of the Swamp Thing ('87, '89)-r/#21-27 (1st & 2nd print)   13.00

...: The Curse (2000, $19.95, TPB) r/#35-42; Bisley-c   20.00

SWAMP THING
DC Comics (Vertigo): May, 2000 - No. 20, Dec, 2001 ($2.50)

1-3-Tefé Holland's return; Vaughan-s/Petersen-a; Hale painted-c.   3.00

4-20: 7-9-Bisley-c. 10-John Constantine-c/app. 10-12-Fabry-c. 13-15-Mack-c 18-Swamp Thing app.   2.50

Preview-16 pg. flip book w/Lucifer Preview   2.25

SWAMP THING
DC Comics (Vertigo): May, 2004 - Present ($2.95)

1-10: 1-Diggle-s/Breccia-a; Constantine app. 2-6-Sargon app. 7,8-Corben-c/a   3.00

...: Bad Seed (2004, $9.95) r/#1-6   10.00

SWING WITH SCOOTER
National Periodical Publ.: June-July, 1966 - No. 35, Aug-Sept, 1971; No. 36, Oct-Nov, 1972

1	9	27	110

	GD	FN	NM-
2,6-10: 9-Alfred E. Newman swipe in last panel	5	15	55
3-5: 3-Batman cameo on-c. 4-Batman cameo inside. 5-JLA cameo			
	5	15	60
11-13,15-19: 18-Wildcat of JSA 1pg. text. 19-Last 12¢-c			
	3	10	35
14-Alfred E. Neuman cameo	4	12	38
20 (68 pgs.)	5	15	55
21-23,25-31	3	9	28
24-Frankenstein-c.	3	10	35
32-34 (68 pgs.). 32-Batman cameo. 33-Interview with David Cassidy.			
34-Interview with Rick Ely (The Rebels)	4	12	50
35-(52 pgs.). 1 pg. app. Clark Kent and 4 full pgs. of Superman			
	8	24	95
36-Bat-signal refererence to Batman	3	10	35

SWORD OF SORCERY
National Periodical Publ.: Feb-Mar, 1973 - No. 5, Nov-Dec, 1973 (20¢)

	GD	FN	NM-
1-Leiber Fafhrd & The Grey Mouser; Chaykin/Neal Adams (Crusty Bunkers) art; Kaluta-c	2	6	22
2,3: 2-Wrightson-c(i); Adams-a(i). 3-Wrightson-i(5 pgs.)	2	6	12
4,5: 5-Starlin-a(p); Conan cameo	1	3	9

TALES CALCULATED TO DRIVE YOU BATS
Archie Publications: Nov, 1961 - No. 7, Nov, 1962; 1966 (Satire)

	GD	FN	NM-
1-Only 10¢ issue; has cut-out Werewolf mask (price includes mask)	13	39	190
2-Begin 12¢ issues	8	24	95
3-6: 3-UFO cover	6	18	70
7-Storyline change	6	18	65
1(1966, 25¢, 44 pg. Giant)-r/#1; UFO cover	6	18	65

TALES OF GHOST CASTLE
National Periodical Publications: May-June, 1975 - No. 3, Sept-Oct, 1975 (All 25¢ issues)

	GD	FN	NM-
1-Redondo-a	3	9	25
2,3: 2-Nino-a. 3-Redondo-a.	2	6	14

TALES OF SUSPENSE (Becomes Captain America #100 on)
Atlas (WPI No. 1,2/Male No. 3-12/VPI No. 13-18)/Marvel No. 19 on:
Jan, 1959 - No. 99, Mar, 1968

	GD	FN	NM-
1-Williamson-a (5 pgs.); Heck-c; #1-4 have sci/fi-c	137	411	2600
2,3: 2-Robot-c. 3-Flying saucer-c/story	50	150	900
4-Williamson-a (4 pgs.); Kirby/Everett-c/a	44	132	750
5,6,8,10: 5-Kirby monster-c begin	33	99	525
7-Prototype ish. (Lava Man); 1 panel app. Aunt May (see Str. Tales #97)	37	111	585
9-Prototype ish. (Iron Man)	38	114	610
11,12,15,17-19: 12-Crandall-a.	27	81	400
13-Elektro-c/story	28	84	410
14-Intro/1st app. Colossus-c/sty	33	99	520
16-1st Metallo-c/story (4/61, Iron Man prototype)	32	96	510

	GD	FN	NM-
20-Colossus-c/story (2nd app.)	28	84	410
21-25: 25-Last 10¢ issue	22	66	320
26,27,29,30,33,34,36-38: 33-(9/62)-Hulk 1st x-over cameo (picture on wall)			
	18	54	265
28-Prototype ish. (Stone Men)	19	57	275
31-Prototype ish. (Dr. Doom)	22	66	320
32-Prototype ish. (Dr. Strange)(8/62)-Sazzik The Sorcerer app.; "The Man and the Beehive" story, 1 month before TTA #35 (2nd Antman), came out after "The Man in the Ant Hill" in TTA #27 (1/62) (1st Antman)-Characters from both stories were tested to see which got best fan response			
	31	93	485
35-Prototype issue (The Watcher)	22	66	320
39 (3/63)-Origin/1st app. Iron Man & begin series; 1st Iron Man story has Kirby layouts	409	1227	9000
40-2nd app. Iron Man (in new armor)	145	435	2750
41-3rd app. Iron Man; Dr. Strange (villain) app.	79	237	1500
42-45: 45-Intro. & 1st app. Happy & Pepper	47	141	800
46,47: 46-1st app. Crimson Dynamo	36	108	575
48-New Iron Man armor by Ditko	41	123	675
49-1st X-Men x-over (same date as X-Men #3, 1/64); also 1st Avengers x-over (w/o Captain America); 1st Tales of the Watcher back-up story & begins (2nd app. Watcher; see F.F. #13)	50	150	900
50-1st app. Mandarin	24	72	350
51-1st app. Scarecrow	20	60	300
52-1st app. The Black Widow (4/64)	30	90	450
53-Origin The Watcher; 2nd Black Widow app.	20	60	300
54-56: 56-1st app. Unicorn	14	42	210
57-Origin/1st app. Hawkeye (9/64)	30	90	450
58-Captain America battles Iron Man (10/64)-Classic-c; 2nd Kraven app. (Cap's 1st app. in this title)	34	102	550
59-Iron Man plus Captain America double feature begins (11/64); 1st S.A. Captain America solo story; intro Jarvis, Avenger's butler; classic-c			
	34	102	550
60-2nd app. Hawkeye (#64 is 3rd app.)	19	57	275
61,62,64: 62-Origin Mandarin (2/65)	11	33	155
63-1st Silver Age origin Captain America (3/65)	27	81	400
65-G.A. Red Skull in WWII stories(also in #66);-1st Silver-Age Red Skull (5/65)	20	60	300
66-Origin Red Skull	15	45	225
67-70: 69-1st app. Titanium Man. 70-Begin alternating-c features w/Capt. America (even #'s) & Iron Man (odd #'s)	9	27	120
71-75, 77,78,81-98: 75-1st app. Agent 13 later named Sharon Carter. 78-Col. Nick Fury app. 81-Intro the Adaptoid by Kirby (also in #82-84). 88-Mole Man app. in Iron Man story. 92-1st Nick Fury x-over (cameo, as Agent of S.H.I.E.L.D., 8/67). 94-Intro Modok. 95-Capt. America's i.d. revealed. 97-1st Whiplash. 98-1st brief app. new Zemo (son?); #99 is 1st full app.	7	21	80
76-Intro Batroc & Sharon Carter, Agent 13 of S.H.I.E.L.D.			
	7	21	90

	GD	FN	NM-
79-Begin 3 part Iron Man Sub-Mariner battle story; Sub-Mariner-c & cameo; 1st app. Cosmic Cube; 1st modern Red Skull	8	24	100
80-Iron Man battles Sub-Mariner story cont'd in Tales to Astonish #82; classic Red Skull-c	8	24	100
99-Captain America story cont'd in Captain America #100; Iron Man story cont'd in Iron Man & Sub-Mariner #1	8	24	105

TALES OF THE LEGION (Formerly Legion of Super-Heroes)
DC Comics: No. 314, Aug, 1984 - No. 354, Dec, 1987

314-354: 326-r-begin			2.50
Annual 4,5 (1986, 1987)-Formerly LSH Annual			3.50

TALES OF THE TEEN TITANS (Formerly The New Teen Titans)
DC Comics: No. 41, Apr, 1984 - No. 91, July, 1988 (75¢)

41,45-49: 46-Aqualad & Aquagirl join			3.00
42-44: The Judas Contract part 1-3 with Deathstroke the Terminator in all; concludes in Annual #3. 44-Dick Grayson becomes Nightwing (3rd to be Nightwing) & joins Titans; Jericho (Deathstroke's son) joins; origin Deathstroke			3.50
50,53-55: 50-Double size; app. Betty Kane (Bat-Girl) out of costume. 53-1st full app. Azrael; Deathstroke cameo. 54,55-Deathstroke-c/stories			3.50
51,52,56-91: 52-1st brief app. Azrael (not same as newer character). 56-Intro Jinx. 57-Neutron app. 59-r/DC Comics Presents #26. 60-91-r/New Teen Titans Baxter series. 68-B. Smith-c. 70-Origin Kole			2.50
Annual 3(1984, $1.25)-Part 4 of The Judas Contract; Deathstroke-c/story; Death of Terra; indicia says Teen Titans Annual; previous annuals listed as New Teen Titans Annual #1,2			4.00
Annual 4-(1986, $1.25)			2.50

TALES OF THE UNEXPECTED (Becomes The Unexpected #105 on)
National Periodical Publications: Feb-Mar, 1956 - No. 104, Dec-Jan, 1967-68

1	92	276	1750
2	46	138	775
3-5	33	99	525
6-10: 6-1st Silver Age issue	28	84	410
11,14,19,20	18	54	260
12,13,15-18,21-24: All have Kirby-a. 15,17-Grey tone-c. 16-Character named 'Thor' with a magic hammer by Kirby (8/57, unlike later Thor)	23	69	340
25-30	15	45	215
31-39	13	39	190
40-Space Ranger begins (8/59, 3rd ap.), ends #82	91	273	1725
41,42-Space Ranger stories	36	108	575
43-1st Space Ranger-c this title; grey tone-c	63	189	1200
44-46	25	75	375
47-50	19	57	275
51-60: 54-Dinosaur-c/story	15	45	225
61-67: 67-Last 10¢ issue	13	39	185
68-82: 82-Last Space Ranger	8	24	105

	GD	FN	NM-
83-90,92-99	6	18	70
91,100: 91-1st Automan (also in #94,97)	6	18	75
101-104	5	15	60

TALES OF THE VAMPIRES (See Buffy the Vampire Slayer and related titles)
Dark Horse Comics: 2003 - No. 5, Apr, 2004 ($2.99, limited series)

1-Short stories by Joss Whedon and others. 1-Totleben-c. 3-Powell-c. 4-Edlund-c			3.00
TPB (11/04, $15.95) r/#1-5; afterword by Marv Wolfman			16.00

TALES TO ASTONISH (Becomes The Incredible Hulk #102 on)
Atlas (MAP No. 1/ZPC No. 2-14/VPI No. 15-21/Marvel No. 22 on: Jan, 1959 - No. 101, Mar, 1968

	GD	FN	NM-
1-Jack Davis-a; monster-c.	137	411	2600
2-Ditko flying saucer-c (Martians); #2-4 have sci/fi-c.	57	171	1075
3,4	44	132	750
5-Prototype issue (Stone Men); Williamson-a (4 pgs.); Kirby monster-c begin	46	138	775
6-Prototype issue (Stone Men)	37	111	585
7-Prototype issue (Toad Men)	37	111	585
8-10	33	99	525
11-14,17-20: 13-Swipes story from Menace #8	27	81	400
15-Prototype issue (Electro)	34	102	550
16-Prototype issue (Stone Men)	29	87	435
21-(7/61)-Hulk prototype	29	87	435
22-26,28-34	20	60	300
27-1st Ant-Man app. (1/62); last 10¢ issue (see Strange Tales #73,78 & Tales of Suspense #32)	318	954	7000
35-(9/62)-2nd app. Ant-Man, 1st in costume; begin series & Ant-Man-c	153	459	3000
36-3rd app. Ant-Man	71	213	1350
37-40: 38-1st app. Egghead	41	123	675
41-43	32	96	500
44-Origin & 1st app. The Wasp (6/63)	41	123	700
45-48: 48-Origin & 1st app. The Porcupine.	20	60	290
49-Ant-Man becomes Giant Man (11/63)	24	72	350
50,51,53-56,58: 50-Origin/1st app. Human Top (alias Whirlwind). 53-Origin Colossus	12	36	180
52-Origin/1st app. Black Knight (2/64)	15	45	220
57-Early Spider-Man app. (7/64)	27	81	400
59-Giant Man vs. Hulk feature story (9/64); Hulk's 1st app. this title	31	93	475
60-Giant Man & Hulk double feature begins	20	60	300
61-69: 61-All Ditko issue; 1st mailbag. 62-1st app./origin The Leader; new Wasp costume. 63-Origin Leader; 65-New Giant Man costume. 68-New Human Top costume. 69-Last Giant Man.	10	30	140
70-Sub-Mariner & Incredible Hulk begins (8/65)	11	33	160
71-81,83-91,94-99: 72-Begin alternating-c features w/Sub-Mariner (even #'s) & Hulk (odd #'s). 79-Hulk vs. Hercules-c/story. 81-1st app. Boomerang.			

	GD	FN	NM-
90-1st app. The Abomination. 97-X-Men cameo	6	18	70
82-Iron Man battles Sub-Mariner (1st Iron Man x-over outside The Avengers			
& TOS); story cont'd from Tales of Suspense #80	7	21	85
92-1st Silver Surfer x-over (outside of Fantastic Four, 6/67); 1 panel cameo			
only	6	18	75
93-Hulk battles Silver Surfer-c/story (1st full x-over)	11	33	150
100-Hulk battles Sub-Mariner full-length story	7	21	85
101-Hulk story cont'd in Incredible Hulk #102; Sub-Mariner story continued in			
Iron Man & Sub-Mariner #1	8	24	100

TARZAN (Continuation of Gold Key series)
National Periodical Publications: No. 207, Apr, 1972 - No. 258, Feb, 1977

207-Origin Tarzan by Joe Kubert, part 1; John Carter begins (origin); 52 pg.			
issues thru #209	5	15	60
208,209-(52 pgs.): 208-210-Parts 2-4 of origin. 209-Last John Carter			
	3	9	30
210-220: 210-Kubert-a. 211-Hogarth, Kubert-a. 212-214: Adaptations from			
"Jungle Tales of Tarzan". 213-Beyond the Farthest Star begins, ends #218.			
215-218,224,225-All by Kubert. 215-part Foster-r. 219-223: Adapts "The			
Return of Tarzan" by Kubert	2	6	20
221-229: 221-223-Continues adaptation of "The Return of Tarzan".			
226-Manning-a	2	6	15
230-DC 100 Page Super Spectacular; Kubert, Kaluta-a(p); Korak begins,			
ends #234; Carson of Venus app.	4	12	42
231-235-New Kubert-a.: 231-234-(All 100 pgs.)-Adapts "Tarzan and the Lion			
Man"; Rex, the Wonder Dog r-#232, 233. 235-(100 pgs.)-Last Kubert issue.			
	4	12	40
236,237,239-258: 240-243 adapts "Tarzan & the Castaways". 250-256 adapts			
"Tarzan the Untamed." 252,253-r/#213	1	4	10
238-(68 pgs.)	2	6	20
Comic Digest 1-(Fall, 1972, 50¢, 164 pgs.)(DC)-Digest size; Kubert-c;			
Manning-a	5	15	55

TARZAN (Lord of the Jungle)
Marvel Comics Group: June, 1977 - No. 29, Oct, 1979

1-New adaptions of Burrough stories; Buscema-a	1	4	10
1-(35¢-c variant, limited distribution)(6/77)	2	6	15
2-29: 2-Origin by John Buscema. 9-Young Tarzan. 12-14-Jungle Tales of			
Tarzan. 25-29-New stories			5.00
2-5-(35¢-c variants, limited distribution)(7-10/77)	1	3	8
Annual 1-3: 1-(1977). 2-(1978). 3-(1979)			5.00

TARZAN FAMILY, THE (Formerly Korak, Son of Tarzan)
National Periodical Publ.: No. 60, Nov-Dec, 1975 - No. 66, Nov-Dec, 1976

60-62-(68 pgs.): 60-Korak begins; Kaluta-r	2	6	16
63-66 (52 pgs.)	2	6	12

TARZAN, LORD OF THE JUNGLE
Gold Key: Sept, 1965 (Giant) (25¢, soft paper-c)

1-Marsh-r	9	27	120

	GD	FN	NM-

TASMANIAN DEVIL & HIS TASTY FRIENDS
Gold Key: Nov, 1962 (12¢)

	GD	FN	NM-
1-Bugs Bunny & Elmer Fudd x-over	15	45	215

TEENAGE MUTANT NINJA TURTLES (Also see Anything Goes, Donatello, First Comics Graphic Novel, Gobbledygook, Grimjack #26, Leonardo, Michaelangelo, Raphael & Tales Of The...)
Mirage Studios: 1984 - No. 62, Aug, 1993 ($1.50/$1.75, B&W; all 44-52 pgs.)

	GD	FN	NM-
1-1st printing (3000 copies)-Origin and 1st app. of the Turtles and Splinter. Only printing to have ad for Gobbledygook #1 & 2; Shredder app. (#1-4: 7-1/2x11") (Prices vary widely on this book. In 2004, a CGC certified 9.2 sold for $1,713, a CGC 8.5 sold for $1,300 and a CGC 7.0 sold for $700)			
1-2nd printing (6/84)(15,000 copies)	2	6	20
1-3rd printing (2/85)(36,000 copies)	2	6	12
1-4th printing, new-c (50,000 copies)			5.00
1-5th printing, new-c (8/88-c, 11/88 inside)			4.00
1-Counterfeit. **Note:** Most counterfeit copies have a half inch wide white streak or scratch marks across the center of back cover. Black part of cover is a bluish black instead of a deep black. Inside paper is very white & inside cover is bright white (no value)			
2-1st printing (1984; 15,000 copies)	6	18	75
2-2nd printing	1	4	10
2-3rd printing; new Corben-c/a (2/85)			5.00
2-Counterfeit with glossy cover stock (no value).			
3-1st printing (1985, 44 pgs.)	4	12	50
3-Variant, 500 copies, given away in NYC. Has 'Laird's Photo' in white rather than light blue	7	21	85
3-2nd printing; contains new back-up story			3.00
4-1st printing (1985, 44 pgs.)	3	10	35
4,5-2nd printing (5/87, 11/87)			2.25
5-Fugitoid begins, ends #7; 1st full color-c (1985)	2	6	18
6-1st printing (1986)	2	6	12
6-2nd printing (4/88-c, 5/88 inside)			2.25
7-4 pg. Eastman/Corben color insert; 1st color TMNT (1986, $1.75-c); Bode Biker back-up story	1	3	8
7-2nd printing (1/89) w/o color insert			2.25
8-Cerebus-c/story with Dave Sim-a (1986)			6.00
9,10: 9 (9/86)-Rip In Time by Corben			5.00
11-15			4.00
16-18: 18-Mark Bode'-a			3.00
18-2nd printing ($2.25, color, 44 pgs.)-New-c			2.50
19-34: 19-Begin $1.75-c. 24-26-Veitch-c/a.			2.50
32-2nd printing ($2.75, 52 pgs., full color)			3.00
35-49,51: 35-Begin $2.00-c.			2.50
50-Features pin-ups by Larsen, McFarlane, Simonson, etc.			3.00
52-62: 52-Begin $2.25-c			2.50
nn (1990, $5.95, B&W)-Movie adaptation			6.00
Book 1,2($1.50, B&W): 2-Corben-c			2.50
...Christmas Special 1 (12/90, $1.75, B&W, 52 pgs.)-Cover title: Michaelangelo			

		GD	FN	NM-

Christmas Special; r/Michaelangelo one-shot plus new Raphael story 2.50
...Special (The Maltese Turtle) nn (1/93, $2.95, color, 44 pgs.) 3.00
...Special: "Times" Pipeline nn (9/92, $2.95, color, 44 pgs.)-Mark Bode-c/a
3.00
Hardcover ($100)-r/#1-10 plus one-shots w/dust jackets - limited to 1000
w/letter of authenticity 100.00
Softcover ($40)-r/#1-10 40.00

TEENAGE MUTANT NINJA TURTLES ADVENTURES (TV)
Archie Comics: 8/88 - No. 3, 12/88; 3/89 - No. 72, Oct, 1995
($1.00/$1.25/$1.50/$1.75)

1-Adapts TV cartoon; not by Eastman/Laird 3.00
2,3,1-5: 2,3 (Mini-series). 1 (2nd on-going series). 5-Begins original stories
not based on TV 2.50
1-11: 2nd printings 2.25
6-72: 14-Simpson-a(p). 19-1st Mighty Mutanimals (also in #20, 51-54).
22-Gene Colan-c/a. 50-Poster by Eastman/Laird. 62-w/poster 2.50
nn (1990, $2.50)-Movie adaptation 2.50
nn (Spring, 1991, $2.50, 68 pgs.)-(Meet Archie) 2.50
nn (Sum, 1991, $2.50, 68 pgs.)-(Movie II)-Adapts movie sequel 2.50
...Meet the Conservation Corps 1 (1992, $2.50, 68 pgs.) 2.50
...III The Movie: The Turtles are Back...In Time (1993, $2.50, 68 pgs.) 2.50
Special 1,4,5 (Sum/92, Spr/93, Sum/93, 68 pgs.)-1-Bill Wray-c 2.50
Giant Size Special 6 (Fall/93, $1.95, 52 pgs.) 2.50
Special 7-10 (Win/93-Fall//94, 52 pgs.): 9-Jeff Smith-c 2.50
NOTE: There are 2nd printings of #1-11 w/B&W inside covers. Originals are color.

TEEN TITANS (See Brave & the Bold #54,60, DC Super-Stars #1, Marvel &
DC Present, New Teen Titans, New Titans, Official...Index and Showcase #59)
National Periodical Publications/DC Comics: 1-2/66 - No. 43, 1-2/73; No.
44, 11/76 - No. 53, 2/78

	GD	FN	NM-
1-(1-2/66)-Titans join Peace Corps; Batman, Flash, Aquaman, Wonder			
Woman cameos	27	81	400
2	12	36	175
3-5: 4-Speedy app.	8	24	100
6-10: 6-Doom Patrol app.; Beast Boy x-over; readers polled on him joining			
Titans	7	21	80
11-18: 11-Speedy app. 13-X-Mas-c	6	18	65
19-Wood-i; Speedy begins as regular	6	18	70
20-22: All Neal Adams-a. 21-Hawk & Dove app.; last 12¢ issue. 22-Origin			
Wonder Girl	7	21	90
23-Wonder Girl dons new costume	4	12	40
24-31: 25-Flash, Aquaman, Batman, Green Arrow, Green Lantern,			
Superman, & Hawk & Dove guests; 1st app. Lilith who joins T.T. West in			
#50. 29-Hawk & Dove & Ocean Master app. 30-Aquagirl app. 31-Hawk &			
Dove app.; last 15¢ issue	4	12	42
32-34,40-43	3	9	26
35-39-(52 pgs.): 36,37-Superboy-r. 38-Green Arrow/Speedy-r; Aquaman/			
Aqualad story. 39-Hawk & Dove-r.	3	9	30
44-(11/76) Dr. Light app.; Mal becomes the Guardian	2	6	14

	GD	FN	NM-
45,47,49,51,52	2	6	14
46,48: 46-Joker's daughter begins (see Batman Family). 48-Intro Bumblebee; Joker's daughter becomes Harlequin	2	6	20
50-1st revival original Bat-Girl; intro. Teen Titans West	2	6	22
53-Origin retold	2	6	16

TEEN TITANS (Also see Titans Beat in the Promotional Comics section)
DC Comics: Oct, 1996 - No. 24, Sept, 1998 ($1.95)

1-Dan Jurgens-c/a(p)/scripts & George Pérez-c/a(i) begin; Atom forms new team (Risk, Argent, Prysm, & Joto); 1st app. Loren Jupiter & Omen; no indicia. 1-3-Origin.	4.00
2-24: 4,5-Robin, Nightwing, Supergirl, Capt. Marvel Jr. app. 12-"Then and Now" begins w/original Teen Titans-c/app. 15-Death of Joto. 17-Capt. Marvel Jr. and Fringe join. 23,24-Superman app.	3.00
Annual 1 (1997, $3.95)-Pulp Heroes story	4.00

TEEN TITANS (Also see Titans/Young Justice: Graduation Day)
DC Comics: Sept, 2003 - Present ($2.50)

1-McKone-c/a;Johns-s	4.00
1-Variant-c by Michael Turner	5.00
1-2nd and 3rd printings	2.50
2-Deathstroke app.	5.00
2-2nd printing	2.50
3-15: 4-Impulse becomes Kid Flash. 5-Raven returns. 6-JLA app.	2.50
16-18: 16-Titans go to 31st Century; Legion and Fatal Five app. 17,18-Future Titans app.	2.50
.../Legion Special (11/04, $3.50) (cont'd from #16) Reis-a; leads into 2005 Legion of Super-Heroes series; LSH preview by Waid & Kitson	3.50
#1/2 (Wizard mail offer) origin of Ravager; Reis-a	8.00
.../Outsiders Secret Files 2003 (12/03, $5.95) Reis & Jimenez-a; pin-ups by various	6.00
A Kid's Game TPB (2004, $9.95) r/#1-7; Turner-c from #1; McKone sketch pages	10.00
Family Lost TPB (2004, $9.95) r/#8-12 & #1/2	10.00

TEEN TITANS GO! (Based on Cartoon Network series) (Also see Free Comic Book Day Edition in the Promotional Comics section)
DC Comics: Jan, 2004 - Present ($2.25)

1-12: 1,2-Nauck-a/Bullock-c/J. Torres-s. 6-Thunder & Lightning app. 8-Mad Mod app.	2.25
13-($2.95) Bonus pages with Shazam! rep.	3.00
... Vol 1: Truth, Justice, Pizza! (2004, $6.95, digest-size) r/#1-5	7.00

TEEN TITANS SPOTLIGHT
DC Comics: Aug, 1986 - No. 21, Apr, 1988

1-21: 7-Guice's 1st work at DC. 14-Nightwing; Batman app. 15-Austin-c(i). 18,19-Millennium x-over. 21-($1.00-c)-Original Teen Titans; Spiegle-a	3.00

TERMINATOR, THE (See Robocop vs. ... & Rust #12 for 1st app.)
Now Comics: Sept, 1988 - No. 17, 1989 ($1.75, Baxter paper)

	GD	FN	NM-
1-Based on movie	1	4	10
2-5			6.00
6-17: 12-($2.95, 52 pgs.)-Intro. John Connor			3.00
Trade paperback (1989, $9.95)			10.00

TERMINATOR, THE: THE BURNING EARTH
Now Comics: V2#1, Mar, 1990 - V2#5, July, 1990 ($1.75, limited series)

	GD	FN	NM-
V2#1: Alex Ross painted art (1st published work)	2	6	15
2-5: Ross-c/a in all	1	4	10
Trade paperback (1990, $9.95)-Reprints V2#1-5			12.00
Trade paperback (ibooks, 2003, $17.95)-Digitally remastered reprint			18.00

30 DAYS OF NIGHT
Idea + Design Works: June, 2002 - No. 3, Oct, 2002 ($3.99, limited series)

1-Vampires in Alaska; Steve Niles-s/Ben Templesmith-a/Ashley Wood-c			30.00
1-2nd printing			10.00
2			12.00
3			6.00
Annual 2004 (1/04, $4.99) Niles-s/art by Templesmith and others			5.00
TPB (2003, $17.99) r/#1-3, foreward by Clive Barker; script for #1			18.00
The Complete 30 Days of Night (2004, $75.00, oversized hardcover with slipcase) r/#1-3; prequel; script pages for #1-3; original cover and promotional materials			75.00

THOR (Journey Into Mystery #1-125, 503-on)(The Mighty Thor #413-490)
Marvel Comics Group: No. 126, Mar, 1966 - No. 502, Sept, 1996

	GD	FN	NM-
126-Thor continues (#125-130 Thor vs. Hercules)	19	57	275
127-130: 127-1st app. Pluto	9	27	110
131-133,135-140: 132-1st app. Ego	7	21	90
134-Intro High Evolutionary	8	24	95
141-150: 146-Inhumans begin (early app.), end #151 (see Fantastic Four #45 for 1st app.). 146,147-Origin The Inhumans. 148,149-Origin Black Bolt in each. 149-Origin Medusa, Crystal, Maximus, Gorgon, Karnak	6	18	75
151-157,159,160	5	15	60
158-Origin-r/#83; 158,159-Origin Dr. Blake (Thor)	9	27	110
161,167,170-179: 179-Last Kirby issue	4	12	50
162,168,169-Origin Galactus; Kirby-a	6	18	65
163,164-2nd & 3th brief app. Warlock (Him)	4	12	50
165-1st full app. Warlock (Him) (6/69, see Fantastic Four #67); last 12¢ issue; Kirby-a	7	21	90
166-2nd full app. Warlock (Him); battles Thor	6	18	75
180,181-Neal Adams-a	5	15	55
182-192: 192-Last 15¢ issue	3	9	30
193-(25¢, 52 pgs.); Silver Surfer x-over	6	18	75
194-199	3	9	24
200	3	9	30
201-206,208-224	2	6	14
207-Rutland, Vermont Halloween x-over	2	6	18
225-Intro. Firelord	2	6	18

	GD	FN	NM-
226-245	1	4	10
246-250-(Regular 25¢ editions)(4-8/76)	1	4	10
246-250-(30¢-c variants, limited distribution)	2	6	15
251-280: 271-Iron Man x-over. 274-Death of Balder the Brave			6.00
260-264-(35¢-c variants, limited distribution)(6-10/77)	1	3	9
281-299: 294-Origin Asgard & Odin			5.00
300-(12/80)-End of Asgard; origin of Odin & The Destroyer			
	1	3	8
301-336,338-373,375-381,383: 316-Iron Man x-over. 332,333-Dracula app.			
340-Donald Blake returns as Thor. 341-Clark Kent & Lois Lane cameo.			
373-X-Factor tie-in			3.00
337-Simonson-c/a begins, ends #382; Beta Ray Bill becomes new Thor			
	1	3	9
374-Mutant Massacre; X-Factor app.			4.00
382-($1.25)-Anniversary issue; last Simonson-a			4.00
384-Intro. new Thor			4.00
385-399,401-410,413-428: 385-Hulk x-over. 391-Spider-Man x-over; 1st Eric			
Masterson. 395-Intro Earth Force. 408-Eric Masterson becomes Thor.			
427,428-Excalibur x-over			2.50
400,411: 400-($1.75, 68 pgs.)-Origin Loki. 411-Intro New Warriors (appears			
in costume in last panel); Juggernaut-c/story			4.00
412-1st full app. New Warriors (Marvel Boy, Kid Nova, Namorita, Night			
Thrasher, Firestar & Speedball)			6.00
429-431,434-443: 429,430-Ghost Rider x-over. 434-Capt. America x-over.			
437-Thor vs. Quasar; Hercules app.;Tales of Asgard back-up stories begin.			
443-Dr. Strange & Silver Surfer x-over; last $1.00-c			2.50
432,433: 432-(52 pgs.)-Thor's 300th app. (vs. Loki); reprints origin & 1st app.			
from Journey into Mystery #83. 433-Intro new Thor			3.00
444-449,451-473: 448-Spider-Man-c/story. 455,456-Dr. Strange back-up.			
457-Old Thor returns (3 pgs.). 459-Intro Thunderstrike. 460-Starlin scripts			
begin. 465-Super Skrull app. 466-Drax app. 469,470-Infinity Watch x-over.			
472-Intro the Godlings			2.50
450-($2.50, 68 pgs.)-Flip-book format; r/story JIM #87 (1st Loki) plus-c plus			
a gallery of past-c; gatefold-c			3.00
474,476-481,483-499: 474-Begin $1.50-c; bound-in trading card sheet.			
459-Intro Thunderstrike. 460-Starlin scripts begin. 472-Intro the Godlings.			
490-The Absorbing Man app. 491-Warren Ellis scripts begins, ends #494;			
Deodato-c/a begins. 492-Reintro The Enchantress; Beta Ray Bill dies.			
495-Wm. Messner-Loebs scripts begin; Isherwood-c/a			2.50
475 ($2.00, 52 pgs.)-Regular edition			2.50
475 ($2.50, 52 pgs.)-Collectors edition w/foil embossed-c			3.00
482 ($2.95, 84 pgs.)-400th issue			3.00
500 ($2.50)-Double-size; wraparound-c; Deodato-c/a; Dr. Strange app.			5.00
501-Reintro Red Norvell			3.00
502-Onslaught tie-in; Red Norvell, Jane Foster & Hela app.			4.00
Special 2(9/66)-See Journey Into Mystery for 1st annual			
	9	27	110
Special 2 (2nd printing, 1994)	2	6	12
King Size Special 3(1/71)	3	10	35

	GD	FN	NM-
Special 4(12/71)-r/Thor #131,132 & JIM #113	3	9	26
Annual 5,6: 5(11/76). 6(10/77)-Guardians of the Galaxy app.			
	2	6	15
Annual 7,8: 7(1978). 8(1979)-Thor vs. Zeus-c/story	1	4	10
Annual 9-12: 9('81). 10('82). 11('83). 12('84)			6.00
Annual 13-19('85-'94, 68 pgs.):14-Atlantis Attacks. 16-3 pg. origin; Guardians of the Galaxy x-over.18-Polybagged w/card			3.00
...Alone Against the Celestials nn (6/92, $5.95)-r/Thor #387-389			6.00
...Legends Vol. 2: Walter Simonson Book 2 TPB (2003, $24.99) r/#349-355,357-359			25.00
...Legends Vol. 3: Walter Simonson Book 3 TPB (2004, $24.99) r/#360-369			25.00
... Visionaries: Mike Deodato Jr. TPB (2004, $19.99) r/#491-494,498-500			20.00
... Visionaries: Walter Simonson TPB (5/01, $24.95) r/#337-348			25.00
...: Worldengine (8/96, $9.95)-r/#491-494; Deodato-c/a; story & new intermission by Warren Ellis			10.00

THOR (Volume 2)
Marvel Comics: July, 1998 - No. 85, Dec, 2004 ($2.99/$1.99/$2.25)

	GD	FN	NM-
1-($2.99)-Follows Heroes Return; Jurgens-s/Romita Jr. & Janson-a; wraparound-c; battles the Destroyer			5.00
1-Variant-c	1	3	8
1-Rough Cut-($2.99) Features original script and pencil pages			3.00
1-Sketch cover			20.00
2-($1.99) Two covers; Avengers app.			3.00
3-11,13-23: 3-Assumes Jake Olson ID. 4-Namor-c/app. 8-Spider-Man-c/app. 14-Iron Man c/app. 17-Juggernaut-c			2.50
12-($2.99) Wraparound-c; Hercules appears			3.00
12-($10.00) Variant-c by Jusko			10.00
24,26-31,33,34: 24-Begin $2.25-c. 26-Mignola-c/Larsen-a. 29-Andy Kubert-a. 30-Maximum Security x-over; Beta Ray Bill-c/app. 33-Intro. Thor Girl			2.25
25-($2.99) Regular edition			3.00
25-($3.99) Gold foil enhanced cover			4.00
32-($3.50, 100 pgs.) new story plus reprints w/Kirby-a; Simonson-a			3.50
35-($2.99) Thor battles The Gladiator; Andy Kubert-a			3.00
36-49,51-61: 37-Starlin-a. 38,39-BWS-c. 38-42-Immonen-a. 40-Odin killed. 41-Orbik-c. 44-'Nuff Said silent issue. 51-Spider-Man app. 57-Art by various. 58-Davis-a; x-over with Iron Man #64. 60-Brereton-c			2.25
50-($4.95) Raney-c/a; back-ups w/Nuckols-a & Armenta-s/Bennett-a			5.00
62-84: 62-Begin $2.99-c. 64-Loki-c/app. 80-Oeming-s begins; Avengers app.			3.00
85-Last issue; Thor dies; Oeming-s/DiVito-a/Epting-c			3.00
...1999 Annual ($3.50) Jurgens-s/a(p)			3.50
...2000 Annual ($3.50) Jurgens-s/Ordway-a(p); back-up stories			3.50
...2001 Annual ($3.50) Jurgens-s/Grummett-a(p); Lightle-c			3.50
...Across All Worlds (9/01, $19.95, TPB) r/#28-35			20.00
Avengers Disassembled: Thor TPB (2004, $16.99) r/#80-85; afterword by Oeming			17.00
...Resurrection ($5.99, TPB) r/#1,2			6.00

	GD	FN	NM-
...: The Dark Gods (7/00, $15.95, TPB) r/#9-13			16.00
...Vol. 1: The Death of Odin (7/02, $12.99, TPB) r/#39-44			13.00
...Vol. 2: Lord of Asgard (9/02, $15.99, TPB) r/#45-50			16.00
...Vol. 3: Gods on Earth (2003, $21.99, TPB) r/#51-58, Avengers #63, Iron			
Man #64, Marvel Double-Shot #1; Beck-c			22.00
...Vol. 4: Spiral (2003, $19.99, TPB) r/#59-67; Brereton-c			20.00
...Vol. 5: The Reigning (2004, $17.99, TPB) r/#68-74			18.00
...Vol. 6: Gods and Men (2004, $13.99, TPB) r/#75-79			14.00

THOR: SON OF ASGARD
Marvel Comics: May, 2004 - Present ($2.99, limited series)

1-10: Teenaged Thor, Sif, and Balder; Tocchini-a. 1-6-Granov-c.			
7-10-Jo Chen-c			3.00
... Vol. 1: The Warriors Teen (2004, $7.99, digest-size) r/#1-6			8.00

3 GEEKS, THE (Also see Geeksville)
3 Finger Prints: 1996 - No. 11, Jun, 1999 (B&W)

1,2 -Rich Koslowski-s/a in all	1	3	8
1-(2nd printing)			2.50
3-7, 9-11			2.50
8-(48 pgs.)			4.00
10-Variant-c			3.50
...48 Page Super-Sized Summer Spectacular (7/04, $4.95)			5.00
...Full Circle (7/03, $4.95) Origin story of the 3 Geeks; "Buck Rodinski" app.			
			5.00
How to Pick Up Girls If You're a Comic Book Geek (color)(7/97)			4.00
When the Hammer Fallls TPB (2001, $14.95) r/#8-11			15.00

THREE MOUSEKETEERS, THE (2nd Series) (See Super DC Giant)
National Periodical Publications: May-June, 1970 - No. 7, May-June, 1971
(#5-7: 68 pgs.)

1-Mayer-r in all	6	18	75
2-4: 4-Doodles Duck begins (1st app.)	4	12	45
5-7:(68 pgs.). 5-Dodo & the Frog, Bo Bunny begin	6	18	70

THREE MUSKETEERS, THE (Also see Disney's The Three Musketeers)
Gemstone Publishing: 2004 ($3.95, squarebound, one-shot)

nn-Adaptation of the 2004 DVD movie; Petrossi-c/a			4.00

THUNDER AGENTS (See Dynamo, Noman & Tales Of Thunder)
Tower Comics: 11/65 - No. 17, 12/67; No. 18, 9/68, No. 19, 11/68, No. 20,
11/69 (No. 1-16: 68 pgs.; No. 17 on: 52 pgs.)(All are 25¢)

1-Origin & 1st app. Dynamo, Noman, Menthor, & The Thunder Squad; 1st			
app. The Iron Maiden	20	60	290
2-Death of Egghead; A-bomb blast panel	11	33	150
3-5: 4-Guy Gilbert becomes Lightning who joins Thunder Squad; Iron			
Maiden app.	8	24	105
6-10: 7-Death of Menthor. 8-Origin & 1st app. The Raven			
	7	21	85
11-15: 13-Undersea Agent app.; no Raven story	6	18	70
16-19	6	18	70

	GD	FN	NM-
20-Special Collectors Edition; all reprints	4	12	45
...Archives Vol. 1 (DC Comics, 2003, $49.95, HC) r/#1-4, restored and recolored			50.00
...Archives Vol. 2 (DC Comics, 2003, $49.95, HC) r/#5-7, Dynamo #1			50.00
...Archives Vol. 3 (DC Comics, 2003, $49.95, HC) r/#8-10, Dynamo #2			50.00
...Archives Vol. 4 (DC Comics, 2004, $49.95, HC) r/#11, Noman #1,2 & Dynamo #3			50.00

THUNDERCATS (TV)
Marvel Comics (Star Comics)/Marvel #22 on: Dec, 1985 - No. 24, June, 1988 (75¢)

	GD	FN	NM-
1-Mooney-c/a begins	2	6	14
2-20: 2-(65¢ & 75¢ cover exists). 12-Begin $1.00-c. 18-20-Williamson-i	1	3	9
21-24: 23-Williamson-c(i)	1	4	10

THUNDERCATS (TV)
DC Comics (WildStorm): No. 0, Oct, 2002 - No. 5, Feb, 2003 ($2.50/$2.95; limited series)

0-($2.50) J. Scott Campbell-c/a			3.00
1-5-($2.95) 1-McGuinness-a/c; variant cover by Art Adams; rebirth of Mumm-Ra			3.00
.../ Battle of the Planets (7/03, $4.95) Kaare Andrews-s/a; 2 covers by Campbell & Ross			5.00
...: Origins-Heroes & Villains (2/04, $3.50) short stories by various			3.50
...Reclaiming Thundera TPB (2003, $12.95) r/#0-5			13.00
... Sourcebook (1/03, $2.95) pin-ups and info on characters; art by various; A. Adams-c			3.00

TICK, THE (Also see The Chroma-Tick)
New England Comics Press: Jun, 1988 - No. 12, May, 1993 ($1.75/$1.95/$2.25; B&W, over-sized)

	GD	FN	NM-
Special Edition 1-1st comic book app. serially numbered & limited to 5,000 copies	6	18	65
Special Edition 1-(5/96, $5.95)-Double-c; foil-c; serially numbered (5,001 thru 14,000) & limited to 9,000 copies			6.00
Special Edition 2-Serially numbered and limited to 3000 copies	5	15	55
Special Edition 2-(8/96, $5.95)-Double-c; foil-c; serially numbered (5,001 thru 14,000) & limited to 9,000 copies	1	3	8
1-Regular Edition 1st printing; reprints Special Ed. 1 w/minor changes	4	12	45
1-2nd printing			6.00
1-3rd-5th printing			3.00
2-Reprints Special Ed. 2 w/minor changes	2	6	22
2-8-All reprints			3.00
3-5 ($1.95): 4-1st app. Paul the Samurai	1	4	10
6,8 ($2.25)			5.00
7-1st app. Man-Eating Cow.			6.00
8-Variant with no logo, price, issue number or company logos.			

	GD	FN	NM-
	2	6	18
9-12 ($2.75)			4.00
12-Special Edition; card-stock, virgin foil-c; numbered edition			
	2	6	22
Pseudo-Tick #13 (11/00, $3.50) Continues story from #12 (1993)			4.00
Promo Sampler-(1990)-Tick-c/story	1	3	8

TITANS (Also see Teen Titans, New Teen Titans and New Titans)
DC Comics: Mar, 1999 - No. 50, Apr, 2003 ($2.50/$2.75)

1-Titans re-form; Grayson-s; 2 covers			3.00
2-11,13-24,26-50: 2-Superman-c/app. 9,10,21,22-Deathstroke app.			
24-Titans from "Kingdom Come" app. 32-36-Asamiya-c. 44-Begin $2.75-c			
			2.75
12-($3.50, 48 pages)			3.50
25-($3.95) Titans from "Kingdom Come" app.; Wolfman & Faerber-s; art by			
Pérez, Cardy, Grummett, Jimenez, Dodson, Pelletier			4.00
Annual 1 ('00, $3.50) Planet DC; intro Bushido			3.50
...Secret Files 1,2 (3/99, 10/00; $4.95) Profile pages & short stories			5.00

TITANS/ LEGION OF SUPER-HEROES: UNIVERSE ABLAZE
DC Comics: 2000 - No. 4, 2000 ($4.95, prestige format, limited series)

1-4-Jurgens-s/a; P. Jimenez-a; teams battle Universo			5.00

TITANS/ YOUNG JUSTICE: GRADUATION DAY
DC Comics: Early July, 2003 - No. 3, Aug, 2003 ($2.50, limited series)

1,2-Winick-s/Garza-a; leads into Teen Titans and The Outsiders series.			
2-Lilith dies			2.50
3-Death of Donna Troy (Wonder Girl)			2.50
TPB (2003, $6.95) r/#1-3; plus previews of Teen Titans and The Outsiders			
series			7.00

TOMB OF DRACULA (See Giant-Size Dracula, Dracula Lives, Nightstalkers,
Power Record Comics & Requiem for Dracula)
Marvel Comics Group: Apr, 1972 - No. 70, Aug, 1979

1-1st app. Dracula & Frank Drake; Colan-p in all; Neal Adams-c			
	15	45	220
2	7	21	85
3-6: 3-Intro. Dr. Rachel Van Helsing & Inspector Chelm. 6-Neal Adams-c			
	6	18	65
7-9	4	12	50
10-1st app. Blade the Vampire Slayer (who app. in 1998, 2002 and 2004			
movies)	12	36	175
11,12,14-16,20:	3	10	35
12-2nd app. Blade; Brunner-c(p)	6	18	65
13-Origin Blade	7	21	85
17,19: 17-Blade bitten by Dracula. 19-Blade discovers he is immune to			
vampire's bite. 1st mention of Blade having vampire blood in him			
	4	12	48
18-Two-part x-over cont'd in Werewolf by Night #15	4	12	38
21,24-Blade app.	3	9	28
22,23,26,27,29	2	6	22

	GD	FN	NM-
25-1st app. & origin Hannibal King	3	9	28
25-2nd printing (1994)	2	6	12
28-Blade app. on-c & inside as an illusion	3	9	28
30,41,42-45-Blade app. 45-Intro. Deacon Frost, the vampire who bit Blade's mother	3	9	24
31-40	2	6	20
43-45-(30¢-c variants, limited distribution)	3	10	36
46,47-(Regular 25¢ editions)(4-8/76)	2	6	12
46,47-(30¢-c variants, limited distribution)	2	6	18
48,49,51-57,59,60: 57,59,60-(30¢-c)	2	6	12
50-Silver Surfer app.	2	6	22
57,59,60-(35¢-c variants)(6-9/77)	2	6	18
58-All Blade issue (Regular 30¢ edition)	3	9	28
58-(35¢-c variant)(7/77)	4	12	42
61-69	2	6	12
70-Double size	3	9	24

TOMB RAIDER: THE SERIES (Also see Witchblade/Tomb Raider)(Also see Promotional Comics section for Free Comic Book Day edition)
Image Comics (Top Cow Prod.): Dec, 1999 - Present ($2.50/$2.99)

1-Jurgens-s/Park-a; 3 covers by Park, Finch, Turner	4.00
2-24,26-29,31-47: 21-Black-c w/foil. 31-Mhan-a. 37-Flip book preview of Stryke Force	3.00
25-Michael Turner-c/a; Witchblade app.; Endgame x-over with Witchblade #60 & Evo #1	3.00
30-($4.99) Tony Daniel-a	5.00
#0 (6/01, $2.50) Avery-s/Ching-a/c	2.50
#1/2 (10/01, $2.95) Early days of Lara Croft; Jurgens-s/Lopez-a	3.00
...: Chasing Shangri-La (2002, $12.95, TPB) r/#11-15	13.00
...Gallery (12/00, $2.95) Pin-ups & previous covers by various	3.00
...Magazine (6/01, $4.95) Hughes-c; r/#1,2; Jurgens interview	5.00
...: Mystic Artifacts (2001, $14.95, TPB) r/#5-10	15.00
...: Saga of the Medusa Mask (9/00, $9.95, TPB) r/#1-4; new Park-c	10.00

TOMB RAIDER/WITCHBLADE SPECIAL (Also see Witchblade/Tomb Raider)
Top Cow Prod.: Dec, 1997 (mail-in offer, one-shot)

	GD	FN	NM-
1-Turner-s/a(p); green background cover	1	4	10
1-Variant-c with orange sun background	1	4	10
1-Variant-c with black sides	1	4	10
1-Revisited (12/98, $2.95) reprints #1, Turner-c			3.00
...: Trouble Seekers TPB (2002, $7.95) rep. T.R./W & W/T.R. & W/T.R. 1/2; new Turner-c			8.00

TOMORROW STORIES
America's Best Comics: Oct, 1999 - No. 12, Apr, 2002 ($3.50/$2.95)

1-Two covers by Ross and Nowlan; Moore-s	3.50
2-12-($2.95)	3.00
Book 1 Hardcover (2002, $24.95) r/#1-6	25.00
Book 2 Hardcover (2004, $24.95) r/#7-12	25.00

TOM STRONG (Also see Many Worlds of Tesla Strong)

	GD	FN	NM-

America's Best Comics: June, 1999 - Present ($3.50/$2.95)

1-Two covers by Ross and Sprouse; Moore-s/Sprouse-a   4.00
2-29-($2.95): 4-Art Adams-a (8 pgs.) 13-Fawcett homage w/art by Sprouse, Baker, Heath. 20-Origin of Tom Stone. 22-Ordway-a   3.00

TOM STRONG'S TERRIFIC TALES
America's Best Comics: Jan, 2002 - Present ($3.50/$2.95)

1-Short stories; Moore-s; art by Adams, Rivoche, Hernandez, Weiss   3.50
2-12-($2.95) 2-Adams, Ordway, Weiss-a; Adams-c. 4-Rivoche-a. 5-Pearson, Aragonés-a. 11-Timm-a   3.00
...: Book One HC ('04, $24.95) r/#1-6, cover gallery and sketch pages 25.00

TOR (See Sojourn)
National Periodical Publications: May-June, 1975 - No. 6, Mar-Apr, 1976

1-New origin by Kubert	2	6	12
2-6: 2-Origin-r/St. John #1			6.00

TOR (3-D)
Eclipse Comics: July, 1986 - No. 2, Aug, 1987 ($2.50)

1,2: 1-r/One Million Years Ago. 2-r/Tor 3-D #2			5.00
...2-D: 1,2-Limited signed & numbered editions	1	3	7

TOR
Marvel Comics (Epic Comics/Heavy Hitters): June, 1993 - No. 4, 1993 ($5.95, limited series)

1-4: Joe Kubert-c/a/scripts   6.00

TOWER OF SHADOWS (Creatures on the Loose #10 on)
Marvel Comics Group: Sept, 1969 - No. 9, Jan, 1971

1-Classic Romita-c, Steranko, Craig-a(p)	7	21	85
2,3: 2-Neal Adams-a. 3-Barry Smith, Tuska-a	4	12	42
4,6: 4-Marie Severin-c. 6-Wood-a	3	9	32
5-B. Smith-a(p), Wood-a; Wood draws himself (1st pg., 1st panel)	3	10	35
7-9: 7-B. Smith-a(p), Wood-a. 8-Wood-a; Wrightson-c. 9-Wrightson-c; Roy Thomas app.	4	12	42
Special 1(12/71, 52 pgs.)-Neal Adams-a; Romita-c	3	10	35

TRANSFORMERS, THE (TV)(See G.I. Joe and...)
Marvel Comics Group: Sept, 1984 - No. 80, July, 1991 (75¢/$1.00)

1-Based on Hasbro Toys	2	6	15
2-5: 2-Golden-c. 3-Spider-Man (black costume)-c/app. 4-Texeira-c	1	4	10
6-10			6.00
11-49: 21-Intro Aerialbots			4.00
50-60: 53-Jim Lee-c. 54-Intro Micromasters			6.00
61-70: 67-Jim Lee-c	1	4	10
71-77: 75-($1.50, 52 pgs.) (Low print run)	2	6	18
78,79 (Low print run)	3	9	28
80-Last issue	4	12	38

TRANSFORMERS DIGEST

	GD	FN	NM-

Marvel Comics: Jan, 1987 - No. 10, July, 1988

	GD	FN	NM-
1,2-Spider-Man-c/s	2	6	15
3-10	2	6	12

TRANSFORMERS/G.I. JOE
Dreamwave Productions: Aug, 2003 - No. 6, Mar, 2004 ($2.95/$5.25)

1-Art & gatefold wraparound-c by Jae Lee; Ney Rieber-s; variant-c by Pat Lee		3.00
1-($5.95) Holofoil wraparound-c by Norton		6.00
2-6-Jae Lee-a/c		3.00
TPB (8/04, $17.95) r/#1-6; cover gallery and sketch pages		18.00

TRANSMETROPOLITAN
DC Comics (Vertigo): Sept, 1997 - No. 60, Nov, 2002 ($2.50)

	GD	FN	NM-
1-Warren Ellis-s/Darick Robertson-a(p)	2	6	12
2,3	1	3	7
4-8			4.00
9-60: 15-Jae Lee-c. 25-27-Jim Lee-c. 37-39-Bradstreet-c			2.50
Back on the Street ('97, $7.95) r/#1-3			8.00
Dirge ('03, $14.95) r/#43-48			15.00
Filth of the City ('01, $5.95) Spider's columns with pin-up art by various			6.00
Gouge Away ('02, $14.95) r/#31-36			15.00
I Hate It Here ('00, $5.95) Spider's columns with pin-up art by various			6.00
Lonely City ('01, $14.95) r/#25-30; intro. by Patrick Stewart			15.00
Lust For Life ('98, $14.95) r/#4-12			15.00
One More Time ('04, $14.95) r/#55-60			15.00
Spider's Thrash ('02, $14.95) r/#37-42; intro. by Darren Aronofsky			15.00
Tales of Human Waste ('04, $9.95) r/Filth of the City, I Hate It Here & story from Vertigo Winter's Edge 2			10.00
The Cure ('03, $14.95) r/#49-54			15.00
The New Scum ('00, $12.95) r/#19-24 & Vertigo: Winter's Edge #3			13.00
Year of the Bastard ('99, $12.95) r/#13-18			13.00

TREEHOUSE OF HORROR (Bart Simpson's...)
Bongo Comics: 1995 - Present ($2.95/$2.50/$3.50/$4.50, annual)

1-(1995, $2.95)-Groening-c; Allred, Robinson & Smith stories	3.50
2-(1996, $2.50)-Stories by Dini & Bagge; infinity-c by Groening	3.00
3-(1997, $2.50)-Dorkin-s/Groening-c	3.00
4-(1998, $2.50)-Lash & Dixon-s/Groening-c	3.00
5-(1999, $3.50)-Thompson-s; Shaw & Aragonés-s/a; TenNapel-s/a	3.50
6-(2000, $4.50)-Mahfood-s/a; DeCarlo-a; Morse-s/a; Kuper-s/a	4.50
7-(2001, $4.50)-Hamill-s/Morrison-a; Ennis-s/McCrea-a; Sakai-s/a; Nixey-s/a; Brereton back-c	4.50
8-(2002, $3.50)-Templeton, Shaw, Barta, Simone, Thompson-s/a	3.50
9-(2003, $4.99)-Lord of the Rings-Brereton-a; Dini, Naifeh, Millidge, Boothby, Noto-s/a	5.00
10-(2004, $4.99)-Monsters of Rock w/Alice Cooper, Gene Simmons, Rob Zombie and Pat Boone; art by Rodriguez, Morrison, Morse, Templeton	5.00

TRUTH RED, WHITE & BLACK
Marvel Comics: Jan, 2003 - No. 6 ($3.50, limited series)

	GD	FN	NM-

1-Kyle Baker-a/Robert Morales-s; the testing of Captain America's
  super-soldier serum ... 3.50
2-7: 3-Isaiah Bradley 1st dons the Captain America costume ... 3.50
TPB (2004, $17.99) r/series ... 18.00

2001, A SPACE ODYSSEY (Movie)
Marvel Comics Group: Dec, 1976 - No. 10, Sept, 1977 (30¢)

	GD	FN	NM-
1-Adaptation of film; Kirby-c/a in all	2	6	16
2-7,9,10	1	3	8
7,9,10-(35¢-c variants, limited distribution)(6-9/77)	2	6	12
8-Origin/1st app. Machine Man (called Mr. Machine)	2	6	18
8-(35¢-c variant, limited distribution)(6,8/77)	3	9	27
...Treasury 1 ('76, 84 pgs.)-All new Kirby-a	3	9	26

UFO FLYING SAUCERS (UFO & Outer Space #14 on)
Gold Key: Oct, 1968 - No. 13, Jan, 1977 (No. 2 on, 36 pgs.)

	GD	FN	NM-
1(30035-810) (68 pgs.)	5	15	55
2(11/70), 3(11/72), 4(11/74)	2	6	22
5(2/75)-13: Bolle-a #4 on	2	6	15

ULTIMATE DAREDEVIL AND ELEKTRA
Marvel Comics: Jan, 2003 - No. 4, Mar, 2003 ($2.25, limited series)

1-4-Rucka-s/Larroca-c/a; 1st meeting of Elektra and Matt Murdock ... 2.25
... Vol.1 TPB (2003, $11.99) r/#1-4, Daredevil Vol. 2 #9; Larroca sketch pages
  ... 12.00

ULTIMATE ELEKTRA
Marvel Comics: Oct, 2004 - No. 5 ($2.25, limited series)

1-4-Carey-s/Larroca-c/a. 2-Bullseye app. ... 2.25

ULTIMATE FANTASTIC FOUR
Marvel Comics: Feb, 2004 - Present ($2.25)

1-Bendis & Millar-s/Adam Kubert-a/Hitch-c ... 2.25
2-13: 2-Adam Kubert-a/c; intro. Moleman 7-Ellis-s/Immonen-a begin; Dr.
  Doom app. 13-Kubert-a ... 2.25
... Vol. 1: The Fantastic (2004, $12.99, TPB) r/#1-6; cover gallery ... 13.00

ULTIMATE MARVEL TEAM-UP (Spider-Man Team-up)
Marvel Comics: Apr, 2001 - No. 16, July, 2002 ($2.99/$2.25)

1-Spider-Man & Wolverine; Bendis-s in all; Matt Wagner-a/c ... 5.00
2,3-Hulk; Hester-a ... 3.50
4,5,9-16: 4,5-Iron Man; Allred-a. 9-Fantastic Four; Mahfood-a. 10-Man-Thing;
  Totleben-a. 11-X-Men; Clugston-Major-a. 12,13-Dr. Strange; McKeever-a.
  14-Black Widow; Terry Moore-a. 15,16-Shang-Chi; Mays-a ... 3.00
6-8-Punisher; Sienkiewicz-a. 7,8-Daredevil app. ... 4.00
TPB (11/01, $14.95) r/#1-5 ... 15.00
HC (8/02, $39.99) r/#1-16 & Ult. Spider-Man Special; Bendis afterword ... 30.00
...: Vol. 2 TPB (2003, $11.99) r/#9-13; Mahfood-c ... 12.00
...: Vol. 3 TPB (2003, $12.99) r/#14-16 & Ultimate Spider-Man Super Special;
  Moore-c ... 13.00

ULTIMATE NIGHTMARE

	GD	FN	NM-

Marvel Comics: Oct, 2004 - No. 5 ($2.25, limited series)

1-3: Ellis-s; Ultimates, X-Men, Nick Fury app. 1,2-Hairsine-a/c			2.25

ULTIMATES, THE (Avengers of the Ultimate line)
Marvel Comics: Mar, 2002 - No. 13, Apr, 2004 ($2.25)

1-Intro. Capt. America; Millar-s/Hitch-a & wraparound-c			6.00
2-Intro. Giant-Man and the Wasp			4.00
3-13: 3-1st Capt. America in new costume. 4-Intro. Thor. 5-Ultimates vs. The Hulk. 8-Intro. Hawkeye			3.00
... Volume 1 HC (2004, $29.99) oversized r/series; commentary pages with Millar & Hitch; cover gallery and character design pages; intro. by Joss Whedon			30.00
... Volume 1: Super-Human TPB (8/02, $12.99) r/#1-6			13.00
... Volume 2: Homeland Security TPB (2004, $17.99) r/#7-13			18.00

ULTIMATES 2
Marvel Comics: Feb, 2005 - Present ($2.99)

1-Millar-s/Hitch-a; Giant-Man becomes Ant-Man			3.00

ULTIMATE SIX (Reprinted in Ultimate Spider-Man Vol.5 hardcover)
Marvel Comics: Nov, 2003 - No. 7, June, 2004 ($2.25) (See Ultimate Spider-Man for TPB)

1-The Ultimates & Spider-Man team-up; Bendis-s/Quesada & Hairsine-a; Cassaday-c			5.00
2-7-Hairsine-a; Cassaday-c			2.25

ULTIMATE SPIDER-MAN
Marvel Comics: Oct, 2000 - Present ($2.99/$2.25)

1-Bendis-s/Bagley & Thibert-a; cardstock-c; introduces revised origin and cast separate from regular Spider-continuity	7	21	90
1-Variant white-c (Retailer incentive)			140.00
1-DF Edition			60.00
1-Free Comic Book Day giveaway & Kay Bee Toys variant - (See Promotional Comics section)			
2-Cover with Spider-Man on car	3	10	35
2-Cover with Spider-Man swinging past building	3	9	35
3,4: 4-Uncle Ben killed	3	9	30
5-7: 6,7-Green Goblin app.	3	10	35
8-13: 13-Reveals secret to MJ	1	3	9
14-21: 14-Intro. Gwen Stacy & Dr. Octopus			5.00
22-($3.50) Green Goblin returns			3.50
23-32			2.50
33-1st Ultimate Venom-c; intro. Eddie Brock			3.00
34-38-Ultimate Venom			2.50
39-49,51-59: 39-Nick Fury app. 43,44-X-Men app. 46-Prelude to Ultimate Six; Sandman app. 51-53-Elektra app. 54-59-Doctor Octopus app.			2.25
50-($2.99) Intro. Black Cat			3.00
60-Intro. Ultimate Carnage on cover			3.00
61-Intro Ben Reilly; Punisher app.			2.25
62-Gwen Stacy killed by Carnage			3.00

	GD	FN	NM-

63-69: 63,64-Carnage app. 66,67-Wolverine app. 68,69-Johnny Storm app.

			2.25
Collected Edition (1/01, $3.99) r/#1-3			4.00
Hardcover (3/02, $34.95, 7x11", dust jacket) r/#1-13 & Amazing Fantasy #15; sketch pages and Bill Jemas' initial plot and character outlines			35.00
...: Double Trouble TPB (6/02, $17.95) r/#14-21			18.00
...: Learning Curve TPB (12/01, $14.95) r/#8-13			15.00
...: Legacy TPB (2002, $14.99) r/#22-27			15.00
...: Power and Responsibility TPB (4/01, $14.95) r/#1-7			15.00
...Special (7/02, $3.50) art by Bagley and various incl. Romita,Sr., Brereton, Cho, Mack, Sienkiewicz, Phillips, Pearson, Oeming, Mahfood, Russell			3.50
Vol. 6: Venom TPB (2003, $15.99) r/#33-39			16.00
Vol. 7: Irresponsible TPB (2003, $12.99) r/#40-45			13.00
Vol. 8: Cats & Kings TPB (2004, $17.99) r/#47-53			18.00
Vol. 9: Ultimate Six TPB (2004, $17.99) r/#46 & Ultimate Six #1-7			18.00
Vol. 10: Hollywood TPB (2004, $12.99) r/#54-59			13.00
Vol. 11: Carnage TPB (2004, $12.99) r/#60-65			13.00
Volume 2 HC (2003, $29.99, 7x11", dust jacket) r/#14-27; pin-ups & sketch pages			30.00
Volume 3 HC (2003, $29.99, 7x11", dust jacket) r/#28-39 & #1/2; script pages			30.00
Volume 4 HC (2004, $29.99, 7x11", dust jacket) r/#40-45, 47-53; sketch pages			30.00
Volume 5 HC (2004, $29.99, 7x11", dust jacket) r/#46,54-59, Ultimate Six #1-7			30.00
Wizard #1/2	1	4	10

ULTIMATE WAR
Marvel Comics: Feb, 2003 - No. 4, Apr, 2003 ($2.25, limited series)

1-4-Millar-s/Bachalo-c/a; The Ultimates vs. Ultimate X-Men			2.25
Ultimate X-Men Vol. 5: Ultimate War TPB (2003, $10.99) r/#1-4			11.00

ULTIMATE X-MEN (Also see Promotional Comics section for FCBD Ed.)
Marvel Comics: Feb, 2001 - Present ($2.99/$2.25)

1-Millar-s/Adam Kubert & Thibert-a; cardstock-c; introduces revised origin and cast separate from regular X-Men continuity	3	9	25
1-DF Edition			30.00
1-DF Sketch Cover Edition			45.00
2	2	6	20
3-6	2	6	14
7-10			6.00
11-24,26-33: 13-Intro. Gambit. 18,19-Bachalo-a. 23,24-Andrews-a			2.25
25-($3.50) leads into the Ultimate War mini-series; Kubert-a			3.50
34-Spider-Man-c/app.; Bendis-s begin; Finch-a			2.25

35-53: 35-Spider-Man app. 36,37-Daredevil-c/app. 40-Intro. Angel. 42-Intro. Dazzler. 44-Beast dies. 46-Intro. Mr. Sinister. 50-53-Kubert-a; Gambit app

			2.25
...: The Tomorrow People TPB (7/01, $14.95) r/#1-6			15.00
...: Return to Weapon X TPB (4/02, $14.95) r/#7-12			15.00
Vol. 3: World Tour TPB (2002, $17.99) r/#13-20			18.00

	GD	FN	NM-
Vol. 4: Hellfire and Brimstone TPB (2003, $12.99) r/#21-25			13.00
Vol. 5 (See Ultimate War)			
Vol. 6: Return of the King TPB (2003, $16.99) r/#26-33			17.00
Vol. 7: Blockbuster TPB (2004, $12.99) r/#34-39			13.00
Vol. 8: New Mutants TPB (2004, $12.99) r/#40-45			13.00
Vol. 9: The Tempest TPB (2004, $10.99) r/#46-49			11.00
Volume 1 HC (8/02, $34.99, 7x11", dust jacket) r/#1-12 & Giant-Size X-Men #1; sketch pages and Millar and Bendis' initial plot and character outlines			35.00
Volume 2 HC (2003, $29.99, 7x11", dust jacket) r/#13-25; script for #20			30.00
Volume 3 HC (2003, $29.99, 7x11", dust jacket) r/#26-33 & Utimate War #1-4			30.00
Wizard #1/2	2	6	15

UNCANNY X-MEN, THE (See **X-Men, The**, 1st series, #142-on)

UNCANNY X-MEN AND THE NEW TEEN TITANS (See Marvel and DC Present...)

UNCLE SCROOGE (Disney) (Becomes Walt Disney's... #210 on)
Gold Key #40-173/Whitman #174-209: No. 40, Dec, 1962 - No. 209, July, 1984

	GD	FN	NM-
40-X-Mas-c	11	33	160
41-60: 48-Magica De Spell-c/story (3/64). 49-Sci/fi-c. 51-Beagle Boys-c/story (8/64)	10	30	130
61-63,65,66,68-71:71-Last Barks issue w/original story (#71-Barks only storyboarded the script)	9	27	120
64-Barks Vietnam War story "Treasure of Marco Polo" banned for reprints by Disney from 1977-1989 because of its Third World revolutionary war theme. It later appeared in the hardcover Carl Barks Library set (4/89) and Walt Disney's Uncle Scrooge Adventures #42 (1/97)	12	36	175
67,72,73: 67,72,73-Barks-r	9	27	110
74-84: 74-Barks-r(1pg.). 75-81,83-Not by Barks. 82,84-Barks-r begin	6	18	70
85-110	5	15	60
111-120	4	12	40
121-141,143-152,154-157	3	10	35
142-Reprints Four Color #456 with-c	4	12	38
153,158,162-164,166,168-170,178,180: No Barks	2	6	20
159-160,165,167	2	6	22
161(r/#14), 171(r/#11), 177(r/#16),183(r/#6)-Barks-r	2	6	22
172(1/80),173(2/80)-Gold Key. Barks-a	3	9	26
174(3/80),175(4/80),176(5/80)-Whitman. Barks-a	3	10	35
177(6/80),178(7/80)	4	12	38
179(9/80)(r/#9)-(Very low distribution)	38	114	600
180(11/80),181(12/80), r/4-Color #495) pre-pack?	5	15	55
182-195: 184,185,187,188-Barks-a. 182,186,191-194-No Barks. 189(r/#5), 190(r/#4), 195(r/4-Color #386)	2	6	22
196(4/82),197(5/82): 196(r/#13)	3	9	26
198-209 (All #90038 on-c; pre-pack; no date or date code): 198(4/83), 199(5/83), 200(6/83), 201(6/83), 202(7/83), 203(7/83), 204(8/83),			

205(8/83), 206(4/84), 207(5/83), 208(6/84), 209(7/84). 198-202,204-206: No Barks. 203(r/#12), 207(r/#93,92), 208(r/U.S. #18), 209(r/U.S. #21)-Barks-r   3   9   30

Uncle Scrooge & Money(G.K.)-Barks-r/from WDC&S #130 (3/67)

    5   15   60

Mini Comic #1(1976)(3-1/4x6-1/2")-r/U.S. #115; Barks-c

    2   6   12

UNCLE SCROOGE THE LEMONADE KING
Whitman Publishing Co.: 1960 (A Top Top Tales Book, 6-3/8"x7-5/8", 32 pgs.)

2465-Storybook pencilled by Carl Barks, finished art adapted by Norman McGary   40   120   640

UNDERDOG (TV)
Charlton Comics/Gold Key: July, 1970 - No. 10, Jan, 1972; Mar, 1975 - No. 23, Feb, 1979

	GD	FN	NM-
1 (1st series, Charlton)-1st app. Underdog	9	27	120
2-10	5	15	60
1 (2nd series, Gold Key)	7	21	85
2-10	4	12	42
11-20: 13-1st app. Shack of Solitude	3	9	32
21-23	3	10	35

UNEXPECTED, THE (Formerly Tales of the...)
National Per. Publ./DC Comics: No. 105, Feb-Mar, 1968 - No. 222, May, 1982

	GD	FN	NM-
105-Begin 12¢ cover price	6	18	75
106-113: 113-Last 12¢ issue (6-7/69)	4	12	50
114,115,117,118,120-125	3	10	35
116 (36 pgs.)-Wrightson-a?	4	12	38
119-Wrightson-a, 8pgs.(36 pgs.)	5	15	55
126,127,129-136-(52 pgs.)	3	10	35
128(52 pgs.)-Wrightson-a	5	15	55
137-156	2	6	20
157-162-(100 pgs.)	4	12	45
163-188: 187,188-(44 pgs.)	2	6	15
189,190,192-195 ($1.00, 68 pgs.): 189 on are combined with House of Secrets & The Witching Hour	2	6	16
191-Rogers-a(p) ($1.00, 68 pgs.)	2	6	18
196-222: 200-Return of Johnny Peril by Tuska. 205-213-Johnny Peril app. 210-Time Warp story. 222-Giffen-a	1	3	9

UNKNOWN SOLDIER (Formerly Star-Spangled War Stories)
National Periodical Publications/DC Comics: No. 205, Apr-May, 1977 - No. 268, Oct, 1982 (See Our Army at War #168 for 1st app.)

	GD	FN	NM-
205	2	6	20
206-210,220,221,251: 220,221 (44pgs.). 251-Enemy Ace begins	2	6	14
211-218,222-247,250,252-264	1	4	10
219-Miller-a (44 pgs.)	2	6	18

248,249,265-267: 248,249-Origin. 265-267-Enemy Ace vs. Balloon Buster.

	GD	FN	NM-
	1	4	10
268-Death of Unknown Soldier	2	6	22

UNLIMITED ACCESS (Also see Marvel Vs. DC))
Marvel Comics: Dec, 1997 - No. 4, Mar, 1998 ($2.99/$1.99, limited series)

1-Spider-Man, Wonder Woman, Green Lantern & Hulk app.		3.50
2,3-($1.99): 2-X-Men, Legion of Super-Heroes app. 3-Original Avengers vs. original Justice League		2.50
4-($2.99) Amalgam Legion vs. Darkseid & Magneto		3.00

UNTOLD TALES OF SPIDER-MAN (Also see Amazing Fantasy #16-18)
Marvel Comics: Sept, 1995 - No. 25, Sept, 1997 (99¢)

1-Kurt Busiek scripts begin; Pat Olliffe-c/a in all (except #9).		2.50
2-22, -1(7/97), 23-25: 2-1st app. Batwing. 4-1st app. The Spacemen (Gantry, Orbit, Satellite & Vacuum). 8-1st app. The Headsman; The Enforcers (The Big Man, Montana, The Ox & Fancy Dan) app. 9-Ron Frenz-a. 10-1st app. Commanda. 16-Reintro Mary Jane Watson. 21-X-Men-c/app. 25-Green Goblin		2.25
...'96-(1996, $1.95, 46 pgs.)-Kurt Busiek scripts; Mike Allred-c/a; Kurt Busiek & Pat Olliffe app. in back-up story; contains pin-ups		2.25
...'97-(1997, $1.95)-Wraparound-c		2.25
...: Strange Encounters ('98, $5.99) Dr. Strange app.		6.00

USAGI YOJIMBO (See Albedo, Doomsday Squad #3 & Space Usagi)
Fantagraphics Books: July, 1987 - No. 38 ($2.00/$2.25, B&W)

	1	3	9
1			
1,8,10-2nd printings			2.25
2-9			4.00
10,11: 10-Leonardo app. (TMNT). 11-Aragonés-a			6.00
12-29			3.00
30-38: 30-Begin $2.25-c			3.00
Color Special 1 (11/89, $2.95, 68 pgs.)-new & r			3.50
Color Special 2 (10/91, $3.50)			3.50
Color Special 3 (10/92, $3.50)-Jeff Smith's Bone promo on inside-c			3.50
Summer Special 1 (1986, B&W, $2.75)-r/early Albedo issues			3.00

USAGI YOJIMBO
Mirage Studios: V2#1, Mar, 1993 - No. 16, 1994 ($2.75)

V2#1-16: 1-Teenage Mutant Ninja Turtles app.		3.00

USAGI YOJIMBO
Dark Horse Comics: V3#1, Apr, 1996 - Present ($2.95/$2.99, B&W)

V3#1-78: Stan Sakai-c/a	3.00
Color Special 4 (7/97, $2.95) "Green Persimmon"	3.00
Daisho TPB ('98, $14.95) r/Mirage series #7-14	15.00
Demon Mask TPB ('01, $15.95)	16.00
Grasscutter TPB ('99, $16.95) r/#13-22	17.00
Gray Shadows TPB ('00, $14.95) r/#23-30	15.00
Seasons TPB ('99, $14.95) r/#7-12	15.00
Shades of Death TPB ('97, $14.95) r/Mirage series #1-6	15.00
The Brink of Life and Death TPB ('98, $14.95) r/Mirage series #13,15,16 &	

	GD	FN	NM-
Dark Horse series #1-6			15.00
The Shrouded Moon TPB (1/03, $15.95) r/#46-52			16.00

VAMPIRELLA (Magazine)(See Warren Presents)
Warren Publishing Co./Harris Publications #113: Sept, 1969 - No. 112, Feb, 1983; No. 113, Jan, 1988? (B&W)

	GD	FN	NM-
1-Intro. Vampirella in original costume & wings; Frazetta-c/intro. page; Adams-a; Crandall-a	41	123	650
2-1st app. Vampirella's cousin Evily-c/s; 1st/only app. Draculina, Vampirella's blonde twin sister	14	42	200
3 (Low distribution)	36	108	575
4,6	11	33	145
5,7,9: 5,7-Frazetta-c. 9-Barry Smith-a; Boris/Wood-c	11	33	150
8-Vampirella begins by Tom Sutton as serious strip (early issues-gag line)	11	33	160
10-No Vampi story; Brunner, Adams, Wood-a	6	18	75
11-Origin & 1st app. Pendragon; Frazetta-c	7	21	90
12-Vampi by Gonzales begins	7	21	90
13-15: 14-1st Maroto-a; Ploog-a	7	21	90
16,22,25: 16-1st full Dracula-c/app. 22-Color insert preview of Maroto's Dracula. 25-Vampi on cocaine-s	7	21	80
17,18,20,21,23,24: 17-Tomb of the Gods begins by Maroto, ends #22. 18-22-Dracula-s	7	21	80
19 (1973 Annual) Creation of Vampi text bio	8	24	100
26,28,34-36,39,40: All have 8 pg. color inserts. 28-Board game inside covers. 34,35-1st Fleur the Witch Woman. 39,40-Color Dracula-s. 40-Wrightson bio	4	12	50
27 (1974 Annual) New color Vampi-s; mostly-r	5	15	60
29,38,45: 38-2nd Vampi as Cleopatra/Blood Red Queen of Hearts; 1st Mayo-a.	4	12	50
30-32: 30-Intro. Pantha; Corben-a(color). 31-Origin Luana, the Beast Girl. 32-Jones-a	4	12	50
33-Wrightson ends; Pantha ends	4	12	50
36,37: 36-1st Vampi as Cleopatra/Blood Red Queen of Hearts. 37-(1975 Annual)	5	15	55
41-44,47,48: 41-Dracula-s	4	12	40
46-(10/75) Origin-r from Annual 1	4	12	48
49-1st Blind Priestess; The Blood Red Queen of Hearts storyline begins; Poe-s	4	12	40
50-Spirit cameo by Eisner; 40 pg. Vampi-s; Pantha & Fleur app.; Jones-a	4	12	40
51-53,56,57,59-62,65,66,68,75,79,80,82-86,88,89: 60-62,65,66-The Blood Red Queen of Hearts app. 60-1st Blind Priestess-c	3	9	28
54,55,63,81,87: 54-Vampi-s (42 pgs.); 8 pg. color Corben-a. 55-Gonzales-a(r). 63-10 pgs. Wrightson-a	3	9	28
58,70,72: 58-(92 pgs.) 70-Rook app.	3	10	35
64,73: 64-(100 pg. Giant) All Mayo-a; 70 pg. Vampi-s. 73-69 pg. Vampi-s; Mayo-a	4	12	38
67,69,71,74,76-78-All Barbara Leigh photo-c	3	10	35
90-99: 90-Toth-a. 91-All-r; Gonzales-a. 93-Cassandra St. Knight begins,			

	GD	FN	NM-
ends #103; new Pantha series begins, ends #108	3	9	28
100 (96 pg. r-special)-Origin reprinted from Ann. 1; mostly reprints; Vampirella appears topless in new 21 pg. story	7	21	90
101-104,106,107: All lower print run. 101,102-The Blood Red Queen of Hearts app. 107-All Maroto reprint-a issue	5	15	55
105,108-110: 108-Torpedo series by Toth begins; Vampi nudity splash page. 110-(100 pg. Summer Spectacular)	5	15	55
111,112: Low print run. 111-Giant Collector's Edition ($2.50) 112-(84 pgs.) last Warren issue	6	18	75
113 (1988)-1st Harris Issue; very low print run	29	87	425
Annual 1(1972)-New definitive origin of Vampirella by Gonzales; reprints by Neal Adams (from #1), Wood (from #9)	27	81	400
Special 1 (1977) Softcover (color, large-square bound)-Only available thru mail order	15	45	225
Special 1 (1977) Hardcover (color, large-square bound)-Only available through mail order (scarce)(500 produced, signed & #'d)	35	105	560
#1 1969 Commemorative Edition (2001, $4.95) reprints entire #1			5.00
...Crimson Chronicles Vol. 1 (2004, $19.95, TPB) reprints stories from #1-10			20.00

VAMPIRELLA (Also see Cain/... & Vengeance of...)
Harris Publications: Nov, 1992 - No. 5, Nov, 1993 ($2.95)

	GD	FN	NM-
0-Bagged			5.00
0-Gold	3	9	30
1-Jim Balent inks in #1-3; Adam Hughes c-1-3	2	6	20
1-2nd printing			5.00
1-(11/97) Commemorative Edition			3.00
2	2	6	15
3-5: 4-Snyder III-c. 5-Brereton painted-c	1	3	8
Trade paperback nn (10/93, $5.95)-r/#1-4; Jusko-c	1	3	7
NOTE: Issues 1-5 contain certificates for free *Dave Stevens* Vampirella poster.			

VAMPIRELLA (THE NEW MONTHLY)
Harris Publications: Nov, 1997 - No. 26, Apr, 2000 ($2.95)

	GD	FN	NM-
1-3-"Ascending Evil" -Morrison & Millar-s/Conner & Palmiotti-a. 1-Three covers by Quesada/Palmiotti, Conner, and Conner/Palmiotti			3.00
1-3-($9.95) Jae Lee variant covers			10.00
1-($24.95) Platinum Ed.w/Quesada-c			25.00
4-6-"Holy War"-Small & Stull-a, 4-Linsner variant-c			3.00
7-9-"Queen's Gambit"-Shi app. 7-Two covers. 8-Pantha-c/app.			3.00
7-($9.95) Conner variant-c			10.00
10-12-"Hell on Earth"; Small-a/Coney-s. 12-New costume			3.00
10-Jae Lee variant-c	1	4	10
13-15-"World's End" Zircher-p; Pantha back-up, Texeira-a			3.00
16,17: 16-Pantha-c;Texeira-a; Vampi back-up story. 17-(Pantha #2)			3.00
18-20-"Rebirth": Jae Lee-c on all. 18-Loeb-s/Sale-a. 19-Alan Davis-a. 20-Bruce Timm-a			3.00
18-20-($9.95) Variant covers: 18-Sale. 19-Davis. 20-Timm			12.00
21-26: 21,22-Dangerous Games; Small-a. 23-Lady Death-c/app.;			

	GD	FN	NM-
Cleavenger-a. 24,25-Lau-a. 26-Lady Death & Pantha-c/app.			3.00
0-(1/99) also variant-c with Pantha #0; same contents			3.00
TPB ($7.50) r/#1-3 "Ascending Evil"			8.00
Ascending Evil Ashcan (8/97, $1.00)			2.25
Hell on Earth Ashcan (7/98, $1.00)			2.25
The End Ashcan (3/00, $6.00)			6.00
...30th Anniversary Celebration Preview (7/99) B&W preview of #18-20			10.00

VAMPIRELLA
Harris Publications: June, 2001 - No. 22, Aug, 2003 ($2.95/$2.99)

	GD	FN	NM-
1-Four covers (Mayhew w/foil logo, Campbell, Anacleto, Jae Lee) Mayhew-a; Mark Millar-s			3.00
2-22: 2-Two covers (Mayhew & Chiodo). 3-Timm var-c. 4-Horn var-c. 7-10-Dawn Brown-a; Pantha back-up w/Texeira-a. 15-22-Conner-c			3.00
Giant-Size Ashcan (5/01, $5.95) B&W preview art and Mayhew interview			6.00
...: Halloween Trick & Treat (10/04, $4.95) stories & art by various; three covers			5.00
... : Nowheresville Preview Edition (3/01, $2.95)- previews Mayhew art and photo models			3.00
...Nowheresville TPB (1/02, $12.95) r/#1-3 with cover gallery			13.00

VENOM
Marvel Comics: June, 2003 - No. 18, Nov, 2004 ($2.25)

	GD	FN	NM-
1-7-Herrera-a/Way-s. 6,7-Wolverine app.			2.25
8-18-($2.99): 8-10-Wolverine-c/app.; Kieth-c. 11-Fantastic Four app.			3.00
... Vol. 1: Shiver (2004, $13.99, TPB) r/#1-5			14.00
... Vol. 2: Run (2004, $19.99, TPB) r/#6-13			20.00
... Vol. 3: Twist (2004, $13.99, TPB) r/#14-18			14.00

VENOM: LETHAL PROTECTOR
Marvel Comics: Feb, 1993 - No. 6, July, 1993 ($2.95, limited series)

	GD	FN	NM-
1-Red holo-grafx foil-c; Bagley-c/a in all			5.00
1-Gold variant sold to retailers			15.00
1-Black-c (at least 23 copies have been authenticated by CGC since 2000)			
	11	33	150
NOTE: Counterfeit copies of the black-c exist and are valueless			
2-6: Spider-Man app. in all			3.00

V FOR VENDETTA
DC Comics: Sept, 1988 - No. 10, May, 1989 ($2.00, maxi-series)

	GD	FN	NM-
1-10: Alan Moore scripts in all			3.00
Trade paperback (1990, $14.95)			15.00

WALT DISNEY'S COMICS AND STORIES
Dell Publishing Co./Gold Key #264-473/Whitman #474-510/Gladstone #511-547/Disney Comics #548-585/Gladstone #586-633/Gemstone Publishing #634 on:
#140, 5/52 - #263, 8/62; #264, 10/62 - #510, 7/84; #511, 10/86 - #633, 2/99; #634, 7/03 - Present

	GD	FN	NM-
140-(5/52)-1st app. Gyro Gearloose by Barks; 2nd Barks Uncle Scrooge-c; 3rd Uncle Scrooge cover app.	16	48	230

	GD	FN	NM-

141-150-All Barks-a. 143-Little Hiawatha begins, ends #151,159

	7	21	85
151-170-All Barks-a	6	18	75
171-199-All Barks-a	6	18	65
200	6	18	75

201-240: All Barks-a. 204-Chip 'n' Dale & Scamp begin

	5	15	60

241-283: Barks-a. 241-Dumbo x-over. 247-Gyro Gearloose begins, ends
#274. 256-Ludwig Von Drake begins, ends #274 · 5 · 15 · 55

284,285,287,290,295,296,309-311-Not by Barks	3	9	25

286,288,291-294,297,298,308-All Barks stories; 293-Grandma Duck's Farm
Friends. 297-Gyro Gearloose. 298-Daisy Duck's Diary-r

	3	9	32
289-Annette-c & back-c & story; Barks-s	4	12	40

299-307-All contain early Barks-r (#43-117). 305-Gyro Gearloose

	3	10	35
312-Last Barks issue with original story	3	10	35
313-315,317-327,329-334,336-341	2	6	22
316-Last issue published during life of Walt Disney	2	6	22
328,335,342-350-Barks-r	2	6	22

351-360-With posters inside; Barks reprints (2 versions of each with & without
posters) · 4 · 12 · 45

351-360-Without posters...	2	6	22
361-400-Barks-r	2	6	22
401-429-Barks-r	2	6	20
430,433,437,438,441,444,445,466-No Barks	1	4	10
431,432,434-436,439,440,442,443-Barks-r	2	6	14
446-465,467-473-Barks-r	1	4	10
474(3/80),475-478 (Whitman)	2	6	18
479(8/80),481(10/80)-484(1/81) pre-pack only	4	12	50
480 (8-12/80)-(Very low distribution)	10	30	135
485-499: 494-r/WDC&S #98	2	6	18

500-510 (All #90011 on-c; pre-packs): 500(4/83), 501(5/83), 502&503(7/83),
504-506(all 8/83),507(4/84), 508(5/84), 509(6/84), 510(7/84). 506-No Barks

	2	6	20

511-Donald Duck by Daan Jippes (1st in U.S.; in all through #518); Gyro
Gearloose Barks-r begins (in most through #547); Wuzzles by Disney
Studio (1st by Gladstone) · 3 · 9 · 30

512,513	2	6	16
514-516,520	1	3	9

517-519,521,522,525,527,529,530,532-546: 518-Infinity-c. 522-r/1st app.
Huey, Dewey & Louie from D. Duck Sunday. 535-546-Barks-r. 537-1st
Donald Duck by William Van Horn in WDC&S. 541-545-52 pgs.
546,547-68 pgs. 546-Kelly-r. 547-Rosa-a · 5.00

523,524,526,528,531,547: Rosa-s/a in all. 523-1st Rosa 10 pager

	2	6	14

548-($1.50, 6/90)-1st Disney issue; new-a; no M. Mouse · 6.00

549,551-570,572,573,577-579,581,584 ($1.50): 549-Barks-r begin, ends
#585, not in #555, 556, & 564. 551-r/1 story from F.C. #29. 556,578-r/

	GD	FN	NM-

Mickey Mouse Cheerios Premium by Dick Moores. 562,563,568-570,572,
  581-Gottfredson strip-r. 570-Valentine issue; has Mickey/Minnie centerfold.
  584-Taliaferro strip-r   4.00
550 ($2.25, 52 pgs.)-Donald Duck by Barks; previously printed only in The
  Netherlands (1st time in U.S.); r/Chip 'n Dale & Scamp from #204   5.00
571-($2.95, 68 pgs)-r/Donald Duck's Atomic Bomb by Barks from 1947
  Cheerios premium   6.00
574-576,580,582,583 ($2.95, 68 pgs.): 574-r/1st Pinocchio Sunday strip
  (1939-40). 575-Gottfredson-r, Pinocchio-r/WDC&S #64. 580-r/Donald
  Duck's 1st app. from Silly Symphony strip 12/16/34 by Taliaferro;
  Gottfredson strip-r begin; not in #584 & 600. 582,583-r/Mickey Mouse on
  Sky Island from WDC&S #1,2   5.00
585 ($2.50, 52 pgs.)-r/#140; Barks-r/WDC&S #140   5.00
586,587: 586-Gladstone issues begin again; begin $1.50-c; Gottfredson-r
  begins (not in #600). 587-Donald Duck by William Van Horn begins   4.00
588-597: 588,591-599-Donald Duck by William Van Horn   3.00
598,599 ($1.95, 36 pgs.): 598-r/1st drawings of Mickey Mouse by Ub Iwerks
      3.00
600 ($2.95, 48 pgs.)-L.B. Cole-c(r)/WDC&S #1; Barks-r/WDC&S #32 plus
  Rosa, Jippes, Van Horn-r and new Rosa centerspread   4.00
601-611 ($5.95, 64 pgs., squarebound, bi-monthly): 601-Barks-c, r/Mickey
  Mouse V1#1, Rosa-a/scripts. 602-Rosa-c. 604-Taliaferro strip-r/1st Silly
  Symphony Sundays from 1932. 604,605-Jippes-a. 605-Walt Kelly-c;
  Gottfredson "Mickey Mouse Outwits the Phantom Blot" r/F.C. #16   6.00
612-633 ($6.95): 633-(2/99) Last Gladstone issue   7.00
634-651: 634-(7/03) First Gemstone issue; William Van Horn-c   7.00

WALT DISNEY'S DONALD DUCK ADVENTURES (D.D. Adv. #1-3)
Gladstone: 11/87-No. 20, 4/90 (1st Series); No. 21,8/93-No. 48, 2/98(3rd Series)

	1	3	7

2-r/F.C. #308   3.00
3,4,6;7,9-11,13,15-18: 3-r/F.C. #223. 4-r/F.C. #62. 9-r/F.C. #159, "Ghost of
  the Grotto". 11-r/F.C. #159, "Adventure Down Under." 16-r/F.C. #291;
  Rosa-c. 18-r/FC #318; Rosa-c   3.00
5,8-Don Rosa-c/a   5.00
12($1.50, 52pgs)-Rosa-c/a w/Barks poster   6.00
14-r/F.C. #29, "Mummy's Ring"   4.00
19($1.95, 68 pgs.)-Barks-r/F.C. #199 (1 pg.)   3.00
20($1.95, 68 pgs.)-Barks-r/F.C. #189 & cover-r; William Van Horn-a   3.00
21,22: 21-r/D.D. #46. 22-r/F.C. #282   3.00
23-25,27,29,31,32-($1.50, 36 pgs.): 21,23,29-Rosa-c. 23-Intro/1st app.
  Andold Wild Duck by Marco Rota. 24-Van Horn-a. 27-1st Pat Block-a,
  "Mystery of Widow's Gap." 31,32-Block-c   2.50
26,28($2.95, 68 pgs.): 26-Barks-r/F.C. #108, "Terror of the River".
  28-Barks-r/F.C. #199, "Sheriff of Bullet Valley"   4.00
30($2.95, 68 pgs.)-r/F.C. #367, Barks' "Christmas for Shacktown"   4.00
33($1.95, 68 pgs.)-r/F.C. #408, Barks' "The Golden Helmet;" Van Horn-c 3.00
34-43: 34-Resume $1.50-c. 34,35,37-Block-a/scripts. 38-Van Horn-c/a   2.50
44-48-($1.95-c)   2.50

	GD	FN	NM-

WALT DISNEY'S DONALD DUCK ADVENTURES (2nd Series)
Disney Comics: June, 1990 - No. 38, July, 1993 ($1.50)

1-Rosa-a & scripts   5.00
2-21,23,25,27-33,35,36,38: 2-Barks-r/WDC&S #35; William Van Horn-a
    begins, ends #20. 9-Barks-r/F.C. #178. 9,11,14,17-No Van Horn-a. 11-Mad
    #1 cover parody. 14-Barks-r. 17-Barks-r. 21-r/FC #203 by Barks.
    29-r/MOC #20 by Barks   3.00
22,24,26,34,37: 22-Rosa-a (10 pgs.) & scripts. 24-Rosa-a & scripts.
    26-r/March of Comics #41 by Barks. 34-Rosa-c/a. 37-Rosa-a; Barks-r 4.00

WALT DISNEY'S DONALD DUCK ADVENTURES (Take-Along Comic)
Gemstone Publishing: July, 2003 - Present ($7.95, 5" x 7-1/2")

1-9-Mickey Mouse & Uncle Scrooge app. 9-Christmas-c   8.00

WALT DISNEY'S DONALD DUCK AND FRIENDS
Gemstone Publishing: No. 308, Oct, 2003 - Present ($2.95)

308-322: 308-Numbering resumes from Gladstone Donald Duck series;
    Halloween-c   3.00

WALT DISNEY'S MICKEY MOUSE ADVENTURES (Take-Along Comic)
Gemstone Publishing: Aug, 2004 - Present ($7.95, 5" x 7-1/2")

1-Goofy, Donald Duck & Uncle Scrooge app.   8.00

WALT DISNEY'S MICKEY MOUSE AND FRIENDS
Gemstone Publishing: No. 257, Oct, 2003 - Present ($2.95)

257-271: 257-Numbering resumes from Gladstone Mickey Mouse series;
    Halloween-c   3.00

WALT DISNEY'S UNCLE SCROOGE (Formerly Uncle Scrooge #1-209)
Gladstone #210-242/Disney Comics #243-280/Gladstone #281-
318/Gemstone #319 on: No. 210, 10/86 - No. 242, 4/90; No. 243, 6/90 - No.
318, 2/99; No. 319, 7/03 - Present

210-1st Gladstone issue; r/WDC&S #134 (1st Beagle Boys)	2	6	16
211-218: 216-New story ("Go Slowly Sands of Time") plotted and partly scripted by Barks. 217-r/U.S. #7, "Seven Cities of Cibola"	2	6	15
219-"Son Of The Sun" by Rosa	3	9	25
220-Don Rosa-a/scripts	1	3	8
221-223,225,228-234,236-240			4.00
224,226,227,235: 224-Rosa-c/a. 226,227-Rosa-a. 235-Rosa-a/scripts			5.00
241-($1.95, 68 pgs.)-Rosa finishes over Barks-r			6.00
242-($1.95, 68 pgs.)-Barks-r; Rosa-a(1 pg.)			6.00
243-249,251-260,264-275,277-280,282-284-($1.50): 243-1st by Disney Comics. 274-All Barks issue. 275-Contains centerspread by Rosa. 279-All Barks issue; Rosa-c. 283-r/WDC&S #98			3.00
250-($2.25, 52 pgs.)-Barks-r; wraparound-c			4.00
261-263,276-Don Rosa-c/a			5.00
281-Gladstone issues start again; Rosa-c			6.00
285-The Life and Times of Scrooge McDuck Pt. 1; Rosa-c/a/scripts	1	4	10

	GD	FN	NM-

286-293: The Life and Times of Scrooge McDuck Pt. 2-8; Rosa-c/a/scripts.
293-($1.95, 36 pgs.)-The Life and Times of Scrooge McDuck Pt. 9 .... 6.00
294-299, 301-308-($1.50, 32 pgs.): 294-296-The Life and Times of Scrooge
 McDuck Pt. 10-12. 297-The Life and Times of Uncle Scrooge Pt. 0;
 Rosa-c/a/scripts 3.00
300-($2.25, 48 pgs.)-Rosa-c; Barks-r/WDC&S #104 and U.S. #216; r/U.S.
 #220; includes new centerfold. 4.00
309-318-($6.95) 318-(2/99) Last Gladstone issue 7.00
319-336: 319-(7/03) First Gemstone issue; The Dutchman's Secret by
 Don Rosa 7.00

WALT DISNEY'S UNCLE SCROOGE ADVENTURES
(Uncle Scrooge Advs. #1-3)
Gladstone Publishing: Nov, 1987 - No. 21, May, 1990; No. 22, Sept, 1993 -
No. 54, Feb, 1998

1-Barks-r begin, ends #26	1	3	8
2-4			4.00

5,9,14: 5-Rosa-c/a; no Barks-r. 9,14-Rosa-a 5.00
6-8,10-13,15-19: 10-r/U.S. #18(all Barks) 3.00
20,21 ($1.95, 68 pgs.) 20-Rosa-c/a. 21-Rosa-a 5.00
22 ($1.50)-Rosa-c; r/U.S. #26 .... 5.00
23-($2.95, 68 pgs.)-Vs. The Phantom Blot-r/P.B. #3; Barks-r 4.00
24-26,29,31,32,34-36: 24,25,29,31,32-Rosa-c. 25-r/U.S. #21 .... 2.50
27-Guardians of the Lost Library - Rosa-c/a/story; origin of Junior
 Woodchuck Guidebook 3.00
28-($2.95, 68 pgs.)-r/U.S. #13 w/restored missing panels 4.00
30-($2.95, 68 pgs.)-r/U.S. #12; Rosa-c 4.00
33-($2.95, 64 pgs.)-New Barks story 3.00
37-54 .... 2.50

WANTED
Image Comics (Top Cow): Dec, 2003 - No. 6 ($2.99)

1-Three covers; Mark Millar-s/J.G. Jones-a; intro Wesley Gibson .. 3.00
1,2-Death Row Edition; r/#1,2 with extra sketch pages and deleted panels
 .... 3.00
2-5: 2-Cameos of DC villains 3.00
...Dossier (5/04, $2.99) Pin-ups and character info; art by Jones, Romita Jr.
 & others 3.00

WATCHMEN
DC Comics: Sept, 1986 - No. 12, Oct, 1987 (maxi-series)

1-Alan Moore scripts & Dave Gibbons-c/a in all	1	3	7
2-12			5.00

Hardcover Collection-Slip-cased-r/#1-12 w/new material; produced by
 Graphitti Designs 70.00
Trade paperback (1987, $14.95)-r/#1-12 .... 18.00

WEB OF SPIDER-MAN (Replaces Marvel Team-Up)
Marvel Comics Group: Apr, 1985 - No. 129, Sept, 1995

1-Painted-c (5th app. black costume?)	2	6	15
2,3			5.00

	GD	FN	NM-
4-8: 7-Hulk x-over; Wolverine splash			4.00
9-13: 10-Dominic Fortune guest stars; painted-c			4.00
14-17,19-28: 19-Intro Humbug & Solo			3.00
18-1st app. Venom (behind the scenes, 9/86)			3.00
29-Wolverine, new Hobgoblin (Macendale) app.	1	3	8
30-Origin recap The Rose & Hobgoblin I (entire book is flashback story); Punisher & Wolverine cameo			4.00
31,32-Six part Kraven storyline begins			5.00
33-37,39-47,49: 36-1st app. Tombstone			3.00
38-Hobgoblin app.; begin $1.00-c			4.00
48-Origin Hobgoblin II(Demogoblin) cont'd from Spectacular Spider-Man #147; Kingpin app.	1	3	9
50-($1.50, 52 pgs.)			3.50
51-58			2.50
59-Cosmic Spidey cont'd from Spect. Spider-Man			3.50
60-89,91-99,101-106: 66,67-Green Goblin (Norman Osborn) app. as a super-hero. 69,70-Hulk x-over. 74-76-Austin-c(i). 76-Fantastic Four x-over. 78-Cloak & Dagger app. 81-Origin/1st app. Bloodshed. 84-Begin 6 part Rose & Hobgoblin II storyline; last $1.00-c. 86-Demon leaves Hobgoblin; 1st Demogoblin. 93-Gives brief history of Hobgoblin. 93,94-Hobgoblin (Macendale) Reborn-c/story, parts 1,2; MoonKnight app. 94-Venom cameo. 95-Begin 4 part x-over w/Spirits of Venom w/GhostRider/Blaze/ Spidey vs. Venom & Demogoblin (cont'd in Ghost Rider/Blaze #5,6). 96-Spirits of Venom part 3; painted-c. 101,103-Maximum Carnage x-over. 103-Venom & Carnage app. 104-106-Nightwatch back-up stories			2.50
90-($2.95, 52 pgs.)-Polybagged w/silver hologram-c, gatefold poster showing Spider-Man & Spider-Man 2099 (Williamson-i)			3.50
90-2nd printing; gold hologram-c			3.00
100-($2.95, 52 pgs.)-Holo-grafx foil-c; intro new Spider-Armor			4.00
107-111: 107-Intro Sandstorm; Sand & Quicksand app.			2.50
112-116, 118, 119, 121-124, 126-128: 112-Begin $1.50-c; bound-in trading card sheet. 113-Regular Ed.; Gambit & Black Cat app. 118-1st solo clone story; Venom app.			2.25
113-($2.95)-Collector's ed. polybagged w/foil-c; 16 pg. preview of Spider-Man cartoon & animation cel			3.00
117-($1.50)-Flip book; Power & Responsibility Pt.1			2.25
117-($2.95)-Collector's edition; foil-c; flip book			3.00
119-($6.45)-Direct market edition; polybagged w/ Marvel Milestone Amazing Spider-Man #150 & coupon for Amazing Spider-Man #396, Spider-Man #53, & Spectacular Spider-Man #219			7.00
120 ($2.25)-Flip book w/ preview of the Ultimate Spider-Man			2.50
125 ($3.95)-Holodisk-c; Gwen Stacy clone			4.00
125,129: 25 ($2.95)-Newsstand. 129-Last issue			3.00
Annual 1 (1985)			3.00
Annual 2 (1986)-New Mutants; Art Adams-a	1	3	8
Annual 3-10 ('87-'94, 68 pgs.): 4-Evolutionary War x-over. 5-Atlantis Attacks; Captain Universe by Ditko (p) & Silver Sable stories; F.F. app. 6-Punisher back-up plus Capt. Universe by Ditko; G. Kane-a. 7-Origins of Hobgoblin I, Hobgoblin II, Green Goblin I & II & Venom; Larsen/Austin-c. 8-Part 3 of			

	GD	FN	NM-
Venom story; New Warriors x-over. 9-Bagged w/card			3.00
Super Special 1 (1995, $3.95)-flip book			4.00

WEBSPINNERS: TALES OF SPIDER-MAN
Marvel Comics: Jan, 1999 - No. 18, Jun, 2000 ($2.99/$2.50)

	GD	FN	NM-
1-DeMatteis-s/Zulli-a; back-up story w/Romita Sr. art			3.00
1-($6.95) DF Edition			7.00
2,3: 2-Two covers			2.50
4-11,13-18: 4,5-Giffen-a; Silver Surfer-c/app. 7-9-Kelly-s/Sears and Smith-a.			
10,11-Jenkins-s/Sean Phillips-a			2.50
12-($3.50) J.G. Jones-c/a; Jenkins-s			3.50

WEIRD WAR TALES
National Periodical Publ./DC Comics: Sept-Oct, 1971 - No. 124, June, 1983 (#1-5: 52 pgs.)

	GD	FN	NM-
1-Kubert-a in #1-4,7; c-1-7	23	69	340
2,3-Drucker-a: 2-Crandall-a. 3-Heath-a	10	30	130
4,5: 5-Toth-a; Heath-a	7	21	90
6,7,9,10: 6,10-Toth-a. 7-Heath-a	5	15	60
8-Neal Adams-c/a(i)	6	18	75
11-20	3	9	30
21-35	2	6	20
36-(68 pgs.)-Crandall & Kubert-r/#2; Heath-r/#3; Kubert-c			
	3	9	24
37-50: 38,39-Kubert-c	2	6	12
51-63: 58-Hitler-c/app. 60-Hindenburg-c/s	1	4	10
64-Frank Miller-a (1st DC work)	3	9	30
65-67,69-89,91,92: 89-Nazi Apes-c/s.	1	3	7
68-Frank Miller-a (2nd DC work)	2	6	22
90-Hitler app.	1	3	8
93-Intro/origin Creature Commandos	1	3	9
94-Return of War that Time Forgot; dinosaur-c/s	1	4	10
95,96,98,102-123: 98-Sphinx-c. 102-Creature Commandos battle Hitler.			
110-Origin/1st app. Medusa. 123-1st app. Captain Spaceman			
	1	3	7
97,99,100,101,124: 99-War that Time Forgot. 100-Creature Commandos in			
War that Time Forgot. 101-Intro/origin G.I. Robot	1	3	8

WEIRD WESTERN TALES (Formerly All-Star Western)
National Per. Publ./DC Comics: No. 12, June-July, 1972 - No. 70, Aug, 1980

	GD	FN	NM-
12-(52 pgs.)-3rd app. Jonah Hex; Bat Lash, Pow Wow Smith reprints; El			
Diablo by Neal Adams/Wrightson	12	36	175
13-Jonah Hex-c & 4th app.; Neal Adams-a	9	27	110
14-Toth-a	6	18	75
15-Adams-c/a; no Jonah Hex	4	12	40
16,17,19,20	4	12	40
18,29: 18-1st all Jonah Hex issue (7-8/73) & begins. 29-Origin Jonah Hex			
	5	15	55
21-28,30: Jonah Hex in all	3	9	25
31-38: Jonah Hex in all. 38-Last Jonah Hex	2	6	20

	GD	FN	NM-
39-Origin/1st app. Scalphunter & begins	2	6	18
40-47,50-69: 64-Bat Lash-c/story	1	3	8
48,49: (44 pgs.)-1st & 2nd app. Cinnamon	1	3	9
70-Last issue	2	6	12

WEIRD WORLDS (Also see Ironwolf: Fires of the Revolution)
National Periodical Publications: Aug-Sept, 1972 - No. 9, Jan-Feb, 1974; No. 10, Oct-Nov, 1974 (All 20¢ issues)

	GD	FN	NM-
1-Edgar Rice Burrough's John Carter Warlord of Mars & David Innes begin (1st DC app.); Kubert-c	2	6	22
2-4: 2-Infantino/Orlando-c. 3-Murphy Anderson-c. 4-Kaluta-a	2	6	14
5-7: .5-Kaluta-c. 7-Last John Carter.	1	4	10
8-10: 8-Iron Wolf begins by Chaykin (1st app.)	1	3	9

WELCOME BACK, KOTTER (TV) (See Limited Collectors' Edition #57 for unpublished #11)
National Periodical Publ./DC Comics: Nov, 1976 - No. 10, Mar-Apr, 1978

	GD	FN	NM-
1-Sparling-a(p)	3	9	25
2-10: 3-Estrada-a	2	6	14

WEREWOLF BY NIGHT (See Giant-Size..., Marvel Spotlight #2-4 & Power Record Comics)
Marvel Comics Group: Sept, 1972 - No. 43, Mar, 1977

	GD	FN	NM-
1-Ploog-a cont'd. from Marvel Spotlight #4	10	30	130
2	5	15	55
3-5	4	12	40
6-10	3	9	26
11-14,16-20	2	6	18
15-New origin Werewolf; Dracula-c/story cont'd from Tomb of Dracula #18; classic Ploog-c	3	9	30
21-31	2	6	12
32-Origin & 1st app. Moon Knight (8/75)	10	30	125
33-2nd app. Moon Knight	5	15	55
34,36,38-43: 35-Starlin/Wrightson-c	1	4	10
37-Moon Knight app; part Wrightson-c	1	3	15
38,39-(30¢-c variants, limited distribution)(5,7/76)	2	6	22

WEST COAST AVENGERS
Marvel Comics Group: Sept, 1984 - No. 4, Dec, 1984 (lim. series, Mando paper)

1-Origin & 1st app. W.C. Avengers (Hawkeye, Iron Man, Mockingbird & Tigra)			4.00
2-4			3.00

WEST COAST AVENGERS (Becomes Avengers West Coast #48 on)
Marvel Comics Group: Oct, 1985 - No. 47, Aug, 1989

V2#1-41			3.00
42-47: 42-Byrne-a(p)/scripts begin. 46-Byrne-c; 1st app. Great Lakes Avengers			3.00
Annual 1-3 (1986-1988): 3-Evolutionary War app.			3.00

	GD	FN	NM-

Annual 4 (1989, $2.00)-Atlantis Attacks; Byrne/Austin-a   3.00

WE3
DC Comics (Vertigo): Oct, 2004 - No. 3, May, 2005 ($2.95, limited series)

1-3-Domestic animal cyborgs: Grant Morrison-s/Frank Quitely-a   3.00

WHAT IF? (1st Series) (What If? Featuring... #13 & #?-33)
Marvel Comics Group: Feb, 1977 - No. 47, Oct, 1984; June, 1988 (All 52 pgs.)

1-Brief origin Spider-Man, Fantastic Four	3	9	30
2-Origin The Hulk retold	2	6	14
3-5: 3-Avengers. 4-Invaders. 5-Capt. America	1	4	10
6-10,13,17: 8-Daredevil; Spidey parody. 9-Origins Venus, Marvel Boy, Human Robot, 3-D Man. 13-Conan app.; John Buscema-c/a(p). 17-Ghost Rider & Son of Satan app.	1	3	9
11,12,14-16: 11-Marvel Bullpen as F.F.			6.00
18-26,29: 18-Dr. Strange. 19-Spider-Man. 22-Origin Dr. Doom retold			5.00
27-X-Men app.; Miller-c	2	6	20
28-Daredevil by Miller; Ghost Rider app.	2	6	14
30-"What If...Spider-Man's Clone Had Lived?"	1	3	9
31-Begin $1.00-c; featuring Wolverine & the Hulk; X-Men app.; death of Hulk, Wolverine & Magneto	2	6	22
32-34,36-47: 32,36-Byrne-a. 34-Marvel crew each draw themselves. 37-Old X-Men & Silver Surfer app. 39-Thor battles Conan			4.00
35-What if Elektra had lived?; Miller/Austin-a.	1	3	8
Special 1 ($1.50, 6/88)-Iron Man, F.F., Thor app.			3.00

WHAT IF...? (2nd Series)
Marvel Comics: V2#1, July, 1989 - No. 114, Nov, 1998 ($1.25/$1.50)

V2#1-...The Avengers Had Lost the Evol. War   4.00
 2-5: 2-Daredevil, Punisher app.   3.00
 6-X-Men app.   4.00
 7-Wolverine app.; Liefeld-c/a(1st on Wolvie?)   5.00
 8,10,11,13-15,17-30: 10-Punisher app. 11-Fantastic Four app. 13-Prof. X; Jim Lee-c. 14-Capt. Marvel; Lim/Austin-c.15-F.F.; Capullo-c/a(p). 17-Spider-Man/Kraven. 18-F.F. 19-Vision. 20,21-Spider-Man. 22-Silver Surfer by Lim/Austin-c/a 23-X-Men. 24-Wolverine; Punisher app. 25-(52 pgs.)-Wolverine app. 26-Punisher app. 27-Namor/F.F. 28,29-Capt. America. 29-Swipes cover to Avengers #4. 30-(52 pgs.)-F.F.   3.00
 9,12-X-Men   3.50
 16-Wolverine battles Conan; Red Sonja app.; X-Men cameo   4.00
 31-104: 31-Cosmic Spider-Man & Venom app.; Hobgoblin cameo. 32,33-Phoenix; X-Men app. 35-Fantastic Five (w/Spidey). 36-Avengers vs. Guardians of the Galaxy. 37-Wolverine. 38-Thor; Rogers-p(part). 40-Storm; X-Men app. 41-(52 pgs.)-Avengers vs. Galactus. 42-Spider-Man. 43-Wolverine. 44-Venom/Punisher. 45-Ghost Rider. 46-Cable. 47-Magneto. 49-Infinity Gauntlet w/Silver Surfer & Thanos. 50-(52 pgs.)- Foil embossed-c; "What If Hulk Had Killed Wolverine" 52-Dr. Doom. 54-Death's Head. 57-Punisher as Shield. 58-"What if Punisher Had Killed Spider-Man" w/cover similar to Amazing S-M #129. 59-...Wolverine led

Alpha Flight. 60-X-Men Wedding Album. 61-bound-in card sheet.
61,86,88-Spider-Man. 74,77,81,84,85-X-Men. 76-Last app. Watcher in title.
78-Bisley-c. 80-Hulk. 87-Sabretooth. 89-Fantastic Four. 90-Cyclops &
Havok. 91-The Hulk. 93-Wolverine. 94-Juggernaut. 95-Ghost Rider.
97-Black Knight. 100-($2.99, double-sized) Gambit and Rogue, Fantastic
Four   3.00

| 105-Spider-Girl debut; Sienkiewicz-a | 2 | 6 | 20 |

106-114: 106-Gambit. 108-Avengers. 111-Wolverine. 114-Secret Wars   2.25
#(-1) Flashback (7/97)   3.00

WHAT THE- -?!
Marvel Comics: Aug, 1988 - No. 26, 1993 ($1.25/$1.50/$2.50, semi-annual #5
on)

1-All contain parodies   3.00
2-24: 3-X-Men parody; Todd McFarlane-a. 5-Punisher/Wolverine parody;
Jim Lee-a. 6-Punisher, Wolverine, Alpha Flight. 9-Wolverine. 16-EC back-c
parody. 17-Wolverine/Punisher parody. 18-Star Trek parody w/Wolverine.
19-Punisher, Wolverine, Ghost Rider. 21-Weapon X parody. 22-Punisher/
Wolverine parody   2.25
25-Summer Special 1 (1993, $2.50)-X-Men parody   2.50
26-Fall Special ($2.50, 68 pgs.)-Spider-Ham 2099-c/story; origin Silver
Surfer; Hulk & Doomsday parody; indica reads "Winter Special."   2.50

WILDC.A.T.S: COVERT ACTION TEAMS
Image Comics (WildStorm Productions): Aug, 1992 - No. 4, Mar, 1993; No.
5, Nov, 1993 - No. 50, June, 1998 ($1.95/$2.50)

1-1st app; Jim Lee/Williams-c/a & Lee scripts begin; contains 2 trading cards
(Two diff versions of cards inside); 1st WildStorm Productions title   4.50
1-All gold foil signed edition   12.00
1-All gold foil unsigned edition   8.00
1-Newsstand edition w/o cards   3.00
1-"3-D Special"(8/97, $4.95) w/3-D glasses; variant-c by Jim Lee   5.00
2-($2.50)-Prism foil stamped-c; contains coupon for Image Comics #0 &
4 pg. preview to Portacio's Wetworks (back-up)   4.50
2-With coupon missing   2.25
2-Direct sale misprint w/o foil-c   3.00
2-Newsstand ed., no prism or coupon   2.25
3-Lee/Liefeld-c (1/93-c, 12/92 inside)   3.50
4-($2.50)-Polybagged w/Topps trading card; 1st app. Tribe by Johnson &
Stroman; Youngblood cameo   3.50
4-Variant w/red card   6.00
5-7-Jim Lee/Williams-c/a; Lee script   3.00
8-X-Men's Jean Grey & Scott Summers cameo   4.00
9-12: 10-1st app. Huntsman & Soldier; Claremont scripts begin, ends #13.
11-1st app. Savant, Tapestry & Mr. Majestic.   3.00
11-Alternate Portacio-c, see Deathblow #5   5.00
13-19,21-24: 15-James Robinson scripts begin, ends #20. 15,16-Black
Razor story. 21-Alan Moore scripts begin, end #34; intro Tao & Ladytron;
new WildC.A.T.S team forms (Mr. Majestic, Savant, Condition Red (Max
Cash), Tao & Ladytron). 22-Maguire-a   3.00

	GD	FN	NM-

20-($2.50)-Direct Market, WildStorm Rising Pt. 2 w/bound-in card 3.00
20-($1.95)-Newsstand, WildStorm Rising Part 2 2.25
25-($4.95)-Alan Moore script; wraparound foil-c. 5.00
26-49: 29-(5/96)-Fire From Heaven Pt 7; reads Apr on-c. 30-(6/96)-Fire From Heaven Pt. 13; Spartan revealed to have transplanted personality of John Colt (from Team One: WildC.A.T.S.). 31-(9/96)-Grifter rejoins team; Ladytron dies 2.50
40-($3.50)Voyager Pack bagged w/Divine Right preview 6.00
50-($3.50) Stories by Robinson/Lee, Choi & Peterson/Benes, and Moore/Charest; Charest sketchbook; Lee wraparound-c 4.00
50-Chromium cover 6.00
Annual 1 (2/98, $2.95) Robinson-s 3.00
Compendium (1993, $9.95)-r/#1-4; bagged w/#0 10.00
Sourcebook 1 (9/93, $2.50)-Foil embossed-c 2.50
Sourcebook 1-($1.95)-Newsstand ed. w/o foil embossed-c 2.25
Sourcebook 2 (11/94, $2.50)-wraparound-c 2.50
Special 1 (11/93, $3.50, 52 pgs.)-1st Travis Charest WildC.A.T.S-a 3.50
...A Gathering of Eagles (5/97, $9.95, TPB) r/#10-12 10.00
.../ Cyberforce: Killer Instinct TPB (2004, $14.95) r/#5-7 & Cyberforce V2 #1-3 15.00
...Gang War ('98, $16.95, TPB) r/#28-34 17.00
...Homecoming (8/98, $19.95, TPB) r/#21-27 20.00

WILDCATS
DC Comics (WildStorm): Mar, 1999 - No. 28, Dec, 2001 ($2.50)

1-Charest-a; six covers by Lee, Adams, Bisley, Campbell, Madureira and Ramos; Lobdell-s 3.00
1-($6.95) DF Edition; variant cover by Ramos 7.00
2-28: 2-Voodoo cover. 3-Bachalo variant-c. 5-Hitch-a/variant-c. 7-Meglia-a. 8-Phillips-a begins. 17-J.G. Jones-c. 18,19-Jim Lee-c. 20,21-Dillon-a 2.50
Annual 2000 (12/00, $3.50) Bermejo-a; Devil's Night x-over 3.50
...: Battery Park ('03, $17.95, TPB) r/#20-28; Phillips-c 18.00
... Ladytron (10/00, $5.95) Origin; Casey-s/Canete-a 6.00
... Mosaic (2/00, $3.95) Tuska-a (10 pg. back-up story) 4.00
...: Serial Boxes ('01, $14.95, TPB) r/#14-19; Phillips-c 15.00
...: Street Smart ('00, $24.95, HC) r/#1-6; Charest-c 25.00
...: Street Smart ('02, $14.95, SC) r/#1-6; Charest-c 15.00
...: Vicious Circles ('00, $14.95, TPB) r/#8-13; Phillips-c 15.00

WILDC.A.T.S TRILOGY
Image Comics (WildStorm Productions): June, 1993 - No. 3, Dec, 1993 ($1.95, lim. series)

1-($2.50)-1st app. Gen 13 (Fairchild, Burnout, Grunge, Freefall) Multi-color foil-c; Jae Lee-c/a in all 5.00
1-($1.95)-Newsstand ed. w/o foil-c 2.25
2,3-($1.95)-Jae Lee-c/a 2.25

WITCHBLADE (Also see Cyblade/Shi, Tales Of The..., & Top Cow Classics)
Image Comics (Top Cow Productions): Nov, 1995 - Present ($2.50/$2.99)

0 1 3 8

	GD	FN	NM-
1/2-Mike Turner/Marc Silvestri-c.	4	12	40
1/2 Gold Ed., 1/2 Chromium-c	4	12	40
1/2-(Vol. 2, 11/02, $2.99) Wohl-s/Ching-a/c			3.00
1-Mike Turner-a(p)	4	12	40
1,2-American Ent. Encore Ed.	1	3	7
2,3	2	6	20
4,5	2	6	16
6-9: 8-Wraparound-c. 9-Tony Daniel-a(p)	1	3	9
9-Sunset variant-c	2	6	12
9-DF variant-c	2	6	20
10-Flip book w/Darkness #0, 1st app. the Darkness	2	6	12
10-Variant-c	2	6	15
10-Gold logo	3	9	30
10-($3.95) Dynamic Forces alternate-c	1	3	8
11-15			5.00
16-19: 18,19-"Family Ties" Darkness x-over pt. 1,4			4.00
18-Face to face variant-c, 18-American Ent. Ed., 19-AE Gold Ed.			
	1	3	8
20-25: 24-Pearson, Green-a. 25-($2.95) Turner-a(p)			3.00
25 (Prism variant)			30.00
25 (Special)			15.00
26-39: 26-Green-a begins			2.50
27 (Variant)			10.00
40-49,51-53: 40-Begin Jenkins & Veitch-s/Keu Cha-a. 47-Zulli-c/a			2.50
40-Pittsburgh Convention Preview edition; B&W preview of #40			3.00
41-eWanted Chrome-c edition			5.00
49-Gold logo	1	3	8
50-($4.95) Darkness app.; Ching-a; B&W preview of Universe			5.00
54-59: 54-Black outer-c with gold foil logo; Wohl-s/Manapul-a			2.50
55-Variant Battle of the Planets Convention cover			3.00
60-74,76-80: 60-($2.99) Endgame x-over with Tomb Raider #25 & Evo #1.			
64,65-Magdalena app. 71-Kirk-a. 77-Land-c. 80-Four covers			3.00
75-($4.99) Manapul-a			5.00
...: Animated (8/03, $2.99) Magdalena & Darkness app.; Dini-s/Bone, Bullock, Cooke-a/c			3.00
...: Blood Oath (8/04, $4.99) Sara teams with Phenix & Sibila; Roux-a			5.00
...: Blood Relations TPB (2003, $12.99) r/#54-58			13.00
.../Darkchylde (7/00, $2.50) Green-s/a(p)			2.50
.../Dark Minds (6/04, $9.99) new story plus r/Dark Minds/Witchblade #1			10.00
.../Darkness: Family Ties Collected Edition (10/98, $9.95) r/#18,19 and Darkness #9,10			10.00
.../Darkness Special (12/99, $3.95) Green-c/a			4.00
...: Demon 1 (2003, $6.99) Mark Millar-s/Jae Lee-c/a			7.00
...: Distinctions (See Tales of the Witchblade)			
... Gallery (11/00, $2.95) Profile pages and pin-ups by various; Turner-c			3.00
Infinity (5/99, $3.50) Lobdell-s/Pollina-c/a			3.50
.../Lady Death (11/01, $4.95) Manapul-c/a			5.00
...: Prevailing TPB (2000, $14.95) r/#20-25; new Turner-c			15.00
...: Revelations TPB (2000, $24.95) r/#9-17; new Turner-c			25.00

	GD	FN	NM-
.../Tomb Raider #1/2 (7/00, $2.95) Covers by Turner and Cha			3.00
Wizard #500			10.00
.../Wolverine (6/04, $2.99) Basaldua-c/a; Claremont-s			3.00

WITCHING HOUR ("The ..." in later issues)
National Periodical Publ./DC Comics: Feb-Mar, 1969 - No. 85, Oct, 1978

	GD	FN	NM-
1-Toth-a, plus Neal Adams-a (2 pgs.)	12	36	170
2,6: 6-Toth-a	6	18	70
3,5-Wrightson-a; Toth-p. 3-Last 12¢ issue	6	18	75
4,7-12: Toth-a in all. 8-Toth, Neal Adams-a	4	12	45
13-Neal Adams-c/a, 2pgs.	4	12	50
14-Williamson/Garzon, Jones-a; N. Adams-c	5	15	55
15	3	9	26
16-21-(52 pg. Giants)	3	9	32
22-37,39,40	2	6	18
38-(100 pgs.)	5	15	55
41-60	2	6	14
61-83,85	1	4	10
84-(44 pgs.)	2	6	12

WOLVERINE (See Alpha Flight, Daredevil #196, 249, Ghost Rider; Wolverine; Punisher, Havok &..., Incredible Hulk #180, Incredible Hulk &..., Kitty Pryde And..., Marvel Comics Presents, New Avengers, Power Pack, Punisher and..., Spider-Man vs... & X-Men #94)

WOLVERINE (See Incredible Hulk #180 for 1st app.)
Marvel Comics Group: Sept, 1982 - No. 4, Dec, 1982 (limited series)

	GD	FN	NM-
1-Frank Miller-c/a(p) in all	6	18	65
2-4	4	12	50
Trade paperback 1(7/87, $4.95)-Reprints #1-4 with new Miller-c.			
	2	6	18
Trade paperback nn (2nd printing, $9.95)-r/#1-4	2	6	12

WOLVERINE
Marvel Comics: Nov, 1988 - No. 189, June, 2003
($1.50/$1.75/$1.95/$1.99/$2.25)

	GD	FN	NM-
1	4	12	45
2	2	6	22
3-5: 4-BWS back-c	2	6	16
6-9: 6-McFarlane back-c. 7,8-Hulk app.	1	4	10
10-1st battle with Sabretooth (before Wolverine had his claws)			
	3	9	30
11-16: 11-New costume	1	3	8
17-20: 17-Byrne-c/a(p) begins, ends #23	1	3	7
21-30: 24,25,27-Jim Lee-c. 26-Begin $1.75-c			5.00
31-40,44,47			4.00
41-Sabretooth claims to be Wolverine's father; Cable cameo			6.00
41-Gold 2nd printing ($1.75)			2.50
42-Sabretooth, Cable & Nick Fury app.; Sabretooth proven not to be Wolverine's father	1	3	8
42-Gold ink 2nd printing ($1.75)			2.50
43-Sabretooth cameo (2 panels); saga ends			5.00

	GD	FN	NM-

45,46-Sabretooth-c/stories — 5.00

48-51: 48,49-Sabretooth app. 48-Begin 3 part Weapon X sequel. 50-(64 pgs.)-Die cut-c; Wolverine back to old yellow costume; Forge, Cyclops, Jubilee, Jean Grey & Nick Fury app. 51-Sabretooth-c & app. — 4.00

52-74,76-80: 54-Shatterstar (from X-Force) app. 55-Gambit, Jubilee, Sunfire-c/story. 55-57,73-Gambit app. 57-Mariko Yashida dies (Late 7/92). 58,59-Terror, Inc. x-over. 60-64-Sabretooth storyline (60,62,64-c) — 4.00

75-($3.95, 68 pgs.)-Wolverine hologram on-c — 5.00

81-84,86: 81-bound-in card sheet — 3.00

85-($2.50)-Newsstand edition — 3.00

85-($3.50)-Collectors edition — 5.00

87-90 ($1.95)-Deluxe edition — 3.00

87-90 ($1.50)-Regular edition — 2.50

91-99,101-114: 91-Return from "Age of Apocalypse," 93-Juggernaut app. 94-Gen X app. 101-104-Elektra app. 104-Origin of Onslaught. 105-Onslaught x-over. 110-Shaman-c/app. 114-Alternate-c — 3.00

100 ($3.95)-Hologram-c; Wolverine loses humanity | 1 | 3 | 9

100 ($2.95)-Regular-c. — 4.00

115-124: 115- Operation Zero Tolerance — 2.50

125-($2.99) Wraparound-c; Viper secret — 3.00

125-($6.95) Jae Lee variant-c — 7.00

126-144: 126,127-Sabretooth-c/app. 128-Sabretooth & Shadowcat app.; Platt-a. 129-Wendigo-c/app. 131-Initial printing contained lettering error. 133-Begin Larsen-s/Matsuda-a. 138-Galactus-c/app. 139-Cable app.; Yu-a. 142,143-Alpha Flight app. — 2.50

145-($2.99) 25th Anniversary issue; Hulk and Sabretooth app. — 3.00

145-($3.99) Foil enhanced cover (also see Promotional section for Nabisco mail-in ed.) — 4.00

146-149: 147-Apocalypse: The Twelve; Angel-c/app. 149-Nova-c/app. — 2.50

150-($2.99) Steve Skroce-s/a — 3.00

151-174,176-182,184-189: 151-Begin $2.25-c. 154,155-Liefeld-s/a. 156-Churchill-a. 159-Chen-a begins. 160-Sabretooth app. 163-Texeira-a(p). 167-BWS-c. 172,173-Alpha Flight app. 176-Colossus app. 185,186-Punisher app. — 2.50

175,183-($3.50) 175-Sabretooth app. — 3.50

#(-1) Flashback (7/97) Logan meets Col. Fury; Nord-a — 2.50

Annual nn (1990, $4.50, squarebound, 52 pgs.)-The Jungle Adventure; Simonson scripts; Mignola-c/a — 5.00

Annual 2 (12/90, $4.95, squarebound, 52 pgs.)-Bloodlust — 5.00

Annual nn (#3, 8/91, $5.95, 68 pgs.)-Rahne of Terror; Cable & The New Mutants app.; Andy Kubert-c/a (2nd print exists) — 6.00

Annual '95 (1995, $3.95) — 4.00

Annual '96 (1996, $2.95)- Wraparound-c; Silver Samurai, Yukio, and Red Ronin app. — 3.00

Annual '97 ($2.99) - Wraparound-c — 3.00

Annual 1999, 2000 ($3.50) : 1999-Deadpool app. — 3.50

Annual 2001 ($2.99) - Tieri-s; JH Williams-c — 3.00

...Battles The Incredible Hulk nn (1989, $4.95, squarebound, 52 pg.) r/Incr. Hulk #180,181 — 5.00

	GD	FN	NM-

Best of Wolverine Vol. 1 HC (2004, $29.99) oversized reprints of Hulk #181, mini-series #1-4, Capt. America Ann, #8, Uncanny X-Men #205 & Marvel Comics Presents #72-84   30.00

...Black Rio (11/98, $5.99)-Casey-s/Oscar Jimenez-a   6.00

...Blood Debt TPB (7/01, $12.95)-r/#150-153; Skroce-c   13.00

...Blood Hungry nn (1993, $6.95, 68 pgs.)-Kieth-r/Marvel Comics Presents #85-92 w/ new Kieth-c   7.00

...: Bloody Choices nn (1993, $7.95, 68 pgs.)-r/Graphic Novel; Nick Fury app.   8.00

... Cable Guts and Glory (10/99, $5.99) Platt-a   6.00

.../Deadpool: Weapon X TPB (7/02, $21.99)-r/#162-166 & Deadpool #57-60   22.00

... Doombringer (11/97, $5.99)-Silver Samurai-c/app.   6.00

... Evilution (9/94, $5.95)   6.00

...: Global Jeopardy 1 (12/93, $2.95, one-shot)-Embossed-c; Sub-Mariner, Zabu, Ka-Zar, Shanna & Wolverine app.; produced in cooperation with World Wildlife Fund   3.00

...:Inner Fury nn (1992, $5.95, 52 pgs.)-Sienkiewicz-c/a   6.00

...: Judgment Night (2000, $3.99) Shi app.; Battlebook   4.00

...: Killing (9/93)-Kent Williams-a   6.00

...: Knight of Terra (1995, $6.95)-Ostrander script   7.00

... Legends Vol. 2: Meltdown (2003, $19.99) r/Havok & Wolverine: Meltdown #1-4   20.00

... Legends Vol. 3 (2003, $12.99) r/#181-186   13.00

... Legends Vol. 4,5: 4-(See Wolverine: Xisle). 5-(See Wolverine: Snikt!)

... Legends Vol. 6: Marc Silvestri Book 1 (2004, $19.99) r/#31-34, 41-42,48-50   20.00

.../ Nick Fury: The Scorpio Connection Hardcover (1989, $16.95)   25.00

.../ Nick Fury: The Scorpio Connection Softcover(1990, $12.95)   15.00

...: Not Dead Yet (12/98, $14.95, TPB)-r/#119-122   15.00

...: Save The Tiger 1 (7/92, $2.95, 84 pgs.)-Reprints Wolverine stories from Marvel Comics Presents #1-10 w/new Kieth-c   3.00

...Scorpio Rising ($5.95, prestige format, one-shot)   6.00

.../Shi: Dark Night of Judgment (Crusade Comics, 2000, $2.99) Tucci-a   3.00

...Triumphs And Tragedies-(1995, $16.95, trade paperback)-r/Uncanny X-Men #109,172,173, Wolverine limited series #4, & Wolverine #41,42,75   17.00

...Typhoid's Kiss (6/94, $6.95)-r/Wolverine stories from Marvel Comics Presents #109-116   7.00

...Vs. Spider-Man 1 (3/95, $2.50) -r/Marvel Comics Presents #48-50   2.50

.../Witchblade 1 (3/97, $2.95) Devil's Reign Pt. 5   4.00

Wizard #1/2 (1997) Joe Phillips-a(p)   10.00

WOLVERINE (Volume 3)
Marvel Comics: July, 2003 - Present ($2.25)

1-Rucka-s/Robertson-a   3.00

2-19: 6-Nightcrawler app. 13-16-Sabretooth app.   2.25

20-Millar-s/Romita, Jr.-a begin, Elektra app.   3.00

21,22: 21-Elektra-c/app.   2.25

...Vol. 1: The Brotherhood (2003, $12.99) r/#1-6   13.00

...Vol. 2: Coyote Crossing (2004, $11.99) r/#7-11   12.00

	GD	FN	NM-

WOLVERINE: THE ORIGIN
Marvel Comics: Nov, 2001 - No. 6, July, 2002 ($3.50, limited series)

1-Origin of Logan; Jenkins-s/Andy Kubert-a; Quesada-c			40.00
1-DF edition			60.00
2			15.00
3			9.00
4-6			5.00
HC (3/02, $34.95) r/#1-6; dust jacket; sketch pages and treatments			35.00
SC (2002, $14.95) r/#1-6; afterwords by Jemas and Quesada			15.00

WONDER WOMAN
National Per. Pub./DC Comics: No. 85, Oct, 1956 - No. 329, Feb, 1986

	GD	FN	NM-
85-90: 85-1st S.A. issue. 89-Flying saucer-c/story	33	99	360
91-94,96,97,99: 97-Last H. G. Peter-a	27	81	285
95-A-Bomb-c	28	84	300
98-New origin & new art team (Andru & Esposito) begin (5/58); origin W.W. id w/new facts	30	90	325
100-(8/58)	30	90	325
101-104,106,108-110	23	69	250
105-(Scarce, 4/59)-W. W.'s secret origin; W. W. appears as girl (no costume yet) (called Wonder Girl)	100	300	1300
107-1st advs. of Wonder Girl; 1st Merboy; tells how Wonder Woman won her costume	33	99	360
111-120	19	57	200
121-126: 121-1st app. Wonder Woman Family. 122-1st app. Wonder Tot. 126-Last 10¢ issue	15	45	160
127-130: 128-Origin The Invisible Plane retold. 129-2nd app. Wonder Woman Family (#133 is 3rd app.)	10	30	125
131-150: 132-Flying saucer-c	8	24	100
151-155,157,158,160-170 (1967): 151-Wonder Girl solo issue	7	21	80
156-(8/65)-Early mention of a comic book shop & comic collecting; mentions DCs selling for $100 a copy	7	21	90
159-Origin retold (1/66); 1st S.A. origin?	9	27	120
171-176	5	15	60
177-W. Woman/Supergirl battle	7	21	85
178-1st new W. Woman	7	21	90
179-Wears no costume to issue #203.	6	18	65
180-195: 180-Death of Steve Trevor. 195-Wood inks	4	12	45
196 (52 pgs.)-Origin-r/All-Star #8 (6 out of 9 pgs.)	4	12	50
197,198 (52 pgs.)-Reprints	4	12	50
199-Jeff Jones painted-c; 52 pgs.	6	18	75
200 (5-6/72)-Jeff Jones-c; 52 pgs.	7	21	85
201,202-Catwoman app. 202-Fafhrd & The Grey Mouser debut.	3	9	32
203,205-210,212: 212-The Cavalier app.	2	6	22
204-Return to old costume; death of I Ching.	3	9	28
211,214-(100 pgs.)	6	18	75
213,215,216,218-220: 220-N. Adams assist	2	6	20

	GD	FN	NM-
217: (68 pgs.)	3	9	32
221,222,224-227,229,230,233-236,238-240	2	6	14
223,228,231,232,237,241,248: 223-Steve Trevor revived as Steve Howard & learns W.W.'s I.D. 228-Both Wonder Women team up & new World War II stories begin, end #243. 231,232: JSA app. 237-Origin retold. 241-Intro Bouncer; Spectre app. 248-Steve Trevor Howard dies (44 pgs.)	2	6	16
242-246,252-266,269,270: 243-Both W. Women team-up again. 269-Last Wood a(i) for DC? (7/80)	1	3	8
247,249-251,271: 247,249 (44 pgs.). 249-Hawkgirl app. 250-Origin/1st app. Orana, the new W. Woman. 251-Orana dies. 271-Huntress & 3rd Life of Steve Trevor begin	1	3	9
250-252,255-262,264-(Whitman variants, low print run, no issue # on cover)	2	6	16
267,268-Re-intro Animal Man (5/80 & 6/80)	1	4	10
272-280,284-286,289,290,294-299,301-325			5.00
281-283: Joker-c/stories in Huntress back-ups	1	3	9
287,288,291-293: 287-New Teen Titans x-over. 288-New costume & logo. 291-293-Three part epic with Super-Heroines			6.00
300-($1.50, 76 pgs.)-Anniv. issue; Giffen-a; New Teen Titans, Bronze Age Sandman, JLA & G.A. Wonder Woman app.; 1st app. Lyta Trevor who becomes Fury in All-Star Squadron #25; G.A. Wonder Woman & Steve Trevor revealed as married			6.00
326-328			6.00
329 (Double size)-S.A. W.W. & Steve Trevor wed	2	6	12

WONDER WOMAN

DC Comics: Feb, 1987 - Present (75¢/$1.00/$1.25/$1.95/$1.99/$2.25)

	GD	FN	NM-
0-(10/94) Zero Hour; released between #90 & #91	1	3	8
1-New origin; Perez-c/a begins	1	3	7
2-5			5.00
6-20: 9-Origin Cheetah. 12,13-Millennium x-over. 18,26-Free 16 pg. story			4.00
21-49: 24-Last Perez-a; scripts continue thru #62			3.00
50-($1.50, 52 pgs.)-New Titans, Justice League			4.00
51-62: Perez scripts. 60-Vs. Lobo; last Perez-c. 62-Last $1.00-c			3.00
63-New direction & Bolland-c begin; Deathstroke story continued from W. W. Special #1			4.00
64-84			2.50
85-1st Deodato-a; ends #100	2	6	12
86-88: 88-Superman-c & app.			5.00
89-97: 90-(9/94)-1st Artemis. 91-(11/94). 93-Hawkman app. 96-Joker-c			4.00
98,99			3.00
100 ($2.95, Newsstand)-Death of Artemis; Bolland-c ends.			4.00
100 ($3.95, Direct Market)-Death of Artemis; foil-c.			6.00
101-119, 121-125: 101-Begin $1.95-c; Byrne-c/a/scripts begin. 101-104-Darkseid app. 105-Phantom Stranger cameo. 106-108-Phantom Stranger & Demon app. 107,108-Arion app. 111-1st app. new Wonder Girl. 111,112-Vs.Doomsday. 112-Superman app. 113-Wonder Girl-c/app; Sugar & Spike app.			2.50

	GD	FN	NM-

120 ($2.95)-Perez-c   3.00
126-149: 128-Hippolyta becomes new W.W. 130-133-Flash (Jay Garrick) &
    JSA app. 136-Diana returns to W.W. role; last Byrne issue. 137-Priest-s.
    139-Luke-s/Paquette-a begin; Hughes-c thru #146   2.50
150-($2.95) Hughes-c/Clark-a; Zauriel app.   3.00
151-158-Hughes-c. 153-Superboy app.   2.25
159-163: 159-Begin $2.25-c. 160,161-Clayface app. 162,163-Aquaman app.
    2.25
164-171: Phil Jimenez-s/a begin; Hughes-c; Batman app. 168,169-Pérez
    co-plot. 169-Wraparound-c.170-Lois Lane-c/app.   2.25
172-Our Worlds at War; Hippolyta killed   3.00
173,174: 173-Our Worlds at War; Darkseid app. 174-Every DC heroine app.
    2.25
175-($3.50) Joker: Last Laugh; JLA app.; Jim Lee-c   3.50
176-199: 177-Paradise Island returns. 184,185-Hippolyta-c/app.; Hughes-c.
    186-Cheetah app. 189-Simonson-s/Ordway-a begin. 190-Diana's new look.
    195-Rucka-s/Drew Johnson-a begin. 197-Flash-c/app. 198,199-Noto-c
    2.25
200-($3.95) back-up stories in 1940s and 1960s styles; pin-ups by various
    4.00
201-210: 203,204-Batman-c/app. 204-Matt Wagner-c   2.25
#1,000,000 (11/98) 853rd Century x-over; Deodato-c   3.00
Annual 1,2: 1 ('88, $1.50)-Art Adams-a. 2 ('89, $2.00, 68 pgs.)-All women
    artists issue; Perez-c(i)/a.   4.00
Annual 3 (1992, $2.50, 68 pgs.)-Quesada-c(p)   3.00
Annual 4 (1995, $3.50)-Year One   3.50
Annual 5 (1996, $2.95)-Legends of the Dead Earth story; Byrne scripts;
    Cockrum-a   3.00
Annual 6 (1997, $3.95)-Pulp Heroes   4.00
Annual 7,8 ('98,'99, $2.95)-7-Ghosts; Wrightson-c. 8-JLApe, A.Adams-c   3.00
...: Challenge of the Gods TPB ('04, $19.95) r/#8-14; Pérez-s/a   20.00
...Donna Troy (6/98, $1.95) Girlfrenzy; Jimenez-a   2.50
...: Down To Earth TPB (2004, $14.95) r/#195-200; Greg Land-c   15.00
... 80-Page Giant 1 (2002, $4.95) reprints in format of 1960s' 80-Page Giants
    5.00
Gallery (1996, $3.50)-Bolland-c; pin-ups by various   4.00
...: Gods and Mortals TPB ('04, $19.95) r/#1-7; Pérez-a   20.00
...: Gods of Gotham TPB ('01, $5.95) r/#164-167; Jimenez-s/a   6.00
Lifelines TPB ('98, $9.95) r/#106-112; Byrne-c/a   10.00
...: Our Worlds at War (10/01, $2.95) History of the Amazons; Jae Lee-c   3.00
...: Paradise Found TPB ('03, $14.95) r/#171-177, Secret Files #3;
    Jimenez-s/a   15.00
...: Paradise Lost TPB ('02, $14.95) r/#164-170; Jimenez-s/a   15.00
Plus 1 (1/97, $2.95)-Jesse Quick-c/app.   3.00
Second Genesis TPB (1997, $9.95)-r/#101-105   10.00
Secret Files 1-3 (3/98, 7/99, 5/02; $4.95)   5.00
Special 1 (1992, $1.75, 52 pgs.)-Deathstroke-c/story continued in Wonder
    Woman #63   4.00
...: The Blue Amazon (2003, $6.95) Elseworlds; McKeever-a   7.00

	GD	FN	NM-

The Challenge Of Artemis TPB (1996, $9.95)-r/#94-100; Deodato-c/a ... 10.00
...: The Once and Future Story (1998, $4.95) Trina Robbins-s/Doran & Guice-a ... 5.00

WONDER WOMAN: SPIRIT OF TRUTH
DC Comics: Nov, 2001 ($9.95, treasury size, one-shot)

nn-Painted art by Alex Ross; story by Alex Ross and Paul Dini ... 10.00

WONDER WOMAN: THE HIKETEIA
DC Comics: 2002 ($24.95, hardcover, one-shot)

nn-Wonder Woman battles Batman; Greg Rucka-s/J.G. Jones-a ... 25.00
Softcover (2003, $17.95) ... 18.00

WORLD'S FINEST COMICS
National Per. Publ./DC Comics: No. 84, Oct, 1956 - No. 323, Jan, 1986

	GD	FN	NM-
84-90: 84-1st S.A. issue. 88-1st Joker/Luthor team-up. 89-2nd Batmen of All Nations (aka Club of Heroes). 90-Batwoman's 1st app. in World's Finest (10/57, 3rd app. anywhere) plus-c app.	29	87	435
91-93,95-99: 96-99-Kirby Green Arrow. 99-Robot-c	22	66	320
94-Origin Superman/Batman team retold	53	159	900
100 (3/59)	36	108	585
101-110: 102-Tommy Tomorrow begins, ends #124	15	45	210
111-121: 111-1st app. The Clock King. 113-Intro. Miss Arrowette in Green Arrow; 1st Bat-Mite/Mr. Mxyzptlk team-up (11/60). 117-Batwoman-c. 121-Last 10¢ issue	12	36	175
122-128: 123-2nd Bat-Mite/Mr. Mxyzptlk team-up (2/62). 125-Aquaman begins (5/62), ends #139 (Aquaman #1 is dated 1-2/62)	10	30	125
129-Joker/Luthor team-up-c/story	11	33	150
130-142: 135-Last Dick Sprang story. 140-Last Green Arrow. 142-Origin The Composite Superman (villain); Legion app.	8	24	95
143-150: 143-1st Mailbag. 144-Clayface/Brainiac team-up; last Clayface until Action #443	6	18	75
151-153,155,157-160: 156-Intro of Bizarro Batman. 157-2nd Super Sons story; last app. Kathy Kane (Bat-Woman) until Batman Family #10	6	18	65
154-1st Super Sons story; last Bat-Woman in costume until Batman Family #10	6	18	75
156-1st Bizarro Batman; Joker-c/story	10	30	140
161,170 (80-Pg. Giants G-28,G-40)	7	21	80
162-165,167,168,171,172: 168,172-Adult Legion app.	4	12	50
166-Joker-c/story	5	15	60
169-3rd app. new Batgirl(9/67)(cover and 1 panel cameo); 3rd Bat-Mite/Mr. Mxyzptlk team-up	5	15	55
173-('68)-1st S.A. app. Two-Face as Batman becomes Two-Face in story	9	27	120
174-Adams-c	5	15	55
175,176-Neal Adams-c/a; both reprint J'onn J'onzz origin/Detective #225,226	5	15	60
177-Joker/Luthor team-up-c/story	5	15	55

	GD	FN	NM-

178,180,182,183,185,186: Adams-c on all. 182-Silent Knight-r/Brave & Bold
   #6. 185-Last 12¢ issue. 186-Johnny Quick-r   4   12   42

179-(80 Page Giant G-52) -Adams-c; r/#94   6   18   70

181,184,187: 187-Green Arrow origin-r by Kirby (Adv. #256)
                                                 4   12   38

188,197:(Giants G-64,G-76; 64 pages)   6   18   65

189-196: 190-193-Robin-r   3   9   30

198,199-3rd Superman/Flash race (see Flash #175 & Superman #199).
   199-Adams-c   9   27   115

200-Adams-c   3   10   35

201-203: 203-Last 15¢ issue.   3   9   26

204,205-(52 pgs.) Adams-c: 204-Wonder Woman app. 205-Shining Knight-r
   (6 pgs.) by Frazetta/Adv. #153; Teen Titans x-over   3   9   30

206 (Giant G-88, 64 pgs.)   5   15   55

207,212-(52 pgs.)   3   9   30

208-211(25¢-c) Adams-c: 208-(52 pgs.) Origin Robotman-r/Det. #138.
   209-211-(52 pgs.)   3   9   32

213,214,216-222,229: 217-Metamorpho begins, ends #220; Batman/
   Superman team-ups resume. 229-r/origin Superman-Batman team
                                                   2   6   16

215-Intro. Batman Jr. & Superman Jr.   3   9   30

223-228-(100 pgs.). 223-N. Adams-r. 223-Deadman origin. 226-N. Adams,
   S&K, Toth-r; Manhunter part origin-r/Det. #225,226. 227-Deadman app.
                                                   4   12   50

230-(68 pgs.)   3   9   28

231-243,247,248: 242-Super Sons. 248-Last Vigilante
                                                   2   6   12

244-246-Adams-c: 244-$1.00, 84 pg. issues begin; Green Arrow, Black
   Canary, Wonder Woman, Vigilante begin; 246-Death of Stuff in Vigilante;
   origin Vigilante retold   2   6   20

249-252 (84 pgs.) Ditko-a: 249-The Creeper begins by Ditko, 84 pgs.
   250-The Creeper origin retold by Ditko. 252-Last 84 pg. issue
                                                   2   6   20

253-257,259-265: 253-Capt. Marvel begins; 68 pgs. begin, end #265.
   255-Last Creeper. 256-Hawkman begins. 257-Black Lightning begins.
   263-Super Sons. 264-Clay Face app.   2   6   12

258-Adams-c   2   6   14

266-270,272-282-(52 pgs.). 267-Challengers of the Unknown app.;
   3 Lt. Marvels return. 268-Capt. Marvel Jr. origin retold. 274-Zatanna
   begins. 279, 280-Capt. Marvel Jr. & Kid Eternity learn they are brothers
                                                   1   4   10

271-(52pgs.) Origin Superman/Batman team retold   2   6   12

283-299: 284-Legion app.   1   3   7

300-($1.25, 52pgs.)-Justice League of America, New Teen Titans & The
   Outsiders app.; Perez-a (3 pgs.)   1   3   8

301-322: 304-Origin Null and Void. 309,319-Free 16 pg. story in each
   (309-Flash Force 2000, 319-Mask preview)   3.00

323-Last issue   6.00

XENA: WARRIOR PRINCESS (TV)

	GD	FN	NM-

Topps Comics: Aug, 1997 - No. 0, Oct, 1997 ($2.95)

1-Two stories by various; J. Scott Campbell-c	1	4	10
1,2-Photo-c	1	4	10
2-Stevens-c			6.00
0-(10/97)-Lopresti-c, 0-(10/97)-Photo-c	1	3	8
...First Appearance Collection ('97, $9.95) r/Hercules the Legendary Journeys #3-5 and 5-page story from TV Guide			10.00

XENA: WARRIOR PRINCESS (TV)
Dark Horse Comics: Sept, 1999 - No. 14, Oct, 2000 ($2.95/$2.99)

1-14: 1-Mignola-c and photo-c. 2,3-Bradstreet-c & photo-c			3.00

X-FACTOR (Also see The Avengers #263, Fantastic Four #286 and Mutant X)
Marvel Comics Group: Feb, 1986 - No. 149, Sept, 1998

1-($1.25, 52 pgs)-Story recaps 1st app. from Avengers #263; story cont'd from F.F. #286; return of original X-Men (now X-Factor); Guice/Layton-a; Baby Nathan app. (2nd after X-Men #201)			6.00
2-4			4.00
5-1st brief app. Apocalypse (2 pages)			4.00
6-1st full app. Apocalypse	1	4	10
7-10: 10-Sabretooth app. (11/86, 3 pgs.) cont'd in X-Men #212; 1st app. in an X-Men comic book			4.00
11-22: 13-Baby Nathan app. in flashback. 14-Cyclops vs. The Master Mold. 15-Intro wingless Angel			3.00
23-1st brief app. Archangel (2 pages)	1	3	7
24-1st full app. Archangel (now in Uncanny X-Men); Fall Of The Mutants begins; origin Apocalypse	1	3	9
25,26: Fall Of The Mutants; 26-New outfits			3.00
27-39,41-83,87-91,93-99,101: 35-Origin Cyclops. 60-X-Tinction Agenda x-over; New Mutants (w/Cable) x-over in #60-62; Wolverine in #62. 62-Jim Lee-c. 68-Baby Nathan is sent into future to save his life. 69,70-X-Men(w/Wolverine) x-over. 71-New team begins (Havok, Polaris, Strong Guy, Wolfsbane & Madrox); Stroman-c/a begins			2.50
40-Rob Liefield-c/a (4/89, 1st at Marvel?)			3.00
84-86 -Jae Lee a(p); 85,86-Jae Lee-c. Polybagged with trading card in each; X-Cutioner's Song x-overs.			3.00
92-($3.50, 68 pgs.)-Wraparound-c by Quesada w/Havok hologram on-c; begin X-Men 30th anniversary issues; Quesada-a.			5.00
92-2nd printing			2.25
100-($2.95, 52 pgs.)-Embossed foil-c; Multiple Man dies.			5.00
100-($1.75, 52 pgs.)-Regular edition			2.25
102-105,107: 102-bound-in card sheet			2.25
106-($2.00)-Newsstand edition			2.25
106-($2.95)-Collectors edition			3.00
108-124,126-148: 112-Return from Age of Apocalypse. 115-card insert. 119-123-Sabretooth app. 123-Hound app. 124-w/Onslaught Update. 126-Onslaught x-over; Beast vs. Dark Beast. 128-w/card insert; return of Multiple Man. 130-Assassination of Grayson Creed. 146,148-Moder-a			2.25
125-($2.95)-"Onslaught"; Post app.; return of Havok			4.00
149-Last issue			3.00

	GD	FN	NM-

#(-1) Flashback (7/97) Matsuda-a — 2.25
Annual 1-9: 1-(10/86-'94, 68 pgs.) 3-Evolutionary War x-over. 4-Atlantis
  Attacks; Byrne/Simonson-a; Byrne-c. 5-Fantastic Four, New Mutants x-over;
  Keown 2 pg. pin-up. 6-New Warriors app.; 5th app. X-Force cont'd from
  X-Men Annual #15. 7-1st Quesada-a(p) on X-Factor plus-c(p). 8-Bagged
  w/trading card. 9-Austin-a(i) — 3.00
...Prisoner of Love (1990, $4.95, 52 pgs.)-Starlin scripts; Guice-a — 5.00

X-FILES, THE (TV)
Topps Comics: Jan, 1995 - No. 41, July, 1998 ($2.50)

-2(9/96)-Black-c; r/X-Files Magazine #1&2 | 1 | 4 | 10
-1(9/96)-Silver-c; r/Hero Illustrated Giveaway | 1 | 4 | 10
0-($3.95)-Adapts pilot episode | | | 4.00
0-"Mulder" variant-c | 1 | 3 | 8
0-"Scully" variant-c | 1 | 3 | 8
1/2-W/certificate | 3 | 9 | 25
1-New stories based on the TV show; direct market & newsstand editions;
  Miran Kim-c on all | 3 | 9 | 30
2 | 2 | 6 | 18
3,4 | 1 | 3 | 8
5-10 | | | 4.00
11-41: 11-Begin $2.95-c. 21-W/bound-in card. 40,41-Reg. & photo-c | | | 3.00
Annual 1,2 ($3.95) | | | 4.00
Afterflight TPB ($5.95) Art by Thompson, Saviuk, Kim | | | 6.00
Collection 1 TPB ($19.95)-r/#1-6. | | | 20.00
Collection 2 TPB ($19.95)-r/#7-12, Annual #1. | | | 20.00
...Fight the Future ('98, $5.95) Movie adaptation | | | 6.00
Hero Illustrated Giveaway | 2 | 6 | 15
Special Edition 1-5 ($4.95)-r/#1-3, 4-6, 7-9, 10-12, 13, Annual 1 | | | 5.00
Star Wars Galaxy Magazine Giveaway (B&W) | 1 | 4 | 10
Trade paperback ($19.95) | | | 20.00

X-FORCE (Becomes X-Statix) (Also see The New Mutants #100)
Marvel Comics: Aug, 1991 - No. 129, Aug, 2002 ($1.00-$2.25)

1-($1.50, 52 pgs.)-Polybagged with 1 of 5 diff. Marvel Universe trading cards
  inside (1 each); 6th app. of X-Force; Liefeld-c/a begins | | | 4.00
1-1st printing with Cable trading card inside | | | 5.00
1-2nd printing; metallic ink-c (no bag or card) | | | 2.25
2-4: 2-Deadpool-c/story. 3-New Brotherhood of Evil Mutants app.
  4-Spider-Man x-over; cont'd from Spider-Man #16; reads sideways | | | 3.00
5-10: 6-Last $1.00-c. 7,9-Weapon X back-ups. 8-Intro The Wild Pack (Cable,
  Kane, Domino, Hammer, G.W. Bridge, & Grizzly); Liefeld-c/a (4); Mignola-a.
  10-Weapon X full-length story (part 3). 11-1st Weapon Prime;
  Deadpool-c/story | | | 3.00
11-15,19-24,26-33: 15-Cable leaves X-Force | | | 2.50
16-18-Polybagged w/trading card in each; X-Cutioner's Song x-overs | | | 3.00
25-($3.50, 52 pgs.)-Wraparound-c w/Cable hologram on-c; Cable returns | | | 4.00
34-37,39-45: 34-bound-in card sheet | | | 2.50
38,40-43: 38-($2.00)-Newsstand edition. 40-43 ($1.95)-Deluxe edition | | | 2.25

	GD	FN	NM-

38-($2.95)-Collectors edition (prismatic) 5.00
44-49,51-67: 44-Return from Age of Apocalypse. 45-Sabretooth app.
   49-Sebastian Shaw app. 52-Blob app., Onslaught cameo.
   55-Vs. S.H.I.E.L.D. 56-Deadpool app. 57-Mr. Sinister & X-Man-c/app.
   57,58-Onslaught x-over. 59-W/card insert; return of Longshot.
   60-Dr. Strange 2.50
50 ($3.95)-Gatefold wrap-around foil-c 4.00
50 ($3.95)-Liefeld variant-c 5.00
68-74: 68-Operation Zero Tolerance 2.50
75,100-($2.99): 75-Cannonball-c/app. 3.00
76-99,101,102: 81-Pollina poster. 95-Magneto-c. 102-Ellis-s/Portacio-a 2.25
103-115: 103-Begin $2.25-c; Portacio-a thru #106. 115-Death of old team 2.25
116-New team debuts; Allred-c/a; Milligan-s; no Comics Code stamp on-c 4.00
117-129: 117-Intro. Mr. Sensitive. 120-Wolverine-c/app. 123-'Nuff Said issue.
   124-Darwyn Cooke-a/c. 128-Death of U-Go Girl. 129-Fregredo-a .. 2.25
#(-1) Flashback (7/97) story of John Proudstar; Pollina-a 2.25
Annual 1-3 ('92-'94, 68 pgs.)-1-1st Greg Capullo-a(p) on X-Force.
   2-Polybagged w/trading card; intro X-Treme & Neurtap 3.00
...And Cable '95 (12/95, $3.95)-Impossible Man app. 4.00
...And Cable '96, ...'97 ('96, 7/97) -'96-Wraparound-c 3.00
...And Spider-Man: Sabotage nn (11/92, $6.95)-Reprints X-Force #3,4 &
   Spider-Man #16 .... 7.00
.../ Champions '98 ($3.50) 3.50
Annual 99 ($3.50) 3.50
...: Famous, Mutant & Mortal HC (2003, $29.99) oversized r/#116-129;
   foreward by Milligan; gallery of covers and pin-ups; script for #123 30.00
...New Beginnings TPB (10/01, $14.95) r/#116-120 .... 15.00
...Rough Cut ($2.99) Pencil pages and script for #102 .... 3.00
...Youngblood (8/96, $4.95)-Platt-c 5.00

X-MAN (Also see X-Men Omega & X-Men Prime)
Marvel Comics: Mar, 1995 - No. 75, May, 2001 ($1.95/$1.99/$2.25)

1-Age of Apocalypse 5.00
1-2nd print 2.25
2-4,25: 25-($2.99)-Wraparound-c 3.00
5-24, 26-28: 5-Post Age of Apocalypse stories begin. 5-7-Madelyne Pryor
   app. 10-Professor X app. 12-vs. Excalibur. 13-Marauders, Cable app.
   14-Vs. Cable; Onslaught app. 15-17-Vs. Holocaust. 17-w/Onslaught
   Update. 18,19-Onslaught x-over. 19-X-Force-c/app; Marauders app.
   20-Abomination-c/app.; w/card insert. 23-Bishop app. 24-Spider-Man,
   Morbius-c/app. 27-Re-appearance of Aurora(Alpha Flight) 2.50
29-49,51-62: 29-Operation Zero Tolerance. 37,38-Spider-Man-c/app.
   56-Spider-Man app. 2.50
50-($2.99) Crossover with Generation X #50 .... 3.00
63-74: 63-Ellis & Grant-s/Olivetti-a begins. 64-Begin $2.25-c 2.25
75 ($2.99) Final issue; Alcatena-a 3.00
#(-1) Flashback (7/97) 2.25
...'96, ...'97-($2.95)-Wraparound-c; '96-Age of Apocalypse 3.00
...: All Saints' Day ('97, $5.99) Dodson-a 6.00
.../Hulk '98 ($2.99) Wraparound-c; Thanos app. 3.00

	GD	FN	NM-

X-MEN, THE (1st series)(Becomes Uncanny X-Men at #142)(The X-Men #1-93; X-Men #94-141) (The Uncanny X-Men on-c only #114-141)
Marvel Comics Group: Sept, 1963 - No. 66, Mar, 1970; No. 67, Dec, 1970 - No. 141, Jan, 1981

	GD	FN	NM-
1-Origin/1st app. X-Men (Angel, Beast, Cyclops, Iceman & Marvel Girl); 1st app. Magneto & Professor X	650	1950	13,000
2-1st app. The Vanisher	153	459	2900
3-1st app. The Blob (1/64)	79	237	1500
4-1st Quicksilver & Scarlet Witch & Brotherhood of the Evil Mutants (3/64); 1st app. Toad; 2nd app. Magneto	82	246	1550
5-Magneto & Evil Mutants-c/story	55	165	1050
6,7: 6-Sub-Mariner app. 7-Magneto app.	50	150	875
8,9,11: 8-1st Unus the Untouchable. 9-Early Avengers app. (1/65); 1st Lucifer. 11-1st app. The Stranger.	41	123	650
10-1st S.A. app. Ka-Zar & Zabu the sabertooth (3/65)	36	108	575
12-Origin Prof. X; Origin/1st app. Juggernaut	44	132	750
13-Juggernaut and Human Torch app.	31	93	485
14,15: 14-1st app. Sentinels. 15-Origin Beast	32	96	500
16-20: 19-1st app. The Mimic (4/66)	18	54	270
21-27,29,30: 27-Re-enter The Mimic (r-in #75); Spider-Man cameo	13	39	190
28-1st app. The Banshee (1/67)(r-in #76)	20	60	300
28-2nd printing (1994)	2	6	12
31-34,36,37,39: 34-Adkins-c/a. 39-New costumes	11	33	150
35-Spider-Man x-over (8/67)(r-in #83); 1st app. Changeling	23	69	340
38,40: 38-Origins of the X-Men series begins, ends #57. 40-(1/68) 1st app. Frankenstein's monster at Marvel	11	33	160
41-49: 42-Death of Prof. X (Changeling disguised as). 44-1st S.A. app. G.A. Red Raven. 49-Steranko-c; 1st Polaris	10	30	125
50,51-Steranko-c/a	10	30	130
52	9	27	110
53-Barry Smith-c/a (his 1st comic book work)	10	30	130
54,55-B. Smith-c. 54-1st app. Alex Summers who later becomes Havok. 55-Summers discovers he has mutant powers	10	30	135
56,57,59-63,65-Neal Adams-a(p). 56-Intro Havok w/o costume. 60-1st Sauron. 65-Return of Professor X.	10	30	130
58-1st app. Havok in costume; N. Adams-a(p)	12	36	175
62,63-2nd printings (1994)	2	6	12
64-1st app. Sunfire	10	30	125
66-Last new story w/original X-Men; battles Hulk	10	30	140
67-93: 67-Reprints begin, end #93. 67-70,72: (52 pgs.). 71-Last 15¢ issue. 73-86-r/#25-38 w/new-c. 83-Spider-Man-c/story. 87-93-r/#39-45 with covers	7	21	85
94 (8/75)-New X-Men begin (see Giant-Size X-Men for 1st app.); Colossus, Nightcrawler, Thunderbird, Storm, Wolverine, & Banshee join; Angel, Marvel Girl & Iceman resign	53	159	1000
95-Death of Thunderbird	14	42	200
96,97	9	27	110

	GD	FN	NM-
98,99-(Regular 25¢ edition)(4,6/76)	8	24	105
98,99-(30¢-c variants, limited distribution)	15	45	225
100-Old vs. New X-Men; part origin Phoenix; last 25¢ issue (8/76)			
	10	30	130
100-(30¢-c variant, limited distribution)	18	54	260
101-Phoenix origin concludes	11	33	150
102-104: 102-Origin Storm. 104-1st brief app. Starjammers; Magneto-c/story			
	6	18	75
105-107-(Regular 30¢ editions). 106-(8/77)Old vs. New X-Men. 107-1st full			
app. Starjammers; last 30¢ issue	6	18	75
105-107-(35¢-c variants, limited distribution)	9	27	120
108-Byrne-a begins (see Marvel Team-Up #53)	7	21	80
109-1st app. Weapon Alpha (becomes Vindicator)	6	18	70
110,111: 110-Phoenix joins	4	12	50
112-116	4	12	50
117-119: 117-Origin Professor X	4	12	40
120-1st app. Alpha Flight, story line begins (4/79); 1st app. Vindicator			
(formerly Weapon Alpha); last 35¢ issue	6	18	70
121-1st full Alpha Flight story	6	18	65
122-128: 123-Spider-Man x-over. 124-Colossus becomes Proletarian			
	3	10	35
129-Intro Kitty Pryde (1/80); last Banshee; Dark Phoenix saga begins; intro.			
Emma Frost (White Queen)	4	12	50
130-1st app. The Dazzler by Byrne (2/80)	3	10	35
131-135: 131-Dazzler app.; 1st White Queen-c. 133-Wolverine app.			
134-Phoenix becomes Dark Phoenix	3	10	35
136,138: 138-Dazzler app.; Cyclops leaves	3	9	28
137-Giant; death of Phoenix	3	10	35
139-Alpha Flight app.; Kitty Pryde joins; new costume for Wolverine			
	3	10	35
140-Alpha Flight app.	3	10	35
141-Intro Future X-Men & The New Brotherhood of Evil Mutants; 1st app.			
Rachel (Phoenix II); Death of Franklin Richards	4	12	40
X-MEN: Titled THE UNCANNY X-MEN #142, Feb, 1981 - Present			
142-Rachel app.; deaths of alt. future Wolverine, Storm & Colossus			
	5	15	55
143-Last Byrne issue	3	10	35
144-150: 144-Man-Thing app. 145-Old X-Men app. 148-Spider-Woman,			
Dazzler app. 150-Double size	2	6	14
151-157,159-161,163,164: 161-Origin Magneto. 163-Origin Binary.			
164-1st app. Binary as Carol Danvers	1	4	10
158-1st app. Rogue in X-Men (6/82, see Avengers Annual #10)			
	2	6	18
162-Wolverine solo story	2	6	14
165-Paul Smith-c/a begins, ends #175	1	4	10
166-170: 166-Double size; Paul Smith-a. 167-New Mutants app. (3/83);			
same date as New Mutants #1; 1st meeting w/X-Men; ties into N.M. #3,4;			
Starjammers app.; contains skin "Tattooz" decals. 168-1st brief app.			
Madelyne Pryor (last page) in X-Men (see Avengers Annual #10)			

	GD	FN	NM-
	1	3	9
171-Rogue joins X-Men; Simonson-c/a	2	6	16
172-174: 172,173-Two part Wolverine solo story. 173-Two cover variations, blue & black. 174-Phoenix cameo	1	3	8
175-(52 pgs.)-Anniversary issue; Phoenix returns	1	4	10
176-185,187-192,194-199: 181-Sunfire app. 182-Rogue solo story. 184-1st app. Forge (8/84). 190,191-Spider-Man & Avengers x-over. 195-Power Pack x-over	1	3	7
186,193: 186-Double-size; Barry Smith/Austin-a. 193-Double size; 100th app. New X-Men; 1st app. Warpath in costume (see New Mutants #16)	1	3	8
200-(12/85, $1.25, 52 pgs.)	1	3	8
201-(1/86)-1st app. Cable? (as baby Nathan; see X-Factor #1); 1st Whilce Portacio-c/a(i) on X-Men (guest artist)	3	9	25
202-204,206-209: 204-Nightcrawler solo story. 2nd Portacio-a(i) on X-Men. 207-Wolverine/Phoenix story	1	3	7
205-Wolverine solo story by Barry Smith	2	6	14
210,211-Mutant Massacre begins	3	9	24
212,213-Wolverine vs. Sabretooth (Mutant Mass.)	3	9	28
214-221,223,224: 219-Havok joins (7/87); brief app. Sabretooth	1	3	7
222-Wolverine battles Sabretooth-c/story	3	9	24
225-242: 225-227: Fall Of The Mutants. 226-Double size. 240-Sabretooth app. 242-Double size, X-Factor app., Inferno tie-in	1	3	7
243,245-247: 245-Rob Liefeld-a(p)	1	3	7
244-1st app. Jubilee	3	9	30
248-1st Jim Lee art on X-Men (1989)	2	6	22
248-2nd printing (1992, $1.25)			2.50
249-252: 252-Lee-c	1	3	7
253-255: 253-All new X-Men begin. 254-Lee-c	1	3	7
256,257-Jim Lee-c/a begins	1	3	9
258-Wolverine solo story; Lee-c/a	1	3	9
259-Silvestri-c/a; no Lee-a	1	3	7
260-265-No Lee-a. 260,261,264-Lee-c	1	3	7
266-1st full app. Gambit (see Ann. #14)-No Lee-a	4	12	45
267-Jim Lee-c/a resumes; 2nd full Gambit app.	2	6	16
268-Capt. America, Black Widow & Wolverine team-up; Lee-a	2	6	18
268,270: 268-2nd printing. 270-Gold 2nd printing			2.50
269,273-275: 269-Lee-a. 273-New Mutants (Cable) & X-Factor x-over; Golden, Byrne & Lee part pencils. 275-(52 pgs.)-Tri-fold-c by Jim Lee (p); Prof. X	1	3	7
270-X-Tinction Agenda begins	1	3	8
271,272-X-Tinction Agenda	1	3	8
275-Gold 2nd printing			2.50
276-280: 277-Last Lee-c/a. 280-X-Factor x-over			6.00
281-(10/91)-New team begins (Storm, Archangel, Colossus, Iceman & Marvel Girl); Whilce Portacio-c/a begins; Byrne scripts begin; wraparound-c (white logo)	1	3	7

	GD	FN	NM-

281-2nd printing with red metallic ink logo w/o UPC box ($1.00-c); does not
   say 2nd printing inside   2.50

282-1st brief app. Bishop (cover & 1 page)   2   6   12

282-Gold ink 2nd printing ($1.00-c)   2.50

283-1st full app. Bishop (12/91)   2   6   12

284-299: 284-Last $1.00-c. 286,287-Lee plots. 287-Bishop joins team.
   288-Lee/Portacio plots. 290-Last Portacio-c/a. 294-Peterson-a(p) begins
   (#292 is 1st Peterson-c). 294-296 ($1.50)-Bagged w/trading card in each;
   X-Cutioner's Song x-overs; Peterson/Austin-c/a on all   4.00

300-($3.95, 68 pgs.)-Holo-grafx foil-c; Magneto app.   6.00

301-303,305-309,311   3.00

303,307-Gold Edition   1   3   8

304-($3.95, 68 pgs.)-Wraparound-c with Magneto hologram on-c; 30th
   anniversary issue; Jae Lee-a (4 pgs.)   6.00

310-($1.95)-Bound-in trading card sheet   3.00

312-$1.50-c begins; bound-in card sheet; 1st Madureira   4.00

313-321   3.00

316,317-($2.95)-Foil enhanced editions   4.00

318-321-($1.95)-Deluxe editions   3.00

322-Onslaught   5.00

323,324,326-346: 323-Return from Age of Apocalypse. 328-Sabretooth-c.
   329,330-Dr. Strange app. 331-White Queen-c/app. 334-Juggernaut app.;
   w/Onslaught Update. 335-Onslaught, Avengers, Apocalypse, & X-Man app.
   336-Onslaught. 338-Archangel's wings return to normal. 339-Havok vs.
   Cyclops; Spider-Man app. 341-Gladiator-c/app. 342-Deathbird cameo;
   two covers. 343,344-Phalanx   2.50

325-($3.95)-Anniverary issue; gatefold-c   5.00

342-Variant-c   1   4   10

347-349:347-Begin $1.99-c. 349-"Operation Zero Tolerance"   2.50

350-($3.99, 48 pgs.) Prismatic etched foil gatefold wraparound-c; Trial of
   Gambit; Seagle-s begin   1   3   8

351-359: 353-Bachalo-a begins. 354-Regular-c. 355-Alpha Flight-c/app.
   356-Original X-Men-c   2.50

354-Dark Phoenix variant-c   4.00

360-($2.99) 35th Anniv. issue; Pacheco-c   3.00

360-($3.99) Etched Holo-foil enhanced-c   4.00

360-($6.95) DF Edition with Jae Lee variant-c   7.00

361-374: 361-Gambit returns; Skroce-a. 362-Hunt for Xavier pt. 1; Bachelo-a.
   364-Yu-a. 366-Magneto-c. 369-Juggernaut-c   2.50

375-($2.99) Autopsy of Wolverine   3.00

376-379: 376,377-Apocalypse: The Twelve   2.25

380-($2.99) Polybagged with X-Men Revolution Genesis Edition preview 3.00

381,382,384-389,391-393: 381-Begin $2.25-c; Claremont-s. 387-Maximum
   Security   2.25

383-($2.99)   3.00

390-Colossus dies to cure the Legacy Virus   3.00

394-New look X-Men begins; Casey-s/Churchill-c/a   3.00

395-399-Poptopia. 398-Phillips & Wood-a   2.25

400-($3.50) Art by Ashley Wood, Eddie Campbell, Hamner, Phillips, Pulido

	GD	FN	NM-
and Matt Smith; wraparound-c by Wood			3.50
401-415: 401-'Nuff Said issue; Garney-a. 404,405,407-409,413-415-Phillips-a			
			2.25
416-421: 416-Asamiya-a begins. 421-Garney-a			2.25
422-($3.50) Alpha Flight app.; Garney-a			3.50
423-(25c-c) Holy War pt. 1; Garney-a/Philip Tan-c			2.25
424-449,452-453: 425,426,429,430-Tan-a. 428-Birth of Nightcrawler.			
437-Larroca-a begins. 444-New team, new costumes; Claremont-s/Davis-a			
begins. 448,449-Coipel-a			2.25
450,451-X-23 app.; Davis-a			2.25
#(-1) Flashback (7/97) Ladronn-c/Hitch & Neary-a			2.50
Special 1(12/70)-Kirby-c/a; origin The Stranger	10	30	125
Special 2(11/71, 52 pgs.)	7	21	85
Annual 3(1979, 52 pgs.)-New story; Miller/Austin-c; Wolverine still in old			
yellow costume	4	12	38
Annual 4(1980, 52 pgs.)-Dr. Strange guest stars	2	6	15
Annual 5(1981, 52 pgs.)	1	3	9
Annual 6-8('82-'84 52 pgs.)-6-Dracula app.			6.00
Annual 9,10('85, '86)-9-New Mutants x-over cont'd from New Mutants Special			
Ed. #1; Art Adams-a. 10-Art Adams-a	1	3	9
Annual 11-13:('87-'89, 68 pgs.): 12-Evolutionary War; A.Adams-a(p).			
13-Atlantis Attacks			4.00
Annual 14(1990, $2.00, 68 pgs.)-1st app. Gambit (minor app., 5 pgs.);			
Fantastic Four, New Mutants (Cable) & X-Factor x-over; Art Adams-c/a(p)			
	3	9	25
Annual 15 (1991, $2.00, 68 pgs.)-4 pg. origin; New Mutants x-over; 4 pg.			
Wolverine solo back-up story; 4th app. X-Force cont'd from New Warriors			
Annual #1			4.00
Annual 16-18 ('92-'94, 68 pgs.)-16-Jae Lee-c/a(p). 17-Bagged w/card			3.00
Annual '95-(11/95, $3.95)-Wraparound-c			4.00
Annual '96,'97-Wraparound-c			3.00
.../Fantastic Four Annual '98 ($2.99) Casey-s			3.00
Annual '99 ($3.50) Jubilee app.			3.50
Annual 2000 ($3.50) Cable app.; Ribic-a			3.50
Annual 2001 ($3.50, printed wide-ways) Ashley Wood-c/a; Casey-s			3.50
...At The State Fair of Texas (1983, 36 pgs., one-shot); Supplement to the			
Dallas Times Herald	2	6	15
...: The Dark Phoenix Saga TPB 1st printing (1984, $12.95)			40.00
...: The Dark Phoenix Saga TPB 2nd-5th printings			30.00
...: The Dark Phoenix Saga TPB 6th-10th printings			20.00
... Days of Future Past TPB (2004, $19.99) r/#138-143 & Annual #4			20.00
...From The Ashes TPB (1990, $14.95) r/#168-176			15.00
...:God Loves, Man Kills ($6.95)-r/Marvel Graphic Novel #5			7.00
...:God Loves, Man Kills - Special Edition (2003, $4.99)-reprint with new			
Hughes-c			5.00
...In The Days of Future Past TPB (1989, $3.95, 52 pgs.)			4.00
...Old Soldiers TPB (2004, $19.99) r/#213,215 & Ann. #11; New Mutants			
Ann. #2&3			20.00
...Poptopia TPB (10/01, $15.95) r/#394-399			16.00

	GD	FN	NM-
Vignettes TPB (9/01, $17.95) r/Claremont & Bolton Classic X-Men #1-13			18.00
... Vol. 1: Hope TPB (2003, $12.99) r/#410-415; Harris-c			13.00
... Vol. 2: Dominant Species TPB (2003, $11.99) r/#416-420; Asamiya-c			12.00
... Vol. 3: Holy War TPB (2003, $17.99) r/#421-427			18.00
... Vol. 4: The Draco TPB (2004, $15.99) r/#428-434			16.00
... Vol. 5: She Lies with Angels TPB (2004, $11.99) r/#437-441			12.00
... Vol. 6: Bright New Mourning TPB (2004, $14.99) r/#435,436,442,443 & (New) X-Men #155,156; Larroca sketch covers			15.00
... - The New Age Vol. 1: The End of History (2004, $12.99) r/#444-449			13.00

UNCANNY X-MEN AND THE NEW TEEN TITANS (See Marvel and DC Present...)

X-MEN (2nd Series)
Marvel Comics: Oct, 1991 - Present ($1.00/$1.25/$1.95/$1.99)

	GD	FN	NM-
1 a-d ($1.50, 52 pgs.)-Jim Lee-c/a begins, ends #11; new team begins (Cyclops, Beast, Wolverine, Gambit, Psylocke & Rogue); new Uncanny X-Men & Magneto app.; four different covers exist			4.00
1 e ($3.95)-Double gate-fold-c consisting of all four covers from 1a-d by Jim Lee; contains all pin-ups from #1a-d plus inside-c foldout poster; no ads; printed on coated stock			5.00
2-7: 4-Wolverine back to old yellow costume (same date as Wolverine #50); last $1.00-c. 5-Byrne scripts. 6-Sabretooth-c/story			5.00
8-10: 8-Gambit vs. Bishop-c/story; last Lee-a; Ghost Rider cameo cont'd in Ghost Rider #26. 9-Wolverine vs. Ghost Rider; cont'd/G.R. #26. 10-Return of Longshot			4.00
11-13,17-24,26-29,31: 12,13-Art Thibert-c/a. 28,29-Sabretooth app.			3.00
11-Silver ink 2nd printing; came with X-Men board game	2	6	15
14-16-($1.50)-Polybagged with trading card in each; X-Cutioner's Song x-overs; 14-Andy Kubert-c/a begins			3.00
25-($3.50, 52 pgs.)-Wraparound-c with Gambit hologram on-c; Professor X erases Magneto's mind	2	6	12
25-30th anniversary issue w/B&W-c with Magneto in color & Magneto hologram & no price on-c	2	6	15
25-Gold			30.00
30-($1.95)-Wedding issue w/bound-in trading card sheet			5.00
32-37: 32-Begin $1.50-c; bound-in card sheet. 33-Gambit & Sabretooth-c/story			3.00
36,37-($2.95)-Collectors editions (foil-c)			5.00
38-44,46-49,51-53, 55-65: 42,43- Paul Smith-a. 46,49,53-56-Onslaught app. 51-Waid scripts begin, end #56. 54-(Reg. edition)-Onslaught revealed as Professor X. 55,56-Onslaught x-over; Avengers, FF & Sentinels app. 56-Dr. Doom app. 57-Xavier taken into custody; Byrne-c/swipe (X-Men,1st Series #138). 59-Hercules-c/app. 61-Juggernaut-c/app. 62-Re-intro. Shang Chi; two covers. 63-Kingpin cameo. 64- Kingpin app.			2.50
45-($3.95)-Annual issue; gatefold-c			5.00
50-($2.95)-Vs. Onslaught, wraparound-c.			4.00
50-($3.95)-Vs. Onslaught, wraparound foil-c.			5.00
50-($2.95)-Variant gold-c.	4	12	40
50-($2.95)-Variant silver-c.	1	3	8

	GD	FN	NM-
54-(Limited edition)-Embossed variant-c; Onslaught revealed as Professor X	3	9	30
66-69,71-74,76-79: 66-Operation Zero Tolerance. 76-Origin of Maggott			2.50
70-($2.99, 48 pgs.)-Joe Kelly-s begin, new members join			3.00
75-($2.99, 48 pgs.) vs. N'Garai; wraparound-c			3.00
80-($3.99) 35th Anniv. issue; holo-foil-c			5.00
80-($2.99) Regular-c			3.00
80-($6.95) Dynamic Forces Ed.; Quesada-c			7.00
81-93,95: 82-Hunt for Xavier pt. 2. 85-Davis-a. 86-Origin of Joseph. 87-Magneto War ends. 88-Juggernaut app.			2.50
94-($2.99) Contains preview of X-Men: Hidden Years			3.00
96-99: 96,97-Apocalypse: The Twelve			2.50
100-($2.99) Art Adams-c; begin Claremont-s/Yu-a			3.00
100-DF alternate-c	1	4	10
101-105,107,108,110-114: 101-Begin $2.25-c. 107-Maximum Security x-over; Bishop-c/app. 108-Moira MacTaggart dies; Senator Kelly shot. 111-Magneto-c. 112,113-Eve of Destruction			2.25
106-($2.99) X-Men battle Domina			3.00
109-($3.50, 100 pgs.) new and reprinted Christmas-themed stories			3.50
114-Title change to "New X-Men," Morrison-s/Quitely-c/a begins			4.00
115-Two covers (Quitely & BWS)			3.00
116-125,127-149: 116-Emma Frost joins. 117,118-Van Sciver-a. 121,122, 135-Quitely-a. 127-Leon & Sienkiewicz-a. 128-Kordey-a. 132,139-141-Jimenez-a. 136-138-Quitely-a. 142-Sabretooth app.; Bachalo-c/a thru #145. 146-Magneto returns; Jimenez-a			2.25
126-($3.25) Quitely-a; defeat of Cassanova			3.25
150-($3.50) Jean Grey dies again; last Jimenez-a			3.50
151-156: 151-154-Silvestri-c/a			2.25
157-164: 157-X-Men Reload begins			2.25
#(-1) Flashback (7/97); origin of Magneto			2.50
Annual 1-3 ('92-'94, $2.25-$2.95, 68 pgs.) 1-Lee-c & layouts; #2-Bagged w/card			4.00
Special '95 ($3.95)			4.00
... '96,...'97-Wraparound-c			3.00
.../ Dr. Doom '98 Annual ($2.99) Lopresti-a			3.00
... Annual '99 ($3.50) Adam Kubert-c			3.50
Annual 2000 ($3.50) Art Adams-c/Claremont-s/Eaton-a			3.50
...2001 Annual ($3.50) Morrison-s/Yu-a; issue printed sideways			3.50
Animation Special Graphic Novel (12/90, $10.95) adapts animated series			11.00
Ashcan #1 (1994, 75¢) Introduces new team members			2.25
Ashcan (75¢ Ashcan Edition) (1994)			2.25
... Archives Sketchbook (12/00, $2.99) Early B&W character design sketches by various incl. Lee, Davis, Yu, Pacheco, BWS, Art Adams, Liefeld			3.00
....: Declassified (10/00, $3.50) Profile pin-ups by various; Jae Lee-c			3.50
...:Fatal Attractions ('94, $17.95)-r/x-Factor #92, X-Force #25, Uncanny X-Men #304, X-Men #25, Wolverine #75, & Excalibur #71			18.00
...Millennial Visions (8/00, $3.99) Various artists interpret future X-Men			4.00
...Millennial Visions 2 (1/02, $3.50) Various artists interpret future X-Men			3.50

	GD	FN	NM-
New X-Men: E is for Extinction TPB (11/01, $12.95) r/#114-117			13.00
New X-Men: Imperial TPB (7/02, $19.99) r/#118-126; Quitely-c			20.00
New X-Men: New Worlds TPB (2002, $14.99) r/#127-133; Quitely-c			15.00
New X-Men: Riot at Xavier's TPB (2003, $11.99) r/#134-138; Quitely-c			12.00
New X-Men: Vol. 5: Assault on Weapon Plus TPB (2003, $14.99) r/#139-145			15.00
New X-Men: Vol. 6: Planet X TPB (2004, $12.99) r/#146-150			13.00
New X-Men: Vol. 7: Here Comes Tomorrow TPB (2004, $10.99) r/#151-154			11.00
New X-Men: Volume 1 HC (2002, $29.99) oversized r/#114-126 & 2001 Annual			30.00
New X-Men: Volume 2 HC (2003, $29.99) oversized r/#127-141; sketch & script pages			30.00
New X-Men: Volume 3 HC (2004, $29.99) oversized r/#142-154; sketch & script pages			30.00
...Pizza Hut Mini-comics-(See Marvel Collector's Edition: X-Men in Promotional Comics section)			
...Premium Edition #1 (1993)-Cover says "Toys 'R' Us Limited Edition X-Men"			2.25
...:Rarities (1995, $5.95)-Reprints			6.00
...:Road Trippin' ('99, $24.95, TPB) r/X-Men road trips			25.00
...:The Coming of Bishop ('95, $12.95)-r/Uncanny X-Men #282-285, 287,288			13.00
...:The Magneto War (3/99, $2.99) Davis-a			3.00
...:The Rise of Apocalypse ('98, $16.99)-r/Rise Of Apocalypse #1-4, X-Factor #5,6			17.00
... Visionaries: Chris Claremont ('98, $24.95)-r/Claremont-s; art by Byrne, BWS, Jim Lee			25.00
... Visionaries: Jim Lee ('02, $29.99)-r/Jim Lee-a from various issues between Uncanny X-Men #248 & 286; r/Classic X-Men #39 and X-Men Annual #1			30.00
... Visionaries: Joe Madureira (7/00, $17.95)-r/Uncanny X-Men #325,326,329, 330,341-343; new Madureira-c			18.00
...: Zero Tolerance ('00, $24.95, TPB) r/crossover series			25.00

X-MEN: HIDDEN YEARS
Marvel Comics: Dec, 1999 - No. 22, Sept. 2001 ($3.50/$2.50)

1-New adventures from pre-#94 era; Byrne-s/a(p)			3.50
2-4,6-11,13-22-($2.50): 2-Two covers. 3-Ka-Zar app. 8,9-FF-c/app.			2.50
5-($2.75)			2.75
12-($3.50) Magneto-c/app.			3.50

X-MEN: THE MOVIE
Marvel Comics: Aug, 2000; Sept, 2000

Adaptation (9/00, $5.95) Macchio-s/Williams & Lanning-a			6.00
Adaptation TPB (9/00, $14.95) Movie adaptation and key reprints of main characters; four photo covers (movie X, Magneto, Rogue, Wolverine)			15.00
Prequel: Magneto (8/00, $5.95) Texeira & Palmiotti-a; art & photo covers			6.00
Prequel: Rogue (8/00, $5.95) Evans & Nikolakakis-a; art & photo covers			6.00
Prequel: Wolverine (8/00, $5.95) Waller & McKenna-a; art & photo covers			6.00

	GD	FN	NM-

TPB X-Men: Beginnings (8/00, $14.95) reprints 3 prequels w/photo-c   15.00

X-MEN 2: THE MOVIE
Marvel Comics: 2003

Adaptation (6/03, $3.50) Movie adaptation; photo-c; Austen-s/Zircher-a   3.50
Adaptation TPB (2003, $12.99) Movie adaptation & r/Prequels Nightcrawler
   & Wolverine   13.00
Prequel: Nightcrawler (5/03, $3.50) Kerschl-a; photo cover   3.50
Prequel: Wolverine (5/03, $3.50) Mandrake-a; photo cover; Sabretooth app.
   3.50

X-MEN UNLIMITED
Marvel Comics: 1993 - No. 50, Sept, 2003 ($3.95/$2.99, 68 pgs.)

1-Chris Bachalo-c/a; Quesada-a.   5.00
2-11: 2-Origin of Magneto script. 3-Sabretooth-c/story. 10-Dark Beast vs.
   Beast; Mark Waid script. 11-Magneto & Rogue   4.00
12-33: 12-Begin $2.99-c; Onslaught x-over; Juggernaut-c/app. 19-Caliafore-a.
   20-Generation X app. 27-Origin Thunderbird. 29-Maximum Security x-over;
   Bishop-c/app. 30-Mahfood-a. 31-Stelfreeze-c/a. 32-Dazzler; Thompson-c/a
   33-Kaluta-c   3.00
34-37,39,40-42-($3.50) 34-Von Eeden-a. 35-Finch, Conner, Maguire-a.
   36-Chiodo-c/a; Larroca, Totleben-a. 39-Bachalo-c; Pearson-a.
   41-Bachalo-c; X-Statix app.   3.50
38-($2.25) Kitty Pryde; Robertson-a   2.25
43-50-($2.50) 43-Sienkiewicz-c/a; Paul Smith-a. 45-Noto-c. 46-Bisley-a.
   47-Warren-s/Mays-a. 48-Wolverine story w/Isanove painted-a   2.50
X-Men Legends Vol. 4: Hated and Feared TPB (2003, $19.99) r/stories by
   various   20.00

X-STATIX
Marvel Comics: Sept, 2002 - No. 26, Oct, 2004 ($2.99/$2.25)

1-($2.99)Allred-a/c; intro. Venus Dee Milo; back-up w/Cooke-a   3.00
2-9-($2.25) 4-Quitely-c. 5-Pope-c/a   2.25
10-26: 10-Begin $2.99-c; Bond-a; U-Go Girl flashback. 13,14-Spider-Man
   app. 21-25-Avengers app. 26-Team dies   3.00
... Vol. 1: Good Omens TPB (2003, $11.99) r/#1-5   12.00
... Vol. 2: Good Guys & Bad Guys TPB (2003, $15.99) r/#6-10 &
   Wolverine/Doop #1&2   16.00
... Vol. 3: Back From the Dead TPB (2004, $19.99) r/#11-18   20.00
... Vol. 4: X-Statix Vs. the Avengers TPB (2004, $19.99) r/#19-26; pin-ups
   20.00

X-TREME X-MEN (Also see Mekanix)
Marvel Comics: July, 2001 - No. 46, Jun, 2004 ($2.99/$3.50)

1-Claremont-s/Larroca-c/a   4.00
2-24: 2-Two covers (Larroca & Pacheco); Psylocke killed   3.00
25-35, 40-46: 25-30-God Loves, Man Kills II; Stryker app.; Kordey-a   3.00
36-39-($3.50)   3.50
Annual 2001 ($4.95) issue opens longways   5.00
... Vol. 1: Destiny TPB (2002, $19.95) r/#1-9   20.00
... Vol. 2: Invasion TPB (2003, $19.99) r/#10-18   20.00

	GD	FN	NM-
... Vol. 3: Schism TPB (2003, $16.99) r/#19-23; X-Treme X-Posé #1&2			17.00
... Vol. 4: Mekanix TPB (2003, $16.99) r/Mekanix #1-6			17.00
... Vol. 5: God Loves Man Kills TPB (2003, $19.99) r/#25-30			20.00
... Vol. 6: Intifada TPB (2004, $16.99) r/#24,31-35			17.00
... Vol. 7: Storm the Arena TPB (2004, $16.99) r/#36-39			17.00
... Vol. 8: Prisoner of Fire TPB (2004, $19.99) r/#40-46 and Ann. 2001			20.00

YOGI BEAR (TV) (Hanna-Barbera) (See Four Color #990)
Dell Publishing Co./Gold Key No. 10 on: No. 1067, 12-2/59-60 - No. 9, 7-9/62; No. 10, 10/62 - No. 42, 10/70

Four Color 1067 (#1)-TV show debuted 1/30/61	12	36	180
Four Color 1104,1162 (5-7/61)	9	27	110
4(8-9/61) - 6(12-1/61-62)	7	21	80
Four Color 1271(11/61)	7	21	80
Four Color 1349(1/62)-Photo-c	10	30	135
7(2-3/62) - 9(7-9/62)-Last Dell	7	21	80
10(10/62-G.K.), 11(1/63)-titled "Yogi Bear Jellystone Jollies" (80 pgs.);			
11-X-Mas-c	8	24	105
12(4/63), 14-20	6	18	65
13(7/63, 68 pgs.)-Surprise Party	8	24	105
21-30	4	12	40
31-42	3	9	32

YOGI BEAR (TV)
Charlton Comics: Nov, 1970 - No. 35, Jan, 1976 (Hanna-Barbera)

1	5	15	60
2-6,8-10	3	9	30
7-Summer Fun (Giant, 52 pgs.)	5	15	60
11-20	3	9	28
21-35: 28-31-partial-r	2	6	20
Digest (nn, 1972, 75¢-c, B&W, 100 pgs.) (scarce)	4	12	38

YOGI BEAR (TV)(See The Flintstones, 3rd series & Spotlight #1)
Marvel Comics Group: Nov, 1977 - No. 9, Mar, 1979 (Hanna-Barbera)

1,7-9: 1-Flintstones begin (Newsstand sales only)	3	9	30
2-6	2	6	20

YOSEMITE SAM (...& Bugs Bunny) (TV)
Gold Key/Whitman: Dec, 1970 - No. 81, Feb, 1984

1	5	15	60
2-10	3	9	28
11-20	2	6	18
21-30	2	6	14
31-50	1	4	10
51-65 (Gold Key)	1	3	8
66,67 (Whitman)	2	6	12
68(9/80), 69(10/80), 70(12/80) 3-pack only	3	9	26
71-78: 76(2/82), 77(3/82), 78(4/82)	2	6	14
79-81 (All #90263 on-c, no date or date code; 3-pack): 79(7/83). 80(8/83).			
81(2/84)-(1/3-r)			
	2	6	22

	GD	FN	NM-

YOUNG JUSTICE (Also see Teen Titans and Titans/Young Justice)
DC Comics: Sept, 1998 - No. 55, May, 2003 ($2.50/$2.75)

1-Robin, Superboy & Impulse team-up; David-s/Nauck-a	4.00
2,3: 3-Mxyzptlk app.	3.00
4-20: 4-Wonder Girl, Arrowette and the Secret join. 6-JLA app. 13-Supergirl x-over. 20-Sins of Youth aftermath	3.00
21-49: 25-Empress ID revealed. 28,29-Forever People app. 32-Empress origin. 35,36-Our Worlds at War x-over. 38-Joker: Last Laugh. 41-The Ray joins. 42-Spectre-c/app. 44,45-World Without YJ x-over pt. 1,5; Ramos-c. 48-Begin $2.75-c	2.75
50-($3.95) Wonder Twins,CM3 and other various DC teen heroes app.	4.00
51-55: 53,54-Darkseid app. 55-Last issue; leads into Titans/Young Justice mini-series	2.75
#1,000,000 (11/98) 853 Century x-over	2.50
...: A League of Their Own (2000, $14.95, TPB) r/#1-7, Secret Files #1	15.00
...: 80-Page Giant (5/99, $4.95) Ramos-c; stories and art by various	5.00
...: In No Man's Land (7/99, $3.95) McDaniel-c	4.00
...: Our Worlds at War (8/01, $2.95) Jae Lee-c; Linear Men app.	3.00
...: Secret Files (1/99, $4.95) Origin-s & pin-ups	5.00
...: The Secret (6/98, $1.95) Girlfrenzy; Nauck-a	2.50

Y: THE LAST MAN
DC Comics (Vertigo): Sept, 2002 - Present ($2.95)

1-Intro. Yorick Brown; Vaughan-s/Guerra-a/J.G. Jones-c			
	2	6	12
2	1	3	8
3-5			6.00
6-29: 16,17-Chadwick-a. 21,22-Parlov-a			3.00
... - Cycles TPB (2003, $12.95) r/#6-10; sketch pages by Guerra			13.00
... - One Small Step TPB (2004, $12.95) r/#11-17			13.00
... - Safeword TPB (2004, $12.95) r/#18-23			13.00
... - Unmanned TPB (2002, $12.95) r/#1-5			13.00

ZERO HOUR: CRISIS IN TIME (Also see Showcase '94 #8-10)
DC Comics: No. 4(#1), Sept, 1994 - No. 0(#5), Oct, 1994 ($1.50, limited series)

4(#1)-0(#5)	4.00
"Ashcan"-(1994, free, B&W, 8 pgs.) several versions exist	2.25
TPB ('94, $9.95)	10.00

ZOT!
Eclipse Comics: 4/84 - No. 10, 7/85; No. 11, 1/87 - No. 36 7/91 ($1.50, Baxter-p)

1	5.00
2,3	4.00
4-10: 4-Origin. 10-Last color issue	3.00
101/2 (6/86, 25¢, Not Available Comics) Ashcan; art by Feazell & Scott McCloud	4.00
11-14,15-35-($2.00-c) B&W issues	3.00
141/2 (Adventures of Zot! in Dimension 101/2)(7/87) Antisocialman app.	3.00
36-($2.95-c) B&W	4.00

Promotional Comics

One of the most intriguing and least recognized factors that influenced the dawn of comics is the concept of the premium or giveaway. Without the concept of the giveaway comic, there would be no comic book industry as we have it today. Well-known now is the story of how in spring 1933 Harry Wildenberg of Eastern Color Printing Company convinced Proctor & Gamble to sponsor the first modern comic book, **Funnies on Parade**, as a premium. Its success led to the first continuing comic book, **Famous Funnies**, and the rest, as they say, is history.

Over the years, free giveaway, mail-in or premium comics have been used to promote everything from sports skills, health, religious causes and tourism to computer knowledge, job-hunting, armed forces recruitment and even how banks operate and birth control methods! Giveaway comics came into their own in World War II, expanded from a purely mercantile promotional tool to an education one as well, and by the '80s and '90s familiar superhero and cartoon characters could be found in free comics discussing everything from the benefits of good dental hygiene to the perils of child abuse and smoking. By the end of the 20th century, the promotional comic as public service was fully established.

Today, you can still find giveaway comics offered in conjunction with countless consumer items and through a multitude of corporations.

	GD	FN	NM-
ACTION COMICS			
DC Comics: 1947 - 1998 (Giveaway)			
1 (1976, 1983) paper cover w/10¢ price, 16 pgs. in color; reprints complete Superman story from #1 ('38)	3	9	25
1 (1976) Safeguard Giveaway; paper cover w/"free", 16 pgs. in color; reprints complete Superman story from #1 ('38)	3	9	28
1 (1987 Nestle Quik; 1988, 50¢)	1	3	9
1 (1993)-Came w/Reign of Superman packs			4.00
1 (1998 U.S. Postal Service, $7.95) Reprints entire issue; extra outer half-cover contains First Day Issuance of 32¢ Superman stamp with Sept. 10, 1998 Cleveland, OH postmark	1	3	8
ACTION ZONE			
CBS Television: 1994 (Promotes CBS Saturday morning cartoons)			
1-WildC.A.T.s, T.M.N.Turtles, Skeleton Warriors stories; Jim Lee-c			2.00

	GD	FN	NM-

ADVENTURES @ EBAY
eBay: 2000 (6 3/4" x 4 1/2", 16 pgs.)

1-Judd Winick-a/Rucka & Van Meter-s; intro to eBay comic buying   2.25

ADVENTURES OF BARRY WEEN, BOY GENIUS, THE
Oni Press: July, 2004 (Free Comic Book Day giveaway)

...: Secret Crisis Origin Files - Judd Winick-s/a   2.25

ADVENTURES OF G. I. JOE
1969 (3-1/4x7") (20 & 16 pgs.)

First Series: 1-Danger of the Depths. 2-Perilous Rescue. 3-Secret Mission to Spy Island. 4-Mysterious Explosion. 5-Fantastic Free Fall. 6-Eight Ropes of Danger. 7-Mouth of Doom. 8-Hidden Missile Discovery. 9-Space Walk Mystery. 10-Fight for Survival. 11-The Shark's Surprise.
Second Series: 2-Flying Space Adventure. 4-White Tiger Hunt. 7-Capture of the Pygmy Gorilla. 12-Secret of the Mummy's Tomb.
Third Series: Reprinted surviving titles of First Series. Fourth Series: 13-Adventure Team Headquarters. 14-Search For the Stolen Idol.

	GD	FN	NM-
each....	3	9	28

ADVENTURES OF KOOL-AID MAN
Marvel Comics: 1983; 1984 (Mail order giveaway)

	GD	FN	NM-
1,2	1	3	7

ADVENTURES OF QUIK BUNNY
Nestle's Quik: 1984 (Giveaway, 32 pgs.)

	GD	FN	NM-
nn-Spider-Man app.	2	6	14

ALICE IN WONDERLAND
Western Printing Company/Whitman Publ. Co.: 1965; 1969; 1982

	GD	FN	NM-
Meets Santa Claus(1950s), nd, 16 pgs.	5	15	40
Rexall Giveaway(1965, 16 pgs., 5x7-1/4) Western Printing (TV, Hanna-Barbera)	3	9	30
Wonder Bakery Giveaway(1969, 16 pgs, color, nn, nd) (Continental Baking Company)	3	9	28

ALL NEW COMICS (Hanna-Barbera)
Harvey Comics: Oct, 1993 (Giveaway, no cover price, 16 pgs.)

1-Flintstones, Scooby Doo, Jetsons, Yogi Bear & Wacky Races previews for upcoming Harvey's new Hanna-Barbera line-up   5.00

AMAZING SPIDER-MAN, THE
Marvel Comics Group

	GD	FN	NM-
Acme & Dingo Children's Boots (1980)-Spider-Woman app.	2	6	18
Adventures in Reading Starring... (1990) Bogdanove & Romita-c/a			4.00
Aim Toothpaste Giveaway (36 pgs., reg. size)-1 pg. origin recap; Green Goblin-c/story	2	6	14
Aim Toothpaste Giveaway (16 pgs., reg. size)-Dr. Octopus app.	2	6	16
All Detergent Giveaway (1979, 36 pgs.), nn-Origin-r	2	6	16

	GD	FN	NM-

Amazing Fantasy #15 (8/02) reprint included in Spider-Man DVD Collector's Gift Set   2.25

Amazing Spider-Man nn (1990, 6-1/8x9", 28 pgs.)-Shan-Lon giveaway; r/ Amazing Spider-Man #303 w/McFarlane-c/a   1   3   9

Amazing Spider-Man #3 Reprint (2004)-Best Buy/Sony giveaway   2.25

Amazing Spider-Man #50 (Sony Pictures Edition) (8/04)-mini-comic included in Spider-Man 2 movie DVD Collector's Gift Set; r/#50 & various ASM covers with Dr. Octopus   2.25

Amazing Spider-Man #129 (Lion Gate Films) (6/04)-promotional comic given away at movie theaters on opening night for The Punisher   2.25

...& Power Pack (1984, nn)(Nat'l Committee for Prevention of Child Abuse) (two versions, mail offer & store giveaway)-Mooney-a; Byrne-c
     Mail offer   2   6   12
     Store giveaway   4.00

...& The Hulk (Special Edition)(6/8/80; 20 pgs.)-Supplement to Chicago Tribune   2   6   16

...& The Incredible Hulk (1981, 1982; 36 pgs.)-Sanger Harris or May D&F supplement to Dallas Times, Dallas Herald, Denver Post, Kansas City Star, Tulsa World; Foley's supplement to Houston Chronicle (1982, 16 pgs.)- "Great Rodeo Robbery"; The Jones Store-giveaway (1983, 16 pgs.)
     2   6   20

...and the New Mutants Featuring Skids nn (National Committee for Prevention of Child Abuse/K-Mart giveaway)-Williams-c(i)   5.00

...Captain America, The Incredible Hulk, & Spider-Woman (1981) (7-11 Stores giveaway; 36 pgs.)   2   6   15

...: Danger in Dallas (1983) (Supplement to Dallas Times Herald) giveaway   2   6   15

...: Danger in Denver (1983) (Supplement to Denver Post) giveaway for May D&F stores   2   6   15

..., Fire-Star, And Ice-Man at the Dallas Ballet Nutcracker (1983; supplement to Dallas Times Herald)-Mooney-p   2   6   15

Giveaway-Esquire Magazine (2/69)-Miniature-Still attached   13   39   185

Giveaway-Eye Magazine (2/69)-Miniature-Still attached   10   30   135

..., Storm & Powerman (1982; 20 pgs.)(American Cancer Society) giveaway   1   3   8

...Vs. The Hulk (Special Edition; 1979, 20 pgs.)(Supplement to Columbus Dispatch)   2   6   20

...Vs. The Prodigy (Giveaway, 16 pgs. in color (1976, 5x6-1/2")-Sex education; (1 million printed; 35-50¢)   3   9   24

Spidey & The Mini-Marvels Halloween 2003 Ashcan (12/03, 8 1/2"x 5 1/2") Giarusso-s/a; Venom and Green Goblin app.   2.25

ANIMANIACS EMERGENCY WORLD
DC Comics: 1995

nn-American Red Cross   4.00

AQUATEERS MEET THE SUPER FRIENDS
DC Comics: 1979

	GD	FN	NM -
nn	2	6	15

ARCHIE'S TEN ISSUE COLLECTOR'S SET (Title inside of cover only)
Archie Publications: June, 1997 - No. 10, June, 1997 ($1.50, 20 pgs.)

1-10: 1,7-Archie. 2,8-Betty & Veronica. 3,9-Veronica. 4-Betty. 5-World of
Archie. 6-Jughead. 10-Archie and Friends   4.00

ASTRO COMICS
American Airlines (Harvey): 1968 - 1979 (Giveaway)

Reprints of Harvey comics. 1968-Hot Stuff. 1969-Casper, Spooky, Hot Stuff,
Stumbo the Giant, Little Audrey, Little Lotta, & Richie Rich reprints.

1970-r/Richie Rich #97 (all scarce)	3	10	36
1973-r/Richie Rich #122. 1975-Wendy. 1975-Richie Rich & Casper	3	9	26
1977-r/Richie Rich & Casper #20. 1978-r/Richie Rich & Casper #25. 1979-r/Richie Rich & Casper #30 (scarce)	3	9	24

ATARI FORCE
DC Comics: 1982 - No. 5, 1983 (Given away with Atari games)

1-3 (1982, 5X7", 52 pgs.)	1	3	7
4,5 (1982-1983, 52 pgs.) (scarcer)	2	6	12

AURORA COMIC SCENES INSTRUCTION BOOKLET (Included with
superhero model kits)
Aurora Plastics Co.: 1974 (6-1/4x9-3/4," 8 pgs., slick paper)

181-140-Tarzan; Neal Adams-a	3	10	36
182-140-Spider-Man.	4	12	50
183-140-Tonto(Gil Kane art). 184-140-Hulk. 185-140-Superman. 186-140-Superboy. 187-140-Batman. 188-140-The Lone Ranger(1974-by Gil Kane). 192-140-Captain America(1975). 193-140-Robin	3	9	30

BACK TO THE FUTURE
Harvey Comics: 1991 (Given away at Universal Studios in Florida)

Special nn (1991, 20 pgs.)-Brunner-c;   5.00

BATMAN
DC Comics: 1966 - Present

Act II Popcorn mini-comic(1998)	3.00
Batman #121 Toys R Us edition (1997) r/1st Mr. Freeze	3.00
Batman #362 Mervyn's edition (1989)	4.00
Batman Adventures #1 Free Comic Book Day edition (6/03) Timm-c	3.00
Batman Adventures #25 Best Western edition (1997)	3.00
Batman and Other DC Classics 1 (1989, giveaway)-DC Comics/Diamond Comic Distributors; Batman origin-r/Batman #47, Camelot 3000-r, Justice League-r('87), New Teen Titans-r	4.00
Batman Beyond Six Flags edition	6.00
Batman: Canadian Multiculturalism Custom (1992)	4.00
Batman Claritan edition (1999)	2.50

Kellogg's Poptarts comics (1966, Set of 6, 16 pgs.); All were folded and
placed in

	GD	FN	NM-

Poptarts boxes. Infantino art on Catwoman and Joker issues.
"The Man in the Iron Mask", "The Penguin's Fowl Play", "The Joker's Happy Victims", "The Catwoman's Catnapping Caper", "The Mad Hatter's Hat Crimes", "The Case of the Batman II"

	GD	FN	NM-
each....	5	15	58
Mask of the Phantasm (1993) Mini-comic released w/video	1	3	7
Onstar - Auto Show Special Edition (OnStar Corp., 2001, 8 pgs.)			2.50
Pizza Hut giveaway (12/77)-exact-r of #122,123; Joker-c/story	2	6	12
Prell Shampoo giveaway (1966, 16 pgs.)- "The Joker's Practical Jokes"			
(6-7/8x3-3/8")	5	14	52
Revell in pack (1995)			3.00

...: The 10-Cent Adventure (3/02, 10¢) intro. to the "Bruce Wayne: Murderer" x-over; Rucka-s/Burchett & Janson-a/Dave Johnson-c; these are alternate copies with special outer half-covers (at least 10 different) promoting comics, toys and games shops   2.50

BATMAN RECORD COMIC
National Periodical Publications: 1966 (one-shot)

	GD	FN	NM-
1-With record (still sealed)	15	45	215
Comic only	9	27	110

BIG JIM'S P.A.C.K.
Mattel, Inc. (Marvel Comics): No date (1975) (16 pgs.)

nn-Giveaway with Big Jim doll; Buscema/Sinnott-c/a	4	12	45

"BILL AND TED'S EXCELLENT ADVENTURE" MOVIE ADAPTATION
DC Comics: 1989 (No cover price)

nn-Torres-a   4.00

BLIND JUSTICE (Also see Batman: Blind Justice)
DC Comics/Diamond Comic Distributors: 1989 (Giveaway, squarebound)

nn-Contains Detective #598-600 by Batman movie writer Sam Hamm, w/covers; published same time as originals?   6.00

BOZO THE CLOWN (TV)
Dell Publishing Co.: 1961

Giveaway-1961, 16 pgs., 3-1/2x7-1/4", Apsco Products	6	18	65

BUGS BUNNY (3-D)
Cheerios Giveaway: 1953 (Pocket size) (15 titles)

	GD	FN	NM-
each....	9	27	75
Mailing Envelope (has Bugs drawn on front)	9	27	75

BUGS BUNNY
DC Comics: May, 1997 ($4.95, 24 pgs., comic-sized)

1-Numbered ed. of 100,000; "1st Day of Issue" stamp cancellation on-c 6.00

BUGS BUNNY POSTAL COMIC
DC Comics: 1997 (64 pgs., 7.5" x 5")

nn -Mail Fan; Daffy Duck app.   4.50

	GD	FN	NM-

CANCELLED COMIC CAVALCADE
DC Comics, Inc.: Summer, 1978 - No. 2, Fall, 1978 (8-1/2x11", B&W) (Xeroxed pgs. on one side only w/blue cover and taped spine)(Only 35 sets produced)

1-(412 pgs.) Contains xeroxed copies of art for: Black Lightning #12, cover to #13; Claw #13, 14; The Deserter #1; Doorway to Nightmare #6; Firestorm #6; The Green Team #2,3.

2-(532 pgs.) Contains xeroxed copies of art for: Kamandi #60 (including Omac), #61; Prez #5; Shade #9 (including The Odd Man); Showcase #105 (Deadman), #106 (The Creeper); Secret Society of Super Villains #16 & 17; The Vixen #1; and covers to Army at War #2, Battle Classics #3, Demand Classics #1 & 2, Dynamic Classics #3, Mr. Miracle #26, Ragman #6, Weird Mystery #25 & 26, & Western Classics #1 & 2.

(A set of Number 1 & 2 was sold in 2002 for $2127.50, then resold for $2590 a month later)

NOTE: *In June, 1978, DC cancelled several of their titles. For copyright purposes, the unpublished original art for these titles was xeroxed, bound in the above books, published and distributed. Only 35 copies were made.*

CAP'N CRUNCH COMICS (See Quaker Oats)
Quaker Oats Co.: 1963; 1965 (16 pgs.; miniature giveaways; 2-1/2x6-1/2")

(1963 titles)- "The Picture Pirates", "The Fountain of Youth", "I'm Dreaming of a Wide Isthmus". (1965 titles)- "Bewitched, Betwitched, & Betweaked", "Seadog Meets the Witch Doctor", "A Witch in Time"   6   18   75

CAPTAIN ACTION (Toy)
National Periodical Publications

...& Action Boy('67)-Ideal Toy Co. giveaway (1st app. Captain Action)
| | 14 | 42 | 205 |

CAPTAIN AMERICA
Marvel Comics Group

...& The Campbell Kids (1980, 36pg. giveaway, Campbell's Soup/U.S. Dept. of Energy)   2   6   12
...Goes To War Against Drugs(1990, no #, giveaway)-Distributed to direct sales shops; 2nd printing exists   6.00
...Meets The Asthma Monster (1987, no #, giveaway, Your Physician and Glaxo, Inc.)   6.00
...Vs. Asthma Monster (1990, no #, giveaway, Your Physician & Allen & Hanbury's)   6.00

CARTOON NETWORK
DC Comics: 1997 (Giveaway)

nn-reprints Cow and Chicken, Scooby-Doo, & Flintstones stories   4.00

CARVEL COMICS (Amazing Advs. of Capt. Carvel)
Carvel Corp. (Ice Cream): 1975 - No. 5, 1976 (25¢; #3-5: 35¢) (#4,5: 3-1/4x5")

	GD	FN	NM-
1-3	1	3	8
4,5(1976)-Baseball theme	2	6	12

CASE OF THE WASTED WATER, THE
Rheem Water Heating: 1972? (Giveaway)

nn-Neal Adams-a	4	12	50

	GD	FN	NM-

CELEBRATE THE CENTURY SUPERHEROES STAMP ALBUM
DC Comics: 1998 - No. 5, 2000 (32 pgs.)

1-5: Historical stories hosted by DC heroes			3.00

CENTIPEDE
DC Comics: 1983

1-Based on Atari video game	1	4	10

DAN CURTIS GIVEAWAYS
Western Publishing Co.:1974 (3x6", 24 pgs., reprints)

1-Dark Shadows	3	9	28
2,6-Star Trek	3	9	28
3,4,7-9: 3-The Twilight Zone. 4-Ripley's Believe It or Not! 7-The Occult Files of Dr. Spektor. 8-Dagar the Invincible. 9-Grimm's Ghost Stories	2	6	18
5-Turok, Son of Stone (partial-r/Turok #78)	3	9	28

DAREDEVIL
Marvel Comics Group: 1993

...Vs. Vapora 1 (Engineering Show Giveaway, 16 pg.) - Intro Vapora			6.00

DC SAMPLER
DC Comics : nn (#1) 1983 - No. 3, 1984 (36 pgs.; 6 1/2" x 10", giveaway)

nn(#1) -3: nn-Wraparound-c, previews upcoming issues. 3-Kirby-a			6.00

DC SPOTLIGHT
DC Comics : 1985 (50th anniversary special) (giveaway)

1-Includes profiles on Batman:The Dark Knight & Watchmen			5.00

DETECTIVE COMICS (Also see other Batman titles)
National Periodical Publications/DC Comics

27 (1984)-Oreo Cookies giveaway (32 pgs., paper-c) r-/Det. #27,#38 & Batman #1 (1st Joker)	5	15	55
38 (1995) Blockbuster Video edition; reprints 1st Robin app.			3.00
38 (1997) Toys R Us edition			3.00
359 (1997) Toys R Us edition; reprints 1st Batgirl app.			3.00

DIG 'EM
Kellogg's Sugar Smacks Giveaway: 1973 (2-3/8x6", 16 pgs.)

nn-4 different issues	1	4	10

EVEL KNIEVEL
Marvel Comics Group (Ideal Toy Corp.): 1974 (Giveaway, 20 pgs.)

nn-Contains photo on inside back-c	4	12	50

FANTASTIC FOUR
Marvel Comics

nn (1981, 32 pgs.) Young Model Builders Club	2	6	12
Vol.2 #60 Baltimore Comic Book Show (10/02, newspaper supplement) 200,000 copies were distributed to Baltimore Sun home subscribers to promote 2002 Baltimore Comic Con			3.00

	GD	FN	NM -

FLOOD RELIEF
Malibu Comics (Ultraverse): Jan, 1994 (36 pgs.)(Ordered thru mail w/$5.00 to Red Cross)

1-Hardcase, Prime & Prototype app.			6.00

FRITO-LAY GIVEAWAY
Frito-Lay: 1962 (3-1/4x7", soft-c, 16 pgs.) (Disney)

nn-Donald Duck "Plotting Picnickers"	6	18	70
nn-Ludwig Von Drake "Fish Stampede"	4	12	40
nn- Mickey Mouse & Goofy "Bicep Bungle"	4	12	45

GENERAL FOODS SUPER-HEROES
DC Comics: 1979, 1980

1-4 (1979), 1-4 (1980)	2	6	12

HAWKMAN - THE SKY'S THE LIMIT
DC Comics: 1981 (General Foods giveaway, 8 pages, 3-1/2 x 6-3/4", oblong)

nn	2	6	15

IRON GIANT
DC Comics: 1999 (4 pages, theater giveaway)

1-Previews movie			3.00

JACKIE JOYNER KERSEE IN HIGH HURDLES (Kellogg's Tony's Sports Comics)
DC Comics: 1992 (Sports Illustrated)

nn			3.00

JUNGLE BOOK FUN BOOK, THE (Disney)
Baskin Robbins: 1978

nn-Ice Cream giveaway	2	6	15

JUSTICE LEAGUE ADVENTURES (Based on Cartoon Network series)
DC Comics: May, 2002

Free Comic Book Day giveaway-Reprints #1 with "Free Comic Book Day" banner on-c	2.25

JUSTICE LEAGUE OF AMERICA
DC Comics: 1999 (included in Justice League of America Monopoly game)

nn - Reprints 1st app. in Brave and the Bold #28	2.50

KELLOGG'S CINNAMON MINI-BUNS SUPER-HEROES
DC Comics: 1993 (4 1/4" x 2 3/4")

4 editions: Flash, Justice League America, Superman, Wonder Woman and the Star Riders each.....	4.00

LIGHTNING RACERS
DC Comics: 1989

1			4.50

LOADED (Also see Re-Loaded)
DC Comics: 1995 (Interplay Productions)

1-Garth Ennis-s; promotes video game	4.00

	GD	FN	NM-

LONE RANGER, THE
Dell Publishing Co.

Doll Giveaways (Gabriel Ind.)(1973, 3-1/4x5")- "The Story of The Lone
  Ranger," "The Carson City Bank Robbery" & "The Apache Buffalo Hunt"

	2	6	20

Legend of The Lone Ranger (1969, 16 pgs., giveaway)-Origin The Lone

Ranger	4	12	45

LOONEY TUNES
DC Comics: 1991, 1998

Claritan promotional issue (1998)			2.50
Colgate mini-comic (1998)			2.50
Tyson's 1-10 (1991)			4.00

MAD MAGAZINE
DC Comics: 1997, 1999

Special Edition (1997, Tang giveaway)			2.50
Stocking Stuffer (1999)			2.50

MAN OF STEEL BEST WESTERN
DC Comics: 1997

nn-Best Western hotels			4.00

MARK STEEL
American Iron & Steel Institute: 1967, 1968, 1972 (Giveaway) (24 pgs.)

1967,1968- "Journey of Discovery with…"; Neal Adams art

	4	12	50
1972- "…Fights Pollution"; N. Adams-a	3	10	35

MARVEL AGE SPIDER-MAN
Marvel Comics: Aug, 2004 (Free Comic Book Day giveaway)

1-Spider-Man vs. The Vulture; Brooks-a			2.25

MARVEL COLLECTOR'S EDITION: X-MEN
Marvel Comics: 1993 (3-3/4x6-1/2")

1-4-Pizza Hut giveaways			5.00

MARVEL COMICS PRESENTS
Marvel Comics: 1987, 1988 (4 1/4 x 6 1/4, 20 pgs.)
...Mini Comic Giveaway

nn-(1988) Alf	1	3	8
nn-(1987) Captain America r/ #250	1	3	7
nn-(1987) Care Bears (Star Comics...)	1	3	7
nn-(1988) Flintstone Kids	1	3	8
nn-(1987) Heathcliffe (Star Comics...)	1	3	7
nn-(1987) Spider-Man-r/Spect. Spider-Man #21	1	3	7
nn-(1988) Spider-Man-r/Amazing Spider-Man #1	1	3	7
nn-(1988) X-Men-reprints X-Men #53; B. Smith-a	1	3	7

MARVEL GUIDE TO COLLECTING COMICS, THE
Marvel Comics: 1982 (16 pgs., newsprint pages and cover)

1-Simonson-c	1	3	7

	GD	FN	NM -

MARVEL MINI-BOOKS
Marvel Comics Group: 1966 (50 pgs., B&W; 5/8x7/8") (6 different issues)
(Smallest comics ever published) (Marvel Mania Giveaways)

	GD	FN	NM -
Captain America, Millie the Model, Sgt. Fury, Hulk, Thor each...	9	27	110
Spider-Man	9	27	120

NOTE: Each came in six different color covers, usually one color: Pink, yellow, green, etc.

MASTERS OF THE UNIVERSE (He-Man)
DC Comics: 1982

1-7			6.00

McDONALDS COMMANDRONS
DC Comics: 1985

nn-Four editions			5.00

MICKEY MOUSE (Also see Frito-Lay Giveaway)
Dell Publ. Co

	GD	FN	NM -
...& Goofy Explore Business(1978)	1	4	10
...& Goofy Explore Energy(1976-1978, 36 pgs.); Exxon giveaway in color; regular size	1	4	10
...& Goofy Explore Energy Conservation(1976-1978)-Exxon	1	4	10
...& Goofy Explore The Universe of Energy(1985, 20 pgs.); Exxon giveaway in color; regular size	1	3	7
The Perils of Mickey nn (1993, 5-1/4x7-1/4", 16 pgs.)-Nabisco giveaway w/ games, Nabisco coupons & 6 pgs. of stories; Phantom Blot app.			5.00

MIGHTY ATOM, THE
Whitman

	GD	FN	NM -
Giveaway (1959, '63, Whitman)-Evans-a	3	9	24
Giveaway ('64r, '65r, '66r, '67r, '68r)-Evans-r?	2	6	14
Giveaway ('73r, '76r)	1	4	10

MIRACLE ON BROADWAY
Broadway Comics: Dec, 1995 (Giveaway)

1-Ernie Colon-c/a; Jim Shooter & Co. story; 1st known digitally printed comic book; 1st app. Spire & Knights on Broadway (1150 print run)			20.00

NOTE: Miracle on Broadway was a limited edition comic given to 1100 VIPs in the entertainment industry for the 1995 Holiday Season.

NEW TEEN TITANS, THE
DC Comics: Nov. 1983

	GD	FN	NM -
nn(11/83-Keebler Co. Giveaway)-In cooperation with "The President's Drug Awareness Campaign"; came in Presidential envelope w/letter from White House (Nancy Reagan)	1	3	7
nn-(re-issue of above on Mando paper for direct sales market); American Soft Drink Industry version; I.B.M. Corp. version			5.00

NOLAN RYAN IN THE WINNING PITCH (Kellogg's Tony's Sports Comics)
DC Comics: 1992 (Sports Illustrated)

nn			4.00

	GD	FN	NM-

OZZIE SMITH IN THE KID WHO COULD (Kellogg's Tony's Sports Comics)
DC Comics: 1992 (Sports Illustrated)

nn-Ozzie Smith app.   5.00

POPEYE
Whitman

Bold Detergent giveaway (Same as regular issue #94) 2   6   14
Quaker Cereal premium (1989, 16pp, small size,4 diff.)(Popeye & the Time Machine, --On Safari, --& Big Foot, --vs. Bluto)   1   4   10

POPEYE
Charlton (King Features) (Giveaway): 1972 - 1974 (36 pgs. in color)

E-1 to E-15 (Educational comics)   2   6   14
nn-Popeye Gettin' Better Grades-4 pgs. used as intro. to above giveaways (in color)   2   6   14

POWER RECORD COMICS
Marvel Comics/Power Records: 1974 - 1978 ($1.49, 7x10" comics, 20 pgs. with 45 R.P.M. record)

PR10-Spider-Man-r/from #124,125; Man-Wolf app. PR18-Planet of the Apes-r. PR19-Escape From the Planet of the Apes-r. PR20-Beneath the Planet of the Apes-r. PR21-Battle for the Planet of the Apes-r. PR24-Spider-Man II-New-a begins. PR27-Batman "Stacked Cards"; N. Adams-a(p). PR30-Batman; N. Adams-r/Det.(7 pgs.).
    With record; each...   5   15   60

PR11-Hulk-r. PR12-Captain America-r/#168. PR13-Fantastic Four-r/#126. PR14-Frankenstein-Ploog-r/#1. PR15-Tomb of Dracula-Colan-r/#2. PR16-Man-Thing-Ploog-r/#5. PR17-Werewolf By Night-Ploog-r/Marvel Spotlight #2. PR28-Superman "Alien Creatures". PR29-Space: 1999 "Breakaway". PR31-Conan-N. Adams-a; reprinted in Conan #116. PR32-Space: 1999 "Return to the Beginning". PR33-Superman-G.A. origin, Buckler-a(p). PR34-Superman. PR35-Wonder Woman-Buckler-a(p)
    With record; each...   4   12   50

PR25-Star Trek "Passage to Moauv". PR26-Star Trek "Crier in Emptiness." PR36-Holo-Man. PR37-Robin Hood. PR39-Huckleberry Finn. PR40-Davy Crockett. PR41-Robinson Crusoe. PR42-20,000 Leagues Under the Sea. PR46-Star Trek "The Robot Masters". PR47-Little Women
    With record; each...   4   12   40

RELOADED (Also see Loaded)
DC Comics: 1996 (Interplay Productions, 16 pgs.)

  1-Promotes video game; Alan Grant-s/John Mueller-a   4.00

RICHIE RICH, CASPER & WENDY NATIONAL LEAGUE
Harvey Publications: June, 1976 (52 pgs.)

  1 (Released-3/76 with 6/76 date)   3   9   24
  1 (6/76)-2nd version w/San Francisco Giants & KTVU 2 logos; has "Compliments of Giants and Straw Hat Pizza" on-c 3   9   24
  1-Variants for other 11 NL teams, similar to Giants version but with different ad on inside front-c   3   9   24

SHAZAM! (Visits Portland Oregon in 1943)
DC Comics: 1989 (69¢ cover)

	GD	FN	NM-

nn-Promotes Super-Heroes exhibit at Oregon Museum of Science and
    Industry; reprints Golden Age Captain Marvel story 2   6   12

SPACE GHOST COAST TO COAST
Cartoon Network: Apr, 1994 (giveaway to Turner Broadcasting employees)

1-(8 pgs.); origin of Space Ghost   6.00

SPIDER-MAN (See Amazing Spider-Man, The)

STAR TEAM
Marvel Comics Group: 1977 (6-1/2x5", 20 pgs.) (Ideal Toy Giveaway)

nn   2   6   20

STAR WARS
Dark Horse Comics: May, 2002; July, 2004 (Free Comic Book Day giveaways)

...: Clone Wars Adventures (7/04) based on Cartoon Network series   2.25
...: Tales - A Jedi's Weapon (5/02, 16 pgs.) Anakin Skywalker Episode 2
    photo-c   2.25

SUGAR BEAR
Post Cereal Giveaway: No date, circa 1975? (2-1/2x4-1/2", 16 pgs.)

"The Almost Take Over of the Post Office", "The Race Across the Atlantic",
    "The Zoo Goes Wild" each...   1   3   8

SUPER FRIENDS
DC Comics: 1981 (Giveaway, no ads, no code or price)

...Special 1 -r/Super Friends #19 & 36   2   6   12

SUPERGEAR COMICS
Jacobs Corp.: 1976 (Giveaway, 4 pgs. in color, slick paper)

nn-(Rare)-Superman, Lois Lane; Steve Lombard app. (500 copies printed,
    over half destroyed?)   24   72   350

SUPERGIRL
DC Comics: 1984, 1986 (Giveaway, Baxter paper)

nn-(American Honda/U.S. Dept. Transportation)   2   6   12

SUPER HEROES PUZZLES AND GAMES
General Mills Giveaway (Marvel Comics): 1979 (32 pgs., regular size)

nn-Four 2-pg. origin stories of Spider-Man, Captain America, The Hulk, &
    Spider-Woman   3   9   24

SUPERMAN
National Periodical Publ./DC Comics

... For the Animals (2000, Doris Day Animal Foundation, 30 pgs.) polybagged
    with Gotham Adventures #22, Hourman #12, Impulse #58, Looney Tunes
    #62, Stars and S.T.R.I.P.E. #8 and Superman Adventures #41   2.50
Kenner: Man of Steel (Doomsday is Coming) (1995, 16 pgs.) packaged with
    set of Superman and Doomsday action figures   3.50
...Meets the Quik Bunny (1987, Nestles Quik premium, 36 pgs.)
                                    1   3   8
Pizza Hut Premiums (12/77)-Exact reprints of 1950s comics except for paid
    ads (set of 6 exist?); Vol. 1-r#97 (#113-r also known)

	GD	FN	NM-
	1	3	10

Radio Shack Giveaway-36 pgs. (7/80) "The Computers That Saved
  Metropolis", Starlin/Giordano-a; advertising insert in Action #509, New
  Advs. of Superboy #7, Legion of Super-Heroes #265, & House of Mystery
  #282. (All comics were 68 pgs.) Cover of inserts printed on newsprint.
  Giveaway contains 4 extra pgs. of Radio Shack advertising that inserts

do not have	1	3	7
Radio Shack Giveaway-(7/81) "Victory by Computer"	1	3	7
Radio Shack Giveaway-(7/82) "Computer Masters of Metropolis"			
	1	3	7

SUPERMAN ADVENTURES, THE (TV)
DC Comics: 1996 (Based on animated series)

1-(1996) Preview issue distributed at Warner Bros. stores			4.00
Titus Game Edition (1998)			2.50

SUPERMAN RECORD COMIC
National Periodical Publications: 1966 (Golden Records)

(With record)-Record reads origin of Superman from comic; came with iron-on
  patch, decoder, membership card & button; comic-r/Superman #125,146

	20	60	230
Comic only	10	30	120

SWORDQUEST
DC Comics/Atari Pub.: 1982, 52pg., 5"x7" (Giveaway with video games)

1,2-Roy Thomas & Gerry Conway-s; George Pérez & Dick Giordano-c/a in			
all	2	6	16
3-Low print	3	9	25

TAZ'S 40TH BIRTHDAY BLOWOUT
DC Comics: 1994 (K-Mart giveaway, 16 pgs.)

nn-Six pg. story, games and puzzles			4.00

TEEN TITANS GO!
DC Comics: Sept, 2004 (Free Comic Book Day giveaway)

1-Reprints Teen Titans Go! #1; 2 bound-in Wacky Packages stickers			2.25

3-D COLOR CLASSICS (Wendy's Kid's Club)
Wendy's Int'l Inc.: 1995 (5 1/2" x 8", comes with 3-D glasses)

The Elephant's Child, Gulliver's Travels, Peter Pan, The Time Machine,			
20,000 Leagues Under the Sea: Neal Adams-a in all each....			3.50

TIME MACHINE, THE
DC Comics: 2002 (10 pgs.)

nn-Promotes the 2002 DreamWorks movie			5.00

TITANS BEAT (Teen Titans)
DC Comics: Aug, 1996 (16 pgs., paper-c)

1-Intro./preview new Teen Titans members; Pérez-a			4.00

2001, A SPACE ODYSSEY (Movie)
Marvel Comics Group

	GD	FN	NM -
Howard Johnson giveaway (1968, 8pp); 6 pg. movie adaptation, 2 pg. games, puzzles; McWilliams-a	2	6	15

ULTIMATE SPIDER-MAN
Marvel Comics: May, 2002

	GD	FN	NM -
Free Comic Book Day giveaway-Reprints #1 with FCBD banner on-c			2.25
1-Kay Bee Toys variant edition	2	6	15

UNTOLD LEGEND OF THE BATMAN, THE
DC Comics: 1989 (28 pgs., 6X9", limited series) (1st & 2nd printings known)

	GD	FN	NM -
1-Batman cereal premium; Byrne-a	1	3	9
2,3	1	3	7

WALT DISNEY'S DONALD DUCK ADVENTURES
Gemstone Publishing: May, 2003 (giveaway promoting 2003 return of Disney Comics)

	GD	FN	NM -
...Free Comic Book Day Edition - cover logo on red background; reprints "Maharajah Donald" & "The Peaceful Hills" from March of Comics #4; Barks-s/a; Kelly original-c on back-c			2.25
...San Diego Comic-Con 2003 Edition - cover logo on gold background			2.25
...ANA World's Fair of Money Baltimore Ed. - cover logo on green bkgd.			2.25
...WizardWorld Chicago 2003 Edition - cover logo on blue background			2.25

WALT DISNEY'S MICKEY MOUSE AND UNCLE SCROOGE
Gemstone Publishing: June, 2004 (Free Comic Book Day giveaway)

	GD	FN	NM -
nn-Flip book with r/Uncle Scrooge #15 and r/Mickey Mouse Four Color #79 (only Barks drawn Mickey Mouse story)			2.25

WOLVERINE
Marvel Comics: 1999 (Nabisco mail-in offer)

	GD	FN	NM -
145-Variant cover by Sienkiewicz	10	30	125
...Son of Canada (4/01, ed. of 65,000) Spider-Man & The Hulk app.			3.00

WONDER WOMAN
DC Comics: 1977

	GD	FN	NM -
Pizza Hut Giveaways (12/77)-Reprints #60,62	2	6	15
... - The Minotaur (1981, General Foods giveaway, 8 pages, 3-1/2 x 6-3/4", oblong)	2	6	20

WORLD'S GREATEST SUPER HEROES
DC Comics (Nutra Comics) (Child Vitamins, Inc.): 1977 (Giveaway, 3-3/4x3-3/4", 24 pgs.)

	GD	FN	NM -
nn-Batman & Robin app.; health tips	2	6	16

X-MEN THE MOVIE
Marvel Comics/Toys R' Us: 2000

	GD	FN	NM -
Special Movie Prequel Edition			5.00

YOGI BEAR (TV)
Dell Publishing Co.

	GD	FN	NM -
Giveaway ('84, '86)-City of Los Angeles, "Creative First Aid" & "Earthquake Preparedness for Children"	1	3	7

Toy Rings

For decades, ring collectors have searched far and wide for the next addition to their collection. Ads in comic books, monster magazines, toy and antique publications occasionally contained ring offerings of interest. Today, older rings are always turning up at antique stores and shows, auctions, comic book conventions, comic book stores, flea markets, toy conventions and of course on the Internet. Getting to know who the key ring dealer/collectors are will increase your chances of obtaining a rare ring whenever one comes up for sale. In the past, the rarest rings were usually passed on from collector to collector or collector/dealer. Over the years the collector would develop a waiting list of buyers for his rarest rings. He only had to privately contact these prospects when it was time to sell. Thanks to the advent of Internet auctions, the market for this collectible category has expanded significantly.

There are many shows that are well worth a search if you're looking for that elusive toy ring purchase. One of the largest, the Atlantique Convention, takes place in Atlantic City in March and again in October. Other important shows for rings and premiums can be found listed on Internet websites devoted to collecting. Rings are a collectible with crossover appeal to many other collectors, so occasionally, comic book and cereal box dealers will also have rings for sale. Ring collectors should check comic book shows around the country as they're also good sources to investigate.

Many toy rings are still offered each year, even though the heyday of the toy ring was decades ago. In the last fifteen years or so, DC produced the Superman Magnet and Green Lantern Squirt rings. Matchbox developed a beautiful set of 68 rings called the "Ring Raiders," and Mattel produced a popular series called "Polly Pockets," with its own styled ring box in the early 1990s. Marvel released an X-Men series of rings, while Image produced Spawn rings. Special rings were released along with comic-themed movies like *The Shadow* and *The Phantom* as well. Rings still appear in blister packs with action figures at major toy stores.

Cereal boxes remain a good source for mail-away ring offers. Lucky Charms offered the Lucky Horseshoe ring in 1985 and Kellogg's Sugar Corn Pops offered a set of 28 football insignia rings in the 1980s and a six ring set of Simpsons Squirt rings in 1997. Disney and Warner Bros. alone have been responsible for the release of many collectible rings.

Ring prices are always changing as the market continues to grow. The wise investor should keep up with the latest sales and discoveries, using this listing only as a guide. We hope this reference work will provide up-to-date information for the collector in this new and exciting hobby.

A word of warning: Because of the popularity of collecting rings, many new fantasy and unlicensed rings are appearing in the market. Reproductions of licensed rings are also prevalent. Rely on experts to tell the difference and protect you from a serious financial miscalculation.

A special thanks to all who helped in the compilation of this listing of those wonderful little collectibles, toy rings!

Grading Toy Rings

Condition plays a large role in determining the value for most rings. The more valuable the ring, the more important condition and accurate grading becomes. Obviously a ring in Mint condition is worth more than one in Good condition, and the value difference could be considerable, as much as 10 times the Good value. For a ring to bring the highest price, it must be complete, original, unrestored and in top condition. Rings should be graded with a keen eye for detail, and close attention should be given to luster, surface wear and defects, color chipping and fading, damage, plastic altered by heat, plating wear, missing parts, replaced parts and restoration before a grade is assigned. The following grades should be used to more accurately describe the condition of your rings.

10 - MINT (MT): Same condition as issued; complete with full luster and no sign of wear. Rarely occurs in 1930s to 1940s rings. In very rare cases, rings have occurred with unbent prongs on otherwise fitted rings and are worth a premium. Rings in this condition could bring considerably more than the Near Mint (NM) listing.

9 - NEAR MINT (NM): Nearly perfect with the slightest evidence of wear and 90% luster to the naked eye. Generally the highest grade reached by most of the metal rings.

8 - VERY FINE (VF): Wear beginning to show on high points, but 70% of the surface shows luster. Very minor color flaking may be evident but the overall appearance is still very desirable.

7 - FINE (FN): Still enough luster to be desirable. General wear beginning to show. Less than 70% and more than 50% luster evident. Slightly above average condition.

5-6 - VERY GOOD (VG): Most of the luster is gone, general wear, tarnishing and fading is the general rule. Prongs can be bent but are still complete. On plated rings, base metal can be seen over much of the ring. Paper (where applicable) could be stained but is still legible and complete. Most rings that have been cleaned will fall into this grade.

3-4 - GOOD (GD): Below average condition. Still complete but prongs can be chipped or bent, color or plating will be gone. Surface abrasion and wear is obvious but all parts must be present.

2 - FAIR (FR): Excessive wear obvious. A minor part may be missing.

1 - POOR (PR): Incomplete and not suited for investment purposes.

Remember: CONDITION IS THE KEY TO VALUE !

History of Toy Rings

Since Man first worked metal and discovered the pleasures of jewelry and adornment, we have been fascinated with rings. Long before science answered many of the world's great mysteries, many even believed in rings that possessed magical powers. From the royal signets once wielded by ancient monarchs to the fictional One Ring in J.R.R. Tolkien's *Lord of the Rings*, we have always been enthralled by the power and beauty of rings.

When Boris Karloff used a ring to bring down his victims in the famous 1933 movie *The Mummy*, illustrator Carl Barks seized on the idea for "The Mummy's Ring" (*Four Color Comics* #29, 1943). In baseball collecting, the Pennant and World Series rings are highly prized by competitors and collectors. No matter what the field of interest, rings have often been a fixture and have grown into a substantial collectible enterprise in their own right.

The earliest known premium rings were given away at the 1893 Columbian Exposition in Chicago. The first ring associated with a cartoon character was the Buster Brown ring dating to the early 1900s. In the 1920s a set of two or three Tarzan rings was offered. These early rings are very scarce in today's market.

By the 1930s the premium ring was given away to children as an early device to trace consumer response to various products. The producers were quick to use words like "mysterious," "mystic," "scarab," "lucky," "cosmic," "ancient," "dragon," "Egyptian," "Aztec," "secret," "magical," etc., reinforcing the ancient belief that rings truly do possess magical and secret properties; of course the only magic at work there was in the marketing office. Cereal companies, sponsors of radio and television shows, beverage companies, food producers, movie studios, comic book companies, toy producers, and sports promoters all gave away rings for this purpose.

The earliest premium ring based on a radio show is the Lone Wolf Tribal ring. This ring is made of sterling silver and was offered in 1932 by Wrigley Gum (the sponsor of the popular *Lone Wolf* radio show) to test listener response. Soon after this historic first, the famous comic strip character *Little Orphan Annie* got her own nationally broadcast radio show. Now known as "Radio" Orphan Annie items, dozens of premiums began appearing on the market, including some of the rarest rings ever offered anywhere. The ROA Altascope (less than 10) was the last ring offered before the radio show was canceled and is the rarest of the ROA rings. The ROA Magnifying and Initial rings are the next most difficult ROA rings to find. Other popular character rings from the 1930s included Buck Rogers, Tom Mix, Frank Buck and Melvin Purvis. The Tom Mix Deputy ring from 1935 was very difficult to acquire and today is one of the 20 rarest rings. Box tops, candy or gum wrappers, and coupons, etc., were required in most cases to receive a premium ring. Some rings were only offered in a limited area while others, like the Kix Atom Bomb, exploded all over the country.

During the 1940s the sponsors of popular radio shows such as *The Shadow, The Lone Ranger, Sky King, Green Hornet* and *Superman* offered premium rings to listeners. The Lone Ranger Atom Bomb, also given away through Kix cereal in 1946, was the most successful premium ever with over 1 million produced. Today this ring is still revered as one of the most beautiful and desirable because of its breathtaking design and eye-catching colors.

The most valuable of these rings is the Supermen of America Membership ring, which was advertised to have shipped to 1,600 winners of the *Action Comics* contest in early 1940. Only 20 complete examples of this ring are known to exist, with all but one in less than Near Mint condition.

The earliest rings were made of metal and usually exhibited excellent quality in design and material; some were even gold plated. Plastic first appeared in 1907 (Bakelite); rings using plastic made their appearance in the late 1930s, and by the 1950s the number of rings made of this cheaper material rivalled then surpassed the metal ones.

After World War II, TV broadcasting exploded, resulting in a huge expansion of the audience for premium offers. Soon, many premiums were being offered through popular television shows. The Clarabelle Face/Hat ring from *Howdy Doody* is the rarest plastic/metal item from this era. Just as in radio, the premiums were used to test viewer response.

Western and space heroes who appeared in comics, on television and on radio also spawned dozens of rings. Gene Autry, Roy Rogers, Gabby Hayes, Hopalong Cassidy, *Space Patrol*, *Captain Video* and others had their rings too.

During the 1960s, dozens of plastic rings based on television shows and celebrities flooded the market. *The Addams Family*, *Dark Shadows*, the Beatles, *Davy Crockett*, *The Munsters*, *Tarzan*, and *Batman* are just a few shows that produced rings. Cereal personalities such as Quisp and Quake also had their series of rings. In fact, the Quisp Figural ring is one of the most valuable post-1959 rings.

The 1970s and '80s saw rings released based on media properties like *Star Wars* (film), *Star Trek* (TV), McDonald's (fast food chain), *Huckleberry Hound* (TV), *Cap'n Crunch* (cereal), and *G.I. Joe* (toys and more). One of the most ambitious ring programs ever initiated was the 1990s *Ring Raiders* set, with an amazing 68 rings in the set.

Today, comic book and collectible companies continue to produce rings, many of which are once again made of metal. Often these are produced specifically for the collectors' market, and many are of high quality in design and manufacture. Rings based on characters like Spider-Man, the X-Men, Batman, Spawn, the Shadow, and many more turn up every year. The saga of the toy ring has only just begun!

Using this Book

This books features a sampling of the many toy rings that one can try to collect. All listings are arranged alphabetically in columns, and should be referenced from top to bottom. Complete ring sets are listed as sets when known, with arrows linking related pictures. Additional pictures may also be used to indicate ring features. Before purchasing a ring, check the illustrations and description in this book to be sure all parts are present.

Price guides exist for antique rings of a generic nature and are quite popular. With the groundswell of interest in the collectibility of comic character-themed and premium rings, this is a perfect time to expand your horizons and discover the fun of collecting toy rings. But how to do it? Read on!

Starting a Collection

Toy rings are still produced today by many comic book and collectible companies, often as mail-away offers. Many of these rings are limited editions and sell out quickly, so be prepared to pay a premium price if you purchase them from dealers or collectors after production is discontinued. Of course, older rings are difficult to find but can be bought from reliable dealers and at toy, comic and collectible shows throughout the country. Before starting your collection, you might want to peruse the rings listings in this book to see if there is any specific character or category that might interest you.

Many premium rings came with a mailing envelope or box and papers ("instructions"). Ring papers are usually scarce, very valuable, and an interesting addition to any ring collection. Other rings appeared in groups attached to cards. Rings were also offered in cereal box promotions, newspaper comic sections and comic book ads. These advertising pages make a ring collection display more colorful and interesting.

Most rings are still inexpensive and affordable. The market is relatively young and new discoveries are always possible for the energetic collector. You may also discover rings that are either omitted from our price guide or incorrectly listed. As always, we're pleased to hear from anyone who has information that can enhance our future publications.

Most Valuable Rings

All prices are for NM rings unless otherwise noted

VALUE	RANK	RING TYPE
$75,000	1	Supermen Of America Prize 1940
$25,500	2	Radio Orphan Annie Altascope 1942
$25,000	3	Superman Secret Compartment with paper Superman image on inside of top (milk) 1941
VF $18,500	4	Superman Secret Compartment with Superman image stamped on top(milk) 1941
$16,000	5	Sky King Kaleidoscope '40s
$15,500	6	Operator Five 1934
$15,000	7	Cisco Kid Secret Compartment 1950s
$8,500	8	Spider 1930s
$8,000	9	Valric of the Vikings 1940s
$6,500	10	Tom Mix Deputy 1935
$6,250	11	Knights of Columbus 1940s
$6,000	12	Lone Ranger (ice cream) 1938

VALUE	RANK	RING TYPE
$5,000	13	Superman Tim 1949
$4,200	14	Buck Rogers Repeller Ray 1930s
$4,200	15	Tom Mix Spinner 1930s
$4,200	16	Tonto Picture (ice cream) 1938
$4,000	17	Frank Buck Black Leopard (World's Fair) 1939
$4,000	18	Lone Ranger Prototype 1942
$4,000	19	Whistle Bomb 1940s
$3,500	20	Green Hornet (plastic) 1930s
$3,500	21	Joe Louis Face 1940s
$3,400	22	Spider-Man (gold) 1993
$3,200	23	Kellogg's Gold Ore 1942
$3,000	24	Clarabelle Face/Hat 1950s
$3,000	25	Frank Buck Black Leopard (unfitted prongs) 1938
$3,000	26	Radio Orphan Annie Initial 1940s
$3,000	27	Radio Orphan Annie Magnifying 1940s
$2,000	28	Bullet Pen 1940s
$2,000	29	Frank Buck Black Leopard (bronze) 1938
$2,000	30	Frank Buck Black Leopard (silver) 1938
$1,800	31	Captain Midnight Mystic Sun God 1947
$1,800	32	Shadow Carey Salt 1947
$1,750	33	Captain Marvel 1940s
$1,650	34	Major Mars Rocket (complete) 1952
$1,600	35	Captain Hawks/Melvin Purvis Scarab 1937
$1,600	36	Space Patrol Cosmic Glow 1950s
$1,500	37	Clyde Beatty Lion's Head 1935
$1,500	38	Don Winslow Member 1938
$1,500	39	Golden Nugget Cave 1950s
$1,500	40	Joe Penner Face Puzzle 1940s
$1,200	41	Buck Rogers Sylvania Bulb 1953
$1,200	42	Sky King Aztec Emerald Calendar 1940s
$1,200	43	Sky King Mystery Picture 1940s
$1,200	44	Ted Williams 1948
$1,100	45	Captain Video Flying Saucer (complete) 1951
$1,000	46	Captain Midnight Signet (1957)
$1,000	47	Green Hornet Seal 1947
$1,000	48	Joe DiMaggio Club 1940s
$1,000	49	Phantom 1950s Rubber Stamp
$1,000	50	Radio Orphan Annie Triple Mystery 1930s

The prices in this guide are in U.S. currency and reflect the market just prior to publication. These reported prices are based on (but not limited to) convention sales, dealers lists, stores, auctions and private sales. The author invites sales lists, sales reports or any other information pertaining to ring information or sales.

> **PRICES IN THIS BOOK ARE FOR ITEMS IN GOOD AND NEAR MINT CONDITION**

Rocket-to-the-Moon

The values listed are for complete examples and represent Good and Near Mint condition where only two prices are shown. All rings valued at $500 or more will show the Good, Fine, and Near Mint values. The more valuable and scarcer rings may have additional grades priced to reflect a wider spread in the value.

Other rings that generally turn up incomplete will be priced in this way with additional prices for the missing parts. Examples are: the **Rocket to the Moon** ring came with 3 rockets–prices are listed for the ring and also for the rockets; the **Captain Video Flying Saucer** ring has prices for the base as well as the saucers, which are usually missing; the **Radio Orphan Annie Triple Mystery** ring is usually found with the top miss-

Captain Video Flying Saucer

ing, so prices for the top and base are given. When rings appear on cards or in sets, both the individual price and the set price may be given.

ROA Triple Mystery

The values in this book are retail prices, not dealers' wholesale prices. Dealers will pay a percentage of the listed prices when buying inventory and this percentage will vary from dealer to dealer. Some dealers are only interested in buying rings in strict near mint or mint condition, while others will buy in all grades.

Ring Pricing Section

Prices listed represent Good and Near Mint condition. Arrow pointing down means follow as links to a set. Arrow pointing up links price to set above.

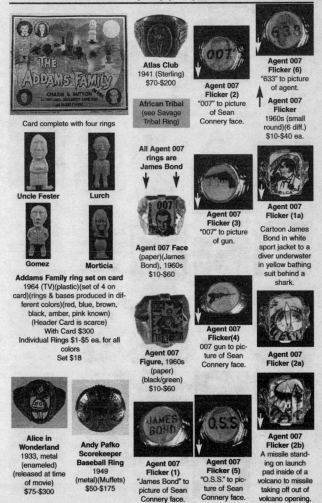

Card complete with four rings

Uncle Fester

Lurch

Gomez

Morticia

Addams Family ring set on card
1964 (TV)(plastic)(set of 4 on card)(rings & bases produced in different colors)(red, blue, brown, black, amber, pink known)
(Header Card is scarce)
With Card $300
Individual Rings $1-$5 ea. for all colors
Set $18

Alice in Wonderland
1933, metal (enameled) (released at time of movie)
$75-$300

Andy Pafko Scorekeeper Baseball Ring
1949 (metal)(Muffets)
$50-$175

Atlas Club
1941 (Sterling)
$70-$200

African Tribal
(see Savage Tribal Ring)

All Agent 007 rings are James Bond

Agent 007 Face
(paper)(James Bond), 1960s
$10-$60

Agent 007 Figure, 1960s (paper) (black/green)
$10-$60

Agent 007 Flicker (1)
"James Bond" to picture of Sean Connery face.

Agent 007 Flicker (2)
"007" to picture of Sean Connery face.

Agent 007 Flicker (3)
"007" to picture of gun.

Agent 007 Flicker(4)
007 gun to picture of Sean Connery face.

Agent 007 Flicker (5)
"O.S.S." to picture of Sean Connery face.

Agent 007 Flicker (6)
"633" to picture of agent.

Agent 007 Flicker
1960s (small round)(6 diff.)
$10-$40 ea.

Agent 007 Flicker (1a)
Cartoon James Bond in white sport jacket to a diver underwater in yellow bathing suit behind a shark.

Agent 007 Flicker (2a)

Agent 007 Flicker (2b)
A missile standing on launch pad inside of a volcano to missile taking off out of volcano opening.

435

Agent 007 Flicker (3a)

Agent 007 Flicker (3)
Dark skinned man with blue hat strapped onto head to same man with veil over face holding a weapon.

Agent 007 Flicker (6a)

Agent 007 Flicker (8b)
Figure in karate outfit with hands together to same man defending himself against a child.

Agent 007 Flicker (6b)
Man in white suit with arms behind his back to same man armed with a sword.

Agent 007 Flicker (11a)

Agent 007 Flicker (11)
White yacht cruising to same yacht moved further along.

Agent 007 Seal
1960s (metal, heavy)
$25-$65

Air Force (see Flight Commander & U.S. Air Force)

Agent 007 Flicker (4a)

Agent 007 Flicker (7a)

Agent 007 Flicker (9a)

Agent 007 Flicker (9b)
Odd-job face to his hat hitting a man in the head.

Agent 007 Flicker (12a)

Agent 007 Flicker (12)
Spaceship in space with cone opening and figure coming out to close-up of figure walking in space.

Agent 007 Flicker (4b)
Picture of two helicopters (1 yellow, 1 white) to close-up of yellow copter.

Agent 007 Flicker (7b)
Face (half white, half flesh with a scar) to same man being punched "POW".

Agent 007 Flicker (10a)

Agent 007 Flicker
1960s (12 diff., (in color, plastic)
Original base -
$10-$45 ea.
Blue base -
$5-$30 ea.

Apollo Flicker (1) Apollo 11 logo to "Apollo 11" cartoon figure of all three figures together.

Apollo Flicker (2) "First Man on the Moon" July 20, 1969 to picture of rocket launching from earth.

Agent 007 Flicker (5a)

Agent 007 Flicker (5)
"007" gun picture to close-up of James Bond holding his gun.

Agent 007 Flicker (8a)

Agent 007 Flicker (10b)
Yellow Aston Martin (sports car) to ejector seat with figure shooting out of sunroof.

Agent 007 Gun
1967 (plastic) (from 007 kit)
$10-$30

Agent 007 Gun,
1960s (metal)
$5-$20

Apollo Flicker (3) "Neil A. Armstrong" to face with space suit on (no helmet).

Apollo Flicker (7) "Columbia" picture to "Eagle" picture.

Apollo Flicker (4) "Edwin E. Aldrin Jr." to face with space suit on (no helmet).

Apollo Flicker (8) "The Eagle has landed" to picture of Eagle landed.

Apollo Flicker (5) "Michael Collins" to face with space suit on (no helmet).

Apollo Flicker (9) "That's one small step for man, one giant leap for mankind" to Armstrong stepping off ladder.

Apollo Flicker (6) Apollo 11 logo to picture of Eagle and Columbia docking.

Apollo Flicker (10) "We came in peace for all mankind" to Armstrong on moon in suit standing by flag.

Apollo Flicker (11) "Apollo 12" angled picture of rocket with moon in background to astronaut on the moon.

Apollo Flicker (12) "Apollo 12" picture of ship on moon to ship taking off of the moon.

Apollo Flicker 1960s, (12 diff.) (scarce set)
Silver base $10-$40 ea.
Blue base- $5-$25 ea.

Apollo Flicker 1960s Armstrong, Aldrin & Collins photograph faces to picture of Eagle sitting on moon with Earth in background $10-$40

Arby's Bugs Bunny Flicker

Arby's Daffy Duck Flicker (obverse & reverse)

Arby's Porky Pig Flicker

Arby's Yosemite Sam Flicker

Arby's Flickers 1987 (set of 4) $15-$65 ea.

Arthur Murray Spinner 1937 (Murray Go Round) (Also see Tom Mix Spinner) (metal) $25-$90

Babe Ruth Club 1934-1936 (gold color metal, Muffets)(glove between crossed bats on side) $60-$250

Barnabas Collins 1969 (Dark Shadows, TV)(Gum) (2 versions)
Plain Base Version
GD $150, FN $400, NM $700
Filigree Base Version
GD $100, FN $300, NM $500

TOY RINGS

Baseball Centennial-Jack Armstrong
(1839-1939)
1939 (gold plated metal) (rare)(also given away by Quaker Puffed Rice later)
GD $250
FN $600
NM $800

Batman Disc
1960s (paper on plastic) (several versions)
$20-$50

Batman Disc
1960s (plastic with paper insert)
$10-$25

Batman Disc
1960s (Batman photograph face (Adam West) to Robin photograph face (Burt Ward))(round)
$25-$70

Batman Flicker (1) "Member Batman Ring Club" to full figure "Batman/Robin" side by side

Batman Flicker (3) "Batman" chest view up to "Bruce Wayne" chest view up

Batman Flicker (4) "Robin" chest view up to "Dick Grayson" chest view up

Batman Flicker (7) "Batmobile" to Batman & Robin swinging on ropes dropping into the Batmobile

Baseball, Cleveland Indians
1950s (metal)
$35-$100

Batman Disc - Joker
1960s (plastic, red on white paper)(red & green base variations)(many different)
$20-$50

Batman Flicker (5) "Batman" face to full figure swinging on rope

Batman Flicker (8a & b) "Batcopter" to close up of Batman & Robin in Batcopter

Batman
1966 (in box) (metal, DC, 3 diff.)
In Box $40
Ring Only $10-$20

Batman Clock Flicker
1960s (silver base)
$25-$75

Batman Flicker (2) "Batman" face to "Robin" face

Batman Flicker (6) "Robin" face to full figure swinging on rope

Batman Flicker (9) "Riddler" face to "BAM" Batman & Riddler fighting

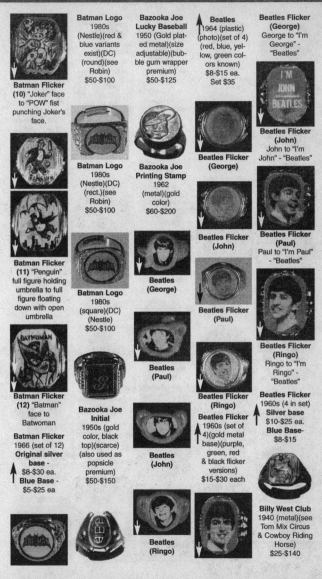

Batman Flicker (10) "Joker" face to "POW" fist punching Joker's face.

Batman Logo 1980s (Nestle)(red & blue variants exist)(DC)(round)(see Robin) $50-$100

Bazooka Joe Lucky Baseball 1950 (Gold plated metal)(size adjustable)(bubble gum wrapper premium) $50-$125

Beatles 1964 (plastic)(photo)(set of 4) (red, blue, yellow, green colors known) $8-$15 ea. Set $35

Beatles Flicker (George) George to "I'm George" - "Beatles"

Beatles Flicker (John) John to "I'm John" - "Beatles"

Batman Logo 1980s (Nestle)(DC)(rect.)(see Robin) $50-$100

Bazooka Joe Printing Stamp 1962 (metal)(gold color) $60-$200

Beatles Flicker (George)

Beatles Flicker (Paul) Paul to "I'm Paul" - "Beatles"

Batman Flicker (11) "Penguin" full figure holding umbrella to full figure floating down with open umbrella

Batman Logo 1980s (square)(DC)(Nestle) $50-$100

Beatles (George)

Beatles Flicker (John)

Beatles Flicker (Paul)

Beatles Flicker (Ringo) Ringo to "I'm Ringo" - "Beatles"

Batman Flicker (12) "Batman" face to Batwoman

Batman Flicker 1966 (set of 12) **Original silver base** - $8-$30 ea. **Blue Base** - $5-$25 ea

Bazooka Joe Initial 1950s (gold color, black top)(scarce) (also used as popsicle premium) $50-$150

Beatles (Paul)

Beatles (John)

Beatles Flicker (Ringo)

Beatles Flicker 1960s (set of 4)(gold metal base)(purple, green, red & black flicker versions) $15-$30 each

Beatles Flicker 1960s (4 in set) **Silver base** $10-$25 ea. **Blue Base-** $8-$15

Billy West Club 1940 (metal)(see Tom Mix Circus & Cowboy Riding Horse) $25-$140

Beatles (Ringo)

Black Flame
1930s (Hi Speed Gas)(metal)(gold color)
$125-$500

Brownies Jumping Elf (1)
1930s-1940s (sterling)
$40-$125

Buck Rogers Repeller Ray
1936 (Cream of Wheat) (green stone) (gold color)
Good - $600
FIne - $1,000
Very Fine - $1,750
Near Mint - $4,200

Bullet Pen
1940s (metal, generic)(very rare)(Robbins archives) (prototype)
$2,000

Buster Brown Flicker, side 2 (Tige)
↑ **Buster Brown Club Flicker**
1950s (Buster to Tige)(color)
$25-$75

Bozo's Circus
1960s (metal)
$30-$100

Brownies Jumping Elf (2)
1940s (sterling)
$20-$60

Buck Rogers Ring of Saturn
1946 (plastic)(red stone)(Post)
GD $100, FN $200, NM $600

Buster Brown Club, 1948 (metal)(fancy and plain band variants)
$25-$80

Br'er Fox Club
1938 (metal-rare)
$75-$150

Buck Jones Club Ring
1937 (Grape Nuts)(metal)
$60-$200

Buster Brown
1900s (metal, rare)
GD $250, FN $500, NM $800

Buzz Corey Space Patrol
1950s (plastic)(photo) (rare)
$225-$450

Bronco Rider Flicker, 1950s (thick top lens)
$25-$75

Buck Rogers Birthstone
1934 (Cocomalt) (birthstones in red, yellow, blue, green & white known)
$150-$500

Buck Rogers Sylvania Bulb
1953, (metal) (glows-in-dark) (Sylvania)(rare)
Good- $250
Fine - $500
Near Mint- $1,200

Buffalo Bill (see Kellogg's Picture Rings)

Buster Brown Big Foot Whistle
1976 (red plastic)(Buster Brown Shoes)
$10-$20

Buzz Corey (Carol)
1950s (sidekick photo)(rare)
$175-$375

Broom Hilda Spinner
1970s (on tree, in package)
In Package $75
Assembled-$20-$75

Buck Rogers Photo
1940s (metal)
$150-$525

Buffalo Bill Jr.
1950 (metal)(TV)
$30-$65

Buster Brown Flicker, side 1 (Buster)

Captain Action Flicker (1)
Full figure Capt. Action to full figure CA logo

Captain Action Flicker (2)
Full figure Capt. Action to full figure Aquaman

Captain Action Flicker (3)
Full figure Capt. Action to full figure Batman

Captain Action Flicker (4)
Full figure Capt. Action to full figure Buck Rogers

Captain Action Flicker (5)
Full figure Capt. Action to full figure Capt. America

Captain Action Flicker (6)
Full figure Capt. Action to full figure Flash Gordon

Captain Action Flicker (7)
Full figure Capt. Action to full figure Green Hornet
$50-$125

Captain Action Flicker (9)
Full figure Capt. Action to full figure Phantom

Captain Action Flicker (10)
Full Figure Capt Action to full figure Spider-Man
$50-$125

Captain Action Flicker (11)
Full figure Capt. Action to full figure Steve Canyon

Captain Action Flicker (12)
Full figure Capt. Action to full figure Superman

Captain Action Flicker (13)
Full figure Capt. Action to full figure Tonto
$30-$80

Captain Action Flicker
1967 (Original silver Hong Kong base)(13 in set)

Green Hornet, Spider-Man - Hong Kong Base- $50-$125
Blue Base- $30-$60;
China Base- $15-$30;

Batman, Buck Rogers, Flash Gordon, Lone Ranger, Phantom, Tonto-Hong Kong base- $30-$80;
Blue Base- $10-$40;
China Base- $5-$20;

All other Captain Action rings-Hong Kong- $30-$80;
Blue Base- $10-$30
China Base- $5-$15

Captain Action Flicker (8)
Full figure Capt. Action to full figure Lone Ranger

Captain Action Doll Box   **Action Boy Doll Box**
1967 (v-based rings included on inside)

Captain America
1980s (metal) (in color) (vitamins)
$60-$250

Captain Bill
1940s (Hills Brothers)(scarce)
$75-$225

Cap'n Crunch Whistle
1970s (cereal)(plastic, diff. colors)(2 views)(also see Whistle Police)
$30-$60

Cap'n Crunch
1970s (similar to Crazy ring)(no indentation on side of base)
$30-$60

Cap'n Crunch Cannon, 1964 (plastic)(cereal) $30-$75

Cap'n Crunch Compass 1964 (cereal) $20-$60

Cap'n Crunch Figural 1964 (plastic)(cereal) $50-$150

Cap'n Crunch Guided Missile 1970s (cereal)(plastic) $50-$150

Cap'n Crunch Carlyle's Rocket Ring 1970s (cereal)(plastic) $50-$150

Cap'n Crunch Drunhilde's Spin-it-ring 1970s (cereal)(plastic) $50-$150

Cap'n Crunch I-Spy ring 1970s (cereal)(plastic) $40-$125

Cap'n Frosty Flicker 1960s "Cap'n Frosty" to "Dairy Clipper" $25-$80

Captain Hawks Air Hawks Membership 1936 (metal)(Captain Franks-Air Hawks on ring) $35-$125

Captain Hawks Sky Patrol 1936, (metal) (rare in NM) $50-$200

Captain Hawks Secret Scarab 1937 (rare in NM)(Post Bran Flakes)(same as Melvin Purvis Secret Scarab) (24k gold finish)(green top) Good - $400 Fine - $800 Near Mint - $1,600

Captain Marvel 1946 (rare) (metal) (red/yellow) Good - $300 Fine - $600 Very Fine - $800 Near Mint - $1,750 3 versions exist, one w/ Japan on compass dial, one w/Japan on back of compass & one w/o Japan.

Captain Midnight Flight Commander 1941 (Ovaltine)(metal) (gold color) GD $125, FN $300, NM $550

Captain Midnight Flight Commander Signet, 1957 (Ovaltine) (plastic) (rare in VF-NM) GD $200 FN $500 NM $1,000

Captain Midnight Initial Printing 1948, (metal) (gold color) (Ovaltine) GD $100 FN $200 NM $500

Captain Midnight Marine Corps, 1942 (metal)(Ovaltine, gold color) $100-$600

Guided missile ring
Shooting this missile calls for a sharp eye and a steady finger. Easy to load. Just attach rubber band as shown in Figure 1. To fire, push down on lever (Figure 2).

I-Spyglass ring
At last, a really handy spyglass! Lets you see faraway things up close, and Attie says, you can look through either end.

Drunhilde's spin-it-ring
To make it to Drunhilde do have a real flip-n-spun ring. In fact, it is a top. And a whistle.

Carlyle's rocket ring
With Carlyle's streamlined rocket you always have a target game of your friends. Comes complete with adjusting elastic.

Cap'n Crunch Cereal box back ad showing 4 plastic rings.

Top slides off to reveal secret compartment

Captain Midnight Secret Compartment
1942 (metal)(Ovaltine) (also see Pilot's Sec. Compt.)
$75-$400

Captain Midnight Whirlwind Whistling
1941 (Ovaltine)(metal)
$150-$850

Captain Video Secret Seal
1951 (copper top)(gold base, metal)
GD $200, FN $400, NM $800

Casper The Friendly Ghost Flicker, 1960s Casper waving to Casper peeking from the corner (original silver base)
$10-$40

Captain Midnight Mystic Sun-God Ring
1947 (metal/plastic)(Ovaltine)
Good - $350
Fine - $900
Very Fine - $1250
Near Mint - $1,800

Captain Midnight Skelly Oil
1940s (red V)(metal)
$100-$400

Captain Video Secret Seal
1951 (gold)(metal)
GD $150, FN $375, NM $675

Captain Video Pendant
1950s (rare)
Complete w/film
Good - $250
Fine - $400
Near Mint - $800
(Subtract $75-$100 if ring base is missing. If picture is missing, reduce price by 80%)

Casper Figure
1950s (plastic)(cereal)
$25-$75

Casper The Friendly Ghost Flicker, 1960s (Casper walking to Casper flying)(original silver base)
$10-$40

Complete ring has string wrapped around top. Pulling string releases saucer to flight

Both saucers are identical except one has florescent paint on underside. Aluminum metal

Casper Figure
1960s (plastic)(black over white)
$25-$85

Chandu The Magician
1940s (metal)
$75-$175

Captain Video Flying Saucer
1951 (gold, aluminum & nickel base versions, 2 saucers) (one glows in dark)(two diff. saucer sets exist w/plastic glow-in-dark & metal glow-in-dark versions)(Post Toasties and Powerhouse candy premium) (rare with saucers & pull string)
Boxed complete $750-$1,100
Ring w/2 saucers - $300-$900
Base Only $75-$200
Day Saucer Only $150-$300
Night Saucer Only $250-$400

Captain Video Picture Ring
1951 (metal)
$75-$275

Casper Figure
1970 (metal, enameled) (original in silver color, cloisonné; repro. in gold color, enameled)
Gold version (fantasy) $1
Silver version $7-$20

Charlie Chaplin
1940s (rare)(metal)
$125-$375

Charlie McCarthy
1940, (metal) (gold color)
$150-$400

Chumley
1960s (plastic)(black over white)
$40-$125

Cinderella
1960s (aluminum)(Disney)
$25-$75

Cisco Kid Secret Compartment
1950 (rare)(metal)
Good - $2,000
Very Good - $3,000
Fine - $5,000
Very Fine - $7,500
Near Mint - $15,000

Clown Flicker
1960s (gold metal)(Hong Kong star)
$10-$20

Compass
1940s (silver metal)(also see Fireball Twigg)
$20-$60

Chief Wahoo
1941 (Goudey Gum)(metal) (also see Indian)
$30-$120

Cisco Kid Club
1950 (gold & silver color versions)(metal)
$60-$200

Clarabelle Horn
1950s (rare in VF-NM) (metal)(complete w/flute inside)
Good $100
Fine $200
Near Mint $375
Flute missing $75-$200

Clyde Beatty Lions Head
(Quaker Crackles)(adj. band)(no jewels in eyes or mouth)(also see Lion's head)
1935 (rare) GD $400, FN $800, NM $1,500

Compass, Wheaties
1940s (metal)
$15-$40

China Clipper
1936 (Quaker)(gold color, metal)
$40-$150

Cisco Kid Hat
1950 (rare) (name on brim)
GD $100, FN $300, NM $500

Compass
1950s (metal)
$20-$60

China Luck
1940s (metal, gold color)
$50-$150

Cisco Kid Saddle, 1950 (rare)("Kid" on back of saddle)
GD $100, FN $200, NM $400

Clarabelle Face/Hat
1950s (rare)(color)
Good - $800
Fine - $1,200
Near Mint - $3,000

Clyde Beatty Jungle Ring
1940s (silver)
$75-$300

Compass, Nabisco
1950s (gold w/red dial) (metal)
$20-$60

Clown Flicker
1950s (thick top)
$30-$90

Compass, Cocomalt
1936 (metal) (rare example w/unbent prongs)
Unbent Prongs - $60-$120
Fitted - $40-$100

Compass
1950s (metal)
$20-$60

Cousin Eerie
1972 (dated
1969) (Warren)
(metal) (gold
color)(also see
Uncle Creepy)
$30-$150

Cowboy Boot
1940s (Goudey
Gum)(metal)
$10-$20

Cowboy Flicker
1950s (thick top)
$30-$90

Cowboy Flicker
1950s (metal)
(in color)
$30-$90

Cowboy Hat
(Goudey)
1940s (metal)
$10-$30

**Cowboy
Riding Horse**
1950s
(metal)(silver)
(gumball)
$2-$15

**Cowboy Riding
Horse**, 1950s
(metal)
(gold version)
(gumball)
$2-$20

Davey Adams
1940, (Lava)
(siren)(metal)
("D.A.S.C." on
side)(scarce)
GD $200, FN
$400, NM $600

**Davy Crockett
Compass**
1950s (elastic
band)
$65-$225

**Davy Crockett
Face**
1950s (raised)
$15-$40

**Davy Crockett
Face**
1950s (metal)
$20-$60

**Davy Crockett
Face**
1950s (metal)
$30-$80

**Davy Crockett
Face**, 1950s
(square, brass)
$20-$60

**Davy Crockett
Face**, 1950s
(raised)(plastic)
(yellow, red)
$15-$40

**Davy Crockett
Face**, 1950s
(copper)
$15-$40

**Davy Crockett
Face**
1950s (bronze)
$15-$40

**Davy Crockett
Fess Parker
Face photo**
1960s
(raised)(silver)
$15-$40

**Davy Crockett
Fess Parker
Figure Photo**
1960s
$15-$40

**Davy Crockett
Face**, 1950s
(green enamel)
$40-$110

**Davy Crockett
Figure**
1950s (silver)
$20-$60

**Davy Crockett
Figure**, 1950s
(silver)(oval)
$15-$45

**Davy Crockett
Figure**
1950s (plastic)
$7-$20

**Davy Crockett
Figure**
1950s (plastic)
$7-$20

**Davy Crockett
Flicker,**
1955 (TV
Screen)
$50-$150

**Davy Crockett
Head**, 1950s
(bronze)(plastic)
$20-$60

Davy Crockett Head, 1950s (silver)(plastic) $20-$60

Davy Crockett 1950s (blue enamel) $40-$125

Good - $100
Fine - $200
Very Fine - $350
Near Mint - $500
Note: A prototype exists from Robbins warehouse.

Disney (Minnie Mouse)

Dennis The Menace, 1970s (Dairy Queen) (rare, on tree) On Tree Only $50 Assembled $10-$30

Davy Crockett Head, 1950s (gold)(plastic) $20-$60

Dennis The Menace (Dennis) 1960s (plastic) (silver over blue) $10-$50

Disney (Peter Pan)

Devil Dogs 1931 (movie) (Quaker Oats) (offered with initial, 3 boxtops) (gold color metal) (rare in NM) $25-$135

Disney (Pinocchio)

Davy Crockett Indian, 1950s (bronze)(plastic) $20-$60

Dennis The Menace (Joey) 1960s (plastic) (black over orange) $10-$50

Dick Tracy Secret Compartment, 1938 (metal)(gold colored brass) $50-$250

Disney (Pluto)

Davy Crockett Rifle 1950s (silver or bronze) $15-$40

Dennis The Menace (Margaret) 1960s (plastic) (silver over red) $10-$50

Dick Tracy Hat 1940 (var. exists w/enamel hat) (hat painted green)(a version exists with no paint) $50-$200

Disney (Donald Duck)

Disney (Snow White)

Disney (Dumbo)

Disney (Sugar Jets) 1950s (8 diff.)(plastic) $15-$60 ea.

Davy Crockett Rifle 1950s (copper) $15-$40

Dennis The Menace (Ruff) 1960s (plastic)(black over yellow) $10-$50

Dick Tracy Monogram 1930s (rare)(metal)

Disney (Mickey)

Dixie (Hanna-Barbera) 1960s (aluminum) $10-$30

Dizzy Dean Winners 1936 (metal) (Post Grapenuts) $100-$350

Dizzy Dean, Win With... 1935 (Post Grapenuts) (metal) $100-$350

Doctor Dolittle Flicker (1) 1970s (Dr. Dolittle to horse)

Doctor Dolittle Flicker (2) 1970s (Pushmi-Pullyu)(both images shown)

Doctor Dolittle Flicker (3) 1970s (both images shown)

Doctor Dolittle Flicker (4) 1970s (Dr. Dolittle face to "Jip" face of dog)

Doctor Dolittle Flicker (5) 1970s ("Chee-Chee" to gorilla sitting on a log)

Doctor Dolittle Flicker 1970s (12 in set) (scarce) Original base $40-$125 ea.

Don Winslow Member, 1938 (Kelloggs)(metal) (each ring carries its own serial number) Good - $300 Fine - $850 Near Mint - $1,500

Donald Duck Figure 1935 (metal w/color)(2nd Donald Duck ring) (Brier Mfg. Co.) $50-$175

Donald Duck Living Toy 1949 (with magnetized Pep box) Complete $100-$300 Ring Only - $40-$100 Pep Box Only - $150

Dorothy Hart 1940s (metal)(rare in NM)("Sunbrite Junior Nurse Corps." on top) $75-$450

Donald Duck 1950s (glow-in-dark) (square top, color & plain) $35-$100

Donald Duck 1950s (glow-in-dark) (Sterling, color & plain, round & square top) $35-$100 ea.

Donald Duck 1950s (sterling, square, no color) $25-$75

Donald Duck Good Luck Portrait 1950s (metal) $50-$150

Egyptian Sphinx (see Lucky Sheik)

Elsie The Cow 1950s (plastic) $15-$30

Elsie The Cow 1950s, (plastic) (gold on white) $10-$40

Elvis Flicker 1960s (metal)(Elvis Presley to Patsy Kline) $30-$90

Elvis Flicker 1960s $40-$120

447

Elvis Flicker
1960s (Elvis Presley (blue) to Patsy Kline (red) (blue)(metal) (Hong Kong Star)
$30-$90

Felix Flicker
1960s Felix kicking a football

Felix Flicker
1960s Felix swinging a bat (set of 3.) (silver base)
$15-$50 ea.

Flying Jet
1948, (plastic in package)
In package $100
Ring only $20-$75

Flying Saucer
(see Quisp & Wheaties)

Car produced in diff. colors: blue, yellow, red, green known

Ford Magno-Power Car
1950s, (Kelloggs)(Cracker Jack's)(1950 Ford scale model with Mystery Control Ring)(hold magnet under a glass to move car across the top)
Ring only $100-$275
Boxed-complete $400

Elvis Photo
1980s (metal)
$10-$40

Fireball Twigg Explorer's
1948 (Post's Grape Nuts) (see Sundial Shoes)(rare in NM)(also see compass)
$25-$110

Felix Face
1983, (in package)
In Package $40
Ring Only $30

Flight Commander
1940s (generic, metal)(also see Captain Midnight Flight Commander)
$10-$30

Fonz, The
1970s (Happy Days TV tie-in) (metal)(photo)
$45-$135

Football
1948 (Bowman gum)(prices vary on gum cards) (Ring is in 2 variant forms; one regular weight, the other a heavier weight)
Heavier Version - $100-$350

Frank Buck Black Leopard Adventurers' Club
1938, (bronze or silver metal)
Good - $500
Fine - $1,000
NM - $2,000

Frank Buck Black Leopard-World's Fair
1939 (rare) (metal)(Jungle-land)(NY)
Good - $750
Fine - $2,000
Near Mint - $4,000

Frank Buck Ivory Initial
1940s (real ivory)(gold initial) (gold metal)
$100-$450

Unfitted prongs

Frank Buck Black Leopard Adventurers' Club
1938, (bronze, rare unbent prongs)(only 2 known)
NM - $3000

Felix Flicker
1960s Felix balancing a chair on his nose

Football
1948 (Later issue) (Bowman gum) (regular weight version)(bronze metal)
Ring Only $35-$100

Frank Buck Movie
(Bring 'Em Back Alive)
1930s (metal)
$75-$375

Frankenberry
(see Monster
Cereal Flicker &
Monster Cereal
Secret
Compartment)

Frankenstein
(see Universal
Monsters)

Freakies (Boss Moss)
1973-1978
(orange plastic)
(Universal
Feat.)(Ralston
Purina Co. cereal
premium)
$75-$275

Freakies (Hamhose)
1973-1978 (blue
plastic)(Universal
Feat.)(Ralston
Purina Co. cereal
premium)
$75-$275

Freakies (Snorkeldorf)
1973-1978 (yel-
low plastic)
(Universal
Feat.)(Ralston
Purina Co. cereal
premium)
$75-$275

Freakies Figural
1978 (green
plastic)(Universal
Features)
$20-$60

Frito Bandito
1969 (plastic)(in
plastic bag)
(warehouse
find?)
$7-$20

Gabby Hayes Cannon, 1951
(gold & silver
versions)
(Quaker, metal)
$100-$350

Gene Autry Eagle
1955 (Gene
Autry Dell comic
book ad premi-
um)(rare)
GD $200
FN $400
NM $700

Gene Autry Face, 1950s
(copper w/
enamel coating)
$50-$150

Gene Autry Face
1950s (copper)
$50-$150

Gene Autry Face
1950s (aluminum
w/gold face)
$85-$250

Gene Autry Face
1950s (silver)
$50-$150

Gene Autry Flag, 1950s
(Dell, gold
& silver versions)
$50-$150

Gene Autry Nail
1950 (on card)
(metal)(also see
Tom Mix
Nail)(nail signed)
On Card - $250
Ring Only
$20-$75

Gleason, James Photo
1940s (metal)
$35-$100

G-Men
1930s (silver
metal)
(name in G)
(also came in
relief on top)(in
diff. colors, red,
blue, & black)
$20-$60

G-Men
1930s
(metal)(name
below G)
$20-$75

Go-Go Discotheque Dancer Rings
1960s, (Flickers)
(plastic)
(6 in Set)(also
see Twist)
(note that all
have "twist" on
the right side)
Ring Only
$20-$65 ea.

Golden Nugget Cave, 1950s
(casino)(rare)
(less than 10
known)(see
Straight Arrow
Nugget)
"Straight Arrow"
is not printed on
the base.
Picture of casino
on inside.
GD $400, FN
$750, NM $1,500

Good Luck Initial
1952 (24k gold-
plated)
(Smith Brothers
Cough Drops)
$40-$150

Graveyard Flicker
(dancing skeleton in a graveyard moving back & forth)(see Penny Kings)
$15-$40

Green Hornet Flicker (3)
"Green Hornet Action ring" to full figure of the green hornet holding sting gun.

Green Hornet Flicker(7)
Full figure of the Green Hornet running from car with sting gun to Hornet rescuing a woman.

Green Hornet Flicker (11)
Hornet sting weapons to "Sting".

Green Hornet Seal
1966
$10-$20

Green Hornet Stamp
1960s (plastic)
$20-$40

Green Hornet
1930s (plastic)(rare) (only 10 known)
Good - $750
Fine - $2,000
Near Mint - $3,500

Green Hornet Flicker(4)

Green Hornet Flicker(8)

Green Hornet Flicker (12)
"Hornet Gun" to a man getting gassed.

Green Hornet Flicker, 1960s (set of 12)
Silver base $10-$35 ea.
Blue base $8-$30 ea.

Guitar Player Flicker
1960s (gold metal, color) (also see Dancing Girl)
$5-$10

Green Hornet Flicker (1)
"The Green Hornet" to small silhouette of the Green Hornet firing hornet gun next to car.

Green Hornet Flicker (5)
Face of Britt Reid to face of the Green Hornet.

Green Hornet Flicker(9)

Guitar Player Flicker
1980s (plastic, color)
$2-$4

Green Hornet Flicker (2)
Picture of the Green Hornet to face of the Green Hornet with mask.

Green Hornet Flicker (6)
Full figure of Kato as butler to full figure Kato in front of car.

Green Hornet Seal
1947 (General Mills radio premium)(Secret Compartment) (base glows-in-dark)
Good - $200
Fine - $400
Near Mint - $1,000

Green Hornet Flicker (10)
Picure of a couple kissing to black beauty driving thru a wall.

Have Gun Will Travel
1960s (Paladin)(white & black top versions)(TV)
On Card $100
Ring Only - $20-$85

Have Gun Will Travel
1960s
(Paladin)(plastic, gold base)
$20-$75

Hopalong Cassidy Compass/Hat
1950s
(metal)(hat fits over compass base)
$100-$300

Howdy Doody Flicker
(Buffalo Bob)

Howdy Doody Flicker
(Mr. Bluster)

Howdy Doody Insert
1950s
(red base)
$50-$150

Red top, yellow base

Howdy Doody Flicker(Chief Thunderthud)

Howdy Doody Flicker
(Princess)

Howdy Doody Flicker
1950s (set of 8)
(Nabisco Rice Honeys cereal premium)
(gray bases)
$7-$35 ea.

Heart-Arrow Flicker
1960s
(plastic)(Cupid)
$5-$10

Heart Throb Flicker
1960s
(silver base)
$15-$50

Howdy Doody Flicker
(Clarabelle)

Yellow top, red base

Hopalong Cassidy Steer Head
1950s (Conchos or ring slide) (rare)(mouth opens so teeth can punch brand on inserted paper)(Grape-Nuts Flakes box-top premium)
$75-$250

Hopalong Cassidy Bar 20
1950s (brass)
$20-$60

Howdy Doody Flicker
(Flubadub)

Howdy Doody Flashlight
1950s
(metal/plastic, color)
Complete w/Battery
$75-$300
Battery Missing
$55-$180

Howdy Doody Jack in Box
1950s (rare)
(red & yellow plastic) (two color versions exist)
Good - $150
Fine - $250
Near Mint - $525

Howdy Doody
(also see Clarabelle)

Hopalong Cassidy Bar 20, 1950s
(sterling silver)(metal)
$60-$250

Howdy Doody Flicker
(Buffalo Bee)

Howdy Doody Flicker
(Howdy)

Howdy Doody Glow Photo
1950s
(metal base)
$50-$200

H.R. Puf'n Stuf
1970s (7 diff.)
$40-$80 ea.

Howdy Doody/ Poll Parrot Flicker
1950s
(Howdy Doody to Poll Parrot flying)(Thick top lens held on by four prongs)
$50-$125

Howdy Doody 3D, 1976 (metal/plastic bust)
$35-$100

Huckleberry Hound/Mr. Jinx
plastic flicker 1960s. Kellogg's cereal (6 in set)
$45-$200

Huskies Club
1936-1937 (rare)(gold color metal, cereal)
GD $100, FN $300, NM $575

Howie Wing Weather
1940s (scarce)(metal)
(also see Lone Ranger & Peter Paul Weather)
GD $100
FN $225
NM $400

Huck Finn Flicker
1950s (shows both images)
$15-$40

Icee Bear
1970s (plastic)
$15-$50

Howdy Doody /Poll Parrot TV Flicker
1950s (blue or orange bases)
(showing Howdy & Poll Parrot)
$50-$160

Huckleberry Hound
1960s (aluminum)
$10-$30

Hush Puppies Flicker, 1960s "Hush Puppies" picture of the dog to "casual shoes" picture of dog looking other way.
$15-$40

Incredible Hulk
1980s, metal (vitamins)(also see Captain America & Spider-Man)
(Marvel Ent. Group)(in color)
$60-$200

Howdy Raised Face, 1950s (silver base)
$50-$150

H.R. Puf'n Stuf (Cling & Clang)

(cloisonné)

Ingersoll
1948 card display (10 rings)
(individual rings are listed and priced under the character names)
Complete $1,200

H.R. Puf'n Stuf (Puf'n Stuf)

Howdy Doody Raised
1950s (Face)(white base)("Poll Parrot" on sides)
$15-$50

H.R. Puf'n Stuf (Witchiepoo)

Huckleberry Hound Club
1960s (2 variations exist, metal cloisonné & plain)
$15-$75 ea.

Indian, Goudey Gum 1940s (silver colored metal) (5 box tops from Indian chewing gum to get ring)(also see Chief Wahoo) $15-$75

James Bond (see Agent 007)

Jimmy Allen "J.A. Cadets" 1930s (metal) (Canadian, rare) $150-$700

Joe E. Brown 1940s (metal) $50-$200

Joe Louis Face 1940s (rare) (nickel metal) (sent in envelope w/photo; less than 10 known) GD $1,000, FN $2,000, NM $3,500

Joe Penner Face Puzzle 1940s (rare) (radio)(metal) (less than 10 known) GD $300 FN $800 NM $1,500

John Wayne Photo, 1950 (rectangle) (metal) (also see Real Photos) $20-$100

Jack Armstrong Dragon's Eye 1940-1941 (green stone)(also see Buck Rogers Ring of Saturn & Shadow Carey Salt)(rarest in high grade of the crocodile set) GD $200, FN $400, NM $1,000

Jiminy Crickett 1960s (aluminum) $15-$35

Jinks (Hanna-Barbera) 1960s (aluminum) (also see Dixie) $10-$30

Joe Louis Figural 1940s (scarce)(Metal) (gold top & silver base) GD $250, FN $500, NM $1,200

John F. Kennedy Flicker 1960s John F. Kennedy 35th president 1917-1963 picture of American Flag to face of JFK. (metal) $10-$30

Junior Fire Marshal, 1950s (bronze metal) $15-$50

Junior Pilot 1955 (American Airlines) (gold stamped metal) (also see Jet-) $15-$50

Jack Armstrong Egyptian Whistle 1940s, (metal) (gold color)(also see Tom Mix Musical) $40-$150

Joe DiMaggio Club, 1940s (metal, silver color) $300-$1000

Jack Armstrong Lead Proof 1939 (Ring was never issued) - Estimate $2,500

Joe Louis Poster 1940s (rare)(shows Louis wearing silver colored ring) $75-$300

Junior Stewardess 1955 (American Airlines)(metal) $15-$50

TOY RINGS

Kellogg's Gold Ore
1942 (offered nationally by Kellogg. Was advertised as having real gold ore from the Comstock lode, but actual contents has not been verified. **Note:** This ring was also offered by General Mills as a **Lone Ranger Meteorite Ring** as a test in the National Defender mailing that lasted for only 2 weeks. Only 45 rings were mailed out. It is unknown if the material in both versions of the ring are the same. Otherwise, both rings are identical.)
Good - $500
Fine - $1,200
Near Mint - $3,200

Kellogg's Picture Rings
1950s (16 in set)(all priced individually)(plastic; each ring came in various colors)

Kellogg's Picture Ring Ad

Airplanes

Kellogg's Picture Douglas DC-6
1950s (plastic)
$15-$40

Kellogg's Picture Pan American Clipper
1950s (plastic)
$15-$40

Kellogg's Picture Douglas F-3D Sky Knight
1950s (plastic)
$15-$40

Kellogg's Picture Republic F-84E Thunderjet
1950s (plastic)
$15-$40

Kellogg's Picture Republic XF-91 Thundercepter
1950s (plastic)
$15-$40

Cowboys

Kellogg's Picture Buffalo Bill
1950s (plastic)
$10-$30

Kellogg's Picture Daniel Boone
1950s (plastic)
$15-$40

Kellogg's Picture Dennis O'Keefe
1950s (plastic)
$7-$20

Indians

Kellogg's Picture Pocahontas
1960s (plastic)
$7-$20

Kellogg's Picture Sitting Bull
1950s (plastic)
$7-$20

Movie Stars

Kellogg's Picture Burt Lancaster
1950s (plastic)
$7-$20

Kellogg's Picture Joanne Dru
1950s (plastic)
$7-$20

Kellogg's Picture Wanda Hendrix
1950s (plastic)
$7-$20

Sport Stars

Kellogg's Picture Baseball, Babe Ruth
1949 (plastic)
$30-$85

Kellogg's Picture Gene Tunney
1950s (plastic)
$15-$40

Kellogg's Picture Jack Kramer
1950s (plastic, orange top, brown base) & (blue top, green base)
$15-$40

Kewpie Figure
1930s (sterling)(not adj.)
$75-$200

Kewpie Kid
1940s (metal)(scarce)
$100-$325

Kill the Jinx Good Luck Signet Ring 1929 (metal) (sold in Johnson Smith & Co. catalogue for $1.00) (Also see Swastika & Navajo Good Luck) (used as Paul Whitman) $75-$350

King Comics Set on card (36 rings),1953 (each ring occurs in diff. colors)(Note: most cards have multiple rings of same characters) Complete Card Set $600

King Comics, Maggie

King Comics, Mama

King Comics, Olive Oyl

King Features 1950s (Mandrake)(in color)(plastic) $25-$85

King Features 1950s (Prince Valiant)(thick top) (in color)(plastic) $25-$85

King Features 1950s (Charles Starrett?)(in color)(plastic) $25-$85

King Comics, Blondie

King Comics, Fritz

King Comics, Inspector

King Comics, Snuffy Smith

King Comics, Captain

King Comics, Hans

King Comics, Jiggs?

King Comics, Swee'pea

King Features 1950s (Sweeney)(thick top)(in color) (plastic) $25-$85

King Comics, Felix

King Comics, Flash Gordon

King Comics, Henry

King Comics, Little Lulu

↑ **King Features Comics** 1953 (set of 20 known)(ceramic material in color) (each ring occurs in diff. colors; Phantom ring has never been verified) $5-$20 ea.

King Features 1950s (Tillie the Toiler) (thick top, in color)(plastic) $25-$85

TOY RINGS

King Vitamin Hologram
1970 (1st hologram ring) (plastic)
$10-$35

Kit Carson TV
1950s (scarce)(metal)
$150-$450

Kix Atomic Bomb (see Lone Ranger --)

Kix Rocket (see Rocket-To-The-Moon)

KKK (see USA/KKK)

Top pivots to reveal glow-in-dark secret compartment with a wax seal over bottom concealing secret message

Krazy Kat
1940s (metal cloisonné)
$75-$225

Knights of Columbus
1940s (radio)(rare)(less than 10 known) View of base used from Green Hornet ring. "G H" (Green Hornet) initials on side of base changed to mean "Holy Ghost."
Good - $1,000
Fine - $3,000
Near Mint - $6,250

Kolonel Keds Space Patrol
1960s (see U.S. Keds) (paper disc)
$50-$165

Kool Aid Aztec Treasure
1930s (metal)
$75-$225

Lassie Friendship
1950s (metal) (20 carat gold plated)
$75-$175

Laugh-In Flicker (1)
(16 diff.) "Laugh-In" to Dan & Dick

Laugh-In Flicker (2)
(16 diff.) Goldie Hawn dancing in bikini

Laugh-In Flicker (3)
(16 diff.) Goldie Hawn figure in bikini dancing side to side.

Laugh-In Flicker (4)
(16 diff.) Ruth Buzzi w/hairnet to Ruth Buzzi w/bonnet

Laugh-In Flicker (5)
(16 diff.) Henry Gibson as Indian to Henry Gibson as a priest

Laugh-In Flicker (6)
(16 diff.) JoAnn Worley sad face to JoAnn Worley screaming

Laugh-In Flicker (7)
(16 diff.) Beauty (Ruth Buzzi w/bonnet) to Beast (Dan Rowan profile)

Laugh-In Flicker (8)
(16 diff.) Artie Johnson as German soldier "Very Interesting" to "But Stupid"

Laugh-In Flicker(9)
(16 diff.) "Here Comes the Judge" to Pigmeat Markham

Laugh-In Flicker (10)
(16 diff.) "Here Comes the Judge" to cartoon judge jumping out of circle

Laugh-In Flicker (11)
(16 diff.) "The Hymns for today are 76, 81, 92, 85, 42..." to Dick Martin cartoon yelling "Bingo"

456

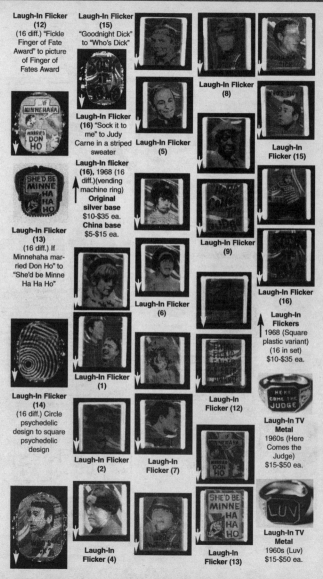

Laugh-In Flicker (12)
(16 diff.) "Fickle Finger of Fate Award" to picture of Finger of Fates Award

Laugh-In Flicker (13)
(16 diff.) If Minnehaha married Don Ho" to "She'd be Minne Ha Ha Ho"

Laugh-In Flicker (14)
(16 diff.) Circle psychedelic design to square psychedelic design

Laugh-In Flicker (15)
"Goodnight Dick" to "Who's Dick"

Laugh-In Flicker (16) "Sock it to me" to Judy Carne in a striped sweater

Laugh-In flicker (16), 1968 (16 diff.)(vending machine ring)
Original silver base $10-$35 ea.
China base $5-$15 ea.

Laugh-In Flicker (5)

Laugh-In Flicker (6)

Laugh-In Flicker (1)

Laugh-In Flicker (2)

Laugh-In Flicker (7)

Laugh-In Flicker (4)

Laugh-In Flicker (13)

Laugh-In Flicker (8)

Laugh-In Flicker (9)

Laugh-In Flicker (12)

Laugh-In Flicker (15)

Laugh-In Flicker (16)

Laugh-In Flickers 1968 (Square plastic variant) (16 in set) $10-$35 ea.

Laugh-In TV Metal 1960s (Here Comes the Judge) $15-$50 ea.

Laugh-In TV Metal 1960s (Luv) $15-$50 ea.

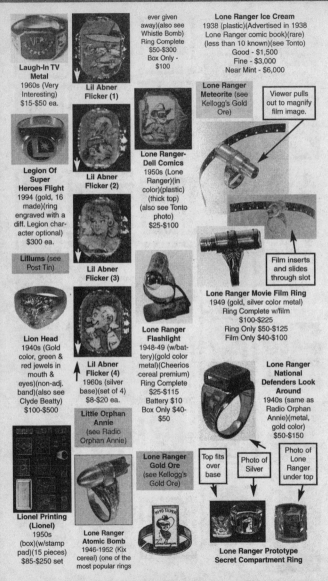

Laugh-In TV Metal
1960s (Very Interesting)
$15-$50 ea.

Legion Of Super Heroes Flight
1994 (gold, 16 made)(ring engraved with a diff. Legion character optional)
$300 ea.

Lil'lums (see Post Tin)

Lion Head
1940s (Gold color, green & red jewels in mouth & eyes)(non-adj. band)(also see Clyde Beatty)
$100-$500

Lionel Printing (Lionel)
1950s (box)(w/stamp pad)(15 pieces)
$85-$250 set

Lil Abner Flicker (1)

Lil Abner Flicker (2)

Lil Abner Flicker (3)

Lil Abner Flicker (4)
1960s (silver base)(set of 4)
$8-$20 ea.

Little Orphan Annie (see Radio Orphan Annie)

Lone Ranger Gold Ore (see Kellogg's Gold Ore)

Lone Ranger Atomic Bomb
1946-1952 (Kix cereal) (one of the most popular rings)

ever given away)(also see Whistle Bomb)
Ring Complete
$50-$300
Box Only -
$100

Lone Ranger-Dell Comics
1950s (Lone Ranger)(in color)(plastic)(thick top)
(also see Tonto photo)
$25-$100

Lone Ranger Flashlight
1948-49 (w/battery)(gold color metal)(Cheerios cereal premium)
Ring Complete
$25-$115
Battery $10
Box Only $40-$50

Lone Ranger Ice Cream
1938 (plastic)(Advertised in 1938 Lone Ranger comic book)(rare)
(less than 10 known)(see Tonto)
Good - $1,500
Fine - $3,000
Near Mint - $6,000

Lone Ranger Meteorite (see Kellogg's Gold Ore)

Viewer pulls out to magnify film image.

Film inserts and slides through slot

Lone Ranger Movie Film Ring
1949 (gold, silver color metal)
Ring Complete w/film
$100-$225
Ring Only $50-$125
Film Only $40-$100

Lone Ranger National Defenders Look Around
1940s (same as Radio Orphan Annie)(metal, gold color)
$50-$150

Top fits over base

Photo of Silver

Photo of Lone Ranger under top

Lone Ranger Prototype Secret Compartment Ring

Has photo of Silver in the top of ring base

Lone Ranger Prototype Secret Compartment Ring
1940 (rare)(gold color metal) (less than 10 known)(complete w/both photos)(photos are rectangular) Only the prototypes were made. Near Mint - $4,000

Lone Ranger Plastic (see Lone Ranger - Dell Comics)

Film slides through saddle

Enlargment of Silver's photo that appears under top of all military rings

with top removed

Lone Ranger Secret Compartment-Marines
1942; 1945 (metal) (scarce) with photos(2) GD $200, FN $400, NM $600

Lone Ranger Sec. Compt.
(All above rings were issued in 1945 without the photos) Value would be 60% less or $200)

Lone Ranger Sec. Comp. rings Includes photos of Silver & Lone Ranger. Beware of repro photos.

Lone Ranger Secret Compartment-Navy,
1942; 1945 (metal)(scarce) with photos (2) GD $200 FN $400 NM $600

Lone Ranger Secret Compartment (see Pilot's Secret Compart.)

Lone Ranger Saddle w/film
1950-51 (gold color metal) Boxed $300
Complete w/film $100-$200
Ring Only $75-$150
Film Only $25-$50
Note: Film with L.R. mask removed exist.

Lone Ranger Seal Print Face
1940s (metal) $75-$300

Lone Ranger Six Shooter Sign
1947-48 (General Mills) $150-$500

Lone Ranger Secret Compt.-Army Air Corps.
1942; 1945 (metal)(scarce) (with a Lone Ranger photo & a Silver photo) GD $200, FN $400, NM $600

Lone Ranger Secret Compartment-Army
1942; 1945 (metal)(scarce) with photos (2)(General Mills, Kix cereal) GD $200, FN $400, NM $600

Lone Ranger Six Shooter
1947-48 (Kix cereal) 1952-59 (Sugar Jets cereal) (metal) (silver color handles) (scarce in NM) $60-$225

Lone Ranger Weather
1946, (metal) (paper changes color)(also see Howie Wing and Peter Paul Weather) (rare in NM) $50-$150

Lone Wolf (see Thunderbird)

Lone Wolf Tribal
1932 Wrigley
(sterling silver)
(radio) (the first
radio premium
ring)
$75-$350

**Looney Tunes
Flicker
Bugs Bunny**
eating a carrot

**Looney Tunes
Flicker
Henry the
Chicken Hawk**
kicking an egg

**Looney Tunes
Flicker
Sam the
Sheepdog**
dancing around

**Looney Tunes
Flicker
Tweety Bird**
looking side to
side

**Lucky Charms
Horseshoe**
1985 (boys)
$7-$30

**Looney Tunes
Flicker
Daffy Duck**
jumping and flap-
ping
his wings

**Looney Tunes
Flicker
PePe LePew**
pinching his
nose

**Looney Tunes
Flicker
Sneezy Mouse**
turning his head
raising his hand
to his ear

**Looney Tunes
Flicker
Wile E. Coyote**
howling

**Lucky Charms
Horseshoe**
1985 (girls)
$10-$50

**Lucky Charms
Figural Spinner
& Ring**
1978 (green
plastic)
In pkg. $35

**Looney Tunes
Flicker
Elmer Fudd**
firing his rifle

**Looney Tunes
Flicker
Porky Pig**
tipping his hat

**Looney Tunes
Flicker
Speedy
Gonzales**
arms out-
stretched, then
points to himself,
then he's gone.
Only his hat
remains.

**Looney Tunes
Flicker
Yosemite Sam**
shooting his
guns

**Looney Tunes
Flicker**
1970s (set of
16)(plastic)
(Original flickers
on original
bases)
$7-$20 ea.

**Looney Tunes
Flicker
Road Runner**
running

**Looney Tunes
Flicker
Sylvester**
tip-toeing

Lucky Buddha
1940s (metal)
$20-$50

**Looney Tunes
Flicker
Boxing
Kangaroo**

**Looney Tunes
Flicker
Foghorn
Leghorn**
walking

Lucky Sheik
1940s (Johnson & Smith)(metal, gold color)(Red & green stones)(adj.)(also see Pharaoh)
$40-$250

Maggie (see Post Tin)

Magic Pup (see Pet Parade)

Mack
1940s (bronze metal) (Mack Truck)
$25-$100

Macy's Santa Flicker
1960s (plastic)(Santa Claus to "Macy's Santa Knows")
$10-$35

Majestic Radio
1930s (Bakelite plastic)(made in regular jewelers ring sizes including adult)
$50-$300
Note: "Majestic" was the trade name of the Grisgsby-Grunow Co. from the late 1920s until the company failed in 1934. The Majestic Radio and Television Corp. carried on the Majestic name beginning in 1937 with many advertising devices including this ring and the 1938 vintage Charlie McCarthy novelty radio show to try and regain the share of the market it once held.

Sun or bulb exposes film to specially treated paper

Flying Wing   Major Mars   The Venusians   F80 Shooting Star

On the Moon   Major Mars Rocket Ship   F84 Thunderjet   A Direct Hit

Major Mars Rocket Film showing all eight negatives

The last four negatives had to be special ordered and are rare

Major Mars Rocket
1952 (w/ 4 negatives, 12 printing papers (in light tight pkg.), a chain to fasten on base, a base in a wax paper pkg., instructions and mailer) (4 additional negatives could be ordered) (Popsicle premium) (sun exposes film to paper)(also see Captain Video Pendant)
Complete $1,650
Ring w/base Only $300-$1,050
Rocket as Pendant (no base)
$200-$800

Man From U.N.C.L.E. Flicker (1)
1960s "U.N.C.L.E." logo to waist up picture of Solo blowing smoke off gun (black & white)
$20-$80

Man From U.N.C.L.E. Flicker (2)
1960s, U.N.C.L.E." smaller logo with picture of three men to full figure being shot through glass (black & white)
$20-$80

Man From U.N.C.L.E. Flicker (3)
1960s (Face of Solo to face of Ilya)
Silver version
$10-$25
Blue version
$8-$20

Man From U.N.C.L.E. Flicker (4)
1960s (Face of Solo to face of Ilya) (square version)
$10-$25

Martin Luther King, Jr. Flicker (1)
"Martin Luther King"
1918-1968 to Face (front view)

Martin Luther King, Jr. Flicker (2)
"I Have Climbed The Mountain" to Face (profile)

Martin Luther King, Jr. Flicker (3a)
"Free at Last" to Face (front view)

Martin Luther King, Jr. Flicker (4a) Picture of American flag to Face (front view)

Martin Luther King, Jr. Flicker (5a)
"1964 Nobel Peace Prize" to Face (profile)

Martin Luther King, Jr. Flicker (6a)
"I Have A Dream" to Face (front view)

Martin Luther King, Jr. Flicker
1964 (set of 6)(plastic)
Silver base
$15-$35 ea.

Marvel Flicker (1) Marvel Super Heroes
"Marvel Super Heroes Ring Club" to 4 faces- Spider-Man, Capt. America, Thor, Thing

Marvel Flicker (2) Captain America
"Captain America" face to "WUM" Captain America punching enemy

Marvel Flicker (3) Dr. Strange Flicker
Dr. Strange face to full figure Dr. Strange w/arms outstretched

Marvel Flicker (4) Fantastic Four
"Fantastic" faces to "Four" 2 faces

Marvel Flicker (5) Hulk
"Hulk" face to "PAM" Hulk fist slamming a wall

Marvel Flicker (6) Human Torch
"Human Torch" face to "Dr. Doom" face

Marvel Flicker (7) Iron Man "Iron Man" face to "Conk" Iron Man punching enemy

Marvel Flicker (10) Sub-Mariner "Sub-Mariner" full figure to "Kop" full figure left handed punch

Marvel Mood Rings 1977 (silver plated metal)(4 diff.)(Spider-Man, Capt. America, Thor, & Hulk) $100-$325 ea.

McDonald's Character Hamburglar 1970s (plastic)(black on yellow)

McDonald's Character Ronald McDonald Die cut face (red/white)

McDonald's Character 1970s (plastic) $5-$15 ea.

Marvel Flicker (11) Thing "Thing" face to full figure Thing w/arms in the air

McCrae, Joel, Photo 1950s (thick top, plastic, color) $25-$85

McDonald's Character Hamburglar (black/yellow)

McDonald's Easter Bunny 1970s (plastic)(blue, green, pink & yellow known) $5-$15

Marvel Flicker (8) Spider-Man "Spider-Man" face to full figure running

McDonald's Character Big Mac 1970s (plastic) (light blue/yellow dark blue/yellow) $5-$10

McDonald's Character McBird (red/yellow)

Marvel Flicker (9) Spider-Man "Spider-Man" full figure on a web to "Pow" throwing a punch

Marvel Flicker (12) Thor "Thor" face to full figure Thor swinging hammer

McDonald's Character McHook (Black/orange or green/orange)

McDonald's 500 Smile Race Car 1985 (top & bottom shown) (plastic)(blue) $5-$15

Marvel Flicker 1966 (plastic) (Marvel Ent. Group) **Silver base** $10-$50 ea. **Blue base** $8-$35

McDonald's Character Grimace (red or orange on purple)

McDonald's Flicker (1) Ronald waving to Ronald on flying hamburger

TOY RINGS

McDonald's Flicker (2)
Ronald on diving board to Ronald splashing as he dives into pool

McDonald's Flicker (3)
Ronald standing with jump rope to Ronald jumping rope

McDonald's Flicker (4)
Ronald juggling balls to same face moving side to side

▲ **McDonald's Flicker**
1970s (original silver base)
$10-$25 ea.

McDonald's Friendship Space Shuttle
1985 (plastic)(blue)
$5-$20

McDonald's Grimace with Hat
1970s (black/green plastic)
$5-$15

McDonald's Grimace
1970s-80s? (metal)(purple enamel over gold)
$10-$30

McDonald's Ronald McDonald Face
1970s (metal, enameled)
$10-$30

McDonald's Horn
1980s (plastic)
$20-$60

McDonald's Ronald McDonald Figural
1970s (yellow or red plastic)
$15-$40

McDonald's QSC Employees
1980s (Balfour stainless steel)
$110

McDonald's Ronald McDonald Disc
1970s (plastic)(red/white)
$7-$20

McDonald's Ronald McDonald 3D face, 1970s (plastic)(red/yellow)
$4-$12

McDonald's Valentine
1970s (plastic)(red & white)
$7-$20

Melvin Purvis Birthstone
1930s (metal)
$125-$425

Melvin Purvis Junior G-Man Corps
1937 (Post)(metal)
$30-$150

Melvin Purvis Secret Operator
1936 (Post)(metal)
$75-$200

Melvin Purvis Secret Scarab
1937 (Post-O) (same as Capt. Hawks Secret Scarab)(rare)(24K gold finish)
Good - $400
Fine - $800
Near Mint - $2,000

Mickey Mouse Club
1950s (red/white/black enamel)(metal)
$20-$70

Mickey Mouse Club Puzzle Dome
1950s (plastic)
$20-$60

Mickey Mouse Club
1960s (plastic)(cookies)
$25-$75

464

Mickey Mouse Club, 1980 (Nestles)(metal) $30-$80

Mickey Mouse Club, 1980 (metal) $30-$80

Mickey Mouse Club, 1980s (round)(metal) $10-$25

Mickey Mouse Face, 1950s (plastic)(oval, paper) $7-$20

Mickey Mouse Figure 1931-1934 (etched metal) (1st Mickey ring)(Cohn & Rosenberger, Inc.) GD $300 FN $450 NM $900

Mickey Mouse Figure 3D Mounted, 1950s (plastic) $20-$50

Mickey Mouse Glass Dome 1940s (rare) (brass)(gold color)(red, black,yellow) (Cleinman & Sons) GD $175 FN $325 NM $500

Mighty Hercules Magic Ring, 1960s (on card)(TV) (scarce) Complete $425 Ring Only $85-$275

Miss Dairylea 1960s (plastic) $20-$45

Mister Softee Flicker 1960s "I Like Mister Softee" to picture of Mr. Softee (silver base) $25-$75

Model Airplane Club 1940s $35-$125

Mickey Mouse Club Flicker 1960s, "Mickey Mouse Club" to Mickey's face with "member" underneath (chocolate chip cookie premium) $15-$40

Mickey Mouse Figure 1935 (Brier Mfg.)(metal cloisonné in color) (2nd Mickey ring)(brass (some came w/Ingersol watch) $175-$550

Mickey Mouse Glow 1950s (square top)(glow-in-dark)(silver) $35-$100

Mr. Peanut 1950s (silver & gold, color, metal) $10-$30

Monkey Flicker 1950s (thick top) $30-$90

Mister Softee 1950s (white plastic)(raised face & name) $10-$20

Monkees Flicker (1a) (side 1) "Davy" face

Mickey Mouse Face 1947 (sterling silver)(store item) $20-$60

Mickey Mouse Figure 1937 (Brier Mfg.) (metal cloisonné in color)(3rd Mickey ring) $150-$400

Mickey Mouse Wedding Band 1970s (metal cloisonné) (2 versions) $10-$30 ea.

Monkees Flicker (1b) (side 2) "Davy" face to full figure playing guitar

Monkees Flicker (2) "Micky" face to full figure playing drums

Monkees Flicker (3a) (side 1) "Mike" face to full figure playing guitar

Monkees Flicker (3b) (side 2) "Mike" face to full figure playing guitar

Monkees Flicker (4) "Peter" face to full figure playing base

Monkees Flicker (5a) Four heads with heart in the middle

Monkees Flicker (5b) "I Love Monkees" logo to four heads w/heart in middle

Monkees Flicker (6) "I Love Monkees" logo w/hearts to four figures in water on surfboard

Monkees Flicker (7) "Peter" & "Micky" full figures playing bass & drums to "Davy" & "Mike" full figures playing guitars

Monkees Flicker (8) "I love Peter Micky" two faces smiling to The Monkees Davy Mike two faces

Monkees Flicker (9) Davy & Micky playing guitar & drums on unicycles to Peter playing base on pogo stick & Mike playing guitar on skate board

Monkees Flicker (10) "Monkees" logo to 4 figures in Monkee Mobile

Monkees Flicker (11) Old fashioned camera w/two guys holding flash to two figures one standing, one sitting

Monkees Flicker (12) "Official member Monkees Ring Club" to four faces in a red heart

Monkees Flicker 1966 (12 different) All rings distributed in cereal boxes sealed in paper
Club Ring $25-$70 ea.
Others $20-$65 ea.

Monster Cartoon Flicker (1) White face phantom to red face Frankenstein looking character

Monster Cartoon Flicker (2a) Fat green one-tooth goon with earrings to skinny white guy with forehead scar

Monster Cartoon Flicker (3) Green face Frankenstein to red face devil with pointed teeth and big ears

Monster Cartoon Flicker 1960s (set of 3) (plastic)
Silver Base $20-$40 ea.
Blue Base $15-$30 ea.

Monster Cereal Secret Compartment-Boo Berry

466

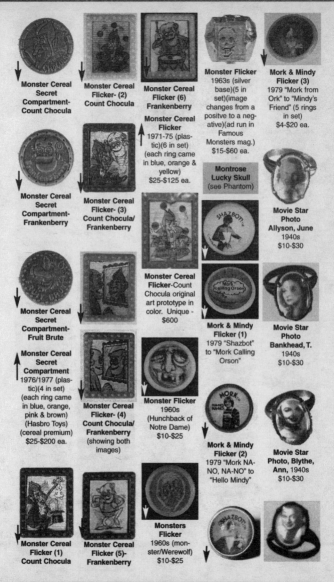

Monster Cereal Secret Compartment- Count Chocula

Monster Cereal Flicker- (2) Count Chocula

Monster Cereal Flicker (6) Frankenberry

Monster Cereal Flicker
1971-75 (plastic)(6 in set) (each ring came in blue, orange & yellow) $25-$125 ea.

Monster Flicker
1963s (silver base)(5 in set)(image changes from a positve to a negative)(ad run in Famous Monsters mag.) $15-$60 ea.

Mork & Mindy Flicker (3)
1979 "Mork from Ork" to "Mindy's Friend" (5 rings in set) $4-$20 ea.

Montrose Lucky Skull (see Phantom)

Monster Cereal Secret Compartment- Frankenberry

Monster Cereal Flicker- (3) Count Chocula/ Frankenberry

Monster Cereal Flicker-Count Chocula original art prototype in color. Unique - $600

Movie Star Photo Allyson, June 1940s $10-$30

Mork & Mindy Flicker (1)
1979 "Shazbot" to "Mork Calling Orson"

Movie Star Photo Bankhead, T. 1940s $10-$30

Monster Cereal Secret Compartment- Fruit Brute

Monster Cereal Secret Compartment
1976/1977 (plastic)(4 in set) (each ring came in blue, orange, pink & brown) (Hasbro Toys) (cereal premium) $25-$200 ea.

Monster Cereal Flicker- (4) Count Chocula/ Frankenberry (showing both images)

Monster Flicker
1960s (Hunchback of Notre Dame) $10-$25

Mork & Mindy Flicker (2)
1979 "Mork NA-NO, NA-NO" to "Hello Mindy"

Movie Star Photo, Blythe, Ann, 1940s $10-$30

Monster Cereal Flicker (1) Count Chocula

Monster Cereal Flicker (5)- Frankenberry

Monsters Flicker
1960s (monster/Werewolf) $10-$25

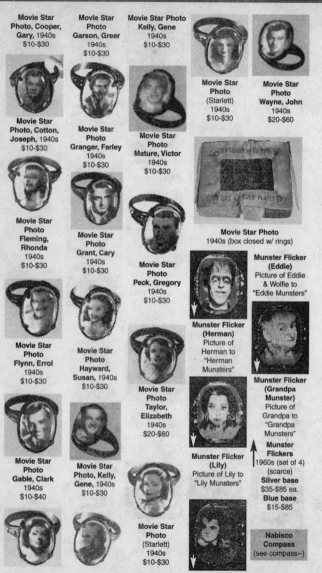

Movie Star Photo, Cooper, Gary, 1940s
$10-$30

Movie Star Photo Garson, Greer 1940s
$10-$30

Movie Star Photo Kelly, Gene 1940s
$10-$30

Movie Star Photo (Starlett) 1940s
$10-$30

Movie Star Photo Wayne, John 1940s
$20-$60

Movie Star Photo, Cotton, Joseph, 1940s
$10-$30

Movie Star Photo Granger, Farley 1940s
$10-$30

Movie Star Photo Mature, Victor 1940s
$10-$30

Movie Star Photo 1940s (box closed w/ rings)

Movie Star Photo Fleming, Rhonda 1940s
$10-$30

Movie Star Photo Grant, Cary 1940s
$10-$30

Movie Star Photo Peck, Gregory 1940s
$10-$30

Munster Flicker (Eddie) Picture of Eddie & Wolfie to "Eddie Munsters"

Movie Star Photo Flynn, Errol 1940s
$10-$30

Movie Star Photo Hayward, Susan, 1940s
$10-$30

Munster Flicker (Herman) Picture of Herman to "Herman Munsters"

Movie Star Photo Taylor, Elizabeth 1940s
$20-$60

Munster Flicker (Grandpa Munster) Picture of Grandpa to "Grandpa Munsters"

Movie Star Photo Gable, Clark 1940s
$10-$40

Movie Star Photo, Kelly, Gene, 1940s
$10-$30

Munster Flicker (Lily) Picture of Lily to "Lily Munsters"

Munster Flickers 1960s (set of 4) (scarce)
Silver base $35-$85 ea.
Blue base $15-$85

Movie Star Photo (Starlett) 1940s
$10-$30

Nabisco Compass (see compass--)

Navajo Good Luck
1930s (metal, silver color) (also see Kill the Jinx, Swastika, and Whitman, Paul)
$35-$125

Ovaltine Signet
1937 (metal) (also see Radio Orphan Annie Signet)
$35-$125

Pet Parade Pup & Magic Ring
1951 (Wheat Chex) (w/magnet ring collar) (very large ring)
$30-$100

P.F. Flyer Decoder
1949 (plastic) (green metal insert) (used in 1960s as a Jonny Quest Magic Ring)
$25-$70

Phantom (see Post Tin, 1949)

Operator 5
1934 (rare) (metal) (12 known examples, 2 in NM, 1 in Mint) (pulp)
Good - $1,500
Very Fine - $3,000
Fine - $5,500
Very Fine - $9,500
Near Mint - $15,500
Box - GD $150
FN $300
NM $600

Perfume Ring
1946 (Betty Crocker Soups) (sterling) (2500 mailed) (cotton under ball will hold perfume)
$50-$175

Perry Winkle (see Post Tin)

Pan American Clipper (see Kellogg's Picture)

Peter Paul Face
1950s (plastic)
$10-$30

Peter Paul Glow-in-Dark Secret Compartment
1940s (metal) (also see Sky King Radar)
$150-$425

Orphan Annie (see Post Tin & Radio--)

Magic magnetic ring collar makes magic pup do tricks

Peter Paul Weather
1950s (also see Howie Wing, Lone Ranger Weather) (metal)
$35-$125

Ovaltine Birthday
1930s (metal) (same as Radio Orphan Annie Birthday)
$100-$425

Phantom
1950s (Australia, Phantom Club gold ring) (Skull and Crossbones in relief, open band, red or white glow in the dark painted eyes) (rare)
$200-$600

No Picture Available

Phantom
1950s (Australia, Phantom Silver plate Skull ring) (skull and crossbones in relief, red eyes. Same style as gold ring above) (rare). No reported sales.
$300-$950

Phantom
1950s (Australia, Phantom Club Rubber Stamper Skulling) (square frame, embossed skull image, "Phantom" printed in relief on closed band. Colors are green or blue) (rare, only 3 known)
$500-$1,000

Phantom
1950s (Swedish plastic glow in the dark skull ring) (closed band, milky white, skull and crossbones in relief) (rare). No reported sales.

Phantom
1948 (U.S.A., plastic Phantom gumball ring (color w/yellow background, set in rectangle frame, pink or gold band) (Scarce)
$75-$150

TOY RINGS

Phantom
1950s (U.S.A.,
plastic Phantom
gumball ring)
(color profile
graphic of
"Devils"-
Phantom's side-
kick-Wolf, pink
tongue, yellow
background, gold
rectangular band
and frame)
$65-$160

Phantom
1950s (U.S.A.,
plastic Phantom
gumball ring)
(color graphic of
"Diana",
Phantom's
sweetheart, with
dark shoulder
length hair. Gold
rectangular band
and frame) (rare)
$50-$225

**Phantom
Flicker**
1967 (Hong
Kong)
$15-$40

**Phantom
Swedish Club**
1970 (copper
finished metal)
(rare)
$75-$250

**Phantom
Swedish Club**
1970 (set of
Metal Skull and
Good mark
rings)(gold finish,
open band)
$35-$100 ea.

Pharaoh
1950s (dark
amber
see-through top)
$20-$75

Pharaoh Skull
1950s (w/eyes
that glow)(also
see Lucky Sheik)
$20-$75

Pinocchio
1940s (metal,
gold color)
$75-$225

**Pinocchio
Figure**
1960s (3D
figure)(rare)
(painted gold
metal in color)
$25-$110

**Pinocchio Tell
The Truth**
1940s (metal
w/plastic nose)
GD $250, FN
$500, NM $800

**Pilot's Secret
Compartment**
1945-46 (same
as Captain
Midnight Secret
Compartment)
(Army Air Corps
star w/pilot's
insignia)(top
slides back to
reveal secret
compartment)
brass
base alloy)
(golden color)
Ring $75-$300

**Pirate Glow
Skull**
1940s (plastic)
$35-$100

**Planet Of The
Apes - Dr. Zaius**

**Planet Of The
Apes - Galen**

**Planet Of The
Apes Rings**
1975 Stan Toy
Co., England
(scarce)(5 rings
in set: Dr. Zaius,
Galen, Zira,
Urko, and
Cornelius or
Caesar)(came in
gold, silver,
green, or black
on iodized
aluminum
base)(similar
rings were made
in Japan in
recent
years)(sold out
of a display box
in England)
(20th Century
Fox film series
started in 1968)
$50-$225 ea.

Pluto
1950s (interna-
tional, silver)
(colored & plain)
$35-$100

Pluto
1950s (glow-in-
dark)
(intl. sterling)
$35-$100

Pocahontas
(see Kellogg's
picture)

Poll Parrot (see
Howdy Doody)

Poll Parrot Face
1950s (gold &
silver versions)
(metal)
$20-$45

**Poll Parrot
Flicker**
1950s (shows
parrot flying
(wings up to
wings down)
$25-$75

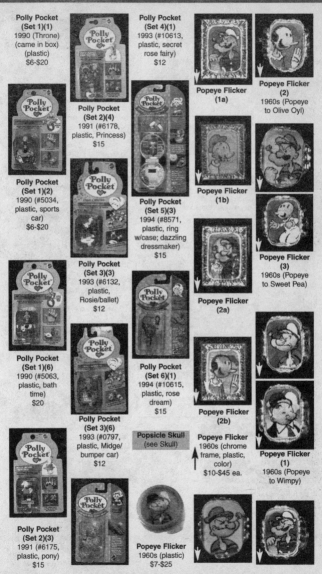

Polly Pocket (Set 1)(1) 1990 (Throne) (came in box) (plastic) $6-$20

Polly Pocket (Set 2)(4) 1991 (#6178, plastic, Princess) $15

Polly Pocket (Set 1)(2) 1990 (#5034, plastic, sports car) $6-$20

Polly Pocket (Set 3)(3) 1993 (#6132, plastic, Rosie/ballet) $12

Polly Pocket (Set 1)(6) 1990 (#5063, plastic, bath time) $20

Polly Pocket (Set 3)(6) 1993 (#0797, plastic, Midge/bumper car) $12

Polly Pocket (Set 2)(3) 1991 (#6175, plastic, pony) $15

Polly Pocket (Set 4)(1) 1993 (#10613, plastic, secret rose fairy) $12

Polly Pocket (Set 5)(3) 1994 (#8571, plastic, ring w/case; dazzling dressmaker) $15

Polly Pocket (Set 6)(1) 1994 (#10615, plastic, rose dream) $15

Popsicle Skull (see Skull)

Popeye Flicker 1960s (plastic) $7-$25

Popeye Flicker (1a)

Popeye Flicker (1b)

Popeye Flicker (2a)

Popeye Flicker (2b)

Popeye Flicker 1960s (chrome frame, plastic, color) $10-$45 ea.

Popeye Flicker (1) 1960s (Popeye to Wimpy)

Popeye Flicker (2) 1960s (Popeye to Olive Oyl)

Popeye Flicker (3) 1960s (Popeye to Sweet Pea)

471

TOY RINGS

Popeye Flicker (4)
1960s (Popeye to
bucktooth nephew)
(silver base)
$10-$40 ea.

Popeye (see
Post Tin &
Wimpy)

Popsicle Boot
1951 (with paper code)
(plastic), Complete $100
Ring Only
$25-$125

Post Tin - Harold Teen, $5-$60

Post Tin - Herby, $5-$60

Post Tin - Lillums, $5-$60

Post Tin Rings

1948 (unbent examples with no rust are rare)
1949, 1952 (cereal premiums)(Post Raisin Bran & Corn
Flakes)(in color)(priced below)

LET'S WEAR THEM! TRADE 'EM! COLLECT 'EM!
NO MONEY! NO BOX TOPS!
FREE
COLORFUL METAL
COMIC
RINGS
ADJUSTABLE... FITS ANY FINGER
ONE PACKED IN EVERY
RING PACKAGE OF...
RAISIN BRAN
12 DIFFERENT COMIC RINGS IN THE SERIES!

Post Tin Display Poster
1948 (color)(large size)
$300-$600

Post Tin - Orphan Annie, $10-$100

Post Tin - Perry Winkle, $5-$60

Post Tin - Skeezix, $5-$60

1948
(All from Post Raisin Bran)

Post Tin - Smilin' Jack, $10-$85

Post Tin - Andy Gump, $5-$60

Post Tin - Smitty, $5-$60

Post Tin - Dick Tracy, $20-$150

Post Tin - Smokey Stover, $5-$60

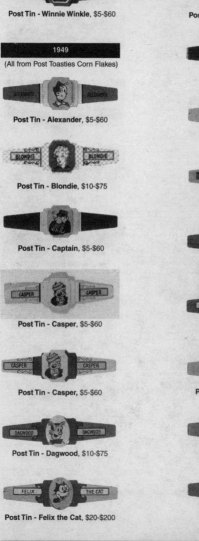

Post Tin - Winnie Winkle, $5-$60

1949
(All from Post Toasties Corn Flakes)

Post Tin - Alexander, $5-$60

Post Tin - Blondie, $10-$75

Post Tin - Captain, $5-$60

Post Tin - Casper, $5-$60

Post Tin - Casper, $5-$60

Post Tin - Dagwood, $10-$75

Post Tin - Felix the Cat, $20-$200

Post Tin - Flash Gordon, $20-$225

Post Tin - Fritz, $5-$60

Post Tin - Hans, $5-$60

Post Tin - Henry, $5-$60

Post Tin - Inspector, $5-$60

Post Tin - Jiggs, $5-$60

Post Tin - Little King, $10-$85

Post Tin - Mac, $5-$60

Post Tin - Maggie, $5-$60

TOY RINGS

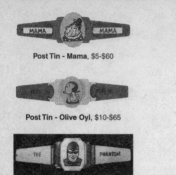

Post Tin - Mama, $5-$60

Post Tin - Olive Oyl, $10-$65

Post Tin - Phantom, $20-$200
(the very first Phantom ring)

Post Tin - Popeye, $20-$175

Post Tin - Snuffy Smith, $10-$60

Post Tin - Swee'pea, $10-$85

Post Tin - Tillie The Toiler, $5-$60

Post Tin - Toots, $10-$60

Post Tin - Wimpy, $10-$65

1953
Roy Rogers Western Rings
(All from Post Raisin Bran)

Post Tin - Bullet (Roy Rogers)
$10-$120

Post Tin - Dale Evans, $10-$150

Post Tin - Dale's Brand
(Roy Rogers), $10-$70

Post Tin - Deputy Sheriff
(Roy Rogers), $10-$100

Post Tin - Roy Rogers, $10-$160

Post Tin - Roy's Boots, $10-$70

Post Tin - Roy's Brand, $10-$70

Post Tin - Roy's Gun, $10-$70

Post Tin - Roy's Holster, $10-$70

Post Tin - Roy's Saddle, front and back view, $10-$70

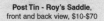

Post Tin - Sheriff (Roy Rogers), $10-$70

Post Tin - Trigger (Roy Rogers), $10-$120

Puzzle (see Quaker Puzzle)

Puzz-L Ring Ad

Puzz-L-Ring
1950s (plastic)(Kellogg's Pep Wheat Flakes cereal)(5 diff.)
$7-$20 ea.

Quake Friendship Figural, Captain,
1960s (plastic, diff. colors) (also see Quisp Figural)(cereal)
In Package $500
Ring Only - $125-$550

Quake Volcano Whistle
1960s (complete in package) (plastic)(cereal)
In Package $300
Ring Only - $100-$325

Quake World Globe
1960s (complete in package) (plastic)(rare) (cereal)
In Package $500
Ring w/Figure $100-$400

Quake Leaping Lava
1960s (green plastic w/clear top)(contains real meteorite) (also see Quisp Meteorite) (cereal)
In Package $325
Ring Only - $100-$300

Quaker Friendship
1950s
$45-$120

Quaker Jingle Bell
1950s
$10-$40

Quaker Puzzle
1950s (tic tac toe)
$10-$40 ea.

Quaker Siren
1950s
$10-$40

Quaker
1940s (metal)(Quaker Oats)
$100-$325

Quaker Water Pistol
1950s
$10-$40

Quaker Whistle
1950s
$10-$40

Quaker Crazy Ring (above)
1950s (10 diff.)
(priced individually)

Quaker Meteor
1950s
(w/meteorite enclosed)
$10-$40

Rabbit Flicker
1950s (thick top)
(plastic)
$30-$90

Radio Orphan Annie (see Post Tin)

Note rare unbent (unfitted) prongs

Radio Orphan Annie Face
1936 (rare unbent prongs)
(metal, gold color)
$120

Quisp Meteorite
1960s (plastic)
In Package $375
Ring Only - $100-$325

Quaker Initial Ring
1939 (metal)
$100-$350

Radio Orphan Annie Birthday
1936 , metal
(gold color)
(same as Ovaltine Birthday)(February shown)
$100-$425

Quisp Space Gun
1965-72 (plastic)
(with 4 bullets)
(diff. colors)
In Package $375
Ring w/Bullet - $100-$325

Quaker Pencil Sharpener
1950s
$10-$40

Quick Draw McGraw
1960s
(w/Huckleberry Hound)
Glove & Ring $150
Ring Only $75

Radio Orphan Annie Mystic Eye, 1930s
(same as Lone Ranger Ntl. Defender)(metal)
$40-$125

Radio Orphan Annie Face
1930s (metal, gold color)
$30-$100

Quaker Puzzle
1950s
$10-$40 ea.

Quisp Space Disk Whistle
1965-72 (plastic)
In Package $375
Ring Only - $100-$325

Small metal plates pivot out to reveal small peep holes for viewing planes

Closed   Open

Quaker Ship-in-Bottle
1950s (Also see Cap'n. Crunch)
$10-$40

Quisp Friendship Figural
1960s (plastic)
In package $1,200
Ring Only $275-$1,000

Radio Orphan Annie Secret Guard Altascope
1942 (very rare)
(Less than 10 known, one in near mint)(World War II premium)
Good - $2,500
Very Good - $4,000
Fine - $8,000
Very Fine - $15,000
Near Mint - $25,500

476

Radio Orphan Annie Secret Guard Initial, 1941, (scarce (gold color metal) (red letter)(also see Walnettos Initial) Good - $500, Fine - $1,200, Near Mint - $3,000

Radio Orphan Annie Secret Guard Magnifying 1941 (scarce)(metal) (also see Valric The Viking) Good - $500 Fine - $1,200 Near Mint - $3,000

Radio Orphan Annie Secret Message 1930s (metal) $75-$300

Radio Orphan Annie Silver Star, 1930s (metal) $100-$325

Radio Orphan Annie Triple Mystery 1930s (secret compartment) Complete - Good - $250, Fine - $500, Near Mint - $1,000 Ring With Top Missing - $50-$100

Radio Orphan Annie 2-Initial Signet 1930s (metal)(also see Ovaltine Signet) $35-$120

Range Rider (TV) 1950s (aluminum w/brown leather tag)(rare) Complete - $100-$350 no tag $200

Range Rider (TV) 1950s (metal) $75-$150

Ranger Rick (TV) 1950s (metal) (2 views shown) $25-$50

Real Photos Card with Rings 1940s, 1950, 1960s (store)(round)(cowboy & T.V. stars) Set $300 Ring $7-$25 ea.

Real Photos Autry, Gene Photo 1950s (plastic)(B&W) $7-$25

Real Photos Benny, Jack Photo 1950s (plastic)(B&W) $7-$25

Real Photos Berle, Milton Photo 1950s (plastic)(B&W) $7-$25

Real Photos Cassidy, Hopalong Photo (William Boyd) 1950s (plastic)(B&W) $10-$30

Real Photos Cooper, Gary Photo 1950s (plastic)(B&W) $7-$25

Real Photos Crosby, Bing Photo 1950s (plastic)(B&W) $7-$25

Real Photos Durante, Jimmy Photo 1950s (plastic)(B&W) $7-$25

TOY RINGS

Real Photos Godfrey, Arthur Photo
1950s (bronze plastic)(B&W)
$7-$25

Real Photos Hayworth, Rita Photo
1950s (bronze plastic)(B&W)
$7-$25

Real Photos Winchell, Paul & Jerry Mahoney Photo
1950s (plastic)(B&W)
$10-$30

Real Photos McCrae, Joel Photo, 1950s (plastic)(B&W)
$7-$25

Real Photos Scott, Randolph Photo, 1950s (plastic)(B&W)
$10-$30

Real Photos Gleason, Jackie Photo
1950s (plastic)(B&W)
$10-$50

Real Photos Hope, Bob Photo 1950s (green plastic base)(B&W)
$7-$30

Real Photos McCrae, Joel 1950s (thick top, plastic)
$25-$75

Real Photos Sinatra, Frank Photo, 1950s (plastic)(B&W)
$7-$30

Real Photos Wayne, John Photo, 1950s (plastic)(B&W)
$15-$60

Real Photos Grable, Betty Photo
1950s (plastic)(B&W)
$10-$30

Real Photos Louis, Joe Photo 1940s (plastic)(B&W)
$15-$50

Real Photos Rogers, Roy Photo, 1950s (plastic)(B&W)
$12-$40

Real Photos Starrett, Charles Photo 1950s (plastic)(B&W) (round)(store)
$7-$25

Red Ball Super Space Decoder 1950s (red plastic)(also offered as Mr. Fix Super Snooper ring in blue, pink & yellow. The only diff. is the color)
In Bag, On Tree $50
Ring Only $10-$40

Real Photos Hayes, Gabby Photo
1950s (plastic)(B&W)
$7-$25

Real Photos MacArthur, Douglas Photo 1950s (plastic)(B&W)
$7-$30

Real Photos Rogers, Roy Photo, 1950s (plastic)(B&W)
$15-$40

Real Photos Sullivan, Ed Photo, 1950s (plastic)(B&W)
$7-$25

Real Photos McCarthy, Charlie Photo 1950s (plastic)(B&W)
$10-$30

Real Photos Scott, Randolph Photo 1950s (profile) (plastic)(B&W)
$7-$25

Red Goose Secret Compartment
1940s (plastic & metal) (some tops are engraved with the customer's name)
$115-$300

Rin Tin Tin (4) Geronimo

Rin Tin Tin (11) Rusty

Rin Tin Tin (12) Sgt. Biff

Robin Hood Shoes
1950s (scarce)(silver)
$125-$300

Rin Tin Tin
1955 (plastic) (12 diff.)(color of plastic base varies)(Nabisco Wheat Honeys cereal premium) (also see Kellogg's Picture Rings)
$10-$30 ea.

Rin Tin Tin (5) Horse

Red Ryder
1940s (metal)
$15-$50

Republic F-84E Thunderjet
(see Kellogg's Picture)

Rin Tin Tin (6) Lt. Rip Masters

Rin Tin Tin Magic Ring
1950s (with pencil)
Complete With Strips Of Paper & Pencil $625
Ring Only $50-$200
Pencil only $40-$175

Robin Logo
1980s
(Nestle)(round)
$40-$75

Republic XF-91 Thundercepter
(see Kellogg's Picture)

Rin Tin Tin (7) Major

Rita Hayworth Photo
(see Real Photo)

Robin Logo
1980s
(Nestle)(square)
$40-$75

No Picture Available

Rin Tin Tin (1) Cochise

RinGun (shoots caps)
1940s (metal)
On Card $50-$75
Ring Only $15-$30

Robin Logo
1980s
(Nestle)(rect.)
$40-$75

Rin Tin Tin (8)

Rin Tin Tin (2) Cpl. Boone

Rin Tin Tin (9)

Luminous rockets can be shot from barrel with the firing bar

Rin Tin Tin (3) Fort Apache

Rin Tin Tin (10) Rinty & Rusty

Rocket-To-The-Moon
1951 (w/3 glow-in-dark rockets)(gold & silver) (red top)(believed to be a Lone Ranger premium) (Kix Cereal). Complete w/papers $900
Rocket Only $150 ea.
Ring $50-$300

Rockettes Flicker
1960s (round, plastic)
$3-$10

Rockettes Flicker 1960s (rectangle)
$3-$10

Rocky & Bulllwinkle Flicker (1a)
1961 (Boris)

Rocky & Bullwinkle Flicker (1b)
1961 (Boris)

Rocky & Bullwinkle Flicker (2b)
1961 (Bullwinkle)

Rocky & Bullwinkle Flicker (3a)
1961 (Dudley)

Rocky & Bullwinkle Flicker (3b)
1961 (Dudley)

Rocky & Bullwinkle Flicker (4a)
1961 (Mr. Peabody)

Rocky & Bullwinkle Flicker (4b)
1961 (Mr. Peabody)

Rocky & Bullwinkle Flicker (5a)
1961 (Rocky)

Rocky & Bullwinkle Flicker (5b)
1961 (Rocky)

Rocky & Bullwinkle Flicker (6a)
1961 (Sherman) (all in color)
Original gold base
$125-$350 ea.
Modern base
$75-$200 ea.

Roger Wilco Magni-Ray
1940s (metal)(two top variations)
$40-$175

Roger Wilco Flying Tigers
1951 (Flying Tigers was a TV serial starring Eric Fleming, later of "Rawhide" fame) (w/metal whistle inside) (red plastic base)
$115-$350

Roger Wilco Rescue
1949 (metal base) (w/metal whistle inside)
$75-$275

Rootie Kazootie TV Flicker
1950s (metal)
$30-$130

Rosalie Gimple
1940s (gold color metal)(scarce)
$200-$625

Romper Room TV, 1960s (silver color) (aluminum)
$7-$20

Romper Room TV, 1960s (gold color) (aluminum)
$20-$60

Rootie Kazootie Lucky Spot
1940s (rare)(metal)
GD $150
FN $400
NM $625

Roy Rogers Branding Iron
1950s, (metal) (white cap)
$75-$275

Roy Rogers Branding Iron
1950s (black cap)(metal)
$75-$275

Roy Rogers Hat
1950s (scarce)(sterling)
GD $200
FN $400
NM $600

Roy Rogers Microscope
1950s (also see Sky King Magni-glo)(metal)
$50-$175

Roy Rogers On Horse
1940s (sterling; non-adjustible band)
$75-$325

Roy Rogers On Horse
1940s (oval)(silver color)(non-adjustable band)
$60-$275

Roy Rogers Photo, (see Post Tin & Real Photos)

Roy Rogers Saddle
1948 (Sterling silver)
GD $225
FN $350
NM $475

Roy Rogers Store
1950s (silver metal)
$35-$120

Rudolph
1940s (metal)(scarce)
$85-$250
Box only $100

Saddle (see Cisco Kid & Walnettos)

Congo

Saddle, Generic
1950s (metal)
$7-$20

French West Africa

Saddle, Goudey Gum
1950s (metal) (saddle spins)
$35-$100

Nigeria

Saddle, Smith Brothers
1951 (Cough Drops premium)(airplane aluminum)(a real scale model of a western saddle)
$12-$50

West Africa

Savage Tribal
1961 (plastic)(set of 6)(Nabisco Wheat or Rice Honeys)
$7-$25 ea.

Scarab (see Capt. Hawks & Melvin Purvis)

Secret Agent Lookaround
1930s (Brass w/same base as R.O.A. Mystic Eye & Lone Ranger National Defenders) (very rare) (a prototype)
GD $150
FN $300
NM $550

Sears Christmas Flicker
1960s ("Sears has everything" picture of four small trees to face of Santa) (silver base) (2 versions)
$10-$30

Secret Compartment (see Pilot's ---)

Secret Service
1950s (gumball) (plastic)
$15-$40

Shadow Blue Coal Ring
1941 (glows-in-dark)(plastic) (blue top resembling a chunk of coal)
GD $100, FN $275, NM $450

1941 Canadian version (stone is reversed)
GD $100, FN $275, NM $500

Shadow Carey Salt
1947 (black stone)(glows-in-dark)(also see Buck Rogers Ring of Saturn, Jack Armstrong Dragon Eye & Shadow Blue Coal)
GD $500
FN $1,000
NM $1,800

Shadow Hologram
1994 (Shadow toy coupon offer)(Kenner) (grey plastic) ring only
$10-$40

Shield
1930s
(metal)(generic)
$15-$45

Shield
1940s
(metal)(blank
top)
$7-$20

Ship in bottle
(see Quaker)

**Shmoo Lucky
Rings,** 1950s
(metal)(on card)
12 rings On Card
$1,500
Ring Only
$20-$75 ea.

Simpson's Squirt Rings
1997 (yellow plastic, cereal
premium)
NM wrapped set (6) $150
NM unwrapped set (6) $100

Siren (see
Quaker)

Skeezix (see
Post Tin)

**Shirley Temple
Face**
1930s (sterling)
(scarce)(gold
plated)(cereal
premium)
GD $175
FN $300
NM $475

**Shirley Temple
Face**
1930s (sterling
w/blue inlay
sides)(scarce)
GD $175
FN $300
NM $475

Skull
1939 (gold w/red
eyes)(metal)
$45-$135

Skull
1940s (gold
w/black eyes)
$45-$135

Skull
1940s (silver
w/green
eyes)(metal)
$45-$135

Skull
1940s (metal)
$45-$135

Skull-Montrose
Lucky (see
Phantom; there
is no Montrose
Lucky ring)

Skull-Popsicle
1949 (silver
w/sparkling
jewel-like
red eyes)
$40-$135

Skull (foreign)
1940s (2 diff.)
(top-green back,
bottom-yellow
back)(metal)
$25-$85 ea.

Sky Bar Pilot
1940s (metal)
$150-$475

Sky Birds
1941 (Army Air
Corps.)
(silver finished
metal w/gold
finished
Air Corps.
insignia)(Sky
Birds Bubble
gum box top
offer)(Goudey
Gum Co.)
$30-$125

**Sky King Aztec
Emerald
Calendar Ring**
1940s,
metal/plastic)
(24 Karat gold
plated)
GD $200, FN
$600, NM $1,200

**Sky King
Electronic
Television
Picture**
1940s
(metal)(with 4
photos of
Clipper, Penny,
Jim & Martha
that can be
placed over por-
trait of Sky King
in base of
ring)(Sky King
picture
glows-in-dark)
Ring Only
$40-$150
Complete
$115-$270
Indiv. Photos -
$25 ea.

Sky King Kaleidoscope
1940s (prototype, metal) (very rare) Near Mint - $16,000

Sky King Navajo Treasure Ring
1950s (turquoise colored stone, silver colored base)(Advertised on back cover of **Danger Trail** comic #1, 1950) $50-$160

Sliding Whistle (see Tom Mix--)

Sliding Whistle
1940s, (generic) (rare)(metal) $100-$300

Smith Brothers (see U.S.--)

Smith Brothers Saddle (see Saddle)

Smith Brothers Good Luck Initial (see Good Luck--)

Smitty (see Post Tin)

Smokey Stover (see Post Tin)

Smile
1950s (Orange flavored drink) (aluminum) $15-$60

Smokey Stover
1964 (still on tree)(Canada Dry & Cracker Jack)(plastic) (also see Smilin' Jack & Terry & the Pirates) On spru $100 Assembled $15-$50

Smile Flicker
1950s (Orange flavored drink) (plastic) $15-$60

Smith Brothers U.S. Army Air Corps.
1940s (Cough Drops)(metal) $30-$80

Sky King Magni-Glo Writing
1940s (also see Super Puff Popcorn & Roy Rogers Microscope) (metal) Ring Only $20-$150

Sky King Radar
1940s (metal)(also see Peter Paul Sec. Compt.) $75-$275

Sky King Tele-Blinker, 1950s (metal)(large size) $75-$200

Smilin' Jack (see Post Tin)

Smith Brothers U.S. Marine
1940s (Cough Drops)(metal) $30-$80

Snap
(white hat) (rubber) GD $75 FN $175 NM $350

Sky King Mystery Picture
1940s (scarce w/picture intact) Complete - GD $400 FN $700 NM $1,200 Complete, no image $125-$300

Sleeping Beauty Prince Phillip
1960s (hard plastic) (Disney)("Truth" & "Virtue" on face of shield) $20-$60

Smilin' Jack
1964 (Canada Dry & Cracker Jack)(plastic) On spru $100 Assembled $15-$50

Smith Brothers U.S. Navy
1940s (Cough Drops)(metal) $30-$80

Crackle
(red hat)(rubber) GD $50 FN $100 NM $250

TOY RINGS

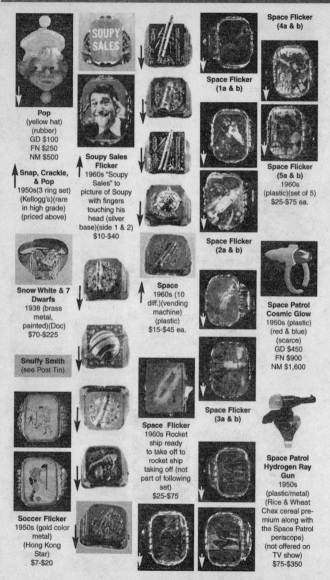

Pop
(yellow hat)
(rubber)
GD $100
FN $250
NM $500

Snap, Crackle, & Pop
1950s (3 ring set)
(Kellogg's) (rare
in high grade)
(priced above)

Soupy Sales Flicker
1960s "Soupy
Sales" to
picture of Soupy
with fingers
touching his
head (silver
base) (side 1 & 2)
$10-$40

Snow White & 7 Dwarfs
1938 (brass
metal,
painted) (Doc)
$70-$225

Snuffy Smith
(see Post Tin)

Soccer Flicker
1950s (gold color
metal)
(Hong Kong
Star)
$7-$20

Space
1960s (10
diff.) (vending
machine)
(plastic)
$15-$45 ea.

Space Flicker
1960s Rocket
ship ready
to take off to
rocket ship
taking off (not
part of following
set)
$25-$75

Space Flicker (1a & b)

Space Flicker (2a & b)

Space Flicker (3a & b)

Space Flicker (4a & b)

Space Flicker (5a & b)
1960s
(plastic) (set of 5)
$25-$75 ea.

Space Patrol Cosmic Glow
1950s (plastic)
(red & blue)
(scarce)
GD $450
FN $900
NM $1,600

Space Patrol Hydrogen Ray Gun
1950s
(plastic/metal)
(Rice & Wheat
Chex cereal pre-
mium along with
the Space Patrol
periscope) (not
offered on
TV show)
$75-$350

484

Space Patrol Printing
1950s (plastic)
W/Stamp Pad -
$350-$850
Ring Only -
$125-$350

Good - $800
Very Good -
$1,300
Fine - $2,500
Very Fine -
$4,500
Near Mint -
$8,500

Space Patrol Siren Whistle
1950s (metal)
(gold & silver versions)
$70-$200

Speak No Evil
1950s (3 monkeys) (metal)
$15-$50

Spider
1934-43 (pulp character)(pulp & theater premium) (scarce)(silver base)(30 known: 7 in gd, 10 in vg, 5 in fn, 5 in vf, 3 in nm)

Spider-Man Face
1960s (Marvel Ent. Group)
Hong Kong base, aluminum)
$15-$80

Spider-Man (vitamins)
1975 (metal)(nickel base)(Marvel Ent. Group)
$30-$150

Spider-Man Face
1980s (green) (Marvel Ent. Group)(see Marvel)(green top, white base)
$20-$60

Spider-Man
1980s (plastic)
$7-$20

Spider-Man (gold) 1993 (limited to 12) (Marvel Ent. Group)
Near Mint - $3,400

Spider-Man (silver) 1993 (limited to 50) (Marvel Ent. Group)
Near Mint - $475

Spider-Man (bronze) 1993 (limited to 50) (Marvel Ent. Group)
Near Mint - $275

Stanley Club
1940s (green stone, gold metal)(radio)
$150-$500

Star Trek
1979 (emblem)

Star Trek
1979 (Enterprise)

Star Trek
1979 (Kirk)

Star Trek
1979 (Mr. Spock) (McDonald's) (plastic, set of 4)
On spru $65 ea.
Assembled $45 ea.

Story Book
1960s (metal)(scarce)
$50-$150

Straight Arrow Gold Arrow Ring (Bandanna slide), 1940s
$20-$60

Straight Arrow Golden Nugget Ring, 1951 (Nabisco Shredded Wheat premium)(w/photo inside)(see Golden Nugget Cave)(Versions exist without photo of sender)
Complete $100-$300
Base Without Insides $15-$20

485

TOY RINGS

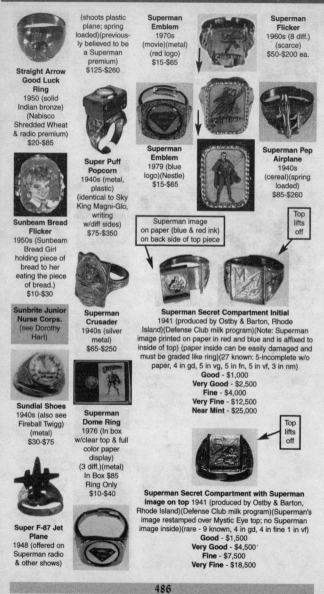

Straight Arrow Good Luck Ring
1950 (solid Indian bronze) (Nabisco Shredded Wheat & radio premium)
$20-$85

Sunbeam Bread Flicker
1950s (Sunbeam Bread Girl holding piece of bread to her eating the piece of bread.)
$10-$30

Sunbrite Junior Nurse Corps.
(see Dorothy Hart)

Sundial Shoes
1940s (also see Fireball Twigg) (metal)
$30-$75

Super F-87 Jet Plane
1948 (offered on Superman radio & other shows)

(shoots plastic plane; spring loaded)(previously believed to be a Superman premium)
$125-$260

Super Puff Popcorn
1940s (metal, plastic) (identical to Sky King Magni-Glo, writing w/diff sides)
$75-$350

Superman Crusader
1940s (silver metal)
$65-$250

Superman Dome Ring
1976 (In box w/clear top & full color paper display) (3 diff.)(metal)
In Box $85
Ring Only $10-$40

Superman Emblem
1970s (movie)(metal) (red logo)
$15-$65

Superman Emblem
1979 (blue logo)(Nestle)
$15-$65

Superman image on paper (blue & red ink) on back side of top piece

Superman Flicker
1960s (8 diff.) (scarce)
$50-$200 ea.

Superman Pep Airplane
1940s (cereal)(spring loaded)
$85-$260

Top lifts off

Superman Secret Compartment Initial
1941 (produced by Ostby & Barton, Rhode Island)(Defense Club milk program)(Note: Superman image printed on paper in red and blue and is affixed to inside of top) (paper inside can be easily damaged and must be graded like ring)(27 known: 5-incomplete w/o paper, 4 in gd, 5 in vg, 5 in fn, 5 in vf, 3 in nm)
Good - $1,000
Very Good - $2,500
Fine - $4,000
Very Fine - $12,500
Near Mint - $25,000

Top lifts off

Superman Secret Compartment with Superman image on top 1941 (produced by Ostby & Barton, Rhode Island)(Defense Club milk program)(Superman's image restamped over Mystic Eye top; no Superman image inside)(rare - 9 known, 4 in gd, 4 in fine 1 in vf)
Good - $1,500
Very Good - $4,500
Fine - $7,500
Very Fine - $18,500

Superman Tim "Good Luck" Ring
1949 (Given away at department stores)(silver color metal)
(25 known: 2 in gd grade, 15 in vg, 5 in fn, 2 in vf, 1 in NM)
Good - $400
Very Good - $900
Fine - $1,500
Very Fine - $3,000
Near Mint - $5,000

Supermen of America Prize Ring
1940 (produced by Ostby & Barton, Rhode Island)(membership)
(rare)(gold plated centerw/red color behind circled letters) (promoted in **Superman** & **Action Comics** & given away w/candy & gum promotions)
(17 known: 2 in pr, 6 in gd, 2 in vg, 3 in fn, 3 in vf, 1 in Mint)
Fair - $1,500
Good - $6,250
Very Good - $9,500
Fine - $15,000
Very Fine - $30,000
Near Mint - $75,000

Swastika Good Luck
1920s (metal)(Symbols of good luck: Swastika, horseshoe, 4-leaf clover)(Also see Kill the Jinx--, Navajo Good Luck & Whitman, Paul)
$20-$75

Tales of the Texas Rangers
1950s (TV) (aluminum) (came w/membership kit)
$25-$100

Target Comics Ring
1920s (sterling silver)
$20-$40
Note: Also known as a Chinese **Good Luck Ring**, sold through Johnson Smith & Co. Catalogues in 1929. Symbols on ring stand for health, happiness, prosperity & prolonged life.
Lrg. Sterling Adj. $75
Lrg. Brass Solid $60
Tiny Girl's Sterling Adj. $75

Tarzan Ape Ring
1920s (metal)(rare)
GD $100
FN $225
NM $450

Tarzan
1920s (metal)(rare)
GD $125
FN $250
NM $500

Tarzan Flicker (not part of set)- Tarzan face to full figure shooting bow & arrow (red letters)
$15-$40

Tarzan Flicker (1)
Tarzan swinging on vine to Tarzan punching out a native

Tarzan Flicker (2)
Tarzan looking over his shoulder at spear throwing natives to Tarzan captured by two jungle natives

Tarzan Flicker (3)
Tarzan lifting a boulder in front of a waterfall to Tarzan punching another guy

Tarzan Flicker (4a)

Tarzan Flicker (4b)
Tarzan squaring off with a gorilla to Tarzan having gorilla in a headlock

Tarzan Flicker (5)
Tarzan yelling to Tarzan caught in vines

TOY RINGS

Tarzan Flicker (6)
Tarzan landing from a vine to Tarzan approaching a jungle native whose back is to us.
$10-$25 ea.

Tarzan Flicker
1960s (silver & gold versions)(plastic)
(all individually priced)

Ted Williams
1948
(metal & plastic)
GD $300
FN $600
NM $1,200

Teenage Mutant Ninja Turtles (April O'Neil)

Teenage Mutant Ninja Turtles (Donatello)
(green rubber)

Teenage Mutant Ninja Turtles (Leonardo)
(green rubber)

Teenage Mutant Ninja Turtles (Michaelangelo)
(green rubber)

Teenage Mutant Ninja Turtles (Raphael)
(green rubber)

Teenage Mutant Ninja Turtles (Rock Steady)

Teenage Mutant Ninja Turtles (Splinter)

Teenage Mutant Ninja Turtles (Shredder)

Teenage Mutant Ninja Turtles
1991 (8 diff.)
(rubber in color)
(cereal premiums; cereal only distr. in Canada)
Turtles - $15 ea.
Others - $20 ea.
In Pkg. add $5
Set (8) - $125

Tennessee Jed Look-Around
1940s
(metal)(rare in VF-NM)
GD $150
FN $350
NM $700

Terry & the Pirates Gold Detector
1947 (metal)
$50-$175

Terry & the Pirates, 1964
(plastic)(Sugar Jets cereal & Cracker Jack)
(also see Smilin' Jack and Smokey Stover)
On spru - $100
Assembled
$15-$50

Three Stooges Flicker (Larry)

Three Stooges Flicker (Curly)

Three Stooges Flicker (Moe)

Three Stooges Flicker
1959 (3 diff.)
(silver base)
$12-$30 ea.

Thunderbird
1930s (rare) (see Lone Wolf)
$150-$400

Tillie The Toller
(see King Features & Post Tin)

Tim (see Superman Tim)

Tim Ring
1930s
(rare)(metal)
(sold at Tim Stores)
GD $100
FN $250
NM $500

Timothy
(Disney)
1950s (oval)
(international sterling)
$35-$100

488

Timothy
(Disney)
1950s (square)
(international
sterling)
$35-$100

**Tom Corbett
Rocket (3)
Rocket Scout**

**Tom Corbett
Rocket (9)
Space Helmet**

Tom Mix Circus
1930s (silver
antiqued
metal)(see Billy
West & Cowboy
Riding Horse)
$7-$20

**Tom Corbett
Rocket (4)
Sound-Ray Gun**

**Tom Corbett
Rocket (10)
Space Suit**

Tom Mix Deputy
1933-35 (rare)(Tom Mix chewing
gum premium)(75 certificates
needed to get ring)(each attached
to a Tom Mix chewing gum wrapper)
(gold & silver)(scarce)
Good - $1,000
Fine - $3,500
Very Fine - $5,000
Near Mint - $6,500

**Tom & Jerry
Flicker**
1970s (blue
plastic base)
(4 diff.)
$15-$40 ea.

**Tom Corbett
Rocket (11)
Strato
Telescope**

**Tom Corbett
Face**
1950s (silver
color metal)
$50-$135

**Tom Corbett
Rocket (6)
Space Cadet
Dress Uniform**

**Tom Corbett
Rocket (12)
Tom Corbet
Space Cadet**

**Tom Corbett
Rocket
1951 (plastic)
(12 diff.)
(Kellogg's Pep
cereal)
$5-$20 ea.
NM set $250**

**Tom Mix Look
Around**
1946 (metal)
$40-$150

**Tom Mix
Magnet Ring**
1947 (metal)
$20-$100

**Tom Corbett
Rocket (1)
Girl's Space
Uniform**

**Tom Corbett
Rocket (7)
Space Cadet
Insignia**

**Tom Mix
Musical Ring**
1944
(metal)(also see
Jack Armstrong
Egyptian
Whistle ring)
Complete In Pkg.
$100-$225
Ring Only
$25-$150

**Tom Mix Lucky
Initial Signet**
1936 (24 kt. gold
plated)
(customer had
his own initial
placed on top of
ring)(came with
and w/o onyx
background)
$100-$325

**Tom Corbett
Rocket (2)
Parallo-Ray
Gun**

**Tom Corbett
Rocket (8)
Space Cruiser**

**Tom Corbett
Rocket
1950s (metal)
$125-$425**

TOY RINGS

Tom Mix Nail
1933
(metal)(same form as Gene Autry Nail) (signed)
$20-$50

Good - $1,000
Fine - $2,400
Near Mint - $4,200

Tom Mix Stanhope Image
1938 metal) (crisp photos of Tom & Tony inside rings are scarce)
$100-$500

Tom Mix Signature
1942 (sterling top)
$100-$325

Tom Mix Target
1937
(metal)(Marlin Guns)
$100-$325

Tom Mix Tiger-Eye
1950 (plastic)
$100-$350

Tonto Photo
1950s (color)(plastic) (see Lone Ranger-Dell)
$25-$85

Twinkie Shoes Elf
1930s sterling
$50-$175

Twist Flicker
1960s (plastic)
$2-$10

Uncle Creepy
1972 (dated 1969), (Warren) (metal)(gold color)(also see Cousin Eerie)
$100-$275

Underdog
1975 (plastic) (black over yellow)
$75-$200

Underdog (Simon Barsinister)
1975 (plastic) (black over yellow)
$25-$75

Tom Mix Sliding Whistle
1949
(metal)(also see Sliding Whistle)
$40-$150

Tom Mix Ralston Logo
1935 (gold Metal)
$60-$150

Tonto Picture
1938 (plastic)(ice cream comic book giveaway) (rare)(also see Lone Ranger Picture) (less than 10 known)
Good - $1,000
Fine - $2,000
Near Mint - $4,200

Universal Monster Flicker (The Creature) (both images shown)

Tom Mix Ralston Logo Variant
1935 (gold Metal) (From Robbins archives) (very rare) (only 6 known)
$175-$600

Tom Mix Spinner/Stamp
1933
(rare)(metal) (used for stamping emblems on paper)(when spinning Tom Mix appears on horse)(less than 10 known)

Twinkie Shoe
1930s (metal) (2 diff.)
$100-$325

Underdog
1975 (plastic) (silver over red)
$75-$225

490

Universal Monster Flicker (Dracula) (both images shown)

Phantom

Universal Monster Flicker (background colors are green, blue,& pink)(scarce) (set of 6)(the 2 Casper flickers may be part of set)(all but Wolfman ring priced below)
Original silver base - $50-$175 ea.
Blue Base - $25-$90 ea.
Silver "china" modern bases - $15-$45 ea.

Universal Monster Flicker 1960s (Phantom of the Opera/ Wolfman) (3 diff. rings known) $15-$50 ea.

U.S. Army Store Card 1950s (plastic) $7-$20

U.S. Marine Corps. Store Card 1950s (plastic) $7-$20

Universal Monster Flicker (Mummy) (both images shown)

USA Astronaut Flicker 1960s (in color)(plastic) $20-$50

U.S.Army Store Card 1950s (3 variations)(plastic) (gold/white/blue) $7-$20 ea.

U.S. Marine Corps. Store Card 1950s (plastic) $7-$20

Wolfman
Original base $75-$250
Blue base $30-$125

Universal Monster Flicker 1960s (Creature from the Black Lagoon/Mr. Hyde)

U.S. Air Force Store Card 1950s (plastic) $7-$20

U.S.Army World War I 1918 (sterling) (childs adj.) $40-$175

Monster

Universal Monster Flicker 1960s (Mummy/ Hunchback)

U.S. Air Force Store Card 1950s (plastic, green) $7-$20

U.S. Army Air Corps. (see Smith Brothers)

U.S. Keds 1960s (metal) (see Kolonel Keds) $60-$125

U.S. Navy Store Card 1950s (3 variations) $7-$25 ea.

TOY RINGS

Walnettos Initial
1940s
(metal)(walnut
flavored
candy)(same
base as R.O.A.
Initial)
$150-$650

Whistle Bomb
1940s (glow-in-dark)(rare)
(3 known)
(metal)
Good $1,000
Fine $2,000
Near Mint $4,000

Wimpy
1950s (silver
color metal)
(in color)(also
see Popeye)
$75-$185

Winnie Winkle
(see Post Tin
1948)

**Wizard Of Oz
Flicker
(Tin Man)**
1967 (plastic)
(shows both
images)

**USA/KKK Ring
(100%)**
1920s (flips to
reveal KKK)
(1st moveable
ring)(rare)(metal)
(2 diff. bases
known)
GD $150, FN
$350, NM $500

**Walnettos Initial
Saddle**
1940s (metal)
$35-$110

**Whistle Space
Ship**
1953 (metal)
$15-$40

**Wizard Of Oz
Flicker
(Dorothy)**
1967 (plastic)
(shows both
images)

**Valric Of The
Vikings
Magnifying**
1941
(All Rye Flakes
premium)(less
than 10 known)
(very rare)
(also see Radio
Orphan Annie
Magnifying)
Good - $2,000
Very Good -
$3,000
Fine - $4,000
Very Fine -
$5,500
Near Mint -
$8,000

Weather Bird
1950s (metal)
(shoes)
$75-$300

**Wheat Chex
Decoder**
1982 (paper)
(plastic base)
$8-$20

Wheaties
(see Compass)

**Whitman, Paul
Good Luck**
1930s
(Bakelite)(band
leader)(Whitman
figure on sides of
ring)(also see
Navajo Good
Luck &
Swastika)(same
as Kill The Jinx
ring)
$75-$350

**William Boyd
(Hopalong
Cassidy)**
(see Real
Photos)

**Wizard Of Oz
Flicker
(Scarecrow)**
1967 (plastic)
(shows both
images)

**Wizard Of Oz
Flicker (Witch)**
1967 (plastic)

Wizard Of Oz Flicker (Wizard)
1967 "Off to See The Wizard" with picture of OZ in background to full cartoon figure of cowardly lion
$10-$35 ea.

Wizard Of Oz Flicker
1967 (plastic)(set of 12)(priced above)(uncut sheets exist from warehouse)

Woman Dancer Flicker
1950s (thick top)
$30-$90

Wonder Bread Smiley Loaf
1960s (blue/white or red/white plastic)
$6-$18

Wonder Woman Logo
1976 (metal)
$50-$100

Wonder Woman Logo
1976 (metal)
$50-$100

Woody Woodpecker Club Stamp
1960s (2 diff. colors)(Kellogg's Rice Krispies cereal premium)(plastic)
$25-$100

World's Fair
1893 Columbia Expo (1492-1892) (sterling)(1st child's adj. premium ring?)(same image used on coin)(rare)
$125-$500

World's Fair
1893 Columbia Expo (sterling)(written in Spanish)
$35-$150

World's Fair
1933 Chicago (metal)
$25-$100

World's Fair
1933 Chicago(silver/blue top)(metal)
$40-$150

World's Fair
1933 Chicago (metal)
$25-$85

World's Fair
1933 Chicago (metal)
$25-$100

World's Fair
1934 Chicago (metal)
$20-$100

World's Fair
1934 Chicago (metal)
$20-$110

World's Fair
1934 Chicago (metal)
$25-$110

World's Fair
1933 Chicago (Indian head) (bronze)
$20-$85

World's Fair
1934 Chicago (Indian head)(pewter)
$20-$85

World's Fair
1934 Chicago (metal)
$20-$100

World's Fair
1934 Chicago (metal)
$20-$100

World's Fair
1934 Chicago (metal)
$20-$75

World's Fair
1934 Hall of Science (Chicago)(metal)
$20-$70

TOY RINGS

World's Fair
1935 San Diego
(metal)
$20-$75

World's Fair
1939 (plastic)
(New York)
(white, blue,
green, orange
tops; silver, gold
metal base
versions)
$50-$200 ea.

X-Men Gold
1993 (Diamond
Comics Dist.)
$750

**Yellow Kid
Collectors' Ring**
1995 (Randy
Bowen)(blue
stones for eyes)
(Limited edition
of 100 came with
statue and litho.)
Ring only - $800

**Yogi Bear's
Jellystone Park**
1960s (metal,
in color)
$15-$40

World's Fair
1939 New York
(metal)
$20-$100

World's Fair
1964 (New York)
(plastic)
$8-$20

X-Men Silver
1993 (Diamond
Comics Dist.)
$125

Yo-Yo/Siren Ring
1960s (Kellogg's Pep)(plastic/metal
siren & string)
Complete In Box w/Papers $400
Ring Only $80-$225
Paper Only $50-$100
Box Only $75

World's Fair
1939 (New York)
(silver metal)
$20-$75

Writer's Club
1940s
(metal)(premium)
$35-$150

World War I (see
U.S. Army)

**X-Men Xavier
Institute Class
Ring,** 1994
Gold (10K, 250
made) $400
Sterling (1,500
made) - $75
Bronze-finished
pewter - $20

**Your Name
Good Luck**
1950s
(metal)(Kellogg's)
(luminous)
$20-$50

Zorro Photo
1960s (plastic)
$10-$40

World's Fair
1939 (New York)
(metal, blue)
$20-$70

**Wyatt Earp
Marshal Initial
Ring**
1958-1960
(metal)
(Cheerios)
$40-$85

World's Fair
1939 (New York)
(plastic top)
$15-$40

**X-Men
Wolverine Mask**
1980s
(rubber)
(black/yellow)
$5-$30

Zorro (Z)
1960s
(plastic)(vending
machine)
$15-$50

**Zorro Logo
Ring**
1960s (vending
machine)
(silver & black
base
versions)
$15-$50

Now that you've had a taste of what awaits you in the world of comic book and toy ring collecting, perhaps you're also interested in other memorabilia categories as well. Below we list some of the other collecting opportunities for anyone looking to expand the scope of their collecting efforts:

Foreign Edition Comics

Many American newspaper and magazine strips are reprinted abroad (in English and other languages) months and even years after they appear in the States. These reprints are often in black and white, and reproduction can be poor.

Newspaper Strips

Collecting newspaper comic strips is somewhat different than collecting comic books, although it can be equally satisfying. Back issues of some newspaper comic strips are also occasionally available from dealers. Prices vary greatly depending on age, condition, and demand.

Original Art

Some enthusiasts collect original comic book and strip art. These mostly black and white, inked drawings are usually done on illustration paper at about 30 percent larger than the original printed panels. Because original art is a one-of-a-kind article, it is highly prized and can be difficult to obtain.

The best way to find the piece you want is to scour cons and get on as many art dealers' mailing lists as possible. Most current work is available at moderate prices, with something for everyone at various costs.

Toys and More

Comic book and toy shows are often dominated by toys and related products. Action figures and limited edition statues based on comic characters are currently the most popular. Statues and figurines, either painted or in kit form, are very popular higher-end collectibles. Numerous other tie-in products based on comic characters are released every year and seem to represent a large percentage of the collectible market today. For much more on toy collecting, see the latest editions of **Hake's Price Guide to Character Toys** and **The Official Price Guide to Disney Collectibles**, which feature over 370 categories of collectibles from a century of print, radio, film and television. Happy hunting!